Microprocessor Systems

Microprocessor Systems

W. Bolton

Pearson Education Limited
Edinburgh Gate
Harlow
Essex CM20 2JE, England
and Associated Companies throughout the world

First published 2000

ISBN 0 582 41881 X

British Library Cataloguing-in-Publication Data

A catalogue record for this book is available from the British Library

Produced by Pearson Education Asia Pte Ltd
Printed in Singapore (KKP)

Contents

Preface

Overview

Microprocessor-based systems are an integral part of the study of all aspiring and practising engineers, whether their discipline is mechanical, electrical, electronic, control, telecommunication or instrumentation engineering. Microprocessor-based systems are a feature of control, measurement and communication systems. This book is an attempt to provide all such readers with sufficient understanding of microprocessor-based systems to enable basic systems to be designed and perhaps extended by more detailed study of systems devoted to particular disciplines.

Readership

The book has been designed to comprehensively cover the *micro-processor systems* unit for the Higher National in Engineering, without assuming that a previous unit in microprocessor systems has been studied. The Higher National in Engineering is a national course of study for higher technicians in England, Wales and Northern Ireland, with clear progression onto degree programmes. It is also envisaged that the book could find use in undergraduate courses as an introduction to microprocessor-based systems for engineers.

Aims

The overall aims of the book are to help the reader:

1. Acquire an understanding of microprocessor-based systems and their use in control, communication and measurement systems.

2. Become capable of designing, building, programming and using simple microprocessor-based systems.

In the various chapters, the book has been written to help the reader achieve the following objectives:

Chapter 1: Introducing microprocessors

Use the binary, octal, hex and BCD number systems.

Describe the basic features of microprocessor architecture and, in particular, the Rockwell 6502, Zilog Z80, Motorola 6800/6802 and Intel 8085A.

Explain the fetch–execute cycle and timing diagrams.

Explain the types of memory chip available.

Explain how, in a multichip system, the system selects which chip to address.

Chapter 2: Microcontrollers

Describe the basic features of microcontrollers and the use of input/output control and status registers, in particular for the Motorola M68HC11, the Intel 8051 and the PIC 16C6x/7x microcontrollers.

Chapter 3: Microprocessor-based systems

Explain the role of microprocessor-based systems in a range of applications: the washing machine, automatic camera, automobile engine management, mobile telephone, smart cards and data acquisition systems.

Review the basic principles of a range of commonly used sensors: switches, encoders, potentiometers, pressure sensors, temperature sensors, light sensors.

Review the basic principles of analogue-to-digital and digital-to-analogue converters,

Review the basic principles of LED displays, stepper motors and the pulse width modulation control of motors.

Chapter 4: Designing programs

Design software in the form of flow charts and pseudocode.

Design software using modular programming.

Use a structured approach to software design.

Chapter 5: Assembly language

Write program instructions in assembly language.

Chapter 6: Assembly language programming

Write programs in assembly language, using looping, subroutines, parameter passing, look-up tables and input/output addressing.

Explain the use of the stack with subroutines.

Chapter 7: C language

Write program instructions in C language.

Use branches, loops, arrays and pointers.

Chapter 8: C programming

Write programs in C language, using header files, bit operations, branches, loops, arrays, pointers and subroutines.

Chapter 9: From debugging to EPROM

Test software using simulation, evaluation boards, and in-circuit emulation.

Transfer programs to EPROM or EEPROM.

Chapter 10: Interfacing

Explain how peripherals can be interfaced to microprocessor-based systems using buffers.

Explain how data can be transferred from peripherals by software synchronisation, handshaking and interrupts.

Explain how peripherals can be interfaced to microprocessor-based systems using programmable parallel and serial interfaces.

Describe the use of the interface standards RS-232, I^2C, CAN, Centronics and IEEE-488.

Chapter 11: Interfacing examples

Explain how switches, LED displays, analogue peripherals, timers, stepper motors and power peripherals can be interfaced to microprocessor-based systems.

Chapter 12: Testing systems

Explain how system hardware can be tested.

Chapter 13: Systems

Design microprocessor-based systems.

Structure of the book

Each chapter of the book is copiously illustrated and contains problems, answers to which are supplied at the end of the book. In particular, the problems given in Chapter 13 can be used as design assignments, with the answers given in the book being possible solutions.

The overall structure of the book is described by the diagram on the following page. Chapters 1, 2 and 3 form a general introduction to basic principles and an overview of systems; parts of them may well be revision. Chapters 4, 5, 6, 7 and 8 are an introduction to programming with Chapter 9 explaining about debugging and putting programs into memory; Chapter 4 covers the basic principles, Chapters 5 and 6 cover assembly language and Chapters 7 and 8 cover C language. Chapters 10 and 11 deal with interfacing. Chapters 12 and 13 round off the book by considering the testing and design of systems.

Acknowledgements

A large debt is owed to the publications of the manufacturers of the microprocessors, microcontrollers and peripherals referred to in the text.

W. Bolton

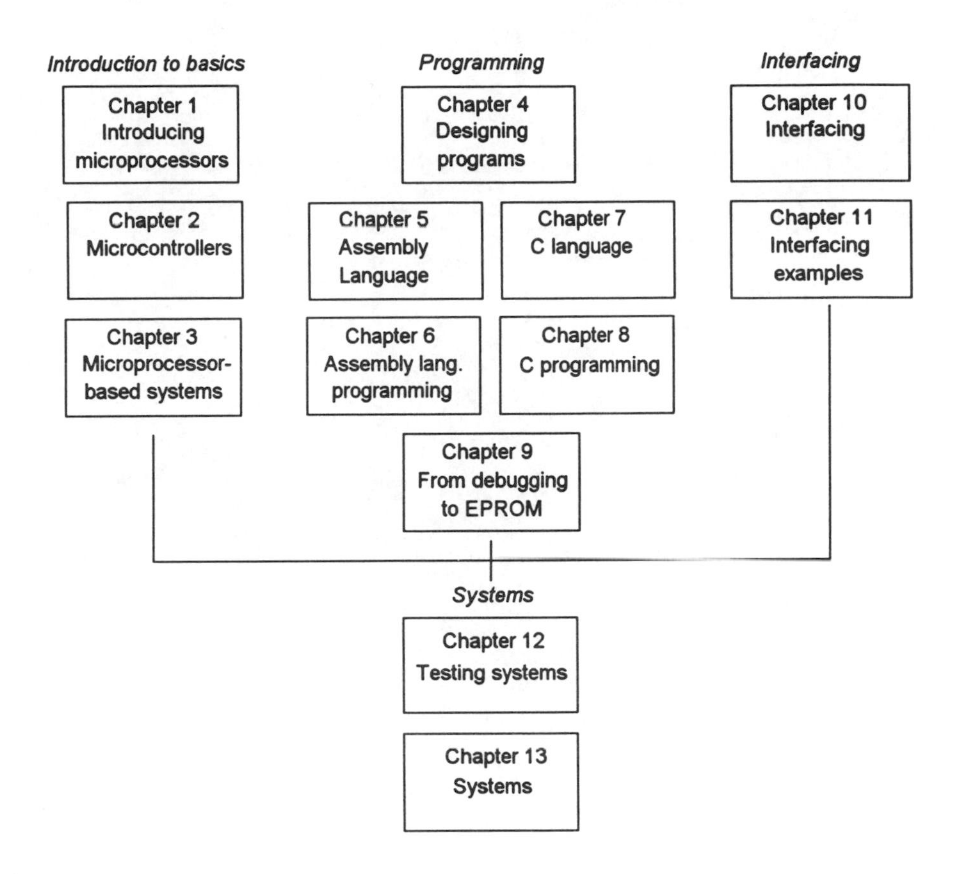

Introduction to basics
Programming
Interfacing
Chapter 1
Introducing
microprocessors
Chapter 4
Designing
programs
Chapter 10
Interfacing
Chapter 2
Microcontrollers
Chapter 5
Assembly
Language
Chapter 7
C language
Chapter 11
Interfacing
examples
Chapter 3
Microprocessor-
based systems
Chapter 6
Assembly lang.
programming
Chapter 8
C programming
Chapter 9
From debugging
to EPROM
Systems
Chapter 12
Testing systems
Chapter 13
Systems

1 Introducing microprocessors

1.1 Introduction

This chapter is a review of the basic features of microprocessors and the terms used in describing their performance. Since the microprocessor first commercially appeared in 1971, it has had a major impact on the design of products such as automatic cameras, toys, washing machines, cars and machine tools. Chapter 3 illustrates such types of applications with a review of microprocessor systems, illustrating in a general way how microprocessors are used in control systems, instrumentation systems and communication systems and examples of sensors and actuators used with microprocessor systems.

1.2 The data bus

Basically a *microprocessor* is a digital device that accepts data from a number of input lines, processes the data according to the dictates of a program and then produces a number of output signals (Fig. 1.1). Each input may be a discrete on/off signal from a sensor and an output may be a signal to switch on or off some device. However, a parallel group of inputs or outputs might be used to represent a value, e.g. the binary number 1000 1100, with each input or output representing one of the bits.

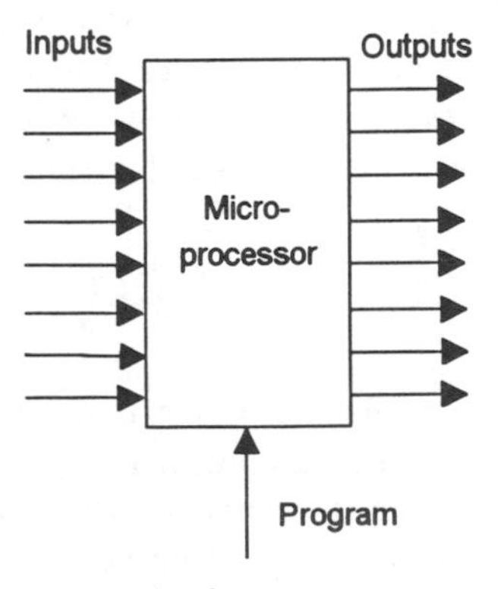

Fig. 1.1 A microprocessor

1.2.1 Bits, words, bytes and nibbles

With a digital system the signals are in one of two states, these being represented by logic 1 and logic 0. These logic 1 and logic 0 states are referred to as binary digits or *bits*. The bits are represented in the microprocessor system by voltage levels; ideally the logic 1 is 5 V and the logic 0 is 0 V. However, the logic levels are influenced by the circuitry used to form the devices; commonly used ones are transistor–transistor logic (TTL) and complementary metal oxide semiconductors (CMOS). With these the logic levels are represented by:

TTL	Inputs:	Low 0 to 0.8 V	High 2.0 to 5.0 V
	Outputs:	Low 0 to 1.5 V	High 3.5 to 5.0 V
CMOS	Inputs:	Low 0 to 1.5 V	High 3.5 to 5.0 V
	Outputs:	Low 0 V	High 5 V

The number of input lines on which data can enter the microprocessor is determined by the width of the data path in the microprocessor; the term *data bus* is used for the lines carrying the data. An 8 bit microprocessor has a data bus with 8 data lines. Such a microprocessor can simultaneously process 8 bits of data at any one time. The term *word* is used for the collection of bits on the input lines and thus, at any given instant of time, the signals on the data lines define a specific data word. The width of the data path is thus the word size. For an 8 bit microprocessor, the data word is made up of the eight bits from data line 0 to line 7, the bit on line 0 being termed the *least significant bit* (LSB) and the bit on line 7 the *most significant bit* (MSB). A data word of 8 bits is called a *byte*, a word of 4 bits is a *nibble*.

The first commercially made microprocessor was the 4 bit Intel 4004 in 1971. Today 4 bit microprocessors are still used in such items as toys, washing machines and central heating system controllers. By the 1980s we had 8 bit microprocessors, e.g. the Intel 8080 and 8050, the Rockwell 6502, the Motorola 6800 and the Zilog Z80. The advent of such 8 bit microprocessors led to the appearance of desktop microcomputers such as the Commodore PET and the Apple. Since then 16 bit, 32 bit and 64 bit microprocessors have become available. The advent of 16 bit microprocessors led to IBM entering the microcomputer market with their personal computer (PC).

1.3 Number systems

The decimal, or denary, system used for everyday counting is based on using ten symbols: 0 to 9. When a number is represented by this system, the digit position in the number indicates that the weight attached to each digit increases by a factor of 10 as we proceed from right to left. With microprocessor-based systems other number systems are used.

1.3.1 Binary system

The *binary system* is based on just two symbols or states: 0 and 1. These are termed *bi*nary digi*ts* or *bits*. When a number is represented by this system, the digit position in the number indicates that the weight attached to each digit increases by a factor of 2 as we proceed from right to left.

...	2^3	2^2	2^1	2^0
	bit 3	bit 2	bit 1	bit 0

For example, the decimal number 15 in the binary system is 1111, i.e. $1 \times 2^3 + 1 \times 2^2 + 1 \times 2^1 + 1 \times 2^0$. In a binary number the bit 0 is termed the *least significant bit* (LSB) and the highest bit the *most significant bit* (MSB).

To convert decimal numbers to binary numbers we can successively divide the decimal number by 2 and note the remainders. Thus, for example, if we have the decimal number 37 then dividing by 2 gives 18 with remainder 1; the 1 becomes the least significant digit; bit 0. Dividing by 2 gives 9 with no remainder; bit 1 is thus 0. Dividing by 2 gives 4 with remainder 1; bit 2 is thus 1. Dividing by 2 gives 2 with no remainder; bit 3 is thus 0. Further dividing by 2 gives 1 with no remainder; bit 4 is thus 0 and bit 5 is 1. The binary number is thus 100101.

Just as a decimal point can be used with a decimal number to separate digits which are multiples of 10 to positive powers, i.e. whole numbers, from those which are multiples of 10 to negative powers, i.e. decimal fractions, so a point can be used with binary numbers to separate the digits which are multiples of 2 to positive powers, i.e. whole binary numbers, from those which are multiples of 2 to negative powers, i.e. binary fractions. Thus the binary number 0.101 is $1 \times 2^{-1} + 0 \times 2^{-2} + 0 \times 2^{-3}$.

To convert decimal fractions to binary fractions, multiply the decimal fraction repeatedly by 2. The whole number part of the product gives the 2^{-1} digit and the fraction part is then further multiplied by 2 with its remainder giving the 2^{-2} digit and so on. Thus, for example, the decimal fraction 0.675 when multiplied by 2 gives 1.350 and so the 10^{-1} digit is 1. The fraction part 0.350 when multiplied by 2 gives 0.700 and so the 10^{-2} digit is 0. The fraction part 0.700 when multiplied by 2 gives 1.400 and so the 10^{-3} digit is 1. The fraction part 0.400 when multiplied by 2 gives 0.800 and so the 10^{-4} digit is 0. The fraction part 0.800 when multiplied by 2 gives 1.600 and so the 10^{-5} digit is 1. The fraction part 0.600 when multiplied by 2 gives 1.200 and so the 10^{-6} digit is 1. The fraction part 0.200 when multiplied by 2 gives 0.400. We can continue this for more digits but to an accuracy of 6 digits the binary number is 0.101011.

1.3.2 The octal system

The *octal system* is based on eight digits: 0, 1, 2, 3, 4, 5, 6, 7. When a number is represented by this system, the digit position in the number indicates that the weight attached to each digit increases by a factor of 8 as we proceed from right to left.

$$\ldots \quad 8^3 \quad 8^2 \quad 8^1 \quad 8^0$$

For example, the decimal number 15 in the octal system is 17, i.e. $1 \times 8^1 + 7 \times 8^0$.

To convert decimal numbers to octal numbers we successively divide by 8 and note the remainders. Thus, for example, the decimal number 241 when divided by 8 gives 30 with remainder 1 and 30 when divided by 8 gives 3 with remainder 6. The octal number is thus 361.

As with decimal and binary numbers, we can use a point to separate digits which are to positive powers of 8 from those which are to negative powers, i.e. octal fractions. To convert a decimal fraction to an octal fraction we multiply repeatedly by 8 and note the whole number part of the resulting product. For example, the decimal fraction 0.52 multiplied by 8 gives 4.16; the 8^{-1} digit is thus 4. Multiplying the fractional part 0.16 by 8 gives 1.28; the 8^{-2} digit is thus 1. Multiplying the fractional part 0.28 by 8 gives 2.04; the 8^{-3} digit is thus 2. Multiplying the fractional part 0.04 by 8 gives 0.32. Thus to an accuracy of three digits the octal number is 0.412.

1.3.3 The hexadecimal system

The *hexadecimal system* is based on 16 symbols: 0, 1, 2, 3, 4, 5, 6, 7, 8, 9, A, B, C, D, E, F with A representing 10, B representing 11, C representing 12, D representing 13, E representing 14 and F representing 15. When a number is represented by this system, the digit position in the number indicates that the weight attached to each digit increases by a factor of 16 as we proceed from right to left.

$$\ldots \quad 16^3 \quad 16^2 \quad 16^1 \quad 16^0$$

For example, the decimal number 268 is 10C in the hex system, i.e. $1 \times 16^2 + 0 \times 16^1 + 12 \times 16^0$. This system is generally used in the writing of programs for microprocessor-based systems since it represents a very compact method of entering data. In such programs, so that it is clear that hex numbers are involved, they are preceded by the symbol $ or followed by an H, e.g. the hex number FF as $FF or FFH.

To convert from decimal numbers to hex we successively divide by 16 and note the remainders. Thus, for example, the decimal number 362 when divided by 16 gives 22 with remainder 10; the 16^0 digit is thus A. Dividing the 22 by 16 gives 1 with remainder 6; the 16^1 digit is thus 6. The hex number is thus 16A.

To convert from binary numbers to hex we group the binary digits in groups of four and replace each group by its equivalent hex digit. For example:

```
1110 1000 1111 0001
  E    8    F    1
```

To convert from hex numbers to binary we reverse the above process and just replace each hex digit by the equivalent binary group of 4.

As with decimal and binary numbers, we can use a point to separate digits which are to positive powers of 16 from those which are to negative powers, i.e. hex fractions.

1.3.4 The binary coded decimal system

The *binary coded decimal system* (BCD) is a widely used system with computers. It is a special form of binary code in which each decimal digit is expressed as a 4 bit binary number. For example, in the most commonly used form of BCD code, each decimal digit is separately written as its binary number and thus the decimal number 15 is 0001 0101. This form of code is termed the 8421 BCD because these numbers represent the weighting attached to successive digits, i.e. 2^3, 2^2, 2^1, 2^0. This code is useful for outputs from microprocessor-based systems where the output has to drive decimal displays, each digit in the display being supplied by the microprocessor with its own binary code.

1.3.5 Review of number systems

Table 1.1 gives examples of numbers in the decimal, binary, BCD, octal and hexadecimal systems.

Table 1.1 Number systems

Decimal	*Binary*	*BCD*	*Octal*	*Hexadecimal*
0	0000	0000 0000	0	0
1	0001	0000 0001	1	1
2	0010	0000 0010	2	2
3	0011	0000 0011	3	3
4	0100	0000 0100	4	4
5	0101	0000 0101	5	5
6	0110	0000 0110	6	6
7	0111	0000 0111	7	7
8	1000	0000 1000	10	8
9	1001	0000 1001	11	9
10	1010	0001 0000	12	A
11	1011	0001 0001	13	B
12	1100	0001 0010	14	C
13	1101	0001 0011	15	D
14	1110	0001 0100	16	E
15	1111	0001 0101	17	F

1.4 Binary arithmetic

Addition of binary numbers follows the following rules:

$0 + 0 = 0$

$0 + 1 = 1 + 0 = 1$

$1 + 1 = 10$ i.e. 0 + carry 1

$1 + 1 + 1 = 11$ i.e. 1 + carry 1

In decimal numbers the addition of 14 and 19 gives 33. In binary numbers this addition becomes:

Augend	01110
Addend	10011
Sum	100001

For bit 0, $0 + 1 = 1$. For bit 1, $1 + 1 = 10$ and so we have 0 with 1 carried to the next column. For bit 3, 1 + 0 + carried 1 = 10. For bit 4, 1 + 0 + carried 1 = 10. We continue this through the various bits and end up with the sum plus a carry 1. The final number is thus 100001. When we have $A + B = C$, then A is termed the *augend*, B the *addend* and C the *sum*.

Subtraction of binary numbers follows these rules:

$0 - 0 = 0$

$1 - 0 = 1$

$1 - 1 = 0$

$0 - 1 = 10 - 1 + \text{borrow} = 1 + \text{borrow}$

When evaluating $0 - 1$, a 1 is borrowed from the next column on the left containing a 1. The following example illustrates this. In decimal numbers the subtraction of 14 from 27 gives 13.

Minuend	11011
Subtrahend	01110
Difference	01101

For bit 0 we have $1 - 0 = 1$. For bit 1 we have $1 - 1 = 0$. For bit 2 we have $0 - 1$. We thus borrow 1 from the next column and so have $10 - 1 = 1$. For bit 3 we have $0 - 1$; remember we borrowed the 1. Again borrowing 1 from the next column, we then have $10 - 1 = 1$. For bit 4 we have $0 - 0 = 0$; remember we borrowed the 1. When subtracting binary numbers A and B to give C, i.e. we have $A - B = C$, then A is termed the *minuend*, B the *subtrahend* and C the *difference*.

Microprocessors have a one-bit flag, i.e. a bit in a register which is either 0 or 1, that saves the carry from the most significant bit of an addition or subtraction and is used to implement carries or borrows between words.

1.4.1 Representing negative numbers

The subtraction of binary numbers is more easily carried out electronically when an alternative method of subtraction is used from that described above. The following techniques indicate how we can specify negative numbers and so turn subtraction into addition. It also enables negative numbers to be specified.

The numbers used so far are referred to as *unsigned*. This is because the number itself contains no indication whether it is negative or positive. A number is said to be *signed* when the most significant bit is used to indicate the sign of the number, a 0 being used if the number is positive and a 1 if it is negative. When we have a positive number then we write it in the normal way with a 0 preceding it. Thus a positive binary number of 10010 would be written as 010010. A negative number of 10010 would be written as 110010. However, this is not the most useful way of representing negative numbers for computers.

A more useful way of representing negative numbers is to use the twos complement method. A binary number has two complements, known as the *ones complement* and the *twos complement*. The ones complement of a binary number is obtained by changing all the 1s in the unsigned number into 0s and the 0s into 1s. The twos complement is then obtained by adding 1 to the ones complement. When we have a negative number, we obtain the twos complement and then sign it with a 1, the positive number being signed by a 0. Consider the representation of the decimal number –3 as a signed twos complement number. We first write the binary number for the unsigned 3 as 0011, then obtain the ones complement of 1100, add 1 to give the unsigned twos complement of 1101, and finally sign it with a 1 to indicate it is negative. The result is thus 11101. The following is another example, the signed twos complement being obtained as an 8 bit number for –6.

Unsigned binary number	000 0110
Ones complement	111 1001
Add 1	1
Unsigned twos complement	111 1010
Signed twos complement	1111 1010

When we have a positive number then we write it in the normal way with a 0 preceding it. Thus a positive binary number of 100 1001 would be written as 01001001. Table 1.2 shows some examples of numbers on this system.

Table 1.2 Signed numbers

Decimal number	*Signed number*	
+127	0111 1111	Just the binary number signed with a 0
etc.		
+8	0000 1000	
+7	0000 0111	
+6	0000 0110	
+5	0000 0101	
+4	0000 0100	
+3	0000 0011	
+2	0000 0010	
+1	0000 0001	
+0	0000 0000	
–1	1111 1111	The twos complement signed with a 1
–2	1111 1110	
–3	1111 1101	
–4	1111 1100	
–5	1111 1011	
–6	1111 1010	
–7	1111 1001	
–8	1111 1000	
etc.		
–127	1000 0000	

Subtraction of a positive number from a positive number involves obtaining the signed twos complement of the subtrahend and then adding it to the signed minuend. Hence, for the subtraction of the decimal number 6 from the decimal number 4 we have

Signed minuend	0000 0100
Subtrahend, signed twos complement	1111 1010
Sum	1111 1110

The most significant bit of the outcome is 1 and so the result is negative. This is the signed twos complement for –2.

Consider another example, the subtraction of 43 from 57. The signed positive number of 57 is 0011 1001. The signed twos complement for –43 is given by:

Unsigned binary number for 43	010 1011
Ones complement	101 0100
Add 1	1
Unsigned twos complement	101 0101
Signed twos complement	1101 0101

Thus we obtain by the addition of the signed positive number and the signed twos complement number:

Signed minuend	0011 1001
Subtrahend, signed twos complement	1101 0101
Sum	0000 1110 + carry 1

The carry 1 is ignored. The result is thus 0000 1110 and since the most significant bit is 0 the result is positive. The result is the decimal number 14.

If we wanted to add two negative numbers, we would obtain the signed twos complement for each number and then add them. Whenever a number is negative we use the signed twos complement, when positive just the signed number. Many microprocessors have a twos complement *overflow flag* that is set when the result of addition or subtraction overflows into the bit position used for the sign.

1.4.2 Addition and subtraction of hex numbers

The following examples illustrate addition of hex numbers:

2 + B = D

F + A = 9 + a carry

A + 2 + a carry = D

Thus if we want to add 20C and AF7 we add them digit by digit, taking account of any carry. Since C + 7 = 13 + a carry, 0 + F + the carry = 0 + a carry and 2 + A + a carry = D then the result is D03.

Hex numbers can be signed like binary numbers. We obtain the 15s complement (equivalent to the ones complement which effectively is obtained by subtraction from 1111 to give the complement) by subtracting a hex number from FFFF. The 16s complement (equivalent to the twos complement) is then obtained by adding 1. Thus to obtain the signed hex number to represent the negative denary number –1000, we first obtain the hex number for 1000 as 03E8. Subtracting this from FFFF gives FC17 and then adding 1 gives FC18 as the 16s complement number.

Consider the decimal number represented by the signed hex number A000. As a 16 bit binary number this is 1010 0000 0000 0000. The 1 for the MSB indicates that the number is negative. The ones complement of the unsigned number is 101 1111 1111. Adding 1 gives 0110 0000 0000 0000 0000 as the twos complement. Hence the decimal number represented by the signed hex number is $-(2^{14} + 2^{13}) = -25\,576$.

1.5 Floating points

In the decimal number system, large numbers such as 120 000 are often written in *scientific notation* as 1.2×10^5 or perhaps 120 ×

10^3 rather than as a number with a fixed location for the decimal point. Likewise 0.000 000 012 can be written as 1.2×10^{-8} or perhaps 12×10^{-9}. Numbers in this form of notation are written in terms of 10 raised to some power.

A similar notation can be used for binary numbers but with them written in terms of 2 raised to some power. For example, we might have 1010 written as 1.010×2^3 or perhaps 10.10×2^2. Because the binary point can be moved to different locations by a choice of the power to which the 2 is raised, this notation is termed *floating point*. The advantage of using floating-point numbers is that, compared with fixed-point representation, a much wider range of numbers can be represented by a given number of digits.

1.5.1 Floating-point arithmetic

If we want to add 2.01×10^3 and 10.2×10^2 we have to make the power (the term *exponent* is generally used) the same for each. Thus we can write $2.01 \times 10^3 + 1.02 \times 10^3$. We can then add them digit by digit, taking account of any carry, to give 2.03×10^3. We adopt a similar procedure for binary floating-point numbers. Thus if we want to add 0.101100×2^4 and 0.111100×2^2 we first adjust them to have the same exponents, e.g. 0.101100×2^4 and 0.001111×2^4, and then add them digit by digit to give 0.111011×2^4.

Likewise for subtraction, digit-by-digit subtraction of floating-point numbers can only occur between two numbers when they have the same exponent. Thus 0.1101100×2^{-4} minus 0.1010100×2^{-5} can be written as $0.01010100 \times 2^{-4} - 0.101010 \times 2^{-4}$ and the result given as 0.1000010×2^{-4}.

1.6 Transmitting alphanumeric characters

When binary information is transmitted by means of an 8-bit word it has to be encoded into a succession of bytes for the microprocessor system and then the output decoded by the receiver. The most commonly used binary code for alphanumeric symbols is the American Standard Code for Information Interchange (ASCII). Up to 128 different characters and control codes are represented using 7 bit binary codes from 000 000 to 111 111, or in hex 00 to 7F. The eighth bit may be used for error-checking purposes.

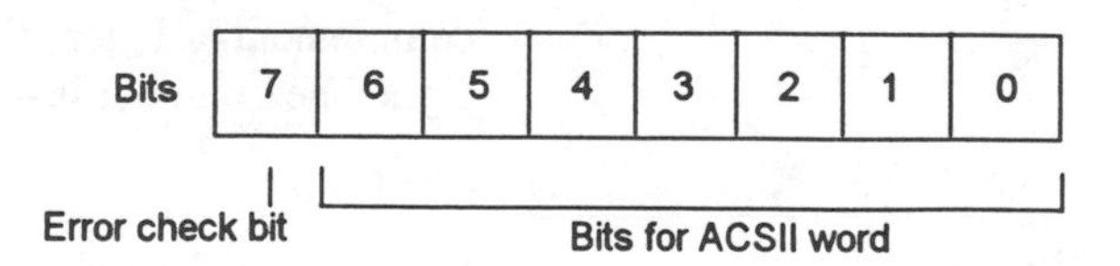

Table 1.3 ASCII code

Hex	*Char.*	*Hex*	*Char.*	*Hex*	*Char.*	*Hex*	*Char.*	*Hex*	*Char.*
00	NUL	1A	SUB	34	4	4E	N	68	h
01	SOH	1B	ESV	35	5	4F	O	69	i
02	STX	1C	FS	36	6	50	P	6A	j
03	ETX	1D	GS	37	7	51	Q	6B	k
04	EOT	1E	RS	38	8	52	R	6C	l
05	ENQ	1F	US	39	9	53	S	6D	m
06	ACK	20	SP	3A	:	54	T	6E	n
07	BEL	21	!	3B	;	55	U	6F	o
08	BS	22	"	3C	<	56	V	70	p
09	HT	23	#	3D	=	57	W	71	q
0A	LF	24	$	3E	>	58	X	72	r
0B	VT	25	%	3F	?	59	Y	73	s
0C	FF	26	&	40	@	5A	Z	74	t
0D	CR	27	'	41	A	5B	[	75	u
0E	SO	28	(	42	B	5C	\	76	v
0F	SI	29	)	43	C	5D	]	77	w
10	DLE	2A	*	44	D	5E	^	78	x
11	DC1	2B	+	45	E	5F	_	79	y
12	DC2	2C	,	46	F	60		7A	z
13	DC3	2D	-	47	G	61	a	7B	{
14	DC4	2E	.	48	H	62	b	7C	|
15	NAK	2F	/	49	I	63	c	7D	}
16	SYN	30	0	4A	J	64	d	7E	~
17	ETB	31	1	4B	K	65	e	7F	DEL
18	CAN	32	2	4C	L	66	f		
19	EM	33	3	4D	M	67	g		

Table 1.4 ASCII codes

Code		*Code*		*Code*	
NUL	All zero	FF	Form feed	CAN	Cancel
SOH	Start of heading	CR	Carriage return	EM	End of medium
STX	Start of text	SO	Shift out	SUB	Substitute
ETX	End of text	SI	Shift in	ESC	Escape
EOT	End of transmission	DLE	Data link escape	FS	File separator
ENQ	Enquiry	DC1	Device control	GS	Group separator
ACK	Acknowledge	DC2	Device control	RS	Record separator
BEL	Audible signal	DC3	Device control	US	Unit separator
BS	Backspace	DC4	Device control	SP	Space
HT	Horizontal tabulation	NAK	Negative acknowledge	DEL	Delete
LF	Line feed	SYN	Synchronous idle		
VT	Vertical tabulation	ETB	End of transmission block		

Table 1.3 shows the code and Table 1.4 the meaning of the code terms. As an illustration of the use of ASCII, suppose we want to transmit the message THE END. The string of codes to be transmitted are 54 48 45 20 45 4E 44. Note that we have to include a code for the space between the words. Likewise if we wanted to include the full stop (.) we would need to add the code for it, i.e. 2E.

1.7 Microprocessor system

The main constituents of a microprocessor system are:

1. The microprocessor, or central processing unit (CPU), to process the data according to a program.
2. Memory to hold program instructions and data.
3. The input and output interfaces to handle communications between the computer and the outside world; the term *port* is used for the interface units.

Digital signals move from one element to another along three buses. A *bus* is just a number of conductors along which electrical signals can be carried.

1. *Data bus*
   This carries the data associated with the processing function of the microprocessor, e.g. a computer word from the memory, or input/output interfaces, to the microprocessor or from the microprocessor to them. There can be problems if we just connect devices to the data bus in that if a device is not in use it may present a low impedance current path for data and prevent the logic levels on the bus from being determined by the device to which they are addressed. To overcome this problem, *tristate output interfaces* are used so that when a device is off it presents a high impedance. The three states the interface can have are thus transmitting a low signal, transmitting a high signal, or presenting a high impedance.
2. *Address bus*
   Each storage location within a memory device has a unique identification, termed its *address*, so that the system is able to select a particular instruction or data item in the memory. Each input/output interface has an address. When a particular address is selected by its address being placed on the address bus, only that location is open to communications from the microprocessor. Devices normally have tristate outputs so that when not enabled for communication they present a high impedance to the data bus. When the address of a device appears on the address bus it becomes *enabled* so that signals can be received or outputted by it. When there are more than a few devices a logic circuit called an *address decoder* is used so that, when the address for a device appears on the bus, the output from the decoder activates the device. This is termed enabling its *chip select* (CS) input.
3. *Control bus*
   This carries the signals relating to the control actions of the microprocessor and the memory devices. For example, it is necessary for the microprocessor to inform memory devices

whether they are to read data from an input
data to an output device. The term *read* is used
signal and *write* for sending a signal. A logic
write line indicates that that a read operation is to be performed from the location whose address is currently on the address bus; a logic 0 on the read/write line indicates that a write operation has to be performed to that location. The convention for indicating these conditions is a horizontal bar. A horizontal bar over the WRITE indicates that the write operation is active when there is a logic 0 on the line; the absence of a bar over the READ indicates that a logic 1 on the line gives the read operation. This is how it is written:

$$\text{READ}/\overline{\text{WRITE}}$$

The control bus is also used to carry the system clock signals; these are used to synchronise all the actions of the microprocessor. The clock is a crystal-controlled oscillator and produces pulses at regular intervals. In older microprocessors, the clock–oscillator is external to the microprocessor; with more recent microprocessors it is usually incorporated within the same chip. The quartz crystal is, however, still required as an external addition.

Figure 1.2 illustrates the general arrangement of a microcomputer system with its address bus, data bus and control bus, a crystal-controlled clock and including two types of memory device, an input/output element and an address decoder.

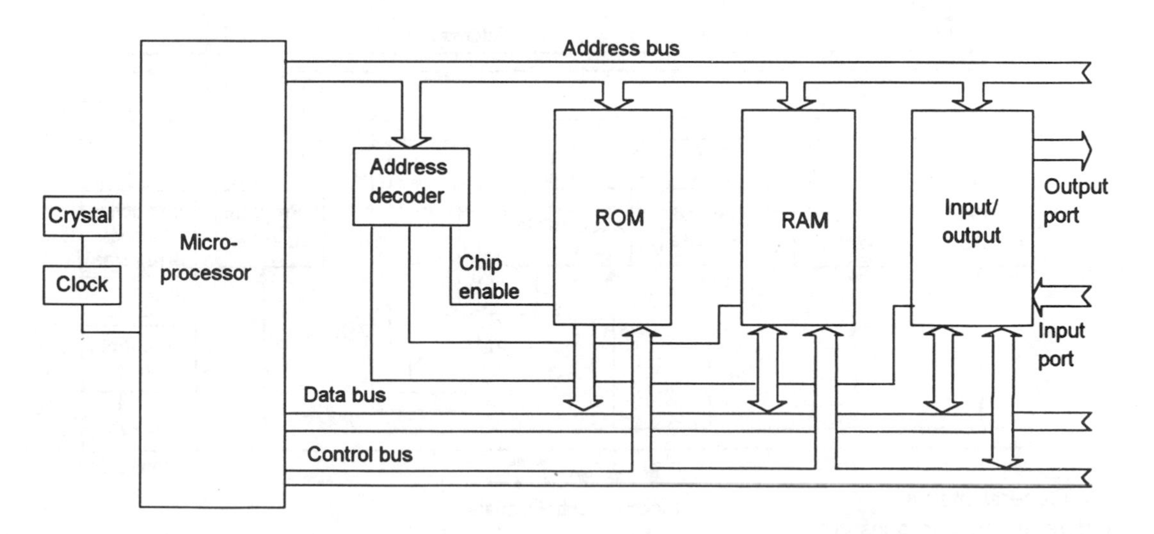

Fig. 1.2 The bus system

Read-only memory (ROM) is a memory used to store contents which are fixed during manufacture and are retained even when the power supply to the system is switched off. *Random access memory* (RAM) is used to store temporary information, i.e. data currently being operated on. The term *random access* is used because you can read any location in the store just as quickly as any other. Such a memory can be read or written to and is generally lost when the power supply is switched off. The address decoder is an element used by the microprocessor to decode its address instructions and determine which of the chips in the system is to be enabled and so addressed. The input/output element is to interface the system with external input/output devices.

Systems which have the processing element, some memory and input/output interfaces all on the same chip are termed *microcontrollers* (see Chapter 2).

1.8 The microprocessor

The microprocessor is generally referred to as the *central processing unit* (CPU). It is responsible for executing arithmetic and logic operations on the binary data being processed and also for controlling the timing and sequencing of operations in the system. The internal structure, the term *architecture* is used, of a microprocessor depends on the microprocessor concerned. Figure 1.3 indicates, in a simplified manner, the general architecture of a microprocessor.

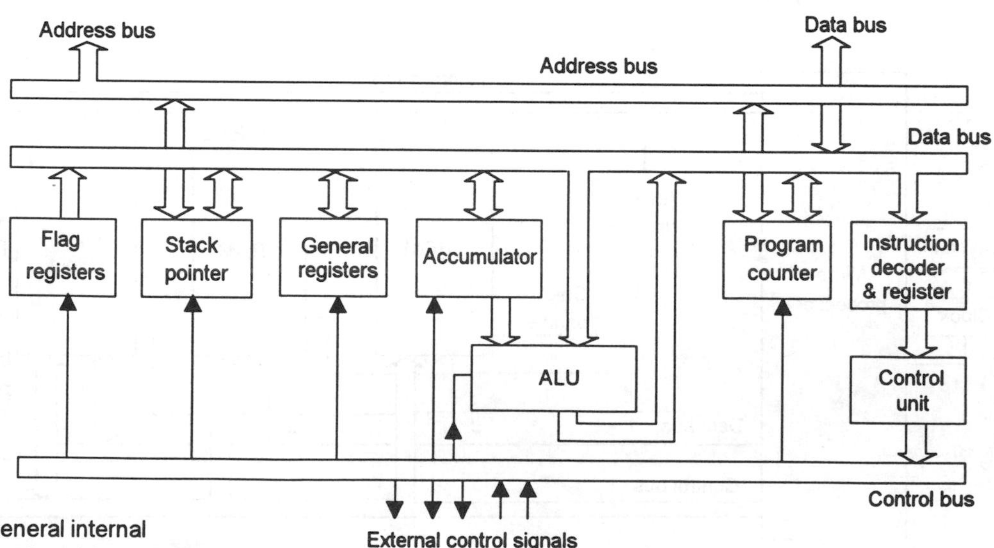

Fig. 1.3 General internal architecture of a microprocessor

1. *Arithmetic and logic unit* (ALU)
   This element is responsible for data manipulation and carries out arithmetic operations of addition and subtraction and logic operations of AND, OR, NOT and EXCLUSIVE-OR.
2. *Registers*
   These are memory locations within the microprocessor and are used to store information involved in program execution. A microprocessor will contain a group of registers, each type of register having a different function.
3. *Control unit*
   This controls the timing of operations within the system.

With an 8 bit microprocessor, the internal data bus can handle 8 bit numbers and the address bus is 16 bits wide (in diagrams the comparative width of a bus is usually indicated by the width of the track shown for it). An 8 bit microprocessor can perform operations between two 8 bit numbers and deliver a corresponding 8 bit result. A 16 bit address bus can handle 2^{16} data locations and so 65 536 different addresses. A 16 bit microprocessor can operate with 16 bit numbers. Generally a 16 bit microprocessor has a 20 bit address bus and so can handle 1 048 576 different addresses.

The number, size and types of registers vary from one microprocessor to another. Here are some of them:

1. *Accumulator*
   The accumulator register (A) is where data for an input to the arithmetic and logic unit is temporarily stored. In order for the microprocessor to be able to access, i.e. read, instructions or data in the memory, it has to supply the address of the required memory word using the address bus. When this has been done, the required instructions or data can be read into the microprocessor using the data bus. Since only one memory location can be addressed at once, temporary storage has to be used when, for example, numbers are combined. For example, in the addition of two numbers, one of the numbers is fetched from one address and placed in the accumulator register while the microprocessor fetches the other number from the other memory address. Then the two numbers can be processed by the arithmetic and logic section of the microprocessor. The result is then transferred back into the accumulator register. The accumulator register is thus a temporary holding register for data to be operated on by the arithmetic and logic unit and also, after the operation, the register for holding the results. It is thus involved in all data transfers associated with the execution of arithmetic and logic operations.

2. *Flag register or status register, or condition code register*
This contains information concerning the result of the latest process carried out in the arithmetic and logic unit. It contains individual bits, called *flags*, with each bit having special significance. The status of the latest operation is indicated by each flag being set or reset. For example, they can be used to indicate whether the last operation resulted in a negative result, a zero result, a carry output (e.g. the sum of two binary numbers such as 101 and 110 has resulted in a result (1)011 which gives a carry of 1), an overflow (used when performing arithmetic on signed numbers and the result causes the sign bit to overflow) or whether the program is allowed to be interrupted so an external event can occur. The following are common flags:

Flag	*Set, i.e. 1*	*Reset, i.e. 0*
Z	result is zero	result is not zero
N	result is negative	result is not negative
C	carry is generated	carry is not generated
V	overflow occurs	overflow does not occur
I	interrupt is ignored	interrupt is processed normally

As an illustration, consider the state of the Z, N, C and V flags for the operation of adding the hex numbers 02 and 06. The result is 08. Since it is not zero then Z is 0. The result is positive so N is 0. There is no carry so C is 0. The unsigned result is within the range –128 to +127 and so there is no overflow and V is 0. Now consider the flags when the hex numbers added are F9 and 08. the result is (1)01. The result is not zero so Z is 0. Since it is positive then N is 0. The unsigned result has a carry and so C is 1. The unsigned result is within the range –128 to +127 and so V is 0.

3. *Program counter register (PC) or instruction pointer (IP)*
This is the register used to allow the microprocessor to keep track of its position in a program. This register contains the address of the memory location that contains the next program instruction. As each instruction is executed the program counter register is updated so that it contains the address of the memory location where the next instruction to be executed is stored. The program counter is incremented by 1 each time so that the microprocessor executes instructions sequentially unless an instruction, such as JUMP or BRANCH, changes the program counter out of that sequence.

4. *General-purpose registers*
These may serve as temporary storage for data or addresses and they may be used in operations involving transfers between various other registers.

5. *Memory address register*
   The term *memory address register* is used for a register that is used to store addresses. For example, in the summing of two numbers the address register is loaded with the address of the first number. The data at this address is then moved to the accumulator. The address of the second number is then loaded into the address register. The data at this address is then added to the data in the accumulator.

6. *Stack pointer register*
   Another form of address register is the *stack pointer register*. The *stack* is a special area of the memory in which program counter values can be stored when a subroutine part of a program is being used. In some microprocessors, e.g. the Rockwell 6502, the stack pointer points to the first free location in the stack; in the Zilog Z80 it points to the last used location.

7. *Special-purpose registers*
   The *index register* allows the original address specified in an instruction to be modified by the contents of this register. Thus instead of stating address 1002 we can state a base address of 1000 and then use the index register to indicate 2 as the second address on from 1000.

8. *Instruction register (IR)*
   This stores an instruction. After fetching an instruction from the memory, the CPU stores it in the instruction register. It can then be decoded and used to execute an operation.

The number and form of the registers, as well as the names used to describe them, depend on the microprocessor concerned. The following sections illustrate this by considering the basic architecture of a number of typical 8 bit microprocessors.

1.8.1 The Rockwell 6502 microprocessor

The Rockwell 6502 is an 8 bit microprocessor and has a bus system directly compatible with the Motorola 6800 series of integrated circuits; Fig. 1.4 shows a functional block diagram representation of the Rockwell 6502 microprocessor, the registers and the pin connections. The 6502 has five internal registers:

1. An 8 bit accumulator.

2. A processor status (flag) register providing the usual flag bits for negative (N), zero (Z), carry (C) and overflow (V). A decimal bit (D) is used to indicate when the accumulator is working in BCD mode and an interrupt bit (I) to set interrupts. The break bit (B) provides a software interrupt facility.

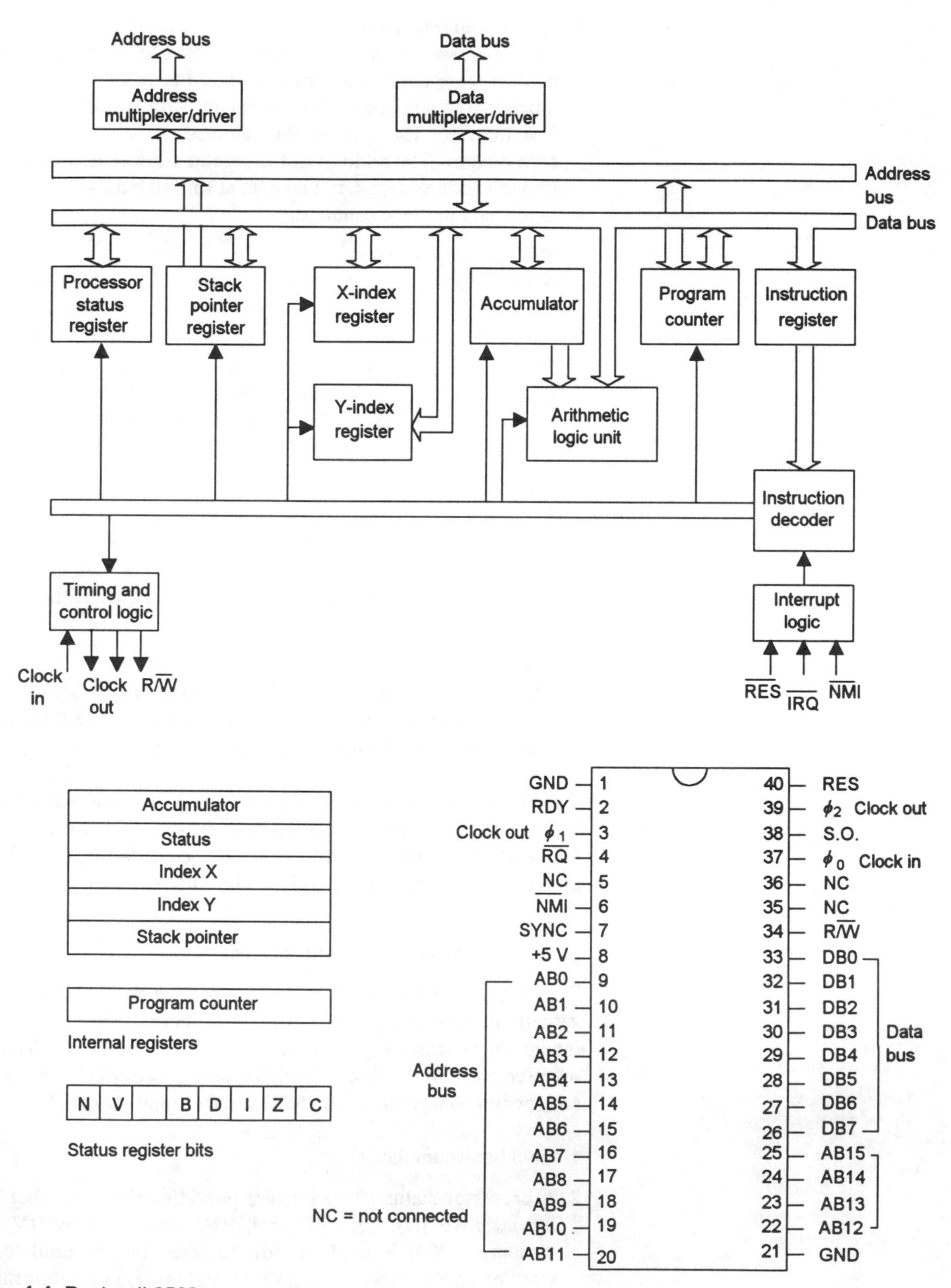

Fig. 1.4 Rockwell 6502

3. Two 8 bit X and Y index registers.
4. A stack pointer
5. A program counter

The 6502 is packaged in a standard 40-pin package. These give the connections:

1. *Address bus*
   A0 to A15 constitute a 16 bit address bus.
2. *Data bus*
   D0 to D7 constitute an 8 bit bidirectional data bus.
3. *System control*
   The R/W pin is taken high, i.e. 1, to read and low, i.e. 0, to write.
4. *Processor control*
   There are three interrupt lines to provide the means of interrupting the microprocessor when it is executing a program. The RES line is used to reset the microprocessor, the IRQ is used for interrupt request and NMI, non-maskable interrupt. The IRQ interrupt may be turned off, i.e. masked, whereas the NMI may not.
5. *Clock*
   The ϕ_0 input is for a single-phase external crystal-controlled oscillator. The ϕ_1 and ϕ_2 clock out signals are used to synchronise operations.

1.8.2 The Z80 microprocessor

The Zilog Z80 is an 8 bit microprocessor based on the Intel 8080, having all the 8080 instructions and some more; Fig. 1.5 shows a functional block diagram representation, details of the registers and Fig. 1.6 the pin connections. The register set includes:

1. Two independent 8 bit accumulators and associated flag registers.
2. Two matched sets of general-purpose registers, each set containing six 8 bit registers that may be used individually as 8 bit registers or as 16 bit register pairs (BC, DE and HL).
3. Two index registers IX and IY. These registers are used to hold 16 bit addresses which are the base addresses for data tables stored in memory. A particular item in the table may then be accessed by adding a number to the index register value, e.g. for the fifth item in the table we just add 5.

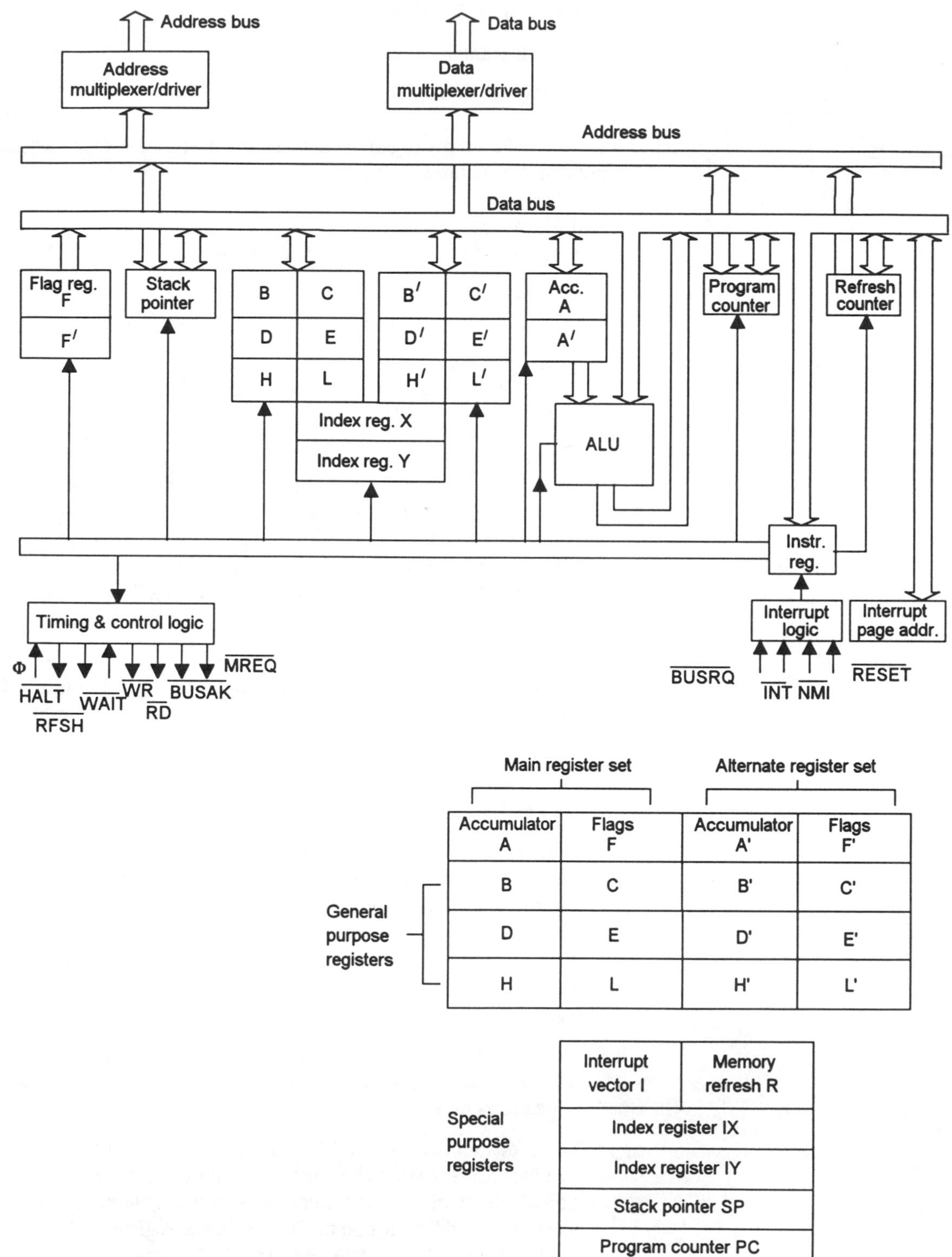

Fig. 1.5 Zilog Z80

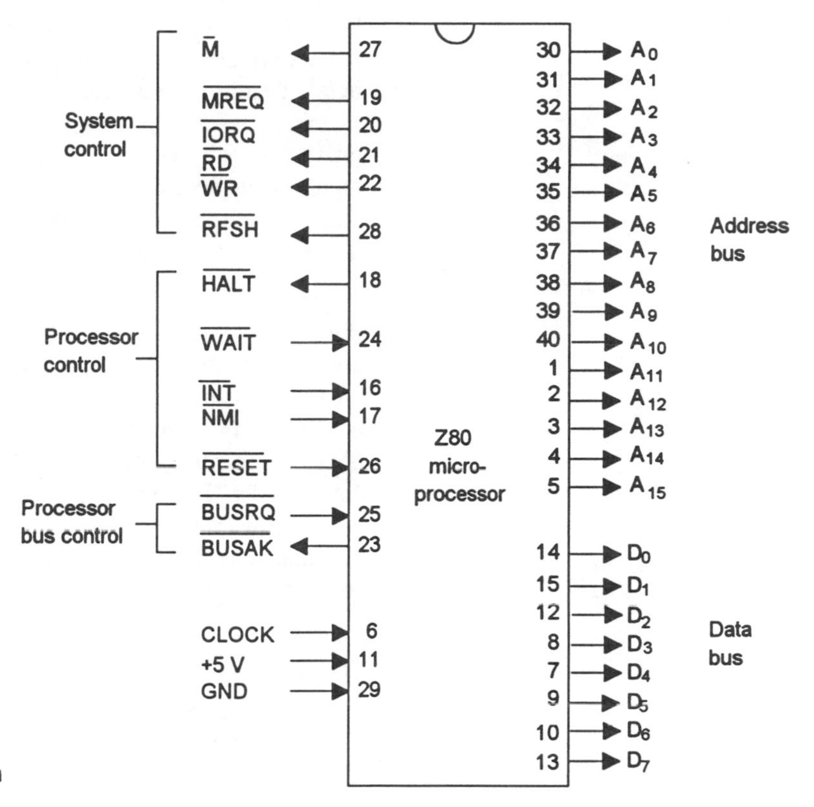

Fig. 1.6 Z80 pin configuration

4. An interrupt vector register; this is used only in a special mode of operation where an indirect call to a memory location is generated in response to an interrupt.

5. The memory refresh register is used to automatically refresh dynamic memories (see Section 1.10.2).

The Z80 is packaged in a standard 40-pin package, the pin connections being:

1. *Address bus*
   A_0 to A_{15} constitute a 16 bit address bus with A_0 the least significant bit and A_{15} the most significant bit of the address. They are tristate outputs and so in a high impedance state when the address bus is disabled.

2. *Data bus*
   D_0 to D_7 constitute an 8 bit bidirectional data bus and are tri-state; D_0 is the least significant bit and D_7 is the most significant bit.

3. *System control*

   Pins 27, 19, 20, 2, 22 and 28 are used for system control. Thus memory request, pin 19, is used to indicate that the address bus holds a valid address for a memory read or write operation. Memory read, pin 21, is used to indicate that the microprocessor wants to read data from memory or an input/output device. Memory write, pin 22, is used to indicate that the microprocessor data bus holds valid data to be stored in the addressed memory or input/output device.

4. *Processor control*

   Pins 18, 24, 16, 17 and 26 are used for signals for microprocessor control. The halt signal is used to indicate that the microprocessor has executed a HALT program instruction. The wait input is used to indicate to the microprocessor that the addressed memory or input/output device is not ready for a data transfer. The interrupt requests on pins 16 and 17 are used by input/output devices to request an interruption of the program. The reset input on pin 26 is used to reset the program counter to zero.

5. *Bus control*

   The input on pin 25 is used to request that the address bus, data bus and tristate output control signals go to a high impedance state. The output on pin 23 is used to indicate that this has happened.

6. *Clock*

   Pin 6, usually denoted by the symbol ϕ, is used for the input of a single-phase clock signal.

1.8.3 The Motorola 6800/6802 microprocessor

The 6800 was the first 8 bit microprocessor from Motorola and needed an external clock generator. The later 6802 has the same basic architecture and instructions as the 6800 but incorporates a built-in clock generator. Figure 1.7(a) shows a functional block diagram representation of the Motorola 6800 microprocessor. It has (Fig. 1.7(b)) two accumulator registers, a status register, an index register, a stack pointer register and a program counter register. The status register has flag bits to show negative N, zero Z, carry C, overflow V, half-carry H and interrupt I. The half-carry flag is used in binary coded decimal arithmetic and is set to logic 1 if a carry is generated between bit 3 and bit 4 of a calculation.

1. *Address bus*

   The 16 pins, labelled A0 to A15, are used for the address bus. They are tristate outputs and so in a high impedance state when the output is disabled.

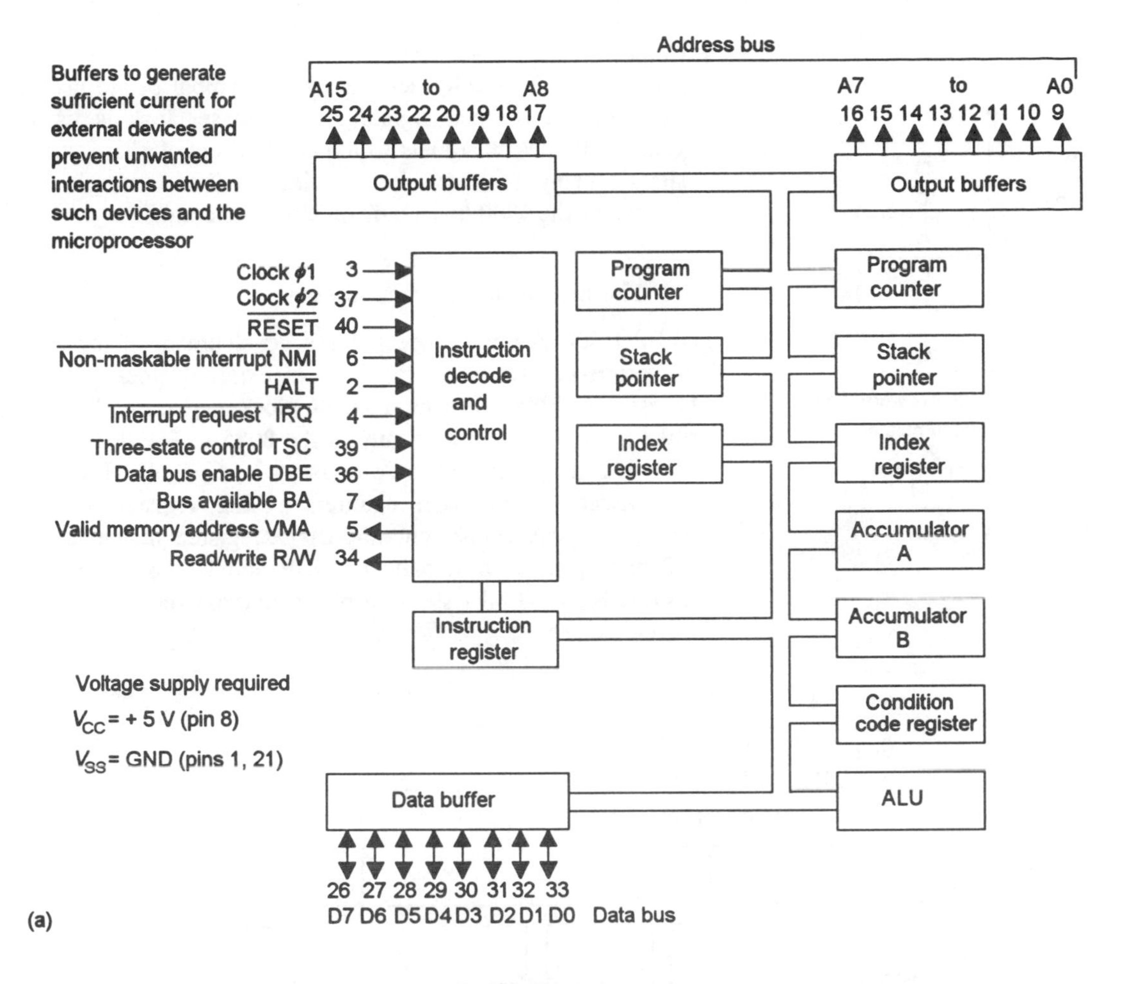

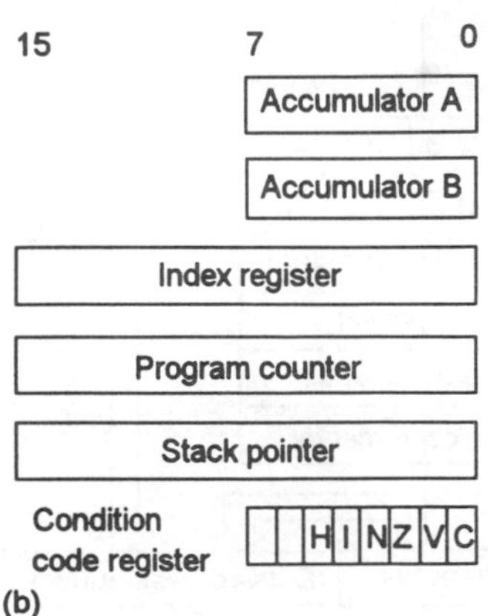

Fig. 1.7 Motorola 6800

2. *Data bus*
   The 8 pins, labelled D0 to D7, are used for the data bus. It is bidirectional and has tristate outputs.

3. *Control*
   Pins 40, 6, 2, 4, 39, 36, 7, 5 and 34 are used for control. When the HALT input occurs, all activity is halted. An input to the three-state control pin causes the address lines and the READ/WRITE line to go into the high impedance state. The READ/WRITE output signals to memory and input/output devices to indicate whether the microprocessor is in a read or write state. The valid memory address output on pin 5 signals to memory or input/output devices that there is a valid address on the address bus. The interrupt requests on pins 4 and 6 are used to request an interruption in the microprocessor program. Reset, on pin 40 is used to reset the program counter to zero. The data bus enable input on pin 36 is used to enable other devices to take control of the data bus; a bus available output on pin 7 indicates that the address bus is available.

4. *Clock*
   Pins 3 and 37, usually denoted by the symbol ϕ, are used for the input of a clock signal. A two-phase clock is used to generate two clock signals which are 180° out of phase, the two signals being used for the two inputs. The Motorola 6802 version of the 6800 has a built-in clock generator.

15	7	0
PSW		A
B		C
D		E
H		L
Stack pointer		
Program counter		

PSW = program status word (flags)
A = primary accumulator

7	6		4		2		0
S	Z		AC		P		CY

Flags in the PSW register

(a)

1.8.4 The Intel 8085A microprocessor

The Intel 8085A microprocessor is a development of the earlier 8080 processor; the 8080 required an external clock generator whereas the 8085A has an in-built clock generator. Programs written for the 8080 can be run on the 8085A. The 8085A (Fig. 1.8(a)) has six general-purpose registers B, C, D, E, H and L, a stack pointer, a program counter, a flag register and two temporary registers. The general-purpose registers may be used as six 8 bit registers or in pairs BC, DE and HL as three 16 bit registers. Figure 1.8(b) shows a block diagram representation of the architecture.

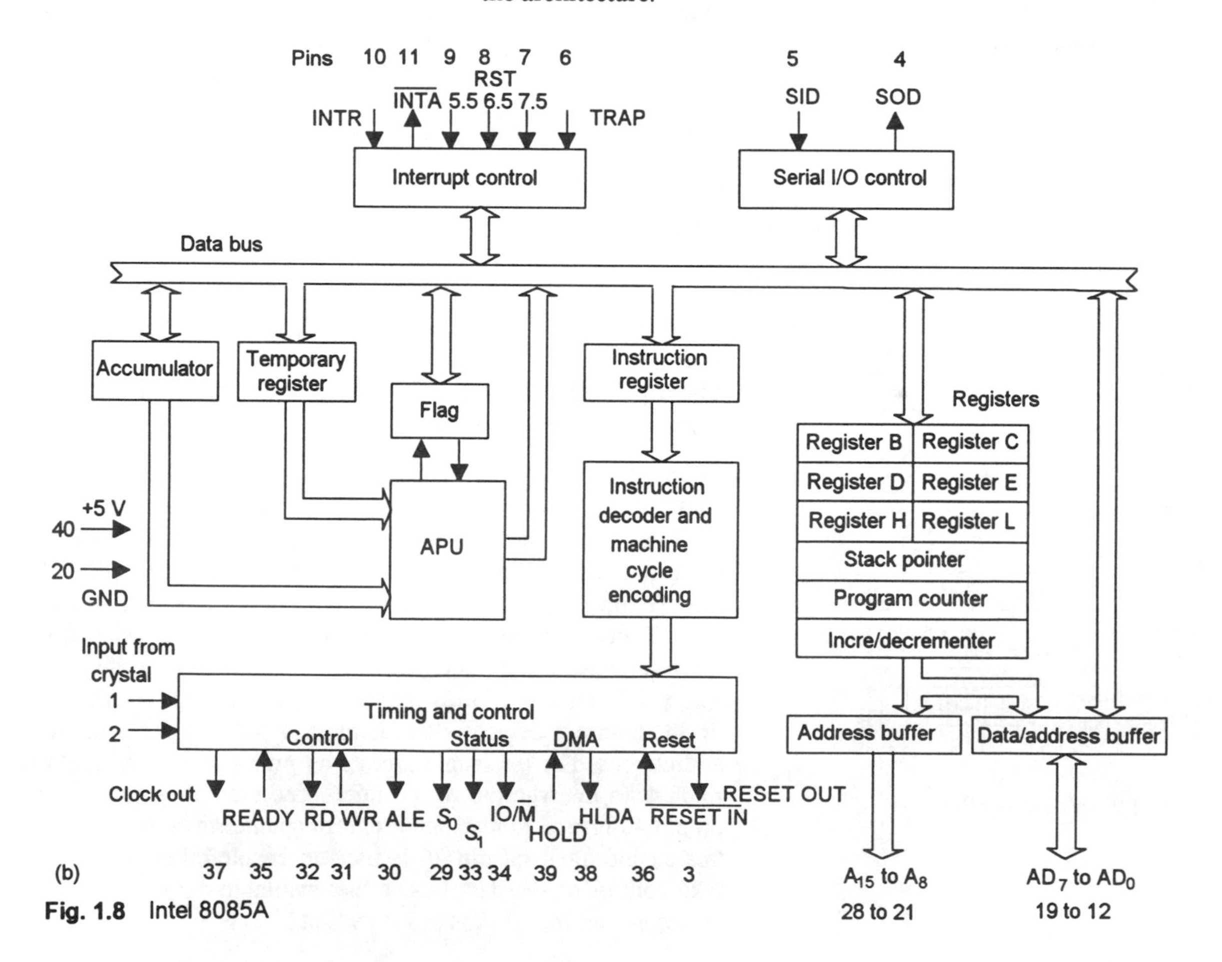

Fig. 1.8 Intel 8085A

The five flags in the flag register are the sign flag S, the zero flag Z, the auxiliary carry flag AC, the parity flag P and the carry flag CY. The zero flag is set if the result is zero. The sign flag is set to the condition of the most significant bit. The auxiliary flag is used to indicate an overflow or carry out of bit 3 of the accumulator and is commonly used in BCD arithmetic. The parity flag is used to test for the number of 1 bits in the accumulator. The carry flag is set or reset by arithmetic operations; an overflow from an 8 bit addition causes it to be set to 1.

1. *Address bus*
   The 8085A has a 16 bit address bus. The eight pins labelled A8 to A15 are used for the most significant bits of the address bus. They are *tristate outputs* giving a high impedance state when the output is disabled.

2. *Input/output data/address bus*
   The signals for the 8 bit data bus share the same set of pins as the lower 8 bits of the address bus. The address/data bus transmits an address when the address latch enable ALE control line is high and data when it is low. It thus provides an output signal for latching, i.e. holding, the low-order byte of the address while the high-order byte is obtained, hence it allows 16 bit addresses to be used.

3. *Timing and control*
   The READ/WRITE output indicates to memory and input/output devices whether the microprocessor is in a read or write state. A high level indicates the data on the data bus is to be read; a low level indicates that the data is to be written. The normal standby state of this signal is high, i.e. read. If READY is high it indicates that the memory or input/output device is ready to receive or send data. HOLD is used to indicate that another master is requesting the use of the address and data buses. HOLD ACKNOWLEDGE (HLDA) is used to indicate that the microprocessor has received the HOLD signal. RESET IN sets the program counter to zero; RESET OUT is used by the microprocessor to indicate that it is being reset.

4. *Interrupt control*
   There are five different forms of interrupt input to request interruptions in a program.

5. *Serial input/output control*
   The serial input SID and the serial output SOD controls are used to input and output data in serial form, rather than parallel. Data from SID is transferred to bit 7 of the accumulator. A single serial bit can be outputted via SOD. The serial output can be used as a one-bit control output.

6. *Clock*
   A complete clock generator is incorporated and just requires the input from a quartz crystal to establish the timing for its operation. The CLOCK OUT pin gives a clock output having a frequency of one-half the frequency of the crystal.

1.9 The fetch–execute cycle

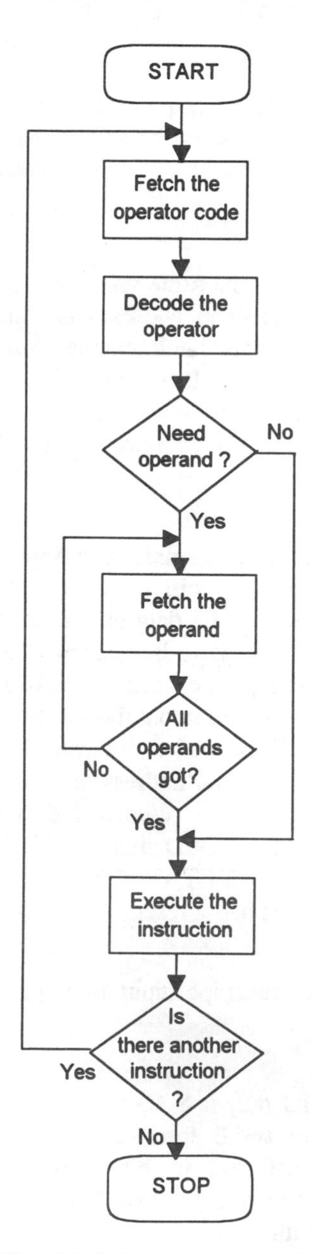

Fig. 1.9 Fetch–execute cycle

The microprocessor program consists of a sequence of instructions, each consisting of an operator code defining the operation to be carried out and an operand code defining the data or location of the data on which the instruction is to operate. The operator code is usually referred to as the *opcode* and is described by one, two or three bytes. Each instruction is carried out by a sequence of operations, known as the *fetch–execute cycle*. This is basically *fetch the next instruction, decode, execute* as the flow chart in Fig. 1.9 indicates:

1. *Fetch* the operator code from memory via the data bus and store it in the instruction register. It does this by providing an address on the address bus and then reading the instruction at this address from the data bus. The address of the instruction is contained in the program counter, and after each part of the operator code has been put into the instruction register, the microprocessor increments the program counter by one. Thus when the entire operator code for an instruction has been put into the instruction register, the program counter may have been incremented by one, two or three, depending upon the size of the operation code. The program counter then points to the next instruction.

2. *Decode* the operator code within the microprocessor's instruction decoder unit to determine the nature of the operation specified by the instruction.

3. *Fetch* further data if necessary.

4. *Execute* the instruction.

5. Following the execution of the instruction, the microprocessor progresses to the fetch phase of the next fetch–decode–execute cycle.

As an illustration of the cycle, consider the Z80 instruction:

```
LD A,(nn)
```

This means copy (LoaD) the contents of memory address nn into the accumulator A. LD A is a mnemonic which when trans- lated into code that the microprocessor can understand, termed *machine code*, is hex 3A. The nn indicates that the address is

Address	Data
1800	3A
1801	01
1802	33
1803	

Fig. 1.10 Memory

located in two memory locations. Thus we might, for example, want to copy the contents at address 3301. We have a three-byte instruction which is stored in memory at three addresses as shown in Fig. 1.10: the machine code for LD A in, say, memory address 1800, the lower byte of the address at which the data is stored at 1801 and the upper byte at 1802. The fetch–execute cycle then involves the following steps:

1. Fetch the opcode 3A from memory via the data bus and transfer it to the instruction register. Increment the program counter by 1.
2. The instruction register passes 3A to the decoder, which determines that 3A is the code for LD A and that a 16 bit, i.e. two-byte, address must follow. The instruction register has thus to increment the program counter two more times before the instruction is complete.
3. Fetch the low byte of the external address, 01 in the above example, from the memory and transfer it to the lower eight bits of the memory address register. Increment the program counter by 1.
4. Fetch the high byte of the external address from the memory, 33 in the above example, and transfer it to the upper eight bits of the memory address register. Increment the program counter by 1.
5. Put the address in the memory address register onto the address bus and transfer the data from this address, via the data bus, to the accumulator.

1.9.1 Timing diagrams

All the microprocessor actions are synchronised by a continuous train of regularly timed pulses known as the *clock*. These clock pulses are generally obtained from an oscillator circuit which has a very stable frequency controlled by a quartz crystal. Each clock period is generally called a *T-state* or *time state*. Thus if the clock frequency is 2.0 MHz then each T-state lasts $1/(2.0 \times 10^6)$ = 500 ns. Each basic operation is called a *machine cycle*. The number of T-states in a machine cycle depends on the instruction which the microprocessor is executing, each taking at least 3 or 4 T-states. An instruction cycle will start with a fetch which is the first machine cycle for the instruction and then it will be followed by further machine cycles to complete the instruction. Figure 1.11 shows the instruction cycle involving a fetch, read and write sequence.

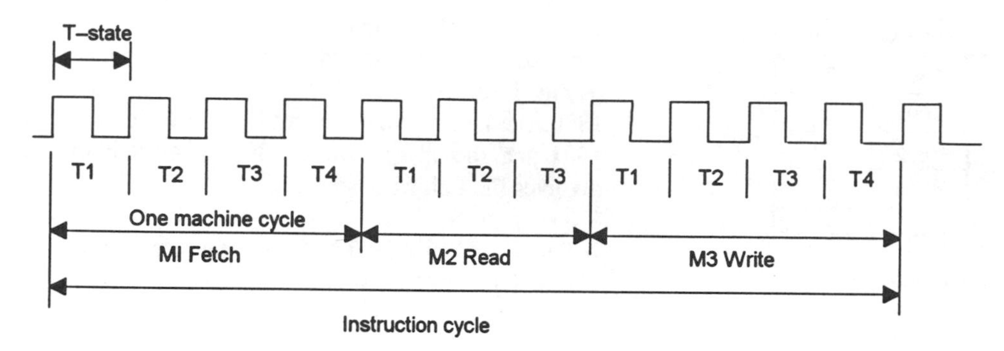

Fig. 1.11 Example of clock cycles

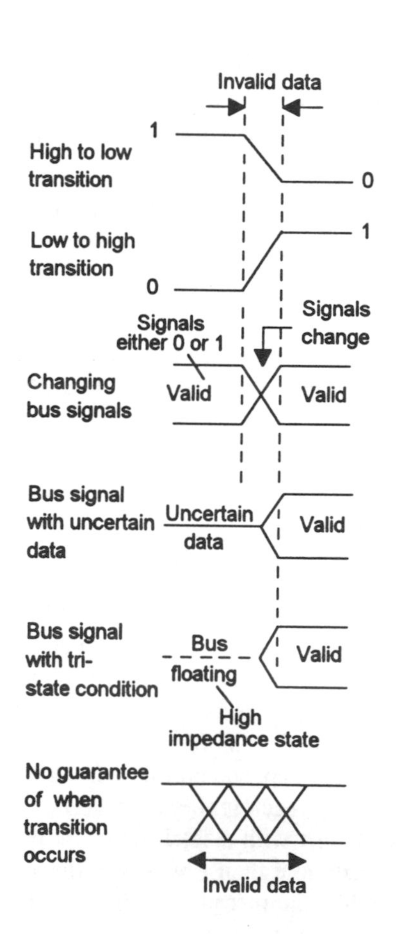

Fig. 1.12 Signal conditions

A *timing diagram* shows in correct time sequence the states of all the bus and control lines during an operation. The diagram shows stable bus signals giving valid data as two lines representing logic low and logic high. During a transition when the bus signals change, the timing diagram indicates how long the transition takes. During the transition the data is invalid. The condition of data on a bus or control line may, at any instant, be either valid, invalid or uncertain. Figure 1.12 shows how these states may be represented diagramatically.

As an illustration, Fig. 1.13(a) shows a timing diagram for that part of an instruction cycle of a Zilog Z80 concerned with the machine cycle for the opcode fetch, Fig. 1.13(b) for read or write. Timing diagrams are given in the information sheets supplied by the manufacturers of the microprocessors.

1. The program counter places an address on the address bus A0–A15 at the beginning of the cycle.
2. After half a clock cycle the memory request signal goes active.
3. The read line also goes active to indicate that the memory should read the data, i.e. the address, on the data bus.
4. The data is put on the line data line D0–D7 and the read signal and memory request signal are then turned off.
5. During T3 and T4 the address signal is refreshed. The memory request signal is used, with the refresh signal, to initiate a refresh read of all memory elements.

If the wait line is activated during the above fetch cycle, the read part of the cycle can be prolonged and thus the time extended to match the access time of a memory device.

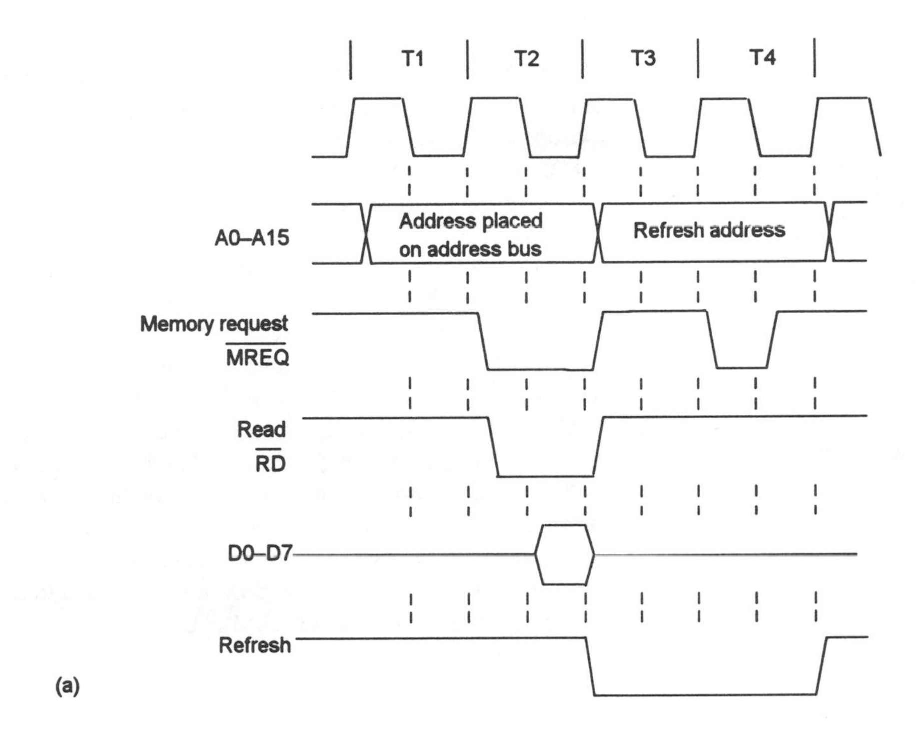

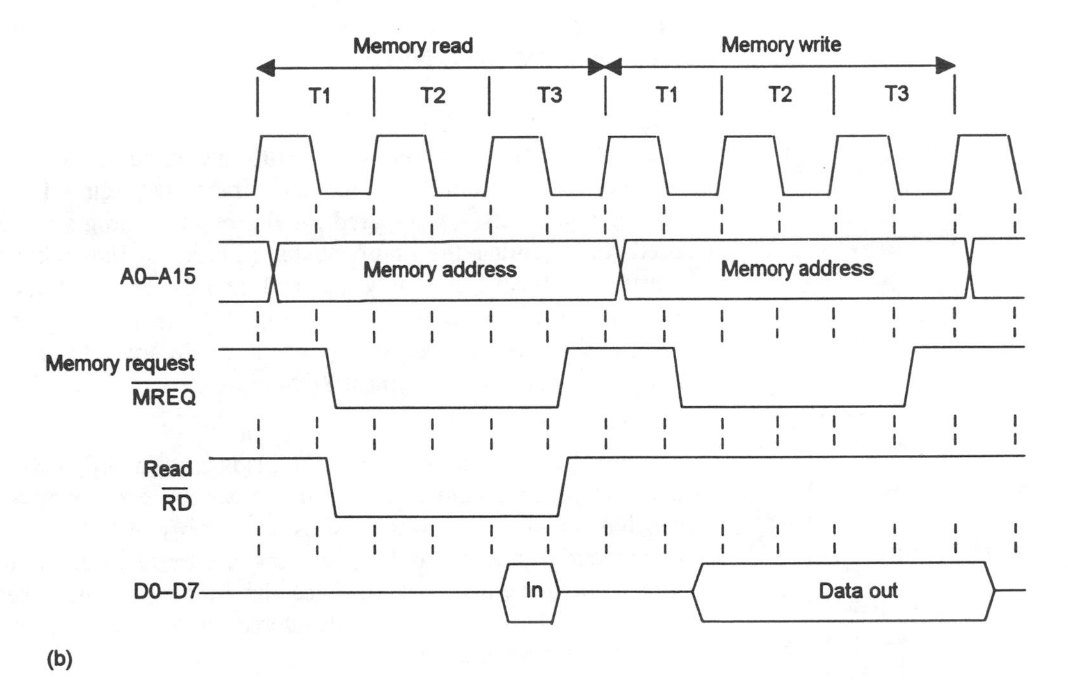

Fig. 1.13 Z80 Timing diagrams:
(a) fetch, (b) read or write

1.10 Memory

The memory unit stores binary data and takes the form of one or more integrated circuits. The memory elements in a unit consist essentially of large numbers of storage cells with each cell capable of storing either a 0 or a 1 bit. The storage cells are grouped in locations with each location capable of storing one word (Fig. 1.14). In order to access the stored word, each location is identified by a unique address. Thus with an 8 bit address bus we can have $2^8 = 256$ different addresses, with each perhaps capable of storing one byte, i.e. a group of eight bits. The number of storage cells is thus $256 \times 8 = 2048$. The size of a memory unit is specified in terms of the number of storage locations available with $1K = 2^{10} = 1024$ locations and thus the above memory is specified as 2K × 8 bit. With a 16 bit address bus we can have 2^{16} = 65 536 different addresses and so we might have, with 8 bit word storage at each address, four 16K × 8 bit memory chips.

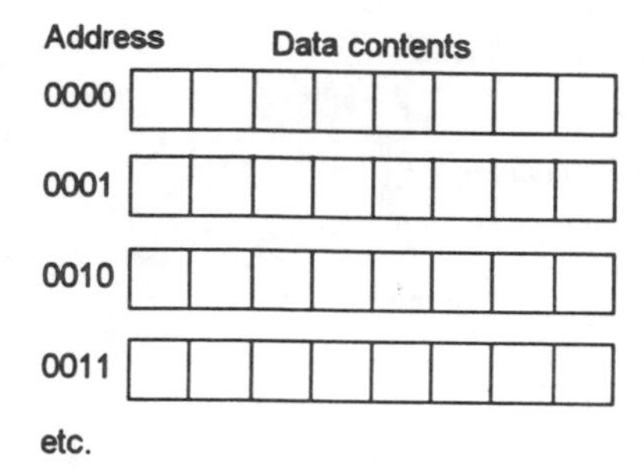

Fig. 1.14 Memory addresses

There are two main types of memory used with a microprocessor system: *read-only memory* (ROM) and *random access memory* (RAM). The major difference between these two types of memory is that ROM does not lose its stored data when the power is switched off but RAM does.

1.10.1 ROM

There are two types of read-only memory; they are termed masked ROM and programmable ROM (PROM). PROM can also occur as EPROM and EEPROM:

1. *Masked ROM*
   Masked ROMs are programmed with the required contents during the manufacture of the integrated circuit. A photographic mask is prepared for the required program and used to determine the on/off status of links in the memory matrix. The data can only be read and is used for fixed programs such as computer operating systems and programs for dedicated microprocessor applications. Figure 1.15 shows the pin connections of a typical ROM chip.

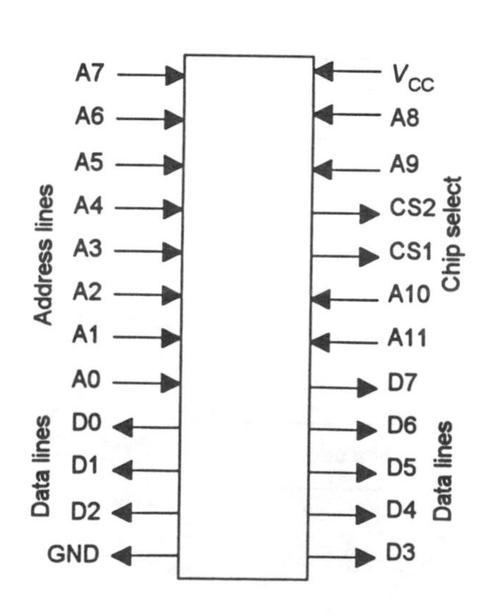

Fig. 1.15 ROM chip

2. *PROM*
   The term *programmable ROM* (PROM) is used for ROM chips that can be programmed by the user. Initially every memory cell has a fusible link which keeps its memory at 0. The 0 is permanently changed to 1 by sending a current through the fuse to permanently open it. Once the fusible link has been opened the data is permanently stored in the memory and cannot be further changed.
3. *EPROM*
   The term *erasable and programmable ROM* (EPROM) is used for ROMs that can be programmed and then altered at a later

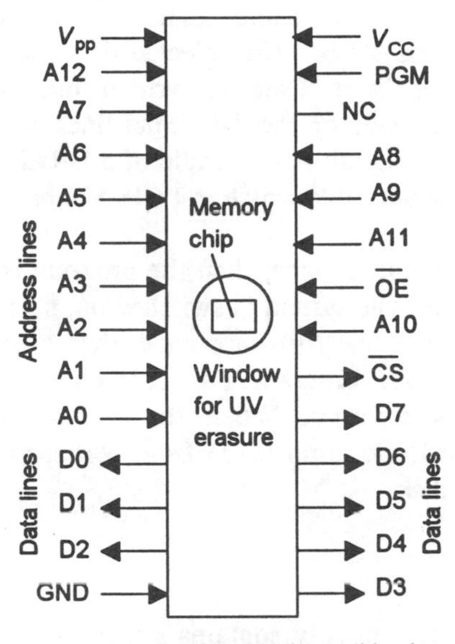

Fig. 1.16 EPROM chip

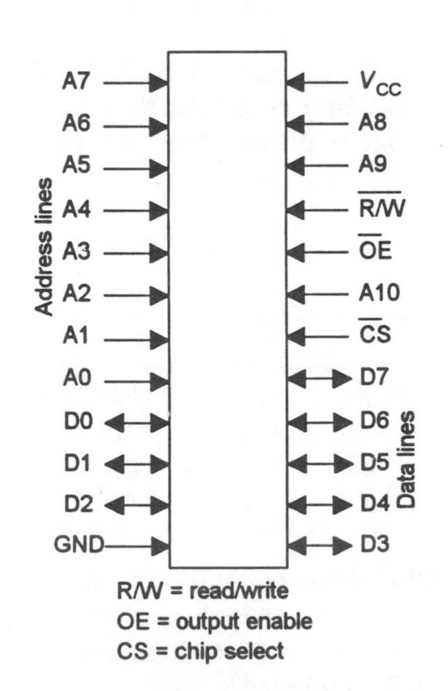

Fig. 1.17 SRAM chip

date. A typical EPROM chip (Fig. 1.16) contains a series of cells, small electronic circuits which can store charge. The program is stored by applying voltages to the integrated circuit connection pins and producing a pattern of charged and uncharged cells. The pattern remains permanently in the chip until erased by shining ultraviolet light through a quartz window on the top of the device. This causes all the cells to become discharged and the entire stored program erased. The chip can then be reprogrammed (see Section 9.5.1 for more details). An example of such a memory is the Intel 2732A 4K × 8 bit. It has 12 address pins and is connected to an 8 bit data bus.

4. *EEPROM*
   Electrically erasable PROM (EEPROM) is similar to EPROM. Erasure is by applying a relatively high voltage rather than using ultraviolet light. Unlike an EPROM, an EEPROM does not have to be completely erased before it can be reprogrammed.

1.10.2 RAM

Temporary data, i.e. data currently being operated on, is stored in a read/write memory referred to as a *random access memory* (RAM). Such a memory can be read or written to. There are two forms of random access memory, termed static and dynamic.

1. *SRAM*
   Static RAM (SRAM) is based on the use of transistor flip-flop elements for temporary storage of 0 or 1 states. Figure 1.17 shows the typical pin connections for a 1K × 8 bit SRAM chip. The chip select pin is used to select the chip for read or write access and the output enable pin is used during a read operation to enable data to be outputted from the data output pins. An example of a SRAM is the Motorola 6810, a 1K × 8 bit memory with 128 addresses and an 8 bit data bus.

2. *DRAM*
   Dynamic RAM (DRAM) uses small capacitors as temporary storage elements. This enables there to be more memory elements per square millimetre of chip than SRAM, where each memory element consists of four or six transistors. SRAM does, however, have the advantage of shorter access time than DRAM. Charge leakage from the capacitors means a loss of stored data and so this type of memory has to be refreshed at frequent intervals, typically about every 2 ms, if data is not to be lost. Figure 1.18 shows the typical pin connections for a 256K × 4 bit DRAM. DRAM cells are generally organised in a square matrix. To read a particular cell, the row address is

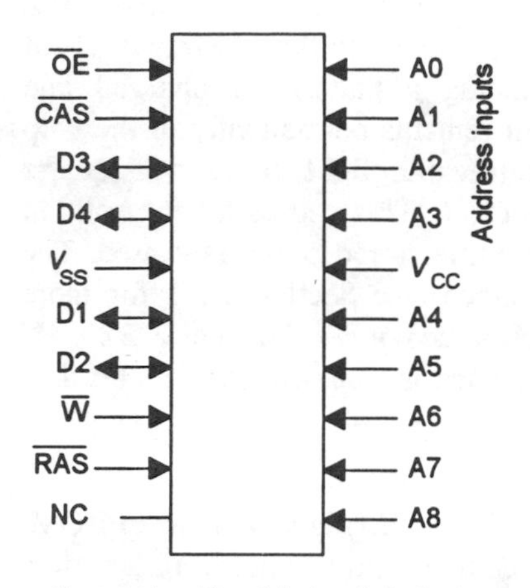

V_{SS} = 0 V D = data inputs/outputs
OE = output enable
CAS = column address strobe input
W = write control input
RAS = row address strobe input

Fig. 1.18 DRAM

provided on the address pins and latched by the row address strobe. This is then followed by the column address which is latched by the column address strobe. The selected data then appears on the data output lines. Data is written into a particular cell by applying the data on the data input lines and by asserting the write control signal. An example of a DRAM is the Texas Instruments TMS4C1924 which is 1 048 576 bit.

When ROM is used for program storage, then the program is available and ready for use when the system is switched on; such programs are termed *firmware*. Some firmware must always be present. When RAM is used for program storage then such programs are referred to as *software*. When the system is switched on, software may be loaded into RAM from perhaps a keyboard, hard disk or floppy disk.

1.10.3 Chip selection

A microcomputer memory system usually contains several RAM and ROM chips and it is thus necessary for the processor to select which chip is to be addressed. Only when a chip has been selected can it communicate with or be communicated with through the data bus. This chip selection can be achieved through an external decoder chip. Thus for a 2 line to 4 line decoder chip, e.g. the 74LS139, a two-bit number can be applied to it from the microprocessor and it will then select one of four connected chips. Table 1.5 shows the truth table for such a decoder; Fig. 1.19(a) shows the pin connections and Fig. 1.19(b) how it can be used to select from two RAM and two ROM chips. The chip select signal input to the decoder is derived from the decoding of the A14 and A15 address lines. The basic address for each device is provided by the A0–A13 address lines. The read/write lines are only connected to the RAM chips since ROMs can only be read.

Table 1.5 Truth table for 2 line to 4 line decoder

Select inputs		*Outputs*			
A15	*A14*	*CS0*	*CS1*	*CS2*	*CS3*
Low	Low	Low	High	High	High
Low	High	High	Low	High	High
High	Low	High	High	Low	High
High	High	High	High	High	Low

Suppose the address 1000 0000 0000 0000 is put on the address bus; this means bit 14 is low and bit 15 high hence CS2 is selected. But with 0000 0000 0000 0000 on the address bus, bit 14 is low and bit 15 is low hence CS0 is selected.

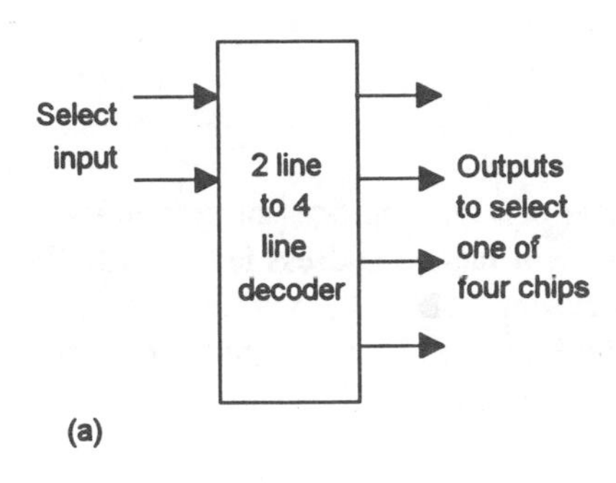

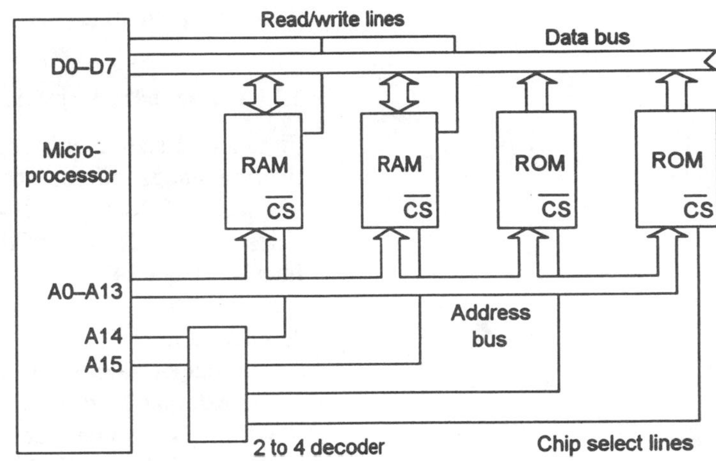

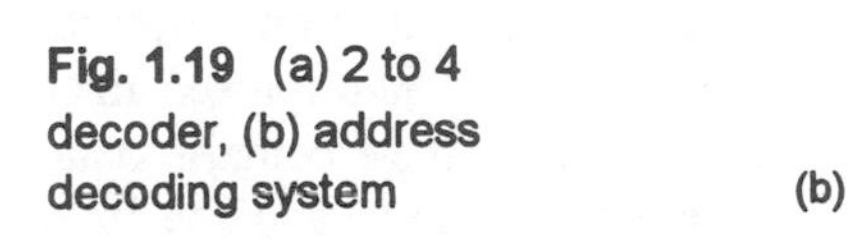

Fig. 1.19 (a) 2 to 4 decoder, (b) address decoding system

Address	
FFFF – C000	16K ROM
BFFF – 8000	16K ROM
7FFF – 4000	16K RAM
3FFF – 0000	16K RAM

Fig. 1.20 Memory map

1.10.4 Memory maps

The addresses of different memory, or input/output, devices can be represented by a *memory map*; this shows which section of addresses is used by which device. The memory map for the system shown in Fig. 1.18, with each of the memory chips being 16K × 8, is broken down into four regions, as shown in Fig. 1.20. The first RAM chip is selected by A15, A14 being 00 and so its addresses start at 0000 0000 0000 0000 or 0000 in hex notation. The second RAM chip is selected by A15, A14 being 01 and so its addresses start at 0100 0000 0000 0000 or 4000 in hex notation. The size of the memory, i.e. 16K, of the first RAM chip is just big enough to occupy all the intervening addresses. The first ROM chip is selected by A15, A14 being 10 and so its addresses start at 1000 0000 0000 0000 or 8000 hex.

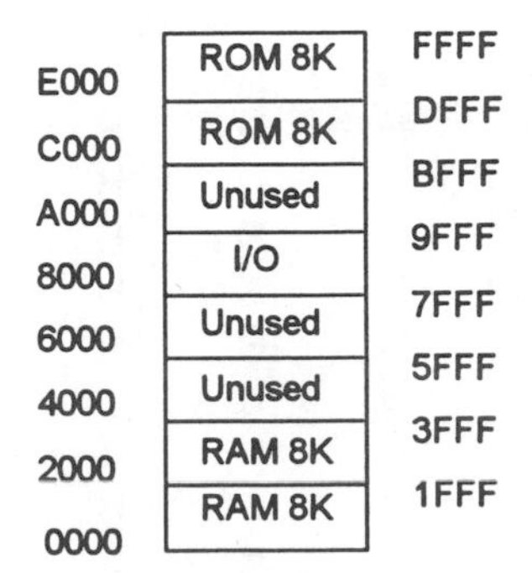

Fig. 1.21 Memory map

1.10.5 Memory-mapped input/output

One method of connecting an input or output device to a microprocessor is to make the interface appear as a memory location within the system. The input/output interface is then said to be *memory mapped*. If data is written into a memory address associated with the input/output interface then it is an output to an external device. If data is read from such an address then it is an input from the input/output interface. So we might have a system with the memory map shown in Fig. 1.21; to write data to the input/output interface the addresses 8000 to 9FFF should be used, and if the first RAM chip is to be addressed then the addresses 0000 to 1FFF should be used. Often not all the addresses are used and so there are unused sections in the memory map.

1.11 Examples of systems

Here are some examples of systems with memory and memory-mapped input/output.

1.11.1 Intel 8085A system

Figure 1.22 shows an example of a microprocessor system using the Intel 8085A microprocessor. It has an address latch 74LS373, a 3 line to 8 line address decoder 74LS138, two 1K × 4 RAM chips 2114, a 2K × 8 EPROM chip 2716 and input and output interface chips 74LS244 and 74LS374.

1. *Address latch*
   The output ALE (address latch enable) provides an output to the external hardware to indicate when the multiplexed lines AD0–AD7 contain addresses and when they contain data. When ALE is made high it activates the latch and the lines A0–A7 pass the lower part of the address to it where it becomes latched. Thus when ALE changes and goes back to being low, so that data can be outputted from the microprocessor, this part of the address remains latched in the 74LS373. The higher part of the address is sent through A8–A15 and is always valid, and the full address is given by the lower part from the latch and the upper part from the microprocessor address bus.

2. *Address decoder*
   The 74LS138 is a 3 line to 8 line decoder and provides an active low at one of its eight outputs; the output selected depends on the signals on its three input lines A, B and C (Table 1.6). Before it can make such a selection it has to be enabled by enable 1 and enable 2 being low and enable 3 high.

Table 1.6 Truth table for the 74LS138

Inputs												
Enable		*Select*			*Outputs*							
E1	*E2/3*	*C*	*B*	*A*	*0*	*1*	*2*	*3*	*4*	*5*	*6*	*7*
X	H	X	X	X	H	H	H	H	H	H	H	H
L	X	X	X	X	H	H	H	H	H	H	H	H
H	L	L	L	L	L	H	H	H	H	H	H	H
H	L	L	L	H	H	L	H	H	H	H	H	H
H	L	L	H	L	H	H	L	H	H	H	H	H
H	L	L	H	H	H	H	H	L	H	H	H	H
H	L	H	L	L	H	H	H	H	L	H	H	H
H	L	H	L	H	H	H	H	H	H	L	H	H
H	L	H	H	L	H	H	H	H	H	H	L	H
H	L	H	H	H	H	H	H	H	H	H	H	L

Note: H = high, L = low, X = does not matter

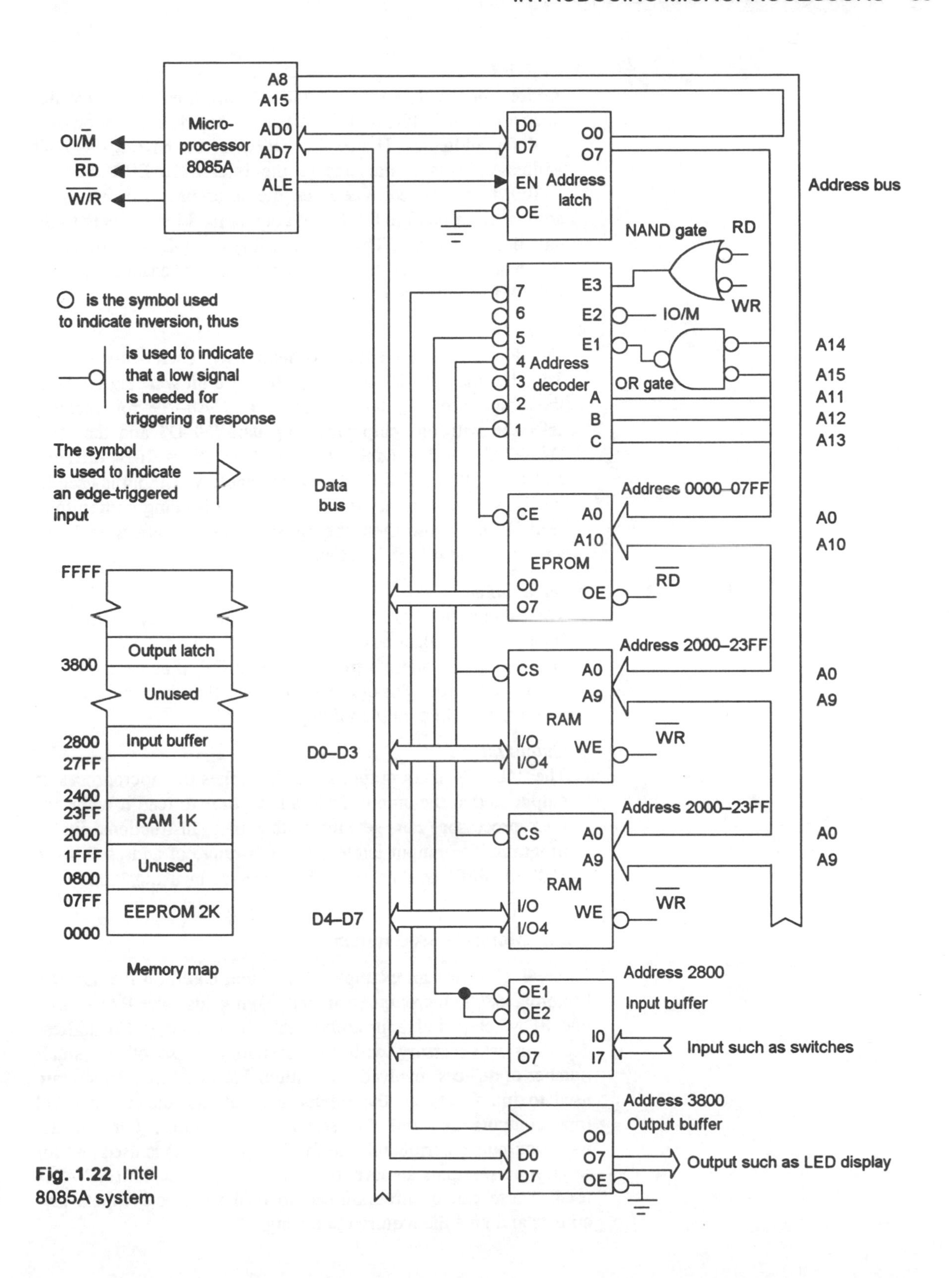

Fig. 1.22 Intel 8085A system

3. *EPROM*
   Address bits A11, A12, A13 and A14 are used to select which device is to be addressed. This leaves the address bits on A0–A10 for addresses. Hence the EPROM can have 2^{11} = 2048 addresses. This is the size of the Intel 2716 EPROM. The EPROM is selected whenever the microprocessor reads an address from 0000 to 07FF and outputs its 8 bit contents to the data bus via O0–O7. The output enable line OE is connected to the read output of the microprocessor to ensure that the EPROM is only written to.

4. *RAM*
   Two RAM chips are shown as being used, each being 1K × 4. Together they provide a memory for an 8 bit wide signal. Both the chips use the same address bits A0–A9 for memory selection with one chip providing data D0–D3 and the other D4–D7. With 10 address bits we have 2^{10} = 1024 different addresses 2000 to 23FF. The write enable WE input is used by the RAM to determine whether the RAM is being written to or read. If it is low then the selected RAM address is being written to and if high it is being read.

5. *Input buffer*
   The input buffer 74LS244 is set to pass the binary value of the inputs over the data bus whenever OE1 and OE2 are low. It is accessed at any address from 2800 to 2FFF, thus we might use the address 2800. The buffer is to ensure that the inputs impose very little loading on the microprocessor.

6. *Output latch*
   The 74LS374 is an output latch. It latches the microprocessor output so that the output devices have time to read it while the microprocessor can get on with other instructions in its program. The output latch is given a range of addresses from 3800 to 3FFF and thus might be addressed by using 3800.

1.11.2 Motorola 6800 system

Figure 1.23 shows an example of a system based on the use of a Motorola 6800 microprocessor and having just one RAM chip, one ROM chip and a programmable input/output. No address decoding is necessary with this system because of the small number of devices involved. Programmable interface adapters are used to interface with the inputs and outputs, one for parallel inputs/outputs and one for serial inputs/outputs. For parallel inputs/outputs a peripheral interface adapter (PIA) is used and for serial inputs/outputs an asynchronous interface adapter (ACIA) is used. These can be programmed to deal with both inputs and outputs and give the required buffering.

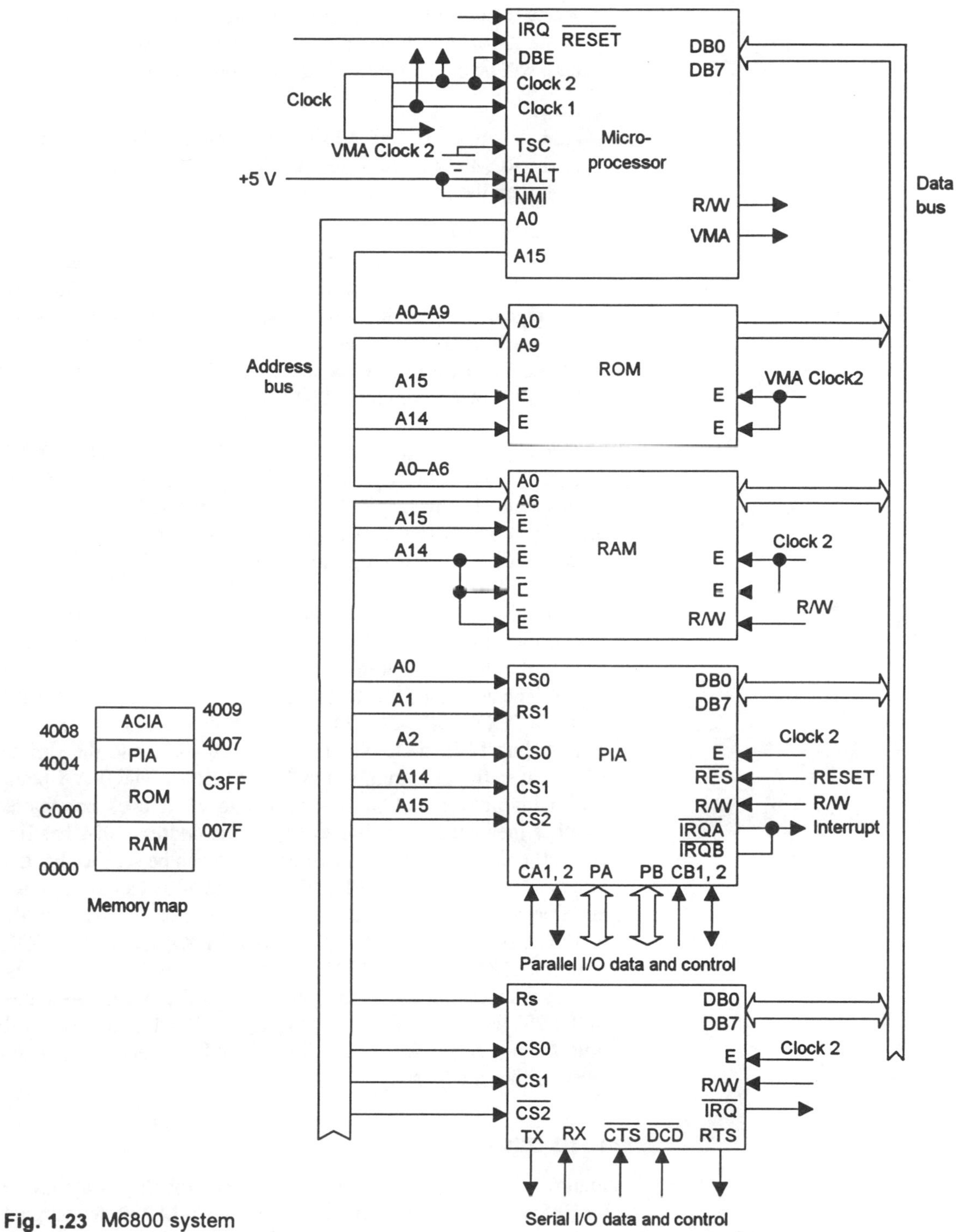

Fig. 1.23 M6800 system

1. *RAM*
   Address lines A14 and A15 are connected to the enable inputs of the RAM chip. When both these lines are low then the RAM chip will be conversing with the microprocessor.
2. *ROM*
   Address lines A14 and A15 are connected to the enable inputs of the ROM chip and when the signals on both these lines are high then the ROM chip is addressed.
3. *Inputs/outputs*
   Address lines A14 and A15 are connected to the enable inputs of the PIA and ACIA. When the signal on line 15 is low and the signal on A14 high then the input/output interfaces are addressed. In order to indicate which of the devices is being enabled, address line A2 is taken high for the PIA and address line A3 is taken high for the ACIA.

The addresses for RAM are 00XX XXXX X000 0000 to 00XX XXXX X1111 1111, i.e. hex 0000 to hex 007F. Thus address lines 14 and 15 are made 00 and the various addresses in RAM given by 0 or 1 being used with lines 6 to 0. For lines 7 to 13 it does not matter whether they are 0 or 1. The addresses for ROM are 11XX XX00 0000 0000 to 11XX XX11 1111 1111, i.e. hex C000 to hex C3FF. Thus address lines 14 and 15 are made 11 and the various addresses in ROM given by 0 or 1 being used with lines 9 to 0. For lines 10 to 13 it does not matter whether they are 0 or 1. The addresses for the PIA are 01XX XXXX XXXX X100 to 01XX XXXX XXXX X111, i.e. hex 4004 to hex 4007. Thus address line 14 is made 0 and line 15 is made 1 and the various addresses in the PIA are given by line 2 being 1, and 0 or 1 being used with lines 1 and 0. For lines 3 to 13 it does not matter whether they are 0 or 1. For example, the address 4004 has line A0 as 0 and line A1 as 1. As a result data can be sent to the data direction register A in the PIA. The address 4005 has line A0 as 1 and line A1 as 1 and data can be sent to control register A in the PIA. The addresses for the ACIA are 01XX XXXX XXXX 1XX0 to 01XX XXXX XXXX 1XX1, i.e. 4008 to 4009. Thus address line 14 is made 0 and line 15 is made 1 and the various addresses in the PIA are given by line 3 being 1, and 0 or 1 being used with line 0. For lines 4 to 13 and lines 1 and 2 it does not matter whether they are 0 or 1.

1.11.3 Z80 system

Figure 1.24 shows a rather basic Z80 system with just a 512 × 8 bit EPROM and a quad data latch, e.g. the 74LS279, for outputs. No external inputs are provided for. No address decoding is necessary because of the small number of devices involved.

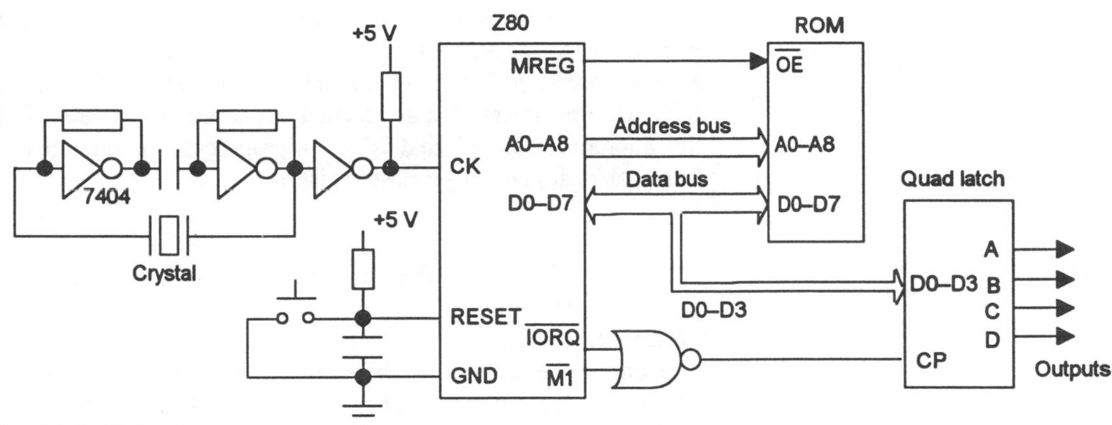

Fig. 1.24 Z80 system

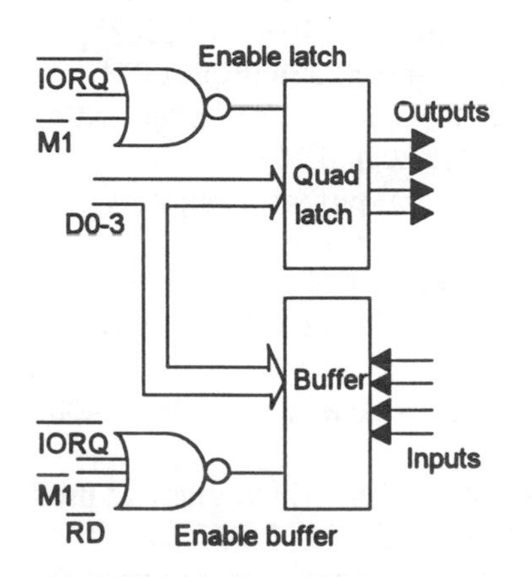

Fig. 1.25 Output/input interfaces

Momentarily closing the reset switch starts the program execution. The program is addressed by addresses XXXX XXXX0 0000 0000 to XXXX XXX1 1111 1111; address lines A9–A15 are not used.

1. *ROM*
   The eight output lines from the ROM connect directly to the Z80 data bus.
2. *Quad latch*
   The output device is a quad latch, i.e. an integrated package containing four latches, which is latched by the D0–D3 lines from the Z80 when an output operation occurs.

We can expand the system so that inputs from external devices can occur, by including tristate buffers, e.g. the 74LS125, as shown in Fig. 1.25 and RAM.

1.12 CISC and RISC

The term *complex instruction set* (CISC) is used to describe microprocessors which have a large number of different instructions, typically between 100 and 250. This large number of instructions necessitates a complex microprocessor and so a larger and more expensive chip. It also reduces processing speed since the instructions take several time cycles. It does, however, keep the amount of program code required, and hence the amount of memory required, to a minimum since quite a complex instruction might be specified by just one instruction instead of stringing together several simpler instructions to generate the complex one. The Z80, Intel 8085A and Motorola 6800 all have this form of architecture. An alternative architecture is used in the *reduced instruction set* (RISC) microprocessor. These have relatively few instructions, each with single-cycle execution. Execution can thus be fast but the amount of program code needed and so the amount of memory required is generally larger. Memory access is limited to just the two instructions LOAD and STORE. Most operations are carried out between registers within the microprocessor so that RISC microprocessors tend to have large banks of general-purpose registers.

Problems

1. What is the basic difference between 4 bit and 8 bit microprocessors?
2. Convert the decimal numbers (a) 27, (b) 31, (c) 42 to binary.
3. Convert the decimal numbers (a) 27, (b) 31, (c) 42 to hex.
4. Convert the decimal numbers (a) 171 and (b) 230 to BCD.
5. Convert the hex numbers (a) A and (b) 10 to BCD.
6. Convert, using the twos complement method, the decimal number –7 to (a) signed 8 bit binary and (b) signed hex.
7. What are (a) 001 010 + 010 101, (b) 000 110 + 011 100?
8. Write 101.001 in floating-point format as a multiple of 2^3.
9. What will be the state of the Z, N, C and V flags after adding the hex numbers (a) 01 and 02, (b) E0 and 20?
10. State the functions of (a) general-purpose registers, (b) instruction registers, (c) memory address registers.
11. With an Intel 8085 microprocessor, which output is used to notify memory or an input/output device that the address/data bus is being used as an address bus?
12. What voltage supply is required to operate an Intel 8085 microprocessor?
13. With the Motoroia 6800 microprocessor, which pins are used for ground connection and which for the +5 V d.c. supply?
14. With the Zilog Z80 microprocessor, which pins are used for (a) the clock input, (b) the data bus, (c) the address bus?
15. In diagrams of pin connections some symbols have bars over them. What does this signify?
16. For the 2 line to 4 line address decoder described in Table 1.1, which chip would be selected by the address bus being given the address 1100 0000 0000 0000?
17. What are the effects with a microprocessor of (a) the write, (b) the read signal being made active?
18. When a 3 line to 8 line decoder is used to decode the highest three address lines of a 16 bit address, for how many 8K blocks of memory can select signals be generated?
19. If two 4K × 8 RAMs are connected in parallel, but with their chip select pins connected to different outputs of an address decoder, what will be the resulting size of RAM?
20. If a program is written for a RISC processor, would you generally expect it to need more or less instructions than a program for a CISC processor?

2 Microcontrollers

2.1 Introduction

For a microprocessor to give a working microcomputer system, which can be used for control tasks, additional chips are necessary, e.g. memory devices for program and data storage and input/output ports to allow it to communicate with the external world and receive signals from it. The *microcontroller* is the integration of a microprocessor with memory and input/output interfaces, and other peripherals such as timers, on a single chip. This chapter is an introduction to microcontrollers.

A microcomputer, such as the IBM PC or Apple Macintosh incorporates a microprocessor with the ROM, RAM and interface circuitry requiring many integrated circuits and does not use microcontrollers. Microcontrollers are, however, mostly found in small applications carrying out control-orientated activities. The use of a microcontroller, rather than a microprocessor with additional chips, reduces the design to the minimum number of components. All that is then required is likely to be a small number of support components and a control program in ROM. Microcontrollers have limited amounts of ROM and RAM and are essentially used for the 'control' of input/output devices whereas a microprocessor system with separate memory and input/output chips is more suited to 'processing' information in computer systems.

2.2 The basic structure of a microcontroller

Figure 2.1 shows a general block diagram of a microcontroller. There are pins on the package for external connections of inputs and outputs, power, clock and control signals. Typically a microcontroller has:

1. *Microprocessor/CPU*

2. *Memory*
   ROM, RAM and EPROM or EEPROM.

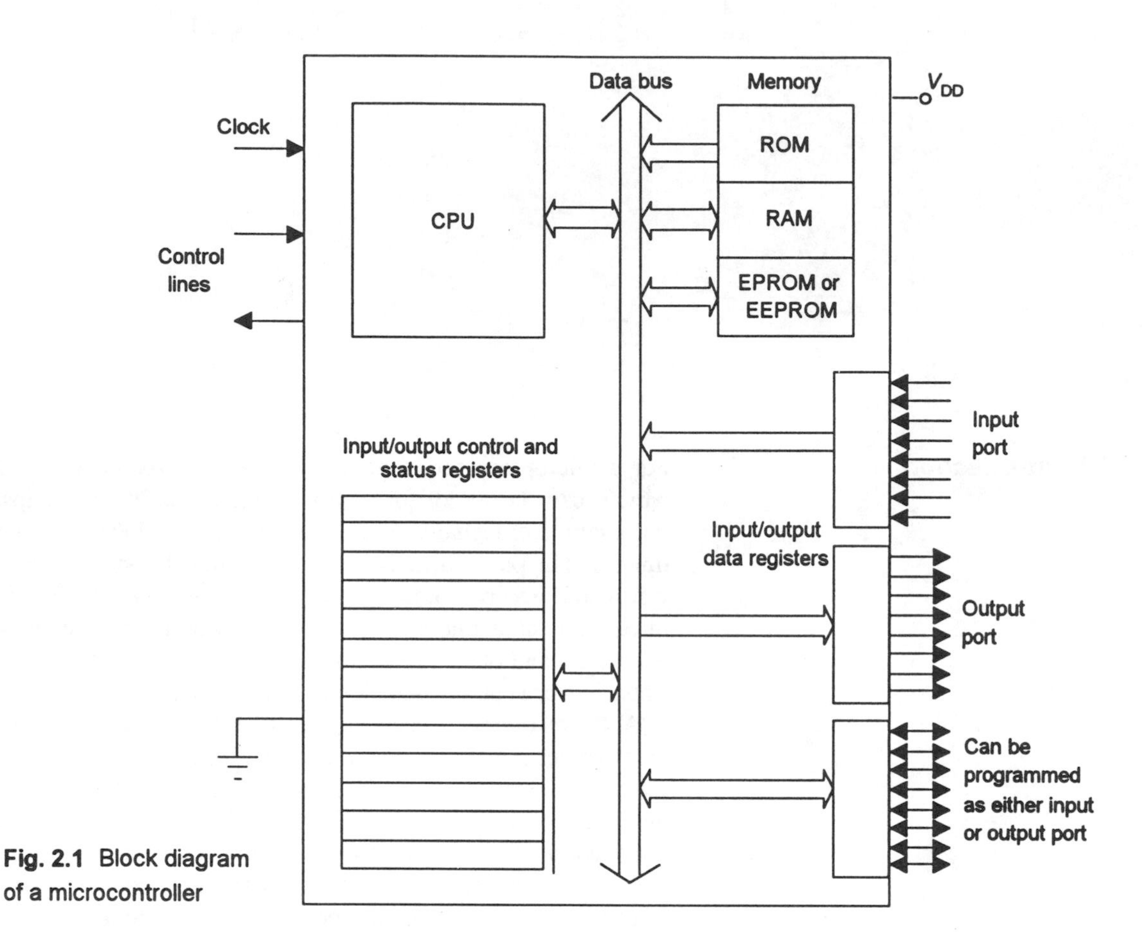

Fig. 2.1 Block diagram of a microcontroller

3. *Input and output ports*
   The pins for the inputs and outputs are grouped into units called input/output ports. Usually such ports have eight lines in order to be able to transfer an 8-bit word of data. Two ports may be used for a 16-bit word, one to transmit the lower 8 bits and the other the upper 8 bits. The ports can be input only, output only or programmable as either input or output. Each input/output data register holds the input/output data associated with its corresponding port. Additionally, an input port might be provided with an analogue-to-digital converter so that analogue inputs can be easily handled and additionally one port might be for use as a serial port.

4. *Input/output control and status registers*
   These control and monitor the microcontroller input/output processes.

The Motorola 68HC11, Intel 8051 and the PIC 16C7x are examples of 8-bit microcontrollers, i.e. the data path is 8 bits wide. The Motorola 68HC16 is an example of a 16 bit microcontroller and the Motorola 68300 a 32-bit microcontroller. These numbers represent families of microcontrollers which differ in their amount of 'enhancements'. Family members differ in such features as the combinations of on-chip ROM or EPROM, on-chip RAM and timing facilities.

2.3 Motorola M68HC11

Motorola offer two basic 8-bit families of microcontrollers, the 68HC05 being the inexpensive core and the 68HC11 the higher performance core. The Motorola M68HC11 family, based on the Motorola 6800 microprocessor, is very widely used for control systems. There are a number of versions, the differences being due to differences in the RAM, ROM, EPROM, EEPROM and configuration register features. For example, one version (68HC11A8) has 8K ROM, 512 bytes EEPROM, 256 bytes RAM, a 16-bit timer system, a synchronous serial peripheral interface and an asynchronous non-return-to-zero serial comm- unication interface, an 8-channel 8-bit analogue-to-digital converter for analogue inputs, and five ports A, B, C, D and E. Figure 2.2 shows a block diagram of the microcontroller and Fig. 2.3 the pin connections and the basic memory map.

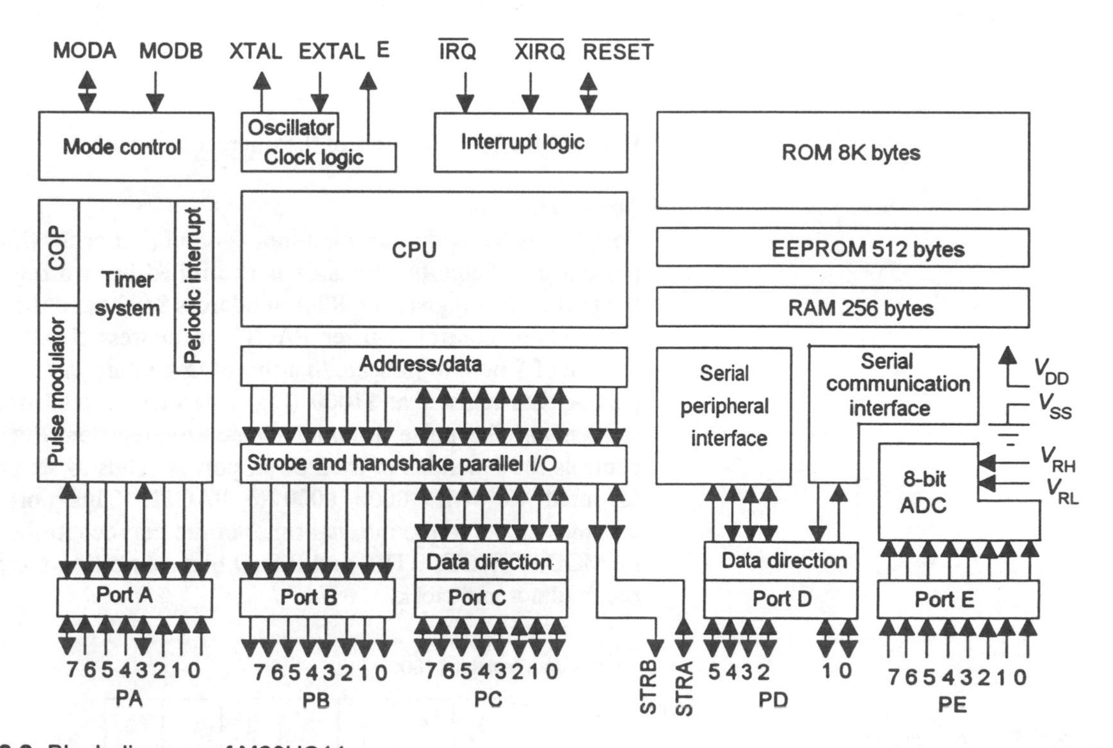

Fig. 2.2 Block diagram of M68HC11

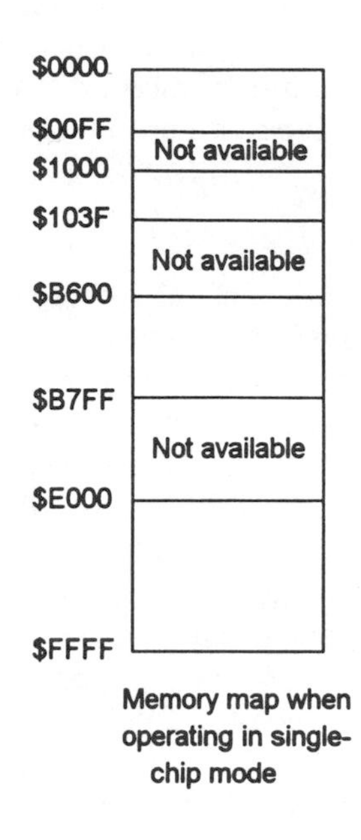

Signal	Pin	Pin	Signal
PA7/PAI/OC1	1	48	V_{DD}
PA6/OC2/OC1	2	47	PD5/$\overline{SS}$
PA5/OC3/OC1	3	46	PD4/SCK
PA4/OC4/OC1	4	45	PD3/MOSI
PA3/OC5/OC1	5	44	PD2/MISO
PA2/IC1	6	43	PD1/TXD
PA1/IC2	7	42	PD0/RXD
PA0/IC3	8	41	$\overline{IRQ}$
PB7/A15	9	40	$\overline{XIRQ}$
PB6/A14	10	39	$\overline{RESET}$
PB5/A13	11	38	PC7/AD7
PB4/A12	12	37	PC6/AD6
PB3/A11	13	36	PC5/AD5
PB2/A10	14	35	PC4/AD4
PB1/A9	15	34	PC3/AD3
PB0/A8	16	33	PC2/AD2
PE0/AN0	17	32	PC1/AD1
PE1/AN1	18	31	PC0/AD0
PE2/AN2	19	30	XTAL
PE3/AN3	20	29	EXTAL
V_{RL}	21	28	STRB/R/$\overline{W}$
V_{RH}	22	27	E
V_{SS}	23	26	STRA/AS
MODB	24	25	MODA/LIR

Fig. 2.3 Motorola M68HC11A8

Here are the basic features of the microcontroller:

1. *Input/output ports*
   Port A may be used as an 8-bit input/output port or for timer or pulse accumulator functions. It is controlled by two registers: the port A data register PORTA at address $1000 and the pulse accumulator control register PACTL at address $1026 (note the use of $ here to indicate that the addresses are in hex). The port A data register at $1000 (Fig. 2.4) may be read from or written to. The pulse accumulator control register (Fig. 2.5) controls the functions of each bit in port A. Thus to set port A as input we write 0000 0000 to PACTL. This port also provides access to the internal timer of the microcontroller, the PAMOD, PEDGE, RTR1 and RTRO bits controlling the pulse accumulator and clock.

Port A data register $1000

Bit	7	6	5	4	3	2	1	0

Fig. 2.4 Port A register

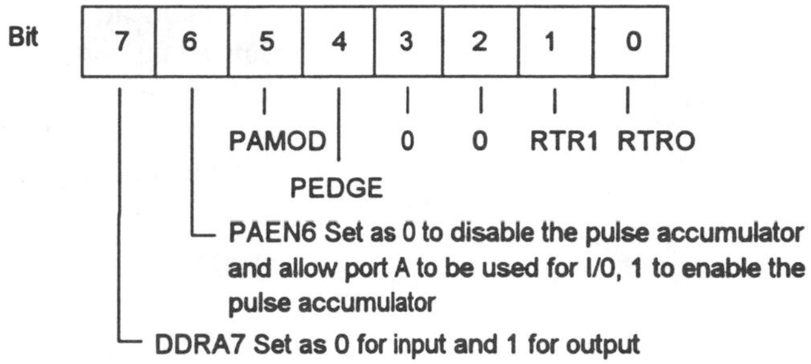

Bit	7	6	5	4	3	2	1	0
	DDRA7	PAEN6	PAMOD	PEDGE	0	0	RTR1	RTRO

PAEN6 Set as 0 to disable the pulse accumulator and allow port A to be used for I/0, 1 to enable the pulse accumulator

DDRA7 Set as 0 for input and 1 for output

Fig. 2.5 Pulse accummulator control register

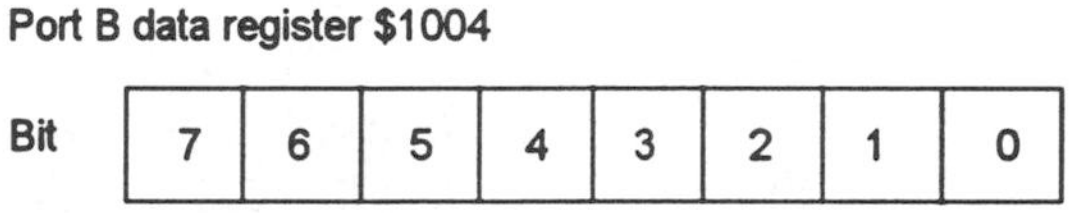

Port B data register $1004

Bit	7	6	5	4	3	2	1	0

Fig. 2.6 Port B register

Port B is output only and has eight output lines. Input data cannot be put on port B pins. Its data register is at the address $1004 (Fig. 2.6) and to output data it has to be written to this memory location.

Port C can be either input or output, data being written or read from its data register at address $1003. Its direction is controlled by the port data direction register at address $1007. The eight bits in this register correspond to the individual bits in port C and determine whether the lines are inputs or outputs; when the corresponding data direction register bit is set to 0 it is an input and when set to 1 an output (Fig. 2.7).

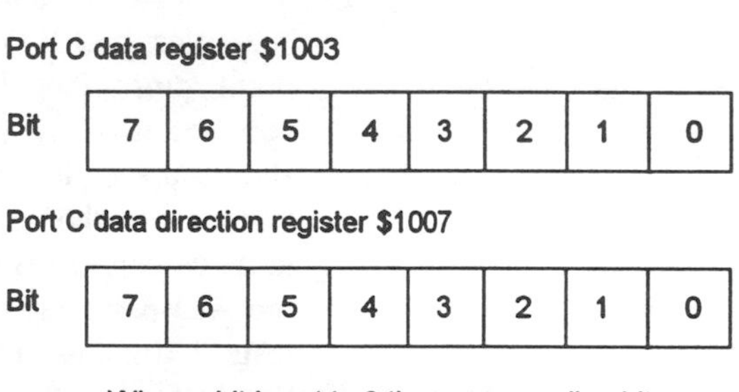

Fig. 2.7 Port C registers

Port D contains just six lines, either input or output, and it has a data register at address $1008; the directions are controlled by a port data direction register at address $1009 with the corresponding bit being set to 0 for an input and 1 for an output (Fig. 2.8). Port D also serves as the connection to the two serial subsystems of the microcontroller. The serial communication interface (SCI), controlled by a register at

$102D, is an asynchronous system which provides serial communication that is compatible with modems and terminals. The serial peripheral interface (SPI), controlled by a register at $1028, is a high speed synchronous system which is designed to communicate at rates between the microcontroller and peripheral components that can access at such rates.

Port D data register $1008

Bit			5	4	3	2	1	0

Port D data direction register $1009

Bit			5	4	3	2	1	0

When a bit is set to 0 the corresponding bit in the port is an input, when set to 1 an output

Fig. 2.8 Port D registers

Port E is an 8-bit input only port, data register at $100A, which can be used as a general-purpose input port or for analogue inputs to the internal analogue-to-digital converter.

Port E data register $100A

Bit	7	6	5	4	3	2	1	0

Fig. 2.9 Port E register

2.*Analogue inputs*

The 68HC11 has an internal analogue-to-digital (A/D) converter; port E bits 0, 1, 2, 3, 4, 5, 6 and 7 are the analogue input pins. Two lines V_{RH} and V_{LH} provide the reference voltages used by the ADC; the high reference voltage V_{RH} should not be lower than V_{DD}, i.e. 5 V, and the low reference voltage V_{LH} should not be lower than V_{SS}, i.e. 0 V. The ADC must be enabled before it can be used. This is done by setting the A/D power-up (ADPU) control bit in the OPTION register (Fig. 2.10), this being bit 7. Bit 6 selects the clock source for the ADC. A delay of at least 100 μs is required after powering up to allow the system to stabilise.

The analogue-to-digital conversion is initiated by writing to the A/D control/status register (ADCTL) after powering up and the stabilisation delay (Fig. 2.11). This involves selecting the channels and operation modes. The conversion will then start one clock cycle later. For example, if single- channel mode is selected by setting MULT = 0 then four successive A/D conversions will occur of the channel selected by the CD–CA bits. The results of the conversion are placed in the A/D result registers ADR1–ADR4.

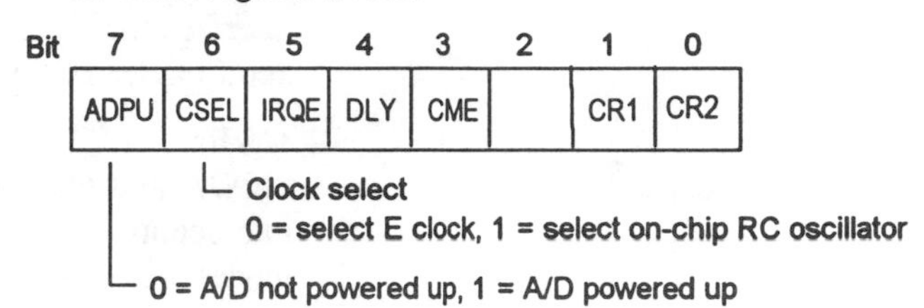

Fig. 2.10 OPTION register

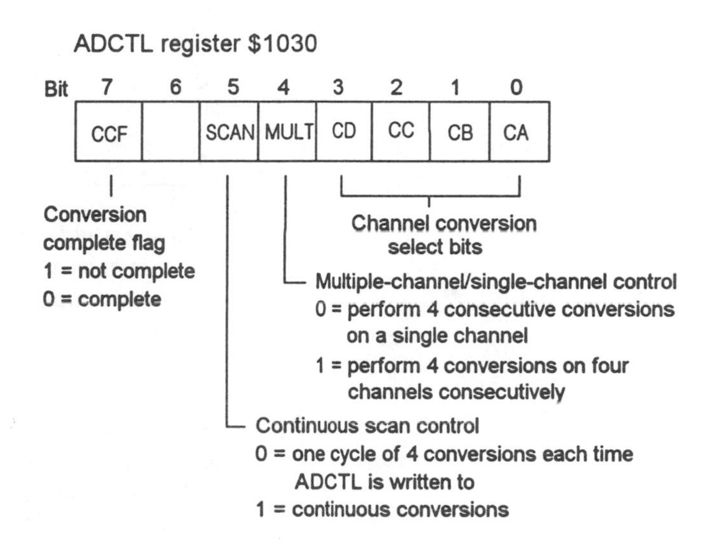

MULT = 0

CD	*CC*	*CB*	*CA*	*Channel converted*
0	0	0	0	PE0
0	0	0	1	PE1
0	0	1	0	PE2
0	0	1	1	PE3
0	1	0	0	PE4
0	1	0	1	PE5
0	1	1	0	PE6
0	1	1	1	PE7

MULT = 1

				A/D result registers			
CD	*CC*	*CB*	*CA*	*ADR1*	*ADR2*	*ADR3*	*ADR4*
0	0	X	X	PE0	PE1	PE2	PE3
0	1	X	X	PE4	PE5	PE6	PE7

Fig. 2.11 ADCTL register

3. *Serial input/output*
The 68HC11 microcontroller has a serial communication (SCI) interface for transmitting and receiving serial communications. See Chapter 10 for discussion of such interfaces.

4. *Modes*
MODA and MODB are two pins that can be used to force the microcontroller into one of four modes at power-up, these modes being special bootstrap, special test, single-chip and expanded.

MODB	*MODA*	*Mode*
0	1	Special bootstrap
0	1	Special test
1	0	Single-chip
1	1	Expanded

In the *single-chip mode* the microcontroller is completely self-contained with the exception of an external clock source and a reset circuit. With such a mode the microcontroller may not have enough resources, e.g. memory, for some applications; however, the *expanded mode* can be used so that the number of addresses can be increased. Ports B and C then provide address, data and control buses. Port B functions as the upper eight address pins and port C as the multiplexed data and low address pins. The *bootstrap mode* allows a manufacturer to load special programs in a special ROM for an M68HC11 customer. When the microcontroller is set in this mode, the special program is loaded. The *special test mode* is primarily used during Motorola's internal production testing.

After the mode has been selected, the MODA pin can be used to determine whether an instruction is starting to execute. The MODB pin has the other function of giving a means of powering the internal RAM of the chip when the regular power is removed.

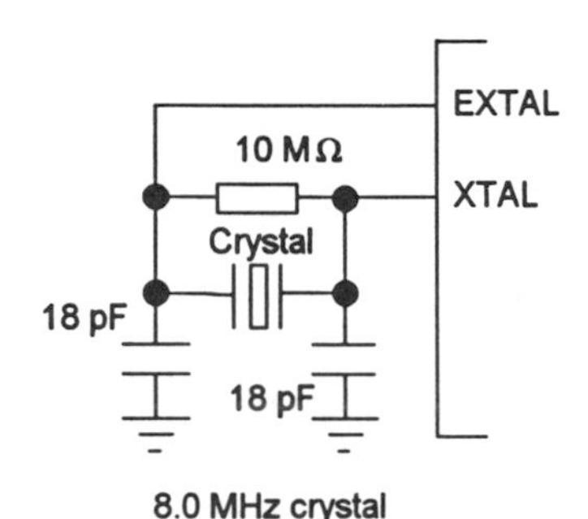

Fig. 2.12 Oscillator input

5. *Oscillator pins*
The oscillator system pins XTAL and EXTAL are the connections needed to access the internal oscillator. Figure 2.12 shows the external circuit that might be used. E is an output from the bus clock and runs at one-quarter of the oscillator frequency and can be used to synchronise external events.

6. *Interrupt controller*
The interrupt controller is to enable interruptions of a program. The two lines IRQ and XIRQ are for the inputs of the interrupt signals. RESET is for resetting. An interrupt is an event that requires the CPU to stop normal program execution and perform some service related to the event.

7. *Timer*
The M68HC11 contains a timer system. This has a free-running counter, five output-compare functions, the ability to capture the time when an external event occurs, a real-time periodic interrupt and a counter, called the pulse accumulator, for external events. The free-running counter, called TCNT, is a 16-bit counter which starts counting at 0000 when the CPU is reset and runs continuously therafter; it cannot be reset by the program. Its value can be read at any time. The source for the counter is the system bus clock and its output can be prescaled by setting the PR0 and PR1 bits at bits 0 and 1 in the timer interrupt register 2, TMSK2, at address \$1024 (Fig. 2.13). With PR0 and PR1 both set to 0 the prescale factor is 0; thus with a bus frequency of 2 MHz a count of 1 takes $1/(2 \times 10^6)$ = 0.5 μs. With PR0 set to 1 and PR1 set to 0 the factor is 4 and a count of 1 then takes 2 μs. Table 2.1 shows the possible prescale factors. The use of the timer functions is discussed in more detail in Section 11.6.

Timer interrupt register 2 at address \$1024

Bit	7	6	5	4	3	2	1	0
							PR1	PR0

Fig. 2.13 TMSK2 register

Table 2.1 Prescale factors

			One count	
		Prescale factor	*Bus frequency*	
PR1	*PR0*		*2 MHz*	*1 MHz*
0	0	1	0.5 μs	1 μs
0	1	4	2 μs	4 μs
1	0	8	4 μs	8 μs
1	1	16	8 μs	16 μs

8. *COP*
Another timer function is COP, the *computer operating properly* function. This is a timer which times out and resets the system if an operation is not concluded in what is deemed a reasonable time. This is often termed a *watchdog timer* because it is watching for unreasonable delays which might occur as a result of a fault in the system.

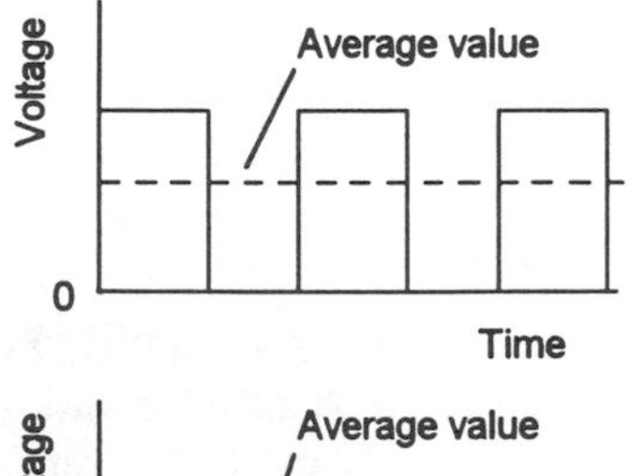

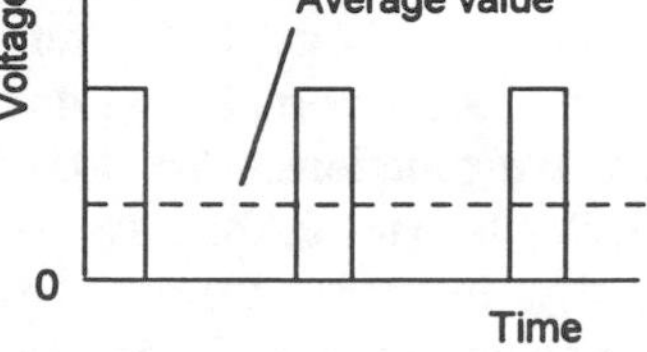

Fig. 2.14 PWM

9. *PWM*
Pulse width modulation (PWM) is used to control the speed of d.c. motors. A square wave signal is generated and the amount of time for which the signal is high is controlled (Fig. 2.14). As a consequence the average value of the signal is controlled, hence the voltage supplied to the motor is also controlled.

Some versions of the M68HC11 have a PWM module and so, after the PWM module has been initialised and enabled, the PWM waveforms can be automatically outputted.

As will be apparent from the above, before a microcontroller can be used it is necessary to initialise it, i.e. set the bits in appropriate input/output control registers so that it will perform as required. Figure 2.15(a) shows the input/output control registers and Fig. 2.15(b) the CPU registers that are used in programming. With the condition code register the flags are S stop disable, X interrupt mask, H half-carry, I interrupt mask, N negative, Z zero, V overflow and C carry.

This gives just a brief indication of the input/output connections to the M68HC11 microcontroller and how they are configured; more will appear in later chapters. For more details the reader is referred to the manuals published by the manufacturer or to texts such as *Software and Hardware Engineering, Motorola M68HC11* by F.M. Cady (Oxford University Press 1997) or *Microcontroller Technology, The 68HC11* by P. Spasov (Prentice Hall 1996, 1992).

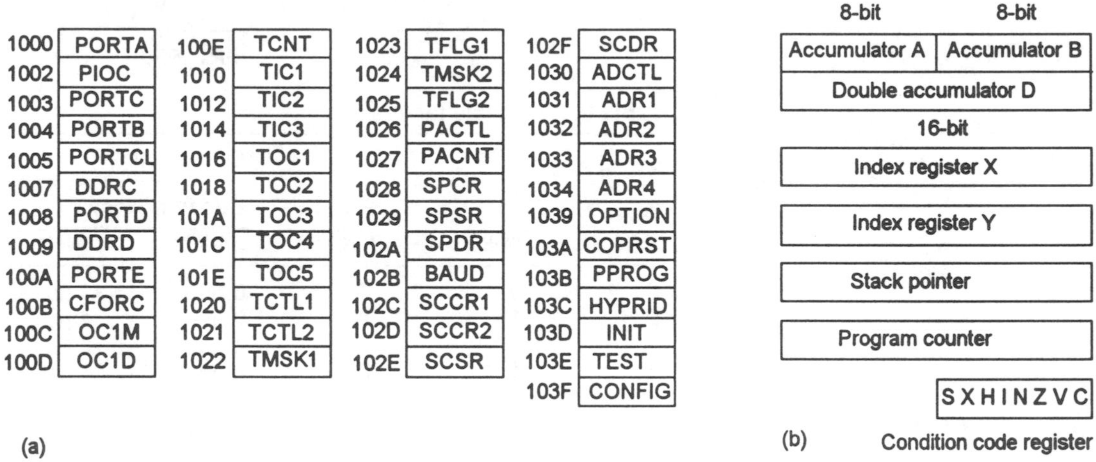
1000 PORTA
1002 PIOC
1003 PORTC
1004 PORTB
1005 PORTCL
1007 DDRC
1008 PORTD
1009 DDRD
100A PORTE
100B CFORC
100C OC1M
100D OC1D
100E TCNT
1010 TIC1
1012 TIC2
1014 TIC3
1016 TOC1
1018 TOC2
101A TOC3
101C TOC4
101E TOC5
1020 TCTL1
1021 TCTL2
1022 TMSK1
1023 TFLG1
1024 TMSK2
1025 TFLG2
1026 PACTL
1027 PACNT
1028 SPCR
1029 SPSR
102A SPDR
102B BAUD
102C SCCR1
102D SCCR2
102E SCSR
102F SCDR
1030 ADCTL
1031 ADR1
1032 ADR2
1033 ADR3
1034 ADR4
1039 OPTION
103A COPRST
103B PPROG
103C HYPRID
103D INIT
103E TEST
103F CONFIG
(a)
8-bit
8-bit
Accumulator A
Accumulator B
Double accumulator D
16-bit
Index register X
Index register Y
Stack pointer
Program counter
S X H I N Z V C
(b)
Condition code register

Fig. 2.15 Registers

2.4 Intel 8051

Another family of microcontrollers is the Intel 8051 family; Fig. 2.16 shows a block diagram of the basic microcontroller and the pin connections and memory map. The basic 8051 microcontroller has four parallel input/output ports, ports 0, 1, 2 and 3. Ports 0, 2 and 3 also have alternative functions. The 8051AH version has 4K × 8 bytes ROM, 128 × 8 bytes RAM, two 16-bit timers and interrupt control for five interrupt sources. Other members of the family have different amounts of RAM and ROM or EPROM, and different numbers of timers and interrupts.

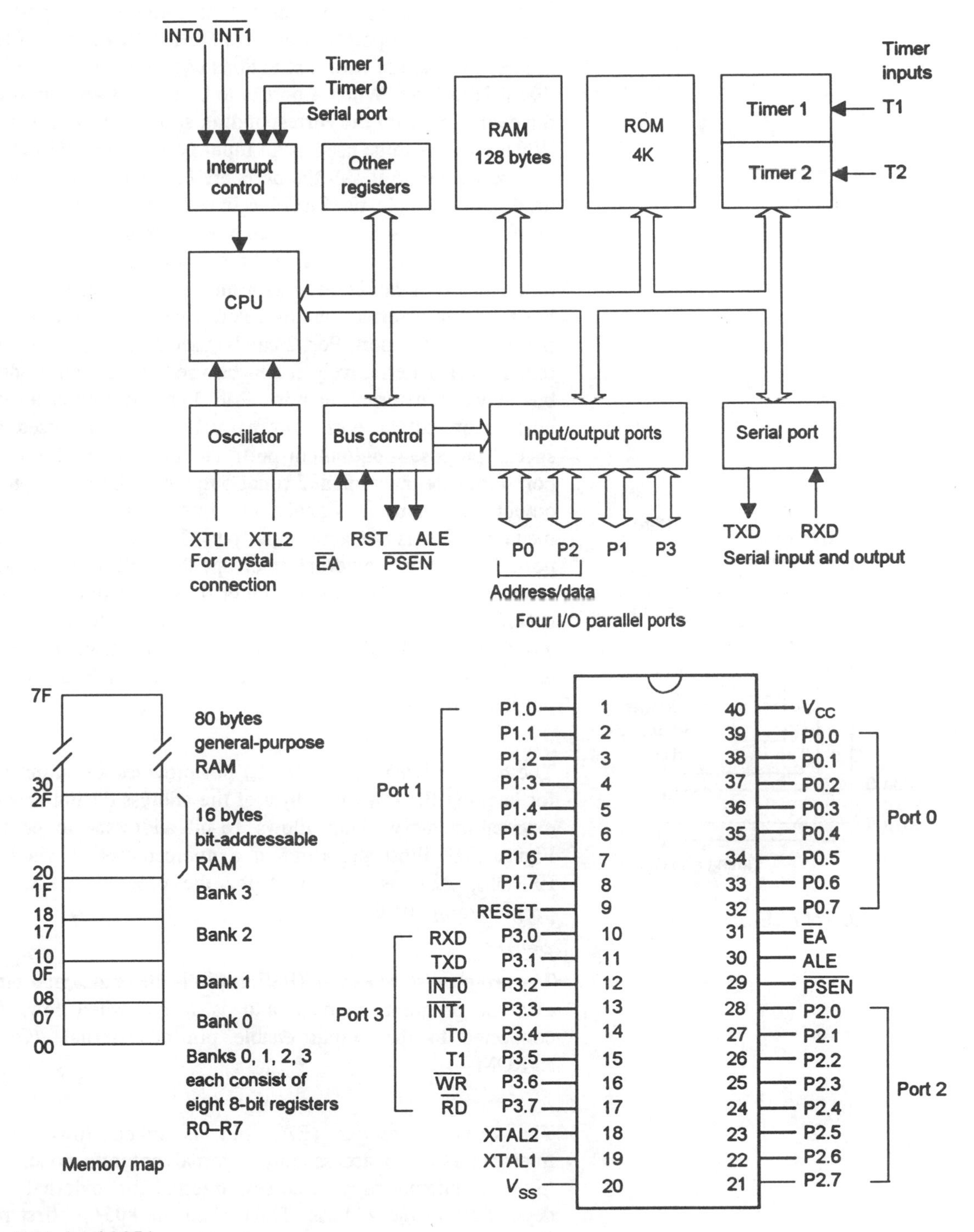

Fig. 2.16 Intel 8051

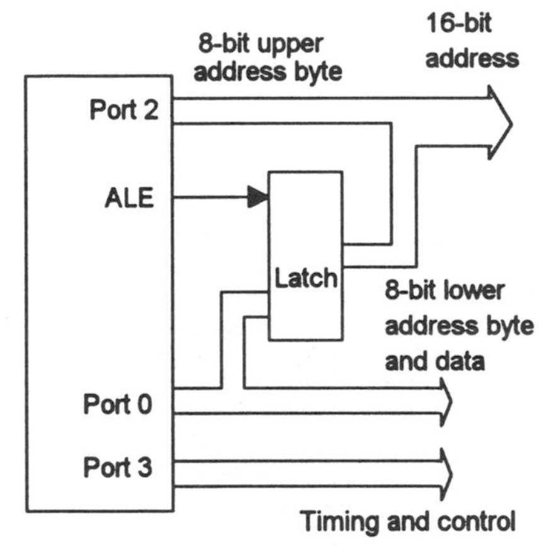

Fig. 2.17 Use of ALE

1. *Input/output ports*
   Port 0 is at address 80H, port 1 at address 90H, port 2 at address A0H and port 3 at address B0H (note the use of H, or h, after the address with instructions used with Intel to indicate that it is in hex). When a port is to be used as an output port, the data is put into the corresponding special function register. When a port is to be used as an input port, the value FFH must first be written to it. All the ports are bit addressable. Thus we might, for example, use just bit 6 in port 0 to switch a motor on or off and perhaps bit 7 to switch a pump on or off.

   Port 0 can be used as an input port or an output port. Alternatively it can be used as a multiplexed address and data bus to access external memory. Port 1 can be used as an input port or an output port. Port 2 can be used as an input port or an output port. Alternatively it can be used for the high address bus to access external memory. Port 3 can be used as an input port or an output port. Alternatively, it can be used as a special-purpose input/output port. The alternative functions of port 3 include interrupt and timer outputs, serial port input and output and control signals for interfacing with external memory. RXD is the serial input port, TXD is the serial output port, INT0 is the external interrupt 0, INT1 is the external interrupt 1, T0 is the timer/counter 0 external input, T1 is the timer/counter 1 external input, WR is the external memory write strobe and RD is the external memory read strobe. The term *strobe* describes a connection used to enable or disable a particular function.

2. *ALE*
   The *address latch enable* (ALE) pin provides an output pulse for latching the low-order byte of the address during access to external memory. This allows 16-bit addresses to be used. Figure 2.17 illustrates this. In a microcontroller which has EPROM, ALE is also used for the program pulse input programming the EPROM.

3. *PSEN*
   The *program store enable* (PSEN) pin is the read signal pin for external program memory and is active when low. It is connected to the output enable pin of external ROM or EPROM.

4. *EA*
   The *external access* (EA) pin is taken low for the microprocessor to access only external program code; when high it automatically accesses internal or external code, depending on the address. Thus when the 8051 is first reset, the program counter starts at $0000 and points to the first program instruction in the internal code memory unless EA is tied low. Then the CPU issues a low on PSEN to enable the

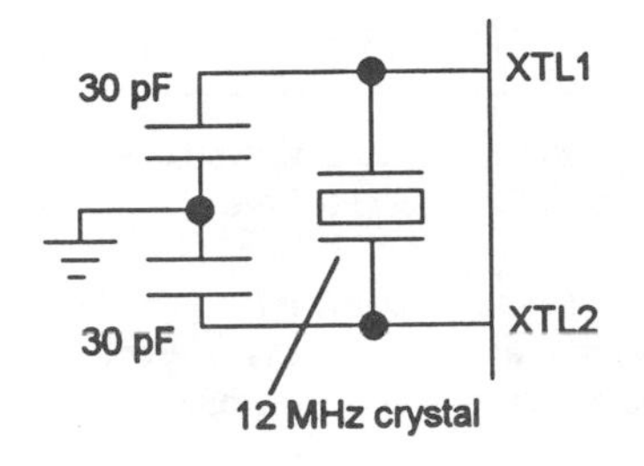

Fig. 2.18 Crystal

external code memory to be used. This pin is also used on a microcontroller with EPROM to receive the programming supply voltage for programming the EPROM.

5. *XTAL1, XTAL2*
   These are the connecting pins for a crystal or external oscillator. Figure 2.18 illustrates how they are used with a crystal. The most commonly used crystal frequency is 12 MHz.

6. *RESET*
   A high signal for a minimum of two machine cycles on this pin resets the microcontroller.

7. *Serial input/output*
   Writing to the serial data buffer SBUF at address 99H loads data for transmission; reading SBUF accesses received data. The bit addressable serial port control register SCON at address 98H is used to control the various modes of operation. See Chapter 10 for a discussion of such interfaces.

8. *Timing*
   The timer mode register TMOD at address 89H is used to set the operating mode for timer 0 and timer 1 (Fig. 2.19). It is loaded at an entity and is not individually bit addressable. The timer control register TCON (Fig. 2.20) contains status and control bits for timer 0 and timer 1. The upper four bits are used to turn the timers on and off or to signal a timer overflow. The lower four bits have nothing to do with timers but are used to detect and initiate external interrupts.

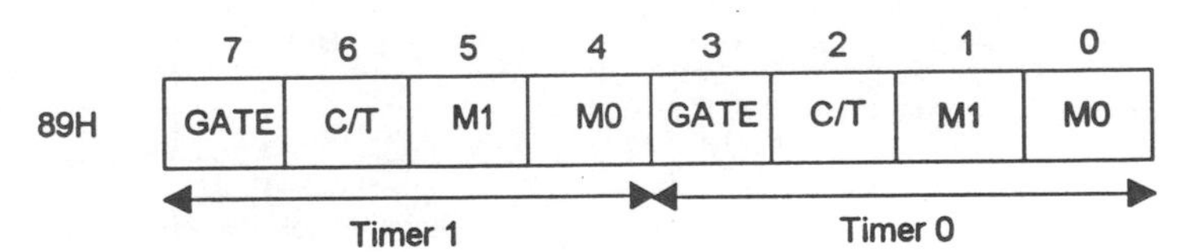

Gate: 0 = timer runs whenever TR0/TR1 set
1 = timer runs only when INT0/INT1 is high along with TR0/TR1
C/T: counter/timer select
0 = input from system clock, 1 = input from TX0/TX1
M0 and M1 set the mode

M1	M0	Mode	
0	0	0	13 bit counter, lower 5 bits of TL0 and all 8 bits of TH0
0	1	1	16 bit counter
1	0	2	8 bit auto-reload timer/counter
1	1	3	TL0 is an 8 bit timer/counter controlled by timer 0 control bits. TH0 is an 8 bit timer controlled by timer 1 control bits. Timer 1 is off.

Fig. 2.19 TMOD register

	7	6	5	4	3	2	1	0
88H	TF1	TR1	TF0	TR0	IE1	IT1	IE0	IT0

TF0, TF1	Timer overflow flag; set by hardware when time overflows and cleared by hardware when the processor calls the interupt routine
TR0, TR1	Timer run control bits: 1 = timer on, 0 = timer off
IE0, IE1	Interrupt edge flag set by hardware when external interupt edge or low level detected and cleared when interrupt processed
IT0, IT1	Interrupt type set by software: 1 = falling edge triggered interrupt, 0 = low level triggered interrupt

Fig. 2.20 TCON register

The source of the bits counted by each timer is set by the C/T bit; if the bit is low the source is the system clock divided by 12 otherwise if high it is set to count an input from an external source. The timers can be started by setting TR0 or TR1 to 1 and stopping by making it 0. Another method of controlling a timer is by setting the GATE to 1 and so allowing a timer to be controlled by the INT0 or INT1 pin on the microcontroller going to 1. In this way an external device connected to one of these pins can control the counter on/off.

9. *Interrupts*
   Interrupts force the program to call a subroutine located at a specified address in memory; they are enabled by writing to the interrupt enable register IE at address A8H (Fig. 2.21).

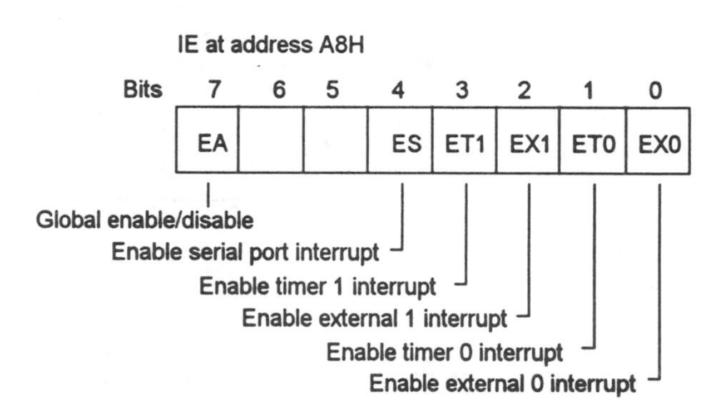

Fig. 2.21 IE register

The term *special function registers* is used for the input/output control registers (Fig. 2.22(a)), like IE above, and these are located at addresses 80 to FF. Accumulator A (ACC) is the major register used for data operations; the B register is used for multiplication and division. P0, P1, P2 and P3 are the latch registers for ports 0, 1, 2 and 3.

Address	Register	Address	Register
8D	TH1	F0	B
8C	TH0	E0	ACC
8B	TL1	D0	PSW
8A	TL0	B8	IP
89	TMOD	B0	P3
88	TCON	A8	IE
87	PCON	A0	P2
83	DPH	99	SBUF
82	DPL	98	SCON
81	SP	90	P1
80	P0		

(a)

	Bank 0		Bank 1		Bank 2		Bank 3
00	R0	08	R0	10	R0	18	R0
01	R1	09	R1	11	R1	19	R1
02	R2	0A	R2	12	R2	1A	R2
03	R3	0B	R3	13	R3	1B	R3
04	R4	0C	R4	14	R4	1C	R4
05	R5	0D	R5	15	R5	1D	R5
06	R6	0E	R6	16	R6	1E	R6
07	R7	0F	R7	17	R7	1F	R7

(b)

Fig. 2.22 Registers

Part of the internal RAM (see the memory map in Fig. 2.16) can be addressed as four register banks 0 to 3, each of which contains eight registers R0 to R7 (Fig. 2.22(b)). Each register can be addressed when its bank is selected: the bank of registers in current use is selected by the setting of the two bank select bits 3 and 4 in PSW (program status word) (Fig. 2.23), by default the bank in use is bank 0. Alternatively a register can be addressed by using its address. For example, if we use the default and then specify register R2, we obtain R2 in bank 0. Alternatively we could specify this register by using its address 02. Besides being used to select the register bank, the PSW register also contains status flags.

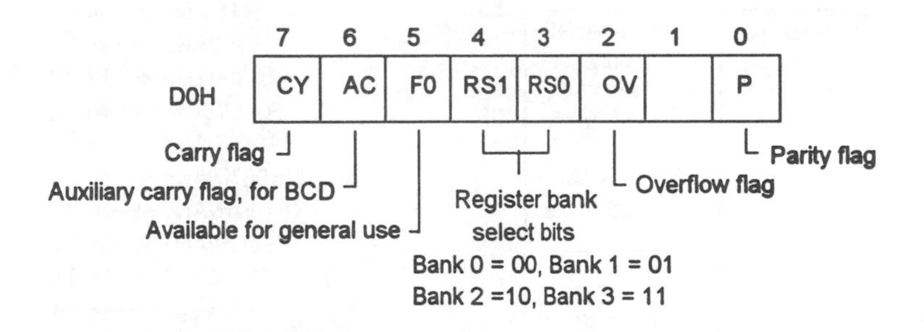

Fig. 2.23 PSW register

For more details regarding the 8051, the reader is referred to the manuals published by the manufacturer or to texts such as *Programming and Interfacing the 8051 Microcontroller* by S. Yeralan and A. Ahluwalia (Addison-Wesley 1993), *The 8051 microcontroller* by I. Scott MacKenzie (Prentice Hall 1999, 1995, 1992) or *The 8051 Family of Microcontrollers* by R.H. Barnett (Prentice Hall 1995).

2.5 PIC microcontrollers

Another widely used family of 8 bit microcontrollers is provided by Microchip as the PIC16C6x/7x family; PIC stands for peripheral interface controller. These use a form of architecture termed *Harvard architecture*. With this architecture, instructions are fetched from program memory using buses that are distinct from the buses used for accessing variables (Fig. 2.24). In the other microcontrollers discussed in this chapter, separate buses are not used and thus program data fetches have to wait for variable read/write and input/output operations to be completed before the next instruction can be received from memory. With Harvard architecture, instructions can be fetched every cycle without waiting, each instruction being executed during the cycle following its fetch. Harvard architecture enables faster execution speeds to be achieved for a given clock frequency.

Figure 2.25 shows the register map and pin connections of the PIC16C74A microcontroller, Fig. 2.26 the architecture.

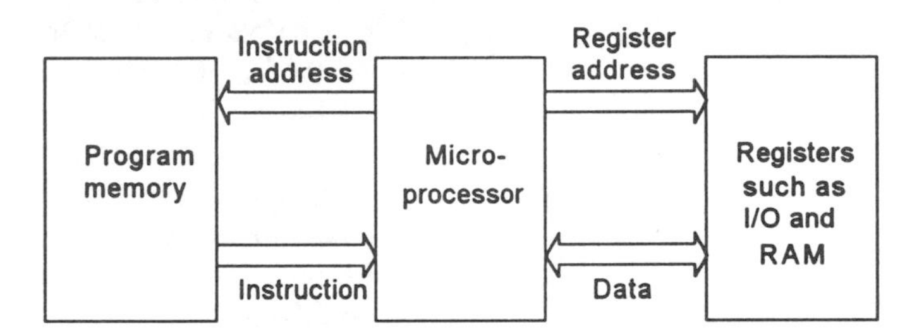

Fig. 2.24 Harvard architecture

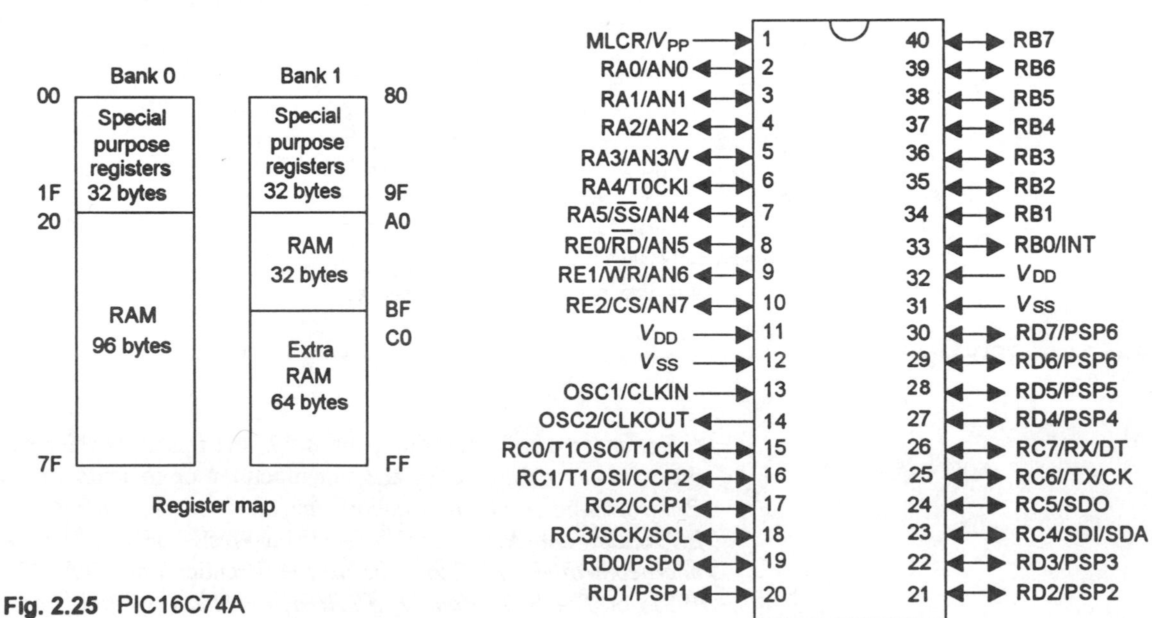

Fig. 2.25 PIC16C74A

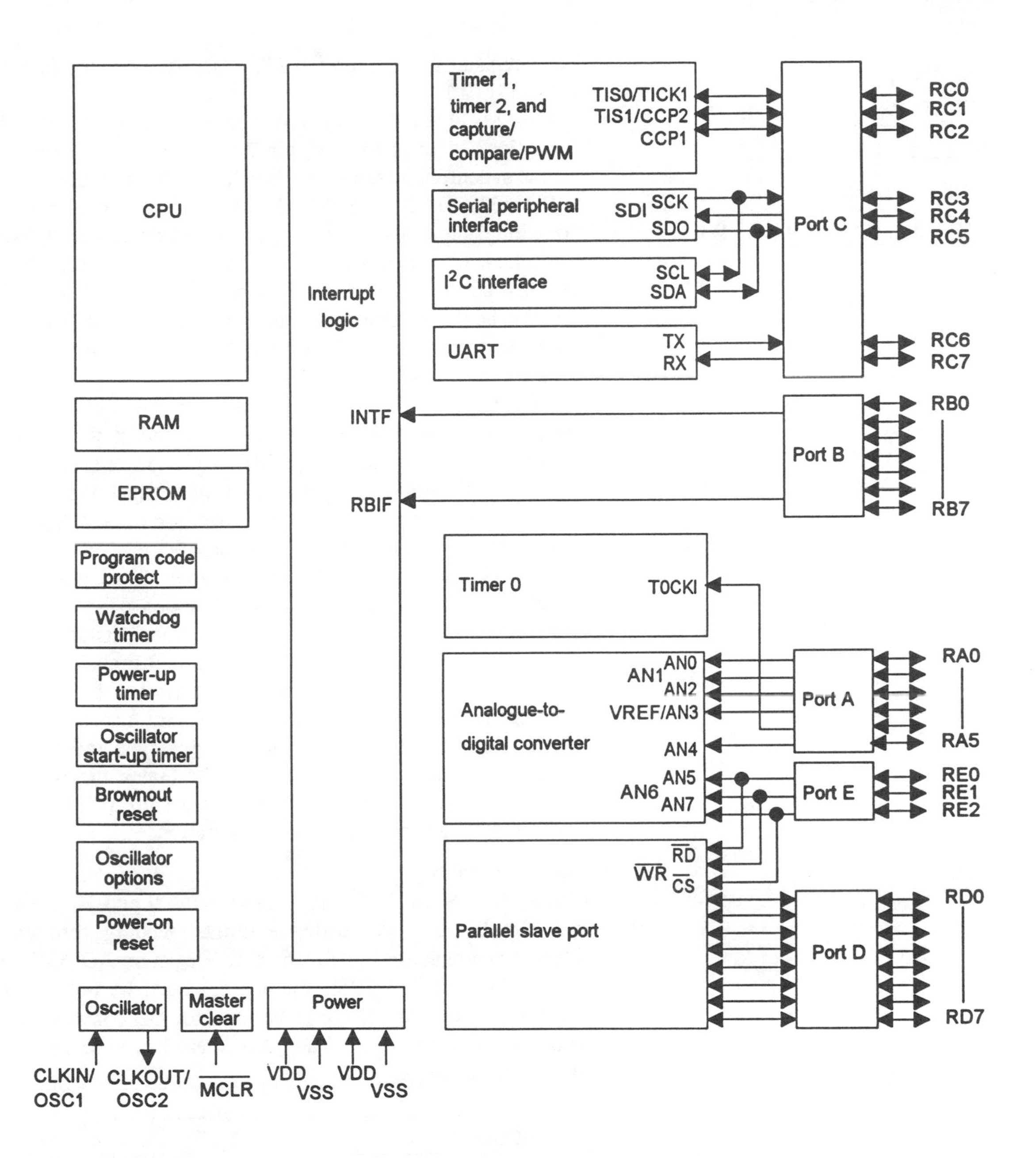

Fig. 2.26 PIC 16C74/74A

Here are the basic features of the microcontroller:

1. *Input/output ports*
   Pins 2, 3, 4, 5, 6 and 7 are for the bidirectional input/output port A. As with the other bidirectional ports, signals are read from and written to via port registers. The direction of the signals is controlled by the TRIS direction registers; there is a

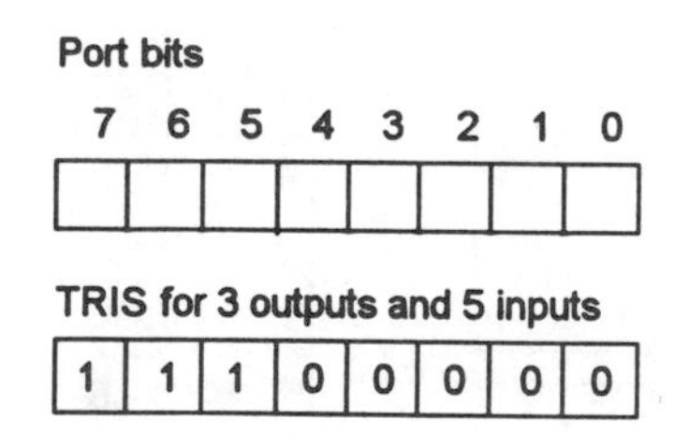

Fig. 2.27 Port direction

TRIS register for each port. TRIS is set as 1 for read and 0 for write (Fig. 2.27)

Pins 2, 3, 4 and 5 can also be used for analogue inputs, pin 6 for a clock input to timer 0; pin 7 can also be the slave select for the synchronous serial port (see later in this section).

Pins 33, 34, 35, 36, 37, 38, 39 and 40 are for the bidirectional input/output port B; the direction of the signals is controlled by a corresponding TRIS direction register. Pin 33 can also be the external interrupt pin. Pins 37, 38, 39 and 40 can also be the interrupt on change pins. Pin 39 can also be the serial programming clock and pin 40 the serial programming data.

Pins 15, 16, 17, 18, 23, 24, 25 and 26 are for the bidirectional input/output port C; the direction of the signals is controlled by a corresponding TRIS direction register. Pin 15 can also be the timer 1 output or the timer 1 clock input. Pin 16 can also be the timer 1 oscillator input or Capture 2 input/Compare 2 output/PWM2 output.

Pins 19, 20, 21, 22, 27, 28, 29 and 30 are for the bidirectional input/output port D; the direction of the signals is controlled by a corresponding TRIS direction register.

Pins 8, 9 and 10 are for the bidirectional input/output port E; the direction of the signals is controlled by a corresponding TRIS direction register. Pin 8 can also be the read control for the parallel slave port or analogue input 5. The parallel slave port is a feature that facilitates the design of personal computer interface circuitry; when in use the pins of ports D and E are dedicated to this operation.

2. *Analogue inputs*
Pins 2, 3, 4, 5 and 7 of port A and pins 8, 9 and 10 of port E can also be used for analogue inputs, feeding through an internal analogue-to-digital converter. Registers ADCON1 and TRISA for port A (TRISE for port E) must be initialised to select the reference voltage to be used for the conversion and select channels as inputs. Then ADCON0 has to be initialised using these settings:

ADCON0 bits			
5	*4*	*3*	*For analogue input on*
0	0	0	Port A, bit 0
0	0	1	Port A, bit 1
0	1	0	Port A, bit 2
0	1	1	Port A, bit 3
1	0	0	Port A, bit 5
1	0	1	Port E, bit 0
1	1	0	Port E, bit 1
1	1	1	Port E, bit 2

3. *Timers*

The microcontroller has three timers: timer 0, timer 1 and timer 2. Timer 0 is an 8-bit counter which can be written to or read from and can be used to count external signal transitions, generating an interrupt when the required number of events have occurred. The source of the count can be either the internal bus clock signal or an external digital signal. The choice of count source is made by the TOCS bit in the OPTION register (Fig. 2.28).

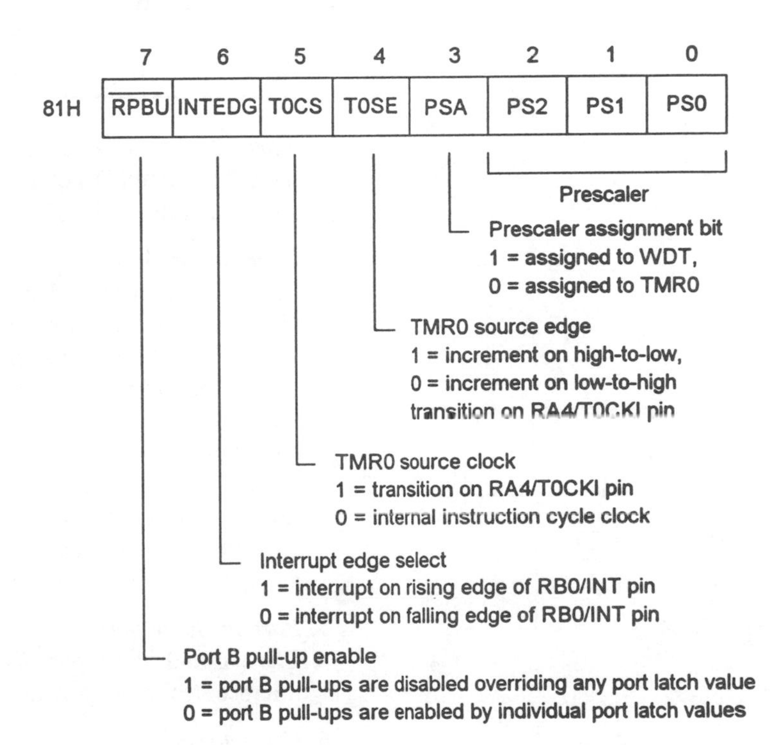

Fig. 2.28 OPTION register

If the prescaler is not selected then the count is incremented after every two cycles of the input source. A prescaler can be used so that signals are only passed to the counter after some other fixed number of clock cycles. Table 2.2 shows the scaling rates possible. WDT gives the scaling factors selected when the watchdog timer is enabled. It is used to time out and reset the system if an operation is not concluded in a reasonable time; the default time is nominally 18 ms.

Timer 1 is the most versatile of the timers and can be used to monitor the time between signal transitions on an input pin or control the precise time of transitions on an output pin. When used with the capture or compare modes, it enables the microcontroller to control the timing of an output on pin 17.

Table 2.2 Prescaler values

Prescalar bit values			*TMRO rate*	*WDT rate*
PS2	*PS1*	*PS0*		
0	0	0	1 : 2	1 : 1
0	0	1	1 : 4	1 : 2
0	1	0	1 : 8	1 : 4
0	1	1	1 : 16	1 : 8
1	0	0	1 : 32	1 : 16
1	0	1	1 : 64	1 : 32
1	1	0	1 : 128	1 : 64
1	1	1	1 : 256	1 : 128

Timer 2 can be used to control the period of a pulse width modulated (PWM) output. Pulse width modulated outputs are supplied at pins 16 and 17.

4. *Serial input/output*
   The PIC microcontroller includes a synchronous serial port (SSP) module and a serial communications interface module (SCI). Pin 18 has the alternative functions of the synchronous serial clock input or output for SPI serial peripheral interface mode and I^2C mode. The I^2C bus provides a two-wire bidirectional interface that can be used with a range of other chips; it can also be used for connecting a master microcontroller to slave microcontrollers. UART, i.e. the universal asynchronous receiver transmitter, can be used to create a serial interface to a personal computer.

5. *Parallel slave port*
   The parallel slave port uses ports D and E and enables the microcontroller to provide an interface with a PC.

6. *Crystal input*
   Pin 13 is for the oscillator crystal input or external clock source input; pin 14 is for the oscillator crystal output. Figure 2.29(a) shows the arrangement that might be used for accurate frequency control. Figure 2.29(b) that which might be used for a low cost frequency control; for a frequency of 4 MHz we can have R = 4.7 kΩ and C = 33 pF. The internal clock rate is the oscillator frequency divided by 4.

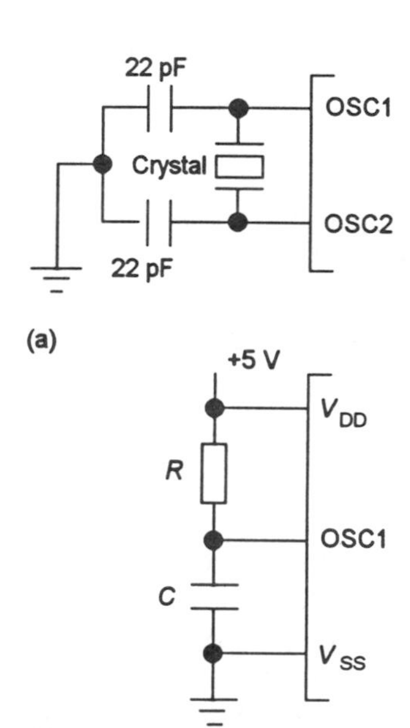

Fig. 2.29 Frequency control

7. *Master clear*
   Pin 1 is the master clear, i.e. reset input, and is taken low to reset the device.

The *special-purpose registers* (Fig. 2.30) are used for input/output control, as illustrated above in relation to a few of these registers. The registers for the PIC16C73/74 are arranged in two banks and before a particular register can be selected, the bank has to be chosen by setting a bit in the status register (Fig. 2.31).

File address	Bank 0	Bank 1	File address
00h	INDF	INDF	80h
01h	TMR0	OPTION	81h
02h	PCL	PCL	82h
03h	STATUS	STATUS	83h
04h	FSR	FSR	84h
05h	PORTA	TRISA	85h
06h	PORTB	TRISB	86h
07h	PORTC	TRISC	87h
08h	PORTD	TRISD	88h
09h	PORTE	TRISE	89h
0Ah	PCLATH	PCLATH	8Ah
0Bh	INTCON	INTCON	8Bh
0Ch	PIR1	PIE1	8Ch
0Dh	PIR2	PIE2	8Dh
0Eh	TMR1L	PCON	8Eh
0Fh	TMR1H		8Fh
10h	T1CON		90h
11h	TMR2		91h
12h	T2CON	PR2	92h
13h	SSPBUF	SSPADD	93h
14h	SSPCON	SSPSTAT	94h
15h	CCPR1L		95h
16h	CCPR1H		96h
17h	CCP1CON		97h
18h	RCSTA	TXSTA	98h
19h	TXREG	SPBRG	99h
1Ah	RCREG		9Ah
1Bh	CCPR2L		9Bh
1Ch	CCPR2H		9Ch
1Dh	CCPR2CON		9Dh
1Eh	ADRES		9Eh
1Fh	ADCON0	ADCON1	9Fh
20h 7Fh	General-purpose registers	General-purpose registers	A0h FFh

Fig. 2.30 PIC registers

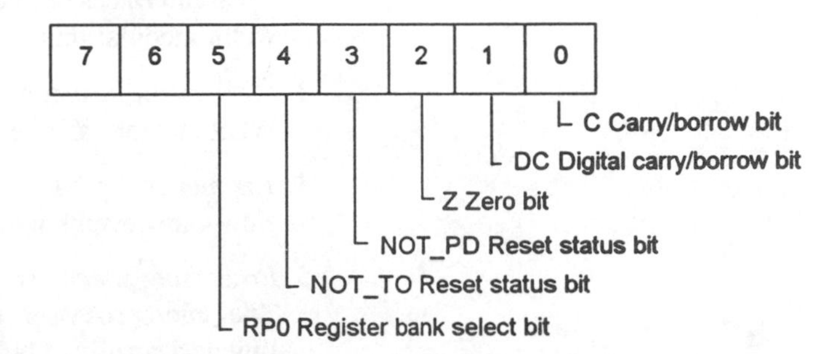

Fig. 2.31 STATUS register

PIC microcontrollers have a CPU with an 8 bit *working register*; this fulfils the functions of accumulators in other microcontrollers.

For more details of PIC microcontrollers, see the publications of the manufacturer or books such as *Design with PIC Microcontrollers* by J.B. Peatman (Prentice Hall 1998) or *Programming and Customizing the PIC Microcontroller* by M. Predko (McGraw-Hill 1998).

2.6 Single or multiple chip

A microcontroller can give a *single-chip system* since it can contain the microprocessor, RAM, EPROM/ROM and input/output ports. A *multiple-chip system* would have separate microprocessor, RAM, EPROM/ROM and input/output port chips. A single-chip microcontroller offers the advantages of simplicity and is likely to be cheaper. However, a microcontroller might not have sufficient input/output pins or sufficient RAM or ROM. With a multiple-chip system, connections must be made between the chips using the data and address buses. The microprocessor then generates an address which is decoded to select a particular chip. The microprocessor can then write data on to the data bus and generate a signal indicating that the selected chip should read the data. Alternatively the microprocessor supplies a signal to tell the selected chip to put data on the data bus for it to read. Examples of multiple-chip systems are given in Section 1.10.5; this chapter gives details of single-chip microcontroller systems.

2.6.1 Selecting a microcontroller

In selecting a microcontroller the following factors need to be considered:

1. *Number of input/output pins*
   How many input/output pins are going to be needed for the task concerned?
2. *Interfaces required*
   What interfaces are going to be required? For example, is pulse width modulation required?
3. *Memory requirements*
   What memory size is required for the task?
4. *The number of interrupts required*
   How many events will need interrupts?
5. *Processing speed required*
   The microprocessor takes time to execute instructions; this time is determined by the processor clock.

Table 2.3 Examples of M68HC11 family

	ROM	*EEPROM*	*RAM*	*ADC*	*Timer*	*PWM*	*I/O*	*Serial*	*E clock MHz*
68HC11A0	0	0	256	8 ch, 8 bit	(1)	0	22	SCI, SPI	2
68HC11A1	0	512	256	8 ch, 8 bit	(1)	0	22	SCI, SPI	2
68HC11A7	8K	0	256	8 ch, 8 bit	(1)	0	38	SCI, SPI	3
68HC11A8	8K	512	256	8 ch, 8 bit	(1)	0	38	SCI, SPI	3
68HC11C0	0	512	256	4 ch, 4 bit	(2)	2 ch, 8 bit	36	SCI, SPI	2
68HC11D0	0	0	192	None	(2)	0	14	SCI, SPI	2

Timer: (1) is 3 input capture, 5 output compare, real-time interrupt, watchdog timer, pulse accumulator, (2) is 3 or 4 input capture, 5 or 4 output compare, real-time interrupt, watchdog timer, pulse accumulator. Serial: SCI is asynchronous serial communication interface, SPI is synchronous serial peripheral interface.

Table 2.4 Examples of Intel 8051 family

	ROM	*EPROM*	*RAM*	*Timers*	*I/O ports*	*Interrupts*
8031AH	0	0	128	2	4	5
8051AH	4K	0	128	2	4	5
8052AH	8K	0	256	3	4	6
8751H	0	4K	128	2	4	5

As an illustration of the variation of microcontrollers available in a family, Table 2.3 shows details of just a few of the M68HC11 family and Table 2.4 details of a few of the Intel 8051 family.

Problems

1. How does a microcontroller differ from a microprocessor?
2. Draw a block diagram of a basic microcontroller and explain the function of each subsystem.
3. Which of the M68HC11 ports is used for (a) the A/D converter, (b) a bidirectional port, (c) a serial input/output, (d) as just an 8-bit output-only port?
4. For the Motorola M68HC11, port C is bidirectional. How is it configured to be (a) an input, (b) an output?
5. The Motorola M68HC11 can be operated in single-chip mode and extended mode. Why are there these modes?
6. What is the purpose of the ALE pin connection with the Intel 8051?
7. What input is required to reset an Intel 8051 microcontroller?
8. What are the functions of the bits in (a) the TMOD and (b) the IE registers of the Intel 8051?
9. PIC microcontrollers use the Harvard architecture. What does this mean?
10. How is the TRIS register used with a PIC microcontroller to set a pin in a port as an input or an output?
11. Which port pins with the PIC16C74/74A microcontroller can be used for analogue inputs?

3 Microprocessor-based systems

3.1 Introduction

Microprocessors and microcontrollers are used in a wide variety of applications which impact directly on our lives. For example, they are in washing machines, cameras, mobile telephones, smart cards, television sets, video recorders, compact disc players, microwave ovens and in automobiles for the engine management system.

This chapter considers the functions of microprocessors and microcontrollers in a range of devices. It also discusses examples of the sensors and actuators used in such systems, i.e. the input devices providing the sensing signals on which the microprocessor or microcontrollers operate and the devices to which the output is directed to produce the required actions.

The term *embedded microprocessor system* is used when the microprocessor system is designed for control purposes and is not built to have its program changed by the end user in the same way that a PC is, i.e. the system is self-contained with its operating program and is not designed to have its functions changed by different software being loaded, whearas a PC can be changed readily from a word processor to a games machine. This chapter is about embedded systems.

3.2 Some examples

Here are some examples of how microprocessors and microcontrollers are used in a range of embedded applications.

3.2.1 Washing machine

With such a machine a number of operations have to be carried out with various valves and pumps switched on and off in the required sequence to achieve the selected wash program, e.g.

1. When the start switch is pressed, valves are opened to allow water into the wash drum.
2. When the full water level is sensed, the valves are closed.

3. The water heater is then switched on.
4. When the correct water temperature is sensed, the washer motor is turned on to rotate the drum.
5. The washer motor is run for a set time.
6. At the end of the set time, the pump is switched on to empty the drum.
7. When empty the pump is switched off.
8. The valves are opened to fill the drum with water.
9. When the full level is sensed, the valves are closed.
10. The rinse action of rotating the drum first one way and then the other is then activated for a set time.
11. Steps 6, 7, 8, 9 and 10 are repeated several times.
12. When the drum is empty after rinsing, the pump is turned off and the drum spun for a set time to remove water from the clothes in the machine and conclude the program.
13. During the running of the wash program, a door catch is actuated and not released until 30 s after the conclusion of the wash program.

Figure 3.1 shows a simplified block diagram of the basic elements of the control system. There are inputs to the controller of the required program, e.g. whether the wash is to be for whites or coloured garments and what temperature is to be used, and from sensors which detect when the machine door is open, the level of the water in the drum and the water temperature. The outputs from the controller are used to actuate the hot water and cold water valves, the water pump, the door lock and the motor speed and its direction of rotation.

Figure 3.2 shows how these inputs and outputs might be organised when a microcontroller is used as the controller. The microcontroller often used is the Motorola M68HC05B6; this is simpler and cheaper than the Motorola M68HC11 microcontroller discussed in the previous chapter and is widely used for low cost applications. The inputs from the sensors for water temperature and motor speed are via the analogue-to-digital input port. Port A provides the outputs for the various actuators used to control the machine and also the input for the water level switch. Port B gives outputs to the display. Port C gives outputs to the display and also receives inputs from the keyboard used to input to the machine the various program selections. The PWM section of the timer provides a pulse width modulated signal to control the motor speed. The entire machine program is interrupted and stopped if the door of the washing machine is opened.

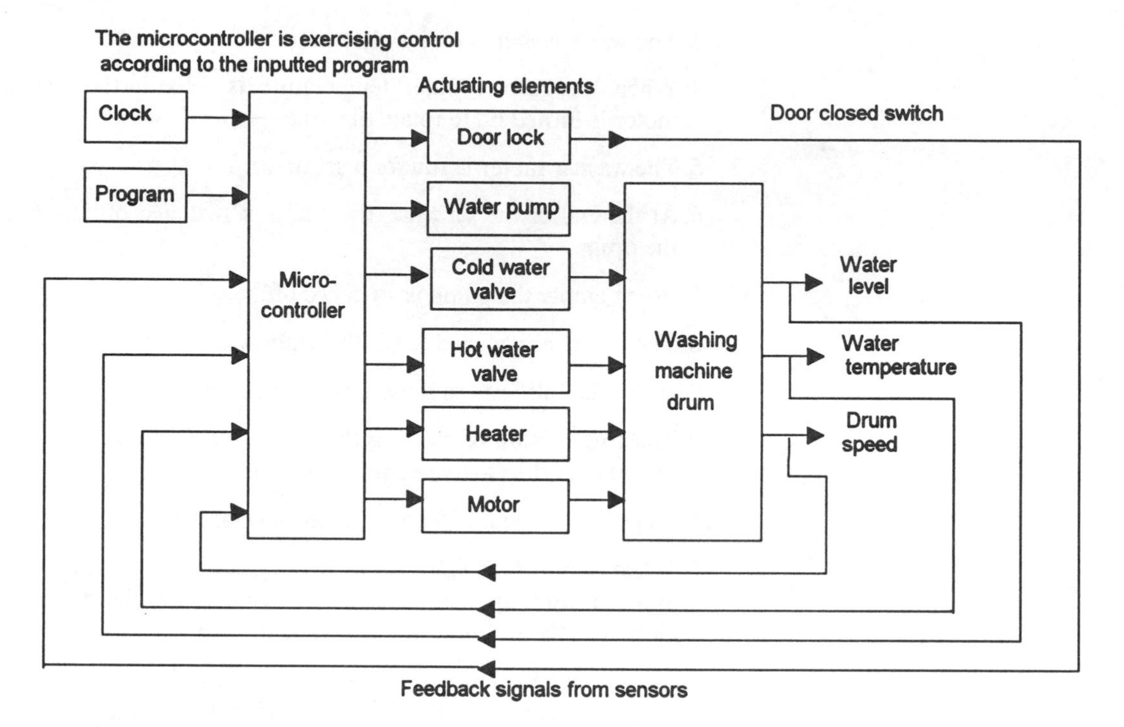

Fig. 3.1 Washing machine system

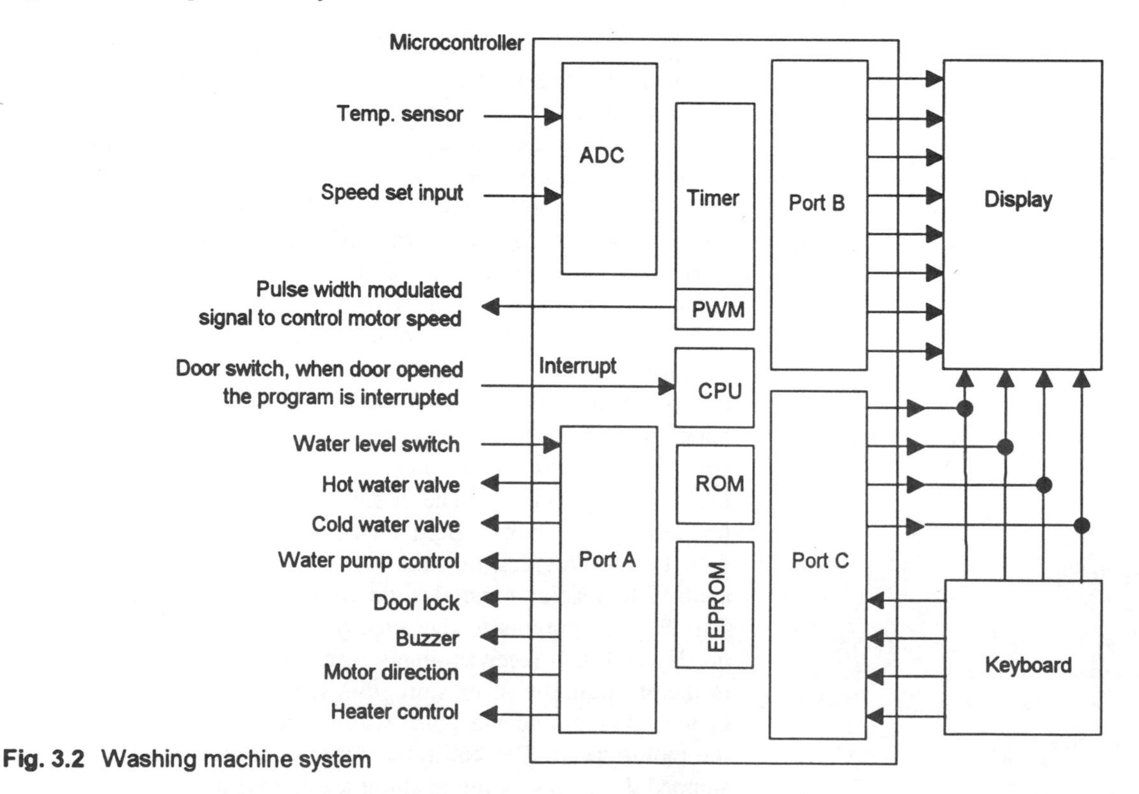

Fig. 3.2 Washing machine system

3.2.2 Automatic camera

The modern film camera is likely to have automatic focusing and exposure. To illustrate the elements involved, Fig. 3.3 shows the basic features of the Canon EOS automatic, autofocus, reflex cameras. The cameras have interchangeable lenses. Consequently, there is a main microcontroller M68HC11 in the camera body and another microcontroller in the lens housing; the two controllers communicate with each other when a lens is attached to the camera body. Figure 3.4 shows a block diagram of the electronic system.

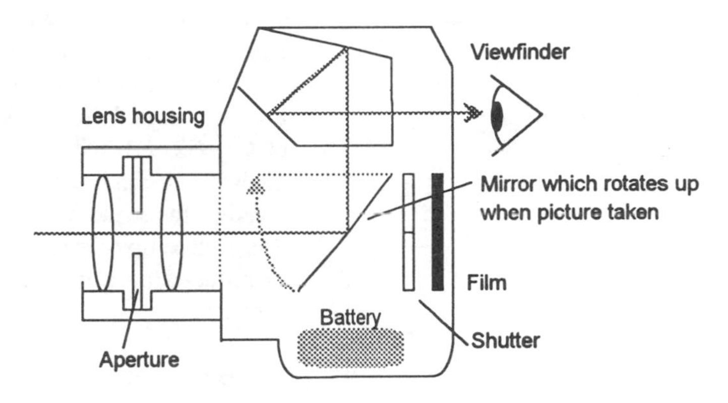

Fig. 3.3 Reflex camera

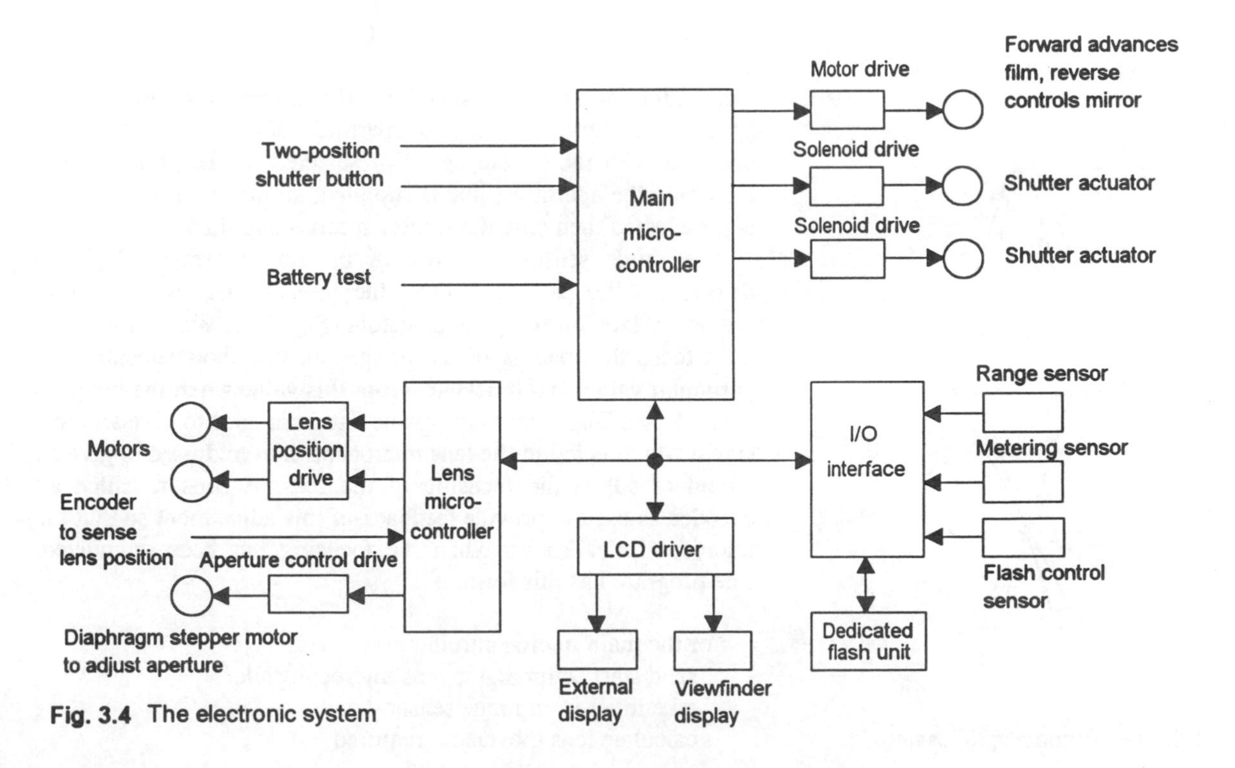

Fig. 3.4 The electronic system

When the photographer presses the shutter button to its first position, i.e. partially depressed, the main microcontroller calculates the shutter speed and aperture settings using the input from the metering sensor and displays them in the viewfinder and an external LCD display. At the same time, the main microcontroller processes the input from the range sensor and sends signals to the lens microcontroller. This issues signals to drive motors to adjust the focusing of the lens. When the photographer presses the shutter button to its second position, i.e. fully depressed, the main microcontroller issues signals to drive the mirror up, change the aperture to the required size, open the shutter for the required exposure time, and, when the shutter has closed, advance the film ready for the next photograph.

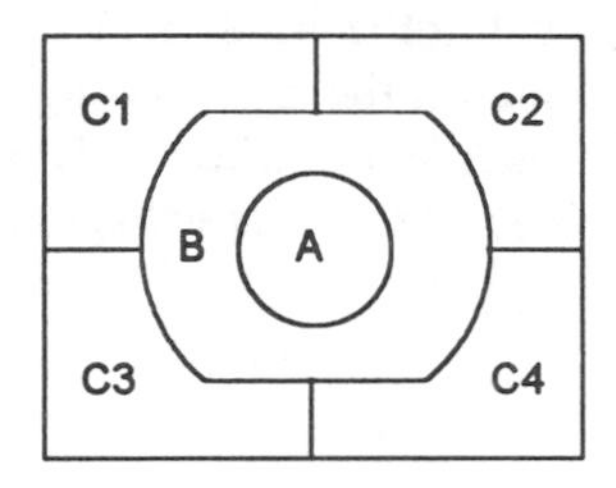

Fig. 3.5 Light sensors

The metering sensor has six light sensors arranged as shown in Fig. 3.5. Signal conditioning is used to obtain the average value of C1, C2, C3 and C4; the A, B and average C value are then analysed to find the required exposure value. This will reveal whether the scene has a relatively constant luminosity or whether it is a close up of a person and therefore has a bright central zone surrounded by a dark background. The type of program that is used is:

if B is equal to A and C minus B is less than 0
  then exposure set on value of A
if B is equal to A and C minus B is 0
  then exposure set on value of C

This information is translated by the microcontroller into an appropriate shutter speed and aperture value. If the camera is operated with the shutter speed preselected by the photographer then only the aperture value is supplied; similarly, if the aperture is preselected then only the shutter speed is supplied.

The range sensor has two 48 bit linear arrays of photodetectors. After passing through the camera lens, the light from the object falls on the photodetectors (Fig. 3.6). When the image is in focus the spacing of the images on the photodetectors is a particular value, and it deviates from this value when the image is out of focus. The amount of this deviation is used to give an error signal which is fed to the lens microcontroller and used to give an output to adjust the focusing of the lens. A sensor, called an encoder, is used to provide feedback of this adjustment so that the microcontroller knows when the focusing has been completed. The program has this form:

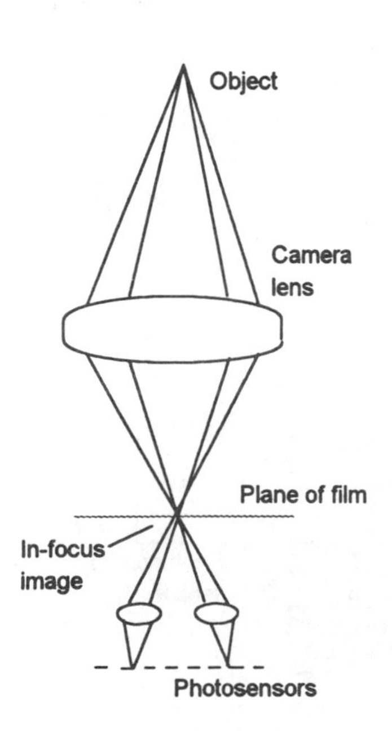

Fig. 3.6 Automatic focussing

For the main microcontroller
  send start command to lens microcontroller
  take input from range sensor
  calculate lens movement required

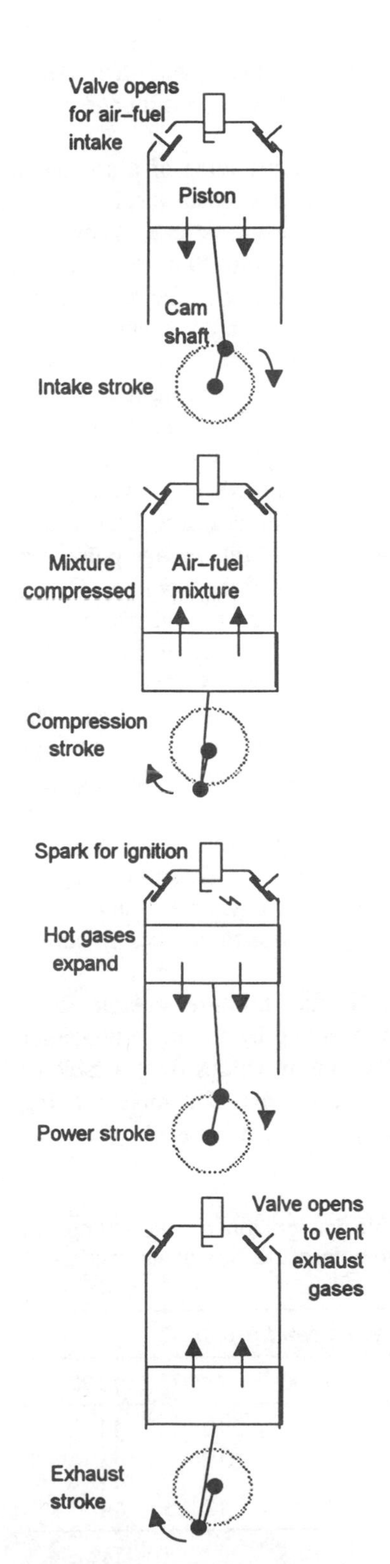

Fig. 3.7 Four-stroke sequence

send lens movement data to lens microcontroller
wait for verification of movement from microcontroller
send in-focus signal to viewfinder display

For the lens microcontroller
wait for start command from main microcontroller
determine initial lens position
wait for lens movement data from main microcontroller
read lens movement data
calculate new lens position
while lens is not in new position, drive the motor
send verification of in-focus signal to main microcontroller

The diaphragm drive system used to determine the lens aperture is a stepper motor (see Section 3.5) which opens or closes a set of diaphragm blades by giving a rotation through an angle determined by the input from the microcontroller. The focusing is achieved by a motor giving a rotation which moves the lens along the optical axis.

3.2.3 Automobile engine management system

A modern car has to give excellent driving performance, good fuel economy and low exhaust emissions under all driving conditions. There are many factors involved in obtaining these conditions. However, when a car is being driven the main factors are the control of the air–fuel mixture ratio and spark timing. The accuracy of the control required to achieve the required performance are such that the modern car uses a microprocessor-based control system. The following is a very simplistic indication of engine management; for more detail the reader is referred to texts such as *Automobile Electrical and Electronic Systems* by T. Denton (Arnold 1995), *Automobile Electronics* by E. Chowanietz (Newnes 1995) or manufacturers' data sheets.

The engine management system of a car is responsible for managing the ignition and fuelling requirements of the engine. With a four-stroke internal combustion engine there are several cylinders, each of which has a piston connected to a common crankshaft and each of which carries out a four-stroke sequence of operations (Fig. 3.7). When the piston moves down a valve opens and the air–fuel mixture, which has been previously mixed in the engine intake, is drawn into the cylinder. When the piston moves up again the valve closes and the air–fuel mixture is compressed. When the piston is near the top of the cylinder the spark plug ignites the mixture with a resulting expansion of the hot gases. This expansion causes the piston to move back down again and so the cycle is repeated. The burnt gases are expelled to the atmosphere on the exhaust stroke and the cylinder is then ready for the next intake of air–fuel mixture. The pistons of each cylinder are connected to a common crankshaft and their power strokes occur at different times so that there is continuous power for rotating the crankshaft.

The air–fuel mixture takes a few thousandths of a second to completely burn and the ignition spark must occur just before the piston reaches the top of its compression stroke, known as *ignition advance*, to allow time for the combustion to occur and the cylinder pressure to reach a maximum just as the piston starts on its expansion stroke. A function of an engine management system is to continually assess the engine operating circumstances and compute the ignition advance to give the timing required for the maximum output torque and then supply an appropriate output to achieve such ignition. The system uses a feedback control system (Fig. 3.8) with a timing wheel providing the feedback pulses to indicate the crankshaft position. The microprocessor then adjusts the timing at which high voltage pulses are sent to the distributor so they occur at the right moments. Figure 3.9 shows the arrangement of an engine management system.

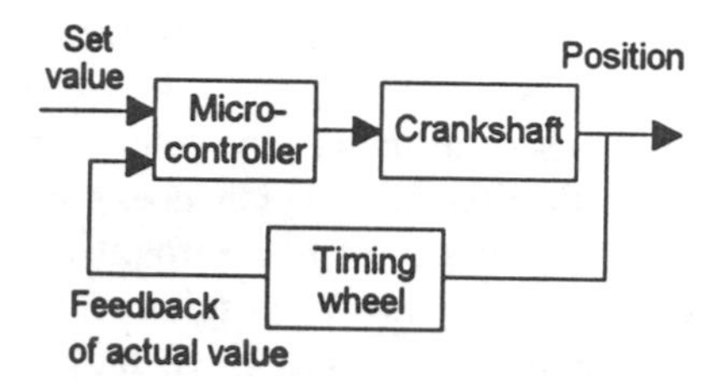

Fig. 3.8 Feedback system

To control the relative amounts of air and fuel in the air–fuel mixture entering a cylinder during the intake strokes, older cars used a carburettor but modern cars use fuel injection. The microprocessor of the engine management system varies the time for which a solenoid is activated to open the valve allowing fuel into the airstream. It does this on the basis of inputs received of the engine temperature and the throttle position. The amount of fuel to be injected into the airstream can be determined by an input from a sensor of the mass rate of airflow, or computed from other measurements, and the microprocessor then gives an output to control a fuel injection valve.

The ignition timing and the air–fuel mixture suitable for a particular situation are generally obtained by the microprocessor using inputs from sensors to select output values from a table of data stored in ROM. Table 3.1 shows part of a table relating engine speed and inlet manifold pressure, a measure of engine load.

Table 3.1 Part of a look-up table for ignition timing settings to give the angle of the crankshaft before the top of its motion at which ignition is to occur

Inlet manifold	*Engine speed (r.p.m.)*				
pressure (bar)	*800*	*1000*	*1200*	*1400*	*1600*
1.0	5	7	9	10	11
0.96	5	7	9	10	11
0.92	8	8	9	11	12
0.88	9	10	11	12	14

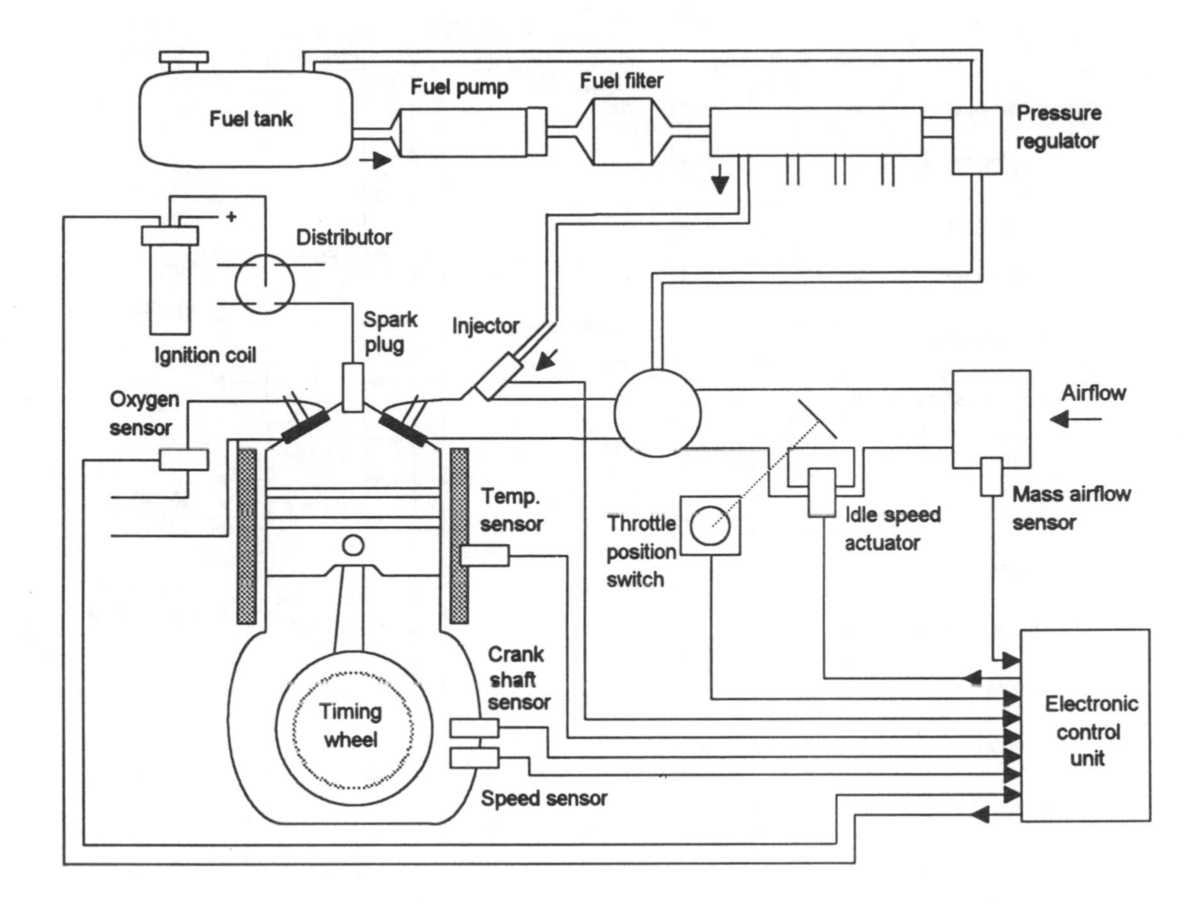

Fig. 3.9 An engine management system

The electronic control unit is basically just a microcontroller. Figure 3.10 shows the type of arrangement involved. After suitable signal conditioning, sensors supply the input signals to the microcontroller, and the microcontroller provides output signals via drivers to actuate actuators. A microcontroller that is used is the Motorola 68HC11. The sensors involved are:

1. The engine speed sensor and the crankshaft position sensors are inductive sensors. The inductance of the sensor coils change as the teeth of the timing wheel pass and this produces a sequence of pulses. The pulses can be used for timing and the engine speed can be found by counting the number of pulses in fixed time intervals. The microcontroller thus obtains an input related to the engine speed.

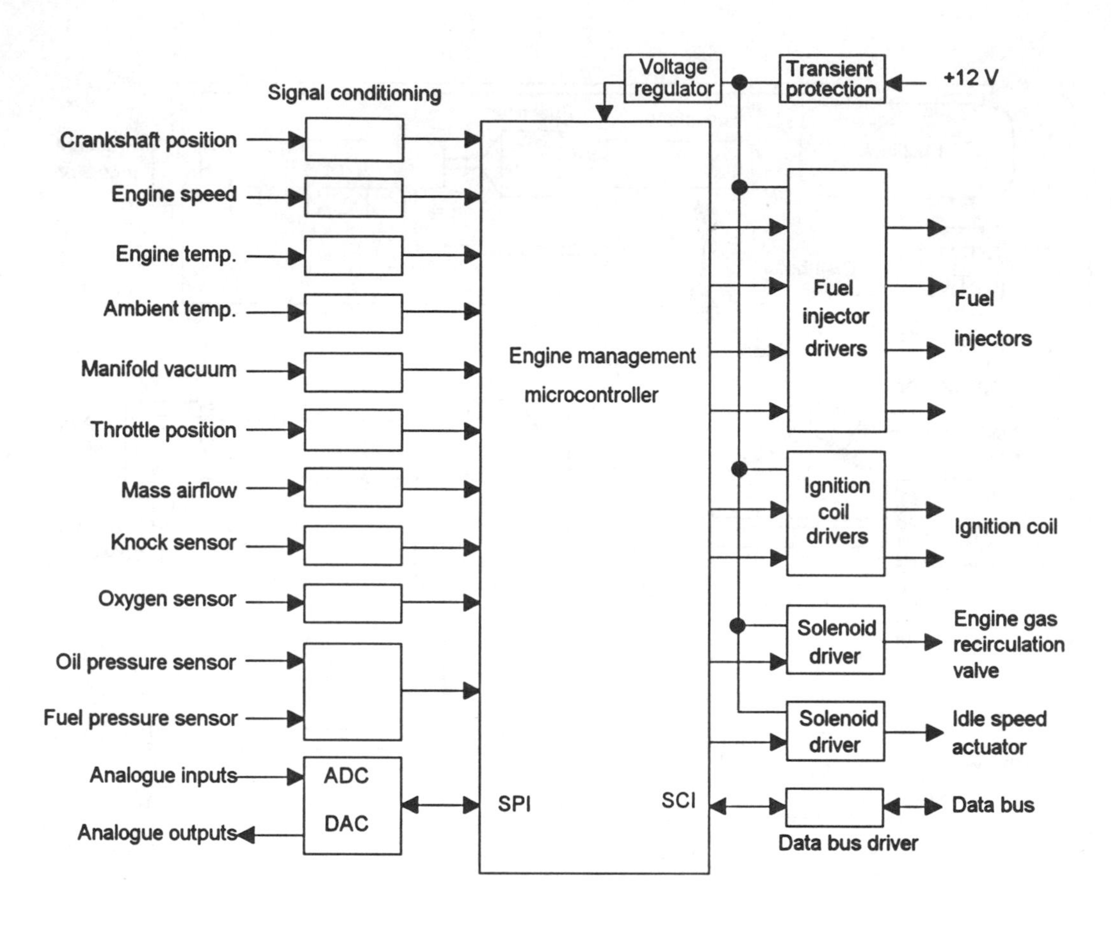

Fig. 3.10 Engine management system

2. The temperature sensor is usually a thermistor. After suitable signal conditioning, it gives an analogue signal to the analogue input port of the microcontroller.

3. The mass airflow sensor may be a hot wire sensor. As air passes over a heated wire it will be cooled, and the amount of cooling depends on the mass rate of flow. This gives an analogue signal which can be inputted to the analogue input port of the microcontroller.

4. The oxygen sensor is generally a closed-ended tube made of zirconium oxide with porous platinum electrodes on the inner and outer surfaces. Above about 300°C the sensor becomes permeable to oxygen ions with the result that a voltage is produced between the electrodes. This gives an analogue signal input to the microcontroller.

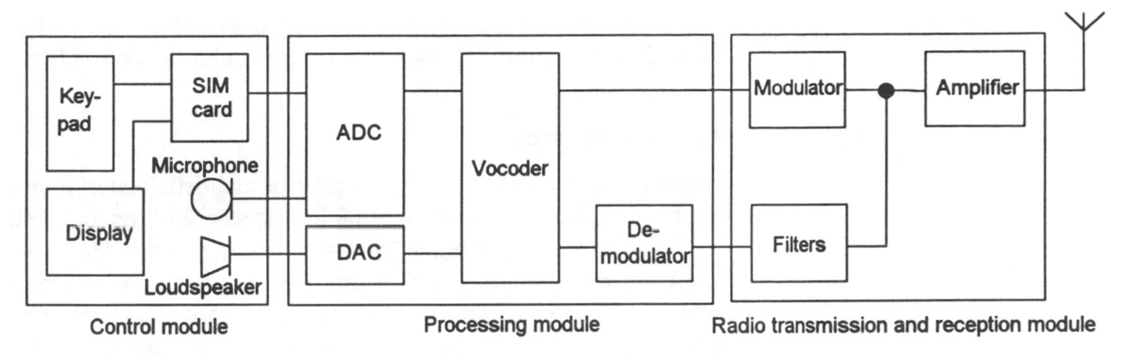

Fig. 3.11 Mobile telephone

3.2.4 Mobile telephone

Figure 3.11 shows the basic elements involved in a mobile telephone:

1. The *control module* controls the user interface.
2. The *processing module* carries out analogue-to-digital conversion and channel coding and decoding.
3. The *radio transmission and reception module* generates, modulates and amplifies the signals for transmission and it filters and amplifies the received signals.

For transmission, the analogue speech signal is converted into a digital signal by the analogue-to-digital converter. This is then coded and used to modulate a radio frequency carrier for transmission. For reception, the received signal is amplified, filtered and demodulated to provide the wanted signal in digital form. A digital-to-analogue converter is then used to provide an analogue output for the loudspeaker.

The subscriber identity module (SIM) (Fig. 3.12) is a smart card (see Section 3.3.5) which contains a microcontroller. The ROM is programmed at the fabrication stage and contains the operating system for the card. The EPROM stores permanent data and electrically configurable data. This includes manufacturer's data such as component and batch numbers, the directory number of the user, subscription information and data which is personalised to determine access to the network. A mobile telephone cannot access the network service unless it can provide a valid access code to enable the network to authenticate the user. The RAM is the working memory of the microprocessor.

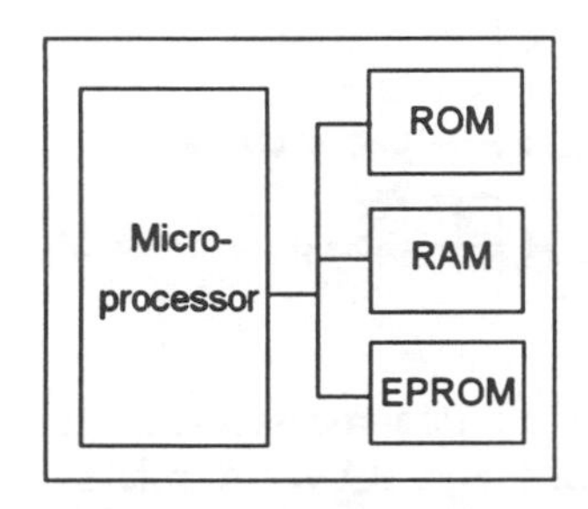

Fig. 3.12 SIM card

The microcontroller has an input from a keypad for the dialled number, interfaces with the processing module and provides an output to a display to give a visual display of the dialled number and other messages.

For more details the reader is referred to specialist texts such as *GSM Cellular Radio Telephony* by J. Tisal (John Wiley 1997).

3.2.5 Smart cards

Magnetic stripe cards consist of a strip of magnetic material on a plastic card. Data, up to about 1000 bits, is stored in the magnetic strip and read by pulling it across a reading head. The main problems with magnetic stripes are the ease with which stored data can be altered; having obtained valid card data, criminals can easily produce duplicates of cards which can then be used in such devices as cash dispensers. But *smart cards* have the advantage that they can be protected against unauthorised access and tampering, besides which they are able to store more data, e.g. 20 Kbytes, they are more more reliable and they have a longer life than magnetic stripe cards.

There are two basic forms of smart card, *memory cards* and *microprocessor cards*. An example of a memory card is a card used for electronic payment where a card is purchased with some initial cash balance stored in it and can then be used for payment; the payment is debited from the balance in the card until all the stored cash is used up, e.g. to pay bus fares by inserting the card in a machine as you enter the bus. Figure 3.13 shows the basic architecture of such a card. The data required for the application, e.g. the cash balance, is stored in the EEPROM. Access to the memory is controlled by the security logic. Data is transmitted to and from the card via the input/output port. Power and clock signals are supplied to the card when it is inserted in the reading machine for a transaction to occur.

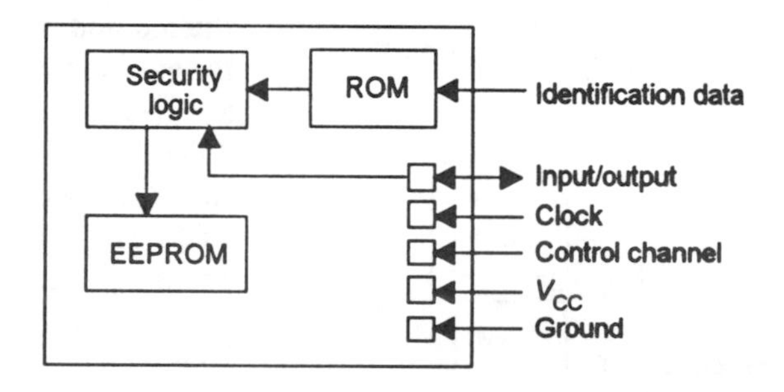

Fig. 3.13 Memory card

Figure 3.14 shows the architecture of a microprocessor card. It has a microprocessor, ROM, EEPROM and RAM. A microcontroller, such as a Motorola MC68HC05SC21, with integral ROM, EEPROM and RAM is often used. The ROM contains the chip operating system. The EEPROM can be written to and read under the control of the operating system and is loaded with the program to run the application for which the card is to be used. The RAM is the working memory for the system. The card also contains an input/output interface. This port is used for serial communications with the data being transferred bit by bit. Power and clock signals are supplied to the card when it is used in a reading or writing machine. When the microprocessor is operating it can be reset by a signal on the reset input.

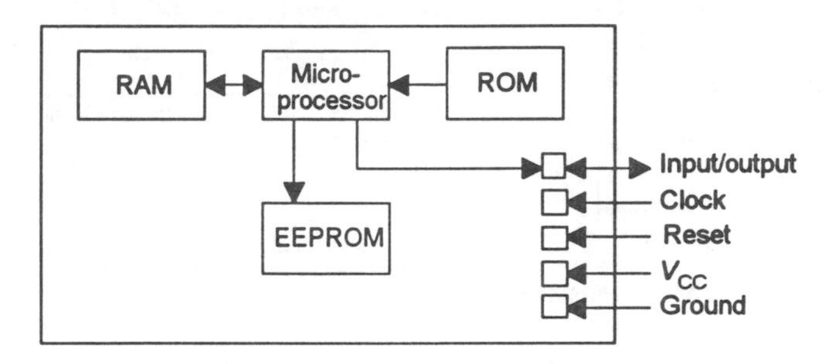

Fig. 3.14 Microprocessor card

The operating sequence that occurs when a smart card is used has this form:

Initialise the hardware, i.e. power supply and clock
Initialise the operating system, i.e. clear RAM, check for errors, select transmission parameters
The microprocessor resets
It then receives signals indicating the format of the message and then the message
It then calls up the program to interpret the message
It interprets the message

Such cards are used for financial transactions where the user is identified by the use of a PIN (personal identification number); code and transactions can then be logged and balances stored. Another application is for security applications where access to specific areas is restricted to those areas for which the user is identified by the smart card as being eligible to enter.

This is just a simple account of smart cards; for more details the reader is referred to specialist texts such as *Smart Card Handbook* by W. Rankl and W. Effing (John Wiley 1997).

3.2.6 Data acquisition systems

Automated data acquisition systems can take the form of a dedicated instrument termed a data logger or a personal computer using plug-in DAQ boards. Figure 3.15 shows the basic elements of a *data logger*. A data logger can monitor the inputs from a large number of sensors; after suitable signal conditioning, they are fed into the multiplexer, which is used to select one signal, and after amplification and conversion to digital, this signal is processed by the microprocessor.

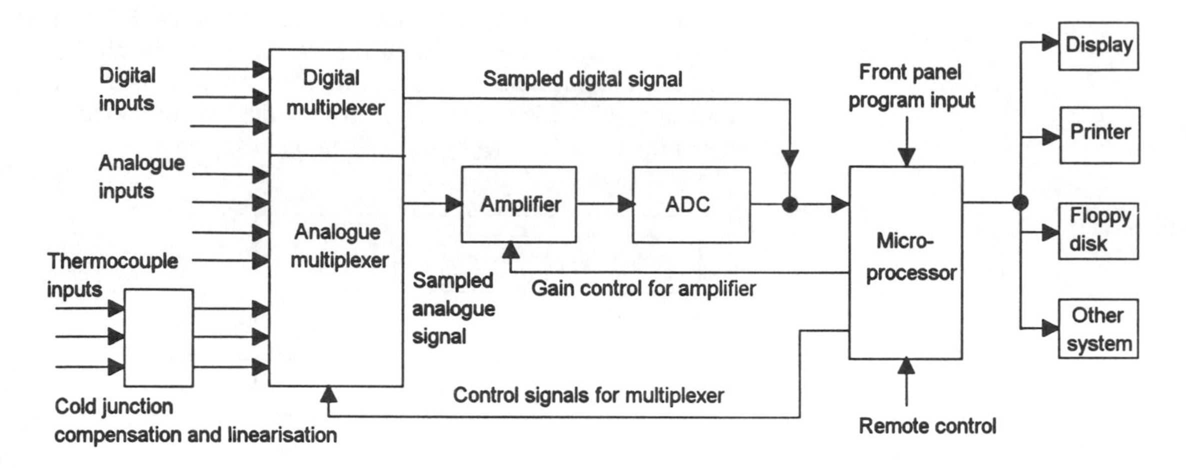

Fig. 3.15 Data logger system

Because data loggers are often used with thermocouples, there are often special inputs for thermocouples; these provide cold junction compensation and linearisation. The multiplexer can be switched to each sensor in turn and so the output consists of a sequence of samples. Scanning of the inputs can be selected by programming the microprocessor to switch the multiplexer so it samples just a single channel, makes a single scan of all channels, a continuous scan of all channels, or perhaps makes a periodic scan of all channels, say every 1, 5, 15, 30 or 60 minutes.

The microprocessor is able to carry out simple arithmetic operations, perhaps taking the average of a number of measurements. The output from the system might be displayed on a digital meter that indicates the output and channel number, used to give a permanent record with a printer, stored on a floppy disk or transferred to a computer. Typically a data logger may handle 20 to 100 inputs, though some may handle considerably more, perhaps 1000. It might have a sample and conversion time of 10 μs and be used to make perhaps 1000 readings per second. The accuracy is typically about 0.01% of full-scale input and linearity is about ±0.005% of full-scale input. Crosstalk is typically 0.01% of full-scale input on any one input. The term *crosstalk* is used to describe the interference that can occur when one sensor is being sampled as a result of signals from other sensors.

Figure 3.16 shows the basic elements of a data acquisition system using plug-in boards with a computer. The signal conditioning prior to the plug-in board depends on the sensors concerned: for thermocouples it can be amplification, cold junction compensation and linearisation; for resistance strain gauges it can be a Wheatstone bridge, voltage supply for the bridge and linearisation; and for resistance temperature detectors it can be a current supply, circuitry and linearisation.

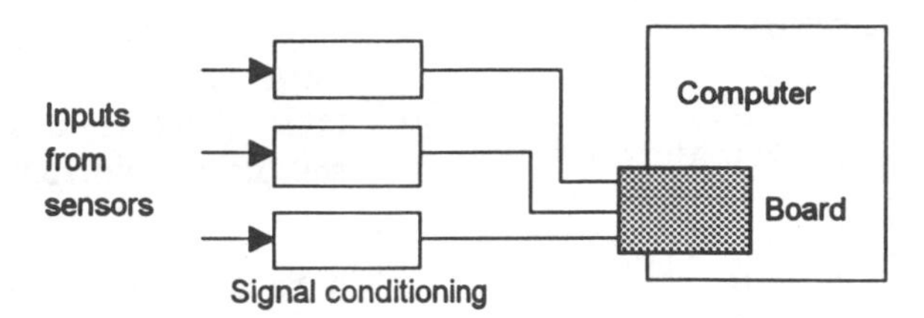

Fig. 3.16 Data acquisition system

The DAQ board is a printed circuit board that, for analogue inputs, provides a multiplexer, amplification, analogue-to-digital conversion, registers and control circuitry so that sampled digital signals are applied to the computer system. Figure 3.17 shows the basic elements of such a board.

Computer software is used to control the acquisition of data via the DAQ board. When the program requires an input from a particular sensor, it activates the board by sending a control word to the control and status register. This indicates the type of operation the board has to carry out. As a consequence the board switches the multiplexer to the appropriate input channel. The input from the sensor connected to that input channel is then passed via an amplifier to the analogue-to-digital converter. After conversion the resulting digital signal is passed to the data register and the word in the control and status register changes to indicate that the signal has arrived.

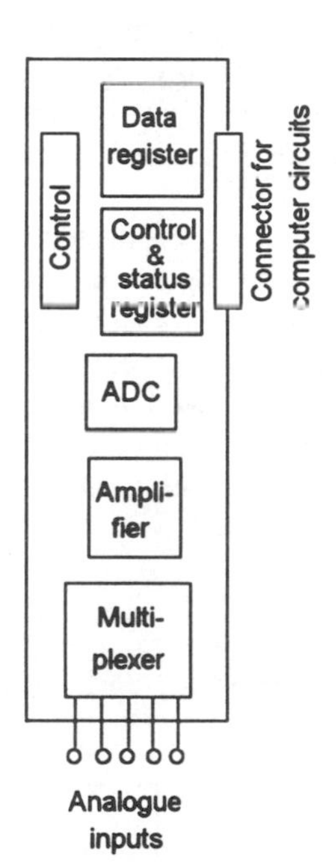

Fig. 3.17 DAQ system

Following that signal, the computer issues a signal for the data to be read and taken into the computer for processing. This signal is necessary to ensure the computer does not wait doing nothing while the board carries out its acquisition of data, but uses this data-to-be-read signal to indicate when the acquisition is complete; the computer can then interrupt any program it is implementing, read the data from the DAQ and then continue with its program. A faster system does not involve the computer in the transfer of the data into memory but transfers the acquired data directly from the board to memory without involving the computer; this is termed *direct memory address* (DMA).

All DAQ boards use software *drivers*, generally supplied by the manufacturer along with a board. The drivers communicate with the computer and tell it what has been inserted and how the computer can communicate with the board. Before a board can be used, three parameters have to be set: the addresses of the input and output channels, the interrupt level, and the channel to be used for direct memory access. With plug-and-play boards for use with Windows software, these parameters are set by the software; otherwise microswitches have to be set on the card in accordance with the instructions supplied with the board.

3.3 Sensors and signal conditioning

Microprocessors have inputs from sensors and often have to use signal conditioning in order to get the signal into the required form before it can be used. This section is a brief overview of the basic elements; Chapters 10 and 11 discuss the interfacing of sensors with microprocessors in more detail.

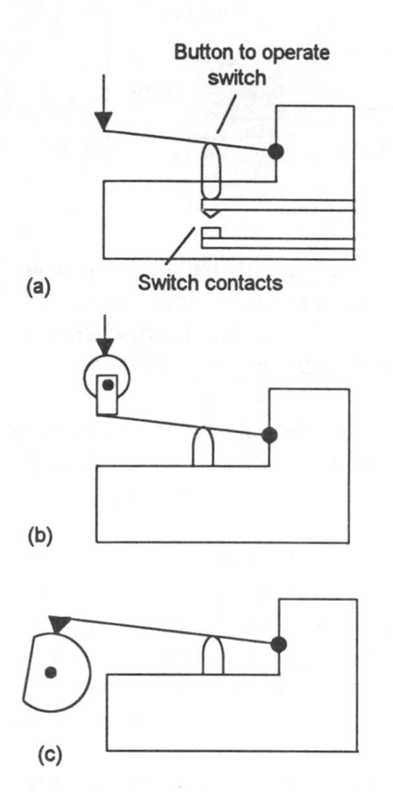

Fig. 3.18 Switches: (a) lever-operated, (b) roller-operated, (c) cam-operated

3.3.1 Digital output sensors

A *switch* is a very basic sensor; its output is a signal which indicates whether the switch has been closed or opened by some mechanical action, e.g. the presence or otherwise of a workpiece on the tool bed of a machine tool being used to activate a switch. Figure 3.18 shows some examples.

Another form of switch is the *reed switch* (Fig. 3.19). It consists of two magnetic switch contacts sealed in a glass tube. When a magnet is brought close to the switch, the magnetic reeds are attracted to each other and close the switch contacts. It is a non-contact proximity switch and is very widely used for checking the closure of doors; the magnet is located in the door and the switch is located in the door frame.

With microprocessors, switches are normally connected so that the inputs are high when the switches are open, and when a switch closes its input goes low; *pull-up resistors* to the +5 V supply are used with the switches connected between the input lines and earth (Fig. 3.20). This form of connection means that when the switch is closed it is connected to the ground and when open it is connected to +5V; this avoids the problem of the input floating when the switch is open.

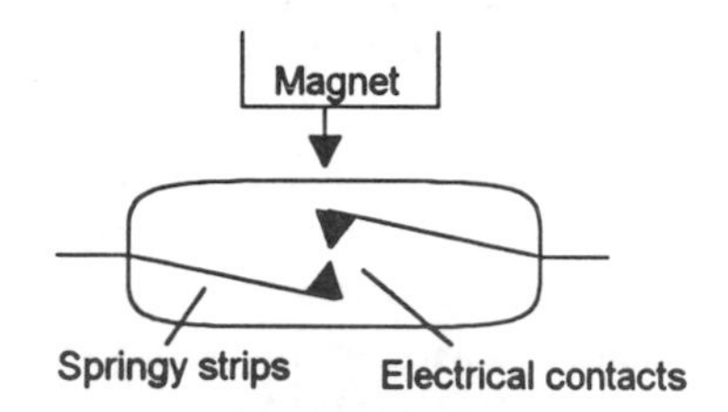

Fig. 3.19 Reed switch

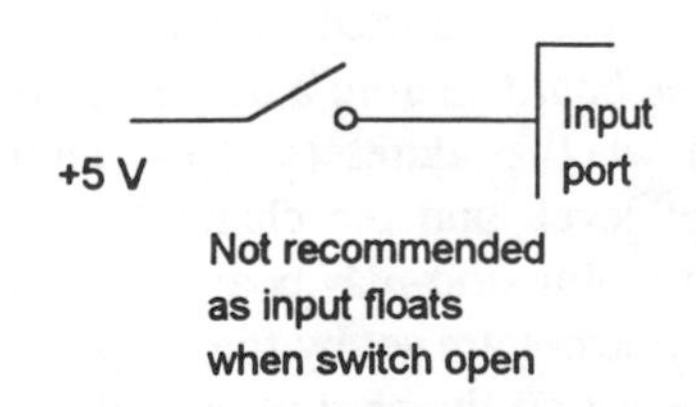

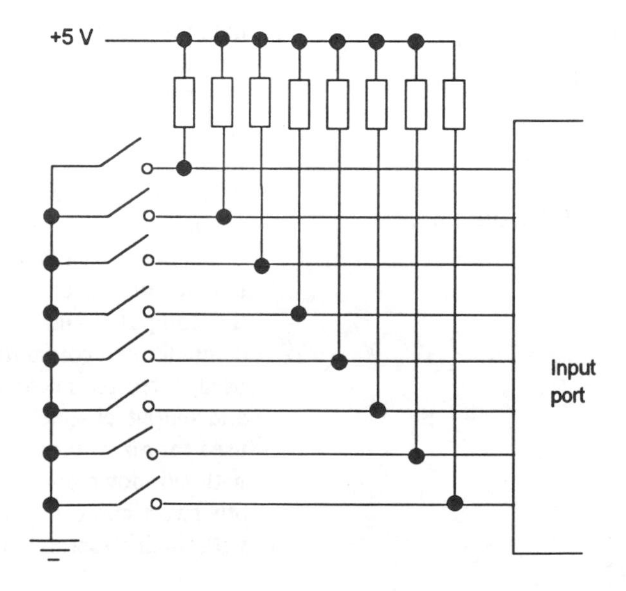

Fig. 3.20 Pull-up resistors

An *encoder* provides a digital output, as a result of a linear or angular displacement, in the form of a stream of pulses; the number of pulses represents the value of the variable being measured. Incremental encoders detect changes in rotation from some datum position and absolute encoders give the actual angular position. Figure 3.21(a) shows the basic form of an *incremental encoder* for the measurement of angular displacement. A beam of light passes through slots in a disc and is detected by a light sensor. When the disc is rotated, a pulsed output is produced by the sensor and the number of pulses is proportional to the angle through which the disc rotates. Thus the angular position of the disc, and hence the shaft rotating it, can be determined by the number of pulses produced since some datum position. In practice three concentric tracks with three sensors are used (Fig. 3.21(b)). The inner track has just one hole and is used to locate the home position of the disc. The other two tracks have a series of equally spaced holes that go completely round the disc but with the holes in the middle track offset from the holes in the outer track by one-half the width of a hole. This offset enables the direction of rotation to be determined. In a clockwise direction the pulses in the outer track lead those in the inner track, in the anticlockwise direction they lag. The resolution is determined by the number of slots on the disc. Since 1 revolution is a rotation of 360°, a disc with 60 slots gives a resolution of 360/60 = 6°.

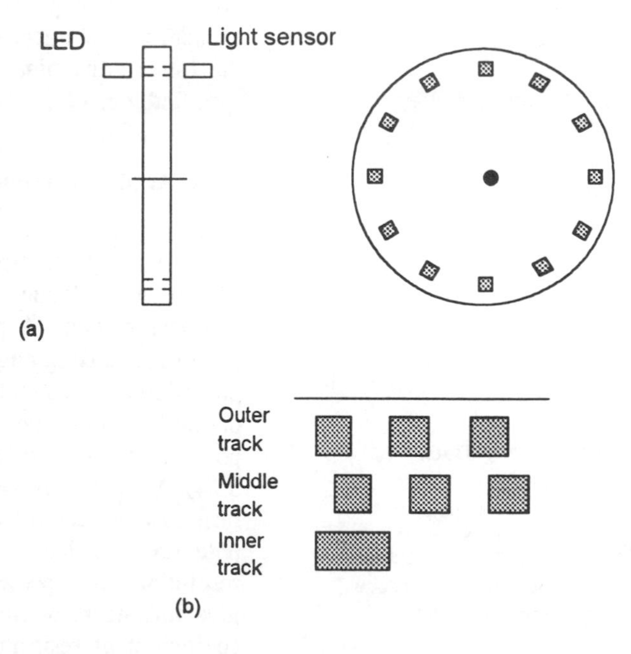

Fig. 3.21 Incremental encoder: (a) the basic principle, (b) concentric tracks

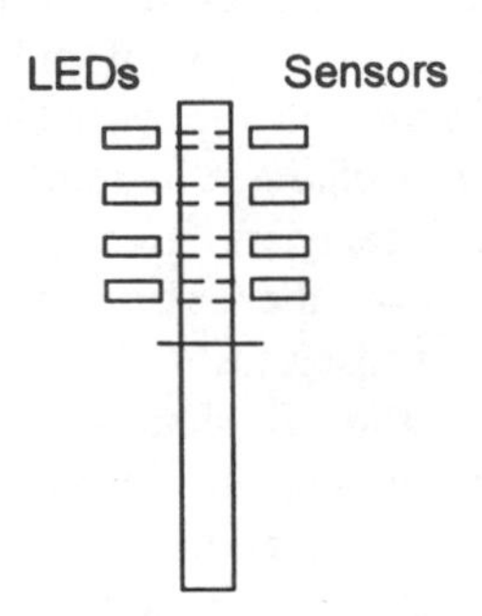

Fig. 3.22 A 3-bit absolute encoder

	Normal binary	Gray code
0	0000	0000
1	0001	0001
2	0010	0011
3	0011	0010
4	0100	0110
5	0101	0111
6	0110	0101
7	0111	0100
8	1000	1100
9	1001	1101
10	1010	1111

□ Hole, so light sensed

▩ Light blocked off

Fig. 3.23 Binary and Gray codes

Figure 3.22 shows the basic form of an *absolute encoder* for the measurement of angular displacement. By having different segments of the disc present different sequences of transmitted and block-off light, so binary codes signals can be generated. This gives an output in the form of a binary number having several digits, and each number represents a particular angular position. The rotating disc shown has four concentric circles of slots and four sensors to detect the light pulses. The slots are arranged in such a way that the sequential output from the sensors is a number in the binary code. The normal form of binary code is generally not used because changing from one binary number to the next can result in more than one bit changing and if, through some misalignment, one of the bits changes fractionally before the others then an intermediate binary number is momentarily indicated and so can lead to false counting. To overcome this the *Gray code* is generally used. With this code only one bit changes in moving from one number to the next. Figure 3.23 shows the tracks with normal binary code and the Gray code.

Typical encoders tend to have up to 10 or 12 tracks. The number of bits in the binary number will be equal to the number of tracks. Thus with 10 tracks there will be 10 bits and so the number of positions that can be detected is 2^{10}, i.e. 1024, a resolution of 360/1024 = 0.35°. Optical encoders, e.g. HEDS-5000 from Hewlett Packard, are supplied for mounting on shafts and contain an LED light source and a code wheel. Interface integrated circuits are also available to decode the encoder and give a binary output suitable for a microprocessor. For an absolute encoder with 7 tracks on its code disc, each track will give one of the bits in the binary number and thus we have 2^7 positions specified, i.e. 128.

3.3.2 Analogue output sensors

Many of the sensors used with microprocessor systems give analogue outputs; these outputs have to be converted to digital signals by analogue-to-digital converters before microprocessors can access them. A potentiometer can be used as an analogue sensor for sensing angular or linear position or displacement; the potentiometer is supplied with a constant voltage and the voltage output from the slider gives a voltage which is related to the slider position or its displacement from some datum position (Fig. 3.24). With a wire-wound track the slider in moving from one turn to another will change the voltage output in steps. If the potentiometer has N turns on its wire-wound track then the resolution, as a percentage, is $100/N$. Conductive plastic tracks give infinite resolution but, as a result of a higher temperature coefficient of resistance, they are more affected by temperature changes. To illustrate their use, a potentiometer can be adapted

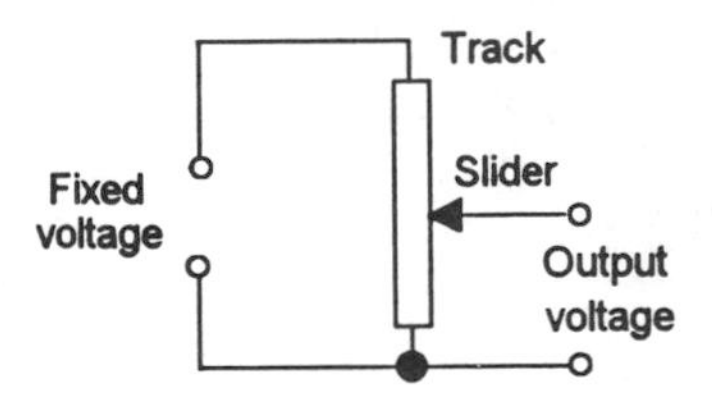

Fig. 3.24 Potentiometer

for measuring the depth of liquid in a container; simply couple a float to the potentiometer slider.

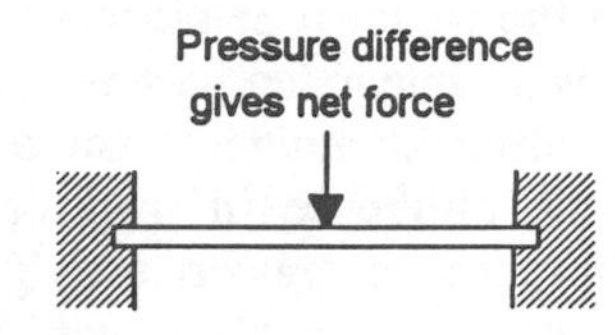

Fig. 3.25 Diaphragm pressure gauge

Many of the sensors for monitoring fluid pressure involve the use of a *diaphragm* (Fig. 3.25). When there is a difference in pressure between the two sides of the diaphragm, the centre of the diaphragm becomes displaced and the amount of the displacement is a measure of the pressure difference. This displacement can be sensed by some form of displacement sensor; electrical resistance strain gauges are often used. Although strain gauges can be stuck on a diaphragm, the more usual procedure is to use a silicon diaphragm with the strain gauges as specially doped areas within the diaphragm. The strain gauge elements can be connected as the arms of a Wheatstone bridge (Fig. 3.26) and the resulting out-of-balance voltage used as a measure of the pressure.

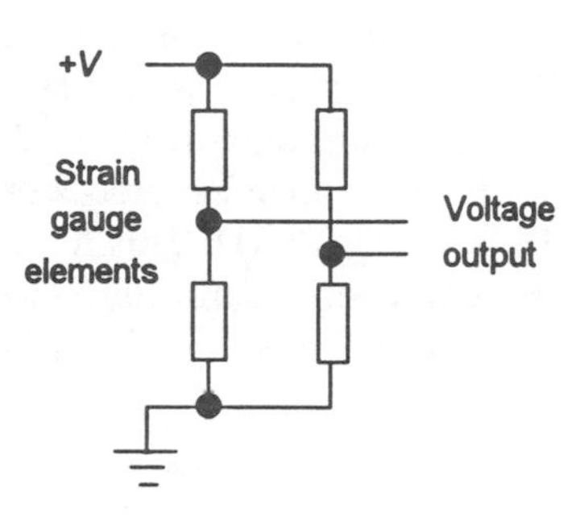

Fig. 3.26 Wheatstone bridge

The *Motorola MPX pressure sensors* have the strain gauge element integrated, together with a resistive network, in a single silicon diaphragm chip. When a current is passed through the strain gauge element and pressure applied at right angles to it, a voltage is produced in a transverse direction (Fig. 3.27). This, together with signal conditioning and temperature compensation circuitry, is packaged as the MPX sensor. The output voltage from the sensor is directly proportional to the pressure. Such sensors are available for use for the measurement of absolute pressure (the MX numbering system ends with A, AP, AS or ASX), differential pressure (the MX numbering system ends with D or DP) and gauge pressure (the MX numbering system ends with GP, GVP, GS, GVS, GSV or GVSX). For example, the MPX2100 series has a pressure range of 100 kPa and, with a supply voltage of 16 V d.c., it gives for the absolute pressure and differential pressure forms a voltage output over the full range of 40 mV. The response time, 10% to 90%, for a step change from 0 to 100 kPa is about 1.0 ms and the output impedance is of the order of 1.4 to 3.0 kΩ. The absolute pressure sensors are used for such applications as altimeters and barometers, differential pressure sensors for airflow measurements and gauge pressure sensors for engine pressure and tyre pressure.

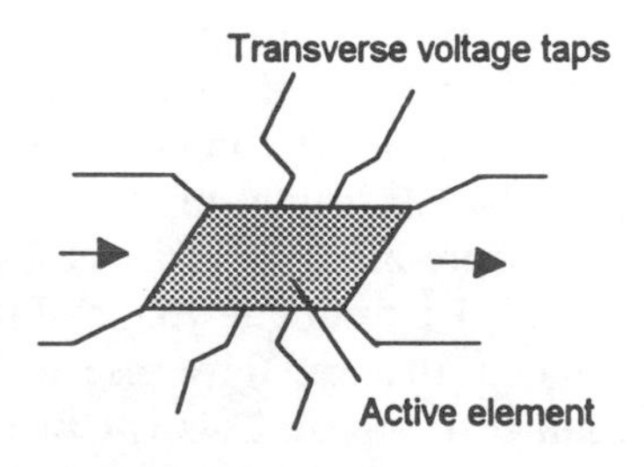

Fig. 3.27 Pressure sensor element

Thermistors are widely used for temperature measurement, their electrical resistance changing when the temperature changes. A simple electrical circuit that can be used to give a voltage output to a microprocessor system is to use a thermistor as an element in a voltage divider circuit (Fig. 3.28).

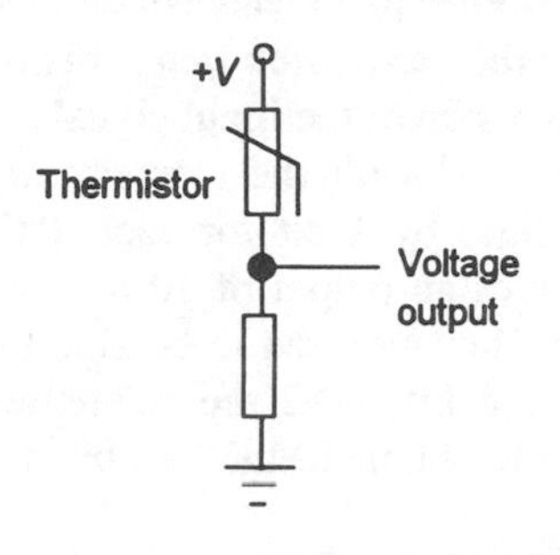

Fig. 3.28 Thermistor circuit

Thermodiodes and *thermotransistors* are used as temperature sensors; temperature affects the rate at which electrons and holes can diffuse across semiconductor junctions. An example of such a sensor is the Motorola MTS101 (Fig. 3.29) which can be used over the range −40°C to +150°C with an accuracy of about ±2°C and gives a base–emitter voltage V_{BE} which is proportional to the temperature, about 2 mV/°C. Another form of thermotransistor

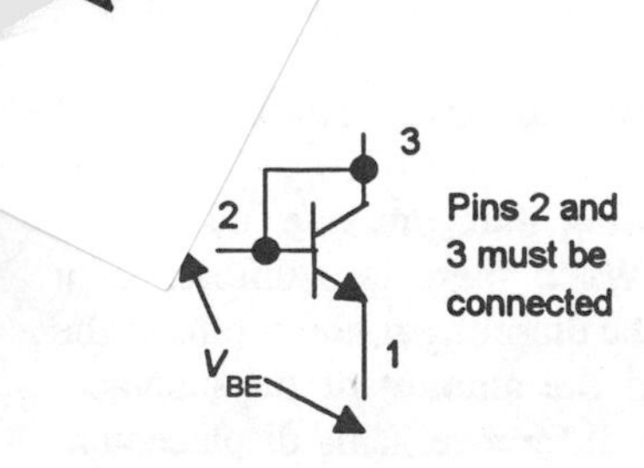

Fig. 3.29 MTS102

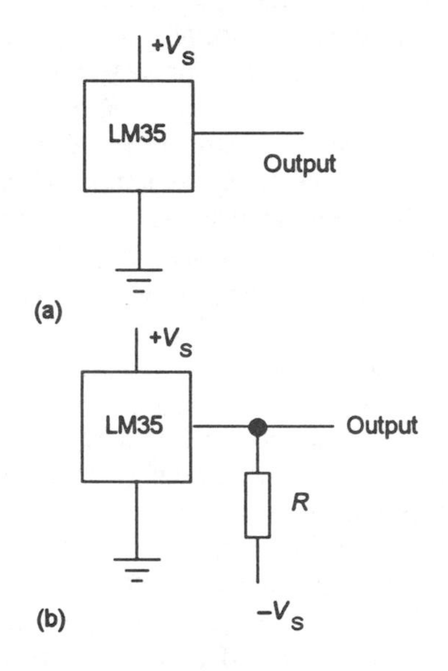

Fig. 3.30 LM35

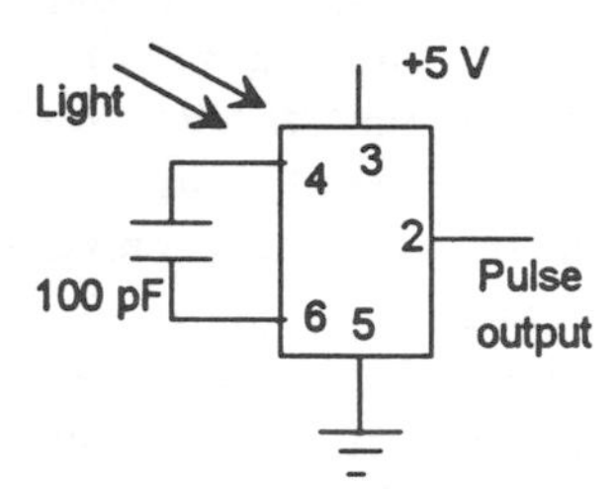

Fig. 3.31 TLS220

sensor that is very frequently used is the National Semiconductor LM35 (Fig. 3.30). This is supplied as an integrated package and uses two transistors operated with different emitter areas and hence different current densities; the difference in their base voltages is then proportional to the absolute temperature. The LM35 sensor can be used in the range –40°C to 110°C with an accuracy of about ±0.8°C and gives an output of 10 mV/°C when the supply voltage is +5V; Fig. 3.29(a) shows the connections for the range 12°C to 110°C and Fig. 3.29(b) shows the connections for –40°C to 110°C.

Photodiodes and *phototransistors* are often used for sensing light levels. They give fairly small analogue signals with a size related to the light level; these signals require amplification. A package that is widely used for interfacing with microprocessor systems is the Texas Instruments TSL220 (Fig. 3.31). This has a photodiode combined with a voltage-to-frequency converter. The output is a fixed-width pulse train with a frequency which is directly proportional to the light intensity.

3.3.3 Analogue-to-digital converters

With analogue sensors the output has to be converted to digital before it can be inputted to a microprocessor; with micro-controllers there is often an analogue-to-digital converter included with one of the input ports. The input to an analogue-to-digital converter is an analogue signal and the output is a binary word that represents the level of the input signal. Typically, ADCs are available to give words lengths of 8 bits, 12 bits or 16 bits. With an 8 bit ADC there are $2^8 = 256$ possible output words, 0000 0000 to 1111 1111, i.e. from 0 to 255, and so the minimum change in input voltage that can give rise to a change in output is 1/255 of the full-scale signal. This is termed the *resolution*. The full-scale analogue signal for the 1111 1111 word is determined by the reference voltage supplied to the ADC. In general the resolution for an n bit ADC is $1/(2^n - 1)$ and so the size of the smallest increment in voltage that will give a change in digital output is $V_{\text{full scale}}/(2^n - 1)$. Another parameter which has to considered in the choice of ADC is the *conversion time*; this is the time required to complete the conversion of the input signal.

Suppose we want to use an 8 bit ADC with the temperature sensor LM35 so that the output changes by 1 bit for each 1°C change in temperature. The LM35 gives an output of 10 mV/°C when it has a supply voltage of 5 V. Thus we need to be able to resolve changes of 10 mV. With the 8 bit ADC the reference voltage is divided into 255 bits and so to obtain 10 mV per bit we need a reference voltage of 2.55 V.

There are three main types of ADC: flash, successive approximations and dual-slope integrating converters. Flash converters give the highest conversion rate; dual-slope converters have a very low conversion rate but have excellent noise rejection. Successive approximations converters are probably the most widely used. A typical 8 bit successive approximations converter, the ZN439, has a conversion time of 5000 ns; the 8 bit flash converter ADC302 has a conversion time of 20 ns. See Section 11.4 for a discussion of the interfacing of ADCs with microprocessors.

3.4 Displays

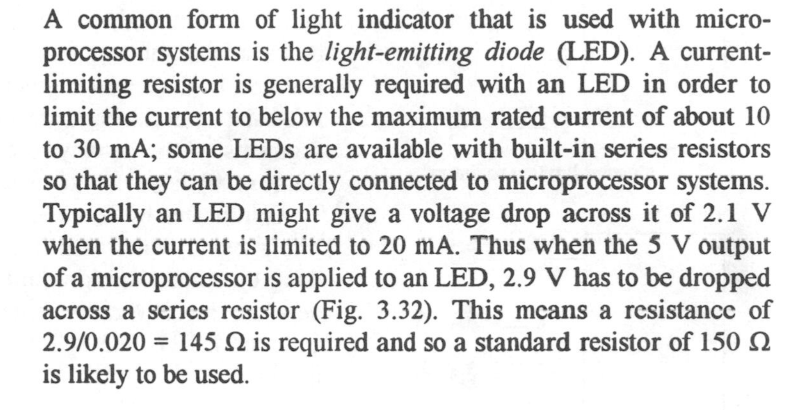

A common form of light indicator that is used with microprocessor systems is the *light-emitting diode* (LED). A current-limiting resistor is generally required with an LED in order to limit the current to below the maximum rated current of about 10 to 30 mA; some LEDs are available with built-in series resistors so that they can be directly connected to microprocessor systems. Typically an LED might give a voltage drop across it of 2.1 V when the current is limited to 20 mA. Thus when the 5 V output of a microprocessor is applied to an LED, 2.9 V has to be dropped across a series resistor (Fig. 3.32). This means a resistance of 2.9/0.020 = 145 Ω is required and so a standard resistor of 150 Ω is likely to be used.

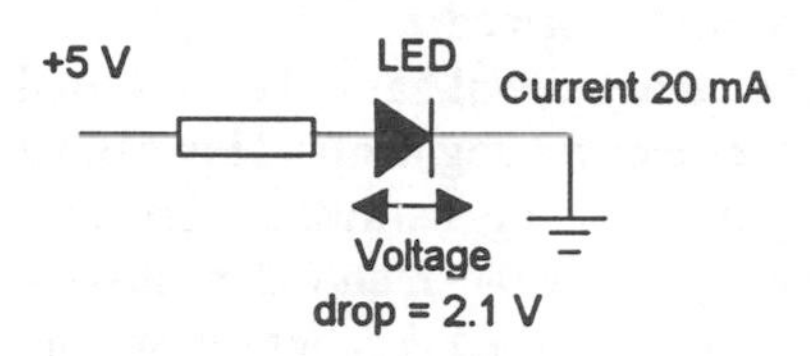

Fig. 3.32 LED with series resistor

3.4.1 Seven-segment displays

The output from many microprocessor systems has to result in a display of alphabetic or numeric characters. One form of such a display uses seven light segments to generate the alphabetic and numeric characters. Figure 3.33 shows the segments, with examples of displays, and Table 3.2 shows the segments that have to be illuminated for a 4 bit binary code input.

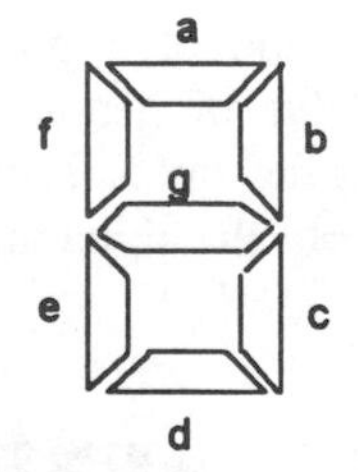

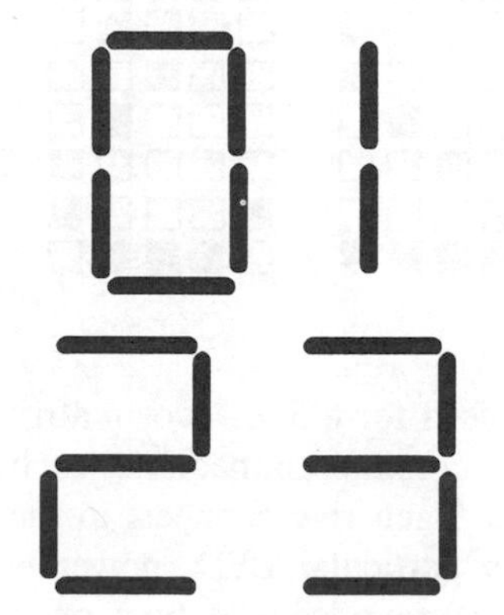

Fig. 3.33 Seven-segment display

Table 3.2 Seven-segment display

Binary signal				*Segments activated* a	b	c	d	e	f	g	*Number displayed*
0	0	0	0	1	1	1	1	1	1	0	0
0	0	0	1	0	1	1	0	0	0	0	1
0	0	1	0	1	1	0	1	1	0	1	2
0	0	1	1	1	1	1	1	0	0	1	3
0	1	0	0	0	1	1	0	0	1	1	4
0	1	0	1	1	0	1	1	0	1	1	5
0	1	1	0	0	0	1	1	1	1	1	6
0	1	1	1	1	1	1	0	0	0	0	7
1	0	0	0	1	1	1	1	1	1	1	8
1	0	0	1	1	1	1	0	0	1	1	9

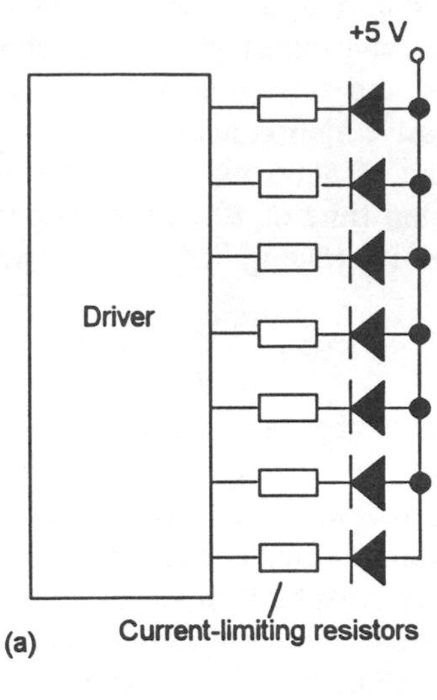

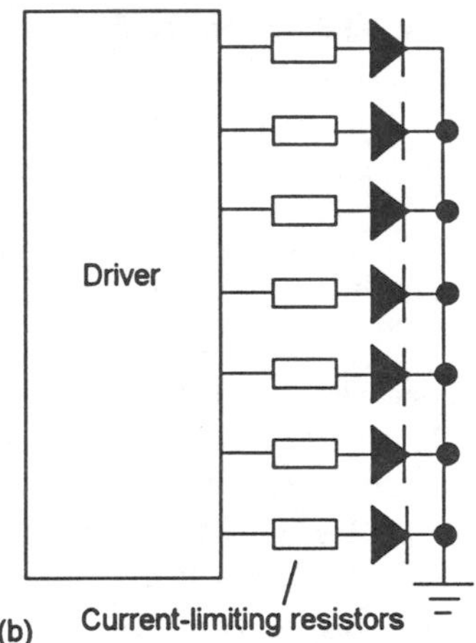

Fig. 3.34 (a) Common anode, (b) common cathode

Figure 3.34(a) shows how seven LEDs, to give the seven segments of a display of the form shown in Fig. 3.33, might be connected to a driver so that when a line is driven low, a voltage is applied and the LED in that line is switched on. Such an arrangement is known as the *common anode* form of connection since all the LED anodes are connected together. An alternative arrangement is the *common cathode* (Fig. 3.34(b)). The elements in common anode form are made active by the input going low; in common cathode form they are made active by the input going high. Examples of LED displays are the seven-segment 7.6 mm and 10.9 mm high intensity displays of Hewlett Packard which are available in common anode or common cathode form. In addition to the seven segments to form the characters, there is a left-hand or right-hand decimal point. By illuminating different segments of the display, the full range of numbers and a small range of alphabetical characters can be formed.

As indicated by Table 3.2, the binary signal has to be converted into a signal which will light the relevant segments. This can be done by suitable programming or by using hardware, termed a *decoder*, to convert the binary signal to the required form (see Section 11.3.1). The 7447 is a commonly used decoder for driving displays.

3.4.2 A 5 × 7 dot matrix LED display

Another type of display has a 7 × 5 or 9 × 7 dot matrix (Fig. 3.35) with the characters generated by the excitation of appropriate dots. Seven-segment displays are only capable of generating a limited number of characters; a 5 × 7 matrix display is, however, more versatile and gives good displays of all alphanumeric characters.

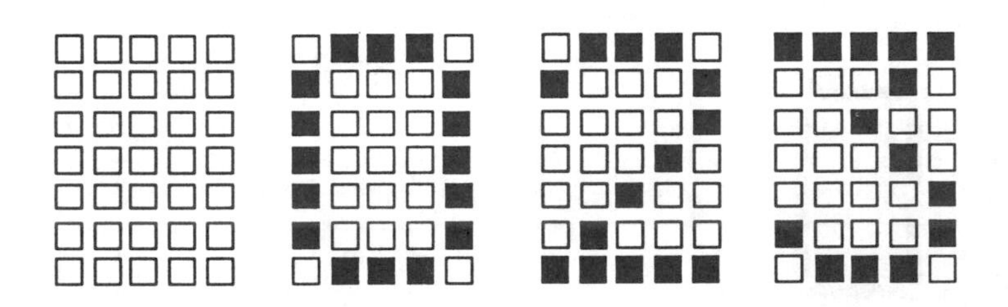

Fig. 3.35 A 7 × 5 dot matrix display

Figure 3.36 shows the basic form used for a 5 × 7 dot matrix display. The array consists of five column connectors, each connecting the anodes of seven LEDs. Each row connects to the cathodes of five LEDs. To turn on a particular LED, power is applied to its column and its row is grounded. To turn on a particular character the required columns are turned on in succession with the relevant rows grounded. To generate the number 2, column 1 is switched on with rows 2 and 7 grounded. Column 2 is switched on with rows 1, 6 and 7 grounded. Column 3 is switched on with rows 1, 5 and 7 grounded. This procedure continues column by column; Fig. 3.37 shows the sequence. Such a task can be achieved by programming the microprocessor or alternatively using hardware to generate the required outputs.

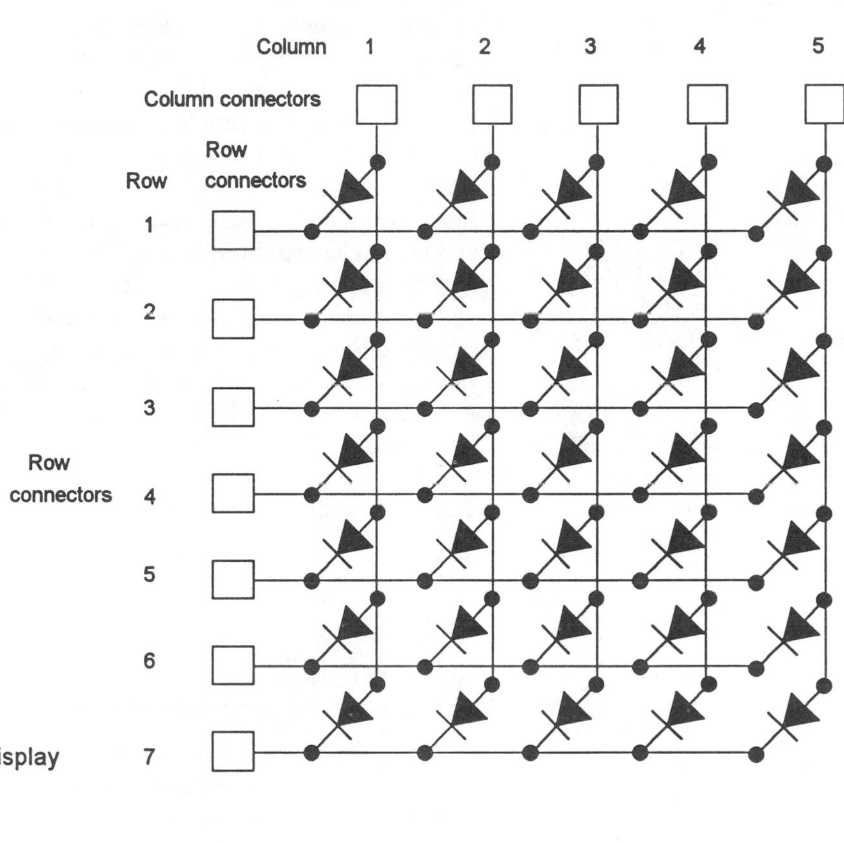

Fig. 3.36 Dot matrix display

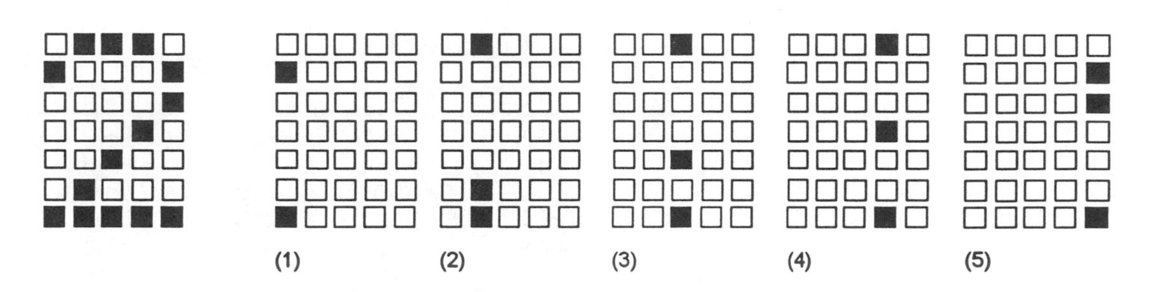

Fig. 3.37 A 7 × 5 dot matrix display

3.5 Motors

Microprocessors are often used to control the motion or position of an object as a result of controlling a motor. The following is a brief overview of the motors most commonly used with microprocessor systems.

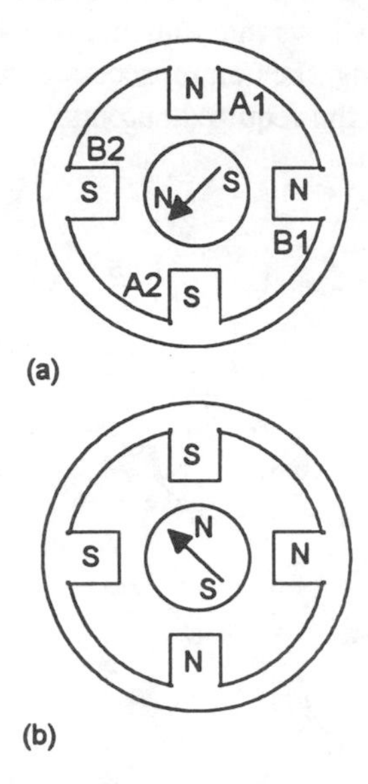

Fig. 3.38 A full-step sequence resulting from the coils round a pair of stator teeth reversing polarity

3.5.1 Stepper motor

The most widely used control motor is the *stepper*; this produces rotation through equal angles, the *steps*, rather than the continuous rotational motion associated with conventional motors. There are several forms of stepper motor; Fig. 3.38 shows the basic form of a simple permanent magnet rotor motor with two pairs of coils, A1–A2 and B1–B2, used to energise the two pairs of stator teeth. The term *phase* is used for the number of independent coils. Two-phase motors thus have two pairs of coils and tend to be used in light-duty applications.

The stepping action is controlled by digital signals that energise magnetic coils within the motor by switching the d.c. supply between coils. Thus, with Fig. 3.38, when the current through one pair of stator coils is reversed, the rotor advances by one step (Table 3.3); this is termed the *full-step mode* of operation.

Table 3.3 Full-step operation

Step	*A1*	*A2*	*B1*	*B2*
1	High	Low	High	Low
2	Low	High	High	Low
3	Low	High	Low	High
4	High	Low	Low	High

A stepper can, however, be made to rotate through half-steps by using independent coils for opposite stator teeth and using the coil-energising sequence shown in Table 3.4; this is termed the *half-step mode* of operation.

Table 3.4 Half-step operation

Step	*A1*	*A2*	*B1*	*B2*
1	High	Low	High	Low
2	Low	Low	Low	High
3	Low	High	High	Low
4	High	Low	Low	Low
5	Low	High	Low	High
6	Low	Low	High	Low
7	High	Low	Low	High
8	Low	High	Low	Low

Programs can be written (see Section 11.8.1) so that a microprocessor gives the required outputs to each of the stepper coils to generate the required step sequence; an alternative is to use hardware (see Section 11.8.2) to produce the required switching action when the digital input changes. Stepper motors can be used to give controlled rotational steps but can also give continuous rotation with their rotational speed controlled by controlling the rate at which pulses are applied to it to cause stepping. This gives a very useful controlled variable speed motor which finds many applications. For more details of stepping motors, the reader is referred to texts such as *Stepping Motors and their Microprocessor Controls* by T. Kenjo (Oxford University Press 1984), *Power Electronics for the Microprocessor Age* by T. Kenjo (Oxford University Press 1990) or *Electrical Machines and Drive Systems* by C.B. Gray (Longman 1989).

3.5.2 Direct current motor

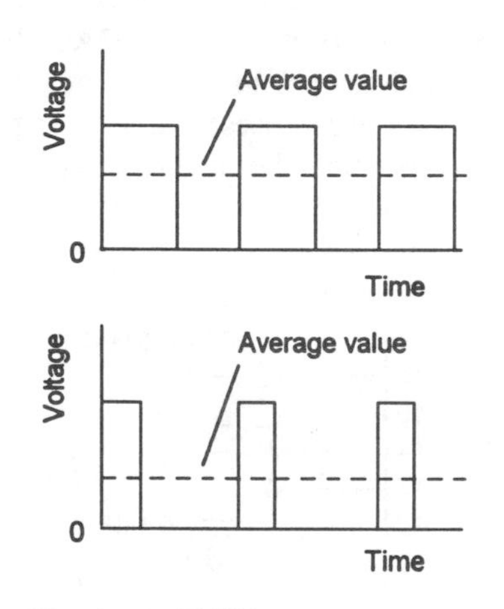

Fig. 3.39 PWM

The speed of rotation of a permanent magnet motor depends on the current through its armature coil. The method commonly used with the digital output from a microprocessor is to use *pulse width modulation* (PWM). PWM works by switching the full voltage of the d.c. power supply to the motor on or off at a fixed frequency. By varying the *duty cycle*, i.e. the portion of the cycle for which the d.c. supply is switched on, so the average voltage to the motor is controlled (Fig. 3.39). Some microcontrollers include a PWM module (see Section 2.3, item 11) to automatically output the PWM waveforms. With other microprocessor systems, the PWM can be achieved by the program; such a program can have the following type of instructions:

switch on the motor
start counting
after the set count has been reached,
  switch off the motor
start counting again
after this set count has been reached,
  loop back to repeat the program

3.6 Digital-to-analogue conversion

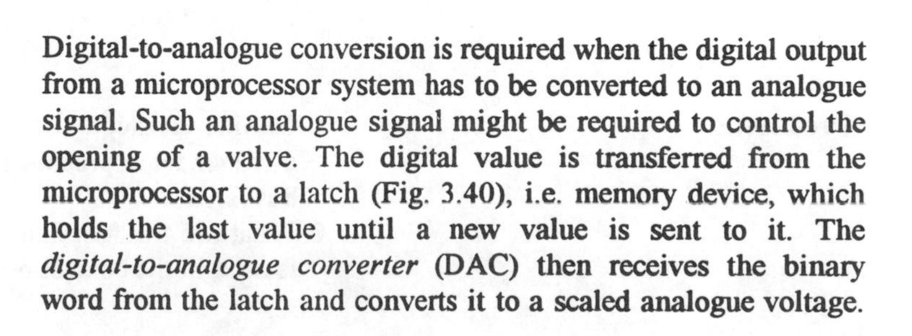
Digital-to-analogue conversion is required when the digital output from a microprocessor system has to be converted to an analogue signal. Such an analogue signal might be required to control the opening of a valve. The digital value is transferred from the microprocessor to a latch (Fig. 3.40), i.e. memory device, which holds the last value until a new value is sent to it. The *digital-to-analogue converter* (DAC) then receives the binary word from the latch and converts it to a scaled analogue voltage.

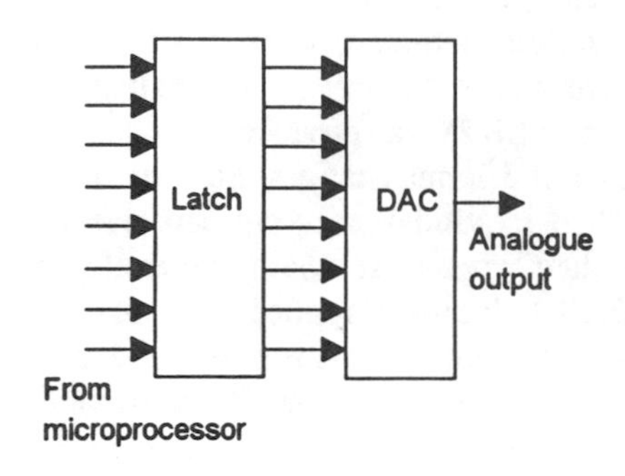

Fig. 3.40 Digital to analogue

Because of the action of the latch, the analogue output is held at a constant value until the next time the microprocessor changes the digital signal.

Fixed reference DACs have a fixed reference voltage and produce an output that is proportional to the digital word input. The fixed reference voltage is derived internally from the fixed power voltage to the DAC chip. *Multiplying DACs* have a variable reference voltage and produce an output signal that is proportional to the product of a variable reference voltage level and the digital word input. The variable reference voltage is derived from an external reference voltage. A major source of error with internally fixed reference voltages is that the voltages drift with temperature; precision external reference voltage integrated circuits can offer less drift and so greater accuracy.

For most microprocessor control purposes an 8 bit DAC is suitable. The output voltage goes up in steps, each step being a change of 1 in the least significant bit. The 8 bit DAC thus gives an output with a resolution of $1/(2^8 - 1)$ of the full-scale output. Higher resolution is given with 12 bit DACs but at a greater cost.

Figure 3.41 shows the AD557 8 bit fixed reference DAC. It operates off a +5 V power supply and has a 0 to +2.55 V output range. Input latches are supplied for microprocessor interfacing. The input latches are controlled by the chip select and chip enable inputs. If the latches are not required, the chip select and chip enable pins are grounded.

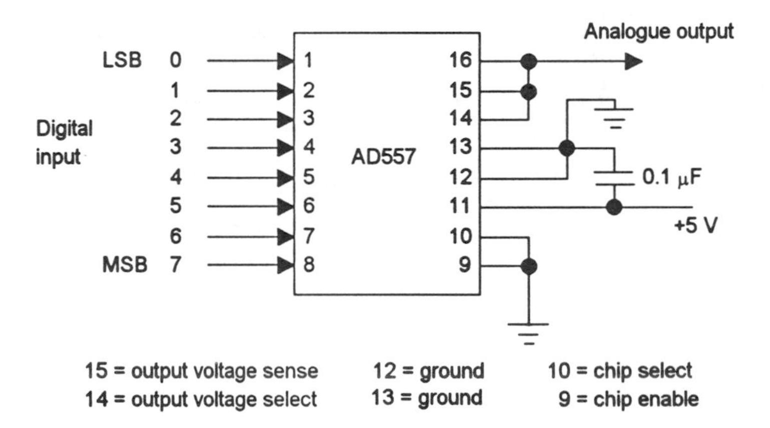

Fig. 3.41 AD557 converter

Problems

1. Outline the steps that might be required in a program used by a reader for a prepaid memory card that is to be used to pay bus fares.
2. What are the functions required of a microcontroller when it is used in the control box of a domestic washing machine?

3. Within an automobile engine management system the micro-controller has to receive an input which relates to the position of the crankshaft. How can this be achieved?
4. Explain how a switch can be connected to the input of a microprocessor system so that it gives a transition from high to low when it is closed.
5. An 8-bit microprocessor system has a bus width which allows for eight parallel inputs. How might the system be adapted so that it can cope with more than eight inputs?
6. Explain how an absolute encoder can be used to give a digital signal which is a measure of the angular position of a shaft.
7. Why is an absolute encoder likely to give an output in the Gray code rather than conventional binary code?
8. What resolution will be given by a 16-bit ADC?
9. Explain the common anode and common cathode method of connecting LEDs to a drive circuit.
10. In a system involving a four-digit display connected to a microcontroller, a decoder is used between the microcontroller and the display. What is its purpose?
11. Explain why a latch is often used with a digital-to-analogue converter connected to a microprocessor.
12. Explain how PWM is used to control the speed of rotation of a d.c. motor.

4 Designing programs

4.1 Introduction

This chapter is concerned with establishing procedures that can be used in the design of programs for use with microprocessor-based systems. A *program* is a sequence of instructions that is used to operate the system to produce a specific result. *Program design* is the stage in the development of a program in which the problem is defined and formulated in the form of a program. *Software* is the term used to describe programs which may be loaded into a microprocessor-based system. This chapter is about program designing, i.e. the designing of the program before it is written into code for use by the microprocessor system.

4.1.1 Machine code and assembly mnemonics

Programs for microprocessor-based systems consist of codes which represent instructions or data. Microprocessors work in binary code and programming instructions written in binary code are termed *machine code*. Originally programmers had to write programs in machine code for direct input to the system. Writing a program in machine code is a skilled and very tedious process. It is prone to errors because the program is just a series of 0s and 1s and the instructions are not easily comprehended from just looking at the patterns of 0s and 1s.

An alternative is to use an easily comprehended form of shorthand code for the pattern of 0s and 1s. Thus a system was developed using what are termed *assembly mnemonics*. For example, LD is used to indicate that the operation required is to load the data that follows; the operation of adding data might be represented by ADD. Such a shorthand code is called a *mnemonic code* – a 'memory aiding' code. Chapter 5 is an introduction to assembly language and Chapter 6 gives some example programs.

4.1.2 High-level languages

Programming has been made even easier by the use of so-called *high-level languages*. The set of instructions that can be used to construct a program is called a *programming language*. These use pre-packaged functions to carry out specific tasks; the pre-packaging allows simple words or symbols to be used which are reasonably descriptive of the function required. Thus the word *read* or *getchar* might be used as an instruction to input some data; the symbol = might be used to indicate an instruction to let some variable equal some value. Examples of programming languages are BASIC, FORTRAN, COBOL, Pascal and C. In this book C will be used. Chapter 7 is an introduction to the language and Chapter 8 gives some example programs.

The reason for the variety of languages is that each has been designed to make it is easy to write programs for specific types of operations. For example, FORTRAN (FORmula TRANslation) was designed for scientific and engineering applications involving the use of algebraic and trigonometric formulas. COBOL (COmmon Business Orientated Language) was designed for business applications. BASIC (Beginners All-purpose Symbolic Instruction Code) was designed as an easy to understand language which did not require detailed knowledge of a specific application. The C language was developed as a general-purpose language to provide a wide range of functions which can be used to develop programs in engineering and science.

However, whatever the language used, the microprocessor still runs on machine code, so the program has to be interpreted for its use. The process of carrying out this interpretation is known as *compiling*. This might be done by hand using the manufacturer's data sheets which list the binary code for each assembly code mnemonic. However, computer programs are available to do the conversion. Thus a program might be written in a high-level language such as C (Chapter 7). It is then run through a compiler program to convert the entire program into machine code, which can then be used by the microprocessor system.

4.2 Program development

Writing, testing and debugging software typically absorbs over 50% of the total design and development costs involved in setting up a microprocessor system. The key to reducing software costs is to adopt methods that improve the ability of a programmer to generate high quality programs in as short a time as possible. Design techniques used to achieve this are likely to involve the following steps:

1. *Definition of what is required of the system*
   This means specifying precisely what the software is required to do, the number of inputs and outputs required, any

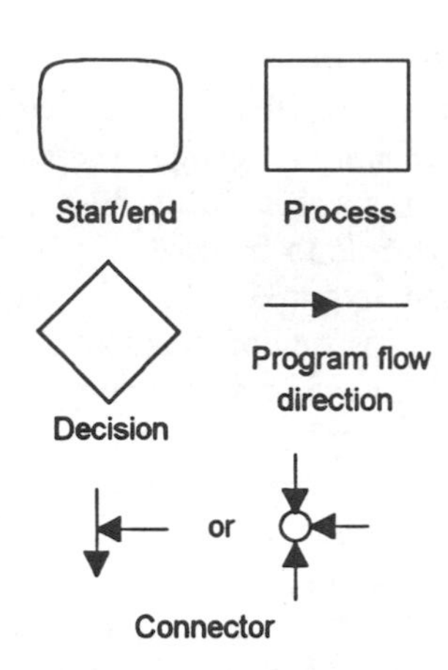

Fig. 4.1 Flow chart symbols

constraints on speed of operation, accuracy, memory, etc., and what action is to be taken if errors occur. For example, a program scanning switches on a control panel has to cope with situations in which a human operates the switches in an unexpected and perhaps incorrect way.

2. *Design initially without using a programming language*
   Define the algorithm to be used. An *algorithm* is a step-by-step sequence which defines a method for solving the problem. A useful aid is to represent the algorithm as a *flow chart*. Figure 4.1 shows the standard symbols used in the preparation of flow charts. Each step of an algorithm is represented by one or more of these symbols and linked together by lines to represent the program flow. Another useful way of describing an algorithm is *pseudocode*. This is a computer-like way of writing programs without bothering about the formal rules of a programming language. It basically involves writing a program as a sequence of functions or operations using the decision elements IF-THEN-ELSE and WHILE-DO. Examples of flow charts and pseudocode are given in Section 4.2.1.

3. *Coding*
   This is the process of translating a flow chart or pseudocode into instructions that a microprocessor can execute and involves writing the instructions in some language, e.g. assembly language or C, and then converting them into machine code, either manually or by means of a computer program.

4. *Testing and debugging*
   Errors in programs are known as *bugs* and the process of tracking them down and eliminating them is called *debugging* (see Section 4.2.2).

5. *Documenting*
   This is supplying information which will tell someone else how a program works so that they can modify the program if problems occur or circumstances change. Most programs are modified at some stage; this is known as *program maintenance*. A program that has been well designed and documented is easier to maintain.

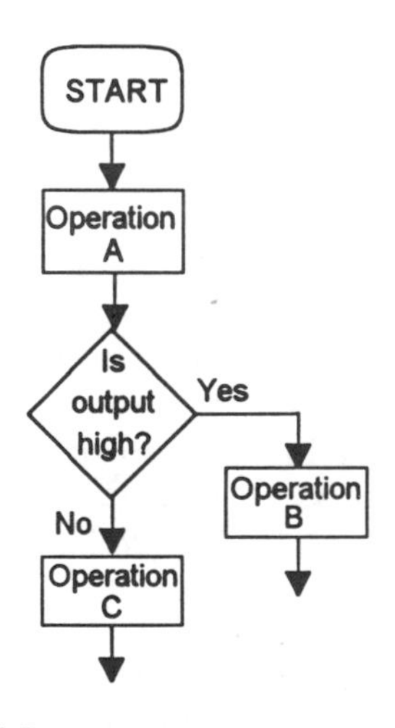

Fig. 4.2 Flow chart

4.2.1 Flow charts and pseudocode

As an illustration of the use of the flow chart symbols, Fig. 4.2 shows part of a flow chart. Following the program start, there is operation A then a branch to either operation B or operation C depending on if the decision to the query is a yes or a no. Thus if the output is high then operation A leads to operation B; if the

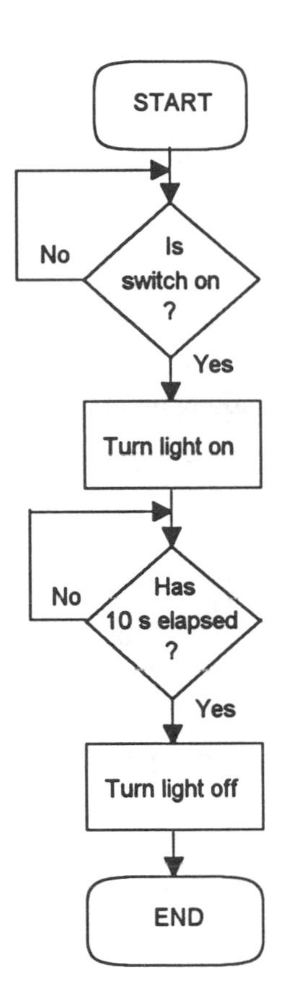

Fig. 4.3 A 10 s response

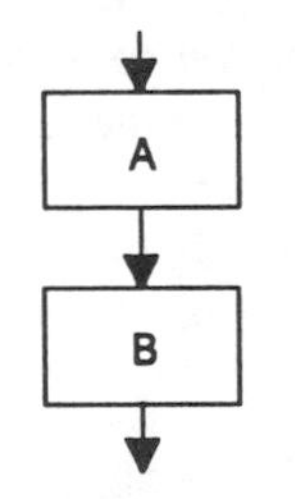

Fig. 4.4 Sequence

output is low then operation A leads to operation C. The basic advantage of using a flow chart to represent an algorithm is that it is a pictorial representation and it is easy to see how the various parts relate. Flow charts are, however, difficult to draw in all except the simplest of situations and can easily become clutterred. As an illustration of a flow chart being used to describe a simple algorithm, consider Fig. 4.3. This is for an algorithm to describe a single switch being used to turn on a light for 10 s and then switch it off.

Pseudocode involves writing a program as a sequence of actions, with selections expressed as IF-THEN-ELSE-ENDIF and repetitions as WHILE-DO-ENDWHILE. All elements must conclude with an END statement and the convention is to write the actions inside a program element so they are indented from the element heading or command; this separates the heading from the contents and makes the code look clearer.

1. *Sequence*
   Suppose we have operation A followed by operation B so that operation B can only start when operation A has finished. Figure 4.4 shows the flow chart and the code would be written as:

```
BEGIN A
   DO ...
END A
BEGIN B
   DO ...
END B
```

   As an illustration, we could use it to express the making of a cup of coffee. The program might be:

```
BEGIN WATER BOILING
   DO Fill kettle with water
   DO Plug kettle into mains supply
   DO Switch on
   DO Wait for water to boil
END WATER BOILING
BEGIN COFFEE MAKING
   DO Get a cup
   DO Put coffee in cup
   DO Add hot water
   DO Add milk
   DO Add sugar
END COFFEE MAKING
```

2. *Decision*
   Where we have a selection required we use the IF-THEN-ELSE-ENDIF elements. Thus we might have this code and the flow chart in Fig. 4.5:

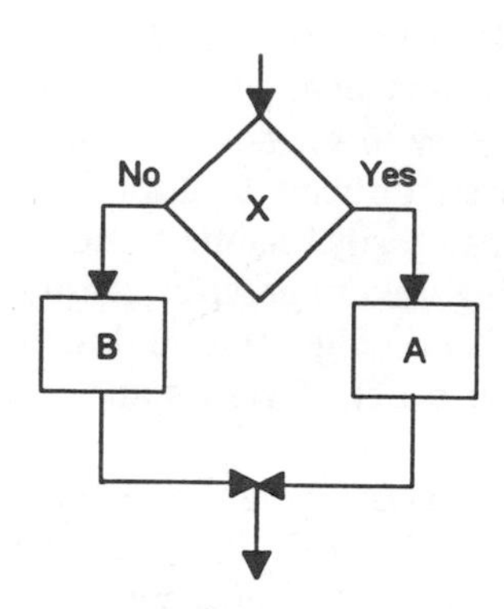

Fig. 4.5 IF-THEN-ELSE

```
IF X
THEN
   BEGIN A
   DO ...
   END A
ELSE
   BEGIN B
   DO ...
   END B
ENDIF X
```

Thus we might include in the coffee-making program:

```
IF sugar required
THEN
   DO Put sugar in the cup
   DO Stir
ELSE
   DO Stir
ENDIF
```

3. *Repetition*
   A repetition is written using the WHILE-DO-ENDWHILE elements as:

```
WHILE X
   BEGIN A
      DO ...
   END A
   BEGIN B
      DO ...
   END B
ENDWHILE X
```

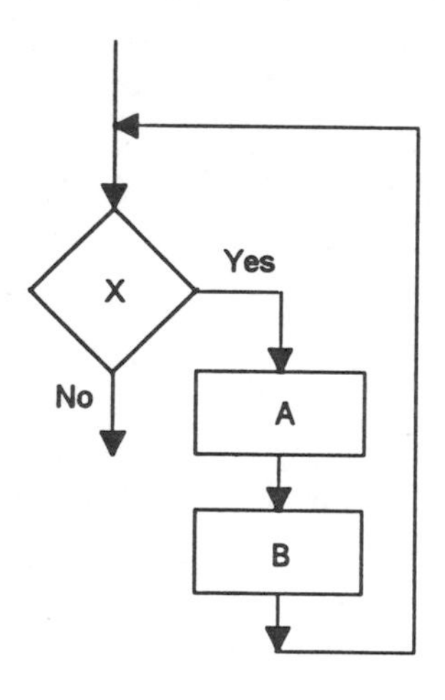

Fig. 4.6 WHILE-DO

While the answer to X is yes, the sequence A followed by B occurs and is then repeated as long as the answer to X is YES. When the answer is NO the loop involving the sequence AB is not followed. Figure 4.6 shows this WHILE-DO operation as a flow chart. As an illustration, the coffee-making program might be modified to allow for another activity while the water is boiling:

```
WHILE Water not boiling
   DO Read the newspaper
ENDWHILE
```

The development of programs in pseudocode is discussed later in this chapter in Section 4.4 where the structured approach to developing programs is discussed.

4.2.2 Testing and debugging

The data used to test a program has to be chosen to reflect as many possibilities as it can. For example, to test a program designed for use with a washing machine it is necessary to try all the combinations of inputs that might occur, and some inputs that should not normally occur but which might occur in the event of the water input not having been switched on or some other unforeseen input condition.

Errors can occur in writing programs and thus debugging it often necessary. To debug a program it is necessary to pin down the point in a program at which an error is occurring. This is discussed in Chapter 9.

4.3 Modular programming

The term *modular programming* is used for the procedure of breaking a programming task down into subtasks or modules. A module is a fairly independent piece of a program with a name and some instructions and data of its own. It is called up from some other module by its name and likewise can call up other modules. As a consequence, programs can be written, tested and debugged for each module before the modules are assembled to give the complete program. This enables program errors to be isolated within single modules and so makes detection and correction easier. It also enables modules to be used many times in the same program and in other programs. Later changes in the task specification then might be accommodated by changes in just one module rather than the entire program having to be rewritten. In C language a module is termed a *function*, in COBOL a *subprogram* and in BASIC a *subroutine*.

How big should a module be? If modules are very big then the benefits of modularisation are lost; if they are too small then we can end up with a proliferation of interconnections between modules, making the program rather complex. Some consider that a module should not occupy more than about 40 to 50 lines in a program and others think about 7 lines.

A basic approach to modularisation is to consider a module being required for each function in the program and being like a black box with an input and output so that we can string together modules without having to worry about what goes on inside each box. Ideally modules should be independent of each other so that if changes are made in the coding in one module then, provided the module still fulfils the same function, there should be no consequential errors introduced into other modules.

As an illustration of modularisation, consider the task of writing a program to switch a light on for 10 s (the flow chart for this was given earlier in Fig. 4.4). We might modularise this into a module giving the program for waiting for the switch to be turned on and then turning the light on, and another module giving the 10 s delay. Because delays occur in many programs it might be that we have a delay module already written and can make use of it without having to write a module from scratch. From the main program we can call up the module for switching the light on, and also from the main program we can call up the second module for the time delay.

4.3.1 Top-down design

The term *top-down design* is used when a programming task is broken down from a top level which defines the main function required of a program. This uses some defined but, as yet unconstructed, subfunctions. These subfunctions form the next level. They use some defined but, as yet unconstructed, sub-subfunctions and these form the next level. In this way we proceed down the levels (Fig. 4.7).

Thus we start at the top level and propose a solution to the problem. As we develop out knowledge about the problem and how to solve it, more detailed levels can be added to the design. Thus we might design at the top level an overall supervisory program module. We then design modules containing the tasks that have to be supervised. Within these modules there may be subtasks to design. We are therefore proceeding down the levels. Each level represents a different level of refinement and describes the program as a whole. Top-down design assumes the use of modular programming.

Note that the term *bottom-up design* assumes that the programmer starts with the fine detail of subsubtasks and then tries to weld them together to accomplish the overall function required of the program. Such an approach involves decisions made at lower levels which may make upper levels difficult to implement and can involve more moving back and forth between levels to change code than would occur with a top-down approach.

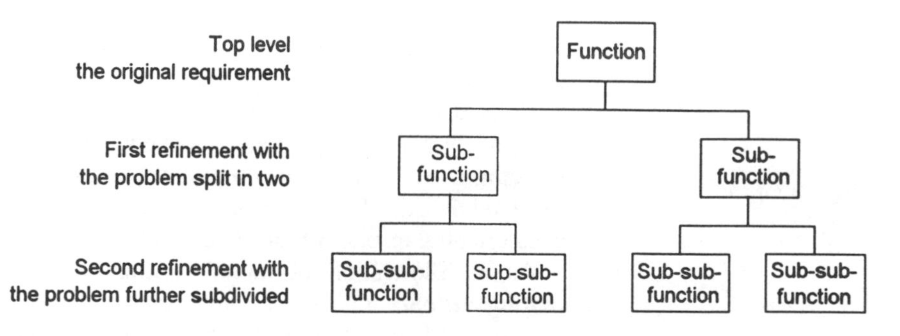

Fig. 4.7 Developing a level structure

As an illustration of top-down design, consider a program that will determine the smallest number from a set of numbers stored in memory and then multiply it by a scaling constant (Fig. 4.8). The top-level description of the program is to compute the scaled number. At the next level of refinement we break the program into two modules, one is to determine the smallest number in the list and the second is to multiply that number by the scaling constant.

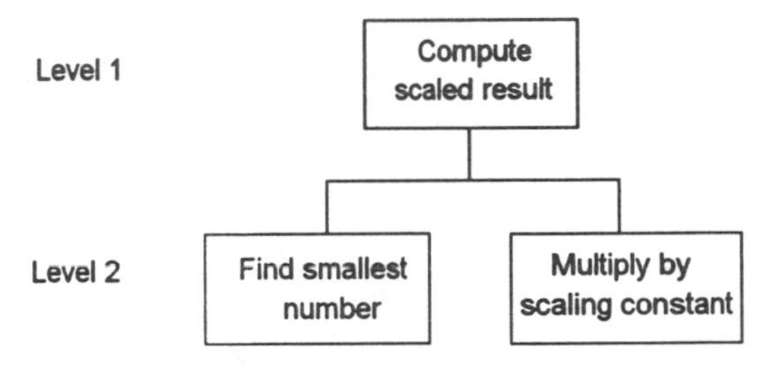

Fig. 4.8 Example of top-down design

4.4 Structured approach

The structured approach to program design involves designing the structure of a program before writing code and only using a few basic structures. *Jackson structured programming* (JSP) is one commonly used method of designing structured programs. It uses level diagrams to show a step-by-step refinement of a program with four basic types of structure, each structural element having just a single entrance and a single exit to link it with other structural elements. The basic structural elements are:

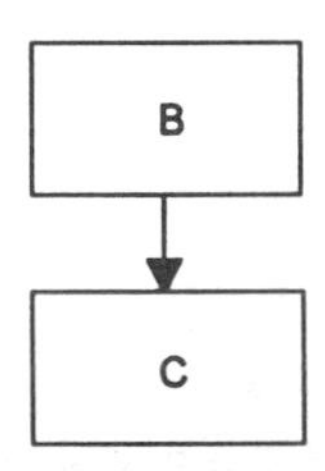

Fig. 4.9 Linear structure on a flow chart

1. *Sequence*
   This is a linear structure in which the program flows in a linear manner from one part to the next. Each part may be a single program statement or complex programs. Figure 4.9 shows how a sequence is represented on a flow chart, subfunction B leading to subfunction C. Figure 4.10 shows the same structure on a JSP diagram; it shows both the levels and the program structure and how function A consists of subfunction B followed by subfunction C. Boxes at the same level represent a sequence. A line drawn downwards below a box means 'consists of', thus A consists of B and C. As an example, for a program to print a page of a report, we might have the print page level subdivided into the two sequential subfunctions of print the page header and print the page text (Fig. 4.11).

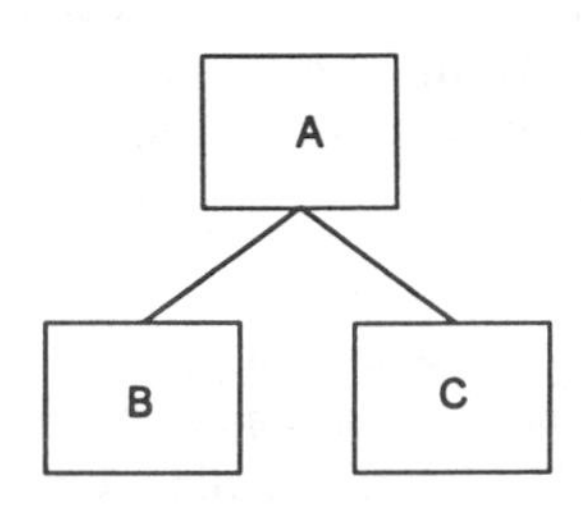

Fig. 4.10 A JSP sequence

2. *Loop* or *iteration*
   The loop or iteration structure is where a program is repeated until some condition obtains. Such structures can be considered as DO-WHILE. Figure 4.12 shows a flow chart for this type of

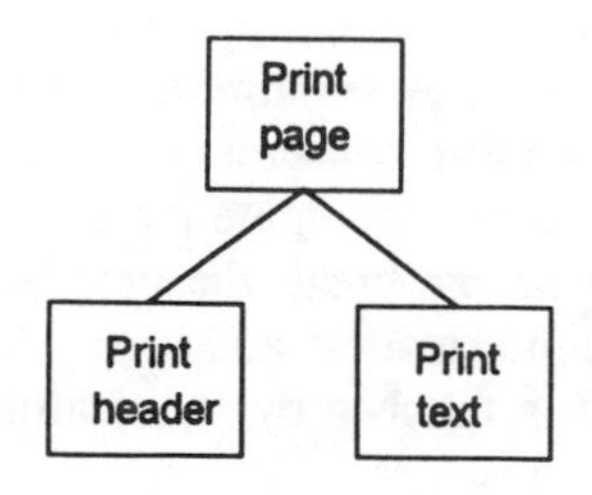

Fig. 4.11 A JSP sequence

structure. C is a condition and E some program element. The microprocessor continually checks C and executes E as long as C is true. Thus we might have the condition that some variable has the value 1; the program then keeps on being repeated until this value changes.

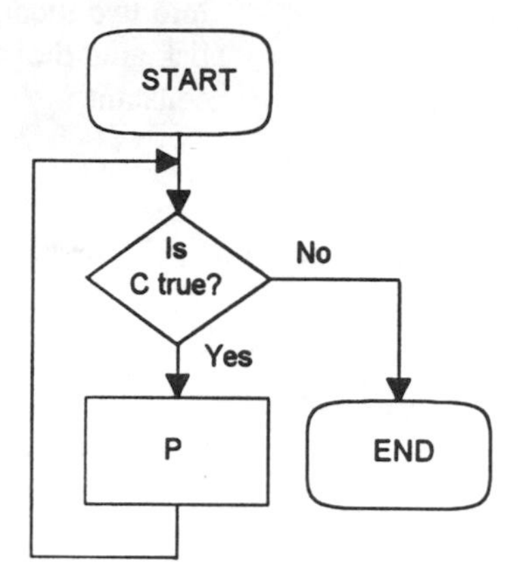

Fig. 4.12 Flow chart for do-while

As an illustration, in pseudocode a loop program to determine the sum of the integers 1, 2, 3, 4, 5, etc. to the *N*th integer could be:

```
I = 0
SUM = 0
WHILE I < N
   DO
   I = I + 1
   SUM = SUM + 1
ENDDO
```

The initial conditions have been set to I = 0 and Sum = 0. The microprocessor then executes the loop as long as I < N and sums the numbers.

Figure 4.13 shows how iteration can be represented on a JSP diagram. Function D is an iteration of subfunction E while condition C is true. Box E includes the asterisk symbol * to signify that D consists of repeated execution of E. With the above program for summing integers the condition is that I is less than N and thus the JSP diagram would involve the subfunction of incrementing and summing being repeated as long as this condition is met (Fig. 4.14).

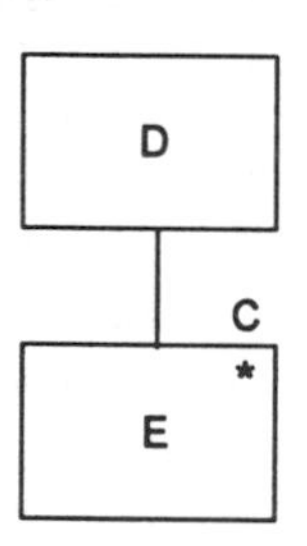

Fig. 4.13 Iteration

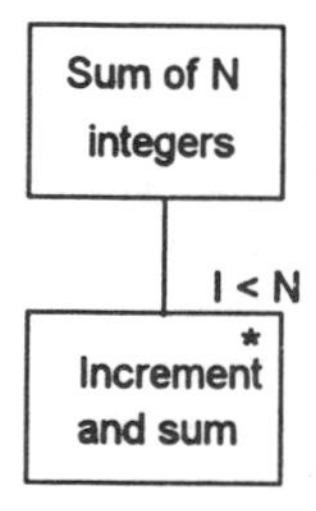

Fig. 4.14 Iteration

3. *Conditional* or *selectional*
   A conditional or selectional structure is one in which the execution of the program depends on a condition such as: if condition C then execute program G, if not C execute program H. Figure 4.15 shows the flow chart. We can describe such a structure as an IF-THEN-ELSE structure.

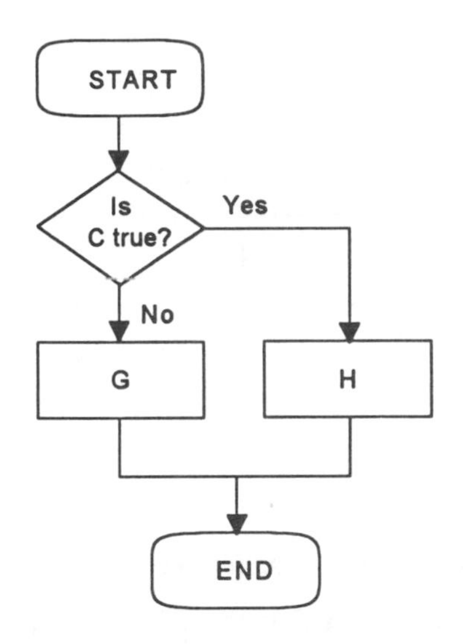

Fig. 4.15 If-then-else flow chart

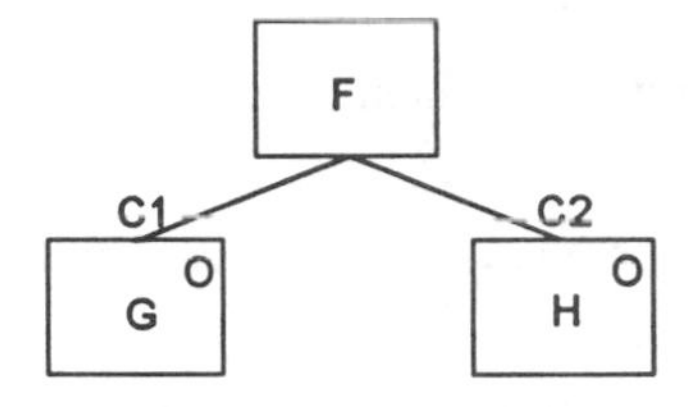

Fig. 4.16 Selection

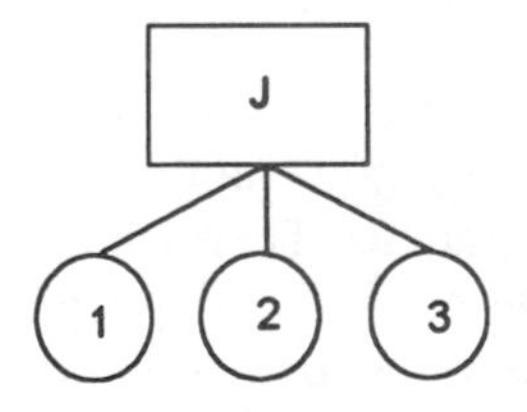

Fig. 4.17 Elementary components

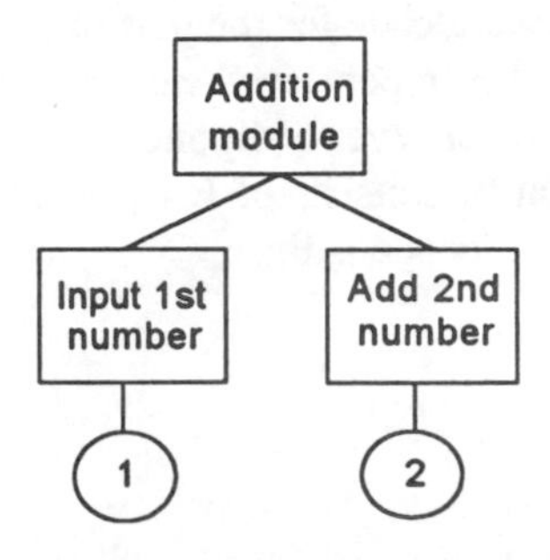

Fig. 4.18 Addition module

In pseudocode the conditional or selectional structure for a program to determine the reciprocal of a positive number might appear as:

```
IF X > 0
THEN
   Y = 1/X
ELSE
   Y = 0
ENDIF
```

Thus if X is greater than 0, i.e. a positive number, then Y is 1/X, else Y = 0. Thus Y is 0 if X is a negative number.

Figure 4.16 shows how a conditional or selectional structure can be represented on a JSP diagram. Function F is a selection of one of the subfunctions G and H depending on the conditions C1 and C2. If condition C1 occurs then the program executes G, if condition C2 occurs it executes H. A circle O is included in the boxes to indicate that F is a selection.

In addition to the above structural elements, JSP charts use *elementary program components*. These are components which are not control functions and represent actions or operations. On JSP diagrams they are generally represented by numbered circles (Fig. 4.17); thus 1, 2 and 3 are elementary program components with J as a sequence of the actions 1, 2 and 3. Each of the actions is linked by a line to the box in the structure which is responsible for it. The same numbered action may occur more than once and be drawn in relation to a number of boxes.

As an example of using the above structures in a program, consider a program module for a microprocessor which is to add two numbers. We require a sequence which is:

Input number 1 to memory
Add second number to contents of the memory

with the actions being:

1. Get first number
2. Get second number

The JSP diagram is thus as shown in Fig. 4.18.

Note that in drawing JSP diagrams, a function cannot be a mixture of different types of structure. Thus the structure shown in Fig. 4.19(a) is not permitted since A cannot be both the sequence B and C and an iteration of C. If we want a sequence B and C with C being iterated then we need to introduce an extra box in the structure and represent it as shown in Fig. 4.19(b). This extra box is often called a *function body*.

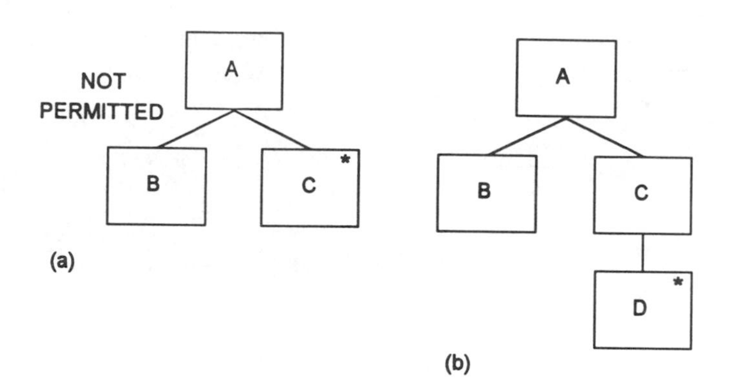

Fig. 4.19 JSP structures: (a) not permitted, (b) permitted

4.4.1 Steps in the JSP procedure for structuring programs

The procedure to be adopted when using the JSP method of structuring a program consists of the following steps:

1. Describe the structure that is required.
2. Draw a diagram showing the structure without bothering about elementary program components.
3. Identify and list the elementary operations, i.e. actions, that the program will have to perform.
4. Place the elementary operations on the program structure diagram.
5. Hence obtain the program structure diagram in a form which can readily be turned into pseudocode.

To derive the pseudocode from a JSP diagram, start at the top level and write down its elementary operations. Then indent the code listing and go down to the next level on the diagram and write the operations and structures present at this level. Repeat this for each level, indenting the code listing each time you move down a level and indicating the end of a structure by the word END.

As an illustration, consider the pseudocode for the part of a JSP diagram shown in Fig. 4.20. At the upper level we have the program component A and at the lower level component B. The asterisk in the box for B shows that A consists of B repeated as long as condition C1 exists. The pseudocode is thus:

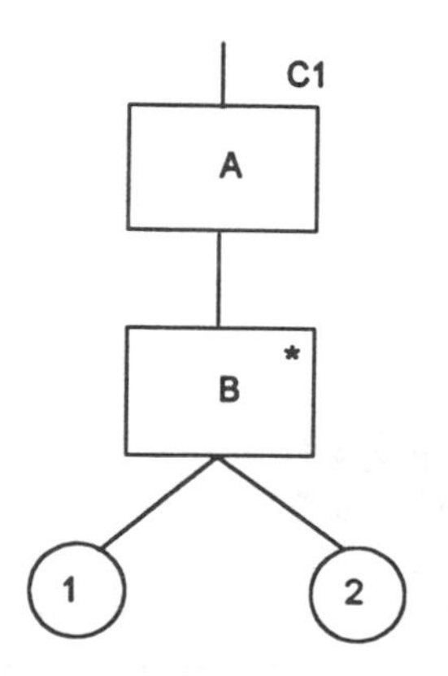

Fig. 4.20 Part of a JSP diagram

```
WHILE C1
   DO 1
   DO 2
ENDWHILE
```

If we have two such structures, as in Fig. 4.21, then because A and D are in sequence they have the same indentation in the pseudocode listing and so the code is:

```
WHILE C1
   DO 1
   DO 2
ENDWHILE
WHILE C2
   DO 3
   DO 4
ENDWHILE
```

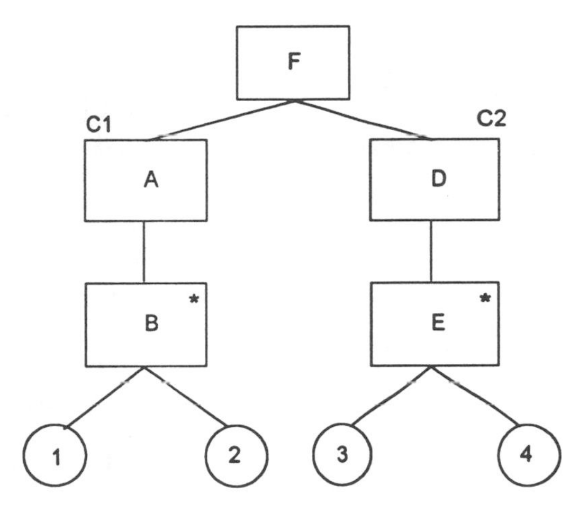

Fig. 4.21 JSP diagram

4.4.2 Examples of JSP structuring

As an example of JSP structuring, consider a program module which is to switch a light on if the input is 1 and off it is 0. This first involves getting the input. Then if a condition is met, the program should give one output; and if it is not met, the program should give another output. Figure 4.22 shows the basic IF-THEN-ELSE structure. We have sequence:

Get input
Output

with the output module having selection subfunctions:

```
If C = 1
   Then
   Light = on
Else
   Light = off
```

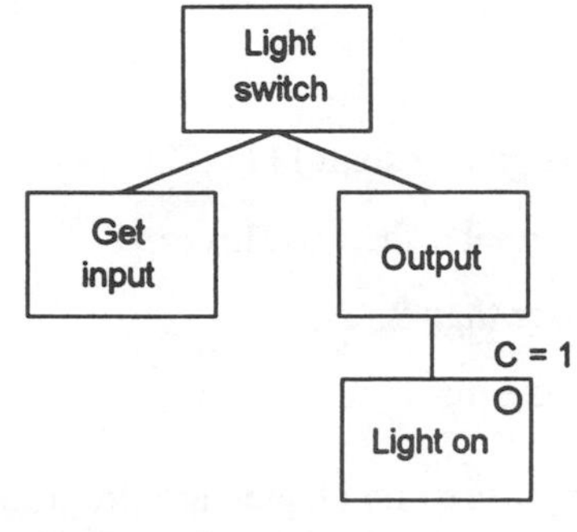

Fig. 4.22 Structure for light switch program

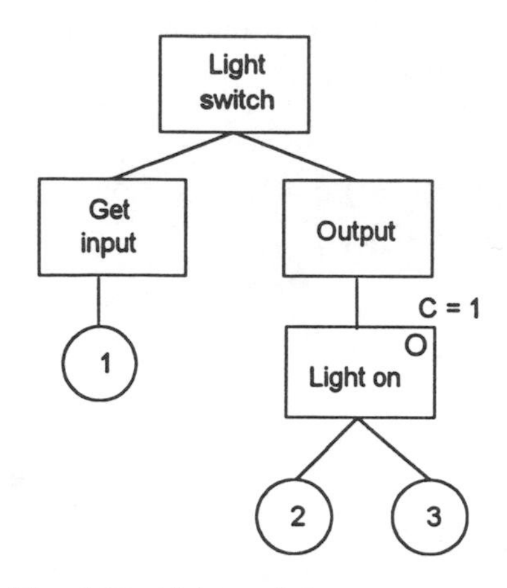

Fig. 4.23 Light switch program

The next step in deriving the JSP diagram is to list the elementary operations the program will have to carry out. They are:

1. Read input
2. Switch light on
3. Switch light off

If we now place these operations on the structure in Fig. 4.22 we obtain the required JSP diagram of Fig. 4.23. Thus Fig. 4.23 gives the pseudocode:

```
DO read input
WHILE output
   IF C = 1
   THEN
      DO switch light on
   ELSE
      DO switch light off
ENDWHILE
END
```

As a another example, consider a program module to read the binary input from eight switches and give an output in binary coded decimal format to a two-digit LED display. We require the program to convert the number and keep on repeating the conversion while the input is less than or equal to 1111, the conversion having the basic sequence:

Get binary input
Convert
Display

with convert requiring the number to be adjusted if it is greater than 1001, i.e. decimal 9. Figure 4.24 shows the program structure.

The basic operations are:

1. Read switches
2. Check if the binary output is greater than 1111
3. Check if the binary input is greater than 1001, i.e. 9
4. Add 6 if the number is greater than 9
5. Display the BCD output on the display

Thus the entire program, with structure and elementary program components, can be represented by the JSP diagram shown in Fig. 4.25. We can write this program in pseudocode as:

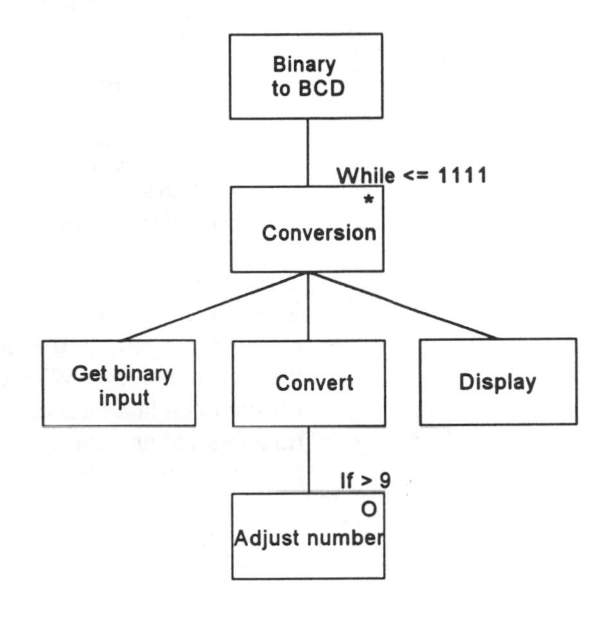

Fig. 4.24 Binary to BCD structure

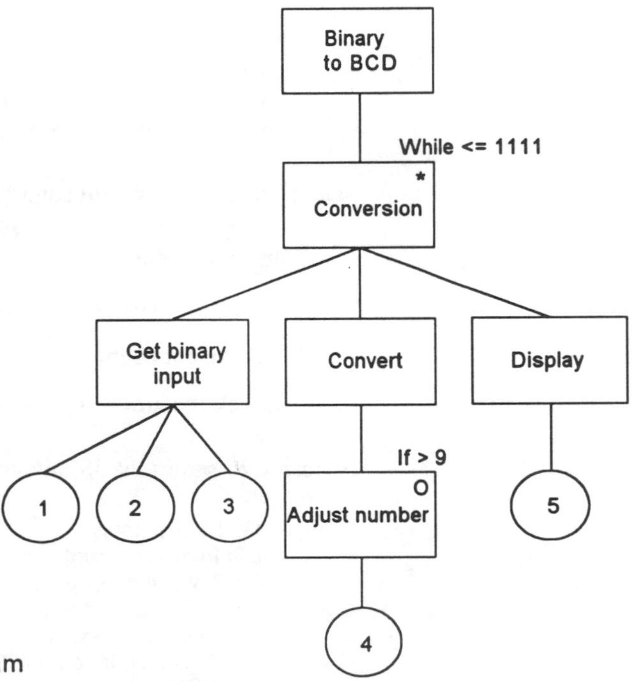

Fig. 4.25 Binary to BCD program

```
BEGIN Binary to BCD
   WHILE Input >=1111
      DO Read Switches
      DO Check for number > 9
           IF number > 9
           THEN
               DO add 06 to input number
           ENDIF
       DO Write BCD to the display
   ENDWHILE
END Binary to BCD
```

As another example, consider the program for a module which is required to produce a short time delay. Such a delay can be achieved by getting the microprocessor to count down to zero from some number. Whenever the microprocessor carries out an instruction it takes a number of clock cycles, so the counting takes time and the amount of time is proportional to the starting value for the countdown. The sequence is thus:

Initialise count
Implement the delay element
End the delay

The delay element is a delay loop which involves:

Read the loop count
Decrement the count
If the count is greater than 0 repeat the loop
End the looping when count = 0

The elementary program components required are:

1. Initialise count
2. Return to main program after delay
3. Decrement count
4. Check if count = 0

Figure 4.26 shows the JSP diagram and the pseudocode is thus:

```
BEGIN Time delay
   DO Initialise count
   BEGIN Delay loop body
      WHILE Count > 0
      DO Decrement count
      DO Check if count > 0
      ENDWHILE
END Delay loop body
   DO Return to main program after delay
END Time delay
```

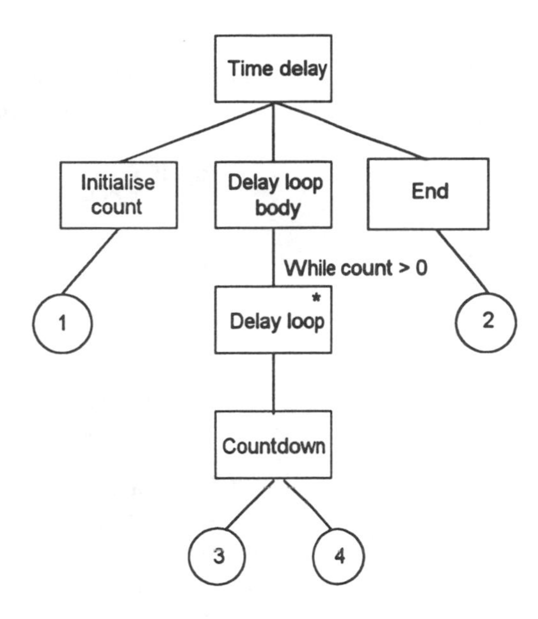

Fig. 4.26 Time delay

Problems

1. Explain what is meant by (a) machine code and (b) mnemonic code.
2. Draw a flow chart to represent the following sequence of operations: operation A is followed by operation B if X is greater than 0, otherwise operation C occurs.
3. Draw a flow chart to represent the sequence of operations which might occur with a burglar alarm system when a four-digit number has to be correctly entered from a keypad to switch off the alarm.
4. Draw a flow chart to describe a program that multiplies the contents of memory location 400 by 5 and stores the result in memory location 500. Hint: multiplication can be achieved by repeated addition.
5. Draw the flow chart and write the pseudocode to represent (a) if A is true then B else C, (b) while A is true do B.
6. Explain what is meant by modular programming.
7. Explain what is meant by top-down program design.
8. What are the three basic elements of Jackson structured programming?
9. Draw the Jackson structures to represent (a) operation A is to involve operation B followed by operation C, (b) operation D involves operation E being repeated until condition C is true, (c) operation F involves operation G if condition C is true otherwise operation H.
10. For the Jackson structure chart in Fig. 4.27 what is the program element represented by (a) block A, (b) the circled numbers 1 and 2?

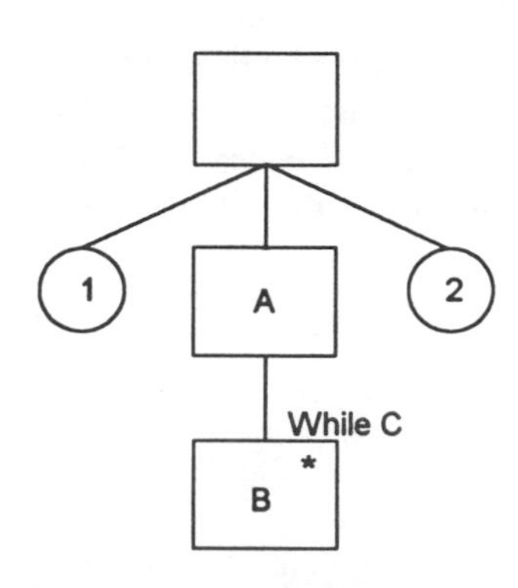

Fig. 4.27 Problem 10

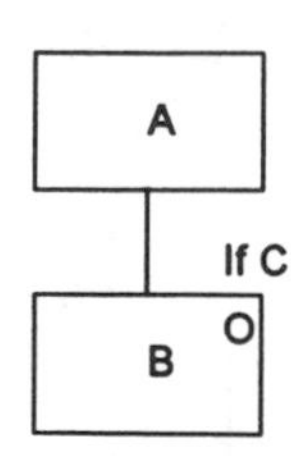

Fig. 4.28 Problem 11

Fig. 4.29 Problem 13

11. For the Jackson structure chart in Fig. 4.28 what is the program element represented?
12. Draw the Jackson structure elements to represent the following parts of programs:

(a)
```
IF C
   DO B
```

(b)
```
IF C
   DO G
ELSE
   DO H
```

(c)
```
WHILE C
   DO E
```

13. Draw a Jackson structure diagram to represent a program which displays on a VDU screen the arrangement of Xs shown in Fig. 4.29.
14. Draw a Jackson structure diagram to represent a program which will add two binary numbers and store the sum in memory, i.e. carry out the following sequence of operations:

    Get number 1
    Get number 2
    Add number 1 to number 2
    Store the sum in memory
    Stop

15. Design a program and represent the result by means of a Jackson structure chart and pseudocode. The program should take two numbers from memory, multiply them and store the result in memory. Hint: multiplication can be achieved by repeated addition.
16. Design a program in pseudocode for a microcontroller used in a car. The program should sound an alarm if the key is in the ignition when the door is open and the motor not running, or if the car lights are on when the key is not in the ignition.
17. Design a program in pseudocode for a microcontroller. The program should give an output which will cause a LED to flash on and off continuously, on for 1 s and then off for 1 s.

5 Assembly language

5.1 Introduction

The inputs to a microprocessor to form its program are termed *instructions* and the set of instructions that a microprocessor recognises is termed its *instruction set*. Different microprocessors have different instruction sets and this chapter details a selection of them. Writing instructions in binary code is a tedious and difficult task since it is not possible by just looking at a program to see what it is meant to be doing. Instructions can, however, be written in a mnemonic form termed *assembly language* and then translated into machine code by the programmer using a conversion table or by a computer program termed an *assembler*. This chapter is an introduction to assembly language and chapter 6 illustrates its use in writing programs.

5.2 Instructions

Each instruction must contain two parts, whether written in machine code or some other language:

1. *Operation*
   The code must detail the *operation* required, i.e. the opcode.

2. *Operand*
   The operation will require some data to operate on and thus an instruction must specify the data or source of data being operated on and its destination after processing; they are known as the *operands*. In principle all instructions require two operands, one to define the source of data prior to processing and one to define the destination for the processed data. Many instructions, however, have operands implied in the mnemonic, so they need not be explicitly specified.

For example, in assembly language an instruction might be LD A,B. The opcode used is LD to specify the operation is to load the operand in register B to the accumulator A.

LD A,B
Operation code for load
Destination
Source

In machine code this is:

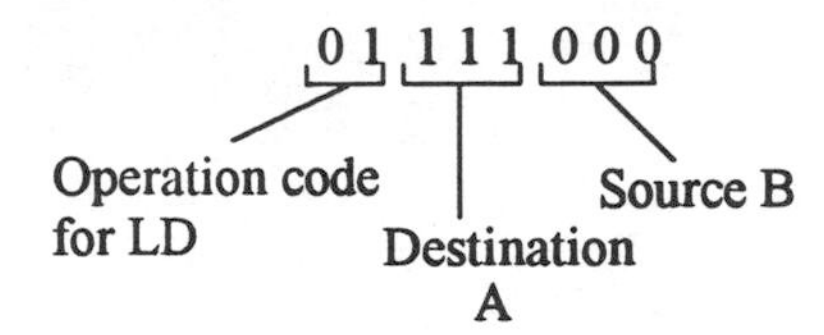

Another example of an instruction is JMP 2000H which has the operation jump with the destination being address 2000H and the source, not explicitly specified but implied by the operation, being the location currently indicated by the program counter.

5.2.1 Operations

In general, though the instructions that can be used depend on the microprocessor concerned, instructions can be classified as falling into four main groups:

1. Data transfer
2. Arithmetic
3. Logical
4. Program control

The following items illustrate the types of operations involved with instructions in these groups, giving the locations of data before and after the operations concerned.

Data transfer

1. *Load/move*
   This instruction reads the contents of a specified memory location and copies it to a specified register location, e.g. the accumulator/working register. Thus we might have:

Before instruction	*After instruction*
Data in memory location 0010	Data still in memory location 0010 Data from 0010 in accumulator

2. *Store*
   This instruction copies the current contents of a specified register into a specified memory location, e.g.

Before instruction	*After instruction*
Data in accumulator	Data still in accumulator Data copied to memory location 0011

Arithmetic

3. *Add*

This instruction adds the contents of a specified memory location to the data in some register, e.g.

Before instruction	*After instruction*
Accumulator with data 0001 Memory location with data 0010	Accumulator with data 0011

4. *Subtract*

This instruction subtracts the contents of a specified memory location from data in some register.

5. *Decrement*

This instruction subtracts 1 from the contents of a specified location, e.g. with the accumulator as the specified location:

Before instruction	*After instruction*
Accumulator with data 0011	Accumulator with data 0010

6. *Increment*

This instruction adds 1 to the contents of a specified location.

7. *Compare*

This instruction indicates whether the contents of a register are greater than, less than or the same as the contents of a specified memory location. The result appears in the status register as flags. Thus if the two are equal we can have the zero flag set to 1 and the carry flag to 0, if greater the zero flag and the carry flag are both 0 and if less than the zero flag is 0 and the carry flag 1.

Logical

8. *AND*

This instruction carries out the logical AND operation bit by bit with the contents of a specified memory location and the data in some register, e.g.

Before instruction	*After instruction*
Accumulator with data 0011 Memory location with data 1001	Accumulator with data 0001

Only in the least significant bit in the above data have we a 1 in both sets of data, hence the AND operation gives a 1 only in the least significant bit of the result. One of the main uses of the AND instruction is to force bits in the accumulator to become 0; this is called *bit masking*. Thus if we have the accumulator content 1010 1111 then ANDing this with mask data 1111 0000 gives the result 1010 0000. Every 0 in the mask data has forced logic 0s into the accumulator data.

9. *OR*

   As with the AND operation, the microprocessor carries out the OR operation bit by bit with the contents of the accumulator and data from a specified memory location. Like the AND operation the OR operation can be used for bit masking. Thus if we have 0011 1000 in the accumulator then ORing it with 1111 0000 results in 1111 1000. Wherever a logic 1 appears in the mask data then the corresponding bit in the accumulator becomes or remains a 1; a logic 0 in the mask data does not change the data in the accumulator.

10. *EXCLUSIVE-OR*

    This instruction carries out the logical EXCLUSIVE-OR (XOR) operation with the contents of a specified memory location and the data in some register, bit by bit. The EXCLUSIVE-OR function gives a 1 if either of the inputs is 1 but it gives a 0 if both are 1. Thus if we have 0110 0101 in the accumulator and XOR it with 1111 0000 then the result is 1001 0101. A logic 1 in the mask data will invert a bit in the accumulator, but a logic 0 will not change the data.

11. *Logical shift (left or right)*

    Logical shift instructions involve moving the pattern of bits in the register one place to the left or right by moving a 0 into the LSB of the number and the overflow bit into the carry. Thus for logical shift left we have:

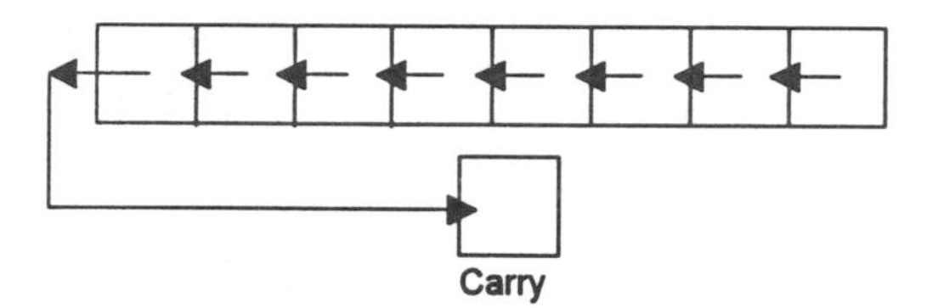

and for logical shift right:

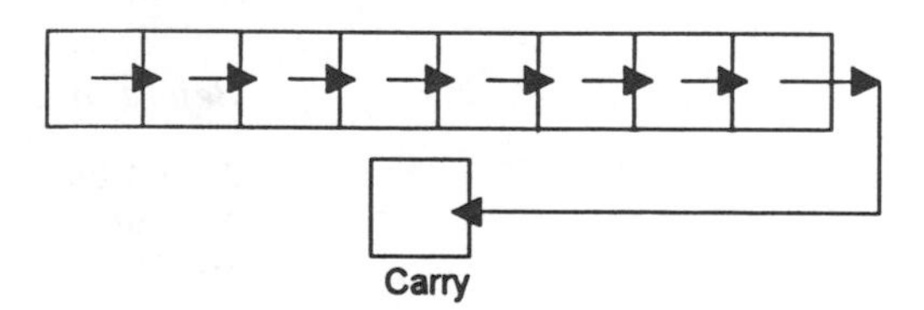

Here is an example for logical shift right:

Before instruction	*After instruction*
Accumulator with data 0011	Accumulator with data 0001 Status register indicates Carry 1

12. *Arithmetic shift (left or right)*
Arithmetic shift instructions involve moving the pattern of bits in the register one place to the left or right but they preserve the sign bit at the left end of the number. The overflow goes into the carry. Thus for arithmetic shift right we have:

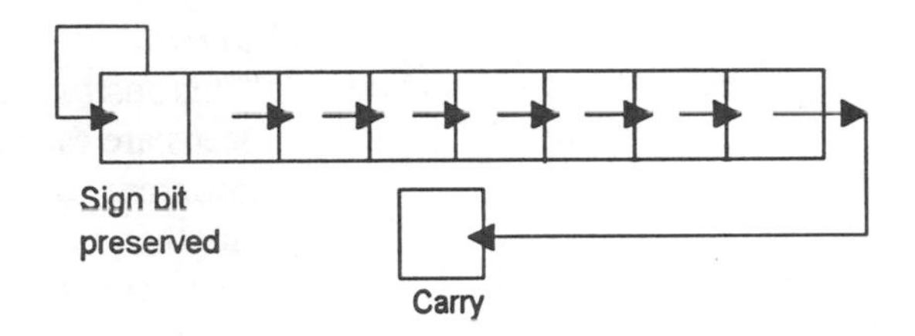

For an arithmetic shift right we might have:

Before instruction	*After instruction*
Accumulator with data 1011	Accumulator with data 1001 Status register indicates Carry 1

and for an arithmetic shift left:

Before instruction	*After instruction*
Accumulator with data 1011	Accumulator with data 1110 Status register indicates Carry 0

13. *Rotate (left or right)*
Rotate instructions involve moving the pattern of bits in the register one place to the left or right through the carry; the bit that spills out is written back into the other end, e.g. for a rotate right:

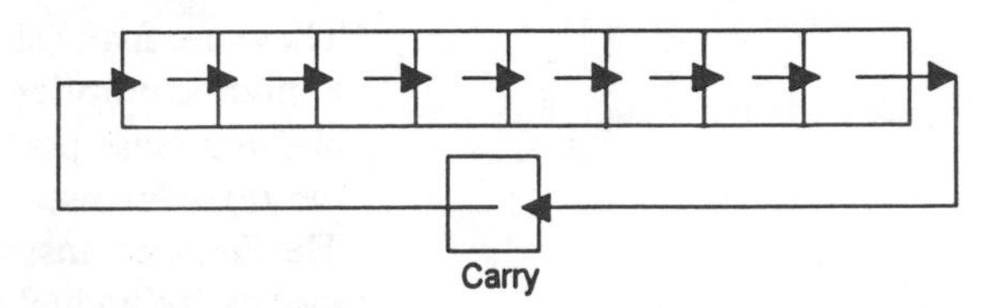

Thus we might have:

Before instruction	*After instruction*
Accumulator with data 0011	Accumulator with data 1001

For a rotate left we have:

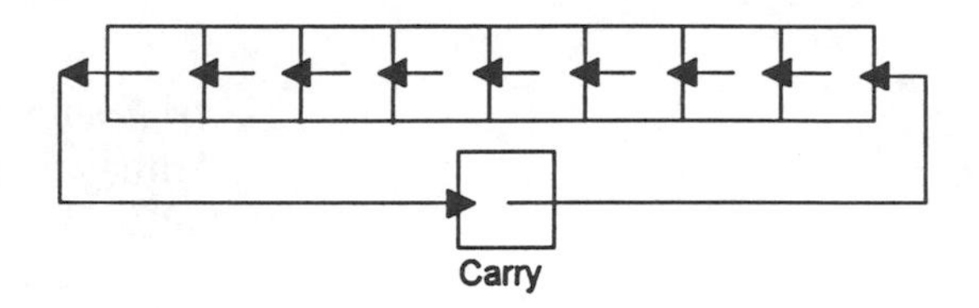

Program control

14. *Jump*
    This instruction changes the sequence in which the program steps are carried out. Normally the program counter causes the program to be carried out sequentially, one instruction after another, in the strict numerical sequence in which the instructions are written. However, the jump instruction causes the program counter to jump to some other specified location in the program. For example, a program might require the following sequence of instructions:

    Decrement the accumulator
    Jump if the accumulator is not zero to instruction ...
    The program then continues from the instruction jumped to

15. *Branch*
    This is a conditional instruction which might be *branch if zero* or *branch if plus.* This branch instruction is followed if the right conditions occur.

16. *End*
    This instruction stops all further microprocessor activity.

17. *No operation*
    This instruction does nothing except use an instruction cycle and increment the program counter. It can therefore be used to provide short delays.

5.2.2 Bit operations

There are many situations where certain bits have to be set, e.g. in a microcontroller register used to determine which pins of a bi-directional port will be an input and which an output, and in the registers used to control the operation of the microcontroller. The Boolean instructions for AND, OR and XOR can be used to modify individual bits. For example, ANDing with 1111 0111 can be used to switch bit 3 from a 1 to a 0, all the other bits remaining unchanged. Other instructions for bit operations include those to set a bit to a 1, e.g. SETB, and to clear a bit to a 0, e.g. CLR. There are also Boolean conditional jumps or branches which depend on the condition of a bit, e.g. branch if bit clear (BRCLR) and jump if bit set (JB).

5.2.3 Instruction sets

The mnemonic codes used for instructions in assembly language depend on the chosen microprocessor or microcontroller. The follow- ing tables show the codes used with some commonly encountered microprocessors and microcontrollers: the Rockwell 6502 micro- processor, the Zilog Z80 microprocessor, the Intel microcontroller 8051 (8085 microprocessor codes are a subset), the Motorola microcontroller M68HC11 (6800 microprocessor codes are a subset) and the Microchip Technology PIC microcontrollers. For full details of these or other instruction sets, see the publications of the manufacturer.

Table 5.1 Instruction set for Rockwell 6502

Instruction	*Mnemonic*	*Instruction*	*Mnemonic*
Add with carry	ADC	Jump to subroutine	JSR
Logical AND	AND	Load accumulator	LDA
Arithmetic shift left	ASL	Load X	LDX
Branch if carry clear	BCC	Load Y	LDY
Branch if carry set	BCS	Logical shift right	LSR
Branch if result equals 0	BEQ	No operation	NOP
Test bit	BIT	Logical OR	ORA
Branch if minus	BMI	Push A	PHA
Branch if not equal to 0	BNE	Push P status	PHP
Branch if plus	BPL	Pull A	PLA
Break	BRK	Pull P status	PLP
Branch if overflow clear	BVC	Rotate left	ROL
Branch if overflow set	BVX	Rotate right	ROR
Clear carry	CLC	Return from interrupt	RTI
Clear decimal flag	CLD	Return from subroutine	RTS
Clear interrupt disable	CLI	Subtract with carry	SBC
Clear overflow	CLV	Set carry	SEC
Compare to accumulator	CMP	Set decimal	SED
Compare to X	CPX	Set interrupt disable	SEI
Compare to Y	CPY	Store accumulator	STA
Decrement memory	DEC	Store X	STX
Decrement X	DEX	Store Y	STY
Decrement Y	DEY	Transfer A to X	TAX
Exclusive OR	EOR	Transfer A to Y	TAY
Increment memory	INC	Transfer stack pointer to X	TSX
Increment X	INX	Transfer X to A	TXA
Increment Y	INY	Transfer X to stack pointer	TXS
Jump	JMP	Transfer Y to A	TYA

Table 5.2 Instruction set for Zilog Z80

Instruction	*Mnemonic*	*Instruction*	*Mnemonic*
Add operand with carry to accumulator	ADC	No operation, increment PC	NOP
Add operand to accumulator	ADD	Logical OR accumulator with operand	OR
Logical AND accumulator with operand	AND	Load output port C with location HL, decrement HL and B	OTDR
Test bit in register or memory location	BIT	Load output port C with location HL, increment HL, decrement B	OTIR
Call subroutine	CALL	Output to port	OUT
Complement carry flag	CCF	Load output port C with location HL, decrement HL and B	OUTD
Compare operand with accumulator	CP	Load output port C with location HL, increment HL, decrement B	OUTI
Compare location HL with accumulator, decrement HL and BC	CPD	Recover data from stack	POP
As for CPD, but repeat until BC = 0	CPDR	Save data on the stack	PUSH
Compare location HL with accumulator, increment HL and BC	CPI	Reset bit in register or memory location	RES
As for CPI but repeat until BC = 0	CPIR	Return from subroutine	RET
Complement accumulator	CPL	Return from maskable interrupt	RETI
Decimal adjust accumulator	DAA	Return from non-maskable interrupt	RETN
Decrement register or contents of memory location	DEC	Rotate left, through carry, data in register or memory location	RL
Disable interrupts	DI	Rotate left, through carry, data in acc.	RLA
Decrement B, jump if not zero	DJNZ	Rotate left circular, data in register or memory location	RLC
Enable interrupts	EI	Rotate left circular accumulator	RLCA
Exchange registers	EX	Rotate digit left and right between acc. and location HL	RLD
Exchange register sets	EXX	Rotate right, through carry, data in register or memory location	RR
Halt, wait for interrupt or reset	HALT	Rotate right, through carry, data in acc.	RRA
Set interrupt mode	IM	Rotate right circular, data in register or memory location	RRC
Input from port	IN	Rotate right circular accumulator	RRCA
Increment register or contents of memory location	INC	Rotate digit right and left between accumulator and location HL	RRD
Load location HL from port C, decrement HL and B	IND	Restart to location in operand	RST
As for IND but repeat until B = 0	INDR	Subtract operand from accumulator with carry	SBC
Load location HL from port C, increment HL, decrement B	INI	Set carry flag	SCF
As for INI but repeat until B = 0	INIR	Set bit in register or memory location	SET
Jump to new location	JP	Arithmetic shift left of operand	SLA
Jump relative to PC	JR	Arithmetic shift right of operand	SRA
Load register or memory location	LD	Logical shift right of operand	SRL
Load location DE with location HL, decrement HL, DE and BC	LDD	Subtract operand from accumulator	SUB
As for LDD but repeat until BC = 0	LDDR	XOR accumulator with operand	XOR
Load location DE with location HL, increment DE and HL, decrement BC	LDI		
As for LDI but repeat until BC = 0	LDIR		
Negate accumulator	NEG		

Table 5.3 Instruction set for Intel 8051

Instruction	*Mnemonic*	*Instruction*	*Mnemonic*
Data transfer		*Logical operations*	
Move data to accumulator	MOV A, #data	AND accumulator to direct byte	ANL direct,A
Move register to accumulator	MOV A, Rn	AND immediate data to direct byte	ANL direct, #data
Move direct byte to accumulator	MOV A, direct	AND immediate data to acc.	ANL A, #data
Move indirect RAM to accumulator	MOV A, @Ri	AND direct byte to accumulator	ANL A, direct
Move accumulator to direct byte	MOV direct, A	AND indirect RAM to accumulator	ANL A, @Ri
Move accumulator to external RAM	MOVX @Ri, A	AND register to accumulator	ANL A, Rn
Move accumulator to register	MOV Rn, A	OR accumulator to direct byte	ORL direct, A
Move direct byte to indirect RAM	MOV @Ri, direct	OR immediate data to direct byte	ORL direct, #data
Move immediate data to register	MOV Rn, #data	OR immediate data to accumulator	ORL A, #data
Move direct byte to direct byte	MOV direct, direct	OR direct byte to accumulator	ORL A, direct
Move indirect RAM to direct byte	MOV direct, @Ri	OR indirect RAM to accumulator	ORL A, @Ri
Move register to direct byte	MOV direct, Rn	OR register to accumulator	ORL A, Rn
Move immediate data to direct byte	MOV direct, #data	XOR accumulator to direct byte	XRL direct, A
Move immediate data to indirect RAM	MOV @Ri, #data	XOR immediate data to acc.	XRL direct, #data
Load data pointer with a 16-bit constant	MOV DPTR, #data16	XOR immediate data to acc.	XRL A, #data
Move code byte relative to DPTR to acc.	MOV A, @A+DPTR	XOR direct byte to accumulator	XRL A, direct
Move external RAM, 16-bit addr., to acc.	MOVX A, @DPTR	XOR indirect RAM to accumulator	XRL A, @Ri
Move acc. to external RAM, 16-bit addr.	MOVX @DPTR, A	XOR register to accumulator	XRL A, Rn
Exchange direct byte with accumulator	XCH A, direct	*Addition*	
Exchange indirect RAM with acc.	XCH A, @Ri	Add immediate data to acc.	ADD A, #data
Exchange register with accumulator	XCH A, Rn	Add direct byte to accumulator	ADD A, direct
Push direct byte onto stack	PUSH direct	Add indirect RAM to accumulator	ADD A, @Ri
Pop direct byte from stack	POP direct	Add register to accumulator	ADD A, Rn
Branching		Add immediate data to acc.	
Absolute jump	AJMP addr 11	with carry	ADDC A, #data
Long jump	LJMP addr 16	Add direct byte to acc. with carry	ADDC A, direct
Short jump, relative address	SJMP rel	Add indirect RAM to acc. with carry	ADDC A, @Ri
Jump indirect relative to the DPTR	JMP @A+DPTR	Add register to acc. with carry	ADDC A, Rn
Jump if accumulator zero	JZ rel	*Subtraction*	
Jump if accumulator is not zero	JNZ rel	Subtract immediate data from acc.	
Compare direct byte to acc. and jump if		with borrow	SUBB A, #data
not equal	CJNE A, direct, rel	Subtract direct byte from acc. with	
Compare immediate to acc. and jump if		borrow	SUBB A, 29
not equal	CJNE A, #data, rel	Subtract indirect RAM from acc.	
Compare immediate to register and		with borrow	SUBB A, @Ri
jump if not equal	CJNE Rn, #data, rel	*Multiplication and division*	
Compare immediate to indirect and		Multiply A and B	MUL AB
jump if not equal	CJNE @Ri, #data, rel	Divide A by B	DIV AB
Decrement register and jump if not zero	DJNZ Rn, rel	*Decimal maths operations*	
Decrement direct byte, jump if not zero	DJNZ A, direct, rel	Exchange low-order digit indirect	
Jump if carry is set	JC rel	RAM with accumulator	XCHD A, @Ri
Jump if carry not set	JNC rel	Swap nibbles within the acc.	SWAP A
Jump if direct bit is set	JB bit, rel	Decimal adjust accumulator	DA A
Jump if direct bit is not set	JNB bit, rel	*Increment and decrement*	
Jump if direct bit is set and clear bit	JBC bit, rel	Increment accumulator	INC A
Subroutine call		Increment direct byte	INC direct
Absolute subroutine call	ACALL addr 11	Increment indirect RAM	INC @Ri
Long subroutine call	LCALL addr 16	Increment register	INC Rn
Return from subroutine	RET	Decrement accumulator	DEC A
Return from interrupt	RETI	Decrement direct byte	DEC direct

(*Continued on next page*)

Instruction	Mnemonic	Instruction	Mnemonic
Bit manipulation		Decrement indirect RAM	DEC @Ri
Clear carry	CLR C	Decrement register	DEC Rn
Clear bit	CLR bit	Increment data pointer	INC DPTR
Set carry but	SETB C	*Clear and complement operations*	
Set bit	SETB bit	Complement accumulator	CPL A
Complement carry	CPL C	Clear accumulator	CLR A
AND bit to carry bit	ANL C,bit	*Rotate operations*	
AND complement of bit to carry bit	ANL C,/bit	Rotate accumulator right	RR A
OR bit to carry bit	ORL C,bit	Rotate accumulator right thro. C	RRC A
OR complement of bit to carry bit	ORL C,/bit	Rotate accumulator left	RL A
Move bit to carry	MOV C,bit	Rotate accumulator left through C	RLC A
Move carry bit to bit	MOV bit,C	*No operation*	
		No operation	NOP

Note: A value preceded by # is a number, #data16 is a 16-bit constant; Rn refers to the contents of a register; @Ri refers to the value in memory where the register points, DPTR is the data pointer, direct is the memory location where data used by an instruction can be found.

Table 5.4 Instruction set for Motorola M68HC11

Instruction	Mnemonic	Instruction	Mnemonic
Loading		*Store registers*	
Load accumulator A	LDAA	Store contents of accumulator A	STAA
Load accumulator B	LDAB	Store contents of accumulator B	STAB
Load double accumulator	LDD	Store contents of double acc.	STD
Load stack pointer	LDS	Store stack pointer	STS
Load index register X	LDX	Store index register X	STX
Load index register Y	LDY	Store index register Y	STY
Pull data from stack and load acc. A	PULA	Push data from acc. A onto stack	PSHA
Pull data from stack and load acc. B	PULB	Push data from acc. B onto stack	PSHB
Pull index register X from stack	PULX	Push index reg. X contents onto stack	PSHX
Pull index register Y from stack	PULY	Push index reg. Y contents onto stack	PSHY
Transfer registers		*Logic*	
Transfer from acc. A to acc. B	TAB	AND with contents of accumulator A	ANDA
Transfer from acc. B to acc. A	TBA	AND with contents of accumulator B	ANDB
From stack pointer to index reg. X	TSX	Exclusive-OR with contents of acc. A	EORA
From stack pointer to index reg. Y	TSY	Exclusive-OR with contents of acc. B	EORB
From index reg. X to stack pointer	TXS	OR with contents of accumulator A	ORAA
From index reg. Y to stack pointer	TYS	OR with contents of accumulator B	ORAB
Exchange double acc. and index reg. X	XGDX	Replace memory with ones complement	COM
Exchange double acc. and index reg. Y	XGDY	Replace acc. A with ones complement	COMA
Decrement/increment		Replace acc. B with ones complement	COMB
Subtract 1 from contents of memory	DEC	*Arithmetic*	
Subtract 1 from contents of acc. A	DECA	Add contents of acc. A to acc. B	ABA
Subtract 1 from contents of acc. B	DECB	Add contents of acc. B to index reg. X	ABX
Subtract 1 from stack pointer	DES	Add contents of acc. B to index reg. Y	ABY
Subtract 1 from index register X	DEX	Add memory to acc. A without carry	ADDA
Subtract 1 from index register Y	DEY	Add memory to acc. B without carry	ADDB
Add 1 to contents of memory	INC	Add mem. to double acc. without carry	ADDD
Add 1 to contents of accumulator A	INCA	Add memory to acc. A with carry	ADCA
Add 1 to contents of accumulator B	INCB	Add memory to acc. B with carry	ADCB
Add 1 to stack pointer	INS	Decimal adjust	DAA
Add 1 to index register X	INX	Subtract contents of acc. B from acc. A	SBA
Add 1 to index register Y	INY	Subtract mem. from acc. A with carry	SBCA

(*Continued on next page*)

Instruction	*Mnemonic*	*Instruction*	*Mnemonic*
Rotate/shift		Subtract mem. from acc. B with carry	SBCB
Rotate bits in memory left	ROL	Subtract mem. from accumulator A	SUBA
Rotate bits in accumulator A left	ROLA	Subtract mem. from accumulator B	SUBB
Rotate bits in accumulator B left	ROLB	Subtract mem. from double acc.	SUBD
Rotate bits in memory right	ROR	Replace acc. A with twos complement	NEGA
Rotate bits in accumulator A right	RORA	Replace acc. B with twos complement	NEGB
Rotate bits in accumulator B right	RORB	Multiply unsigned acc. A by acc. B	MUL
Arithmetic shift bits in memory left	ASL	Unsigned integer divide D by i. reg. X	IDIV
Arithmetic shift bits in acc. A left	ASLA	Unsigned fractional divide D by i. reg. X	FDIV
Arithmetic shift bits in acc. B left	ASLB	*Conditional branch*	
Arithmetic shift bits in memory right	ASR	Branch if minus	BMI
Arithmetic shift bits in acc. A right	ASRA	Branch if plus	BPL
Arithmetic shift bits in acc. B right	ASRB	Branch if overflow set	BVS
Logical shift bits in memory left	LSL	Branch if overflow clear	BVC
Logical shift bits in acc. A left	LSLA	Branch if less than zero	BLT
Logical shift bits in acc. B left	LSLB	Branch if greater than or equal to zero	BGE
Logical shift bits in acc. D left	LSLD	Branch if less than or equal to zero	BLE
Logical shift bits in memory right	LSR	Branch if greater than zero	BGT
Logical shift bits in acc. A right	LSRA	Branch if equal	BEQ
Logical shift bits in acc. B right	LSRB	Branch if not equal	BNE
Logical shift bits in acc. C right	LSRD	Branch if higher	BHI
Data test with setting of condition codes		Branch if lower or same	BLS
Logical test AND between acc. A & memory	BITA	Branch if higher or same	BHS
Logical test AND between acc. B & memory	BITB	Branch if lower	BLO
Compare accumulator A to accumulator B	CBA	Branch if carry clear	BCC
Compare accumulator A and memory	CMPA	Branch if carry set	BCS
Compare accumulator B and memory	CMPB	*Jump and branch*	
Compare double accumulator with memory	CPD	Jump to address	JMP
Compare index register X with memory	CPX	Jump to subroutine	JSR
Compare index register Y with memory	CPY	Return from subroutine	RTS
Subtract $00 from memory	TST	Branch to subroutine	BSR
Subtract $00 from accumulator A	TSTA	Branch always	BRA
Subtract $00 from accumulator B	TSTB	Branch never	BRN
Interrupt		Branch bits set	BRSET
Clear interrupt mask	CLI	Branch bits clear	BRCLR
Set interrupt mask	SEI	*Condition code*	
Software interrupt	SWI	Clear carry	CLC
Return from interrupt	RTI	Clear overflow	CLV
Wait for interrupt	WAI	Set carry	SEC
Complement and clear		Set overflow	SEV
Clear memory	CLR	Transfer from acc. A to condition code reg.	TAP
Clear A	CLRA	Transfer from condition code reg. to acc. A	TPA
Clear B	CLRB	*Miscellaneous*	
Clear bits in memory	BCLR	No operation	NOP
Set bits in memory	BSET	Stop processing	STOP
		Special test mode	TEST

Note: The number of bits in a register depends on the processor. An 8-bit microprocessor generally has 8-bit registers. Sometimes two of the data registers may be used together to double the number of bits. Such a combined register is referred to as a doubled register.

Table 5.5 PIC16Cxx instruction set

Instruction	*Mnemonic*	*Instruction*	*Mnemonic*
Add a number with number in working reg.	addlw number	Move (copy) the number in a file reg. into the working reg.	movf FileReg,w
Add number in working reg. to number in file register and put number in file register	addwf FileReg,f	Move (copy) number into working reg.	movlw number
Add number in working reg. to number in file register and put number in working reg.	addwf FileReg,w	Move (copy) the number in file reg. into the working reg.	movwf FileReg
AND a number with the number in the working reg. and put result in working reg.	andlw number	No operation	nop
AND a number in the working reg. with the number in file reg., and put result in file reg.	andwf FileReg,f	Return from a subroutine and enable global interrupt enable bit	refie
Clear a bit in a file reg., i.e. make it 0	bcf FileReg,bit	Return from a subroutine with a number in the working register	retlw number
Set a bit in a file reg., i.e. make it 1	bsf FileReg,bit	Return from a subroutine	return
Test a bit in a file reg. and skip the next instruction if the bit is 0	btfsc FileReg,bit	Rotate bits in file reg. to the left through the carry bit	rlf FileReg,f
Test a bit in a file reg. and skip the next instruction if the bit is 1	btfss FileReg,bit	Rotate bits in file reg. to the right through the carry bit	rrf FileReg,f
Call a subroutine, after which return to where it left off	call AnySub	Send the PIC to sleep, a low power consumption mode	sleep
Clear, i.e. make 0, the number in file reg.	clrf FileReg	Subtract the number in working reg. from a number	sublw number
Clear , i.e. make 0, the no. in working reg.	clrw	Subtract the no. in working reg. from number in file reg., put result in file reg.	subwf FileReg,f
Clear the number in the watchdog timer	clrwdt	Swap the two halves of the 8 bit no. in a file reg, leaving result in file reg.	swapf FileReg, f
Complement the number in file reg. and leave result in file register	comf FileReg,f	Use the number in working reg. to specify which bits are input or output	tris PORTX
Decrement a file reg., result in file reg.	decf FileReg,f	XOR a number with number in working register	xorlf number
Decrement a file reg. and if result zero skip the next instruction	decfsz FileReg,f	XOR the number in working reg. with number in file reg. and put result in the file reg.	xorwf FileReg,f
Go to point in program labelled	gotot label		
Increment file reg. and put result in file reg.	incf FileReg,f		
OR a number with number in working reg.	iorlw number		
OR the number in working reg. with the number in file reg., put result in file reg.	iorwf FileReg,f		

Note: f is used for the file register, w for the working register and b for bit. The mnemonics indicate the types of operand involved, e.g. movlw indicates the move operation with the lw indicating a literal value, i.e. a number, is involved in the working register w; movwf indicates the move operation when the working register and a file register are involved.

5.2.4 Numerical values

Numerical data may be binary, octal, hex or decimal. Generally in the absence of any indicator the assembler assumes the number is decimal. With PIC microcontrollers the header file has R = DEC for this to be the default. Then for binary the number is enclosed in quotation marks and preceded by B (H for hex). With Intel, numerical values must be preceded by # to indicate a number and by B for binary, O or Q for octal, H or h for hex and D or nothing for decimal. With Motorola, a number is indicated by the prefix #; a binary number is preceded by % or followed by B; an octal number is preceded by @ or followed by O; a hex number is preceded by $ or followed by H; and a decimal number requires no indicating letter or symbol. Rockwell uses the same system as Motorola.

5.2.5 Addressing

When a mnemonic, such as LD or LDA, is used to specify an instruction it will be followed by additional information to specify the source and destination of the data required by the instruction. The data following the instruction is referred to as the *operand*.

There are several different methods that are used for specifying data locations, i.e. addressing, and hence the way in which the program causes the microprocessor to obtain its instructions or data. Different microprocessors have different addressing modes. The Motorola 68HC11 has the six addressing modes of immediate, direct, extended, indexed, inherent and relative; the Intel 8051 has the five modes of immediate, direct, register, indirect and indexed; the PIC microcontroller has the three modes of immediate, direct and indirect with the indirect mode allowing indexing. The following are the commonly used addressing modes:

1. *Immediate addressing*
   The data immediately following the mnemonic is the value to be operated on. This type of instruction with immediate addressing is used with the loading of a predetermined value into a register or memory location.

   For example, with Z80 codes, LD A,25H means load the A register with the number 25, the H indicating that it is a hex number. With the Motorola code, LDA B #$25 means load the number 25 into accumulator B. The # signifies immediate mode and a number, the $ that the number is in hexadecimal notation. The Rockwell 6502 code is similar. With the Intel code we might have MOV A,#25H to move the number 25 to the accumulator A. The # indicates a number and the H indicates a hex number. With the PIC code we might have movlw H'25' to load the number 25 into the working register w, the H indicating it is a hex number.

2. *Direct, absolute, extended or zero-page addressing*
   With this form of addressing the data byte that follows the opcode directly gives an address that defines the location of the data to be used in the instruction. With Motorola the term *direct addressing* is used when the address given is only 8 bits wide; the term *extended addressing* is used when it is 16 bits wide. The term *zero-page addressing* is also used with some microprocessors, e.g. the 6502, to indicate an 8 bit address.

   For example, with Z80 code, LD A,(0400H) means load the accumulator with the data at address 0400. With Motorola code, LDAA $25 means load the accumulator with the contents of memory location 0025, the 00 is assumed; with the Rockwell code this same operation is written as LDA $25. With Intel code, for the same operation, we can have the direct address instruction MOV A,20H to copy the data at address 20 to the accumulator A. With the PIC code we might have movwf Reg1 to copy the contents of Reg1 into the working register, the address of Reg1 having been previously defined.

3. *Implied addressing, or inherent addressing*
   With this mode of addressing, the address is implied in the instruction.
   For example, with Z80 code, Motorola code and Intel code, CLR A means clear accumulator A. With PIC code clrw means clear the working register.

4. *Register*
   With this form of addressing, the operand is specified as the contents of one of the internal registers.
   For example, with Z80 codes we can have ADD A,B to add register B to the accumulator; with Intel ADD R7,A to add the contents of the accumulator to register R7.

5. *Indirect*
   This form of addressing means that that the data is to be found in a memory location whose address is given by the instruction.
   For example, with Z80 code, we might first load the HL register pair with the address of the location of data and then use LD A,(HL) to load the accumulator with the data found in the memory location given by the HL register pair; we can say that the HL register has pointed to the data. With the PIC system the INDF and FSR registers are used. The address is first written to the FSR register and then this serves as an address pointer. A subsequent direct access of INDF with the instruction movf INDF,w will load the working register w using the contents of FSR as a pointer to the data location.

6. *Indexed addressing*
   Indexed addressing means that the data is in a memory location whose address is held in an index register. The first byte of the instruction contains the opcode and the second byte contains the offset; the offset is added to the contents of the index register to determine the address of the operand.
   A Motorola instruction might thus appear as LDA A $FF,X; this means load accumulator A with data at the address given by adding the contents of the index register and FF. Another example is STA A $05,X; this means store the contents of accumulator A at the address given by the index register plus 05. A Z80 example is LD A,(IX+5); this means load the accumulator with the data found in the memory address which is five beyond the address held in the IX register. With the PIC, the method of indirect addressing used allows for INDF to be incremented to get to other addresses.

7. *Relative addressing*

This is used with branch instructions. The opcode is followed with a byte called the relative address. This indicates the displacement in address that has to be added to the program counter if the branch occurs.

For example, Motorola code BEQ $F1 indicates that if the data is equal to zero then the next address in the program is F1 further on. The relative address of F1 is added to the address of the next instruction. With Z80 code, JR F1H means that the number F1 is added to the current program counter value to locate the next address to be used.

Source and destination operands may each have their own separate addressing modes and so an instruction might involve two different addressing modes. For example, with Z80 code, ADD A,(HL) uses indirect addressing to specify the data source and register addressing to specify the location of the data to which the source data must be added. With Intel code we might have MOV A,#7EH; here the data source is specified using immediate addressing and register addressing to specify where the data is to be moved. As an illustration, Table 5.6 shows some instructions with the modes of addressing used in Motorola systems. Note that some of the instructions have mixed modes of addressing.

Table 5.6 Examples of addressing with Motorola

Address mode	*Instruction*	
Immediate	LDAA #$F0	Load accumulator A with data F0
Direct	LDAA $50	Load accumulator A with data at address 0050
Extended	LDAA $0F01	Load accumulator A with data at address 0F01
Indexed	LDAA $CF,X	Load accumulator with data at the address given by the index register plus CF
Immediate	ADDA #$16	Add the hexadecimal value 16 to the accumulator A
Direct	ADDA $00	Add the value stored at memory location with address 0000 to the accumulator A
Extended	ADDD $1030	Add the 16 bit value stored at the memory locations with addresses 1030 and 1031 to the double accumulator D
Indexed	ADDA 10,X	Add the value stored at the memory location pointed to by the sum of 10 and the contents of the index register X to the accumulator A
Inherent	ABA	Add the contents of accumulator B to accumulator A
Relative	BEQ THERE	Branches to the address indicated by the label THERE if equal, i.e. the Z bit in the CCR register is 1 (this flag is set to 1 whenever the result of an operation is zero, otherwise it is set to 0)
Inherent	CLR A	Clear accumulator A
Extended	CLR $2020	Clear address 2020, i.e. store all 0s at address 2020
Indexed	CLR $10,X	Clear the address given by the index register plus 10, i.e. store all 0s at that address

5.2.6 Translating to machine code

A program written in assembly language can be translated to machine code by hand using the manufacturer's instruction set sheet for the microprocessor or microcontroller concerned. Table 5.7 shows information obtained from a Z80 sheet.

Table 5.7 Extract from a Z80 instruction set sheet

		Source															
		Implied		*Reg. indirect*							*Reg. indirect*			*Indexed*		*Ext. add.*	*Imm.*
Destination		*I*	*R*	*A*	*B*	*C*	*D*	*E*	*H*	*L*	*(HL)*	*(BC)*	*(DE)*	*(IX+d)*	*(IY+d)*	*(nn)*	*n*
Reg.	A	ED 57	ED 5F	7F	78	79	7A	7B	7C	7D	7E	0A	1A	DD 7E d	FD 7E d	3A n n	3E n
	B			47	40	41	42	43	44	45	46			DD 46 d	FD 46 d		06 n
	C			4F	48	49	4A	4B	4C	4D	4E			DD 4E d	FD 4E d		0E n
	D			57	50	51	52	53	54	55	56			DD 56 d	FD 56 d		16 n
	E			5F	58	59	5A	5B	5C	5D	5E			DD 66 d	FD 66 d		1E n
	H			67	60	61	62	63	64	65	66			DD 66 d	FD 66 d		26 n
	L			6F	68	69	6A	6B	6C	6D	6E						2E n
Reg. indir.	(HL)			77	70	71	72	73	74	75							36 n
	(BC)			2													
	(DE)			12													
Indexed	(IX+d)			DD 77 d	DD 70 d	DD 71 d	DD 72 d	DD 73 d	DD 74 d	DD 75 d							DD 36 d n
	(IY+d)			FD 77 d	FD 70 d	FD 71 d	FD 72 d	FD 73 d	FD 74 d	FD 75 d							FD 36 d n
Ext. ad.	(nn)			32 n n													
Implied	I			ED 47													
	R			ED 4F													

For example, if we want the machine code for LD E,B, i.e. loading register F from register B, then we look at the source column in Table 5.7 headed B and find the intersection of that column with the row for the destination headed E. The machine code is thus 58. If we want the machine code for the immediate addressing instruction LD A,30H, i.e. load the A register with the hexadecimal value 30, then we use the immediate address column in Table 5.7 and find its intersection with the row for register A. This gives the code 3E n where n is the data to be loaded. The machine code is thus 3E 30. If we want the machine code for LD A,(1A20), i.e. the extended addressing instruction to load the accumulator A from address 1A20, then we look at the column for extended addressing to find the machine code 3A n n. the first n represents the low byte of the address and the second n the high byte. Thus the machine code is 3A 20 1A.

Here is a brief illustration of the type of information that will be found in the Motorola 6800 instruction set sheet:

		Addressing modes					
		IMMED			*DIRECT*		
Operation	*Mnemonic*	*OP*	*~*	*#*	*OP*	*~*	*#*
Add	ADDA	8B	2	2	9B	3	2

~ is the number of microprocessor cycles required and # is the number of program bytes required.

This means that when using the immediate mode of addressing with this processor the Add operation is represented by the mnemonic ADDA. When the immediate form of addressing is used, the machine code for this is 8B and it will take two cycles to be fully expressed. The operation will require two bytes in the program. With the direct mode of addressing, the machine code is 9B and takes three cycles and two program bytes.

For an Intel data sheet the mnemonic MOV A,#data is given with the machine code E4 2F, the number of program bytes # as 2 and the number of microprocessor cycles required as 12. MOV A,direct is given as E5 29, the number of bytes as 2 and microprocessor cycles as 12.

5.3 Examples of assembly codes

Here are some assembly codes for the different microprocessors and microcontrollers whose instruction sets were given earlier in the chapter. They are intended to perform relatively simple tasks.

1. *Z80 tasks*

Load the A register with hex 20:

```
LD A,20H
```

Add E1 to the contents of accumulator A:

```
ADD A,E1
```

Subtract hex 30 from the accumulator:

```
SUB 30H
```

Set the carry flag bit to 1:

```
SCF
```

Add 1 to the H register:

```
INC H
```

Jump to address 1810 if the C flag is set:

```
JP Z,1810H
```

If this instruction is at memory address 1800 and if the C flag is not set, the next memory address is 1803 because the instruction occupies three program bytes; but if the C flag is set then the next memory address is 1810.

2. *6502 tasks*
   Load accumulator A with the data contained in memory address C000:

```
LDA $C000
```

Add the contents of memory address C001 to accumulator A:

```
ADC $C001
```

Subtract, with carry, the contents of address C000 from the accumulator:

```
SBC $C000
```

Store at memory address C002:

```
STA $C002
```

Clear the carry flag bit:

```
CLC
```

3. *8051 tasks*
Load accumulator A with the data contained in memory address 22H:

```
MOV A,22H
```

Add the contents of register 5 to accumulator A:

```
ADD A,R5
```

Subtract, with borrow, hex 30 from the accumulator:

```
SUBB A,#30
```

Set the carry bit to 0:

```
CLR C
```

Increment register R2:

```
INC R2
```

Logical AND thc contents of accumulator A with the data at address 25H:

```
ANL A,25H
```

Change all the 0s to 1s and all the 1s to 0s in the accumulator, i.e. obtain the complement:

```
CPL A
```

Jump to address 0200 if the accumulator is not zero:

```
JNZ 0200H
```

If this instruction is at memory address 0100 and if the accumulator is not zero, the next memory address is 0200; but if the accumulator is zero, the next memory address is 0102 since the instruction takes two program bytes.

4. *PIC tasks*
Load the working register w with 5:

```
movlw 5
```

Add 5 to the contents of the working register:

```
addlw 5
```

Clear the working register, i.e. set to 0:

```
clrw
```

Complement the lower three bits of the working register:

```
xorlw B'00000111'
```

Force the upper four bits of W to 0:

```
andlw B'00001111'
```

Skip the next instruction if bit 0 of TEMP1 equals 0:

```
btfsc  TEMP1,0
```

5. *M68HC11 task*s
Load accumulator A with the data contained in memory address 00AF:

```
LDAA $00AF
```

Add 20 to the contents of accumulator A:

```
ADDA #$20
```

Enter all zeros in accumulator A:

```
CLRA
```

Rotate left the data contained in memory location 00AF:

```
ROL $00AF
```

Store the data contained in accumulator A into memory location 0021:

```
STAA $21
```

Branch forward four places if the result of the previous instruction is zero:

```
BEQ $04
```

If this instruction is at memory address 0010 and if the result is not zero, the next memory address is 0012 since BEQ, in this mode, occupies two program bytes. But if the result is zero then the next address is 0012 + 4 = 0016.

5.3.1 Instruction sequences

Here are some examples of simple instruction sequences. Note that explanatory comments about program instructions are separated from the instructions by semicolons. When the microprocessor reads the program it ignores all that is written to the right of a semicolon.

1. *Z80 sequence*: Add 5 to the accumulator three times. The accumulator is where the Z80 accumulates the results of arithmetic operations. It is the working register, i.e. like a notepad on which the calculations are carried out before the result is transferred elsewhere.

   This can be carried out by adding 5 to the accumulator three times in sequence.

```
LD     A,0   ; start with zero in the accumulator
ADD    A,5   ; add 5 to the accumulator
ADD    A,5   ; add 5 to the accumulator
ADD    A,5   ; add 5 to the accumulator
END
```

2. *PIC sequence*: Add 10 twice and put the result in the working register w.

   Every arithmetic operation that takes place with the PIC has to use the w register. Thus to add two numbers or the contents of two registers, one of the numbers or the contents of one of the registers must first be moved into the working register and then the other number or the contents of the other register can be added to it. For this task, the instruction movlw can be used to load the working register with the number 10. This is copied to the register Reg so that we can then add the values in w and Reg and store the result.

```
movlw   10      ; move 10 to working register w
movwf   Reg     ; copy the 10 to Reg
add     Reg,w   ; add w and Reg and put the result in w
END
```

3. *M68HC11 sequence*: Subtract 5 from three 8 bit numbers stored at addresses $00, $01 and $02.

   The accumulator is where the M68HC11 accumulates the results of arithmetic operations. It is the working register, i.e. like a notepad on which the calculations are carried out before the result is transferred elsewhere. Thus we have to copy data to the accumulator before we can carry out the arithmetic, and so for subtraction or addition the accumulator has to hold one of the values. The steps required are to load a number from the memory location into an accumulator, then subtract 5 from it and store it back into the memory location. This sequence is repeated for each number.

```
LDAA    $00   ; load the first number into accumulator
SUBA    #05   ; subtract 5 from the first number
STAA    $00   ; store the new value at $00
LDAA    $01   ; load the second number into accumulator
SUBA    #05   ; subtract 5 from the second number
STAA    $01   ; store the new value at $01
LDAA    $02   ; load the third number into accumulator
SUBA    #05   ; subtract 5 from the third number
STAA    $02   ; store the new value at $02
END
```

4. *6502 sequence*: Subtract the number stored at address C001 from the number stored at address C000 and store the result at address B001.

   The accumulator is where the 6502 accumulates the results of arithmetic operations. It is the working register, i.e. like a notepad on which the calculations are carried out before the result is transferred elsewhere. Thus we have to copy data to the accumulator before we can carry out the arithmetic, and so for subtraction or addition the accumulator has to hold one of the values. The first operation is to move one of the bytes into the accumulator. Because the subtract instruction subtracts with borrow, we must clear the carry flag since this acts as the borrow bit. Then we can do the subtraction before finally storing the result at address B001.

```
LDA     $C000     ; move number from $C000 to
                  ; accumulator
CLC               ; clear the carry flag
SBC     $C001     ; subtract number at $C001 from
                  ; that in accumulator
STAA    $B001     ; store result at $B001
END
```

5. *8051 sequence*: Subtract the contents of register R6 from register R7 and leave the result in R7.

   The accumulator is where the 8051 accumulates the results of arithmetic operations. It is the working register, i.e. like a notepad on which the calculations are carried out before the result is transferred elsewhere. Thus we have to copy data to the accumulator before we can carry out the arithmetic, and so for subtraction or addition the accumulator has to hold one of the values. Thus the first operation is to move one of the bytes into the accumulator. Because the subtract instruction subtracts with borrow, we must clear the carry flag since this acts as the borrow bit. Then we can do the subtraction before finally storing the result in R7. The program sequence might thus be:

```
MOV    A,R7   ; move byte from R7 to accumulator
CLR    C      ; clear carry flag
SUBB   A,R6   ; subtract register 6 from accumulator
MOV    R7,A   ; store result in register R7
END
```

6. *M68HC11 sequence*: Add the BCD numbers stored at addresses $00 and $01 and store the result at address $02.

We cannot use the sequence of instructions which would be appropriate for adding binary numbers since the result can be in error when the numbers are in BCD. With BCD each decimal digit is coded separately into binary or hex. Consider the problems of adding the numbers 12 and 34. We can add the 2 and the 4 digits to give 6 and then separately add the 1 and 3 digits to give 7. But we have a problem if the sum of a pair of digits is greater than 9; a carry is involved and in BCD addition we do not make use of a carry since we consider each pair of digits independently of any others. We can overcome this by adding 6 to every sum digit greater than 9. For example, consider adding 12 and 08. This gives 1A to which we then add 06 to give 20. Fortunately we do not have to program for this in that the microcontroller has the decimal adjust instruction DAA to take care of this. Thus the program sequence is:

```
LDAA   $00   ; load the first BCD number into acc.
ADDA   $01   ; add the second number to it
DAA          ; decimal adjust the sum
STAA   $02   ; store the sum at address $02
END
```

7. *8051 sequence*: add the hexadecimal numbers 1234 and 4142 and store the result in registers R6 and R7.

This requires the low byte of the sum to be added, with no carry, and the result stored in R6. Then the high byte is added, with any carry set by the first addition, and the result stored in register R7. The program sequence is thus:

```
MOV    A,34H   ; move 34H into accumulator
ADD    A,42H   ; add 42H, with no carry, to the acc.
MOV    R6,A    ; store result in R6
MOV    A,12H   ; move 12H into accumulator
ADDC   A,41H   ; add 41H, with carry, to the acc.
MOV    R7,A    ; store result in R7
END
```

5.4 Programs

An assembly language program consists of a series of instructions to an assembler which will then produce the machine code program. It is written as a sequence of statements, one statement per line. A statement contains from one to four sections or *fields*, these being:

Label Operator Operand ; Comment

A field consists of a group of characters, with the label, operator and operand fields separated from each other by a space and the comment field separated from the operand by a space and a semicolon.

5.4.1 Labels

The *label* is the name by which a particular entry can be referenced by other instructions within a program. Note that a label is not required for each statement and in the absence of a label a space should left. All labels within a program should be unique. Labels may use letters, digits and special characters such as @, ? and $. However, the label must not allow the assembler to confuse it with registers, instruction codes or pseudo-operations (see Section 5.4.2). Their names must not be used as labels. Also to avoid confusion, the first character of any label must not be a digit and it is forbidden to include any spaces in the label.

Thus NUM1 or NUM_1 might be used for a label to define the address where number 1 is to be found. SUM might be used for a statement line which gives the current sum to which the program might later call up in order to add more to it. Another example might be LOOP to indicate which statement a branching instruction later in the program will loop back to. Note that capital letters are generally used for labels. But PIC labels are usually mixed case, e.g. Num1; all capitals is reserved for special register and bit names, and all lower case for instruction mnemonics.

5.4.2 Operators

The *operator field* contains a specification of how data is to be manipulated and this is specified by its mnemonic, e.g. LD; or it contains an assembly directive. The operator field is the only field that must never be empty.

Assembly directives appear in the operator field and are directives to the assembler. These are termed *pseudo-operations* since they appear in the operator field but are not translated into instructions in machine code. They may specify the starting address in the program, define symbols, assign programs and data to certain areas of memory, generate fixed tables and data, indicate the end of the program, etc. The directives that can be used depend on the chosen assembler. Commonly used directives are:

1. ORG
   This defines the starting memory address of the part of the program that follows. For example, we might have the statement, with no label, to specify that the starting memory address is $100 of:

   ```
   ORG $100
   ```

2. END
   End is the last statement; nothing beyond this statement is processed by the assembler.

3. EQU, SET or DEF
   These equate, set or define a symbol for a numerical value or an expression. The format for the directive is:

   ```
   symbol   EQU   expression
   ```

   For example,

   ```
   NUM1   EQU   5
   ```

   indicates that whenever NUM1 is referred to it will be given the value 5.

4. DS or RMB
   These instruct the assembler to define storage or reserve memory bytes; the size of the memory reserved is specified by the number that follows the directive. For example, we might use the following instructions:

   ```
          ORG  $100
   BUFFER RMB  100
   ```

   to reserve a block of 100 bytes starting at the address $100.

5. DBIT
   This is like the DS directive but instructs the assembler to reserve memory bits.

6. BSZ, FCB, FDB and FCC
   These are used to give initial values to a reserved memory block. BSZ, the block storage of zeros directive, causes the assembler to allocate a block of bytes and assign each byte the initial value of zero. FCB, the form constant byte directive,

puts a byte in memory for each of the arguments following the directive. For example:

```
ORG $100
FCB $11,$22,$33
```

will initialise the contents of memory locations at $100 to $11, $101 to $22 and $102 to $33. FDB, the form double byte directive, initialises two consecutive bytes for each argument. FCC, the form constant character directive, will use ASCII to generate the code bytes for the letters in the arguments of the directive.

7. DATA or DSEG
These instruct the assembler to create a data segment which is used to store frequently used program data.
8. CSEG or CODE
This directive instructs the assembler to start a code segment which is used to store program code. The directive DB can be used to initialise code memory with byte values and thus we might have:

```
      CSEG AT 0100H
NUM   DB 0, 1, 2, 3, 4, 5 ;numbers 0 to 5
```

As a result, when assembled, we have:

Address	*Contents*
0100	00
0101	01
0102	02
0103	03
0104	04
0105	05

DE, the define word directive, performs the same function as the DB directive except it assigns two memory locations (16 bits) for each data item.

5.4.3 Operands

The operand field follows the mnemonic field and contains the address or data used by the instruction. A label may be used to represent the address of the data or a symbol to represent a data constant. The field may be empty if the instructions given by the mnemonic do not need any address or data. Some mnemonics allow for multiple operands separated by commas.

5.4.4 Comments

The comment field is preceded by a semicolon and is optional. It is there to allow the programmer to include any comments which may make the program more understandable to a reader. The comment field is ignored by the assembler.

5.4.5 Examples

Here are some examples of very simple programs to illustrate the above points; Chapter 6 goes on to deal with more complex and more useful programs.

1. *Z80 program* to add two numbers stored in memory and store the number back into memory.

```
            ; Addition of two numbers

NUM1    EQU    1900H         ; location of number 1
NUM2    EQU    1901H         ; location of number 2
SUM     EQU    1902H         ; location for the sum

        ORG    1800H         ; address of start of user RAM
START   LD     A,(NUM1)      ; load number 1 into acc. A
        LD     B,A           ; moves the contents of A to B
        LD     A,(NUM2)      ; load number 2 into acc. A
        ADD    A,B           ; add number 1 to A
        LD     (SUM),A       ; save the sum to 1902H
        END
```

2. *6502 program* to add two numbers stored in memory and store the number back into memory.

```
            ; Addition of two numbers

NUM1    EQU    $0030     ; location of number 1
NUM2    EQU    $0031     ; location of number 2
SUM     EQU    $0032     ; location for the sum

        ORG    $0020     ; address of start of user RAM
START   LDA    NUM1      ; load number 1 into acc. A
        ADC    NUM2      ; add number 1 to A
        STA    SUM       ; save the sum to $0032
        END
```

3. *6800 program* to add two numbers stored in memory and store the number back into memory.

```
            ; Addition of two numbers

NUM1    EQU    $0030     ; location of number 1
NUM2    EQU    $0031     ; location of number 2
SUM     EQU    $0032     ; location for the sum
```

```
        ORG   $0020    ; address of start of user RAM
START   LDAA  NUM1     ; load number 1 into acc. A
        ADDA  NUM2     ; add number 1 to A
        STAA  SUM      ; save the sum to $0032
        END
```

4. *M68HC11 program* to add two numbers stored in memory and store the number back into memory.

```
        ; Addition of two numbers

NUM1    EQU   $00      ; location of number 1
NUM2    EQU   $01      ; location of number 2
SUM     EQU   $02      ; location for the sum

        ORG   $C000    ; address of start of user RAM
START   LDAA  $NUM1    ; load number 1 into acc. A
        ADDA  $NUM2    ; add number 2 to A
        STAA  SUM      ; save the sum to $02
        END
```

5. *8051 program* to add two numbers stored in memory and store the number back into memory.

```
        ; Addition of two numbers

NUM1    EQU   20H      ; location of number 1
NUM2    EQU   21H      ; location of number 2
SUM     EQU   22H      ; location for the sum

        ORG   8000H    ; address of start of user RAM
START   MOV   A,NUM1   ; load number 1 into acc. A
        ADD   A,NUM2   ; add number 2 to A
        MOV   SUM,A    ; save the sum to address 22H
        END
```

6. *PIC program* to add two numbers stored in memory and store the number back in memory.

```
        ; Addition of two numbers

Num1    equu   H'20'   ; location of number 1
Num2    equ    H'21'   ; location of number 2
Sum     equ    H'22'   ; location for the sum

        org    H'000'  ; address of start of user RAM
Start   movlw  Num1    ; load number 1 into w
        addlw  Num2    ; add number 2 to w
        movwf  Sum     ; save the sum H'22'
        End
```

Problems

1. Describe the results of the following Motorola 68HC11 instructions: (a) LDAA #10, (b) LDAA $1000, (c) LDAB #10, (d) LDAB $1000, (e) LDD #10, (f) ABA, (g) ABX, (h) ADCA #10, (i) ADCA $10, (j) SBA, (k) SBCA #10, (l) SBCA $10.
2. Describe the results of the following Intel 8051 instructions: (a) MOV A,R7, (b) MOV R1,A, (c) MOV A,20H, (d) MOV A,#20, (e) MOV A,#2EH, (f) MOV R3, 2EH, (g) ADD A,R5, (h) ADD A,#20, (i) ADD A,20, (j) SUBB A,#20.
3. Describe the results of the following Zilog Z80 instructions: (a) LD A,5, (b) LD A,(1000H), (c) LD B,A, (d) LD(BC),A, (e) LD A,(IX+5), (f) ADD A,B, (g) ADD A,(1000H), (h) SUB B.
4. Describe the results of the following PIC instructions: (a) movlw 6, (b) movwf FSR, (c) clrw, (d) movf Reg1,w, (e) addlw 6.
5. Describe the results of the following Rockwell 6502 instructions: (a) LDA $C000, (b) AND #$F0, (c) STA$C001.
6. Describe the results of the following Motorola 68HC11 instructions: (a) CLRA, (b) ASLA when the original value in A is 01110100 and the carry flag is 1, (c) ASRA when the original value in A is 11110110 and the carry flag is 1, (d) ROLA when the original value in A is 10111110 and the carry flag is 1.
7. Describe the results of the following Intel 8051 instructions: (a) CLR A, (b) RL A when the original value in A is 01110100, (c) RR A when the original value in A is 1011 1100, (d) RRC A when the original value in A is 0011 1100 and the carry flag is 1.
8. Describe the results of the following Zilog Z80 instructions: (a) RLCA when the original value in A is 00001111 and the carry flag is 0, (b) RLA when the original value in A is 1100 0010 and the carry flag is 1, (c) SRA A when the original value in A is 0110 0100.
9. What are the Motorola 68HC11 instruction mnemonics for the following operations: (a) increment the accumulator, (b) subtract one from the accumulator, (c) transfer from accumulator A to accumulator B, (d) store contents of accumulator A, (e) branch if less than zero.
10. What are the Intel 8051 instruction mnemonics for the following operations: (a) increment the accumulator, (b) decrement the accumulator, (c) exchange register with accumulator, (d) jump if accumulator zero.
11. What are the Zilog Z80 instruction mnemonics for the following operations: (a) increment accumulator A, (b) decrement the accumulator, (c) jump to new location, (d) complement the accumulator.
12. What are the PIC instruction mnemonics for the following operations: (a) increment a file register, (b) decrement a file

register, (c) jump to new location, (d) complement the number in a file register.

13. What are the results of (a) logical ORing 1100 0011 with 0101 0101, (b) logical ANDing 1100 0011 with 0101 0101, (c) logical XORing 1100 0011 with 0101 0101?
14. Write a Motorola 68HC11 sequence to add the contents of the memory addresses $00 and $01 and store the sum at address $02.
15. Write a Motorola 68HC11 sequence to swap the contents of the memory addresses $00 and $01.
16. Write an Intel 8051 sequence to put a 0 in the accumulator, then 10H and then decimal 20.
17. Write an Intel 8051 sequence to form the twos complement of a number at address 2000 H and store the result in memory at address 2010H.
18. Write a Zilog Z80 sequence to fetch data from address 1900H into the accumulator, add 3 to it and then store the result at address 1901H.
19. Write a Zilog Z80 sequence to add 20H to the contents of the B register.
20. Write a Rockwell 6502 sequence to fetch data from address $0080, multiply it by 5 and then store the result at address $0081. Hint: a shift to the left of one place is equivalent to multiplying by 2.
21. Write a Rockwell 6502 sequence which will change bits 0, 1, 2 and 3 in the data byte stored as address C000 to 1s without affecting the 4, 5, 6 and 7 bits. The result is to be stored at address C000.
22. Write a Z80 sequence which will change bits 0, 1, 2 and 3 in the data byte stored as address 0C80 to 1s without affecting the 4, 5, 6 and 7 bits. The result is to be stored at address 0C80.
23. Write a PIC sequence which will put the number 10 into the working register, then copy it to the register Reg and then add the number in Reg to the working register, so the final result is to have 10 in Reg and 20 in the working register.
24. Write a PIC sequence which will put the binary number 00001111 in the working register and then copy it to the register Reg.
25. What is the outcome of the following program instructions?

```
DATA  EQU 2000H
      LD   A,DATA
```

26. What is the outcome of the following program instruction?

```
ORG 1800H
```

6 Assembly language programming

6.1 Introduction

This chapter follows on from Chapter 5 and considers the development of programs using assembly language. It describes the use of loops, subroutines, the stack, parameter passing and interrupts, and programs are developed to implement simple problems involving microprocessors, particularly the Motorola 68HC11, Intel 8051 and PIC16Cxx microcontrollers.

6.2 Looping

Many programs require a task to be carried out a number of times in succession. Then the program can be designed so that the operation passes through the same section a number of times. This is termed *looping*, and the operation is described by the WHILE-DO program structure.

Figure 6.1 illustrates looping by showing a flow diagram of a loop in which a certain operation has to be performed a number of times before the program proceeds. The number of loops required is first loaded into a register used for a counter. Each time the operation occurs the counter is decremented and the loop repeated until the counter reaches zero. Only then can the program proceed beyond the loop section.

The following examples illustrate how looping programs can be written in assembly language.

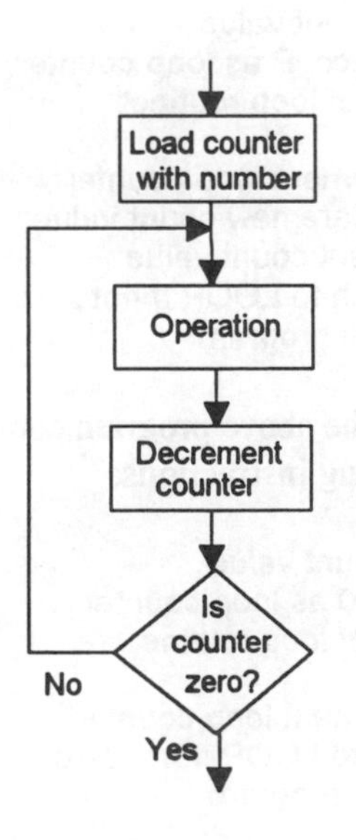

Fig. 6.1 Loop counter

1. *Problem:* Multiply a number stored at some address by 5 and store the result in a different address.

   This can be tackled by repeating a loop five times with the loop involving repeated addition of the same number. The structure of the program can be described as:

```
Multiplicand = 5
Sum = 0
   WHILE loop not equal to 0
      DO loop = loop – 1
      DO sum = sum + number
```

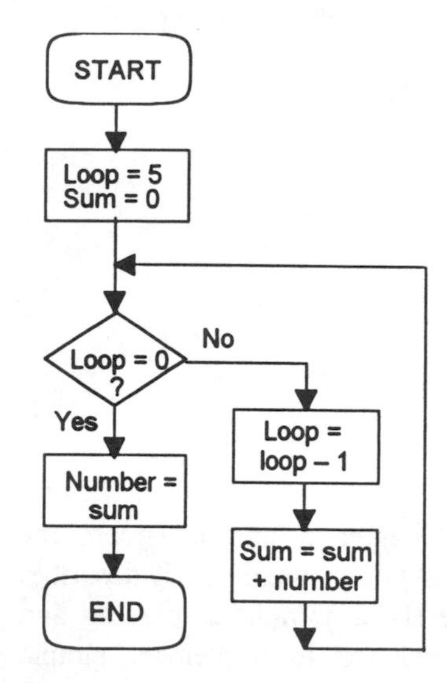

Fig. 6.2 Flow chart

```
    ENDWHILE
    Number = sum
```

Figure 6.2 shows the flow chart. In Z80 assembly code this program is:

```
MULT    EQU     5           ; set loop count to be 5
NUM     EQU     1900H       ; address of number
RES     EQU     2000H       ; address for result
        ORG     1800H       ; start of user RAM
        LD      A,(NUM)     ; get the number
        LD      C,A         ; temporarily store it
        LD      B,(MULT)    ; load multiplicand into B
        LD      D,0         ; load sum = 0 into D
LOOP    LD      A,B         ; get loop number
        CP      0           ; compare 0 to accumulator
        JP      Z,(2000H)   ; jump to 2000H if yes
        DEC     B           ; decrement loop number
        LD      A,D         ; get sum in A
        ADD     A,C         ; sum = sum + number
        JP      (LOOP)      ; jump to loop
        LD      A,D         ; get sum in A
        LD      A,(RES)     ; store at result address
        RST     30H         ; program end, return to
                            ; address 30H
        END                 ; indicates end to assembler
```

With a Motorola 68HC11 the above program could use the following lines for the key looping instructions:

```
MULT        EQU     #5      ; set count value
            LDAB    MULT    ; use acc. B as loop counter
LOOP                        ; start of loop routine
            ...
            DECB            ; decrement loop counter
            CMPB    MULT    ; compare new count value
                            ; with set count value
            BGT     LOOP    ; branch to LOOP if not zero
                            ; rest of program
```

With an Intel 8051 microcontroller the above program could use the following lines for the key looping instructions:

```
MULT    EQU     #5          ; set count value
        MOV     R0,MULT     ; use R0 as loop counter
LOOP                        ; start of loop routine
        ...
        DJNZ    R0,LOOP     ; decrement loop counter,
                            ; jump to LOOP if not zero
                            ; rest of program
```

With a PIC microcontroller the above program could use the following lines for the key looping instructions:

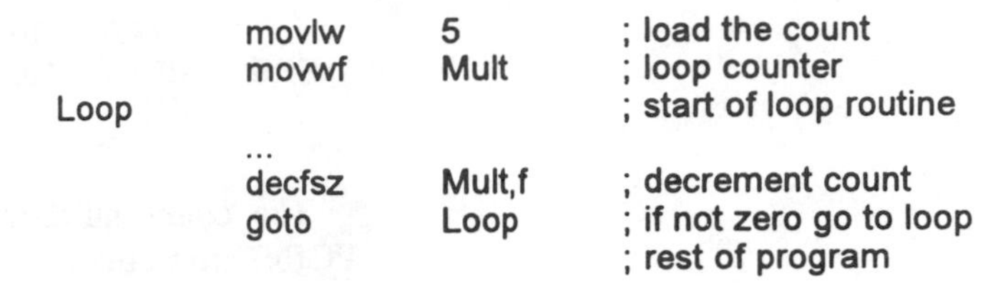

```
        movlw    5         ; load the count
        movwf    Mult      ; loop counter
Loop                       ; start of loop routine
        ...
        decfsz   Mult,f    ; decrement count
        goto     Loop      ; if not zero go to loop
                           ; rest of program
```

2. *Problem*: the addition of numbers located at 10 consecutive addresses (these might be the results of inputs from 10 different sensors).

This involves a loop being repeated 10 times. The structure of the program might thus be described as:

```
Count = 0
Sum = 0
WHILE count not equal to 10
   DO count = count + 1
   DO sum = sum + number
ENDWHILE
Number = sum
```

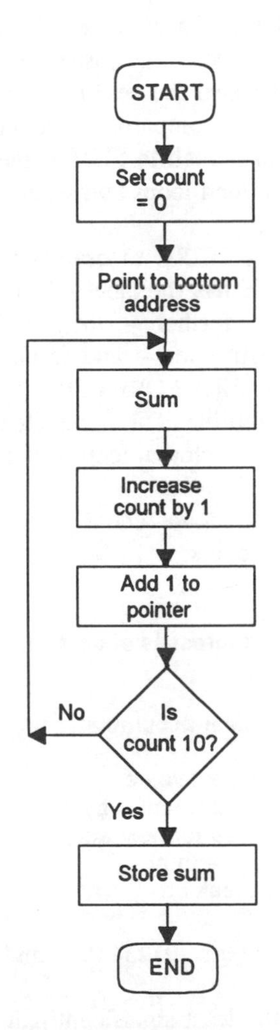

Fig. 6.3 Flow chart

Figure 6.3 shows the flow chart. In terms of an algorithm we might have:

1. Start.
2. Set the count as 0.
3. Point to location of bottom address number.
4. Add value at bottom address number.
5. Decrease the count number by 1.
6. Add 1 to the address location pointer.
7. Is count 10? If no branch to 4. If yes proceed.
8. Store sum.
9. Stop.

A conditional branch instruction can be used to implement such a loop in Motorola 68HC11 assembly language. Using accumulator A to store the sum and accumulator B to store the count, the program might be:

```
COUNT  EQU   #10
POINT  EQU   $0020    ; addresses of data
RESULT EQU   $0100
       ORG   $C000
       LDAB  #0       ; initialise loop count to 0
       LDAA  #0       ; initialise sum to 0
SUM    ADDA  POINT    ; add addend
       INCB           ; add 1 to loop count
       INC   POINT    ; add 1 to address pointer
       CMPB  COUNT    ; compare the count with 10
       BNE   SUM      ; branch to sum while count
                      ; < 10
```

```
        STAA   RESULT ; store at result address
HERE    BRA    HERE   ; end of program
        END
```

The count number of 10 is loaded into accumulator B. POINT gives the initial address of the data being added. After initialisation of the loop count to zero and the sum to zero, the first summation step is to add the contents of the memory location addressed by POINT to the contents of the accumulator. INCB adds 1 to the contents of accumulator B to keep track of the number of numbers added. The instruction INC $POINT adds 1 to the index register so the next location that will be addressed is 0021. CMPB then compares the count with 10. BNE is then the instruction to branch to SUM if the loop count is less than 10. The program then loops and repeats the loop until ACCB is 10.

Note the use of the instruction BRA HERE to branch to HERE where the instruction BRA HERE has the label HERE. This stops the program running any further – the CPU continually executes the same BRA instruction – and is one way to stop a program. The instruction BRA FOREVER may be used to branch to the start of the routine if it is labelled FOREVER; this instruction constitutes a closed loop which keeps on going forever.

With the Rockwell 6502 and the loop count being decremented, the program might look like this:

```
COUNT    EQU    #10
POINT    EQU    $0080     ; addresses of data
RESULT   EQU    $0091
         ORG    $0020
         LDA    #$00      ; clear accumulator
         LDX    COUNT
ADD      ADC    POINT,X   ; select value
         DEX              ; decrement X by 1
         BNE    ADD       ; loop for next addition
         STA    RESULT    ; save total
         BRK              ; break off
```

2. *Problem*: Add the hexadecimal numbers 01234567 and 89ABCDEF.

This can be tackled by first adding the least significant pair of digits, i.e. 67 and EF, then looping to repeat the addition procedure for the next pair of digits, i.e. 45 and CD, and repeating the looping until all the digits have been added. We have four pairs of digits and so four loops are required. The program structure is:

```
WHILE number of loops less than 4
   DO add pairs of digits
```

```
    DO store result
    DO increment pointer to next byte of first number
    DO increment pointer to next byte of second number
    DO decrement loop counter
ENDWHILE
```

The result of the addition may be placed in the addresses of the first number; registers R0 and R1 may be used for pointing to the bytes that are added to each number; and register R3 may be used as a loop counter. Here is an Intel 8051 assembly language program:

```
        ORG     8000H
        MOV     70H,#67H      ; least significant byte of first number
        MOV     71H,#45H      ; next byte of first no.
        MOV     72H,#23H      ; next byte of first no.
        MOV     73H,#01H      ; most significant byte of first number
        MOV     78H,#0EFH     ; least significant byte of second number
                              ; note that the EF has been preceded by a zero to clearly
                              ; indicate that a number is concerned
        MOV     79H,#0CDH     ; next byte of second number
        MOV     7AH,#0ABH     ; next byte of second number
        MOV     7BH,#89H      ; most significant byte of second number
        MOV     R3,#4         ; specify number of bytes (the number has 4 × 2 digits)
        MOV     R0,#70H       ; R0 to point to bytes of first number
        MOV     R1,#78H       ; R1 to point to bytes of second number
                              ; R0 and R1 are used to select the addresses of the bytes to be
                              ; added
        CLR     C             ; clear carry flag
LOOP    MOV     A,@R0         ; get byte of first number
        ADDC    A,@R1         ; add byte of second number and any carry
        MOV     @R0,A         ; store result in byte of first number
        INC     R0            ; increment pointer to next byte of first number
        INC     R1            ; increment pointer to next byte of second number
        DJNZ    R3,LOOP       ; decrement loop counter and jump to LOOP if not zero
        LJMP    0             ; end of program, return to the monitor
        END
```

6.3 Subroutines

It is often the case that a block of programming might be required a number of times in a program. For example, it might be needed to produce a time delay at several places in the program. It would be possible to duplicate this subroutine a number of times in the main program; this, however, is an inefficient use of memory. It is better to have a single copy in the memory and branch or jump to it every time the subroutine is required. But after completion of the subroutine, the problem now is to find wherabouts to resume in the main program. What is required is a mechanism for getting back to the main program and continuing with it from the point at which it was left to carry out the subroutine. To do this we need to store the contents of the program counter at the time of branching to the subroutine so that this value can be reloaded into the program counter when the subroutine is complete. The two instructions which are provided with most microprocessors to enable a subroutine to be implemented in this way are:

1. JSR (jump to subroutine), or CALL, which enables a subroutine to be called.
2. RTS (return from subroutine), or RET (return), which is used as the last instruction in a subroutine and returns it to the correct point in the calling program.

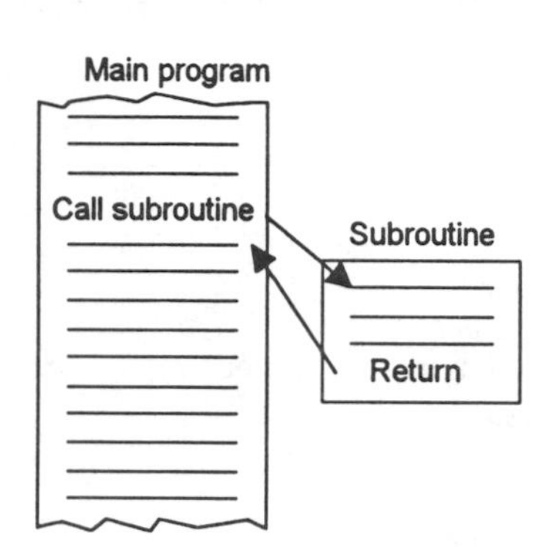

Fig. 6.4 Calling a subroutine

Generally subroutines are entered into the memory after the main program and are then accessed when required by calling the required start address. The call instruction stores the address of the next instruction before it jumps to the beginning of the subroutine, so there is a mechanism for it to return to a particular point in the program. Figure 6.4 illustrates this. The ordinary jump instruction simply jumps to the beginning of the subroutine and there is no mechanism for it to return automatically to a particular point in the program. There are often three types of jumps: long jumps, absolute jumps and relative jumps. The long jump is a jump to an address anywhere in the code; the absolute and relative jumps are jumps relative to the current value of the program counter.

6.3.1 Time delays

Time delays are very frequently used subroutines. They are often required because a microprocessor can produce output changes faster than many output devices can cope with, so pauses have to be introduced to allow time for the devices to react. One way of introducing time delays is for a subroutine to use a loop; set a loop counter register to, say, FFH and allow it to count down until it reaches 0. The loop is executed FFH times; each instruction in the loop takes a finite amount of time. Thus we might have:

```
DELAY   MOV   C,FFH    ; load C with FFH
LOOP    DEC   C        ; decrement C
        JNZ   LOOP     ; jump to LOOP until C = 0
```

To determine how long this delay will be, we need to refer to the manufacturer's data sheet to ascertain how many microprocessor clock cycles are needed for the instructions. The MOV C,FFH instruction takes 12, DEC C takes 12 and JNZ takes 24. Thus the delay is 12 + 255(12 + 24) = 9192 cycles. With a frequency of, say, 4 MHz then the delay is 2.298 ms. We can increase the time delay by inserting further instructions, e.g. NOP, in the loop to occupy more time.

An example of a time delay subroutine for a PIC microcontroller is:

```
        movlw   Value    ; load count value required
        movwf   Count    ; loop counter
Delay   decfsz  Count    ; decrement counter
        goto    Delay    ; loop
```

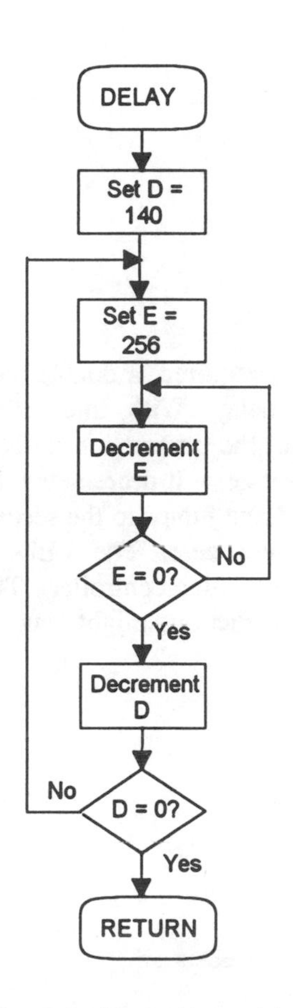

Fig. 6.5 Nested loop delay

The decfsz instruction takes one cycle and the goto instruction takes two cycles. This loop will be repeated (count – 1) times. In addition we have the movlw and movwf instructions, each taking one cycle, and when the count equals 1 we have decfsz which gives a further two cycles. Thus the total number of cycles is:

$$\text{number of instruction cycles} = 3(\text{count} - 1) + 4$$

Each instruction cycle takes four clock cycles and so the number of delay cycles introduced by this subroutine is:

$$\text{number of clock cycles} = 4[2(\text{count} - 1) + 4]$$

With a 4 MHz clock each clock cycle takes $1/(4 \times 10^6)$ s.

Often the delay obtained by using just the single loop described above is not enough. One way to obtain a longer delay is to use a nested loop. Figure 6.5 shows the flow chart for a nested loop delay. The inner loop is the same as the single-loop program described earlier. It will decrement register E 255 times before the looping is completed and the zero flag set. The outer loop causes the inner loop routine to be repeatedly executed as register D is decremented down to zero. Thus with register D initially set with a loop count of, say, 140 then the time delay will be 140 x 2.298 = 321.72 ms. The program is thus:

```
DELAY   MOV   D,8CH   ; set D to 8CH, i.e. 140
OLOOP   MOV   E,FFH   ; set E to FFH, i.e. 255
ILOOP   DEC   E       ; decrement E, i.e. inner loop
                      ; counter
        JNZ   ILOOP   ; repeat ILOOP 255 times
        DEC   D       ;decrement D, i.e. outer loop
                      ; counter
        JNZ   OLOOP   ; repeat OLOOP 140 times
```

Here are some examples of programs where time delay subroutines are involved.

1. *Problem*: Switch a LED on and off repeatedly.

   With this problem a subroutine DELAY is used with loops to provide time delays; the microprocessor takes a finite amount of time to process the instructions in a loop and thus to complete the loop. The structure of the program is:

```
WHILE operating
   IF LED on
      DO turn LED off
```

```
        WHILE LED off
            DO subroutine TIME_DELAY
         ENDWHILE
      ELSE
        DO turn LED on
           DO subroutine TIME_DELAY
      ENDIF
      TIME_DELAY
      WHILE count less than X
        DO an instruction
      ENDWHILE

   ENDWHILE
```

Because of the length of time delay required, a double loop is likely to be used for the time delay. With Intel 8051 programming, it is possible to use the instruction DJNZ, decrement and jump if the result is not zero. It decrements the location indicated by the first operand and jumps to the second operand if the resulting value is not zero. The LED is connected to bit 0 of port 1 of the microcontroller. The program with Intel 8051 assembly instructions might thus be as follows:

```
FLAG      EQU    0FH              ; flag set when LED is on
          ORG    8000H

START     JB     FLAG,LED_OFF     ; jump if LED_OFF bit set, i.e. LED is on
          SETB   FLAG             ; else set FLAG bit
          CLR    P1.0             ; turn LED on
          LCALL  DELAY            ; call up delay subroutine
          SJMP   START            ; jump to START
LED_OFF   CLR    FLAG             ; clear the LED on flag to indicate the LED is off
          SETB   P1.0             ; turn LED off
          LCALL  DELAY            ; call up delay subroutine
          LJMP   START            ; jump to START

DELAY     MOV    R0,#0FFH         ; outer loop delay value
ILOOP     MOV    R1,#0FFH         ; inner loop delay value
OLOOP     DJNZ   R1,ILOOP         ; wait through inner loop
          DJNZ   R0,OLOOP         ; wait through outer loop
          RET                     ; return from subroutine

          END
```

2. *Problem*: Switch on in sequence eight LEDS.

The rotate instruction can be used to successively turn on LEDS so that we have initially the bit pattern 0000 0001 which is then rotated to give 0000 0011, then 0000 0111, and so on. The following is a program in Motorola 68HC11 assembly language that can be used, the LEDS being connected to port B; a short delay is incorporated in the program:

```
COUNT    EQU    8            ; the count gives the number of loops required,
                             ; i.e. the number of bits to be switched on
FIRST    EQU    %00000001    ; turn on 0 bit
PORTB    EQU    $1004        ; address of port B
         ORG    $C000
         LDAA   #FIRST       ; load initial value
         LDAB   #COUNT       ; load count
LOOP     STAA   PORTB        ; turn on bit 1 and so LED 1
         JSR    DELAY        ; jump to delay subroutine
         SEC                 ; set carry bit to rotate into least significant bit to
                             ; maintain bit as 1
         ROLA                ; rotate left
         DECB                ; decrement count
         BNE    LOOP         ; branch to loop eight times

DELAY    RTS                 ; simple short delay

         END
```

6.4 The stack

Subroutines may be called from many different points in a program and thus it is necessary for the microprocessor to remember the address to return to at the end of a subroutine. It does this by storing the program counter contents in such a way that we have a last-in first-out store (LIFO). Such a register is referred to as a *stack*. It is like a stack of plates in that the last plate is always added to the top of the pile of plates and the first plate that is removed from the stack is always the top plate and hence the last plate that was added to the stack. The stack may be a block of registers within a microprocessor or, more commonly, a section of RAM which is defined for that purpose. A special register within the microprocessor, called the *stack pointer register*, is then used to point to the next free address in the area of RAM being used for the stack, i.e. the memory location above the top element. By convention, the stack usually grows from high addresses towards lower addresses.

When a jump to a subroutine occurs, the return address to the main program is stored on the stack. When, in the subroutine, the return from subroutine instruction is met, the address stored on the top of the stack is removed and placed in the program counter.

In addition to the automatic use of the stack when subroutines are used, a programmer can write a program which involves the use of the stack for the temporary storage of data. For example, before a subroutine the data in some registers may have to be saved; after the subroutine, the data is restored. The two instructions that are likely to be involved are:

1. PUSH, which causes data in specified registers to be saved to the next free location in the stack. For example, with M68HC11 the instruction PSHA pushes A onto the stack.

2. PULL, or POP, which causes data to be retrieved from the last used location in the stack and transferred to a specified register. For example, with M68HC11 the instruction PULA pulls A from the stack.

As an illustration, consider the stack shown in Fig. 6.6(a) when the stack pointer is $00FF when pointing to the next free location on the stack. Suppose we now use the instruction PSHA with A being $10. A is pushed onto the top of the stack and the stack pointer decrements by 1 to the next free address of $00FE (Fig. 6.6(b)). Suppose we now use the instruction PSHX to put $30 on the stack. It will go into address $00FE and the stack pointer decrements by 1 to the next free address of $00FD (Fig. 6.6(c)). Anything that is pushed onto the stack must be popped before the subroutine return instruction is reached. Thus at the end of the subroutine we pop the last pushed instruction, the one at the top of the stack, first. For the stack which has been pushed to the state shown in Fig. 6.6(c), the pop sequence is as shown in Fig. 6.7.

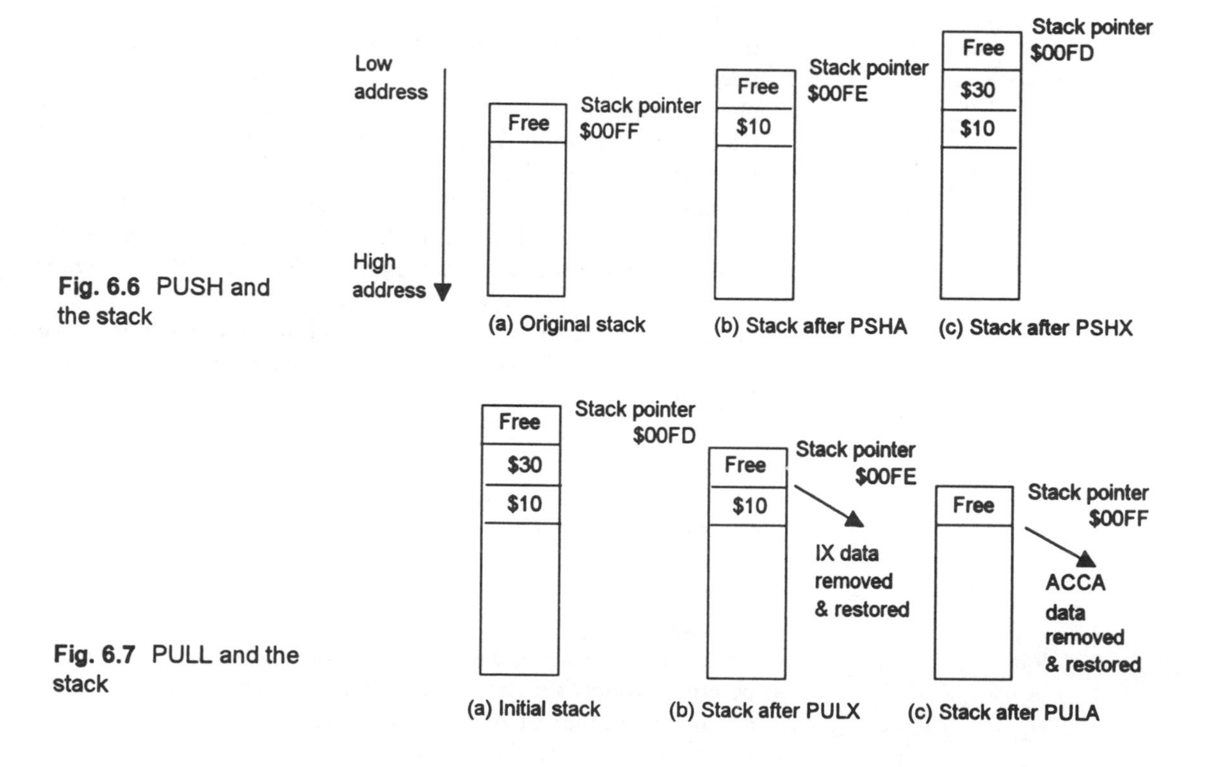

Fig. 6.6 PUSH and the stack

Fig. 6.7 PULL and the stack

As well as being used to store data and addresses when a subroutine is being called, the stack can also be used as a temporary store for the contents of registers – like a piece of paper on which, during some complex arithmetic calculation, intermediate data is jotted so that it is not lost while other operations are carried out. Data and addresses can also be saved during interrupts.

As a simple illustration of the use of the stack, consider the following program instructions for the Intel 8051 when its stack is used as a temporary store for data. Note that with the 8051 the stack pointer points to the top value in the stack and not the empty space above it.

```
        ORG     8000H
BEGIN   MOV     SP,#4FH    ; sets the stack pointer to 4FH
        MOV     A,#20H     ; puts 20H in the accumulator
        PUSH    A          ; pushes the 20H from the
                           ; accumulator onto the stack
                           ; at 50H, the top of the stack
        MOV     B,#0       ; clear the B register
        POP     B          ; pops the top of the stack, i.e.
                           ; the 20H, into the B register
                           ; continues with rest of program
```

As a further example, consider the use of the stack to temporally store an intermediate result in the calculation of the sum of the squares of two integer numbers. The algorithm might be:

1. Determine the square of the first number.
2. Temporally store it on the stack.
3. Determine the square of the second number.
4. Retrieve the first result from the stack and add.

The program for the Motorola 68HC11 might thus be:

```
NUM1    EQU     $1030      ; address of first number
NUM2    EQU     $1031      ; address of second number
        ORG     $E000      ; start address of the program
        LDS     #$FF       ; set initial address of the
                           ; stack pointer
        LDAA    NUM1       ; get first number
        TAB                ; copy it to B
        MUL                ; multiply A by B and put
                           ; result in A
        PSHA               ; push it onto the stack
        LDAA    NUM2       ; get second number
        TAB                ; copy it to B
        MUL                ; multiply A by B and put
                           ; result in A
        PULB               ; retrieve first square to B
        ABA                ; add the two squares
HERE    BRA     HERE       ; stop the program
```

6.4.1 Parameter passing

The term *parameter passing* is used for when a program has to pass values or parameters to subroutines so that they can act upon data that is present in the main program and return values or parameters back to the program. Thus we might have a subroutine for the multiplication of two numbers; it is written as a general multiplication subroutine so that it will multiply any two numbers passed to it. Figure 6.8 illustrates how the subroutine is called, the operands are passed to it and the result is returned to the main program.

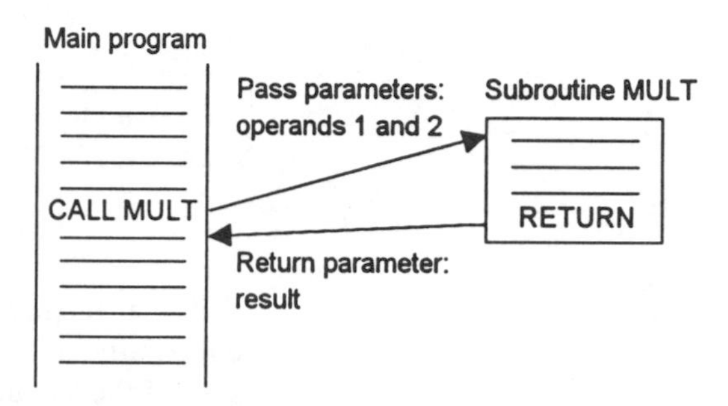

Fig. 6.8 Parameter passing

There are a number of mechanisms by which parameters can be passed. A common method involves placing the parameters that are to be passed into registers before the subroutine call is made. For a multiplication subroutine where the operands to be multiplied have to be passed to the subroutine, the program might do this:

Place operand 1 in register B
Place operand 2 in register C
CALL the subroutine

The multiplication is performed and then the subroutine might:

Place the upper 8 bits of the result in register B
Place the lower 8 bits of the result in register C
RETURN to the main program

In the above illustration, two registers have been used for the return of the result because the product of two 8-bit numbers is likely to be a 16-bit number. An important point to consider is that the subroutine overwrites the operands in the registers with the result, so the operands should be stored in memory before the subroutine is called.

As an illustration of this, consider the following programs for subroutines which involve parameter passing.

1. *Program*: A subroutine to provide a time delay which is determined by a value in a register in the main program.

   The subroutine is required to save the values of the registers before beginning the time delay routine, which is a loop with the loop count determined by the value in the register in the main program. The algorithm for the subroutine has the following basic form:

   1. Call the delay subroutine.
   2. Save the values of the main program registers by pushing them on to the stack.
   3. Start the loop element to generate the time delay, calling up the count from the relevant register.
   4. Restore the main program registers.
   5. Return to main program.

   Here is a Z80 subroutine to do this:

```
        ORG   OC00   ; start address for subroutine
DELAY   PUSH  AF     ; push AF onto stack to save it
        PUSH  BC     ; push BC onto stack to save it
        PUSH  HL     ; push HL onto stack to save it
        LD    B,0    ; clear B
LOOP    DJNZ  LOOP   ; use B as inner loop counter
        DEC   HL     ; decrement HL which is used as
                     ; the outer loop counter to give
                     ; the time delay value parameter
                     ; from the main program
        LD    A,H
        OR    L
        JRNZ  LOOP   ; repeat loop if not zero
        POP   HL     ; restore HL
        POP   BC     ; restore BC
        POP   AF     ; restore AF
        RET          ; return to main program
```

2. *Program*: Determine the squares of numbers in an array.

   Here is the basic algorithm:

   1. In the main program, point to the first number in the array.
   2. Square the number by using a subroutine. This involves the subroutine getting the number from a register in the main program and is an example of parameter passing to a subroutine.
   3. Return to the main program.

4. In the main program, point to the next number in the array.
5. Square the number by using a subroutine. This involves the subroutine getting the number from the main program.
6. Return to the main program.

And so on, until the end of the array is reached.

The following shows how this program might be implemented for the Motorola 68HC11 microcontroller. The main program uses a subroutine called SQUARE to calculate the square of a number which is pointed to in the array.

The numbers are stored in an array which occupies addresses $C000 to $C06F. The subroutine modifies the contents of accumulators A and B, hence their original values are preserved on the stack and then restored at the end of the subroutine.

```
        ORG     $E000     ; start address
MAIN    LDS     #$FF      ; definition of the stack
        LDX     #$C000    ; the initial data pointer, the data being in an array starting at this
                          ; address
LOOP1   JSR     SQUARE    ; square the number pointed to
        INX               ; point to next number
        CPX     #$C070    ; compare index register with memory to check if the end of the array,
                          ; e.g. #$C070, has been reached
        BNE     LOOP1     ; if not, get the next number
HERE    BRA     HERE      ; stop the program

SQUARE  PSHA              ; preserve register
        PSHB              ; preserve register
        LDAA    $0,X      ; get the number to be squared
        TAB               ; copy it to accumulator B
        MUL               ; multiply A by B to square
        ADCA    #$00      ; round it to an 8-bit result
        STAA    $0,X      ; store result
        PULB              ; restore register
        PULA              ; restore register
        RTS               ; return

        END
```

6.4.2 Other parameter-passing methods

With registers being used to pass parameters, the number of values that can be passed to a subroutine is restricted to those that can be contained within the register block, so this method is only suitable for a small number of parameters. Another method that can be used with large numbers of parameters involves the use of program memory. With this method the parameters being passed are stored in the microprocessor system memory. Instead of passing the parameters from the memory to the subroutine, it is usual to pass the start address of the memory block in which the parameters are stored. Thus the program might do this:

Place the parameters in memory
Set the H and L registers to point to the first address
of the parameter area in the memory
CALL the subroutine

To return the subroutine would then do this:

Place the results in memory
Set the H and L registers to point to the first address
of the result area in the memory
RETURN to the main program

Another method that can be used is where the parameters are pushed onto the stack before a subroutine is called. The resulting values are then popped from the stack at the end of the subroutine. Here is the procedure for using a subroutine to multiply two numbers that are passed to it:

PUSH operand 1
PUSH operand 2
CALL the multiply subroutine

To return the results to the main program, the procedure is:

RETURN to the main program
POP lower byte of result
POP upper byte of result

Note that the program must contain the same number of POP instructions as PUSH instructions. If this is not the case, execution of RETURN would pull data out of the stack rather than the return address. Program failure would probably occur.

6.4.3 Nested subroutines

We can have situations where subroutine 1 can call another subroutine 2 and it might in turn call another subroutine 3. Subroutine 2 is said to be nested inside subroutine 1 and subroutine 3 nested within subroutine 2. Figure 6.9 illustrates this. Although 3 is nested within 2, it is still possible for the main program to call 3 without going through 2.

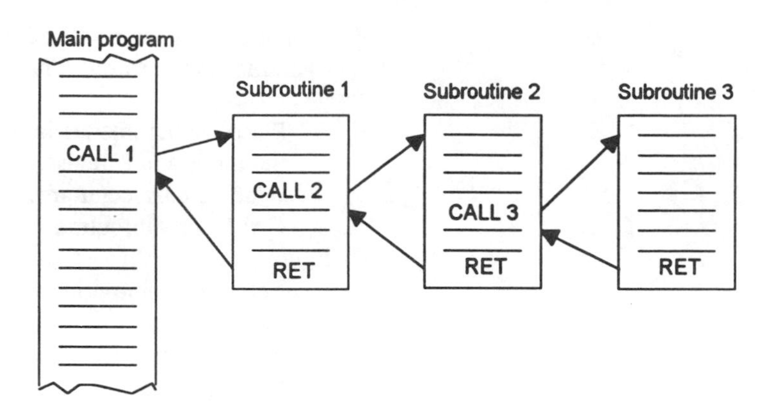

Fig. 6.9 Nested subroutines

6.5 Look-up tables

Indexed addressing (see Section 5.2.43) can be used to enable a program to look up values in a table. For example, in determining the squares of integers, a possible method is to look up the value corresponding to a particular integer in a table of squares, instead of doing the arithmetic to determine the square. Look-up tables are particularly useful when the relationship is non-linear and not described by a simple arithmetic equation, e.g. the engine management system described in Section 3.2.3 and Table 3.1 giving ignition timing settings as a function of the angle of the crankshaft and the inlet manifold pressure. Here the microcontroller has to give a timing signal that depends on the input signals from the speed sensor and crankshaft sensors.

To illustrate how look-up tables are used, consider the problem of determining the squares of integers. We can place a table of squares of the integers 0, 1, 2, 3, 4, 5, 6, ... in program memory and have the entries of the squares 0, 1, 4, 9, 16, 25, 36, ... at successive addresses. If the number to be squared is 4 then this becomes the index for the index address of the data in the table, the first entry being index 0. The program adds the index to the base address of the table to find the address of the entry corresponding to the integer. Thus we have:

Index	0	1	2	3	4	5	6
Table entry	0	1	4	9	16	25	36

For example, with the Motorola 68HC11 microcontroller we might have the following look-up program to determine the squares:

```
REGBAS  EQU    $B600     ; base address for the table
        ORG    $E000
        LDAB   $20       ; load acc. B with the
                         ; integer to be squared
        LDX    #REGBAS   ; point to table
        ABX              ; add contents of acc. B to
                         ; index register X
```

```
LDAA    $00,X           ; load acc. A with the
                        ; indexed value
```

and we could have loaded the table into memory by using the pseudo-operation FDB:

```
ORG     $B600
FDB     $00,$01,$04,$09   ; giving values to the
                          ; reserved memory block
```

With the Intel 8051 microcontroller the instruction MOVC A,@A+DPTR fetches data from the memory location pointed to by the sum of DPTR and the accumulator A and stores it in the accumulator. This instruction can be used to look up data in a table where the data pointer DPTR is initialised to the beginning of the table. As an illustration, suppose we want to use a table for the conversion of temperatures on the Celsius scale to the Fahrenheit scale. The program involves parameter passing of the temperature requiring conversion to a subroutine, so it might include the following instructions:

```
          MOV     A,#NUM                          ; load the value to be converted
          CALL    LOOK_UP                         ; call the LOOK_UP subroutine

LOOK_UP   MOV     DPTR,#TEMP                      ; point to table
          MOVC    A,@A+DPTR                       ; get the value from the table
          RET                                     ; return from the subroutine
TEMP      DB      32, 34, 36, 37, 39, 41, 43, 45  ; giving values to the table
```

Another example of the use of a table is to sequence a number of outputs. This might be a sequence to operate traffic lights to give the sequence red, red plus amber, green, amber. The red light is illuminated when there is an output from RD0, the amber is illuminated from RD1, and the green is illuminated from RD2. The data table might then be:

	Red	Red + amber	Green	Amber
Index	0	1	2	3
	0000 0001	0000 0011	0000 0100	0000 0010

6.6 Input/output addressing

There are two ways microprocessors can select input/output devices. Some microprocessors, e.g. the Zilog Z80, have dedicated instructions for carrying out input/output operations; this being termed *isolated input/output*. With isolated input/output, input instructions such as IN are used to read from an input device and output instructions such as OUT are used to output to an output device. For example, with the Z80 we might have:

```
IN A,(B2)
```

to read input device B2 and put the data in the accumulator A. An output instruction might be:

```
OUT (C), A
```

to write the data in accumulator A to port C.

Other microprocessors do not have separate instructions for input and output; they use the same instructions as they use for reading from or writing to memory. This is termed *memory-mapped input/output*. With this method, each input/output device has an address, just like a memory location. The Motorola 68HC11, Intel 8051 and PIC microcontrollers have no separate input/output instructions and can only use memory mapping. Thus, with memory mapping we might use:

```
LDAA $1003
```

to read the data input at address $1003 (port C address, see Fig. 2.5).

```
STAA $1004
```

to write data to the output at address $1004 (port B).

The following example illustrates how we might use such instructions when we have a simple on/off input. From the input word we might just use the 0 bit as the on/off signal about the state of the input and we might require an output when this bit 0 is set to 1. We can use an AND mask to give an output only when the 0 bit is set.

```
LDAA    $1002           ; get input data
ANDA    #%00000001      ; logical AND so that there is a
                        ; non-zero output only if bit 0 is set
STAA    $1003           ; output if there was an input
                        ; to address $1002
```

Where ports are bidirectional we have to set the bits in the data direction register for the port to be either inputs or outputs; this must be done before we can input or output data from them.

6.6.1 Input/output registers

The Motorola 68HC11 microcontroller has five ports A, B, C, D and E (see Section 2.3). Ports A, C and D are bidirectional and can be used for either input or output. Ports B is output only and port E input only. Whether a bidirectional port is used for input or output depends on the setting of a bit in its control register. For example, port A at address $1000 is controlled by the pulse accumulator control register PACTL at address $1026. To set port

A for input requires bit 7 to be 0; output requires bit 7 to be 1 (see Fig. 2.5). Port C is bidirectional and the eight bits in its register at address $1003 are controlled by the corresponding bits in its port data direction register at address $1007 (see Fig. 2.7) When the corresponding data direction bit is set to 0 it is an input, when set to 1 it is an output. Port D is bidirectional and contains just six input/output lines at address $1008. It is controlled by a port direction register at address $1009. The direction of each line is controlled by the corresponding bit in the control register; it is set to 0 for an input and 1 for an output (see Fig. 2.8). Some of the ports can also be set to carry out other functions by setting other bits in their control registers.

For a fixed-direction port, e.g. port B in the Motorola 68HC11 is output only, the instructions needed to output some value, e.g. $FF, are simply those needed to load the data to that address. The instructions might be:

```
REGBAS  EQU   $1000     ; base address of I/O registers
PORTB   EQU   $04       ; offset of PORTB from REGBAS
        LDX   #REGBAS   ; load index register X
        LDAA  #$FF      ; load $FF into accumulator
        STAA  PORTB,X   ; store value at PORTB address
```

For the fixed-direction port E, which is input only, the instruction to read a byte from it might be:

```
REGBAS  EQU   $1000     ; base address of I/O registers
PORTE   EQU   $0A       ; offset of PORTE from REGBAS
        LDAA  PORTE,X   ; load value at PORTE into
                        ; the accumulator
```

For a bidirectional port such as C, before we can use it for an input we have to configure the port so that it acts as an input. This means setting all the bits to 0. Thus we might have:

```
REGBAS  EQU   $1000     ; base address of I/O registers
PORTC   EQU   $03       ; offset of PORTC from REGBAS
DDRC    EQU   $07       ; offset of data direction
                        ; register from REGBAS
        CLR   DDRC,X    ; set  DDRS to all 0
```

For the Intel 8051 microcontroller (see Section 2.4) there are four parallel bidirectional input/output ports. When a port bit is to be used for output, the data is just put into the corresponding special function register bit; when it is used for input a 1 must be written to each bit concerned, thus FFH might be written for an entire port to be written to. Consider an example of Intel 8051 instructions to light an LED when a push-button is pressed. The push-button provides an input to P3.1 and an output to P3.0; the push-button pulls the input low when it is pressed.

```
        SETB   P3.1      ; make bit P3.1 a 1 and so an input
LOOP    MOV    C,P3.1    ; read the state of the push-button
                         ; and store it in the carry flag
        CPL    C         ; complement the carry flag
        MOV    P3.0, C   ; copy state of carry flag to output
        SJMP   LOOP      ; keep on repeating the sequence
```

With PIC microcontrollers the direction of the signals at its bidirectional ports is set by the TRIS direction registers (see Section 2.5). TRIS is set as 1 for read and 0 for write. The registers for the PIC16C73/74 are arranged in two banks (see Fig. 2.30) and before a particular register can be selected the bank has to be chosen by setting bit 5 in the STATUS register (see Fig. 2.31). This register is in both banks and so we do not have to select the bank in order to use this register. The TRIS registers are in bank 1 and the PORT registers in bank 0. Thus to set port B as output we have to first select bank 1 and then set TRISB to 0. We can then select bank 0 and write the output to PORTB. The bank is selected by setting a bit in the STATUS register. The instructions to select port B as an output are thus:

```
Output  clrf   PORTB          ; clear all the bits in port B
        bsf    STATUS,RP0     ; use status register to
                              ; select bank 1 by setting
                              ; RP0 to 1
        clrf   TRISB          ; clear bits so output
        bcf    STATUS,RP0     ; use status register to
                              ; select bank 0
                              ; port B is now an output
                              ; set to 0
```

6.7 Header files

Assemblers need to know the definitions of each of the labels used in a program in order that they can correctly translate the assembly mnemonics in machine code. This can be done by a list of declarations at the beginning of the program, for example:

```
REGBAS  EQU  $1000
PORTC   EQU  $0A
etc.
```

We can avoid having to repeat such a listing for each program by the assembler having available to it a collection of files giving such declarations for a range of microcontrollers and we then tell the assembler, by using a *header file* statement, which of its files it should use.

For example, with the PIC assembler it first needs to know which microcontroller it is working with and so the first line of the program has to tell it. Thus we might have:

```
list P=16C74A
```

This is followed by a line telling it to include a particular file, e.g.

```
include "C:\MPLAB\PICC74A.INC"
```

This gives, for the microcontroller concerned, the addresses of each of the special-purpose registers and the named bits in them.

Problems

1. Explain how multiplication of two numbers can be programmed by using a loop.
2. A program for the Intel 8051 terminates with the instruction LJMP 0. What does this do?
3. Describe the operation of the following M68HC11 program:

```
        ORG     $E000
        LDAA    $00
        BEQ     THERE
        LDAB    $01
        STAB    $00
THERE   STAA    $01
HERE    BRA     HERE
```

4. Describe the operation of the following Intel 8051 program:

```
        ORG     8000H
START   MOV     C,P1.0
        MOV     P1.1,C
        SJMP    START
```

5. Devise a program for a Motorola 68HC11 to add all the contents of the locations starting from $C100 and continuing to $C120 if the result of the addition could be a two-byte number and is to be stored in locations $C121 and $C122.
6. Devise a program for a Zilog Z80 to carry out 16-bit binary addition using the 8-bit ADD instruction for data stored in memory locations 1900H to 1903H and store the sum in 1904H and 1905H.
7. Devise a program for a Motorola 68HC11 to shift left the value in accumulator A by the number of times specified by the number stored in accumulator B.
8. State the instructions that can be used to enable the main program to carry out a subroutine and then return to the main program at the point where it left off.
9. Explain how the stack register is used to enable a program to carry out a subroutine and return to the main program at the point where it left off.
10. State the effect of the following program instructions:

```
PUSH AF
POP  BC
```

11. Explain what is meant by parameter passing and its use in programs.
12. Describe the operation of the following program instructions which involve the use of a subroutine labelled as SEND to output data:

```
LDAA    #$61    ; ASCII code for a
JSR     SEND
LDAA    #$62    ; ASCII code for b
JSR     SEND
LDAA    #$63    ; ASCII code for c
JSR     SEND
```

13. Explain how the time delay produced by a delay subroutine can be calculated.
14. Explain how nested loops can be used to obtain longer time delay subroutines than are feasible with a single delay loop.
15. Devise a subroutine for the Motorola 68HC11 to give a time delay of 100 ms. Try a solution using the LDX instruction which takes 2 cycles to load the required loop count, NOP instruction 2 cycles, DEX 3 cycles and BNE 3 cycles and assume the microcontroller is running at 2 MHz.
16. Modify the solution to Problem 15 by using a nested loop in order to create a delay of 10 s.
17. A microcontroller has six LEDs connected to its output port. The LEDs are connected to their supply voltage so that they are on when there is a 0 output. Devise a program for a Motorola 68HC11 to switch a LED off long enough for the eye to detect it and to sequentially switch LEDs off. Use a delay subroutine.
18. Devise programming instructions which will use a table to convert a binary number into its BCD equivalent.
19. Write the instructions needed to read the value from a bank of eight switch inputs connected to port E of the Motorola 68HC11 microcontroller.
20. Write the instructions needed to output the value $04 from port B of the Motorola 68HC11 microcontroller.
21. Write the instructions needed to obtain low outputs from port D of a PIC16C74 microcontroller.
22. Write a header file to enable the labels STATUS, PORTA, PORTB, PORTC, PORTD, PORTE, TRISA, TRISB, TRISC, TRISD and TRISE to be used in programs.
23. Write a program for an Intel 8051 microcontroller which will give an output from P4.0 when the input to P4.1 goes low.
24. Write a program for an Intel 8051 microcontroller which will give an output from P4.0 when either the input to P4.1 or to P4.2 goes low.

7 C language

7.1 Introduction

C is a high-level language that is often used in place of assembly language for the programming of microprocessors. It has the advantages, when compared with the assembly language, of being easier to write as well as more readable and comprehensible, and the same program can be used with different microprocessors since all that is necessary is to use the relevant conversion program, termed the *compiler*, to translate the C program into the machine language for the microprocessor concerned. Assembly language is different for the different microprocessors and so, while the procedures are generally the same, different mnemonics have to be used to write the program for the different microprocessors. However, C language is standardised, the standard being set by the American National Standards Institute (ANSI), so the same terms and approach can be used for all microprocessors..

This chapter is intended to give an introduction to the C language and the writing of programs; Chapter 8 gives examples of programs written for microprocessors and microcontrollers. For a more detailed consideration of writing programs in C, the reader is referred to texts such as *Teach Yourself C Programming in 21 Days* by P. Aitken and B.L. Jones (Sams Publishing 1995) or *C for Engineers and Scientists* by G. Bronson (West 1993) and, specifically for writing programs for microcontrollers, *Programming Microcontrollers in C* by T. Van Sickle (High Text 1994) and *C and the 8051*, volumes 1 and 2, by Tom Schultz (Prentice Hall 1998).

7.2 C program structure

C programs are built up from modules, each module being designed to perform a specific task and thus receive data, process the data and return a result. In assembly language terms, a module is a small subroutine. Since each subroutine has a function within the overall program, in a C program it is called a function rather than a subroutine. A *function* is thus a self-contained block of program code which performs a specific set of actions and has a name by which it can be referred to and called up.

A function is given a name that conveys some idea of what is does, e.g. add_num. Function names must begin with a letter or an underline, and only letters, digits or underlines may follow the initial letter. Blank spaces are not allowed, thus an underline is used to separate words in a name consisting of multiple words. Note that C is a case-sensitive language and distinguishes between upper case and lower case letters. Thus Add_num would be regarded as a different function from add_num or ADD_NUM. Generally lower case letters are used for all functions. A function name cannot be one of the *keywords* in Table 7.1; these are words that are used in C for specific purposes and can only be used for those purposes.

Table 7.1 Keywords

auto	double	int	struct
break	else	long	switch
case	enum	register	typedef
char	extern	return	union
const	float	short	unsigned
continue	for	signed	void
default	goto	sizeof	volatile
do	if	static	while

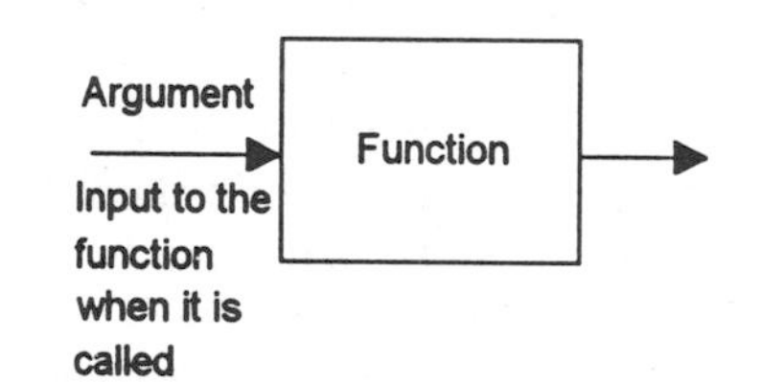

Fig. 7.1 Function principle

All function names are followed by brackets, i.e. name( ). The brackets enclose *arguments*; a function's argument is a value that is passed to the function when the function is called. Figure 7.1 illustrates this principle. A function is executed through calling it up by its name in the program statement. For example, we might have the statement

```
printf("Mechatronics");
```

This would mean that the word Mechatronics, i.e. the argument for the function, is passed to the function printf( ) and, as a result, the word is printed onscreen. In order to indicate that characters form a sequence, e.g. those making up the word Mechatronics, they are enclosed within double quotes. A sequence of characters enclosed within double quotes, i.e. " ", is termed a *string*. As the term implies, the characters within the double quotes are treated as a linked entity

7.2.1 Statements and variables

C functions are made up from *statements*, every statement being terminated by a semicolon. The statements making up a function

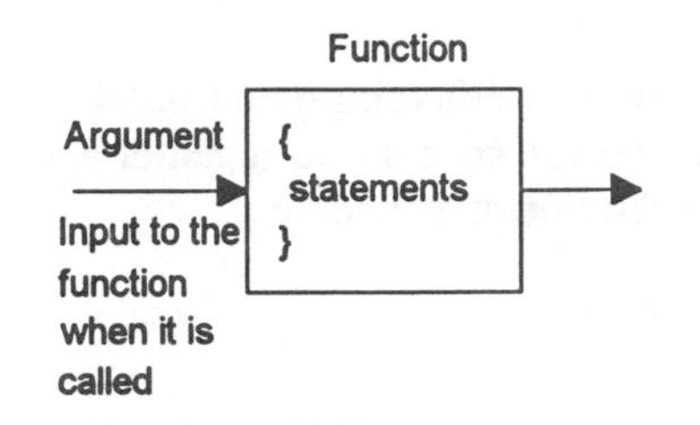

Fig. 7.2 Function principle

are always grouped by putting them between braces (parentheses), i.e. { }. Thus for a two-statement function we have:

```
function( )
{
    statement 1;
    statement 2;
}
```

Figure 7.2 illustrates the principle of using statements to determine what a function will do. In assembly language terms, you can think of { and } enclosing the instructions which make up the subroutine.

The term *variable* is used for a name which describes a memory address. A variable name is selected by the same rules as described earlier for the selection of function names. Thus we might have the name num1 to describe a particular memory address at which the first number is to be found, num2 for where the second number can be found. We then might have the statements:

```
num1 = 20;
num2 = 10;
total  = num1 + num2;
```

Each of the above statements tells the computing system to assign, i.e. store, a value into the memory address which is described by the variable. *Assignment statements* always have an equals (=) sign. An assignment statement assigns the value of the expression to the right of the = sign to the variable on its left. Blank spaces have been inserted into the statements for readability. Except for messages contained within " ", function names and the reserved words, C ignores all blank spaces.

Before storing a value in a variable we must define the type of data that is to be stored in it by using a *declaration statement*. Variables that can hold a character are specified using the keyword *char*, such a variable being 8 bits long and generally used to store a single character. Signed integers, i.e. numbers with no fractional parts and which are signed to indicate positive or negative, are specified using the keyword *int*. The keyword *float* is used for floating-point numbers. The keyword *double* is also used for floating-point numbers but provides about twice the number of significant digits as *float*. To declare a variable the type is inserted before the variable name, e.g.

```
int total;
```

This declares the variable total to be of integer type. As another example we might have:

```
float num1;
```

This indicates that the variable num1 is a floating-point number. Variables having the same data type can be grouped together and declared by means of a single declaration statement, e.g.

```
int num1, num2;
```

Declaration statements within a function appear immediately after the opening brace of a function and, as with all other C statements, must end with a semicolon. Thus we might have:

```
{
   int num1, num2, total;
   num1 = 20;
   num2 = 10;
   total  = num1 + num2;
}
```

7.2.2 The main function

The C program consists of a main program in which there are subroutines, i.e. functions. We use a function called main( ) to combine the subroutine functions in the required order. Every C program must have a function called main( ) in which the other functions are to be located. Execution starts with its first statement. Other functions may be called up within statements, each one is executed in turn and control is passed back to the main function (Fig. 7.3).

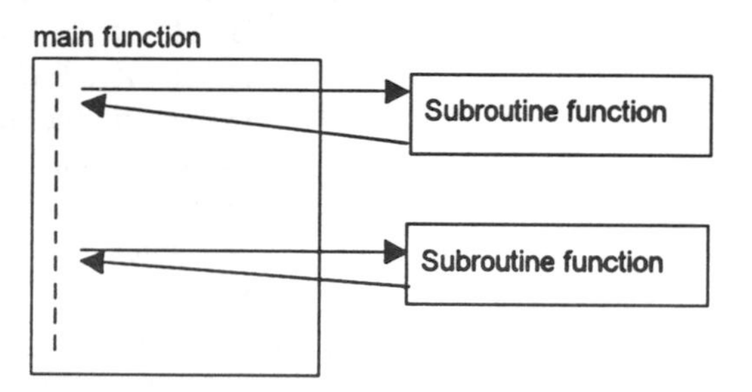

Fig. 7.3 The main function

For example, we might have a main function to calculate the cost of a meal in a restaurant, itself composed of a number of functions. We might thus have:

```
main( )
{
   input_cost ( );
   service_charge ( );
   total ( );
}
```

The { and } indicate the beginning and end of the main function. Within the main function there are three functions input_cost ( ), service_charge ( ) and total ( ) and they are called up in the order in which they appear in the main function. Each of these functions may be defined by its own statements enclosed between its own { and }.

7.2.3 Function definitions and declaration

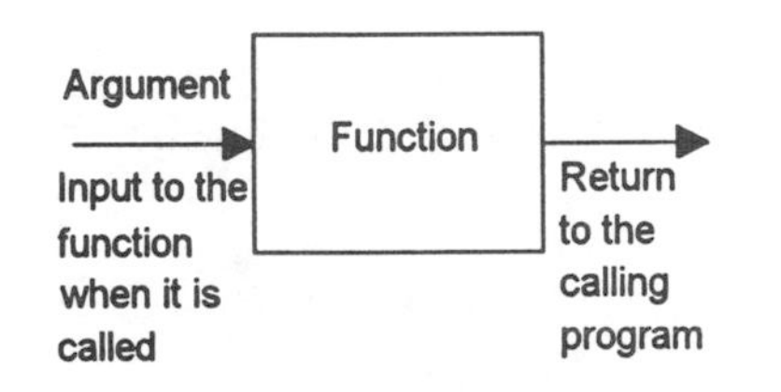

Fig. 7.4 Function principle

The purpose of a C function is to receive data, operate on the data and then return no more than a single value to the program that called the function (Fig. 7.4). A function is called up by giving its name and in the brackets following the name any data to be passed to the function:

```
function_name(data passed to function);
```

So that the compiler knows what it meant when a subroutine function name is called, it is necessary to give a definition of it. Each function is defined once in a program and can then be used by any other function that calls it. A function is defined by a *function header* and a *function body*:

```
function header
{
   function body;
}
```

The function header identifies the function name, the arguments with the names and types expected by the function and the type of data to be returned to the calling function. Thus we might have the function header:

```
int findmax(int x, int y)
```

to head a function used to determine the maximum number from two numbers x and y. This declares that the function findmax expects two integer values to be sent to it and that it will return an integer value. Note that there is no semicolon after a function header; the next thing that follows is the opening brace { of the function body. The function body gives the statements to operate on the passed data and return at most a single value to the function that called up the function. The ***return type*** appears in front of the function name; this specifies the type of value to be returned to the calling function when execution of the function is completed. To return a value from a function back to the calling point, the keyword return is used and the return statement terminates the function. Thus a function that calls up the function findmax to determine the maximum number of the two integer numbers x and y to get back the integer maximum number might be:

```
int findmax(int x, int y)
{
   int maxnum;
   if (x >= y);
      maxnum = y;
   else
      maxnum = y;
   return(maxnum);
}
```

The return type may be specified as void if the function does not return a value, e.g.

```
void main( )
```

By convention a return value of 0 from main( ) is used to indicate normal program termination, i.e. the entry:

```
return 0;
```

7.2.4 Pre-processor

The *pre-processor* is a program that is identified by *pre-processor commands* so that it is executed prior to compilation. All such commands are identified by having # at the beginning of the line. Thus we might have:

```
# include < >
```

to include the file named between the angle brackets < >. When this command is reached the specified file will be inserted into the program. It is frequently used to add the contents of standard header files, which give a number of declarations and definitions that enable standard library functions to be used. The entry would then be:

```
# include <stdio.h>
```

As an illustration, consider the simple program:

```
# include <stdio.h>

main( )
{
   printf("Microprocessors");
}
```

Before starting the main program the file stdio.h is added. Thus when the main program starts, we are able to access the function printf( ) without the need to define it, since the stdio.h file has already defined it. Hence we can display the word 'Microprocessors' on the screen.

Another type of pre-processor command is one used to define values that will be inserted whenever a particular symbol is encountered in the program, for example:

```
# define pi 3.14
```

Whenever pi is encountered the value 3.14 will be used.

Yet another use of the pre-processor command # define is to create a *function macro*. This is a type of shorthand way of representing something more complex. A simple example is:

```
# define square(x) (x)*(x)
```

which will replace the term square(x) in the program by (x)*(x). Note that there must be no white space between square and (x), otherwise square will be defined as (x) (x)*(x).

7.2.5 Standard library functions

C packages are supplied with libraries containing a large number of predefined functions that have already been written; this saves you the effort of having to write them. These functions can be called up by just naming them. In order to use the contents of any particular library, that library has to be specified in a header file. Examples of such library files are:

math.h for mathematical functions
stdio.h for input and output functions
time.h for date and time functions

For example, the function printf( ) is a function that can be called up from the stdio.h library and is the function for printing to the screen of the monitor. Another function is scanf( ); this can be used to read data from a keyboard. An example of a mathematical function is double sqrt(double num); this is used to return the square root of num. The type double is used to indicate a double-precision floating-point number. Thus we might have:

```
printf("%f", sqrt(16.0));
```

and the result printed to the screen is 4.0. Other mathematical functions included are log10(x) for the logarithm to base 10, log(x) for the natural logarithm, exp(x) for e^x, sin(x), cos(x), tan(x), asin(x) for the inverse sine of x, acos(x), atan(x), sinh(x), cosh(x), tanh(x) and pow(x,y) for x^y. All angles as arguments or return values are in radians.

7.2.6 Comments

The symbols /* and */ are used to enclose comments. Comments are ignored by the compiler and are used to enable a programmer to more easily comprehend the program. Thus we might have an entry such as:

```
/* Main program follows */
```

Comments can span more than one line, e.g.

```
/* An example of a program used to
   illustrate programming */
```

7.2.7 Program example

The following simple program illustrate points made in the previous sections.

```
#include <stdio.h> /*identifies the function library that
                    is to be used*/

main( )
{
   printf("Microprocessor systems");
}
```

The first line of the program is a pre-processor command to include the named file, i.e. stdio.h, in the program. The stdio.h file is termed a *header file* because it is placed at the head of the C program. With the pre-processor command is a comment to help readers understand what is being attempted. Following the pre-processor command is the main function; this has just one statement. The statement calls the function printf( ) and passes it one argument, the message. The message is a string of characters with the beginning and end marked by double quotation marks. When a message is passed to printf( ) the function prints the message on the screen.

7.3 Escape sequences and format specifiers

The combination of a backslash \ and certain characters is termed an *escape sequence*. Escape sequences means that the characters 'escape' from the standard interpretation of characters and are being used to control the location of output on a display by moving the screen cursor or indicating special treatments. Thus we might have:

```
printf("\nSum = %d", d);
```

with the \n indicating that a new line is to be used when it is printed on the screen. Escape sequences commonly used are:

```
\a      sound a beep
\b      backspace
\n      new line
\t      horizontal tab
\\      backslash
\?      question mark
\'      singe quotation
```

As an illustration of a *format specifier*, we might have:

```
printf("Sum = %d", x);
```

The argument in ( ) specifies what is passed to the print function. There are two arguments, separated by a comma. The first argument is the string between the double quotes and specifies how the output is to be presented, the %d specifying that the variable is to be displayed as a decimal integer. The other argument x specifies the value that is to be displayed. Other format specifiers are:

```
%c      character
%d      signed decimal integer
%e      scientific notation
%f      decimal floating point
%o      unsigned octal
%s      string of characters
%u      unsigned decimal integer
%x      unsigned hexadecimal
%%      prints a % sign
```

As another example, the statement:

```
scanf("%d", &x);
```

reads a decimal integer from the keyboard and assigns is to the integer variable x. The & symbol in front of x is used to represent the term 'address of' operator. When placed before the name of a variable, it returns the address of the variable. The command thus scans for data and stores the item using the address given. Thus we might have:

```
scanf("%f", &num1);
```

This will read the decimal floating-point number and store it at the address defined for num1.

Here is an example of a program to illustrate the above; it uses the defined function findmax to determine the maximum of two numbers entered on the screen following a request message:

```
#include <stdio.h>
main( )
{
   int num1, num2, maxnum;
   int findmax(int, int);

   printf("Enter the first number: "); /*request for first
                                              number*/
   scanf("%u", &num1);
   printf("\n Enter the second number: "); /* , following a
                  line space a request for second number*/
   scanf(%d", &num2);
   maxnum = findmax(num1, num2); /*calls the function
                                              findmax*/
   printf("\n The maximum number is %u", maxnum);
                                    */ displays the result*/
}

/* the following is the function findmax */
int findmax{int x, int y) /* function header*/
{
   int maxnum;
   if (x >= y)
      maxnum = x; /* max. number is x if x greater than
                        or equal to y */
   else
      maxum = y;
   return(maxnum); /* return the value to the calling
                           function*/
}
```

7.4 Operators

This section describes how to program arithmetical, relational, logical and bitwise operations.

7.4.1 Arithmetic operators

The arithmetic operators used are:

```
addition +
subtraction –
multiplication *
division /
modulus %
increment + +
decrement – –
```

Increment operators increase the value of a variable by 1, decrement operators decrease it by 1. The normal rules of arithmetic hold for the precedence of operations. For example,

2*4 + 6/2 gives 11. A useful rule to ensure that the intended sequence of operations occur is to use brackets. Thus we might write (2*4) + (6/2). The value of any arithmetic operation can be displayed by using the printf( ) function.

The division of two integers to give an integer return will neglect any fractional parts. For example, 5/3 will return a value of 1. There are times when we wish to retain the remainder of such a division and this can be achieved by the use of the modulus operator %. This operator can only be used with integers. If we have 5 % 3 then the value returned is the remainder, which is 2. If we have 6 % 3 then the value returned is 0 since there is no remainder.

The following is an example of a program involving arithmetic operators to determine the area of a circle.

```
/* program to determine area of a circle*/

#include <stdio.h>  /*identifies the function library*/

int radius, area  /*variables radius and area are integers*/

int main(void )  */starts main program, the int specifies
      that an integer value is returned, the void indicates
      that main( ) has no parameters*/
{
     printf("Enter radius:");  */ "Enter radius" on screen*/
     scanf("%d", &radius);  */Reads an integer from
          keyboard and assigns it to the variable radius*/
     area = 3.14 * radius * radius; */Calculates area*/
     printf("\n Area = %d", area); */On new line prints Area
          = and puts in numerical value of the area*/
     return 0;  */returns to the calling point*/
}
```

7.4.2 Relational operators

Relational operators are used to compare expressions, asking questions like these: Is *x* equal to *y*? Is *x* greater than 10?. The relational operators are:

is equal to = =
is not equal to !=
less than <
less than or equal to <=
greater than >
greater than or equal to >=

For example, we might have the question 'Is *x* equal to 2?' and represent this by (x = = 2). Note that = = has to be used when asking whether two variables are the same, but = is used when you are assigning a value to some variable.

With relational expressions the value can only be 0 or 1, defined respectively to be interpreted as false and true. We might want to know whether the temperature variable is greater than 50, so we would write temp > 50. If it is greater than 50, we will obtain the value 1, otherwise we will obtain the value 0. If we want to know whether the temperature is equal to 50 then we write temp = = 50. If we want to know whether the temperature is not equal to 50 then we write temp != 50.

7.4.3 Logical operators

The logical operators are:

<table>
<tr><th>Operator</th><th>Symbol</th></tr>
<tr><td>AND</td><td>&&</td></tr>
<tr><td>OR</td><td>||</td></tr>
<tr><td>NOT</td><td>!</td></tr>
</table>

Thus we might write:

```
(voltage > 10) && (current < 20);
```

to establish whether the voltage has a value more than 10 and the current a value less than 20. If the answer is yes than the value returned is 1, otherwise it is 0.

7.4.4 Bitwise operators

The bitwise operators treat their operands as a series of individual bits rather than a numerical value, comparing corresponding bits in each operand, and they only work with integer variables. The operators are:

<table>
<tr><th>Bitwise operation</th><th>Symbol</th></tr>
<tr><td>AND</td><td>&</td></tr>
<tr><td>OR</td><td>|</td></tr>
<tr><td>EXCLUSIVE-OR (XOR)</td><td>^</td></tr>
<tr><td>NOT</td><td>~</td></tr>
<tr><td>Shift right</td><td>>></td></tr>
<tr><td>Shift left</td><td><<</td></tr>
</table>

As an illustration, consider the two binary numbers 1010 0011 and 1101 0101 which are to be ANDed. Each bit in one number is compared with bit occupying the same position in the other number and the result is a 1 if the two bits are 1s and 0 if not.

```
  1010 0011
& 1101 0101
  ---------
  1000 0001
```

AND operations can be used to eliminate selected bits from an operand. This is because ANDing any bit with a 0 forces the resulting bit to be 0, whereas ANDing any bit with a 1 leaves the original bit unchanged.

As an illustration of an OR operation, consider the two binary numbers 1010 0011 and 1101 0101 which are to be ORed. Each bit in one number is compared with the bit occupying the same position in the other number; the result is a 1 if either bit is a 1 and 0 if both bits are 0.

```
  1010 0011
| 1101 0101
-----------
  1111 0111
```

OR operations can be used to force selected bits to take on a 1 value and pass other bit values through unchanged. As an illustration of the OR bitwise operator with a microprocessor system, we might have the statement:

```
portA = portA | 0x0c;
```

The prefix 0x is used to indicate that the 0c is a hex value, being 0000 1100 in binary. The value ORed with port A is thus a binary number that forces bits 2 and 3 on, all the other bits remaining unchanged.

The EXCLUSIVE OR (XOR) operator ^ returns a 1 as a result of comparing bits if only one of the bits being compared is a 1, otherwise it returns 0. Thus we can have:

```
  1010 0011
^ 1101 0101
-----------
  0111 0110
```

Since this operation means that XORing any bit with a 1 forces it to return the opposite value, XOR operations can be used to return the opposite value of any individual bit in a variable. Thus we might have:

```
portA = portA ^ 1;
```

This statement causes all the bits except for bit 1 of port A to remain unchanged. If bit 0 is 1 in port A then the XOR will force it to 0; if it is 0 then the XOR will force it to 1.

The complement operator ~ changes each 1 bit in the operand to 0 and each 0 bit to 1, e.g.

```
~ 1010 0011
-----------
  0101 1100
```

The shift operators cause the bits in an operand to be shifted by a given amount, any vacated bits being filled with a zero. For example, a shift left of four bits for the operand 1010 0011 gives:

```
<<4  1010 0011
     ---------
     0011 0000
```

7.4.5 Example of a C program

An example of a simple program to illustrate the use of some of the above terms is:

```
/* A simple program in C*/

# include <stdio.h>

void main(void)
{
   int a, b, c, d;  /*a, c, c and d are integers*/
   a = 4;  /*a is assigned the value 4*/
   b = 3; /*b is assigned the value 3*/
   c = 5; /*c is assigned the value 5*/
   d = a * b * c;  /*d is assigned the value of  a % b % c*/
   printf("a * b * c = %d\n", d);
}
```

The statement int a, b, c, d; declares the variables a, b, c and d to be integer types. The statements a = 4, b = 3, c = 5 assign initial values to the variables, the = sign being used to indicate an assignment. The statement d = a * b * c directs that a is to be multiplied by b and then by c and stored as d. The printf in the statement printf("a * b * c = %d\n", d) is the display on screen function. The argument contains %d and this indicates that it is to be converted to a decimal value for display. Thus it will print a * b * c = 60. The character \n at the end of the string is to indicate that a new line is to be inserted at that point.

7.5 Branches and loops

Statements to enable branching and looping in programs are *if*, *if/else*, *for*, *while* and *switch*.

7.5.1 If

The *if* statement allows branching (Fig. 7.5). For example, if an expression is true then the statement is executed, if not true it is not executed and the program proceeds to the next statement. Thus we might have statements of the form:

```
if(condition 1= = condition 2);
printf("\nCondition is OK.");
```

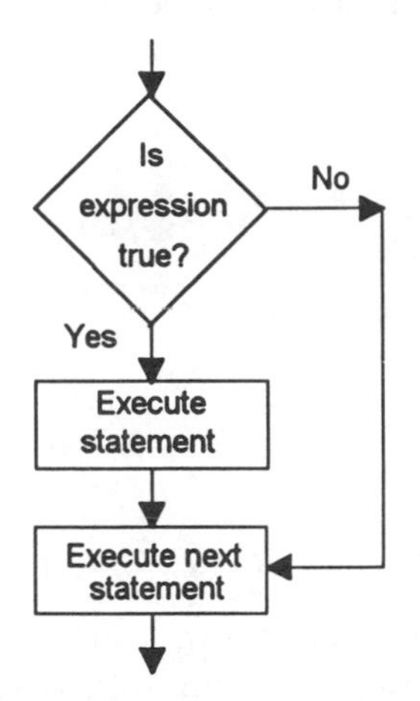

Fig. 7.5 If

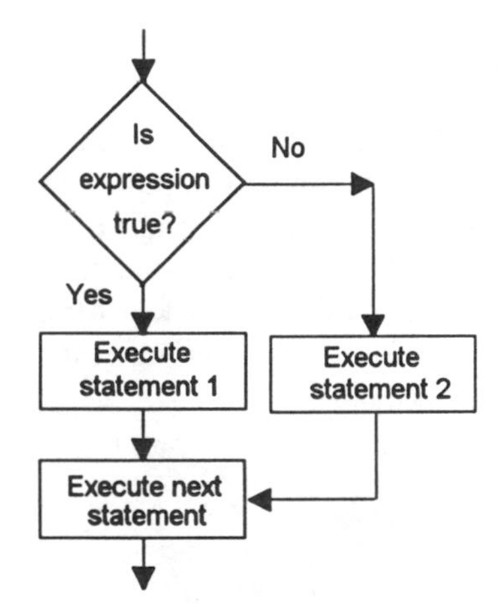

Fig. 7.6 If/else

An example of a program involving *if* statements is:

```
#include <studio.h>

int x, y;
main( )
{
   printf("\nInput an integer value for x: ");
   scanf("%d", &x);
   printf("\nInput an integer value for y: ");
   scanf(%d", &y);
   if(x = = y)
      printf("x is equal to y");
   if(x > y)
      printf("x is greater than y");
   if(x < y)
      printf("x is less than y");
   return 0;
}
```

The screen shows 'Input an integer value for x:' and then a value is to be keyed in. The screen then shows 'Input a value for y:' and then a value is to be keyed in. The *if* sequence then determines whether the keyed-in values are equal or which one is greater than the other and then it displays the result on the screen.

7.5.2 If/else

The *if* statement can be combined with the *else* statement. This allows one statement to be executed if the result is yes and another if it is no (Fig. 7.6). Thus we might have a program to give a warning if a temperature is more than 50 or satisfactory if less:

```
#include <studio.h>

main( )
{
   int temp;
   if(temp > 50)
      printf("Warning");
   else
      printf("System OK");
}
```

7.5.3 For

The term *loop* is used for the execution of a sequence of statements until a particular condition reaches the required condition of being true or false. Figure 7.7 illustrates this. One way of writing statements for a loop is to use the function *for*. The general form of the statement is:

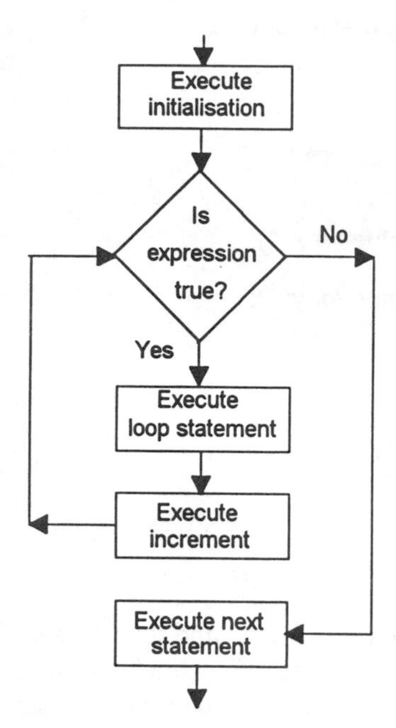

Fig. 7.7 For

```
for(initialising expression; test expression; increment
    expression)
loop statement;
```

Thus we might have:

```
#include <studio.h>

int count
main( )
{
   for(count = 0; count < 7; count ++)
   printf("\n%d", count);
}
```

Initially the count is 0 and will be incremented by 1 and then looped to repeat the *for* statement as long as the count is less than 7. The result is that the screen shows 0 1 2 3 4 5 6 with each number being on a separate line.

7.5.4 While

Another way of writing statements for a loop is to use *while*. The *while* statement allows for a loop to be continually repeated as long as the expression is true (Fig. 7.8). When the expression becomes false then the program continues with the statement following the loop. As an illustration we could have the following program where the *while* statement is used to count as long as the number is less than 7, displaying the results:

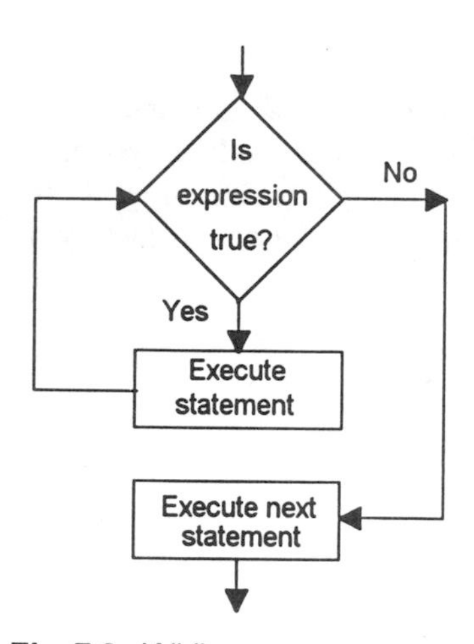

Fig. 7.8 While

```
#include <studio.h>

int count;
int main( );
{
   count = 1;
   while(count < 7)
     {
        printf("\n%d", count);
        count++;
     }
   return 0;
}
```

The variable *count* starts at 1 and is incremented while it remains less than 7; during this time the program loops through the *while* loop. The resulting display on the screen is 1 2 3 4 5 6 with each number on a separate line.

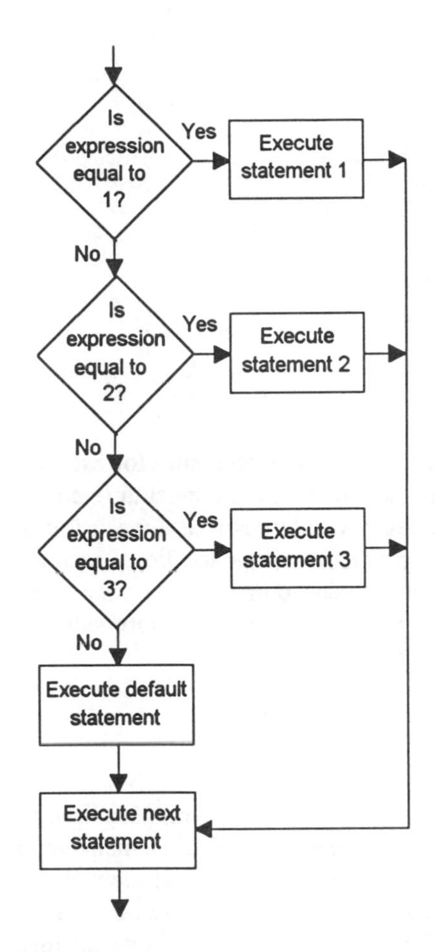

Fig. 7.9 Switch

7.5.5 Switch

The *switch* statement allows selection between several alternatives, the test condition being in parentheses. The possible choices are identified by case labels which identify the expected values of the test condition. For example, we might have the situation where if case 1 occurs we execute statement 1, if case 2 occurs we execute statement 2, etc. If the expression is not equal to any of the cases then the default statement is executed. The keywords used with a switch are *switch*, *case*, *default* and *break*. The keyword *case* is used to identify or label individual values. The *switch* expression's value is then compared with each of these case values in the order they are listed until a match is found. After each case statement there is normally a *break* statement to transfer execution to the statement after the switch and stop the switch continuing down the list of cases. If the value of the expression does not match any of the case values, the program begins with the statement following the keyword *default*. The sequence is thus (Fig. 7.9):

```
switch(expression)
{
   case 1;
      statement 1;
      break
   case 2;
      statement 2;
      break;
   case 3;
      statement 3;
      break;
   default;
      default statement;
}
next statement
```

Here is an example of a program which recognises the numbers 1, 2 and 3 and will display whichever one is entered from the keyboard.

```
#include <stdio.h>

int main ( );
{
   int x;

   printf("Enter a number 1, 2 or 3:  ");
   scanf("%d", &x);

   switch (x)
   {
      case 1:
```

```
        printf("1");
        break;
      case 2:
        printf("2");
        break;
      case 3:
        printf("3");
        break;
      default;
        printf("Not 1, 2 or 3");
      }
    return 0;
  }
```

7.6 Arrays

Suppose we want to record the midday temperature for each day for a week and then later be able to find the temperature corresponding to any one particular day. This can be done using an array. An *array* is a collection of data storage locations, each one having the same data type and referenced through the same name. To declare an array with the name temperature to store values of type float we use the statement:

```
float temperature[7];
```

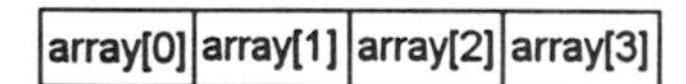

Fig. 7.10 A four-element sequential array

The size of the array is indicated between square brackets [ ] immediately after the array name. In this case 7 has been used for the data for the seven days of the week. Individual elements in an array are referenced by an index number. The first element has the index number 0, the second 1, and so on, to the last element in an n-sequence, which will be $n - 1$. Figure 7.10 shows the form of a sequential array. To store values in the array we can write:

```
temperature[0] = 22.1;
temperature [1] = 20.4;
etc.
```

with temperature[0] referring to the first temperature stored in the array, temperature[1] to the second temperature, and so on.

Here is an example of a simple program to store and display the squares of the numbers 0, 1, 2, 3 and 4. It uses the *for* loop to sequence through an array.

```
#include <stdio.h>

int main(void)
{
  int sqrs[5];
  int x;

  for(x = 1; x<5; x++)
```

```
        sqrs[x – 1] = x * x;
    for(x = 0; x < 4; x++)
        printf("%d", sqrs[x]);
    return 0;
}
```

If you want to use scanf( ) to input a value into an array element, put & in front of the array name, e.g.

```
scanf("%d", &temperature [3]);
```

This will put the value at the address of element 3 in the array.

Arrays can be given initial values when first declared, e.g.

```
int array[7] = {10, 12, 15, 11, 10, 14, 12};
```

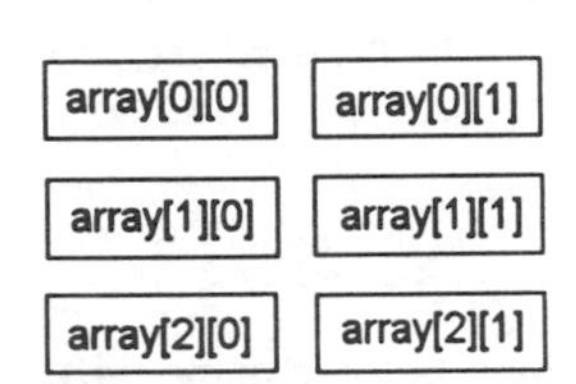

Fig. 7.11 Two-dimensional array

If you omit the array size, the compiler will create an array just large enough to hold the initialisation values.

```
int array[ ] = {10, 12, 15, 11, 10, 14, 12};
```

Multidimensional arrays can be used. For example, a table of data is a two-dimensional array (Fig. 7.11), where x represents thc row and y thc column, and is written as:

```
array[x][y];
```

A three-dimensional array can be considered as a book with tables on each page, where x represents the page number, y the row in a table on that page and z the column in that table:

```
array[x][y][z];
```

Here is a program which takes a two-dimensional array and multiplies each of its values by 5.

```
#include <stdio.h>

main( )
{
    i, j, val[3][4] = {4, 19, 12, 6,
                      5, 12, 8, 15,
                      9, 10, 13, 5};

    /* multiply each element by 5 and display it*/

    printf("\n\nDisplay of multiplied array\n");
    for (i = 0; i < 3; ++1)
    {
        for (j = 0; j < 4; ++j)
        {
```

```
                val[i][j] = val[i][j] * 5;
                printf("%3d  ", val[i][j]);
            }
        }
    }
```

7.7 Pointers

Each memory location has a unique address and this provides the means by which data stored at a location can be accessed. A *pointer* is a special kind of variable that can store the address of another variable. Thus if a variable called p contains the address of another variable called x, then p is said to *point* to x. For example, if x were at the address 100 in the memory then p would have the value 100. A pointer is a variable and, as with all other variables, it has to be declared before it can be used. A pointer declaration takes the form:

```
type *name;
```

The * should be followed immediately by a pointer name with no white space between the * and the name. It indicates that the name refers to a pointer and the * can be read as indicating 'the variable whose address is stored in'. Thus *num_addr means that variable whose address is stored in num_addr. Often names used for pointers are written with the prefix p, i.e. in the form pname. Thus we might have:

```
int *pnumber;
```

To initialise a pointer and give it an address to point to, we use the address operator & in front of the variable name; the & is read as meaning 'the address of':

```
pointer = &variable;
```

The following short program illustrates this:

```
#include <stdio.h>

int main(void)
{
   int *p, x;
   x = 12;
   p = &x;   /* assigns p the address of x*/
   printf("%d", *p);  /*displays the value of x using pointer*/
   return 0;
{
```

The program thus displays the number 12 on the screen. Accessing the contents of a variable by using a pointer, as above, is called *indirect access*. The process of accessing the data in the variable pointed to by a pointer is termed *dereferencing* the pointer.

7.7.1 Pointer arithmetic

Pointer variables can have the arithmetic operators +, –, + + and – – applied to them. Incrementing or decrementing a pointer results in it pointing to the next element or the previous element in an array. Thus to increment a pointer to the next element in an array we can use:

```
pa++;  /*using the increment by 1 operator*/
```

or

```
pa = pa + 1;   /*adding 1*/
```

7.7.2 Pointers and arrays

Pointers can be used to access individual elements in an array; the following program shows one way to do this:

```
#include <stdio.h>

int main(void)
{
   int x[5] = (0, 2, 4, 6, 8);
   int *p;
   p = x;   /*assigns to p the address of the start of x*/
   printf("%d %d", x[0], x[2]);
   return 0;
}
```

The statement printf("%d %d", x[0], x[2]); results in pointing to the address given by x and hence the values at the addresses [0] and [2] being displayed, i.e. 0 and 4, on separate lines.

7.8 Program development

The program development cycle involves a number of steps:

1. *Creating the source code*
   Creating the source code means writing the sequence of statements in C that will constitute the program. Many compilers come with an editor which can be used to enter the source code, otherwise a program such as Notepad with Microsoft Windows can be used. Using a word processor program can present problems in that additional formatting information is included which can prevent compilation unless the file is saved without the formatting information.

2. *Compiling the source code*
   Compiling the source code is its translation into machine code. Before the compilation process starts, all the pre-processor commands are executed. The compiler can detect several different forms of error during the translation and generate messages indicating the errors. Sometimes a single error may result in a cascading sequence of errors all following from that single first error. Errors usually involve going back to the editor stage and re-editing the source code.
3. *Linking to create an executable file*
   Linking is the process of bringing together everything into a single executable file, adding the library functions where necessary.
4. *Execute the program*
   The executable file should have the .EXE extension.

Problems

1. The following questions are all concerned with components of programs.

   (a) Explain what is indicated by int in the statement:

   ```
   int counter;
   ```

   (b) Explain what the following statement indicates:

   ```
   num = 10;
   ```

   (c) What will be the result of the following statement?

   ```
   printf("Name");
   ```

   (d) What will be the result of the following statement?

   ```
   printf("Number %d", 12);
   ```

   (e) What is the effect of the following statement?

   ```
   #include <stdio.h>
   ```

   (f) State the purpose of the words between /* and */ in a program, e.g.

   ```
   main( ) /*this program prints the book title*/
   ```

2. Write a C program that calls up the following functions in the order listed here.

old_value( ), correction( ), new_value( )

3. For the following program, what are the reasons for including the line (a) #include <stdio.h>, (b) the { and }, (c) the /d, and (d) what will appear on the screen when the program is executed?

```
#include <stdio.h>

main( )
{
   printf(/d"problem 3");
}
```

4. State what will be displayed on the screen with the program:

```
#include <stdio.h>

int main(void );
{
   int num;
   num = 20;
   printf("The number is %d", num);
   return 0;
}
```

5. State the output displayed on the screen with the program:

```
#include <stdio.h>

main( )
{
   printf("answer is the integer %d", 5/2);
}
```

6. Determine the values returned with the following when x = 5, y = 2 and z = 4: (a) x > y, (b) x = = y, (c) x != y, (d) x * y, (e) x * y = = z, (f) x % y
7. Determine the values returned with: (a) 1100 1100 & 1001 1011, (b) 1100 1100 | 1001 1011, (c) 1100 1100 ^ 1001 1011
8. Write a program to compute the area of a rectangle given its length and width at screen prompts for the length and width, then display the answer preceded by the words 'The area is'.
9. Write a program that displays the numbers 1 to 15, each on a separate line.
10. Explain the reasons for the statements in the following program for the division of two numbers:

```
#include <stdio.h>

int main(void);
{
```

```
    int num1, num2;
    printf("Enter first number:");
    scanf("%d", &num1);
    printf("Enter second number: ");
    scanf("%d", &num2);
    if(num2 = = 0)
      print f("Cannot divide by zero")
    else
      printf("Answer is: %d", num1/num2);
    return 0;
}
```

11. Write a program that prompts the user to type in the value of a voltage and if the value entered is greater than 10 the program should print the message 'the voltage is satisfactory', otherwise the message printed should be 'the voltage is low'.
12. Write a program that prompts the user to type in the code number of a sensor and the value it is indicating. If the value is greater than a limit of 100.0 the program should print the message 'the sensor is over the limit'.
13. Write a program to determine the square roots of a quadratic equation and display the values if the equation has real roots, otherwise indicate that it has no real roots.
14. Write a program to input eight integer numbers into an array named temp. As each number is inputted, it should be added into a total. After all the eight numbers have been inputted, the numbers should be displayed along with their average value.
15. Write a program to prompt the user to enter the noonday temperatures for a month. The program should then determine the average temperature, the minimum temperature and the maximum temperature for the month.
16. If sum is a variable, what is meant by &sum?
17. What will be printed to the display by the following program:

```
#include <stdio.h>;

int main(void)
{
   int a[10] = (1, 2, 3, 4, 5, 6, 7, 8, 9, 10);
   int *p;
   p = a;
   printf("%d %d %d", *p, *(p+1));
   return 0;
}
```

18. As exercises in using the <math.h> library of functions, write programs to (a) print the natural logarithms for the numbers 1 to 10, (b) print the sines of the angles –1 to +1 radians when taken in increments of 0.1.

8 C programming

8.1 Introduction

This chapter uses the C language for programs for microprocessor systems; in particular, the examples relate to the Intel 8051 and the Motorola 68HC11 microcontrollers. C language has the great advantage over assembler code in being easier to write, fewer lines generally being required to get the system to perform some action. However, the machine code program produced by the C compiler is likely to be significantly longer than the program produced from assembly language. Thus if a high execution speed is required, it is better to write the program in assembly language rather than C.

8.1.1 Some style points

In writing programs in C the following points must be borne in mind:

1. Individual statements do not have to be on separate lines since C pays no attention to line breaks.
2. Except for messages contained within double quotes, function names and special words, C ignores all blank spaces on lines.
3. For readability, the function name is usually written on one line and the opening brace { of the function body follows on the next line and is placed under the first letter of the function name. Similarly, the closing function brace } is placed on a line by itself under the opening brace. This enables the function to be seen as a single unit. Within the function, all program statements are usually indented to show that they are within the function. Indentation is not necessary but does make a program easier to read.
4. Comments can be written on the same line as a program statement or on separate lines. One comment must not contain another comment within itself.

5. C is a case-sensitive language, distinguishing between upper case and lower case letters. Thus NUM would be regarded as a different function to Num.
6. The word *main* in a C program tells the microprocessor system where the program starts. Every C program must contain a main function and only one.

8.1.2 Common programming errors

Common errors that occur in writing C programs are:

1. Forgetting the opening or closing braces for a function.
2. Forgetting to add a semicolon at the end of each statement.
3. Forgetting that a pre-processor command must not have a semicolon.
4. Forgetting to enclose messages in double quotes.
5. Misspelling the name of a function or not using the same capital and/or lower case letters.
6. Typing the letter O for the digit zero or vice versa.

8.2 Header files

Pre-processor commands are used at the beginning of a program to define the functions used in that program; this is so they can be referred to by simple labels. To use standard functions it is not necessary to define them, since they have already been coded in a library which is recognised by the compiler. All that is necessary is to indicate which file of standard functions should be used by the compiler; this file being is a *header* since it comes at the head of the program. Header files are also available to define the registers and ports of microcontrollers and save the programmer having to define each register and port by writing pre-processor lines for each. Thus for an Intel 8051 micro- controller we might have the header:

```
#include <reg51.h>
```

and for a Motorola M68HC11E9 the header:

```
#include <hc11e9.h>
```

The Intel 8051 header defines registers, e.g. the ports P0, P1, P2, and P3, and individual bits in bit-addressable registers, e.g. bits TF1, TR1, TF0, TR0, IE1, IT1, IE0 and IT0 in register TCON. Thus we have definitions such as:

```
/* BYTE register */
sfr P0 = 0x80;
sfr P1 = 0x90;
sfr P2 = 0xA0
sfr P3 = 0xB0;
/* BIT register */
/* TCON */
sbit TF1 = 0x8F;
sbit TR1 = 0x8E;
sbit TF0 = 0x8D;
sbit TR0 = 0x8C;
etc.
```

with sfr used to indicate that specific bytes are involved, and sbit used to indicate specific bits. Thus we can write instructions referring to port 0 inputs/outputs by purely using the label P0 or TF1 to refer to the TF1 bit in register TCON.

Similarly, the Motorola M68HC11E9 header defines registers, e.g. PORTA, PORTB, PORTC and PORTD, and individual bits in bit-addressable registers, e.g. bits STAF, STAI, CWOM, HNDS, OIN, PLS, EGA and INVB in register PIOC. Thus we have definitions such as:

```
unsigned int Register_Set = 0x1000;
#define PORTA (*(volatile Register*)(Register_Set+0))
#define PIOC (*(Register*)(Register_Set+2))
#define PORTC (*(volatile Register*)(Register_Set+3))
```

The first line gives the initial location of the variable Register_Set and the instructions that follow indicate the addresses of registers offset from this. Thus we can write instructions referring to port A inputs/outputs by purely using the label PORTA.

8.3 Bit operations

With inputs and outputs to microcontrollers it is often necessary to read or write to just one bit; also in using the control registers it is necessary to address individual bits. The modification of a variable with the result assigned back to the original variable can be achieved using a statement like this:

```
PORTA = PORTA & 0xbf
```

This assignment modifies the port A register by ANDing it with the hex number bf; with C the 0x indicates that bf is a hex value. A shorter way of writing the same operation is as follows:

```
PORTA &= 0xbf;
```

The operators that can be used to modify individual bits are termed *bitwise operators* (see Section 7.4.4):

1. *Bitwise AND*
   Since 0 ANDed with 0 and 1 ANDed with 0 both give 0, ANDing any bit with a 0 forces the resulting bit to be 0. Since 0 ANDed with 1 gives 0 and 1 ANDed with 1 gives 1, ANDing with a 1 leaves the original bit unchanged. The AND bitwise operator is &, thus we might have:

   ```
   PORTA = PORTA & 0xbf;
   ```

   With C, the 0x indicates that bf is a hex value, in this case 1011 1111 in binary. ANDing with this forces bit 6 to be 0.

2. *Bitwise OR*
   Since 0 ORed with 0 is 0 and 0 ORed with 1 is 1, we can use the bitwise OR operator | to force a bit to take on a 1 value by ORing it with a 1. Thus we might have:

   ```
   PORTA = PORTA | 0x0c;
   ```

   With C, the 0x indicates that 0c is a hex value, in this case 0000 1100 in binary. ORing this with port A forces bits 2 and 3 to be 1s, all the other bits remaining unchanged.

3. *Bitwise EXCLUSIVE-OR (XOR)*
   XORing any bit with a 1 forces it to return the opposite value. The XOR bitwise operator is ^ and so we might have:

   ```
   PORTA = PORTA ^ 1;
   ```

   This causes all the bits except for bit 1 of port A to remain unchanged; bit 1 changes to a 0 if it was a 1 and to a 1 if it was a 0.

4. *Bitwise complement*
   The complement operator ~ changes each bit which is 1 to 0 and each bit which is 0 to 1.

5. *Bitwise shift*
   The shift operators, >> for shift right and << for shift left, cause the bits to be shifted by a specified amount; any vacated bit is filled with a zero and any bit falling off the other end is discarded. Thus we might have:

   ```
   new = new<<4;
   ```

   to shift all the bits in new to the left by 4 places. Thus if we had new originally as 0001 1001 then after the operation we would have 1001 0000.

8.3.1 Examples of instructions

The following are examples of instructions involving the bitwise operators.

1. Define bit 7 of PORT1 to be the output pin.
   This can be done by using the XOR operator ^ so that all the pins other than pin 7 are unaffected. Thus, for Intel 8051, we might have:

```
sbit OUT = P1^7;
```

   The sbit is used to indicate that it is a single bit definition.

2. Switch off bit PB0.
   This can be done by defining the on state as 1, so to switch off there needs to be a 0. Thus, for the Motorola M68HC11, we might have:

```
#define ON 1
PORTB.PB0 &=~ON;
```

   or

```
#define ON 1
PORTB.PB0 = PORTB.PB0 & ~ON;
```

   PB0 is ANDed with the complement of ON, i.e. 0.

3. Switch on bit PB0.
   This can be done by defining the on state as 1, so to switch on there needs to be a 1. Thus, for the Motorola M68HC11, we might have:

```
#define ON 1
PORTB.PB0 |=ON;
```

   or

```
#define ON 1
PORTB.PB0 = PORTB.PB0 | ON;
```

   PB0 is switched on by ORing it with 1.

8.4 Branches and loops

In Section 7.5 the principles of branching and looping were introduced using the instructions if, if/else, for, while and switch.

1. *If*
   The *if* statement allows branching and selection of a particular statement if some condition occurs. Thus we might have:

```
if (P1!=0)
   C=0;
```

If port 1 is not 0 then C is 0.

2. *If/else*
   The *if/else* statement allows the selection of a sequence of one or more instructions based on the results of a comparison giving a yes or no answer. Thus we might have:

```
if (P1==0)
   C = 1;
else
   C=0;
```

   If port 1 is 0 then C is 1, otherwise C is 0.

3. *For*
   The *for* statement is used for loops and involves the repeated execution of a sequence of statements until a particular condition is reached. Thus we might have:

```
for (i=1; i<=10; i++)
{
   delay;
}
```

   Thus, for i starting at the initial value 1 and being incremented each time the statement is repeated until i reaches the value 10, the delay subprogram is repeated.

4. *While*
   The *while* statement is used for loops. It involves the program testing an expression and, while it has a non-zero value, executing the statement that follows; it then returns to the beginning of the loop to test the expression again. When the zero value occurs, the *while* statement is exited. Thus we might have:

```
while
   (ADCI==0);
return ADAT;
}
```

   The program keeps checking the condition and waiting for it to be realised. When ADCI is equal to 0 it then proceeds to the return statement. The statement:

```
while(1)
```

   is used to keep the system continually running, since it is always true.

Time delays can be produced by looping using the *while* statement (see Section 6.3.1). For a nested double-loop time delay (see Fig. 6.5) we might have:

```
void delay(unsigned int x)
{
    unsigned char j;
    while (x-->0)
    {
    for (j=0; j<125; j++);
    }
}
```

The *while* condition is to decrement each loop until x becomes 0. This gives the outer loop condition. The inner loop is specified by the *for* statement. This starts with j equal to 0, j incrementing each inner loop repetition until j reaches 125. Thus if we give x the value of 20 then the delay is 20 times the time delay produced by the inner loop. Instructions with the 8051 take 12 or 24 clock cycles to complete. Until the program is compiled, it is not obvious how many instructions are involved in the *for* statement and therefore how many clock cycles are involved. The *for* statement will involve instructions such as DEC A and JNZ, and depending on the choice of compiler, it takes about 96 cycles. With a 12 MHz clock this is 8 μs for each loop. Thus the inner loop takes $125 \times 8 = 1000$ μs = 1 ms and with x = 20 we have a total delay of 20 ms.

The above statement can be described as a *while ... do ...* loop. But there is also a *do ... while ...* loop. This executes a block of statements as long as a specified condition is true; the condition is tested at the end of the loop rather than at the beginning:

```
do
    statement
while (condition);
```

For example, we might have the instructions:

```
main( )
{
    do
    {
        pump=run;
        LED=green;
    }
    while(x<temp);
}
```

The pump will run and the LED will give green while x is less than the set temperature.

5. *Switch*
   The *switch* statement allows the selection between several alternatives. An example of the switch instruction in a program is where the bits in an input port are each tested and the system breaks if one of them is a 1.

8.4.1 Examples of programs

The following examples illustrate how to apply the above statements to microcontroller programs.

1. *Motor speed control*: Two switches are to be used to control the speed of a motor, one to give high speed and one low speed. In addition there is to be an on/off switch.
   With one speed being set by the input to P1.0, the other to P1.1 and the on/off switch from the motor to P1.2, an Intel 8051 program might look this:

```
#include <reg51.h>
#define ON 1
sbit MOTOR = P1^2; /* defines the pin for motor switch
                       on/off */
sbit SPEED1 = P1^0; /* defines the pin for speed1 switch */
sbit SPEED2 = P1^1; /* defines the pin for speed2 switch */

void speed1( ) /* the speed1 control */
void speed2( ) /* the speed2 control */

main( )
{
   do
   {
      if SPEED1==ON
         speed1( ); /* speed 1 subprogram occurs */
      if SPEED2==ON
         speed2( ); /* speed 2 subprogram occurs */
      MOTOR==~ON; /* turns motor off */
   }
}
```

   sbit is used to indicate that it is a single bit definition. Thus sbit MOTOR = P1^2; is used to define MOTOR as bit 2 in port 1, the ^ operation (XOR) causes all the bits except for bit 7 to remain unchanged when there is an input. If the SPEED1 input is switched on then the speed1( ) subprogram runs, if SPEED2 then speed2( ). Otherwise the motor is switched off, the input being the complement of ON.

2. *Motor on/off control*: Two switches are to be used to control a motor, one to switch it on and one to switch it off.
   The following is written for the Motorola M68HC11 microcontroller. It is designed to start a motor when a switch

connected to PC0 is operated and to stop when a switch connected to PC1 is operated. When a switch is operated there is a 0 input, when not operated a 1. The output to drive the motor is taken from PB0.

```
#include <hc11e9.h>
#define ON 1

main( )
{
   PORTB.PB0 &=~ON; /* motor initially off */
   DDRC=0; /* makes port C input */
   while (1)
      {
         if (PORTC.PC0==0)
            PORTB.PB0 |=ON; /* switch motor on */
         else
            if (PORTC.PC1==0)
                PORTB.PB0 &=~ON; /* motor off */
      }
}
```

3. *Stepper motor control*: Program a stepper motor to give controlled step-by-step rotation.

   In order to rotate the coil of a stepper motor (see Sections 3.5.1 and 11.8) through its angular steps, the output values to its coils must follow a prescribed sequence. Thus, for a motor having four coils, when it moves whole steps each time, the required sequence of inputs to the motor coils is given in Table 8.1. To rotate the coil step by step in one direction, the outputs from a controlling microcontroller must follow the sequence 1010, 1001, 0101, 0110. For rotation in the opposite direction we need the reverse sequence: 0110, 0101, 1001, 1010. One way of obtaining the required sequence is by using a special motor driver interface chip; here, however, we will obtain the sequence by programming an Intel 8051 to give continuous rotation. Time delays are needed between each microcontroller step output to allow time for the motor to complete the step, since a microcontroller can change its step outputs much faster than the motor can cope with.

Table 8.1 Stepper motor drive sequence

Step	*Bit 3*	*Bit 2*	*Bit 1*	*Bit 0*	*Hex code*
1	1	0	1	0	A
2	1	0	0	1	9
3	0	1	0	1	5
4	0	1	1	0	6

```
#include <reg51.h>
#define STEPPER P1
main ( )
{
   do
   {
      STEPPER = 0x0a; /* sends first byte to stepper */
         DELAY( ); /* delay subroutine */
      STEPPER = 0x09; /* sends second byte */
         DELAY( ); /* delay subroutine */
      STEPPER = 0x05; /* sends third byte */
         DELAY( ); /* delay subroutine */
      STEPPER = 0x06; /*sends fourth byte */
         DELAY( ); /* delay subroutine */
   }
   while(1);
}
```

4. *Reading an ADC channel of a microcontroller*: Program a microcontroller containing an internal analogue-to-digital (ADC) converter connected to one of its ports, e.g. the Motorola M68HC11, so that a single channel can be read.

   The M68HC11 contains an eight-channel multiplexed, 8 bit, successive approximations ADC with inputs via port E and outputs through the ADR registers (Fig. 8.1). Here we are considering there will be an input through just one of the channels PE0 to PE7. The ADC control/status register ADCTL contains the conversion complete flag CCF at bit 7 and other bits to control the multiplexer and the channel scanning (Fig. 8.2(a)). When CCF = 0 the conversion is not complete and when CCF = 1 it is complete. The analogue-to-digital conversion is initiated by writing a 1 to the ADPU bit in the OPTION register (Fig. 8.2(b)). However, the ADC must have been turned on for at least 100 μs before reading a value.

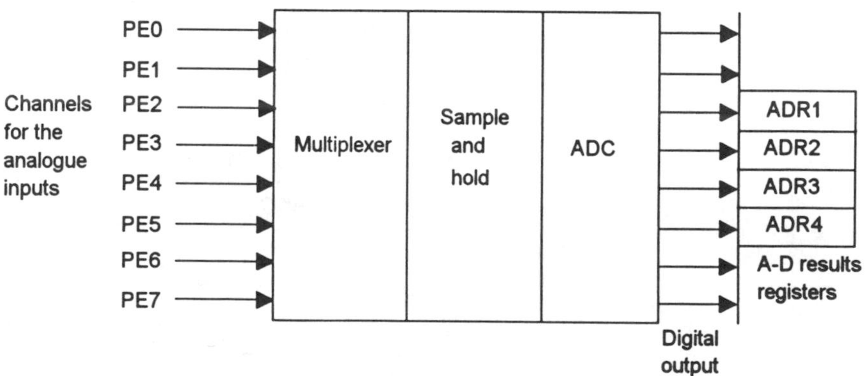

Fig. 8.1 ADC converter

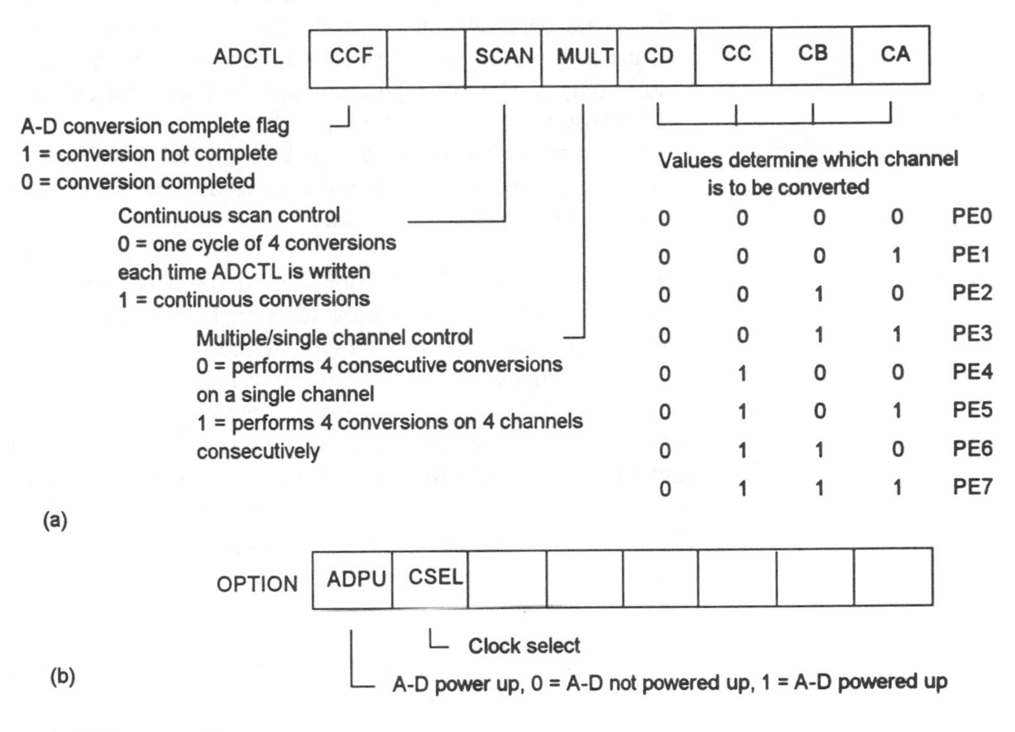

Fig. 8.2 ADC conversion

To convert the analogue input to PE0, the first four bits in the ADCTL register, i.e. CA, CB, CC and CD, must all be set to 0. When operating to convert just a single channel, bit 5 SCAN might be set to 0 and bit 4 MULT to 0. After powering up the ADC, a simple program to read a particular channel might thus involve turning all the bits in the ADCTL register to 0s, putting in the channel number and then reading the input while CCF is 0. Consequenly the program might look like this:

```
#include <hc11e9.h>

void main(void)
{
    unsigned int k; /* this enters the channel number*/

    OPTION=0; /*this and following line turns the ADC on*/
    OPTION.ADPU=1;

    ADCTL &=~0x7;  /*clears the bits*/
    ADCTL |=k; /*puts the channel number to be read*/
    while (ADCTL.CCF= =0);
    return ADR1; /*returns converted value to address 1*/
}
```

The action of the complement operator ~ is to reverse every bit in its operand, changing all the 0s to 1s and vice versa. Thus bit 7 is set. | is the OR operator and sets a bit in the result to 0 only if the corresponding bits in both operands are 0, otherwise it sets to 1. It is used to turn on, or set, one or more bits in a value. In this case with k = 1 it just sets CA to 1. A delay subroutine can be included to ensure that after power-up the value is not read too quickly.

8.5 Arrays and pointers

Arrays were introduced in Section 7.6. An *array* is a collection of data storage locations with each location having the same data type and referenced through the same name.

A common use of an array is for a *look-up table* in which values corresponding to particular table addresses can be obtained. In assembly language an array is accessed by storing a start address for the collection and then adding to the value of an index to point to the required address (see Section 6.5 for a discussion of the use of assembly language for look-up tables). A similar procedure can be used with C.

Pointers were introduced in Section 7.7. The data at a particular location in an array can be accessed by using a *pointer* to point to it. A pointer is a special kind of variable that can store the address of another variable.

An example of the use of a pointer with an array might be a program for a stepper motor where rotation is required to a particular angle. Table 8.1 (see above) can be stored in an array labelled as steptab by the statement:

```
unsigned char steptab [ ] = {0xa, 0x9, 0x5, 0x6};
```

We might then use a pointer to point at the start of the array and be incremented until the increment count reaches the required number of steps (see next section for an example program).

8.6 Subroutines

In earlier program examples in this chapter some of the instructions for a routine, e.g. a time delay, have been packaged separately from the main program. In assembly language such separate packages are called subroutines. These subroutines are called up from the main program and after execution they return control to the main program. In C the term *function* is used for a subroutine.

As an illustration consider a program for a stepper motor. We can write a function – we might call it step – which will drive the stepper from its current step to the next one. The step function will increment the array pointer to point to the next array entry, and when it reaches the end of the array it will go back to the beginning. It will output to the stepper and follow each step with a time delay. After use it returns to the main program. Here is a possible program for an Intel 8051:

```
#include <reg51.h>
unsigned char steptab[ ] = {0xa, 0x9, 0x5, 0x6};
void step(void)
{
   static unsigned char i;
   P1=steptab[i=++i&3]; /* increments to next entry in table
         and when reaches last entry goes back to start */
   delay; /* uses time delay function which is separately
           specified */
}
```

The unsigned char i has the prefix static, this term ensures that the function remembers values between function calls. Thus the latest value is retained so that when each time step is called it starts from where it left off the last time it was called. By omitting the term static or including the term auto, for automatic, the variable i is automatically stored for use while the step function is being used, but it will be lost when the function returns control to the calling function.

In the main program involving the use of the stepper we might call it up a number of times, perhaps the first time it is called it rotates through 10 steps and the next time it is called through 15 steps. For the 10-step call we can have:

```
for(i=1; i<11; i++)
{
   step( );
}
```

and for 15 steps:

```
for(i=1; i<16; i++)
{
   step( );
}
```

8.6.1 Passing parameters

In C the function header (see Section 7.2.3) is a single line which identifies the function name, the arguments with the names and types expected by the function and the type of data to be returned to the calling function. Note that only one value can be returned by a function. The arguments are the parameters that can be passed to the function. Thus the function header:

```
int num(int x, int y)
```

states that two integers x and y are to be passed to the function num and it will return an integer value. The compiler in translating the C code into assembly code will use the stack, passing the parameters onto the stack (see Section 6.4). When writing in assembly language we have to write the instructions to achieve this, in C we can leave it to the compiler. For example, the following program, discussed earlier in this chapter, has the parameter x passed to it from the main program to determine the length of the time delay:

```
void delay(unsigned int x)
{
   unsigned char j;
   while (x-->0)
   {
      for (j=0; j<125; j++);
   }
}
```

Problems

1. State the reason for the inclusion in programs of lines such as:

```
include <hc11e9>
```

2. The following brief program does not include any comments or definitions. Explain what the program is doing and state the definitions required.

```
main( )
{
   motoroff( );
   while (TRUE)
      {
      if (stop)
         motoroff( );
      else
         if (start)
            motoron( );
      }
}
```

3. Write a program line to force a bit to be 0, e.g. bit 7 in port B of a Motorola M68HC11 microcontroller or bit 7 in port 1 of an Intel 8051 microcontroller.
4. Write a program line to force a bit to 1, e.g. bit 4 in port B of a Motorola M68HC11 microcontroller or bit 4 in port 1 of an Intel 8051 microcontroller.
5. Write a program line to force a bit to return the opposite value, e.g. bit 3 in port B of a Motorola M68HC11 microcontroller or bit 3 in port 1 of an Intel 8051 microcontroller.

6. Write an instruction to change port A from 0001 0000 to 0010 0000.
7. If we define ON as 1, what instruction can be written to switch bit 0, defined as BIT0, off?
8. Write a program line to use BIT0, which is 1, to set FLAG which is 0 to 1, both BIT0 and FLAG having been defined.
9. Write a program line to use BIT0, which is 0, to set FLAG which is 1 to 0, both BIT0 and FLAG having been defined.
10. Write a program line to use BIT0, which is 1, to set FLAG which is 1 to 0, both BIT0 and FLAG having been defined.
11. Write a program for a stepper motor to rotate forward 3 steps and then reverse 3 steps.
12. Write a program to switch a LED on and off repeatedly. The LED is switched on by an output of 0.
13. Write a subroutine to convert a temperature on the Celsius scale to one on the Fahrenheit scale by using a look-up table.

9 From debugging to EPROM

9.1 Introduction

Although we can wire up a microprocessor or microcontroller system, burn the program into EPROM/EEPROM and then try it, the program is very likely to contain bugs and each bug can only be corrected by correcting the code and preparing another EPROM/EEPROM. A better technique, which is less time-consuming, is to try to find any bugs before this stage is reached by testing a program using a simulator, an evaluation board with a monitor program or an emulator. *Debugging* is the term used for finding errors that occur in software and correcting them so that the software performs as required. This chapter is about debugging and then entering programs into EPROM/EEPROM.

9.2 Simulation

Instead of testing a program by running it with an actual microcontroller, we can test it by running it with a computer program that simulates the microcontroller. This can also assist in the debugging of the program code. A simulator allows the code to be tried and monitored during its execution and is very good for checking the general performance of the program code. Typically, the display screen is divided into a number of windows in which information such as the source code is displayed as it is executed, the CPU registers and flags with their current states, the input/output ports, registers and timers, and the memory situation. Figure 9.1 shows the typical form of display on the computer screen.

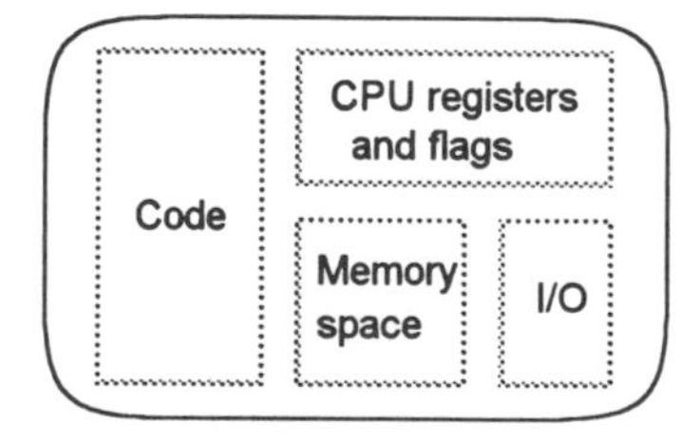

Fig. 9.1 Simulation screen

The limitations of simulators need to be recognised. They only test software; they do not test the microprocessor or microcontroller systems as an entity. Also, they do not run in real time. This means that they are not able to determine correct functioning if there is a critical time relationship between the program and the functioning of external hardware, e.g. a program used to determine a sequence of events where the events are to be switched on in sequence but each event takes a finite time and problems can occur if switching takes place before an event is completed. Thus there can still be a need, after using a simulator, to test the program with the hardware.

9.3 Evaluation board

A relatively cheap way of developing a system is to use an *evaluation board*. Evaluation boards are available for all the main microcontrollers or can be specifially made up. An evaluation board contains:

1. An identical microprocessor or microcontroller to the device running the program in the system under development.
2. Memory chips which the microprocessor or microcontroller can use for data and program memory.
3. An input/output port to enable access to all the input/output signals.
4. A communications port to enable communications between the microcontroller monitor program and a personal computer. The program code can be written in a host computer and then downloaded through either a serial or a parallel link into the memory on the board. The microprocessor or microcontroller then operates as though this program is contained within its own internal memory.
5. The board is already programmed with a monitor system which enables the operation of a program to be monitored at a terminal. It also allows the contents of memory, registers, input/output ports to be checked and modified.

Figure 9.2 shows the general arrangement of the connections to an evaluation board.

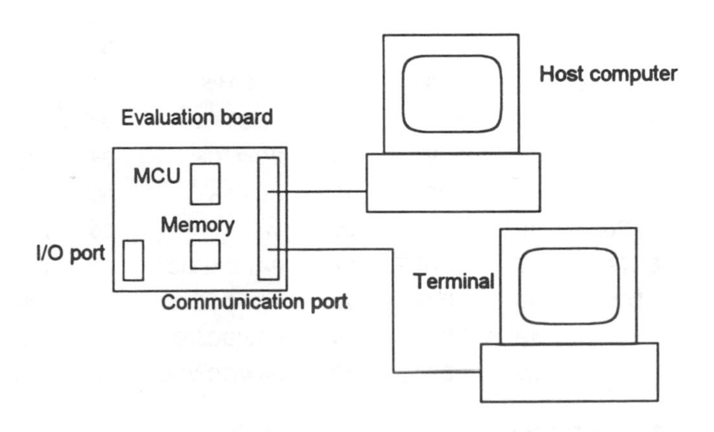

Fig. 9.2 Using an evaluation board

Figure 9.3 shows the basic elements of a typical evaluation board, the MC68HC11EVB provided by Motorola. Connections can be made to the input/output ports via a 60-pin connector. Figure 9.4 shows the memory map for the board. An MC6850 asynchronous communications interface adapter (ACIA) (see Chapter 10) is used for interfacing parallel and serial lines. A partial RS-232 interface is supplied with each of the two serial ports for connection to the host computer and the monitoring terminal. The board uses a monitor program called *Bit User Fast Friendly Aid to Logical Operations* (BUFFALO), and it is stored in the 8K EPROM. Though RAM addresses go from \$0000 to \$00FF, only \$0000 to \$003F can be used for user programs since BUFFALO uses the other addresses. This program is discussed in the next section. For more details of this evaluation board, the reader is referred to the *M68HC11EVB Evaluation Board User's Manual* (Motorola 1986).

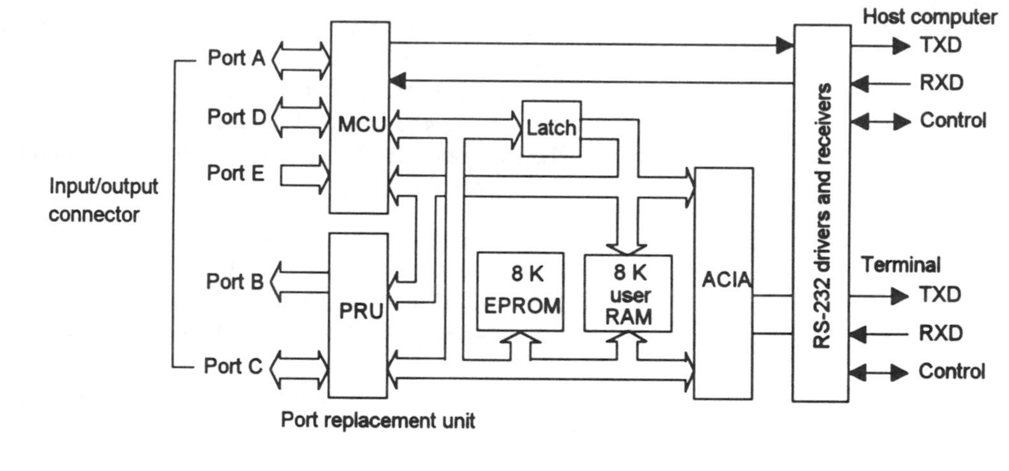

Input/output port connections

1	GND	11	PC2	21	PD1/TXD	31	PA3/OC5/OC1	41	PB1	51	V_{RH}
2	MODB	12	PC3	22	PD2/MISO	32	PA2/IC1	42	PB0	52	NC
3	NC	13	PC4	23	PD3/MOSI	33	PA1/IC2	43	PE0	53	NC
4	STRA	14	PC5	24	PD4/SCK	34	PA0/IC3	44	PE4	54	NC
5	E	15	PC6	25	PD5/SS	35	PB7	45	PE1	55	NC
6	STRB	16	PC7	26	V_{DD}	36	PB6	46	PE2	56	NC
7	EXTAL	17	$\overline{RESET}$	27	PA7/PAI/OC1	37	PB5	47	PE6	57	NC
8	XTAL	18	$\overline{XIRQ}$	28	PA6/OC2/OC1	38	PB4	48	PE3	58	NC
9	PC0	19	$\overline{IRQ}$	29	PA5/OC3/OC1	39	PB3	49	PE7	59	NC
10	PC1	20	PD0/RXD	30	PA4/OC4/OC1	40	PB2	50	V_{RL}	60	NC

Fig. 9.3 MC68HC11EVB

9.3.1 Monitor program

The monitor program enables user programs to be downloaded from a computer and/or assembled from mnemonics, the programs to be run and debugged, and memory locations to be inspected and modified. As an illustration of these stages, consider the BUFFALO monitor program.

The BUFFALO prompt on the screen display is a > and the command line format is to enter first the command mnemonic after the prompt, then parameters such as an expression or address and then to terminate the line by using the enter key. All numerical values will be in hex without $ having to be used to indicate this. The following is a brief outline of how some of the features of the program are used:

1. *Assembling a program from mnemonics*
   The instruction:

   ASM *address*

   is used to enter instructions directly into the RAM of the evaluation board. For example, to enter the instruction ADDA #$10 at $C000 we type, after the prompt:

   ASM C000

   The current instruction at C000 is displayed, then the indented prompt waiting for the new instruction, i.e. ADDA #$10, to be entered. The instruction will then be assembled into machine code and displayed. Further instructions can then be entered. When all have been entered, the control and A keys are simultaneously pressed to exit from the assembler.
2. *Downloading a program from a PC*
   The program is entered into the PC using a text editor, then assembled into the S-record format. This format is generated by a 68HC11 assembler and besides the program, it includes some formatting information. The command:

   LOAD T

   can then be used to download the program from the host computer.
3. *Running a program*
   To start executing a program, the command:

   >G *start address*

is used to go to the specified address and run the program starting there.

4. *Debugging using breakpoints*
   Breakpoints are points placed in a program to cause it to breakoff and return control to the monitor. These points are used to divide a program into segments so that the running of the program can be checked at each breakpoint. In this way bugs can be located to particular segments. By suitable choice of breakpoints, outputs and inputs can be checked as they occur, calculation algorithms can be checked for correct functioning, loops can be checked to determine whether the program is stuck in an endless loop, and branches can be checked for correct functioning. With BUFFALO, up to four breakpoints can be inserted at any one time. They are inserted by using the command:

   BR *address*

   BUFFALO sets breakpoints by inserting the software interrupt instruction SWI in the program. The contents of the registers are then displayed. The program will continue from a breakpoint when the proceed command:

   P

   is used. The command to remove breakpoints is:

   BR-*address*

5. *Debugging using trace*
   The trace command:

   T*n*

   can be used to trace *n* steps of a program, *n* having a value between 1 and FF. This command causes the contents of the registers to be displayed on the completion of each instruction.

6. *Filling memory addresses*
   To fill a block of memory with constant data, the following command is used:

   BF *address1 address2 data*

   To display a block of memory, the following command is used:

   MD *address1 address2*

To display and modify memory, the command is:

MM *address*

To copy a block of memory to a destination, the command is:

MOVE *address1 address2 destination*

7. *Modifying registers*
   To display and modify the contents of registers, the command to be used is:

   RM [p,x,y,a,b,c,s]

   The letters inside the brackets are p for program counter, x and y index registers, a and b accumulators, c the condition code register and s the stack pointer. To see all the registers, the bracketed term is omitted.
8. *Getting help*
   If the following command is typed, the screen shows all the monitor commands:

   H

Similar monitor programs are available for use with the evaluation boards of other manufacturers. For example, Microchip supply a development kit, PICSTART-16C, consisting of an evaluation board with a PIC16C64 microcontroller, an assembler, a simulator and host software.

9.4 In-circuit emulation

A microprocessor or microcontroller *in-circuit emulator* is a tool that enables code to be developed and debugged while running the program with the actual hardware to be used for the system. The microcontroller in the system is replaced by having a special pod which will behave as though it is the microprocessor or microcontroller in the system with the program burnt into its EPROM, hence it is able to test the program. Figure 9.4 shows the general arrangement of system and emulator and Fig. 9.5 shows the general connections to an emulator. The evaluation board referred to in Section 9.3 can be used as a low cost emulator. Emulators are very good at determining bugs but those which can match the microcontroller speed do have the disadvantage of being expensive.

A low cost emulator is likely to have:

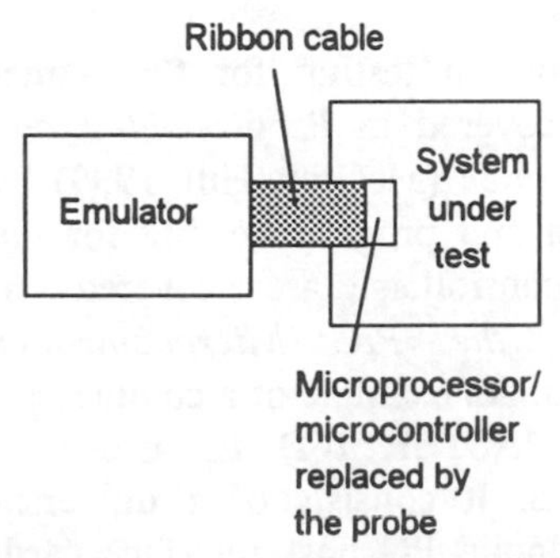

Fig. 9.4 Connecting the emulator to the system under test

1. An identical microprocessor or microcontroller to the device running the program in the system under development.

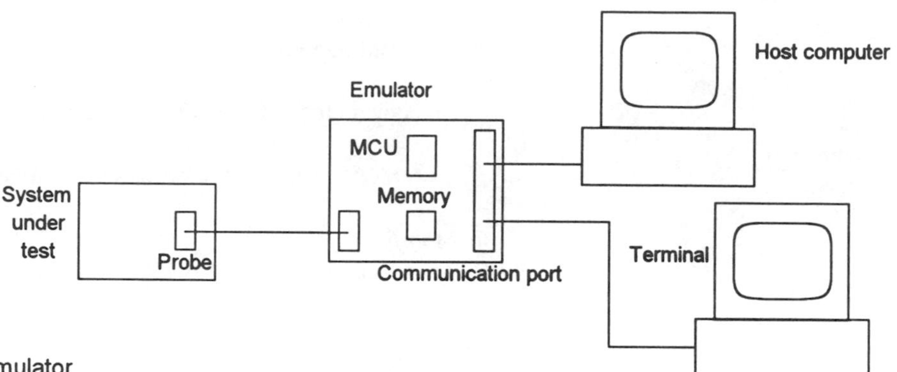

Fig. 9.5 Using an emulator

2. Memory chips which the microprocessor or microcontroller can use for data and program memory.
3. An input/output port to enable connections to be made with the hardware of the system under test. The input/output lines of the board are connected via a ribbon cable from its input/output port to a pod. The microprocessor or microcontroller in the system being tested is removed and the pod plugged in. The system under test then operates as though the microprocessor or microcontroller is plugged into it. The emulator is already programmed with a monitor program which enables the application program to be monitored at a terminal and the contents of memory, registers, and input/output ports to be checked and modified.
4. A communications port to enable communications between the microcontroller monitor program and a personal computer. The program code can be written in a host computer and then downloaded through either a serial or a parallel link into the memory on the board. The microcontroller then operates as though this program is contained within its own internal memory.

Emulator construction and program testing for the Atmel AT89C2051 microcontroller are covered in *Programming and Customising the 8051 Microcontroller* (McGraw-Hill 1999) by M. Predko. Emulator construction and program testing for the PIC16C61 and 16C71 microcontrollers are covered in *Programming and Customising the PIC Microcontroller* (McGraw-Hill 1998) by M. Predko. An example of a commercial emulator is the Microchip PICMASTER 16D for use with PIC16C71 microcontroller systems. It consists of a universal emulator pod, universal power supply, PC host interface card, connecting cables and an assembler.

9.5 EPROM programming

Having obtained a debugged application program, the next step for its use in an embedded system is to arrange for a manufacturer to make a ROM containing the program – only economical if there is a need for a large number of these chips – or to transfer it to the EPROM/EEPROM of the application hardware. This might involve the EPROM/EEPROM within a microcontroller or separate EPROMs in the system.

9.5.1 Programming an EPROM

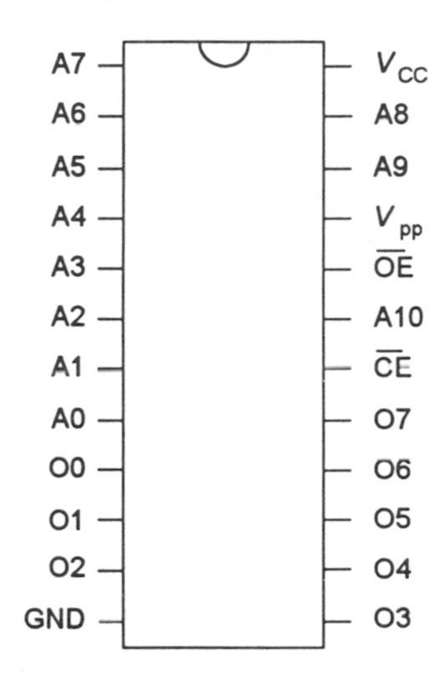

Fig. 9.6 Intel 2716

An example of an EPROM that might be used with a microprocessor system is the Intel 2716 (Fig. 9.6) (see Fig. 1.22 for a system using such a chip). Initially, and after an erasure, the bits are all 1. Data is introduced by selectively programming 0s into the desired bit locations. Erasure, i.e. the changing of 0s to 1s, is by exposure to ultraviolet light. To program:

1. Set the programming voltage pin V_{pp} to 25 V and OE to high.
2. Set up the address of the location to be programmed on A0–10.
3. Set up the 8 bit data to be programmed on the O_0–O_7 outputs.
4. Apply a 50 ms active-low TTL pulse (see Section 1.2) to the CE input.
5. Repeat steps 2, 3 and 4 until all locations have been programmed.

The above sequence is normally carried out using an EPROM programmer. Software supplied with the programmer enables a binary file to be copied into the EPROM. To read the EPROM and verify the program:

1. OE is tied to ground, i.e. held low, and V_{pp} is tied to 5 V.
2. The address is sent to the address bus A0–A10 using the instruction LDA.
3. The chip enable pin CE is brought low.

9.5.2 Programming the EPROM of a microcontroller

The Intel 8051 microcontroller has its own EPROM. To program it, the arrangement shown in Fig. 9.7 is required. There must be a 4–6 MHz oscillator input. The procedure is then as follows:

1. The address of an EPROM location, to be programmed in the range 0000H to 0FFFH, is applied to port 1 and pins P2.0 and P2.1 of port 2; at the same time, the code byte to be programmed into that address is applied to port 0.

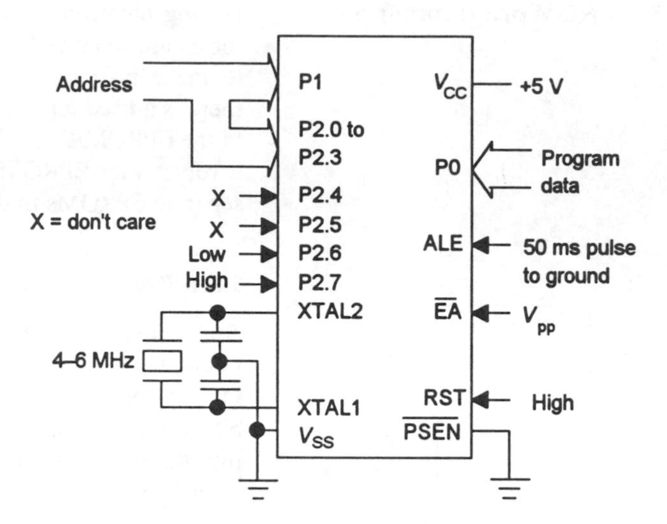

Fig. 9.7 Programming the 8051

2. Pins P2.7, RST and ALE should be held high, pins P2.6 and PSEN low. For pins P2.4 and P2.5 it does not matter whether they are high or low.
3. Pin EA/V_{pp} is held at a logic high until just before ALE is to be pulsed, then it is raised to +21 V, ALE is pulsed low for 50 ms to program the code byte into the addressed location, and then EA is returned to a logic high.

Verification of the program, i.e. reading out of the program, is achieved by the arrangement shown in Fig. 9.8.

1. The address of the program location to be read is applied to port 1 and pins P2.0 to P2.3 of port 2.
2. Pins EA/V_{pp}, RST and ALE should be held high, pins P2.7, P2.6 and PSEN low. For pins P2.4 and P2.5 it does not matter whether they are high or low.
3. The contents of the addressed location come out on port 0.

A security bit can be programmed to deny electrical access by any external means to the on-chip program memory. Once this bit has been programmed, it can only be cleared by the full erasure of the program memory. The same arrangement is used as for programming (Fig. 9.7) but P2.6 is held high. Erasure is by exposure to ultraviolet light. Since sunlight and fluorescent lighting contain some ultraviolet light, prolonged exposure (about 1 week in sunlight or 3 years in room-level fluorescent lighting) should be avoided and the chip window should be shielded by an opaque label.

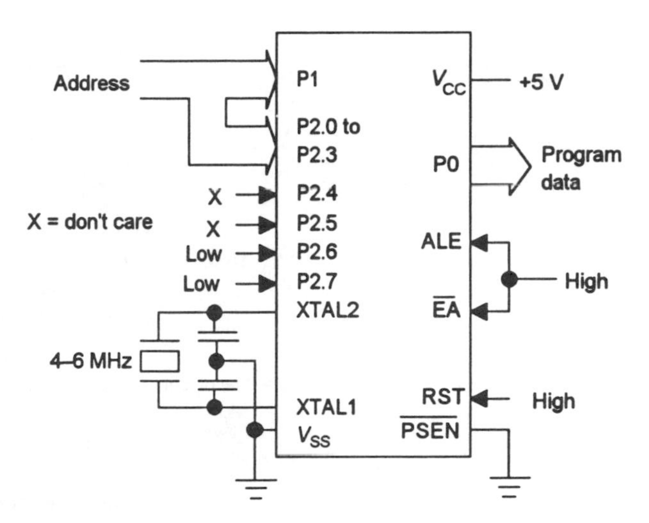

Fig. 9.8 Verification with the 8051

To aid in carrying out the above steps to program an internal EPROM, a separate programmer can be used. This involves running a program on a PC. The application program that is to be loaded into the EPROM is loaded into the PC memory and then, by typing in appropriate commands or using a mouse to select commands from menus in a Windows form of programmer, the erasure and loading can proceed. One such program is used with PIC microcontrollers. From the PICSTART menu ENABLE PROGRAMMER is selected. In one display window you can see the program currently in memory. In another window you can set up the details of how the PIC is to be programmed, selecting such details as the type of PIC and the type of oscillator to be used. The next step is to select IMPORT and then DOWNLOAD TO MEMORY, find the .hex file which the assembler has produced and click OK. A window will emerge showing the progress of the programming.

9.5.3 Programming the EEPROM of the Motorola 68HC11

The Motorola 68HC11 microcontroller is available with an internal electrically erasable programmable read-only memory (EEPROM). The EEPROM is located at addresses $B600 to $B7FF. Like an EPROM, a byte is erased when all the bits are 1 and programming involves making particular bits 0. The EEPROM is enabled by setting the EEON bit in the CONFIG register (Fig. 9.9) to 1 and disabled by setting it to 0. Programming is controlled by the EEPROM programming register (PPROG) (Fig. 9.10). The procedure for programming is:

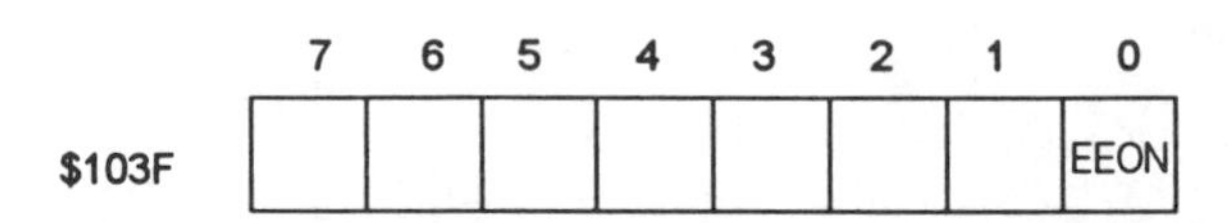

Fig. 9.9 CONFIG

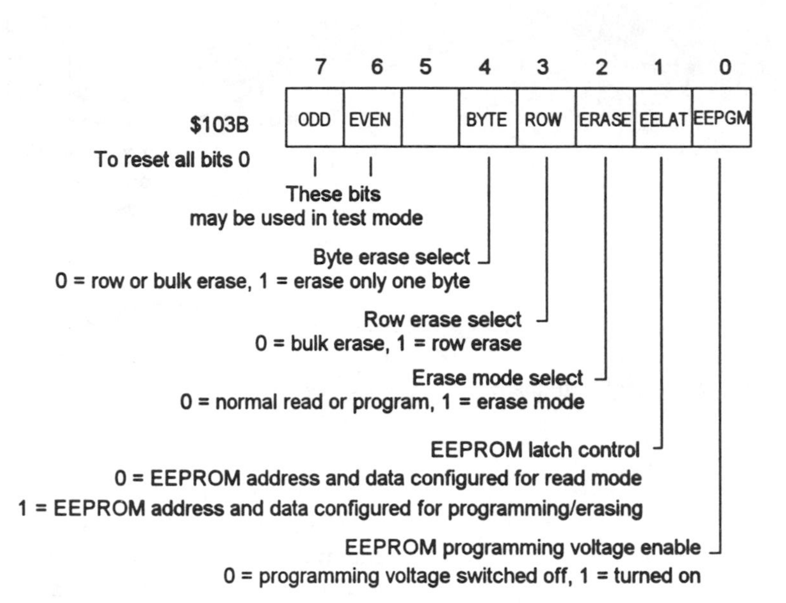

Fig. 9.10 PPROG

1. Write to the PPROG register to set the EELAT bit to 1 for programming.
2. Write data to the EEPROM address selected. This latches in the address and data to be programmed.
3. Write to the PPROG register to set the EEPGM bit to 1 to turn on the programming voltage.
4. Delay for 10 ms.
5. Write to the PPROG register to turn off, i.e. to 0, all the bits.

The procedure for erasure is:

1. Write to the PPROG register to select for erasure of a byte, row or the entire EEPROM.
2. Write to an EEPROM address within the range to be erased.
3. Write a 1 to the PPROG register to turn on the EEPGM bit and hence the erase voltage.
4. Delay for 10 ms.
5. Write 0s to the PPROG register to turn off all the bits.

Here, in assembly language, is a programming sub- routine for use with the MC68HC11:

```
EELAT       EQU    %00000010    ; EELAT bit
EEPGM       EQU    %00000001    ; EEPGM bit
PPROG       EQU    $1028        ; address of PPROG register

EEPROG
            PSHB
            LDAB   #EELAT
            STAB   PPROG        ; set EELAT = 1 and EEPGM = 0
            STAA   0,X          ; store data X to EEPROM address
            LDAB   #%00000011
            STAB   PPROG        ; set EELAT = 1 and EEPGM = 1
            JSR    DELAY_10     ; jump to delay 10 ms subroutine
            CLR    PPROG        ; clear all the PPROG bits and return to the read mode
            PULB
            RTS

; subroutine for approximately 10 ms delay
DELAY_10
            PSHX
            LDX    #2500        ; count for 20 000 cycles
DELAY       DEX
            BNE    DELAY
            PULX
            RTS
```

Here is a subroutine for bulk EEPROM erasure:

```
ROW         EQU    %00001000    ; ROW bit
ERASE       EQU    %00000100    ; ERASE bit
EELAT       EQU    %00000010    ; EELAT bit
EEPGM       EQU    %00000001    ; EEPGM bit
PPROG       EQU    $1028        ; PPROG register address
EEPROM      EQU    $B600        ; EEPROM location

BULK_ERASE
            PSHB
            LDAB   #%00000110
            STAB   PPROG        ; set EELAT = 1, ERASE = 1, EEPGM = 0 for bulk erase
            STAB   EEPROM       ; store data to any location
            LDAB   #%00000111
            STAB   PPROG        ; turn on voltage for erasure
            JSR    DELAY_10     ; delay for 10 ms
            CLR    PPROG        ; clear all bits to return to read mode
            PULB
            RTS

; subroutine for approximately 10 ms delay
DELAY_10
            PSHX
            LDX    #2500        ; count for 20 000 cycles
DELAY       DEX
            BNE    DELAY
            PULX
            RTS
```

This subroutine is to erasure a row in EEPROM:

```
ROW          EQU    %00001000     ; ROW bit
ERASE        EQU    %00000100     ; ERASE bit
EELAT        EQU    %00000010     ; EELAT bit
EEPGM        EQU    %00000001     ; EEPGM bit
PPROG        EQU    $1028         ; PPROG register address
EEPROM       EQU    $B600         ; EEPROM location

EEROW_ERASE
             PSHB
             LDAB   #%00001110
             STAB   PPROG         ; set ROW = 1, ERASE = 1, EELAT = 1 for row erase
             STAB   0,X           ; set row address to be erased
             LDAB   #%00001111
             STAB   PPROG         ; turn on erase voltage
             JSR    DELAY_10      ; 10 ms delay
             CLR    PPROG         ; clear all bits
             PULB
             RTS

; subroutine for approximately 10 ms delay
DELAY_10
             PSHX
             LDX    #2500         ; count for 20 000 cycles
DELAY        DEX
             BNE    DELAY
             PULX
             RTS
```

This subroutine is to erase a byte in EEPROM:

```
BYTE         EQU    %00010000     ; BYTE bit
ERASE        EQU    %00000100     ; ERASE bit
EELAT        EQU    %00000010     ; EELAT bit
EEPGM        EQU    %00000001     ; EEPGM bit
PPROG        EQU    $1028         ; PPROG register address
EEPROM       EQU    $B600         ; EEPROM location

EEROW_ERASE
             PSHB
             LDAB   #%00010110
             STAB   PPROG         ; set BYTE = 1, ERASE = 1, EELAT = 1 for byte erase
             STAB   0,X           ; set byte address to be erased
             LDAB   #%0010111
             STAB   PPROG         ; turn on erase voltage
             JSR    DELAY_10      ; 10 ms delay
             CLR    PPROG         ; clear all bits
             PULB
             RTS

; subroutine for approximately 10 ms delay
DELAY_10
             PSHX
             LDX    #2500         ; count for 20 000 cycles
```

```
DELAY       DEX
            BNE     DELAY
            PULX
            RTS
```

Problems

1. What are the limitations of simulation for testing software?
2. Explain how you could use an evaluation board and monitor program to test a program you have written.
3. What is the reason for introducing breakpoints in software that is being tested?
4. What is the logic level of an erased bit in EPROM?
5. How is the data in an EPROM erased?
6. Outline the steps needed to program an EPROM chip.
7. What is the purpose of programming the security bit of the EPROM in the Intel 8051 microcontroller?
8. Why is the chip window of the Intel 8051 microcontroller likely to be covered with an opaque label?
9. Some microcontrollers have EEPROM and not EPROM. What is the difference?
10. What is the logic level of an erased bit in EEPROM?
11. Which bits should be set for programming the EEPROM of a Motorola 68HC11 microcontroller to (a) select to erase a byte, (b) select to erase a row, (c) select to program address and data, (d) turn on the programming voltage.
12. Write a subroutine to program a byte into the EEPROM of a Motorola 68HC11 microcontroller.
13. Write a subroutine to erase a byte in the EEPROM of a Motorola 68HC11 microcontroller.

10 Interfacing

10.1 Introduction

When a microprocessor is used to control some system it has to accept input information, respond to it and produce output signals to implement the required control action. Thus there can be inputs from sensors to feed data in and outputs to external devices such as relays and motors. The term *peripheral* is used for a device, such as a sensor, keyboard, actuator, etc., which is connected to a microprocessor. It is, however, not normally possible to connect directly such peripheral devices to a microprocessor bus system due to a lack of compatibility in signal forms and levels. Because of such incompatibility, a circuit known as an *interface* is used between the peripheral items and the microprocessor. Figure 10.1 illustrates the arrangement. The interface is where this incompatibility is resolved.

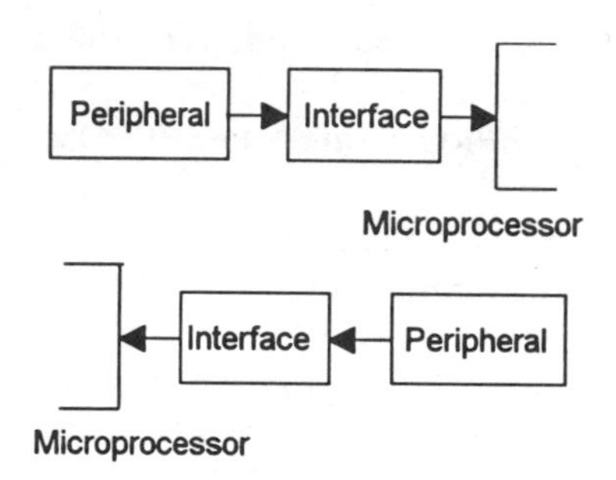

Fig. 10.1 The interfaces

This chapter is about the principles involved in interfacing microprocessors and microcontrollers with peripherals; Chapter 11 follows with further examples of commonly encountered input/output systems.

10.2 Input/output systems

Input/output systems are used to interface a microprocessor with peripheral devices. These may be constructed from individual chips and/or make use of a programmable universal interface. Microcontrollers are designed to include programmable input/output interfaces.

Both programmable input/output chips and microcontrollers handle input/output processing using registers. A register is used to store the next data to be sent out from the system; a register holds the most recently read data from an input.

10.2.1 Addressing inputs and outputs

One way of accessing a peripheral device which is connected to a microprocessor is for the peripheral device to look like a memory location to the microprocessor. With such a *memory-mapped* system, the input/output ports function as though they are memory, with each port being assigned one or more addresses; microprocessors generally use the same buses for both memory and input/output transfers. Thus with assembly language (see Section 6.6) for the Motorola 68HC11 the instruction to write data to an output port at address $1004 is:

```
STAA $1004
```

and to read data from an input port:

```
LDAA $1004
```

With C language we would just write statements to put the value in the output port address or statements to read the input port address, having first defined the port address in perhaps the header file. Thus for the output and input we can write:

```
PortB = 0x34h;  /*writes 34h to port B*/

x = PortB;  /*reads port B*/
```

Alternatives to memory mapping are *isolated input/output* in which memory and input/output addresses are separately decoded and *attached input/output* in which the input/output ports are activated by special instructions. The memory-mapped system is probably the most common and can be used with any microprocessor; the isolated input/output approach is only possible with those microprocessors that are specifically designed for this approach and have separate IN and OUT instructions, e.g. the Zilog Z80 (see Section 6.6).

10.2.2 Functions of input/output systems

Input/output systems may have to cope with data being transmitted as parallel or serial signals. Parallel systems require one data line for each bit, serial systems use only a single line. Buffering may be required to provide signals at the required current or voltage level. Also there may be a need to isolate the microprocessor or microcontroller from high voltages or high currents. Timing control can be needed when the data transfer rates of the peripheral and the microprocessor are different, e.g. when interfacing a microprocessor to a slower peripheral.

10.3 Buffers

The peripherals connected to the bus of a microprocessor system may require more current than can be supplied by the microprocessor. This problem may be overcome by connecting the peripherals to the bus by means of a *buffer* which acts as a current

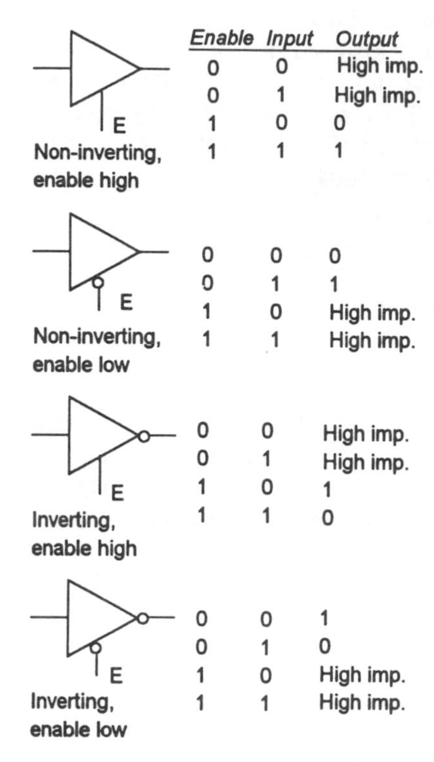

Fig. 10.2 Three-state buffers

amplifier. Thus, if the output of a microprocessor is connected to the base of a transistor, the base current required to switch the transistor is likely to be greater than the current which can be supplied by the microprocessor, so a buffer can be used to step up the current and also provide isolation between the microprocessor and the higher power system.

A conventional buffer would have an output which is one of two different logic states. However, often a number of peripheral devices have to share the same data lines from the microprocessor, i.e. they are connected to the data bus, and thus there is a need for the microprocessor to be able to enable just one of the devices at a time with the others disabled. This is achieved by using *tristate buffers*. The term *tristate* occurs because the output can be low, high or floating. This floating state is high impedance so that the output looks like an open circuit to anything connected to it. Figure 10.2 shows the symbols used.

A unidirectional buffer may be used where the data flow is either just out from or into the microprocessor, but bidirectional buffers will be needed where the data transfers have to take place in both directions. Figure 10.3 shows the basic circuit of a bidirectional buffer. When the enable input to the buffer is 0 then both buffers are high impedance. When enable is 1 then the direction of the data transfer may be selected by using the direction input. The term *bidirectional transceiver* is often used to describe such buffers.

Buffers are available as integrated packages. For example, the Texas Instruments SN74LS244 has eight non-inverting, enable high, buffers. The Texas Instruments SN74LS240 has eight inverting, enable high, buffers. The Texas Instruments SN74LS245 has eight bidirectional, enable high, buffers.

Figure 10.4 shows how buffers can be used with a microprocessor. Enabling of the bidirectional buffer can be under the control of the microprocessor; or EN can be earthed and so enabled and the direction is set via WR and RD. The other buffers are set in an enabled state.

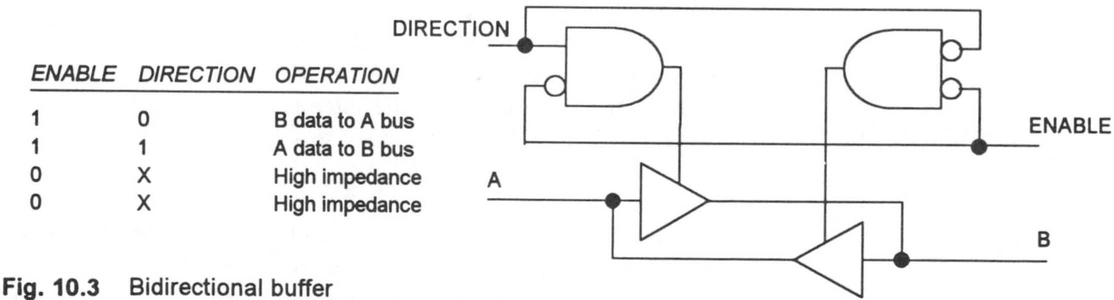

ENABLE	DIRECTION	OPERATION
1	0	B data to A bus
1	1	A data to B bus
0	X	High impedance
0	X	High impedance

Fig. 10.3 Bidirectional buffer

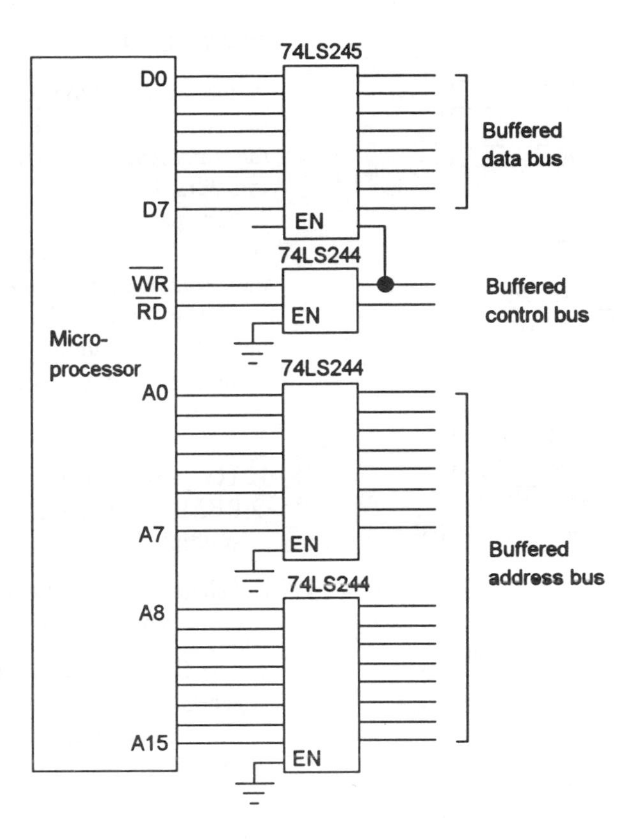

Fig. 10.4 Buffered microprocessor

10.4 Data transfer

Consider the problem of data transfer from or to a peripheral device. The CPU and the peripheral device must be synchronised so that the reading and writing occurs when the other is ready to transmit or receive the data. There are a number of methods by which this can be realised.

10.4.1 Software synchronisation

Consider the problem of using the output from a microprocessor or microcontroller to rotate a stepper motor. An output to rotate the stepper by one step cannot be followed immediately by an output to rotate by the next step since the stepper motor needs time to rotate. A simple solution is to insert a time delay in the program so that after rotating by one step the delay occurs before the next instruction to rotate by the next step. A software delay has thus been used to match the CPU to the timing requirements of the peripheral device. The problem with this approach is that the CPU cannot do anything else while it is wasting time in the delay subroutine.

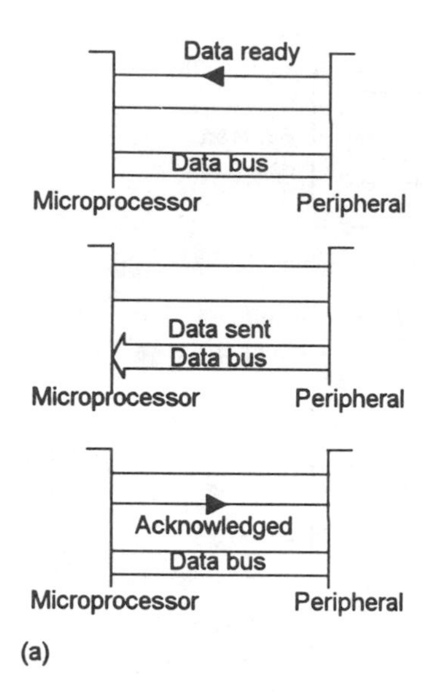

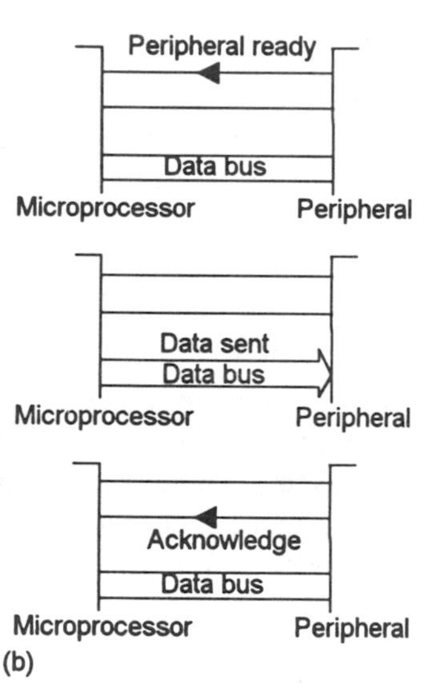

Fig. 10.5 Handshaking

10.4.2 Handshaking

A hardware method that can be used to achieve synchronisation is to use input/output lines, termed *handshake lines*, between the microprocessor and the peripheral to control the timing of data transfers; the process is termed *handshaking*.

For parallel data transfer, *strobe-and-acknowledge* is the commonly used form of handshaking. Readiness to receive is indicated then the data is sent. While it is being received the receiving device indicates not ready for further data; the receiver indicates ready again when the transfer has been completed. Here is the sequence for an input to a microprocessor from a peripheral (Fig. 10.5(a)):

1. The peripheral puts data on the data bus and sends a DATA READY signal, also called the strobe, to the microprocessor system.
2. When the CPU receives the DATA READY signal it knows there is data on the data bus.
3. The CPU then reads the data from the input/output section and sends an INPUT ACKNOWLEDGED signal to the peripheral. This signal indicates that the transfer has been completed and the peripheral can send more data.

Figure 10.6 illustrates the timing diagram for such a strobe-and-acknowledge handshaking.

Here is the sequence for an output from a microprocessor to a peripheral (Fig. 10.5(b)):

1. The peripheral sends an OUTPUT REQUEST or PERIPHERAL READY signal to the input/output section.
2. The CPU sees that the PERIPHERAL READY signal is active and sends the data to the peripheral.
3. The peripheral may then send an acknowledge signal or the next PERIPHERAL READY signal may be used to inform the CPU that the transfer has been completed.

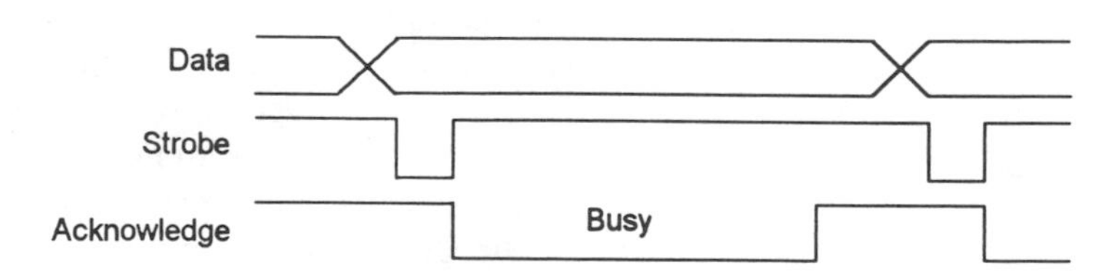

Fig. 10.6 Handshaking

We can implement handshaking with a microprocessor system by designating two of the input/output lines for the strobe and acknowledge signals. For example, with an Intel 8051 microcontroller we might use port 1 for the data transfer, port 3 bit 0 for the strobe signal and port 3 bit 1 for the acknowledge signal. The program would then have instructions such as:

```
DATA    EQU   P1
STROBE  EQU   P3.0
ACK     EQU   P3.1

        ...                 ; initial part of program
        ORL   P3,#03H       ; set strobe and ack. high
        ...                 ; get and output data
        CLR   STROBE        ; start strobe pulse
        SETB  STROBE        ; finish strobe pulse
WAIT    JNB   ACK,WAIT      ; wait for ack. signal
        ...                 ; continue program
```

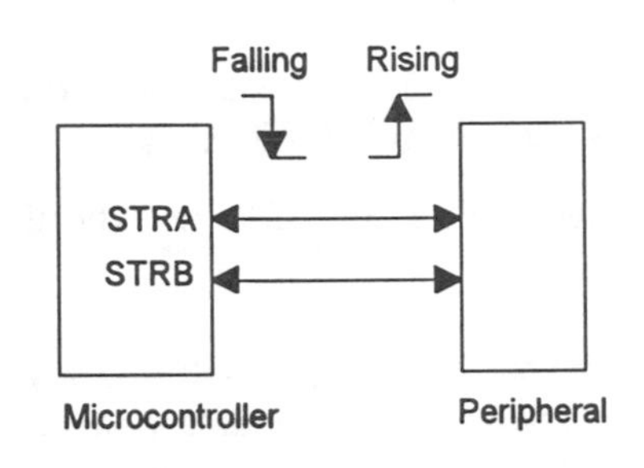

Fig. 10.7 Handshaking control

With the microcontroller MC68HC11, the handshaking control signals use pins STRA and STRB (Fig. 10.7), port C is used for the strobed input and port B for the strobed output. Before handshaking can occur, the parallel input/output register PIOC at address $1002 has to be first configured. Figure 10.8 shows the required states for the relevant bits in that register.

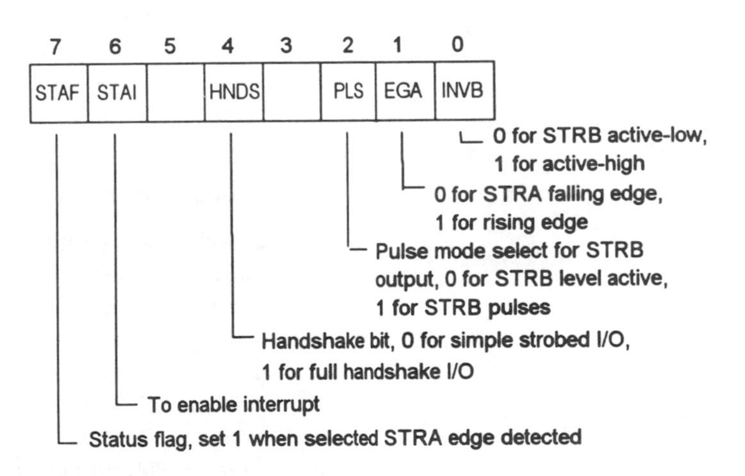

Fig. 10.8 PIOC

The basic strobed output operates as follows:

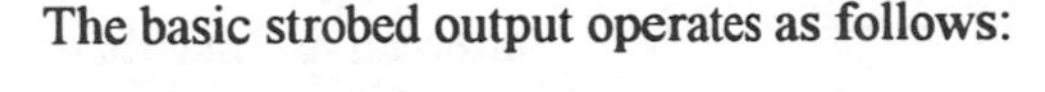

1. When data is ready to be sent by the microcontroller, a pulse is produced at STRB and sent to the peripheral device.
2. When the microcontroller receives either a rising or falling edge to a signal on STRA, the peripheral ready signal, then the microcontroller sends the data to the peripheral.

The basic strobed input operates as follows:

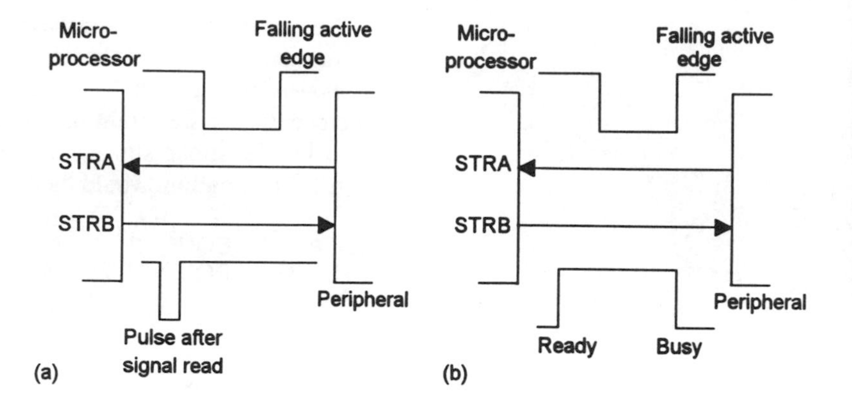

Fig. 10.9 Full handshaking: (a) pulsed, (b) interlocked

1. When data is ready to be transmitted to the microcontroller, the peripheral sends an edge signal on STRA that it is ready.
2. A pulse signal on STRB is then used by the CPU to indicate readiness to receive.

Full handshake input/output involves two signals being sent along STRB, the first indicates ready to receive data and the second indicates that the data has been read. This mode of operation requires that in PIOC the HNDS bit is set to 1. If PLS is set to 0 then the full handshake is said to be pulsed; whereas if PLS is set to 1 then it is interlocked. With pulsed operation a pulse is sent as acknowledgement, with interlocked STRB there is a reset (Fig.10.9).

10.4.3 Interrupts

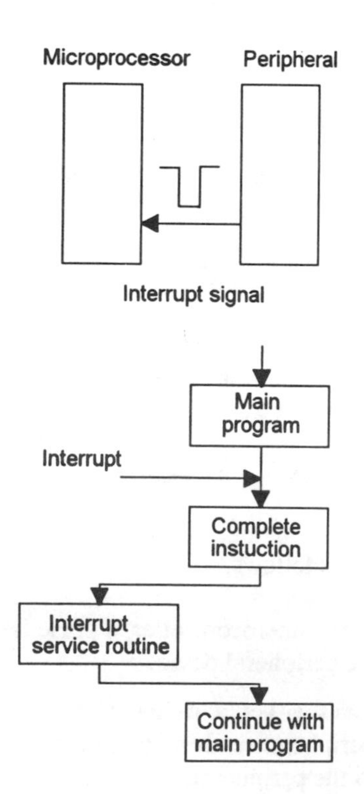

Fig. 10.10 Interrupt request

Another way peripherals and the CPU can be synchronised is by means of interrupts. Consider the problem of some event, such as the pressing of a key on a keyboard, being used as an input and having to initiate some action. We could write a program involving a loop with the system going round and round the loop and checking each time it reaches the input instruction as to whether there is an input. This repeated checking is termed *polling*. Polling may mean there is a significant time delay before obtaining a response to the input. There is, however, an alternative, and that is to use an interrupt. An *interrupt* is an event that requires the microprocessor to stop normal program execution when an interrupt event occurs, in order to handle the interrupt (Fig. 10.10). When an interrupt occurs:

1. The CPU waits until the end of the instruction it is currently executing before dealing with the interrupt.

2. All the CPU registers are pushed onto the stack and a bit set to stop further interrupts occurring during this interruption.
3. The CPU then determines the address of the interrupt service routine to be executed. Some microprocessors have dedicated interrupt pins and the pin that is chosen determines which address is to be used. Other microprocessors have only one interrupt pin and the interrupting device must then supply data that tells the microprocessor where the interrupt service routine is located. Some microprocessors have both kinds of interrupt inputs. The starting address of an interrupt service routine is called an *interrupt vector*. The block of memory assigned to store the vectors is known as the *vector table*. Vector addresses are fixed by the chip manufacturer.
4. The CPU branches to the interrupt service routine.
5. After completion of this routine, the CPU registers are returned from the stack and the main program continues from the point it left off.

Unlike a subroutine call, which is located at a specific point in a program, an interrupt can be called from any point in the program. Note that the program does not control when an interrupt occurs; control lies with the interrupting event.

Input/output operations frequently use interrupts since often the hardware cannot wait. For example, a keyboard may generate an interrupt input signal when a key is pressed. The microprocessor then suspends the main program to handle the input from the keyboard; it processes the information and then returns to the main program to continue from where it left off. This ability to code a task as an interrupt service routine and tie it to an external signal simplifies many control tasks, enabling them to be handled without delay.

For some interrupts it is possible to program the microprocessor to ignore the interrupt request signal unless an enable bit has been set. Such interrupts are termed *maskable*.

10.5 External interrupts

The following examples illustrate how external interrupts can be used with a range of microprocessors and microcontrollers.

1. *Zilog Z80*
   With the Zilog Z80, the non-maskable input NMI cannot be masked by the programmer and will always be executed on completion of the instruction currently being executed. The NMI is initiated by a negative-going transition and causes the interrupt service routine which follows from the interrupt vector 0066H to be executed. The return from the routine occurs when the instruction RETN is reached.

The other Z80 interrupt INT is maskable and is enabled by the enable interrupt instruction EI and disabled by the disable interrupt instruction DI. At the end of an interrupt service routine the instruction RETI is used to return to the main program. INT may operate in one of three modes: mode 0 is when the Z80 responds by asking the peripheral generating the interrupt for a single instruction, this is generally a branch to some specific location; mode 2 is when the interrupt service routine at address 0038H is to be executed; mode 2 is when the peripheral supplies a pointer to the address where the interrupt service routine can be found.

2. *Rockell 6502*
   The non-maskable interrupt is initiated by a negative-going transition input to the NMI pin and will always be executed on completion of the instruction currently being executed. When the NMI interrupt occurs, the CPU jumps to the interrupt service routine program whose interrupt vector is held at address $FFFE/F (the low and high bytes of the address). The other interrupt is the IRQ interrupt, initiated by a negative-going transition, and this is maskable. The interrupt vector is held at address $FFFA/B.

3. *Motorola 6800*
   The non-maskable interrupt is initiated by a negative-going transition input to the NMI pin and will always be executed on completion of the instruction currently being executed. When the NMI interrupt occurs, the CPU jumps to the interrupt service routine whose interrupt vector is held at address $FFFC/D (the low and high bytes of the address). The other interrupt is the IRQ interrupt, initiated by a negative-going transition, and this is maskable The interrupt vector is held at address $FFF8/9. To enable the interrupt, a clear interrupt mask instruction CLI must be used, and to mask it a set interrupt mask instruction SEI is used.

4. *Motorola 68HC11*
   The Motorola 68HC1 has two external interrupt request inputs. XIRQ is a a non-maskable interrupt and will always be executed on completion of the instruction currently being executed. When the XIRQ interrupt occurs, the CPU jumps to the interrupt service routine whose interrupt vector is held at address $FFF4/5 (the low and high bytes of the address). IRQ is a maskable interrupt. When the microcontroller receives a signal at the interrupt request pin IRQ by it going low, the microcontroller jumps to the interrupt service routine indicated by the interrupt vectors $FFF2/3. IRQ can be masked by the instruction set interrupt mask SEI and unmasked by the instruction clear interrupt mask CLI. At the end of an interrupt

service routine the instruction RTI is used to return to the main program.

5. *Intel 8051*
   With the Intel 8051, interrupt sources are individually enabled or disabled through the bit-addressable register IE (interrupt enable) at address 0A8H (Fig. 10.11). In addition there is a global enable/disable bit in the IE register that is set to enable all external interrupts or cleared to disable all external interrupts. The TCON register (Fig. 10.12) is used to determine the type of interrupt input signal that will initiate an interrupt.

7	6	5	4	3	2	1	0
EA		EA2	ES	ET1	EX1	ET0	EX0

EA	0 = disable all interrupts, 1 = enable all unmasked interrupts
ET2	0 = disable timer interrupt 2 interrupts, 1 = enable them
ES	0 = disable serial port interrupts, 1 = enable them
ET0, ET1	0 = disable timer overflow interrupt, 1 = enable
EX0, EX1	0 = disable external interrupts, 1 = enable

Fig. 10.11 IE register

7	6	5	4	3	2	1	0
TF1	TR1	TF0	TR0	IE1	IT1	IE0	IT0

TF0, TF1	Overflow flag, set and cleared by hardware
TR0, TR1	Run control bit set by software: 0 = timer off, 1 = timer on
IE0, IE1	Interrupt edge flag set by hardware
IT0, IT1	Interrupt type set by software: 1 = falling edge triggered, 0 = low level triggered

Fig. 10.12 TCON register

6. *PIC microcontroller*
   With the PIC microcontrollers, interrupts are controlled by the INTCON register (Fig. 10.13). To use bit 0 of port B as an interrupt, it must be set as an input and the INTCON register must be initialised with a 1 in INTE and a 1 in GIE. If the interrupt is to occur on a rising edge then INTEDG (bit 6) in the OPTION register (Fig. 10.14, also see Fig. 2.28) must be set to 1; if on a falling edge it must be set to 0. When an interrupt occurs, INTF is set. It can be cleared by the instruction bcf INTCON,INTF.

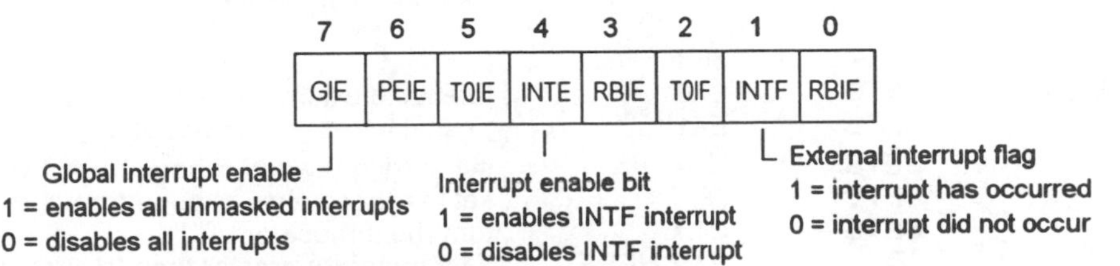

Fig. 10.13 INTCON

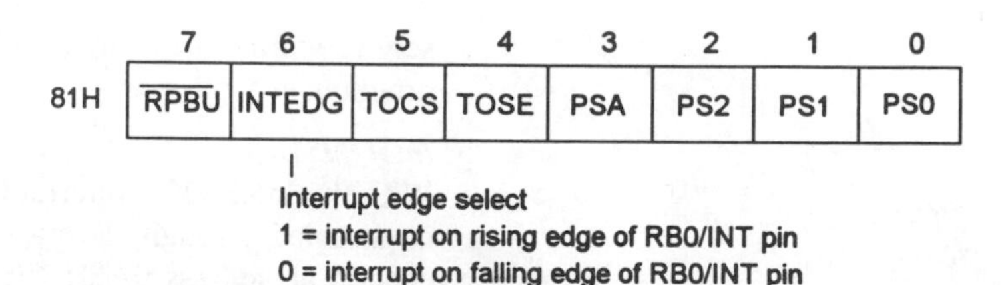

Fig. 10.14 OPTION register

As an illustration of a program involving external interrupts, consider a simple on/off control program for a central heating system involving an Intel 8051 microcontroller (Fig. 10.15). The central heating furnace is controlled by an output from P1.7 and two temperature sensors are used, one to determine when the temperature falls below, say, 20.5°C and the other when it rises above 21.0°C. The sensor for the 21.0°C temperature is connected to interrupt INT0, port 3.2, and the sensor for the 20.5°C temperature is connected to interrupt INT1, port 3.3 (see Fig. 2.16). By selecting the IT1 bit to be 1 in the TCON register, the external interrupts are edge-triggered, i.e. activated when there is a change from 1 to 0. When the temperature rises to 21.0°C the external interrupt INT0 has an input which changes from 1 to 0 and the interrupt is activated to give the instruction CLR P1.7 for a 0 output to turn the furnace off. When the temperature falls to 20.5°C the external interrupt INT1 has an input which changes from 0 to 1 and the interrupt is activated to give the instruction SETB P1.7 for a 1 output to turn the furnace on. The MAIN program is just a set of instructions to configure and enable the interrupts, establish the initial condition of the furnace to be on if the temperature is less than 21.0° or off if above, and then to wait doing nothing until an interrupt occurs. With the program, a header file has been assumed.

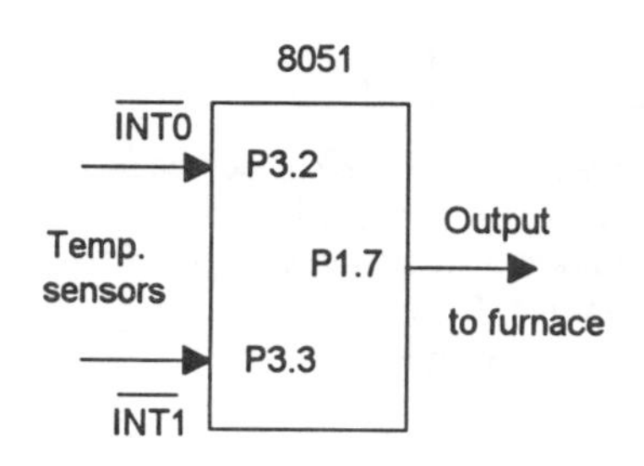

Fig. 10.15 Central heating system

```
        ORG     0
        LJMP    MAIN

        ORG     0003H      ; gives the entry address for ISR0
ISR0    CLR     P1.7       ; interrupt service routine to turn the furnace off
        RETI               ; return from interrupt

        ORG     0013H      ; gives the entry address for ISR1
ISR1    SETB    P1.7       ; interrupt service routine to turn furnace off
        RETI               ; return from interrupt

        ORG     30H
MAIN    SETB    EX0        ; to enable external interrupt 0
        SETB    EX1        ; to enable external interrupt 1
        SETB    IT0        ; set to trigger when change from 1 to 0
        SETB    IT1        ; set to trigger when change from 1 to 0
        SETB    P1.7       ; turn the furnace on
        JB      P3.2,HERE  ; if temperature greater than 21.0°C jump to HERE and
                           ; leave furnace on
```

```
        CLR     P1.7        ; turn the furnace off
HERE    SJMP    HERE        ; just doing nothing until an interrupt occurs
        END
```

10.5.1 Multiple interrupts

Microprocessors and microcontrollers have very few external interrupt pins and often there is a need for a greater number of different interrupting peripherals. One way this can be solved is for a number of peripherals to share the same interrupt pin; they are connected via an OR gate (Fig. 10.16) so that a high from any one of the peripherals will give a low to the interrupt. When an interrupt request is received then the microprocessor polls each peripheral to determine the source of the interrupt.

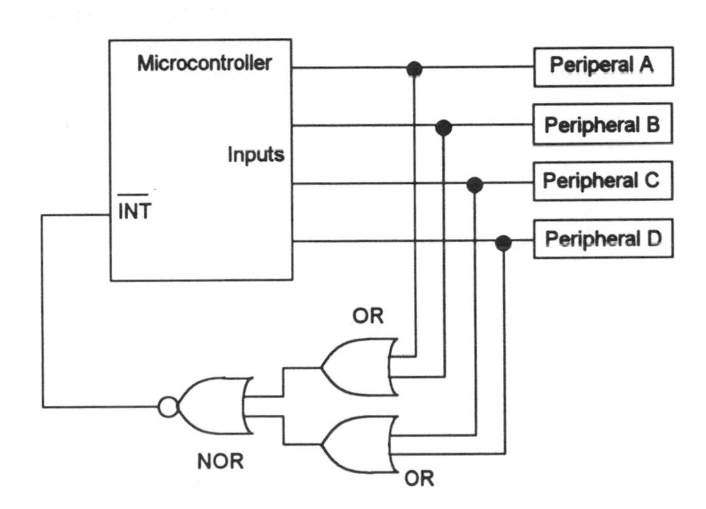

Fig. 10.16 Multiple peripherals

10.5.2 Interrupt priority

With a multiple-interrupt system a situation might arise where two peripherals simultaneously issue interrupt signals and thus a priority system is required. Non-maskable interrupts always have priority over maskable interrupts; the non-maskable interrupt is usually reserved for emergency routines that need to occur in the case of events such as power failure. But how can we order the priorities of maskable interrupts?

With a microcontroller such as the Intel 8051, which has a number of maskable interrupts, each interrupt source can be programmed to one of two priority levels by setting bits in interrupt priority register IP (Fig. 10.17). Clearing the register sets all to the lowest priority, then setting some of the bits makes those interrupts highest priority. A high priority interrupt will always take priority over a low priority interrupt.

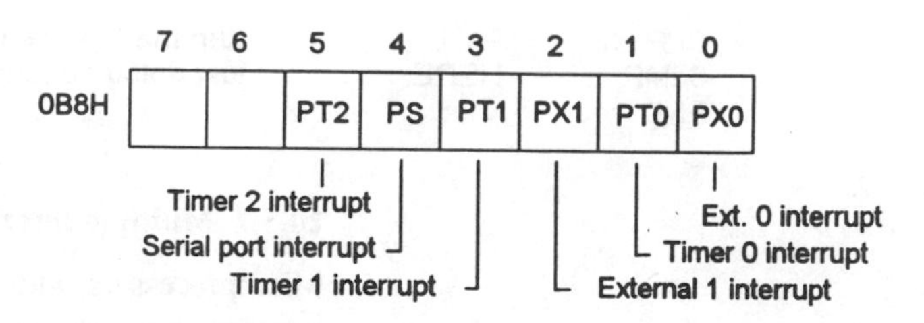

Fig. 10.17 IP register

In general with microprocessor systems, priorities can be allocated using a *priority encoder* such as the 74LS148. This has eight interrupt inputs 0 to 7, each of which is active low. Input 7 has the highest priority, input 1 the lowest. When one of the inputs is taken low, its corresponding three-bit binary code appears on the A0–A2 outputs and is used as part of the interrupt vector 0000xxx0. Also, the GS output is taken low to request an interrupt. Figure 10.18 shows how such a priority encoder might be used with a Z80 operating in mode 2.

Inputs									*Outputs*				
EI	*0*	*1*	*2*	*3*	*4*	*5*	*6*	*7*	*A2*	*A1*	*A0*	*GS*	*E0*
1	x	x	x	x	x	x	x	x	1	1	1	1	1
0	1	1	1	1	1	1	1	1	1	1	1	1	0
0	x	x	x	x	x	x	x	0	0	0	0	0	1
0	x	x	x	x	x	x	0	1	0	0	1	0	1
0	x	x	x	x	x	0	1	1	0	1	0	0	1
0	x	x	x	x	0	1	1	1	0	1	1	0	1
0	x	x	x	0	1	1	1	1	1	0	0	0	1
0	x	x	0	1	1	1	1	1	1	0	1	0	1
0	x	0	1	1	1	1	1	1	1	1	0	0	1
0	0	1	1	1	1	1	1	1	1	1	1	0	1

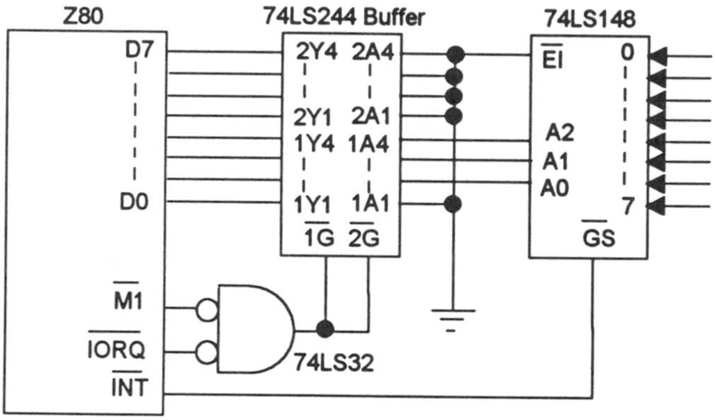

Fig. 10.18 Z80 with priority encoder

10.5.3 Resets

A *reset* is a special type of interrupt. When a reset signal occurs, the main program stops running and usually the registers and memory are reinitialised. It's a 'let's start all over again' signal. The Motorola 68HC11 microcontroller has four possible types of reset:

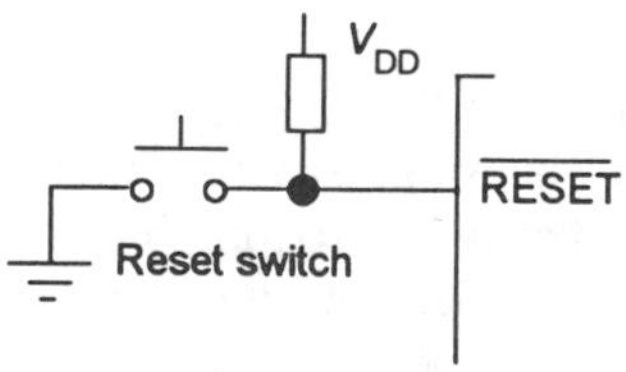

Fig. 10.19 Manual reset

1. *External reset pin*
   A low signal to this pin causes a reset action. Figure 10.19 shows a basic external reset circuit; the resistor is to maintain the pin high when the switch is open. A better circuit is shown in Fig. 10.20. MC34064 is a low voltage sensing circuit and

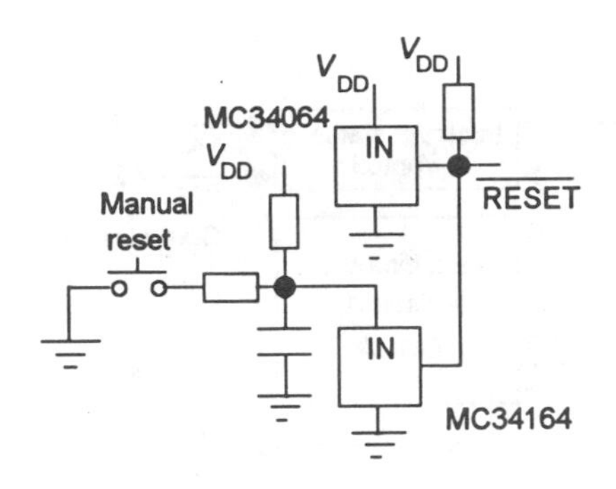

Fig. 10.20 External reset

holds reset low whenever V_{DD} is below the minimum operating voltage level for the microcontroller; MC34164 and the *RC* circuit provide a delay circuit with the manual reset switch. This delay is to allow time before the microcontroller starts operating for the power supply and crystal oscillator to stabilise after switching on. With PIC microcontrollers, the reset pin is designated master clear (MCLR).

2. *Power-on reset*
   This reset begins a short time after power has been applied to the microprocessor.
3. *Computer operating properly (COP)*
   The microcontroller has an internal watchdog timer. This is a timer which times out and resets the system if an operation is not concluded in what has been deemed a reasonable amount of time. It thus watches for those unreasonable delays which might occur as a result of a fault in the system.
4. *Clock monitor reset*
   This reset is triggered if the microcontroller clock drops below a frequency of 10 kHz.

10.6 Parallel interfaces

Output ports need to hold data ready for collection by peripherals, so they can be constructed using a latch, e.g. the 74LS373. Input ports do not require data storage, so they need only consist of tristate buffers, e.g. the LS244. Microcontrollers can be considered as microprocessors with input/output ports incorporated on the same chip. Microprocessors can have their input/output interfaces provided by discrete components or by a separate chip termed a *programmable peripheral interface*. Figure 10.21 shows the basic functions of these interfaces which provide two ports with handshake lines

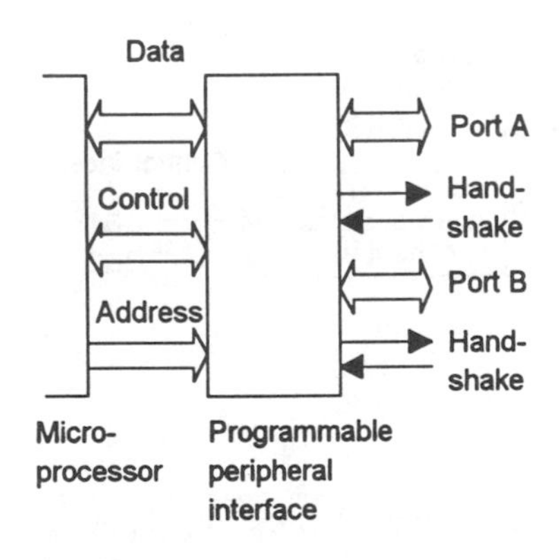

Fig. 10.21 Programmable peripheral interface

10.6.1 Motorola MC6821

A commonly used dedicated *peripheral interface adapter* (PIA) for use with microprocessors is the *Motorola MC6821*. It is part of the MC6800 family and thus can be directly attached to Motorola MC6800 and MC68HC11 buses. The device can be considered essentially as two parallel input/output ports, with their control logic, to link up with the host microprocessor. Figure 10.22 shows the basic structure of the MC6821 PIA and the pin connections. The PIA contains two 8 bit parallel data ports, termed A and B. Each port has:

1. *A peripheral interface register*
   This register is used temporarily to store data for output to a peripheral.

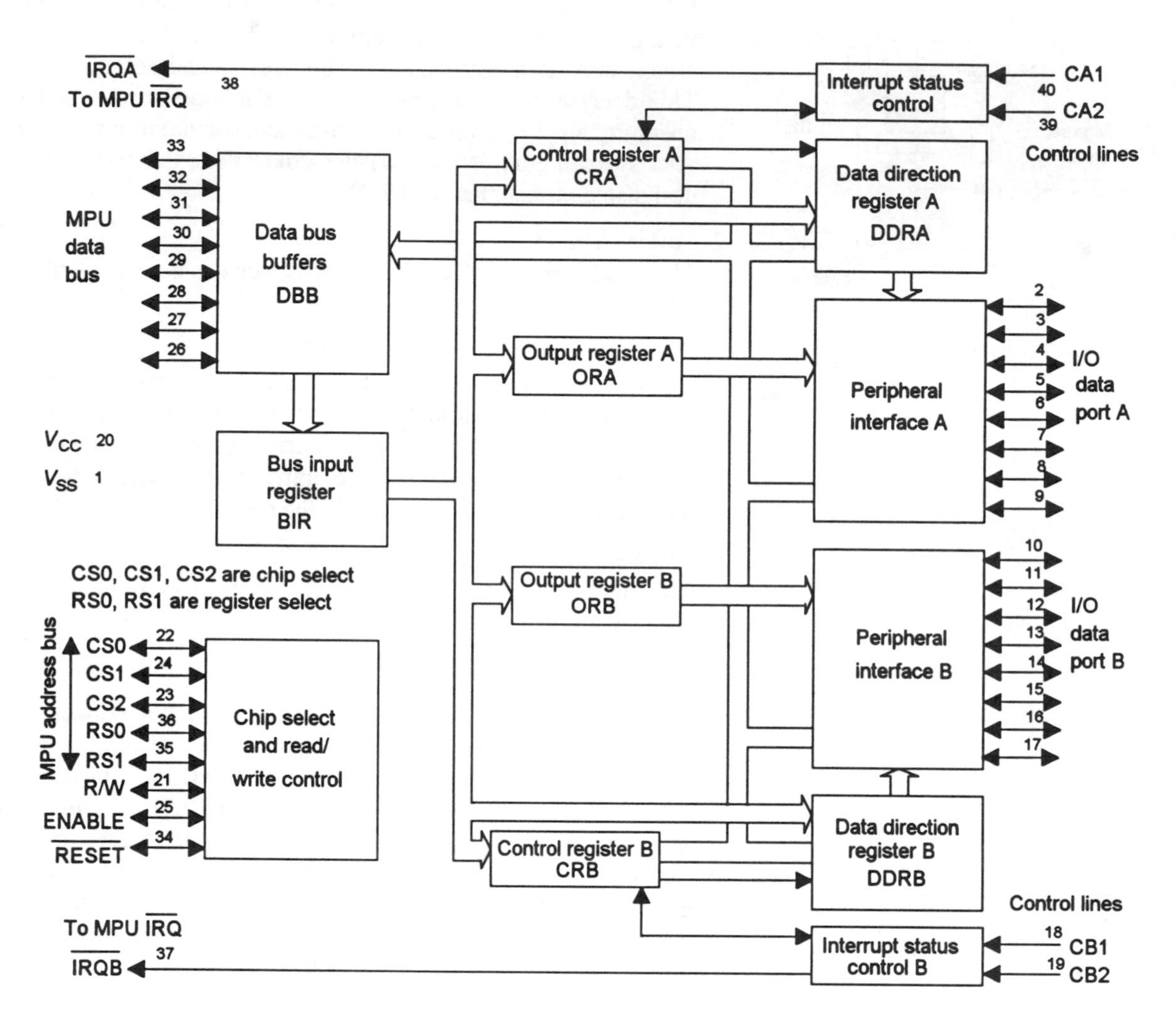

Fig. 10.22 MC6821 PIA

2. *A data direction register*
   This determines whether the input/output lines are inputs or outputs.

3. *A control register*
   Bits in this register are used to control the operations of the input/output ports.

4. *Two control lines*
   These are CA1 and CA2 or CB1 and CB2; they are used to control interrupts.

Two microprocessor address lines are connected to the PIA through the two register select lines RS0 and RS1. This gives the

PIA four addresses for the six registers. When RS1 is low then side A is addressed, and when RSI is high then side B. RS0 addresses registers on a particular side, i.e. A or B. When RS0 is high the control register is addressed, when RS0 is low it is the data register or the data direction register. For a particular side, the data register and the data direction register have the same address. Which of them is addressed is determined by bit 2 of the control register. Each of the bits in the A and B control registers is concerned with some features of the operation of the ports. Thus, for the A control register, we have the bits shown in Fig. 10.23. A similar pattern is used for the B control register.

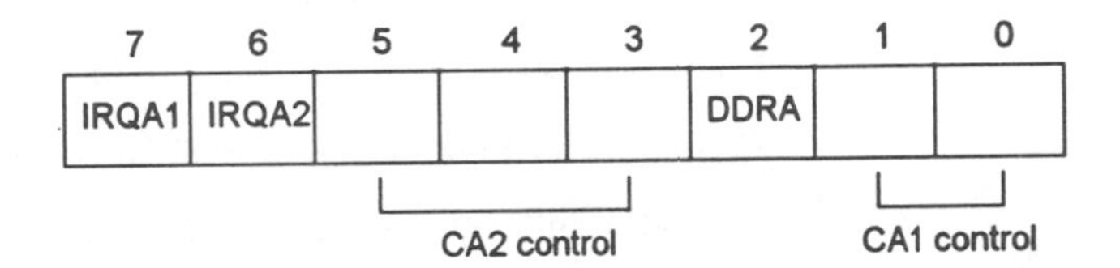

Bits 0 and 1
Bit 0 determines whether the interrupt output is enabled. B0 = 0 disables the IRQA(B) microprocessor interrupt, B0 = 1 enables the interrupt. CA1 and CB1 are not set by the static level of the input but are edge triggered, i.e. set by a changing signal. Bit 1 determines whether bit 7 is set by a high-to-low transition (a trailing edge) or a low-to-high transition (a leading edge): B1 = 0 a high-to-low transition, B1 = 1 a low-to-high transition.

Bit 2
Bit 2 determines whether data direction registers or peripheral data registers are addressed: B2 = 0 data direction registers, B2 = 1 peripheral data registers.

Bits 3, 4 and 5
These bits allow the PIA to perform a variety of functions. Bit 5 determines whether control line 2 is an input or an output. If bit 5 = 0 control line 2 is an input, if bit 5 = 1 it is an output. In input mode, both CA2 and CB2 operate in the same way. Bits 3 and 4 determine whether the interrupt output is active and which transitions set bit 6.
With B5 = 0: B3 = 0 disables IRQA(B) microprocessor interrupt by CA2(CB2), B3 = 1 enables IRQA(B) microprocessor interrupt by CA2(CB2); B4 = 0 determines that the interrupt flag IRQA(B), bit B6, is set by a high-to-low transition on CA2(CB2), B4 = 1 determines that it is set by a low-to-high transition.
With B5 = 1: CA2 and CB2 behave differently. For CA2: with B4 = 0 and B3 = 0, CA2 goes low on the first high-to-low ENABLE (E) transition following a microprocessor read of peripheral data register A and is returned high by the next CA1 transition; B4 = 0 and B3 = 1, CA2 goes low on the first high-to-low ENABLE transition following a microprocessor read of the peripheral data register A and is returned to high by the next high-to-low ENABLE transition. For CB2: with B4 = 0 and B3 = 0, CB2 goes low on the first low-to-high ENABLE transition following a microprocessor write into peripheral data register B and is returned to high by the next CB1 transition; B4 = 0 and B3 = 1, CB2 goes low on the first low-to-high ENABLE transition following a microprocessor write into peripheral data register B and is returned high by the next low-to-high ENABLE transition. With B4 = 1 and B3 = 0, CA2(CB2) goes low as the microprocessor writes B3 = 0 into the control register. With B4 = 0 and B3 = 1, CA2(CB2) goes high as the microprocessor writes B3 = 1 into the control register.

Bit 6
This is the CA2(CB2) interrupt flag, being set by transitions on CA2(CB2). With CA2(CB2) as an input (B5 = 0), it is cleared by a microprocessor read of the data register A(B). With CA2(CB2) as an output (B5 = 1), the flag is 0 and is not affected by CA2(CB2) transitions.

Bit 7
This is the CA1(CB1) interrupt flag, being cleared by a microprocessor read of data register A(B).

Fig. 10.23 Control register

The process of selecting which options are to be used is termed *configuring* or *initialising* the PIA. Before the PIA can be used, this initialisation program has to set the conditions for the desired peripheral data flow, so it is placed at the beginning of the main program; thereafter, the microprocessor can read peripheral data. Therefore the initialisation program is only run once.

The initialisation program to set which port is to be input and which is to be output can have the following steps:

1. Clear bit 2 of each control register by a reset so that data direction registers are addressed; data direction register A is addressed as XXX0 and data direction register B as XXX2.
2. For A to be an input port, load all 0s into direction register A.
3. For B to be an output port, load all 1s into direction register B.
4. Load 1 into bit 2 of both control registers so that peripheral data registers are addressed; peripheral data register A is now addressed as XXX0 and peripheral data register B as XXX2.

Thus, following a reset, an initialisation program in assembly language to make side A an input and side B an output could be:

```
INIT    LDAA    #$00     ; load 0s
        STAA    $2000    ; make side A input port
        LDAA    #$FF     ; load 1s
        STAA    $2000    ; make side B output port
        LDAA    #$04     ; load 1 into bit 2, all other bits 0
        STAA    $2000    ; select port A data register
        STAA    $2002    ; select port B data register
```

Peripheral data can now be read from input port A with the instruction LDAA 2000 and the microprocessor can write peripheral data to output port B with the instruction STAA 2002.

Figure 10.24 shows a basic arrangement of how the PIA might be interfaced with a 6802 microprocessor; the PIA is not connected for any handshaking or interrupts but just to provide two input/output ports. With this arrangement, the address line A14 must be 1 and A15 must be 0. The registers in the PIA are selected by address lines A0 and A1. Thus the addresses used for the PIA are 0100 0000 0000 to 0100 0000 0011, i.e. in hex 4000 to 4003.

The Motorola MC6821 PIA has two connections IRQA and IRQB through which interrupt signals can be sent to the microprocessor so that an interrupt request from CA1, CA2 or CB1, CB2 can drive the IRQ pin of the microprocessor to the active-low state. When the initialisation program for a PIA was considered above, only bit 2 of the control register was set as 1, the other bits being 0. These 0s disabled interrupt inputs.

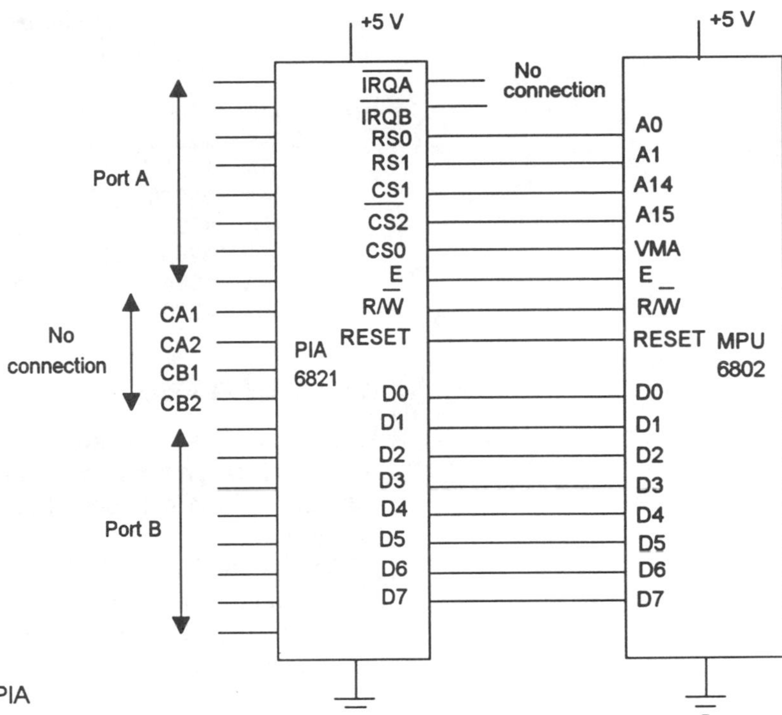

Fig. 10.24 Interfacing with a PIA

In order to use interrupts, the initialisation step which stores $04 into the control register must be modified. The form of the modification will depend on the type of change in the input which is required to initiate the interrupt. Suppose we want CA1 to enable an interrupt when there is a high-to-low transition, with CA2 and CB1 not used and CB2 enabled and used for a set/reset output. For CA the control register format to meet this specification is:

B0 is 1 to enable interrupt on CA1.
B1 is 0 so that the interrupt flag IRQA1 is set by a high-to-low transition on CA1.
B2 is 1 to give access to the data register.
B3, B4, B5 are 0 because CA2 is disabled.
B6, B7 are read-only flags and thus a 0 or 1 may be used.

Hence the format for CA1 can be 00000101, which is 05 in hexadecimal notation. The control register format for CB2 is:

B0 is 0 to disable CB1.
B1 may be 0 or 1 since CB1 is disabled.
B2 is 1 to give access to the data register.
B3 is 0, B4 is 1 and B5 is 1, to select the set/reset.
B6, B7 are read-only flags and thus a 0 or 1 may be used.

Hence the format for CA1 can be 00110100, which is 34 in hex notation. The initialisation program might then read:

```
INIT  LDAA  #$00   ; load 0s
      STAA  $2000  ; make side A input port
      LDAA  #$FF   ; Load 1s
      STAA  $2000  ; Make side B output port
      LDAA  #$05   ; Load the required control register format
      STAA  $2000  ; Select port A data register
      LDAA  #$34   ; Load the required control register format
      STAA  $2002  ; Select port B data register
```

10.6.2 Zilog Z80 PIO

Another example of a programmable parallel interface is the *Zilog Z80 PIO* (programmable input/output). Figure 10.25 shows a diagram of the pin connections and a block diagram of the architecture.

The Z80 PIO has two bidirectional ports, A and B, which can be programmed for input or output. In addition to the two sets of eight bidirectional input/output lines, there are two sets of lines for handshaking between the input/output device and the PIO. Six control lines to the microprocessor control the PIO operations. PORT A/B SEL selects port A or port B. CONTROL/DATA SEL selects the transfer of either control data or operand data to the PIO. CHIP ENABLE is the signal to the PIO that is used to indicate that the PIO address has been selected. M1, IORQ and RD are connected to the corresponding pins on a Z80 microprocessor to supply control signals. There are three interrupt control signals. The clock input signal is the clock signal from the microprocessor.

Each port may operate in one of four modes, selected by the contents of the mode-control registers: mode 0 is byte output, mode 1 is byte input, mode 2 is byte bidirectional bus and mode 3 is bit mode. Port A may operate in any one of these modes, port B in all except mode 2. Each port has an input/output select register which is used to specify which of the bits in each port are to be inputs and which outputs. A 0 in a bit position is used to give an output, a 1 an input. There is also a mask control register which is used in mode 3 to allow input/ output lines to operate as interrupt inputs. With the Z80 PIO all the control words are sent to the same input/output address and it is the sequencing of the words sent which indicates to the PIO which control register is being configured.

To set the mode, bits 0, 1, 2 and 3 of the control word (Fig. 10.26) are set to 1s to indicate that the control word is setting the mode, and bits 6 and 7 of the control word are used to indicate which mode.

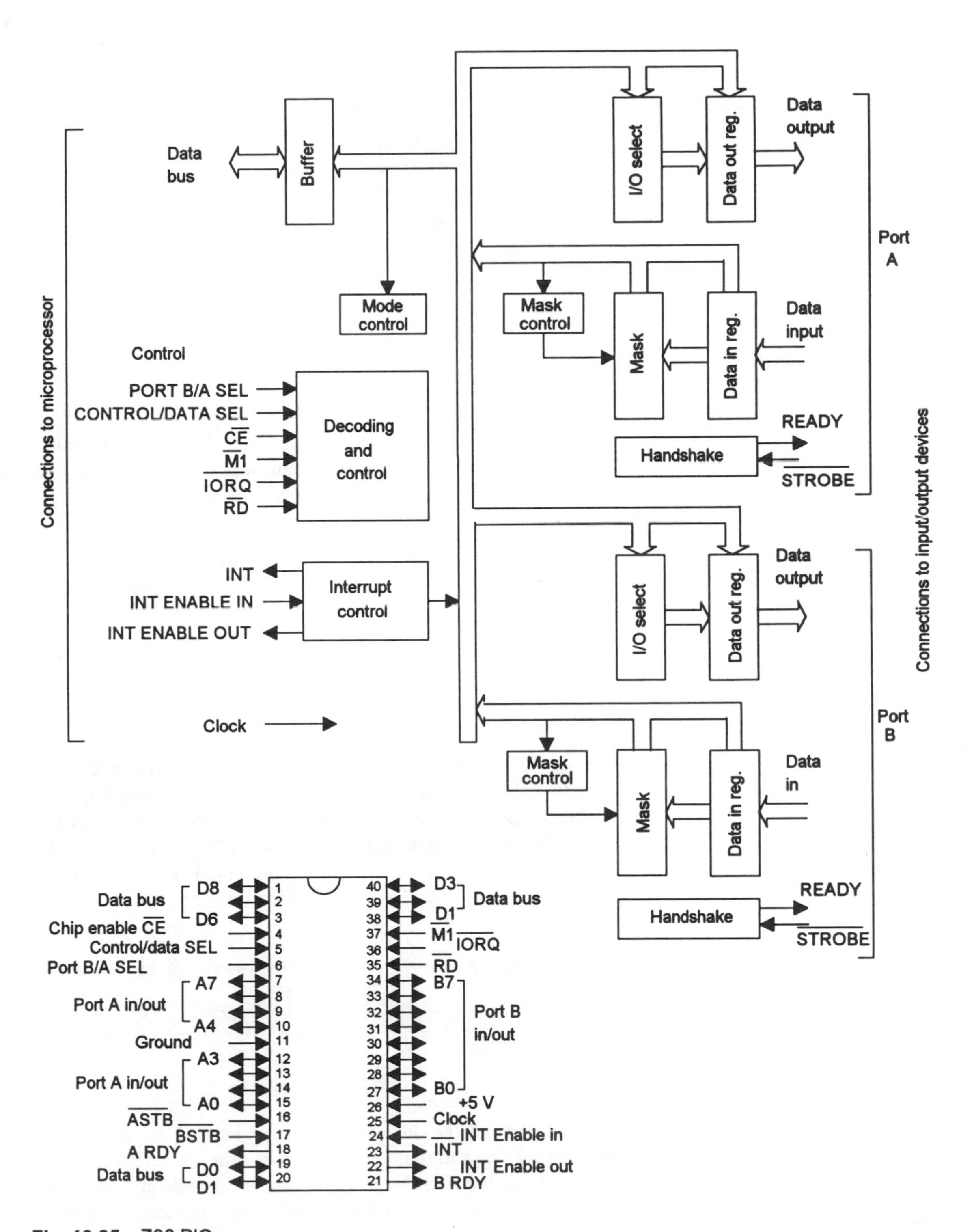

Fig. 10.25 Z80 PIO

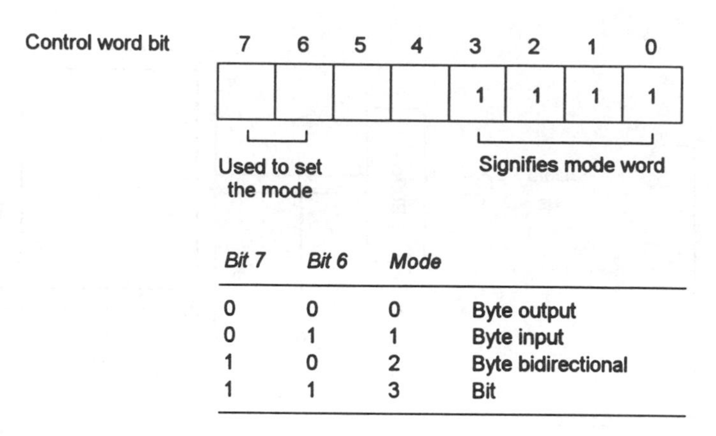

Bit 7	*Bit 6*	*Mode*	
0	0	0	Byte output
0	1	1	Byte input
1	0	2	Byte bidirectional
1	1	3	Bit

Fig. 10.26 Mode setting

1. *Mode 0* is the output mode. In mode 0 the 8 bit data output register is active and the 8 bit data input register is inactive. Data may be written to the output register by addressing the port.
2. *Mode 1* is the input mode. When a port is in this mode, the data input register is active and the data output register is inactive.
3. *Mode 2* is the bidirectional mode and only port A may be used for this mode. With this mode, the port A handshake lines are used for the output operations and the port B handshake lines for the input operations.
4. *Mode 3* is used for bit, rather than byte, operations. After setting the mode by the control word, a second control word is then loaded to the PIO address. In this word, each bit corresponds to a port input/output line (Fig. 10.27). If the control bit is 0 then the corresponding bit in the port is an output; if the control bit is 1 then the correspodning bit is an input.

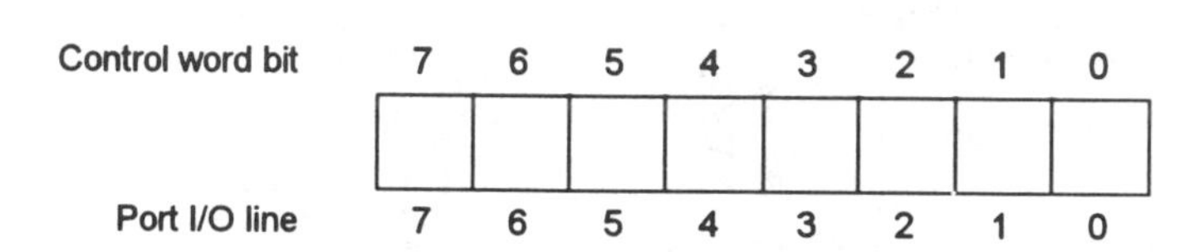

Fig. 10.27 Mode 3 I/O programming

Each port of the PIO may be programmed to provide an external interrupt to the microprocessor. When a load instruction for a control word with the port address is used and the 8 bit control word has a 0 in bit 0, then any subsequent mode 2 interrupts generated from the PIO port will use the interrupt vector of the control word stored in the port. Interrupts are enabled by setting bit 7 of the interrupt control word, indicated by bits 0, 1 and 2 being 1 (Fig. 10.28); if bit 7 is 1 then interrupts are enabled. Bits 4, 5 and 6 are used only with mode 3. Bit 4 is set to 1 to indicate that a mask word follows. Bit 5 determines the active state for the interrupt, with a 1 for interrupt active high and a 0 for interrupt active low. Bit 6 set as 1 means that all unmasked inputs have to be active to generate an interrupt; and bit 6 set as 0 means that any unmasked input generates an interrupt.

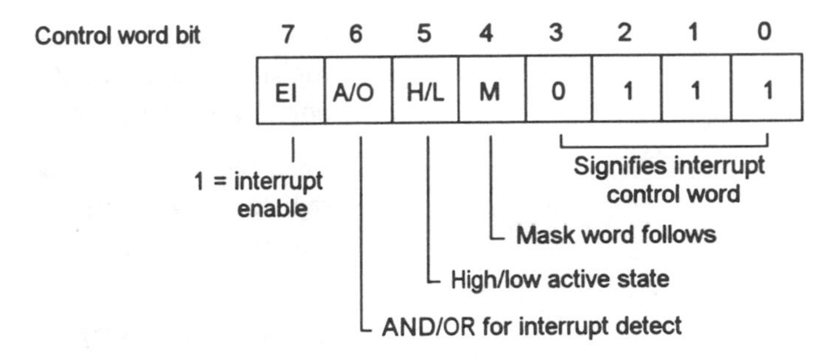

Fig. 10.28 Interrupt control word

Figure 10.29 shows a system involving a Z80 microprocessor and the Z80 PIO. The input/output (I/O) capability has effectively been doubled from the single port of the microprocessor to the two ports given by the PIO. With just the single PIO the decoder is not really necessary. However, by using the other I/O lines from the address decoder, other PIOs can be used and the I/O capability still further increased.

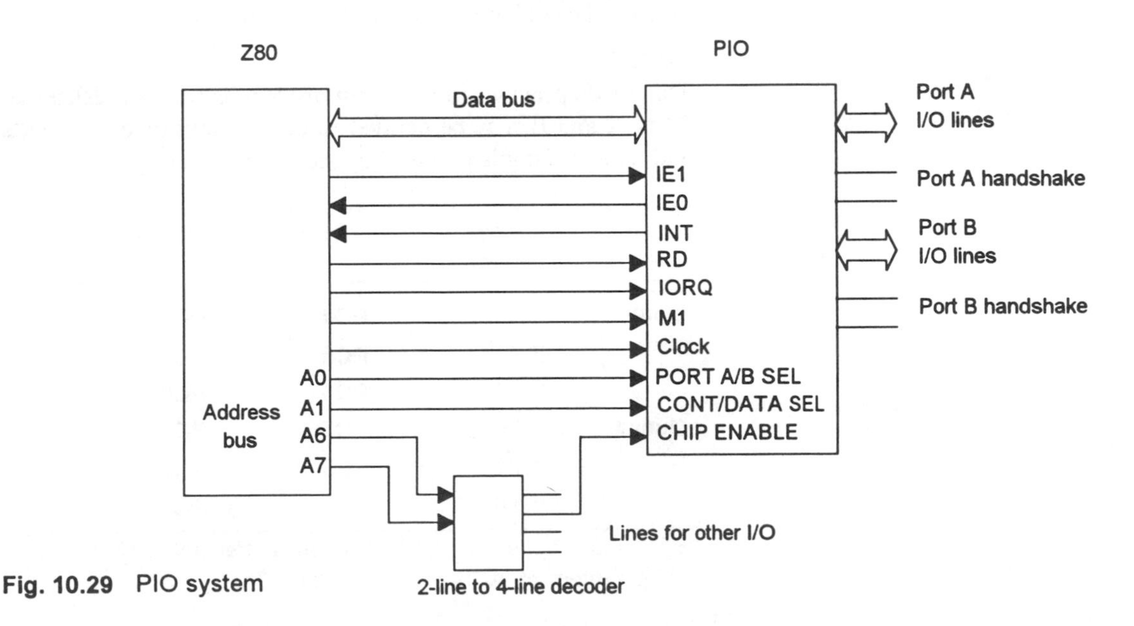

Fig. 10.29 PIO system

With the arrangement shown in Fig. 10.29, the PIO is enabled by the address 01XXXXXX. The address 01XXXX00 is used for port A data, 01XXXX01 for port B data, 01XXXX10 for port A command, and 01XXXX11 for port B command. To set up port A as an output port and port B as an input port, when not under interrupt control, the procedure is:

1. Load the interrupt control word 07 into the CPU register. Then output this to addresses 01000010 and 01000011.
2. Load the operating mode control word 00001111 into the CPU register. Then output this to address 01000001. This makes port A an output port.
3. Load the operating mode control word 01001111 into the CPU register. Then output this to address 01000011. This makes port B an input port.

10.6.3 Intel 8255 PPI

Another example of a programmable parallel peripheral interface is the *Intel 8255 PPI*. Figure 10.30 shows a block diagram of the PIA and the pin connections. The 8255 has three 8-bit input/output ports A, B and C, with C split into two halves, and three operation modes:

1. *Mode 0*
   This is the basic input/output mode. Ports A, B and each half of C can be configured entirely as input or output.
2. *Mode 1*
   This mode provides input/output operations with handshaking. Ports A and B may be defined as either input or output ports and handshaking is provided by the two halves of port C:

	Control function	*Port A*	*Port B*
Input	$\overline{\text{STB}}$	PC4	PC2
	IBF	PC5	PC1
	INTR	PC3	PC0
Output	$\overline{\text{OBF}}$	PC7	PC1
	$\overline{\text{ACK}}$	PC6	PC2
	INTR	PC3	PC0

IBF = input buffer full, OBF = output buffer full, STB = strobe, INTR = interrupt, ACK = acknowledge

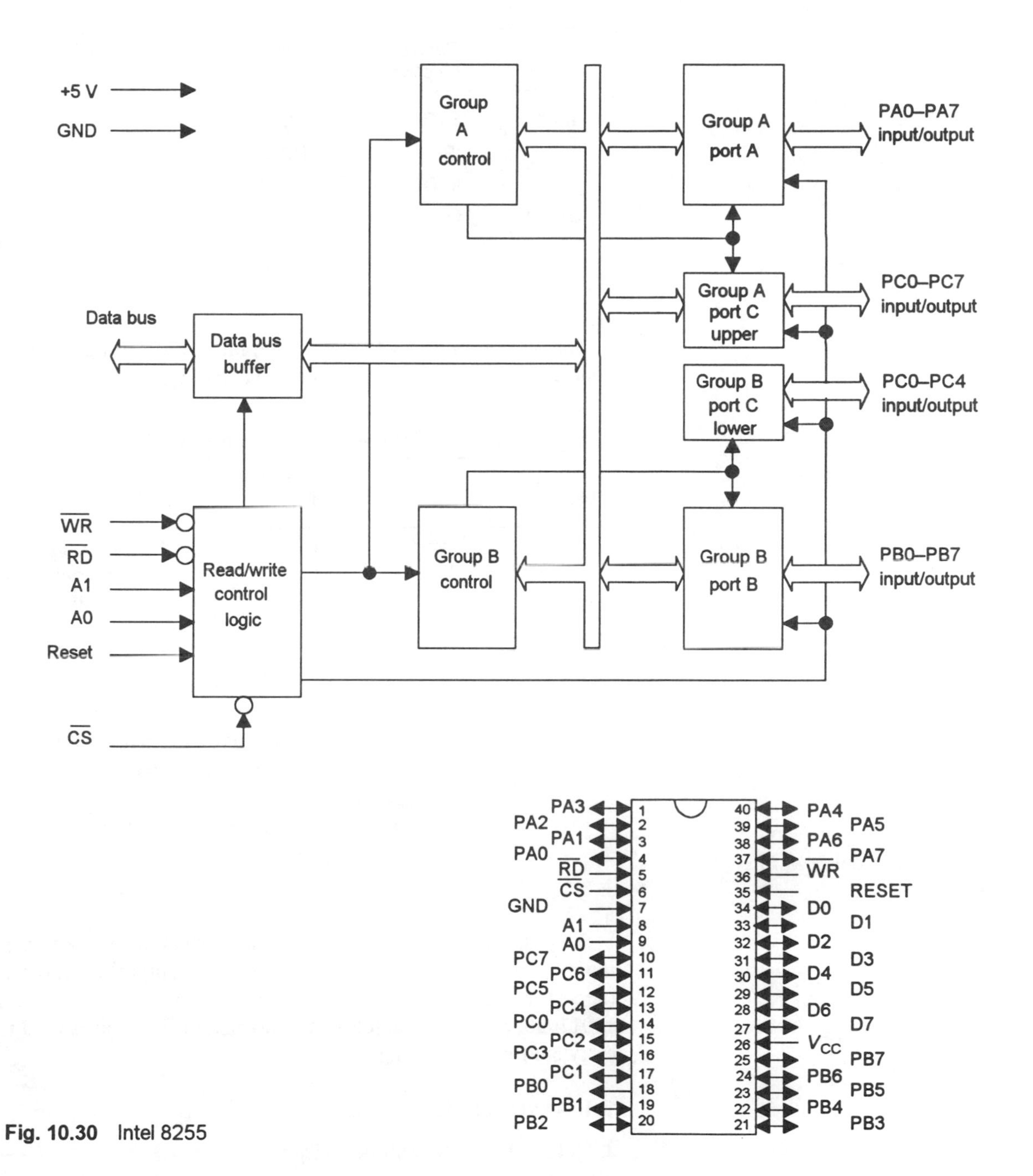

Fig. 10.30 Intel 8255

3. *Mode 2*
   This mode provides bidirectional input/output operations on port A only. Handshaking is provided by port C.

	Control function	*Port A*
Input	$\overline{STB}$	PC4
	IBF	PC5
	INTR	PC3
Output	$\overline{OBF}$	PC7
	$\overline{ACK}$	PC6
	INTR	PC3

The modes of the 8255 are configured by writing an 8-bit control word to the control register (Fig. 10.31).

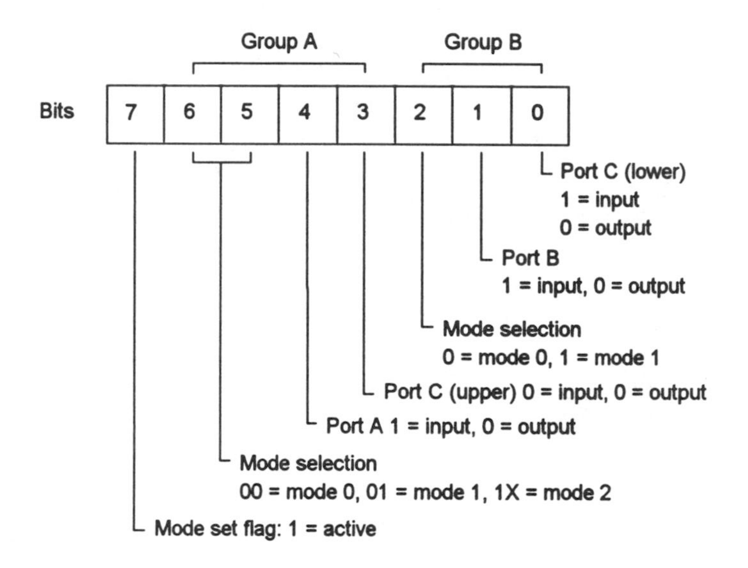

Fig. 10.31 Control word

Suppose we want the 8255 to operate in mode 0 with port A as input, port B as output, port C (lower) as output and port C (upper) as input. The binary control word required is thus 10011000, i.e. 98H. The following instruction sequence is used to carry out this configuring:

1. Load 98H into CPU register.
2. Output this to the control register.

For normal mode selection, bit 7 of the control word is set to 1 and ensures that data sent to the control address is stored in the mode definition register. But if bit 7 is 0 then any of the eight bits of port C can be set or reset. Figure 10.32 shows the functions of the bits in the control word for this situation. Thus if the control word is 0000 0101 then bit 7 as a 0 indicates that the word is selecting the bit set/reset function. Bit 0 as 1 indicates set. Bits 1, 2 and 3 as 010 indicate that bit PC2 is to be set.

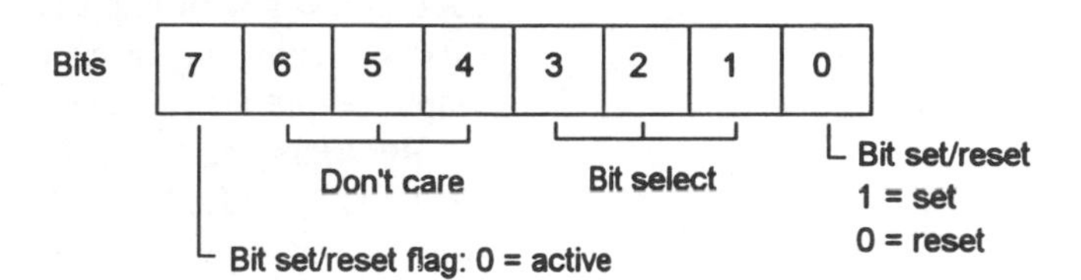

Fig. 10.32 Control word

As an illustration, Fig. 10.33 shows an 8255 used with an Intel 8086 microprocessor and Fig. 10.34 shows an 8255 used with a Z80 microprocessor. The decoder is to permit the connection of further 8255 chips and so further expansion in the number of ports.

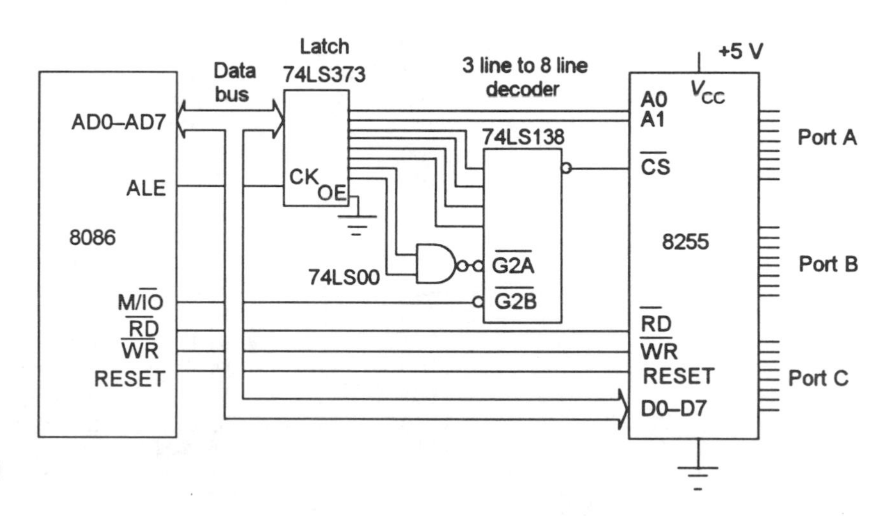

Fig. 10.33 8086 system

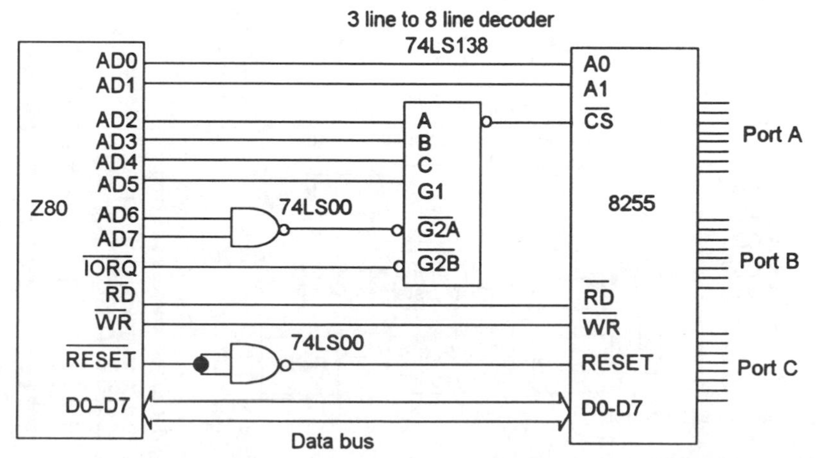

Fig. 10.34 Z80 system

10.6.4 Rockwell versatile interface adapter

The 6521 versatile interface adapter contains two 8 bit input/output ports with handshaking lines. The 6522 VIA (Fig. 10.35) also contains two 16 bit timers and a shift register. Here only the input/output facilities will be discussed.

Registers are selected by using four address lines connected to RS0, 1, 2, 3 (Table 10.1). Each port has a *data direction register* and a *data register*. The ports are configured for input or output on an individual line basis by setting the appropriate bits in the port data direction register, a 1 giving an output and a 0 an input. Data is outputted by writing data to the data register and inputted by reading from it.

Table 10.1 Register select

RS0-3	*Address offset*	*Register*	
0000	0	DRB	Data register B
0001	1	DRA	Data register A
0010	2	DDRB	Data direction register B
0011	3	DDRA	Data direction register A
0100	4	T1C-L	Timer 1 counter/latch low byte
0101	5	T1C-H	Timer 1 counter high byte
0110	6	T1L-L	Timer 1 latch low byte
0111	7	T1L-H	Timer 1 latch high byte
1000	8	T2C-L	Timer 2 counter/latch low byte
1001	9	T2C-H	Timer 2 counter high byte
1010	10	SR	Shift register
1011	11	ACR	Auxiliary control register
1100	12	PCR	Peripheral control register
1101	13	IFR	Interrupt flag register
1110	14	IER	Interrupt enable register
1111	15	DRA-N	DRA without handshaking

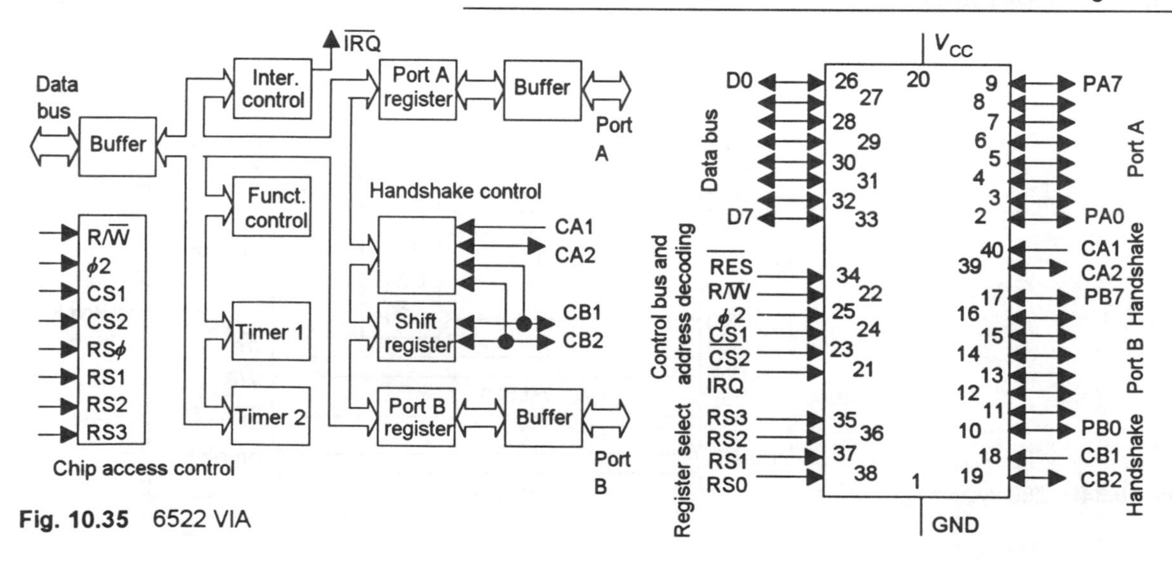

Fig. 10.35 6522 VIA

Bits 0 and 1 of the *auxiliary control register* can be used to enable (1) or disable (0) latches for ports A and B, the other bits being used for the timer/counters and the shift register. When latching is enabled, an active transition on the CA1 or CB1 line causes the data present at the port to be latched into the data register. When it is disabled, the data input is whatever exists at the instant when the microprocessor reads the input port.

The *peripheral control register* (Fig. 10.36) is used to configure the handshake lines. An active transition on one of the handshake lines sets a flag in the *interrupt flag register* (Fig. 10.37). An active flag may be cleared by writing a 1 into the appropriate bit of the interrupt flag register. Each bit in the interrupt flag register has a parallel bit in the *interrupt enable register*; a 1 being used to enable an interupt and a 0 to disable it.

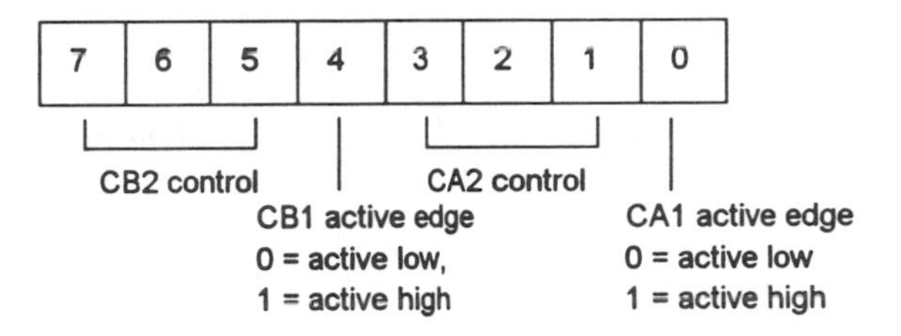

Bit 7/3	Bit 6/2	Bit 5/1	CB2/CA2
0	0	0	Input: interrupt on negative transition, cleared on read/write of data register
0	0	1	Input: interrupt on negative transition, cleared by read/write to the flag register
0	1	0	Input: interrupt on positive transition, cleared on read/write of data register
0	1	1	Input: interrupt on positive transition, cleared on read/write to the flag register
1	0	0	Output: low following a write, high after an active transition on CA1/CB1
1	0	1	Output: low for one cycle after write of data register
1	1	0	Output: low
1	1	1	Output: high

Fig. 10.36 Peripheral control register

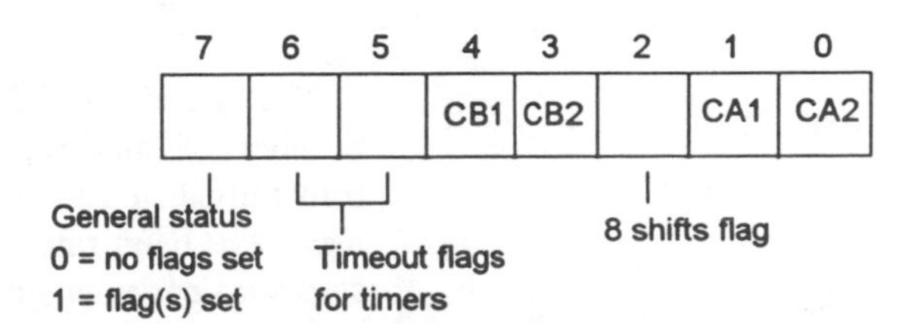

Fig. 10.37 Interrupt flag register

10.7 Serial input/output

With the parallel transmission of data, one line is used for each bit; with serial transmission a single line is used to transmit data as sequential bits. Thus serial data transmission is not as rapid as parallel data transmission. It does, however, have the advantage of not requiring so many wires for transmission and is less susceptible to degradation.

With serial transmission, successive data transmissions are unrelated in time and thus there is a problem of a receiver knowing what is the beginning and what is the end of a particular data transmission. This can be achieved in the following ways:

1. *Synchronous*
   With synchronous transfer, one of the communicating devices controls the data transfer by constantly transmitting its clock signals to synchronise the transfer of each bit. Thus the receiver knows the time intervals in which bits will be sent.

2. *Asynchronous*
   With asynchronous transfer, the receiver and the transmitter of the data each have their own clock signals. Thus there is a need for the transmitter to inform the receiver when a word starts or stops. This can be done by each transmitted word carrying its own start and stop bits to indicate the beginning and end of a word. When there is no transmission the serial link is maintained at a logic 1 level. When this level falls to zero it indicates either a fault in the system, in which case the 0 is continuous, or the start of a word, in which case it is followed by the eight bits of the word. Following the word is a parity bit that is used to check for errors and one or two stop bits before any further data is transmitted. The parity bit is 1 if the total number of 1s in the data is even and 0 if the total is odd; it thus provides a check as to whether a bit has been corrupted in the transfer. Figure 10.38 illustrates this. All the bits take the same length of time.

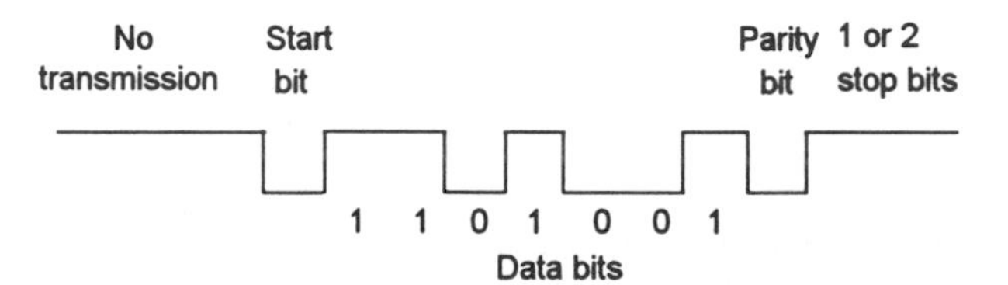

Fig. 10.38 Asynchronous transmission

The rate of serial data transmission is measured in terms of the number of bits transmitted per second. Thus if n bits are transmitted in a time T then the rate is n/T. The *baud* is the unit used. The baud rate of transmission does not distinguish between stop/start/parity bits and data bits, so when such bits are used the actual rate of data transmission is less than the baud rate.

The following sections describe some special chips which can be used to interface microprocessors with peripherals when serial data transfer is required. They also consider the serial transfer facilities that are built into microcontrollers.

10.7.1 Universal asynchronous receiver/tranmitters

The *universal asynchronous receiver/transmitter* (UART) is used to change serial data to parallel data for input to a microprocessor and parallel data to serial data for the output from a microprocessor. One commonly used programmable form of UART is the Motorola MC6850 *asynchronous communications interface adapter* (ACIA); Fig. 10.39 shows a block diagram of the constituent elements.

1. *Data flow* between the microprocessor and the ACIA is via eight bidirectional lines D0 to D7. The direction of the data flow is controlled by the microprocessor through the read/write input to the ACIA.

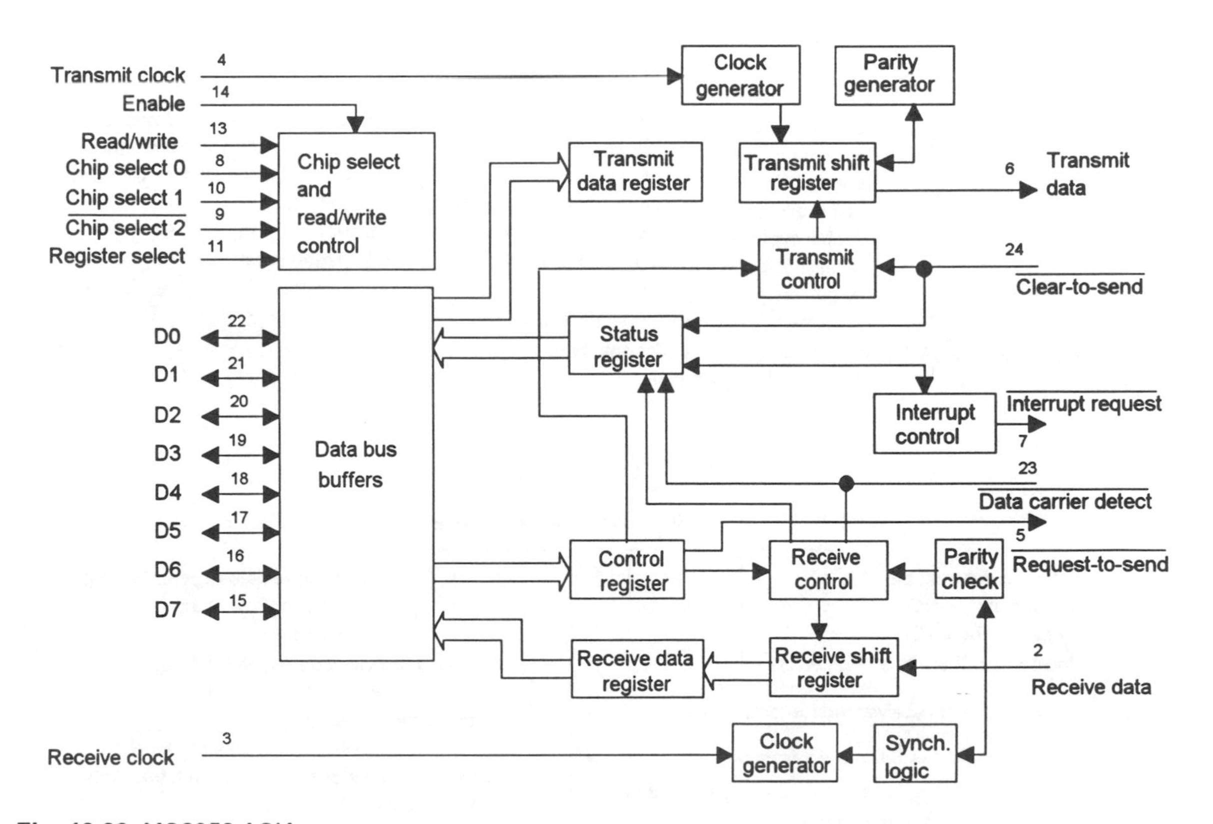

Fig. 10.39 MC6850 ACIA

2. The three *chip select lines* are used for addressing a particular ACIA.

3. The *register select line* is used to select particular registers within the ACIA; if the register select line is high then the data transmit and data receive registers are selected, if low then the control and status registers are selected. The status register contains information on the status of serial data transfers as they occur and is used to read the data carrier detect and clear-to-send lines. The control register is initially used to reset the ACIA and subsequently to define the serial data transfer rate and the data format.

4. The peripheral side of the ACIA includes two *serial data lines* and three *control lines*. Data is sent by the transmit data line and received by the receive data line. The control signals are provided by clear-to-send, data carrier detect and request-to-send. Figure 10.40 shows the bit format of the control register and Fig. 10.41 the status register.

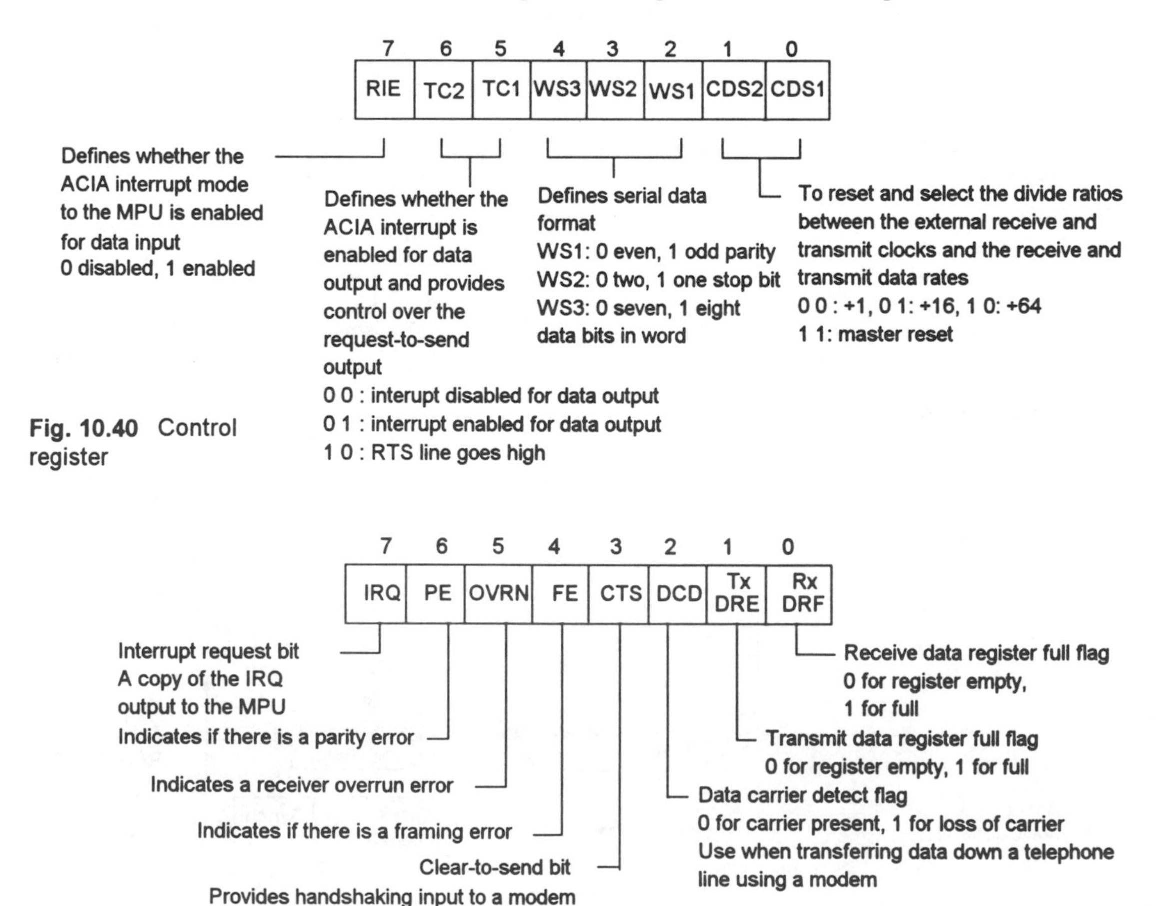

Fig. 10.40 Control register

Fig. 10.41 Status register

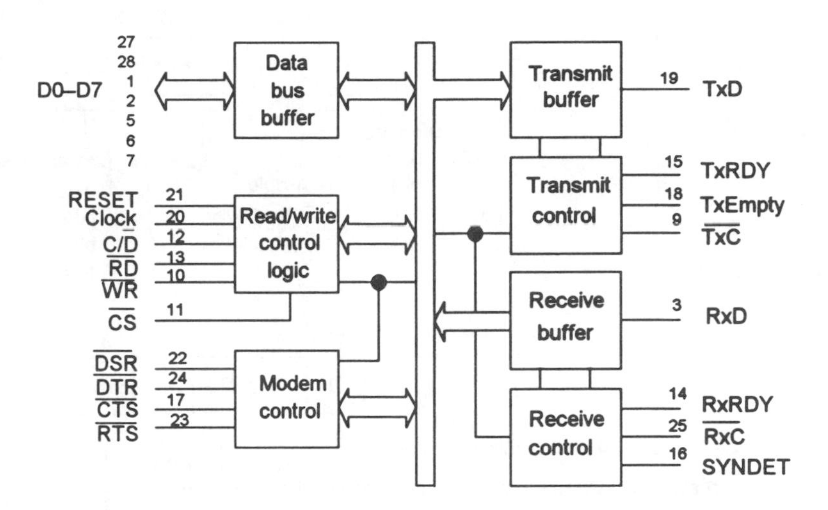

Fig. 10.42 8251 UART

Another example of a UART is the *Intel 8251*; Fig. 10.42 shows a block diagram. It can operate in asynchronous mode and in synchronous mode, and it contains separate parallel-to-serial (transmitter, T) and serial-to-parallel (receiver, R) sections.

1. For the read/write control logic, it has a single *chip select* input (CS) for addressing and this must be low for the device to operate.
2. A single *register select* line (C/D) is used to select either the control and status registers or the data registers. When C/D is at 1 the status register is selected for write operations and the control register by write operations. The C/D input is usually connected to an address line, e.g. A0 or A1, so that the two sets of registers have different addresses.
3. The RD and WR signals are used to select whether reading or writing is involved. If both RD and WR are 1, the data bus lines are disabled.

The 8251 has four control registers which need to be programmed: the MODE register, two 8 bit registers for the SYNCH word and the COMMAND register. In addition there is a STATUS register.

Before transmission, a mode byte (Fig. 10.43) is sent to the UART to determine the transmission characteristics required. The mode byte indicates by bits 0 and 1 whether synchronous or asynchronous working is required. For synchronous working, both bits must be 0; for asynchronous they are codes 01, 10 or 11 depending on the baud rate factor required.

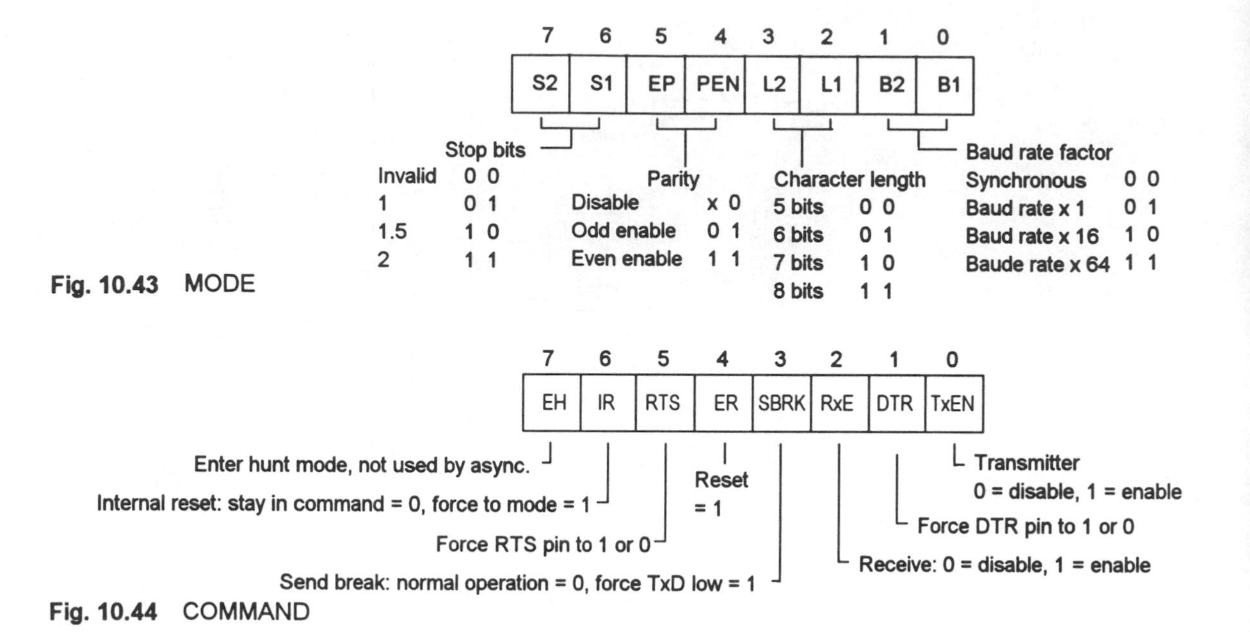

Fig. 10.43 MODE

Fig. 10.44 COMMAND

Once data has been written to the mode register, the other registers are automatically selected in sequence. With asynchronous mode selected, the next register is the command register (Fig. 10.44). The command instruction byte is used to clear error flags, enable or disable interrupts, control RTS and reset the UART so that it awaits a new mode byte.

For asynchronous operation, the selection is made by the mode byte then this is followed automatically by one or two SYNC bytes. These are characters which are transmitted at the start of a message. Next comes the command byte and finally the data byte.

The STATUS register (Fig. 10.45) uses flags to indicate the status of signals transmitted and received. The following sequence illustrates how the UART might be programmed:

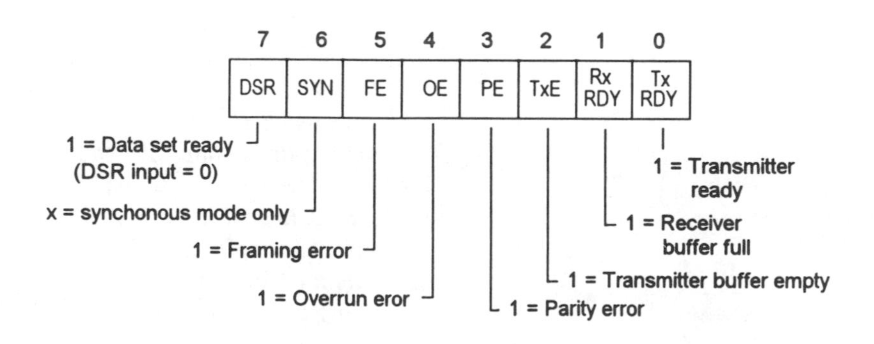

Fig. 10.45 STATUS

1. Internal reset; this causes the COMMAND register to be selected.
2. Set bit 6 in the COMMAND register to force to MODE.
3. Load the MODE register with the required byte, e.g. 01001110.
4. The COMMAND register automatically follows and can be loaded with the required byte, e.g. 00110111.
5. The STATUS register can be read to determine when to transfer data.

Asynchronous serial data transfer is generally used for communications between two computers, with or without a modem, or a computer and a printer.

10.7.2 Serial interfaces with microcontrollers

Many microcontrollers have serial interfaces, i.e. built-in UARTs. For example, the Motorola M68HC11 has a serial peripheral interface (SPI) and a serial communication interface (SCI).

The SPI is a synchronous interface and the same clock signal is used by the microcontroller and the externally connected device or devices (Fig. 10.46). The SPI allows interconnection of several microcontrollers which have this facility; one of them acts as the master and the others act as slaves. Four of the 68HC11 port D pins are associated with SPI transfers: SS/PD5, SCK/PD4, MOSI/PD3 and MISO/PD2. When data is to be transmitted from the master to the slave, a clock signal is generated by the master on SCK to synchronise the transfer of the data. The slave select signal on SS must be low to select a microcontroller or device as a slave and high for a master. MISO, master-in slave-out, is configured as an input in a master device and as an output in a slave device; it is used to transfer serial data from master to slave. MOSI, master-out slave-in, is configured as an output in a master device and as an input in a slave device; it is used to transfer serial data from slave to master.

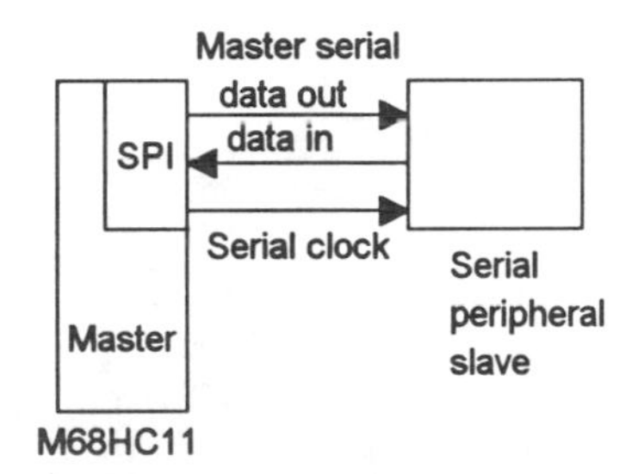

Fig. 10.46 SPI

Figure 10.47 shows one way an SPI system can be arranged with a master and two slaves. The master has its SS pin tied to high. When the master communicates with a slave it drives its SS pin low.

The SPI is initialised by bits in the SPI control register SPCR (Fig. 10.48) and the port D data direction control register DDRD (Fig. 10.49). The SPI status register SPSR (Fig. 10.50) contains status and error bits. Data is written to and read from the SPI data register SPDR at memory location $1024.

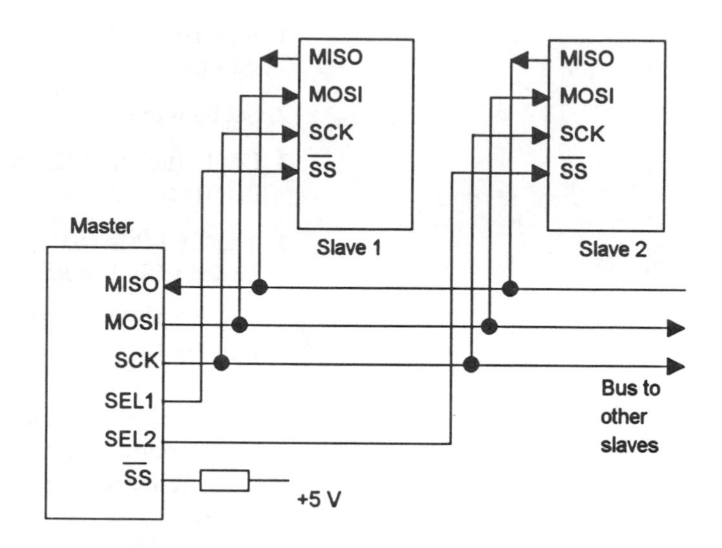

Fig. 10.47 Master and slaves

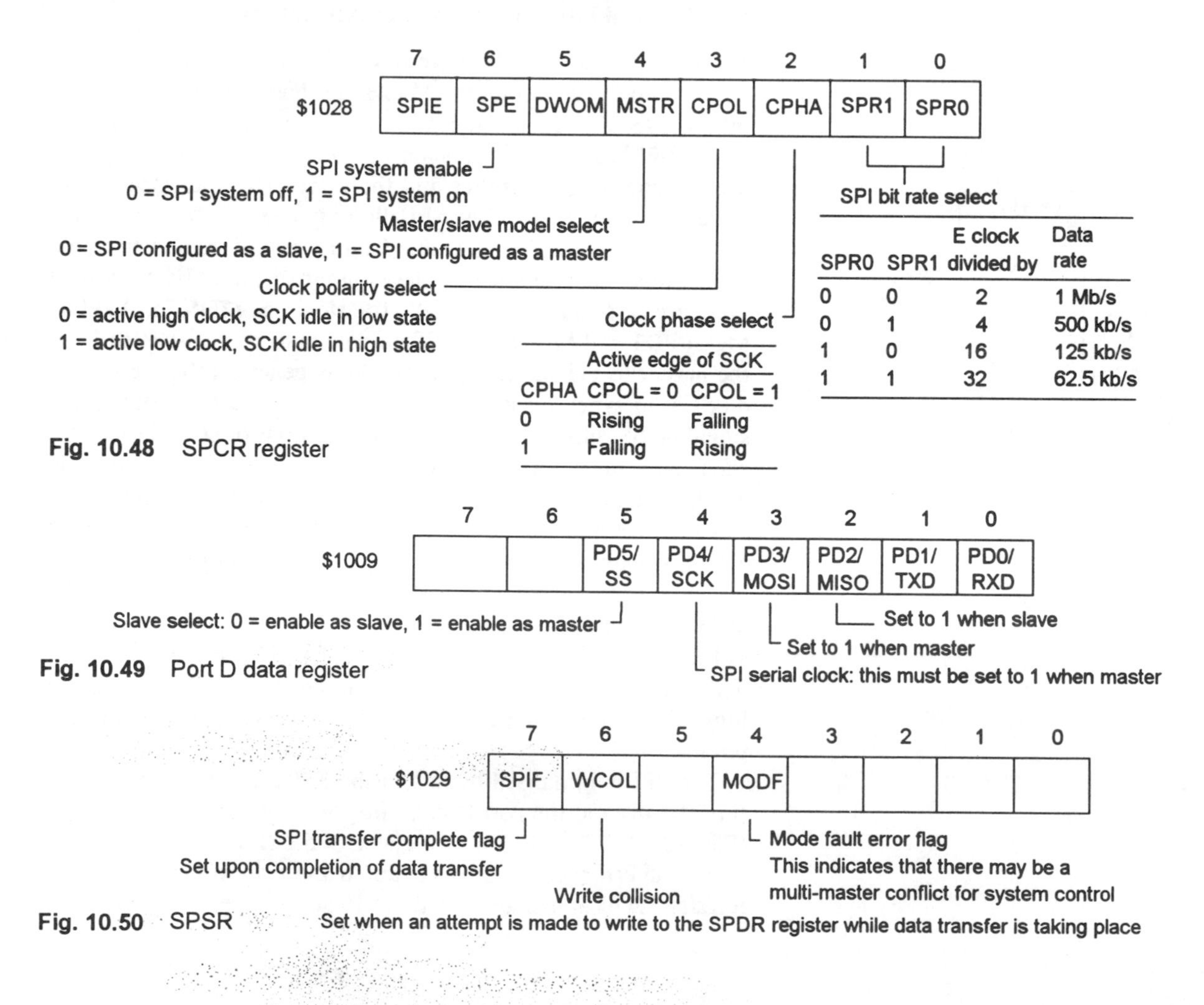

CPHA	Active edge of SCK CPOL = 0	CPOL = 1
0	Rising	Falling
1	Falling	Rising

SPR0	SPR1	E clock divided by	Data rate
0	0	2	1 Mb/s
0	1	4	500 kb/s
1	0	16	125 kb/s
1	1	32	62.5 kb/s

Fig. 10.48 SPCR register

Fig. 10.49 Port D data register

Fig. 10.50 SPSR

Instructions for a master to transfer data from a master to a slave are:

```
REGBAS  EQU   $1000      ; base address
SPDR    EQU   $2A        ; offset of SPDR from REGBAS
SPCR    EQU   $28        ; offset of SPCR from REGBAS
SPSR    EQU   $29        ; offset of SPSR from REGBAS
DDRD    EQU   $09        ; offset of DDRD from REGBAS
        ORG   $00
        LDX   #REGBAS
        LDAA  #$38       ; value to set SPI pin directions,
                         ; set SS, SCK and MOSI pins
                         ; for output and remaining
                         ; D pins for input
        STAA  DDRD,X     ; sets directions of SPI pins
        LDAA  #$54       ; value to initialise the SPI,
                         ; enable SPI, make master,
                         ; active high clock, falling edge,
                         ; data rate 1 Mb/s
        STAA  SPCR,X     ; initalise SPI
        LDAA  DATA       ; load the data to be sent
        STAA  SPDR,X     ; start the SPI transfer
WAIT    LDAB  SPCR,X     ; check bit 7 for completion of
                         ; SPI transfer
        BPL   WAIT
```

Instruction for a master to read data from a slave SPI device are:

```
        LDX   #REGBAS
        LDAA  #$38
        STAA  DDRD,X
        LDAA  #$54
        STAA  SPCR,X
        STAA  SPDR,X     ; start the SPI transfer
HERE    LDAB  SPCR,X     ; wait until character transferred
        BPL   HERE
        LDAA  SPDR,X     ; load the character in A
```

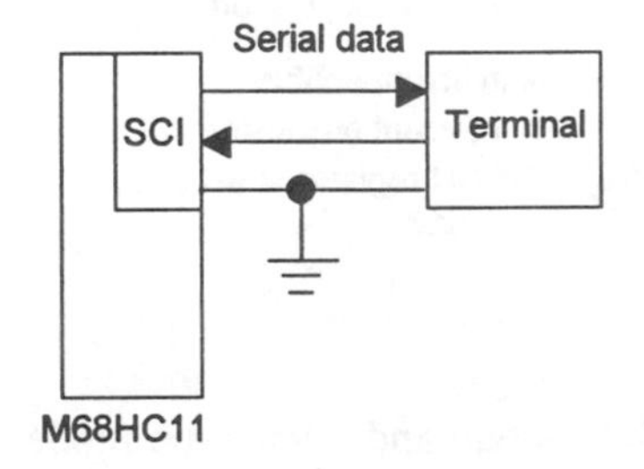

Fig. 10.51 SCI

The Motorola 68HC11 serial communication interface SCI is a full-duplex asynchronous serial communications interface, so it allows different clock signals to be used by the SCI system and the externally connected device (Fig. 10.51). A full-duplex interface is where data may be simultaneously transmitted and received. The SCI and SPI share serial input and output pins with the port D input/output register and the pins for SCI are 0 and 1, RXD and TXD (Fig. 10.52). It is initialised by using the SCI control register 1 (Fig. 10.53), the SCI control register 2 (Fig. 10.54) and the baud rate control register (Fig. 10.55). Status flags are in the SCI status register (Fig. 10.56). Data is written to and read from the SCI data register at memory location $102F.

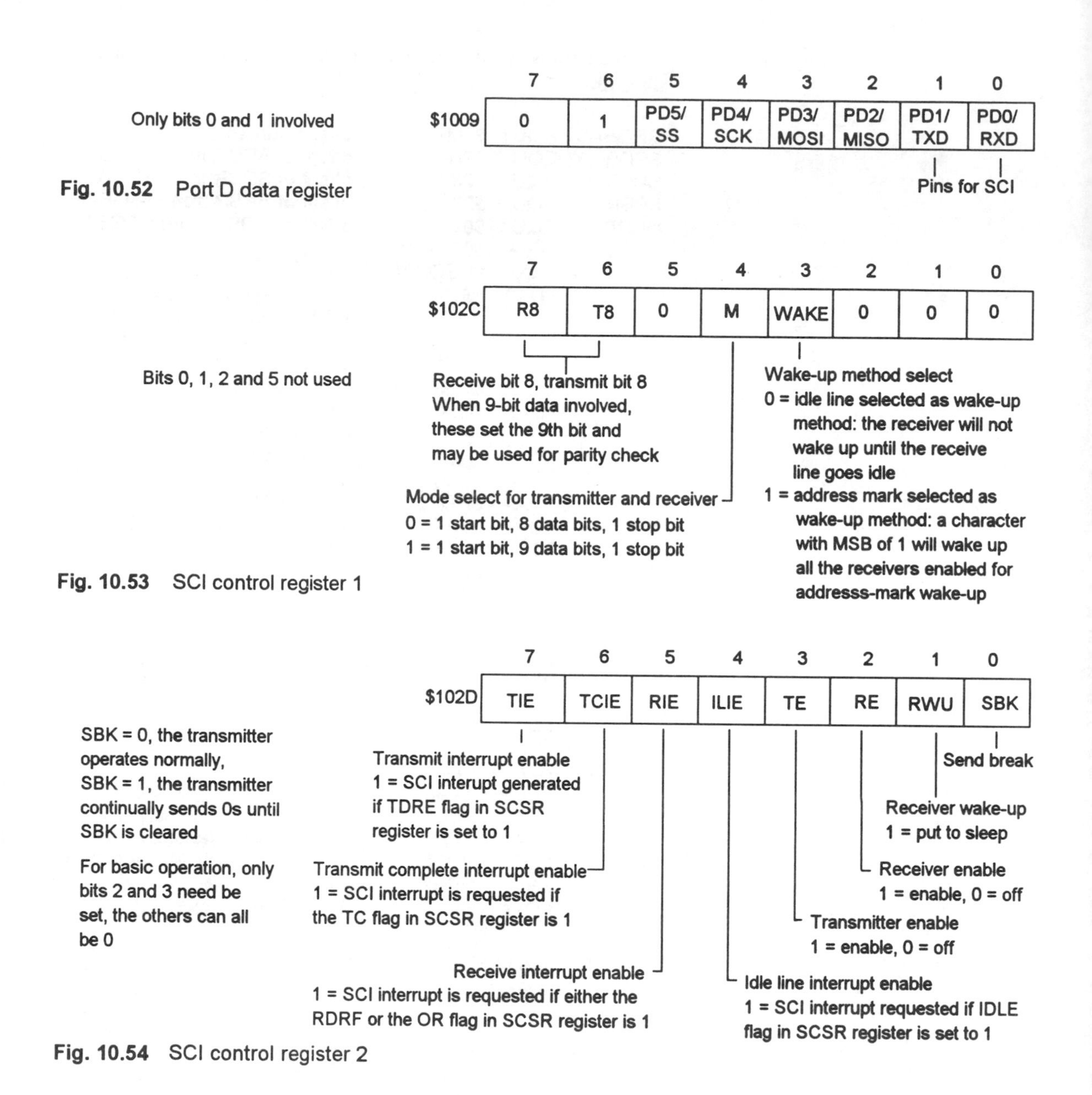

Fig. 10.52 Port D data register

Fig. 10.53 SCI control register 1

Fig. 10.54 SCI control register 2

The Motorola SCI features a sleep mode and a wake-up mode. They can be used in applications where one M68HC11 is sending data to many serial receivers. Software in each receiver is put to sleep until the programmed wake-up sequence is received. Receivers that are asleep do not respond to data sent from the transmitter. The wake-up mode and the receiver wake-up enable are controlled by bits in the SCCR1 and SCCR2 registers.

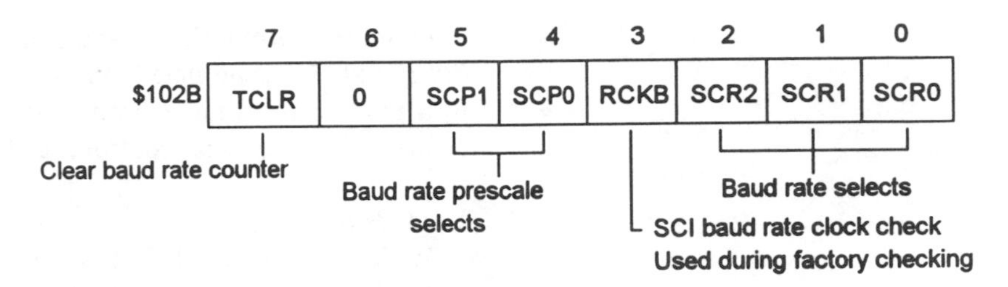

Baud rate prescale selects

SCP1	*SCP0*	*Divide processor clock by*
0	0	1
0	1	3
1	0	4
1	1	13

Baud rate selects

SCR2	*SCR1*	*SCR0*	*Divide prescale output by*
0	0	0	1
0	0	1	2
0	1	0	4
0	1	1	8
1	0	0	16
1	0	1	32
1	1	0	64
1	1	1	128

Example of standard baud rates with a bus frequency of 2 MHz

SCP1	*SCP0*	*SCR2*	*SCR1*	*SCR0*	*Baud rate*
0	0	0	0	0	125K
1	1	0	0	0	9600
1	1	0	0	1	4800
1	1	0	1	0	2400
1	1	0	1	1	1200
1	1	1	0	0	600
1	1	1	0	1	300
1	1	1	1	0	150
1	1	1	1	1	75

Fig. 10.55 BAUD rate control register

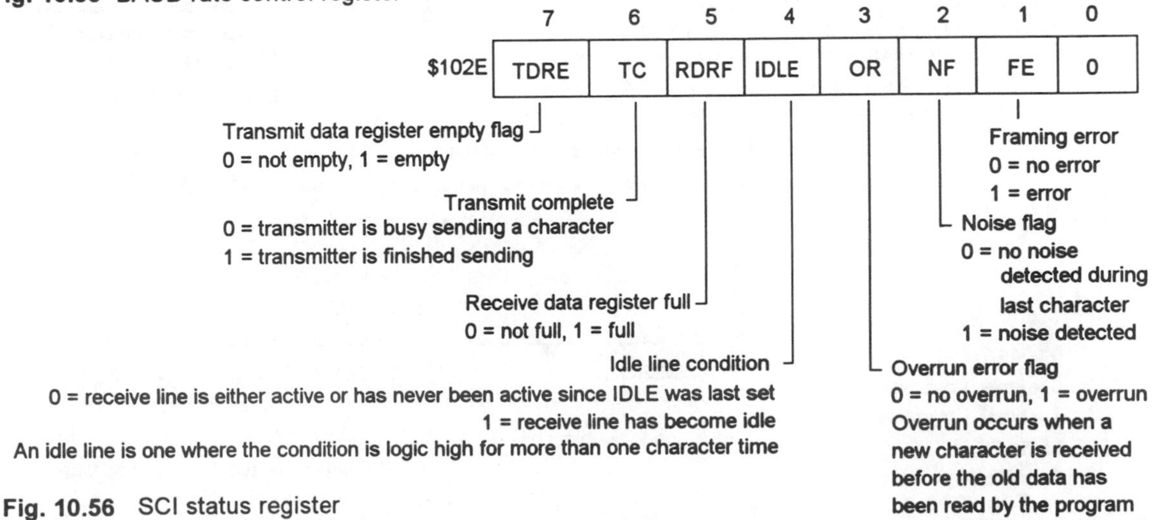

Fig. 10.56 SCI status register

Other microcontrollers have similar serial interfaces. The *Intel 8051* is able to send data both synchronously and asynchronously in a number of different transmission modes. All the modes are controlled by the serial control register SCON (Fig. 10.57).

1. *Mode 0*
   With mode 0, serial data is transmitted and received through the RXD pin while pin TXD provides the clock signal. This is the synchronous mode. The baud rate is the oscillator frequency divided by 12, i.e. the instruction clock frequency. The other modes provide asynchronous transmission.

2. *Mode 1*
   With mode 1, which is probably the most commonly used, the transmission consists of a start bit (0), the 8 data bits and a stop bit (1). The baud rate is variable and controlled by an internal microcontroller timer. Timer 1 should be configured in mode 2, 8 bit auto-reload mode (see Chapter 11); each time the timer reloads it provides a clock pulse to the serial port. The value of the SMOD bit in the power control register PCON (Fig. 10.58) helps to determine the baud rate.

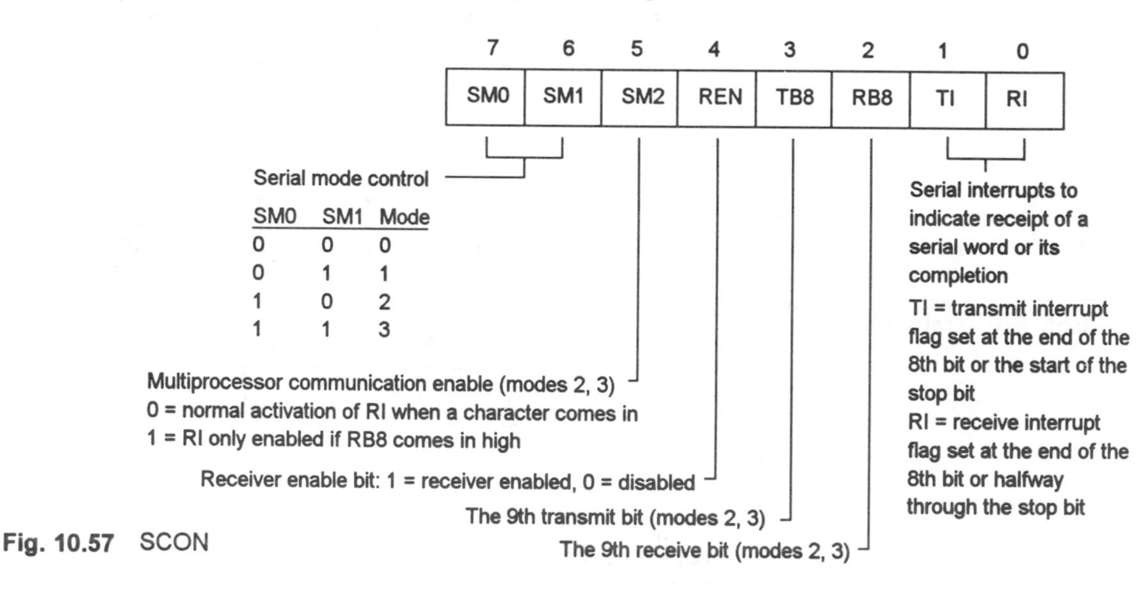

Fig. 10.57 SCON

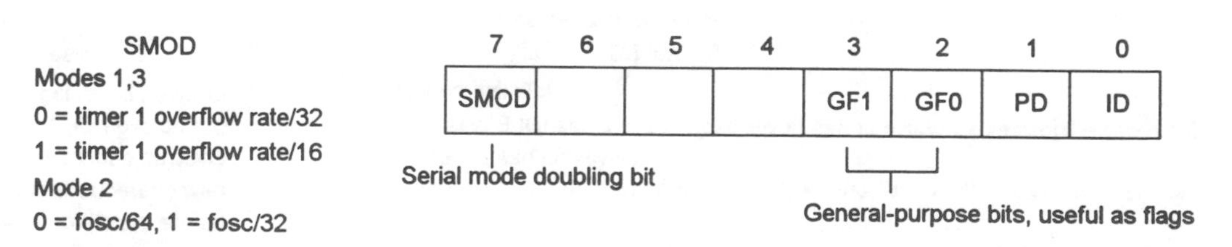

Fig. 10.58 PCON

With SMOD as 0, its usual value is used, the following formula can be used to determine the reload value TH1 that will produce a particular baud rate:

$$256 - \text{TH1} = \frac{\text{fosc}/12}{32 \times \text{baud rate}}$$

Thus with an oscillator frequency (fosc) of 12 MHz, a baud rate of 9600 is obtained when TH1 is 253, i.e. hex FD. Initialisation of the microcontroller might then this form:

```
INIT    MOV     TMOD,#29H      ; set timer 1
        MOV     TH1,#0FDH      ; set for 9600 baud
        MOV     TCON,#00H      ; clear all bits
        MOV     SCON,#42H      ; 8-bit asynchronous
        SETB    TR1            ; timer on
```

3. *Modes 2 and 3*
   With modes 2 and 3 there are 9 data bits; the ninth bit is a parity bit calculated in software and loaded into the TB8 bit of the SCON register. Mode 2 has baud rates of the oscillator frequency divided by either 64 or 32; mode 3 has a variable baud rate controlled by an internal microcontroller timer.

Many *PIC 16 microcontrollers* include a universal asynchronous receiver transmitter (UART) module. To transmit a data byte from the RC6/TX pin, the byte is written to the register TXREG. The byte is there framed by a start bit (0) and a stop bit (1) before transmission from the pin. Data is received at the RC7/RX pin; the start and stop bits are extracted and the byte is then transferred to the register RCREG. Initialisation involves setting the data direction bits associated with the RC6/TX and the RC7/RX pins as inputs, i.e. 1s in bits 6 and 7 of the TRISC register. The UART's baud rate and its transmit and receive functions are then initialised by writing data to the SPBRG register and setting bits in the TXSTA (Fig. 10.59) and RCSTA (Fig. 10.60) registers, e.g. TXSTA 00100?10, RCSTA 10010??0.

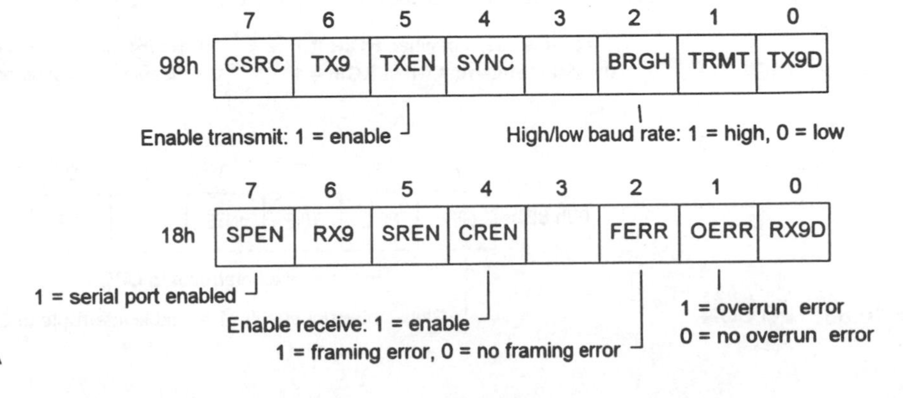

Fig. 10.59 TXSTA

Fig. 10.60 RCSTA

The SPRG register has a number written to it to generate the required baud rate. The value depends on the setting of the BRGH bit in the TXSTA register. For BRGH = 1:

$$\text{baud rate} = \frac{\text{fosc}}{16(\text{SPBRG} + 1)}$$

and for BRG = 0:

$$\text{baud rate} = \frac{\text{fosc}}{64(\text{SPBRG} + 1)}$$

Table 10.2 shows typical values.

Table 10.2 SPRG values

Baud rate	*OSC = 4 MHz*		*OSC = 10 MHz*		*OSC = 20 MHz*	
	BRGH	*SPRG*	*BRGH*	*SPRG*	*BRGH*	*SPRG*
9600	1	25	1	64	1	129
19200	1	12	1	32	1	64

The flag and interrupt bits of the PIR1 (Fig. 10.61), PIE1 (Fig. 10.62) and INTCON (Fig. 10.63) registers control the timing of the interactions of the CPU with the UART.

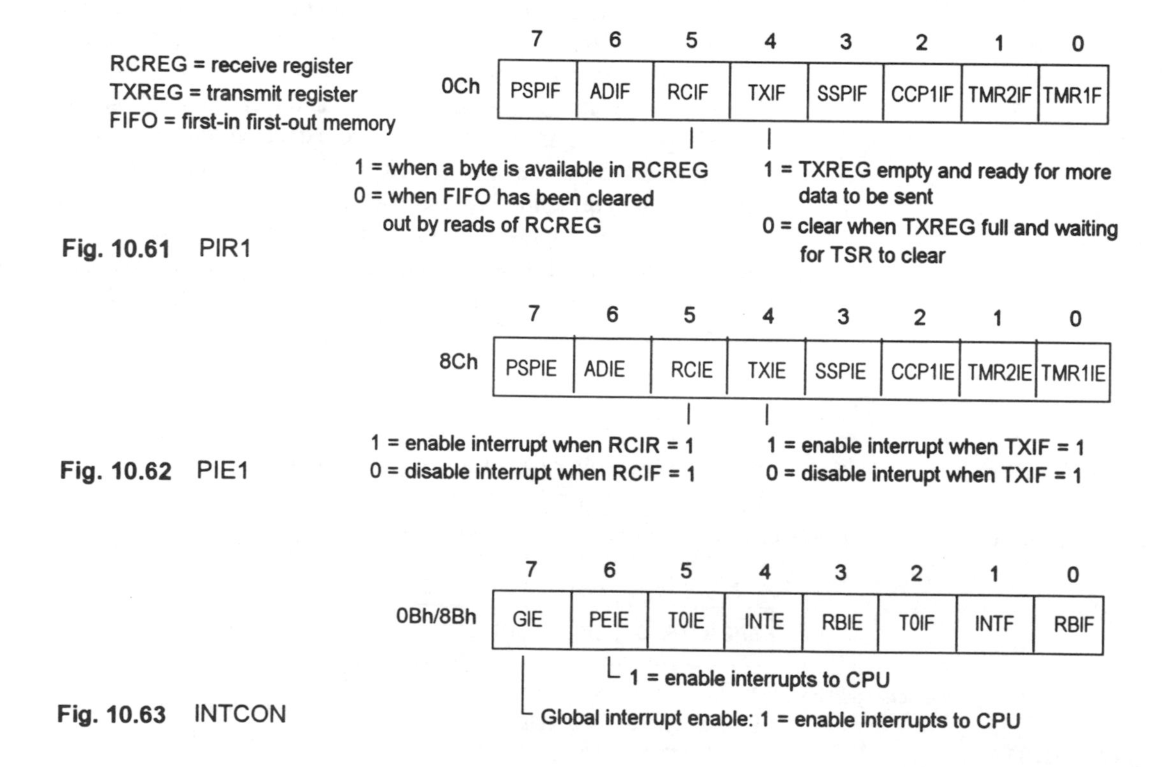

Fig. 10.61 PIR1

Fig. 10.62 PIE1

Fig. 10.63 INTCON

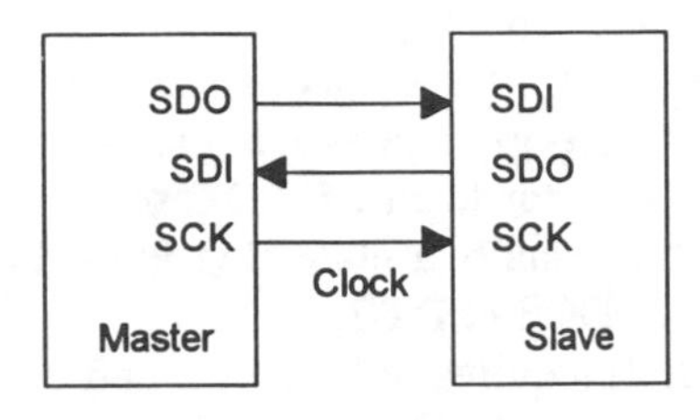

Fig. 10.64 SPI master–slave

PIC16 microcontrollers also have a synchronous peripheral interface (SPI). The three pins associated with this interface are RC5/SDO, RC4/SDI and RC3/SCK. Figure 10.64 shows the connections involved with a master–slave set-up. For the master, the SCK pin must be an output. Data is received and transmitted via the SSPBUF register in synchronism with the clock signals. Initialisation involves setting bits in the SSPCON and SSPSTAT registers. In register PIR1 (Fig. 10.61), SSPIF is 1 when the transfer is completed and has to be cleared before the beginning of each transfer.

10.8 Interface standards

Interface standards have been specified to simplify interconnections between different devices, perhaps supplied by different manufacturers. The standards specify mechanical connections, pin assignments, signal levels, signal timing and framing formats. With serial communications the main standards are *RS-232* and *I²C*, though for automobiles CAN is widely used. With parallel communications commonly used standards are the *Centronics parallel interface* and the *general-purpose interface bus* (GPIB) (IEEE-488).

10.8.1 Serial communication interface

The most commonly used interface for asynchronous serial communication is RS-232; this was first defined by the American Electronic Industries Association (EIA) in 1962. The standard relates to data terminal equipment (DTE) and data circuit-terminating equipment (DCE). Data terminal equipment, e.g. a microcontroller can send or receive data via the interface. Data circuit-terminating equipment is used to facilitate communication; a typical example is a modem. Modems provide an essential link between microcomputers and conventional analogue telephone lines. RS-232 signals can be grouped into three categories:

1. *Data*
   RS-232 provides two independent serial data channels, termed primary and secondary, both are used for full-duplex operation.

2. *Handshake control*
   Handshaking signals are used to control the flow of serial data over the communication path.

3. *Timing*
   For synchronous operation, clock signals pass between transmitters and receivers.

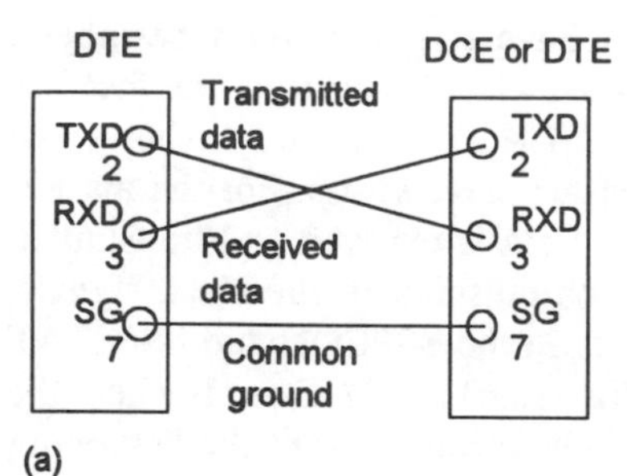

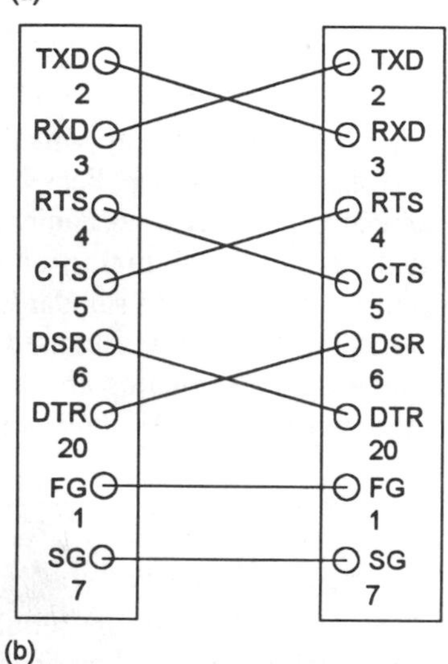

Fig. 10.65 RS-232 connections: (a) minimum, (b) more complex

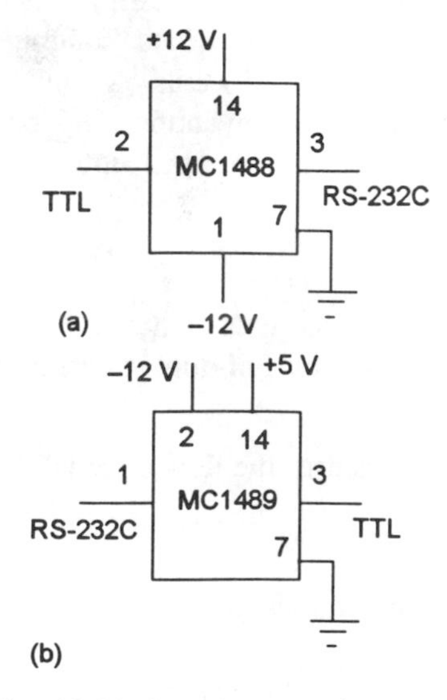

Fig. 10.66 Level conversion

Table 10.3 gives the RS-232C connector pin numbers and signals for which each is used; not all the pins and signals are necessarily used in a particular set-up. The signal ground wire allows for a return path. The connector to an RS-232C serial port is via a 25-pin D-type connector; usually a male plug is used on cables and a female socket on the DCE or DTE.

The simplest bidirectional link requires only lines 2 and 3 for transmitted data and received data, with signal ground (7) for the return path of these signals (Fig. 10.58(a)). A more complex set-up involves pins 1, 2, 3, 4, 5, 6, 7 and 20 (Fig. 10.58(b)). The signals sent through pins 4, 5, 6 and 20 are used to check that the receiving end is ready to receive a signal; and to check the transmitting end is ready to send and the data is ready to be sent.

The RS-232C standards are +12 V for logic 0 and −12 V for logic 1 whereas microcontrollers such as the Motorola 68HC11 and the Intel 8051 use transistor–transistor logic (TTL) for which logic 0 is 0 V and logic 1 is +5 V. The signal levels must therefore be converted. This can be achieved using devices such as the MC1488 for TTL to RS-232C conversion and the MC1489 for RS-232C to TTL conversion (Fig. 10.66).

Table 10.3 RS-232 pin assignments

Pin	*Abbreviation*	*Direction*	*Signal/function*
1	FG		Frame/protective ground
2	TXD	To DCE	Transmitted data
3	RXD	To DTE	Received data
4	RTS	To DCE	Request to send
5	CTS	To DTE	Clear to send
6	DSR	To DTE	DCE ready
7	SG		Signal ground/common return
8	DCD	To DTE	Received line detector
12	SDCD	To DTE	Secondary received line signal detector
13	SCTS	To DTE	Secondary clear to send
14	STD	To DCE	Secondary transmitted data
15	TC	To DTE	Transmit signal timing
16	SRD	To DTE	Secondary received data
17	RC	To DTE	Received signal timing
18		To DCE	Local loop back
19	SRTS	To DCE	Secondary request to send
20	DTR	To DCE	Data terminal ready
21	SQ	To DEC/DTE	Remote loop back/signal quality detector
22	RI	To DTE	Ring indicator
23		To DEC/DTE	Data signal rate selector
24	TC	To DCE	Transmit signal timing
25		To DTE	Test mode

10.8.2 I²C bus

The *inter-IC communication bus*, referred to as the I²C bus, is a data bus designed by Philips for use in communications between integrated circuits on the same circuit board or between equipment when the joining cable is relatively short. The bus allows data and instructions to be exchanged between devices by means of just two wires and so it gives a considerable simplification of any circuits. Some microcontrollers have I²C interfaces, e.g. PIC16C/74.

The two lines are a bidirectional serial data line (SDA) and a serial clock line (SCL). With the PIC microcontroller they are supplied by pins RC3/SCK/SCL and RC4/SDI/SDA. Both lines are connected to the positive power supply via resistors (Fig. 10.67). The device that controls the bus operation is the master, and the devices it controls are the slaves.

When the bus is in the idle state with no input, both the clock and the data lines are pulled high. To initiate a data transfer, the transmitter pulls down the SDA bus followed by the SCL bus line. This gives the start signal. The data is then sent. Receipt, and so the end of the data byte, is indicated by an acknowledge signal. To send an acknowledge, the receiver takes the SCL line high then the data line SDA. There is one clock pulse per data bit transferred with no limit on the number of data bytes that can be transferred between the start and stop conditions; after each byte of data the receiver acknowledges with a ninth bit. This can then be followed by the transmission of the next byte. When the end of the message is reached, a stop signal is sent by taking SCL high then SDA high. Figure 10.68 illustrates this by showing the form of this clock signal and the outputs of a transmitter and a receiver.

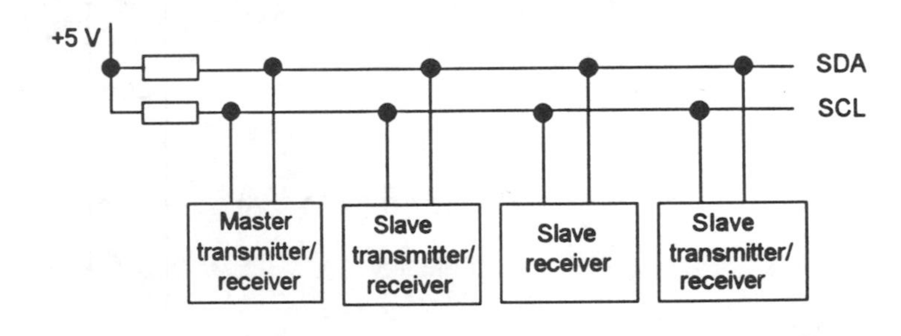

Fig. 10.67 I²C bus

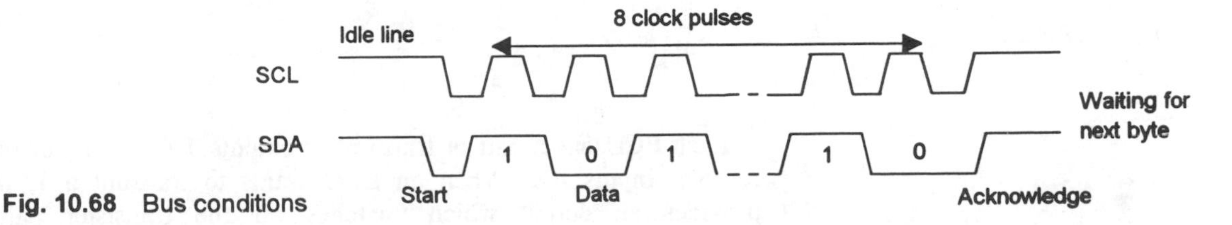

Fig. 10.68 Bus conditions

10.8.3 CAN

The *controller area network* (CAN) was developed by Bosch for use in automobile computerised control systems. CAN is a high speed serial data bus that can transfer up to 1 million data bits per second. It is used to interconnect the systems microcontrollers (electronic control units, ECUs) so that a sensor input to one can be communicated to others and operate actuators; it is a multi-master system. It uses a common bus line of two wires, termed CAN_L and CAN_H. Figure 10.69 shows how the ECUs are connected to the CAN bus.

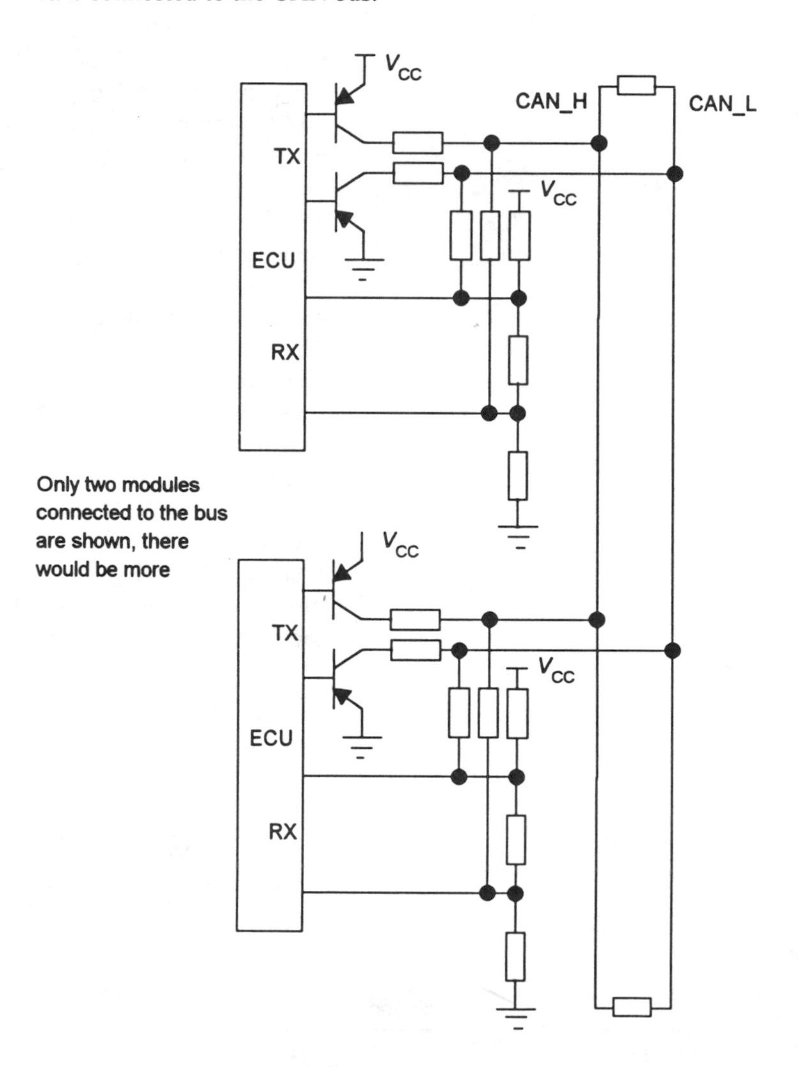

Fig. 10.69 CAN

Each ECU has a pair of transmitter outputs TX and a pair of receiver inputs RX. When an ECU wants to transmit a 1, it provides an output which switches off the transistor pair connected to the TX outputs. As a result, both the CAN_L and

CAN_H wires assume approximately the same voltage level. As a consequence, a 1 input is provided to the RX terminals of other ECUs. If the transistors are switched on, a current is produced through the bus wires and a voltage difference is produced between them. As a consequence, a 0 input is provided to the RX terminals of other ECUs. With CAN, devices are not given specific addresses but the messages are identified using bits and the ECUs wait for messages which have the relevant identifier bits for them.

10.8.4 Centronics parallel interface

The Centronics parallel interface is commonly used for the parallel interface to a printer. Table 10.4 shows the pin assignments using an Amphenol 36-way connector. The signal levels used for the Centronics interface are transistor–transistor logic (TTL).

Figure 10.70 shows how a printer can be connected via a Centronics bus to a Motorola 68HC11 microcontroller. Port C is set up for the output of data to the printer. The microcontroller sends a strobe pulse every time it sends data to the printer, STRB is used to provide the strobe signal input to the printer. Handshaking involves two printer signals, ACK and BUSY. When the printer receives the strobe pulse it sets its BUSY line high; and after the data has been received it sends back an acknowledge pulse, indicating it is ready for more data, and sets BUSY low. The acknowledgement of receipt of signal ACK by the printer gives an input to the microcontroller STRA pin; the BUSY signal is not used in the example illustrated by the figure. The select state SLCT signal is provided by PE7; a low indicates that the printer is effectively disconnected from the micro-controller and a high indicates that the printer can communicate with the microcontroller. The error signal ERROR is inputted to PE6, which goes low when the printer detects a fault.

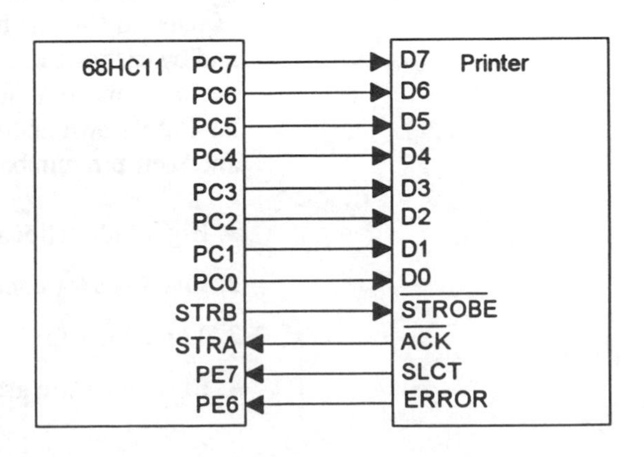

Fig. 10.70 Interfacing with a Centronics printer

Table 10.4 Centronics pin assignments

Signal pin	*Return pin*	*Signal*	*Function*
1	19	STROBE	Strobe pulse to read data in
2	20	DATA 1	Data bit 1 (LSB)
3	21	DATA 2	Data bit 2
4	22	DATA 3	Data bit 3
5	23	DATA 4	Data bit 4
6	24	DATA 5	Data bit 5
7	25	DATA 6	Data bit 6
8	26	DATA 7	Data bit 7
9	27	DATA 8	Data bit 8 (MSB)
10	28	ACK	Acknowledge pulse to indicate data has been received and printer ready for new data
11	29	BUSY	Printer busy, a high signal indicating printer cannot receive data
12		PO	Goes high when printer out of paper
13		SLCT	Select status, high when printer can communicate, low when not
14		AUTO FEED	Auto linefeed, if low a linefeed is added to a carriage return
16		SG	Signal ground
17		FG	Frame ground
18		+5 V	
31	30	PRIME	Used to initialise printer, when low the printer resets
32		ERROR	Error status line, low when printer detects a fault
33		SG	Signal ground

10.8.5 General-purpose instrument bus

The standard interface commonly used for parallel communications is the *general-purpose instrument bus* (GPIB), the IEEE-488 standard, originally developed by Hewlett Packard to link their computers and instruments and thus often referred to as the *Hewlett Packard instrumentation bus*. Each of the devices connected to the bus is termed a listener, talker or controller (Fig. 10.71). Listeners are devices that accept data from the bus, talkers place data, on request, on the bus and controllers manage the flow of data on the bus by sending commands to talkers and listeners and by carrying out polls to see which devices are active. Up to 15 devices can be attached to the bus at any one time, each device having its own address. Table 10.5 lists the functions of the lines and their pin numbers in a 25-way D-type connector. There are:

1. Eight bidirectional lines to carry data and commands
2. Five lines for control and status signals
3. Three lines for handshaking between devices
4. Eight lines are ground return lines

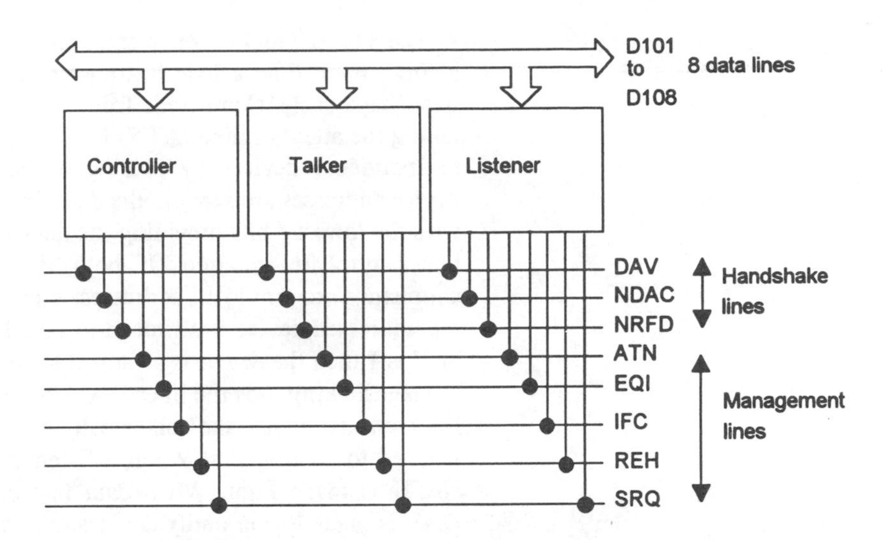

Fig. 10.71 GPIB bus

Table 10.5 IEEE-488 bus system

Pin	Signal group	Abbreviation	Function
1	Data	D101	Data line 1
2	Data	D102	Data line 2
3	Data	D103	Data line 3
4	Data	D104	Data line 4
5	Management	EOI	End Or Identify: used either to signify the end of a message sequence from a talker or by the controller to ask a device to identify itself
6	Handshake	DAV	Data Valid: when low then the information on the data bus is valid and acceptable
7	Handshake	NRFD	Not Ready For Data: used by listener devices taking it high to indicate that they are ready to accept data
8	Handshake	NDAC	Not Data Accepted: used by listeners taking it high to indicate that data is being accepted
9	Management	IFC	Interface Clear: used by the controller to reset all the devices of the system to the start state
10	Management	SRQ	Service Request: used by devices to signal to the controller that they need attention
11	Management	ATN	Attention: used by the controller to signal that it is placing a command on the data lines
12		SHIELD	Shield
13	Data	D105	Data line 5
14	Data	D106	Data line 6
15	Data	D107	Data line 7
16	Data	D108	Data line 8
17	Management	REN	Remote Enable: to enable a device to indicate that it is to be selected for remote control rather than by its own control panel
18		GND	Ground/common (twisted pair with DAV)
19		GND	Ground/common (twisted pair with NRFD)
20		GND	Ground/common (twisted pair with NDAC)
21		GND	Ground/common (twisted pair with IFC)
22		GND	Ground/common (twisted pair with SRG)
23		GND	Ground/common (twisted pair with ATN)
24		GND	Signal ground

The 8 bit parallel data bus can transmit data as one 8 bit byte at a time. Each time a byte is transferred the bus goes through a handshake cycle. Commands from the controller are signalled by taking the attention line (ATN) low. Commands are then directed to individual devices by placing addresses on the data lines; device addresses are sent via the data lines as a parallel 7 bit word with the lowest 5 bits providing the device address and the other 2 bits control information. If both these bits are 0 then the commands are sent to all addresses; if bit 6 is 1 and bit 7 is 0 then the addressed device is switched to be a listener; if bit 6 is 0 and bit 7 is 1 then the device is switched to be a talker.

Handshaking uses the lines DAV, NRFD and NDAC, the three lines ensuring that the talker will only talk when it is being listened to by listeners. When a listener is ready to accept data, NRFD is made high. When data has been placed on the line, DAV is made low to notify devices that data is available. When a device accepts a data word, it sets NDAC high to indicate that it has accepted the data and NRFD low to indicate that it is now not ready to accept data. When all the listeners have set NDAC high, the talker cancels the data valid signal, DAV going high. This then results in NDAC being set low. The entire process can then be repeated for another word being put on the data bus.

Problems

1. Explain the purpose of buffers in interfaces.
2. What are the three states of a tristate buffer.
3. For parallel data transfer, strobe-and-acknowledge is often used for handshaking. Describe how this gives handshaking.
4. Explain the use of interrupts in the programs.
5. What is the result of activating the reset pin on a microcontroller?
6. Assuming a header file, what instruction could be used to set an Intel 8051 microcontroller to enable external interrupt 0?
7. Assuming a header file, what instruction could be used to set a Motorola 68HC11 microcontroller to globally enable all interrupts?
8. What instruction should be used to enable the maskable interrupt with (a) a Zilog Z80 microprocessor, (b) a Motorola 6800 microprocessor?
9. Assuming a header file, what instruction could be used to enable all the unmaskable interrupts for an Intel 8051 microcontroller?
10. Assuming a header file, what instruction could be used to set an Intel 801 microcontroller so that interrupts occur on falling edge changes.
11. What instructions should be used to enable INTF interrupts with a PIC16 microcontroller?

12. What instruction should be used with a PIC16 microcontroller for interrupts to occur on the rising edge of the signal to the INT pin?
13. Explain the function of the internal watchdog timer in microcontroller systems.
14. For a Motorola MC6821 PIA, what value should be stored in the control register if CA1 is to be disabled, CB1 is to be an enabled interrupt input and set by a low-to-high transition, and CB2 is to be enabled and go low on the first low-to-high E transition following a microprocessor write into peripheral data register B then return high by the next low-to-high E transition.
15. Write, in assembly language, a program to initialise the Motorola MC6821 PIA to achieve the specification given in Problem 14.
16. Write, in assembly language, a program to initialise a Motorola MC6821 PIA to read in eight bits of data from port A.
17. Write, in assembly language, a program to initialise the Z80 PIO so that port A is an input port and port B is in bit mode with bits 0 to 4 as inputs and bits 5 to 7 as outputs.
18. What control words should be used with an Intel 8255 PPI to give (a) ports A, B and C as outputs, (b) port A as input and ports B and C as outputs, (c) port A as output, port B as output, C0 to C3 as inputs and C4 to C7 as outputs.
19. Explain how programmable peripheral interfaces can be used to expand the number of input/output ports of a microprocessor.
20. Explain the difference between synchronous and asynchronous serial transmissions.
21. What will be the serial data format for the output from a Motorola MC6850 UART when the following bits are set in the control register: (a) bit 2 as 0, bit 3 as 0, bit 4 as 0, (b) bit 2 as 1, bit 3 as 0, bit 4 as 0, (c) bit 2 as 0, bit 3 as 0, bit 4 as 1?
22. How can the synchronous or asynchronous mode be selected with an Intel 8251 UART?
23. Explain how the Motorola 68HC11 microcontroller can be connected to give synchronous serial interfaces with peripherals.
24. Write a program, for a Motorola 68HC11 microcontroller, to transfer by synchronous serial transmission one byte of data from a master to a slave if the slave is always enabled and the baud rate is to be the E clock rate divided by 32.
25. With a bus frequency of 2 MHz, what settings should be used with BAUD, the baud rate control register of a Motorola 68HC11, for it to give asynchronous serial transmission with a baud rate of 4800.

26. How is the character format selected, e.g. one start bit, 8 data bits and one stop bit, for asynchronous transmissions with the Motorola 68HC11 microcontroller?
27. Write a program to initialise a Motorola 68HC11 to operate with asynchronous transmission at 9600 baud, to give a format of one start bit, eight data bits and one stop bit, no interrupt for receive or transmit, enable receive and transmit, idle-line wake-up and no break to be sent.
28. How can an Intel 8051 microcontroller be set for synchronous serial signal operation?
29. Write a program in assembly language to initialise an Intel 8051 microcontroller to operate as an 8 bit asynchronous UART at 2400 baud; the clock is 12 MHz. The receiver should be enabled and the transmit interrupt flag set at the end bit 8.
30. Write a program in C to initialise an Intel 8051 microcontroller to operate as an 8 bit UART at 9600 baud. The receiver should be enabled and serial interrupts enabled. Assume a header file.
31. What values can be written to the SPRG and TXSTA registers of a PIC16 microcontroller for asynchronous serial transmission if it is to have a baud rate of 9600 with an oscillator of frequency 10 MHz?
32. What values should be written to a PIC16 microcontroller's registers if it is to have pins RC6 and RC7 configured for asynchronous transmission and reception at a baud rate of 9600. Interrupts to the CPU should be enabled.
33. If a microcontroller is to be used with the RS-232 bus, what interface is needed?
34. CAN is a bus often used with automobiles. Explain how it functions.
35. In general, can a microcontroller be directly connected to a Centronics bus without any adjustment of signal levels?

11 Interfacing examples

11.1 Introduction

This chapter is a continuation from Chapter 10 and considers the design of interfaces in applications involving switches, LEDs, timers and analogue signals, stepper motors and power devices.

11.2 Interfacing switches

Switches are generally interfaced to an input port of a peripheral interface adapter (PIA) or a microcontroller with the aid of a pull-up resistor (Fig. 11.1(a)). This enables the switch to supply a logic 0 when closed and a logic 1 when open; when closed the input is connected to ground and when open the input is connected via a resistor to +5 V. The alternative of just putting the switch in the 5 V line (Fig. 11.1(b)) presents problems in that when the switch is open the input floats.

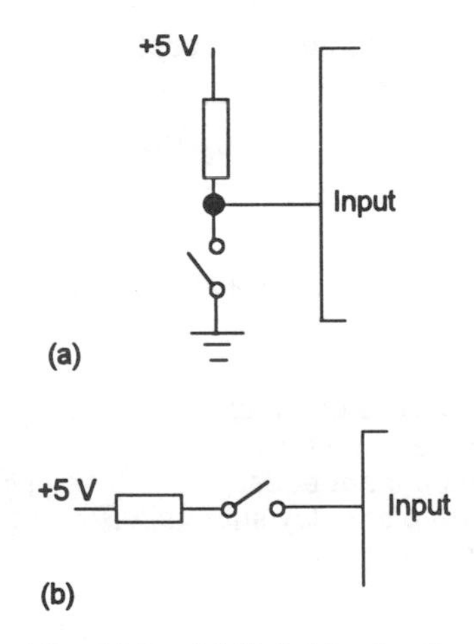

Fig. 11.1 (a) Suitable circuit, (b) unsuitable circuit

The PIC 16 microcontroller can have the bits of port B initialised as inputs by setting bits in TRISB. The pins set as inputs can include an optional pull-up resistor if the NOT_RBPU bit of the OPTION register (Fig. 11.2) is made 0. They thus provide inputs for switches, the pin being held high until a switch attached to it is closed.

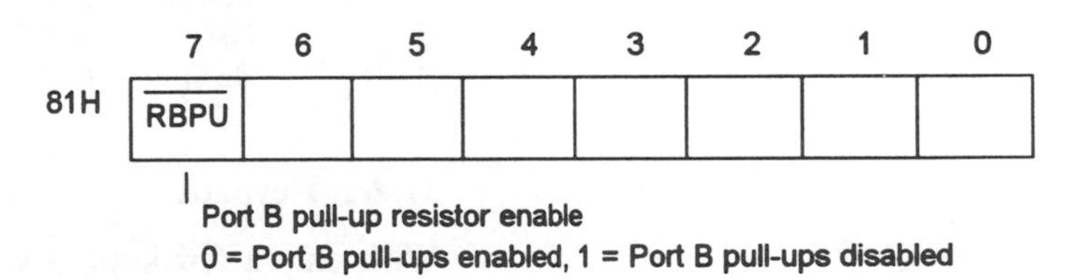

Fig. 11.2 OPTION register

11.2.1 Debouncing

Whenever a mechanical switch is opened or closed, there is a very short period of time during which the contacts open and close a number of times, the term used is *bounce*, before completely opening or closing (Fig. 11.3). Although this bouncing only takes

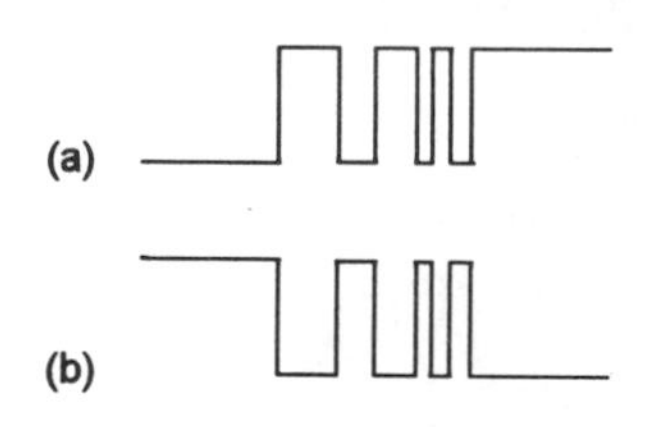

Fig. 11.3 Bouncing with switch: (a) opening, (b) closing

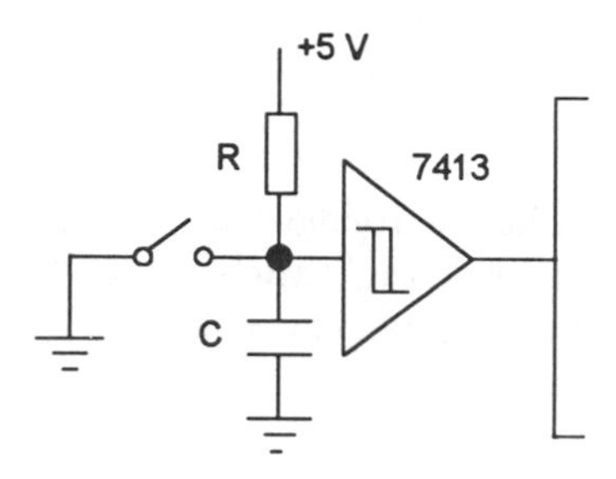

Fig. 11.4 Schmitt trigger

place over a few milliseconds, it can present a problem with microprocessor systems if they detect a single opening or closing as multiple openings and closings.

There are several hardware methods that can be used to debounce switches. One commonly used method for a single-pole single-throw switch involves using a *Schmitt trigger*. As the input to the trigger rises from a low value, the output from the trigger remains low until the on threshold is reached. The output then jumps to a high and remains high until the off threshold is reached. With the circuit shown in Fig. 11.4, when the switch is opened the supply voltage charges the capacitor; any bouncing merely prolongs the time taken to charge the capacitor to the on threshold. When the switch is closed, the first bounce discharges the capacitor and the output from the trigger goes low; the rest of the bounces do not last long enough to charge up the capacitor to cause the trigger to switch.

An alternative to using hardware for debouncing is to use software. Essentially the procedure is to:

1. Detect switch closure.
2. Since small switches do not bounce for more than about 20 ms, wait 20 ms before checking the switch again.
3. If the output is still low, the program assumes the switch has indeed been closed and the program continues.

A possible program to debounce a switch which is active low and at address $2000 is thus of the form:

```
LOOP    LDAA    $2000     ; address of switch
        CMPA    #$FF      ; detect closure
        BEQ     LOOP      ; loop if not equal
        JSR     DELAY     ; jump to delay subroutine
        LDAA    $2000     ; repeat check
        CMPA    #$FF
        BEQ     LOOP
```

11.2.2 Keypads

With only a few keys, a keypad can be arranged as an array of switches with each having its own input to the microcontroller or PPI. However, for more than a few keys it is generally necessary to arrange the switches as a matrix. Figure 11.5 shows the basic form of a 16-key keypad. Such a keypad has four column rails and four row rails. Each switch has one terminal connected to a column rail and one to a row rail. One way the keypad can be used is to connect the rows to inputs of a microcontroller or PIA and the columns to outputs. This sequence can then be followed:

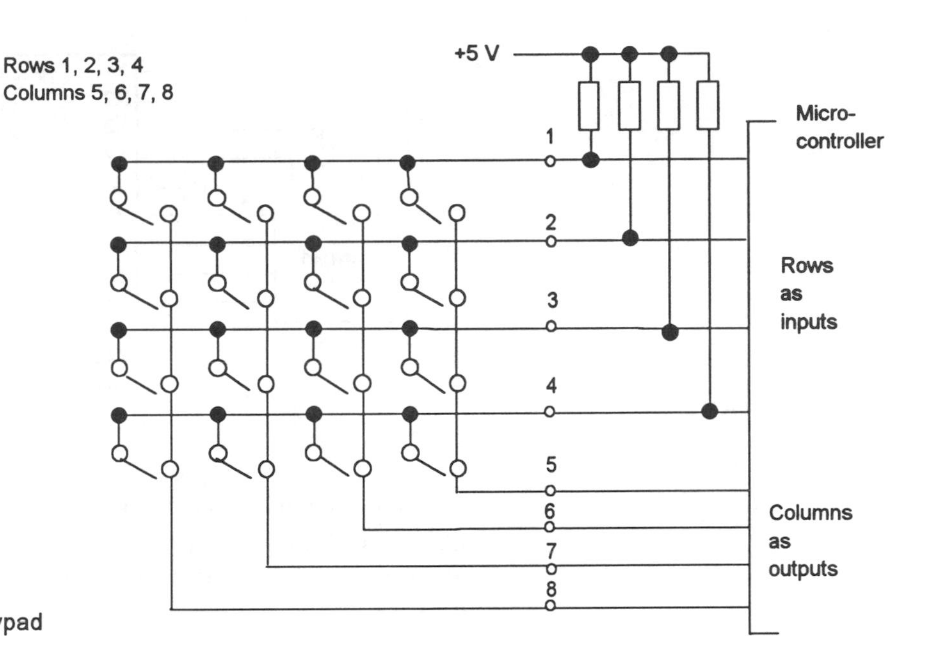

Fig. 11.5 A 16 way keypad

1. Bits PB0, PB1, PB2 and PB3 of the microcontroller are set as input bits, bits PB4, PB5, PB6 and PB7 as outputs.
2. Make all the columns 0. Read each input in turn until a 0 is found to indicate a closed key. The four row bits are thus read, the result being 1110, 1101, 1011 or 0111. Save the value.
3. Loop through the column outputs making, one at a time, a column 0 with all the other columns 1. The sequence of outputs is thus 1110, 1101, 1011, 0111. Only when the column in which the closed key is located is made 0 is its row rail 0.
4. Use the row PB0–PB3 and the column PB4–PB7 values to determine the key pressed by going to a look-up table.

An alternative is to use an encoding chip (Fig. 11.6) to determine which key has been closed. The keypad is connected to the encoder which then gives a high output on one line DAV (data available) when any key is pressed. There is then a 4 bit output to indicate which key has been closed. The program sequence is then:

1. Wait for DAV to be 0, indicating that no key is closed.
2. When DAV is 1, indicating a key is pressed, read the 4-bit data. A look-up table can then be used.

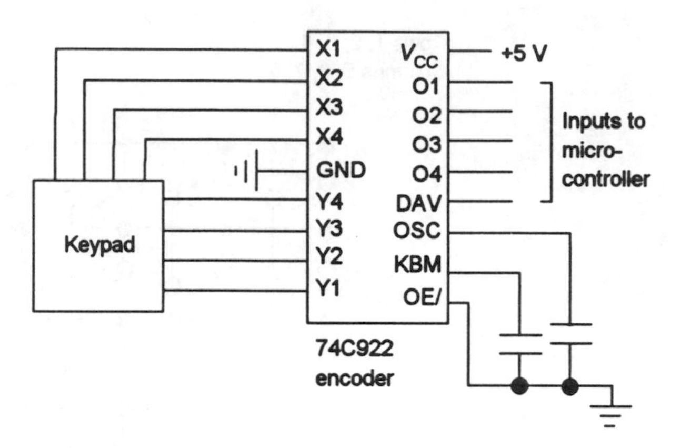

Fig. 11.6 Encoder

In Fig. 11.6 the circuit is shown for direct connection to the input port of a microcontroller with no interrupt facility. To use an interrupt, the DAV line going high can be used to trigger the interrupt.

11.3 Interfacing LEDs

A light-emitting diode (LED) will be illuminated if it is forward-biased and there is enough current flowing through it. Typically a current of a few milliamps up to 20 mA is required. The voltage drop across a forward-biased LED ranges from about 1.6 V to 2.5 V. LEDs are simple to interface with a microprocessor, provided the interface circuit can give sufficient current. Connection between a microcontroller or PIA output port (Fig. 11.7(a)) and earth to drive the LED by a 1 output will not work satisfactorily because the output will not provide enough current. A far better option is the circuit shown in Fig. 11.7(b) with an inverter buffer. When the inverter buffer receives a 1 input, it is enabled to sink the LED current. If we assume 10 mA is required for the LED and the forward voltage drop across it is 1.7 V then 3.3 V will be dropped across the series resistor and so the required resistance to give 10 mA is 3.3/0.010 = 330 Ω.

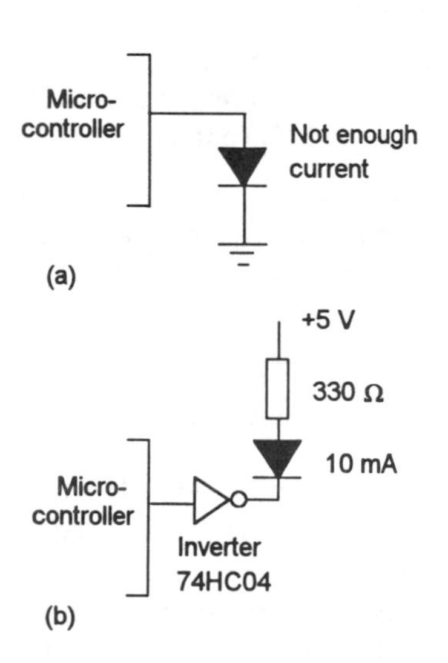

Fig. 11.7 Connecting an LED to a microcontroller

11.3.1 Seven-segment LEDs

Seven-segment displays contain seven LEDs in a figure-eight arrangement (see Section 3.4). The seven LEDs are always connected together so that one end is a common anode and the elements are made active by the input going low, or it is a common cathode and the elements are made active by the input going high (see Fig. 3.34). Common anode is probably more usual. The seven-segment display requires a certain set of 7 bits, i.e. code, to be applied to its pins for each character to be displayed.

Figure 11.8(a) shows how a seven-segment display can be connected to the port of a microcontroller in the common anode arrangement; if a microprocessor with a PIA is used then buffer/latch is provided by the PIA. To display the required character, the correct code for each character must be latched and outputted from the microcontroller; the software has to take the program data and compute the code required for the display by perhaps using a look-up table. With a voltage drop across an LED segment of, say, 1.7 V and an output high from the 74LS244 of 5 V, the voltage drop across a resistor is 3.3 V and if the current is to be limited to, say, 15 mA then the resistors need to be about 220 Ω.

An alternative is to use hardware coding. Decoder/drivers are devices which take a BCD number, decode it for the display and provide ample current to drive the segments. A popular choice for a seven-segment display is the 7447 (Fig. 11.8(b)).

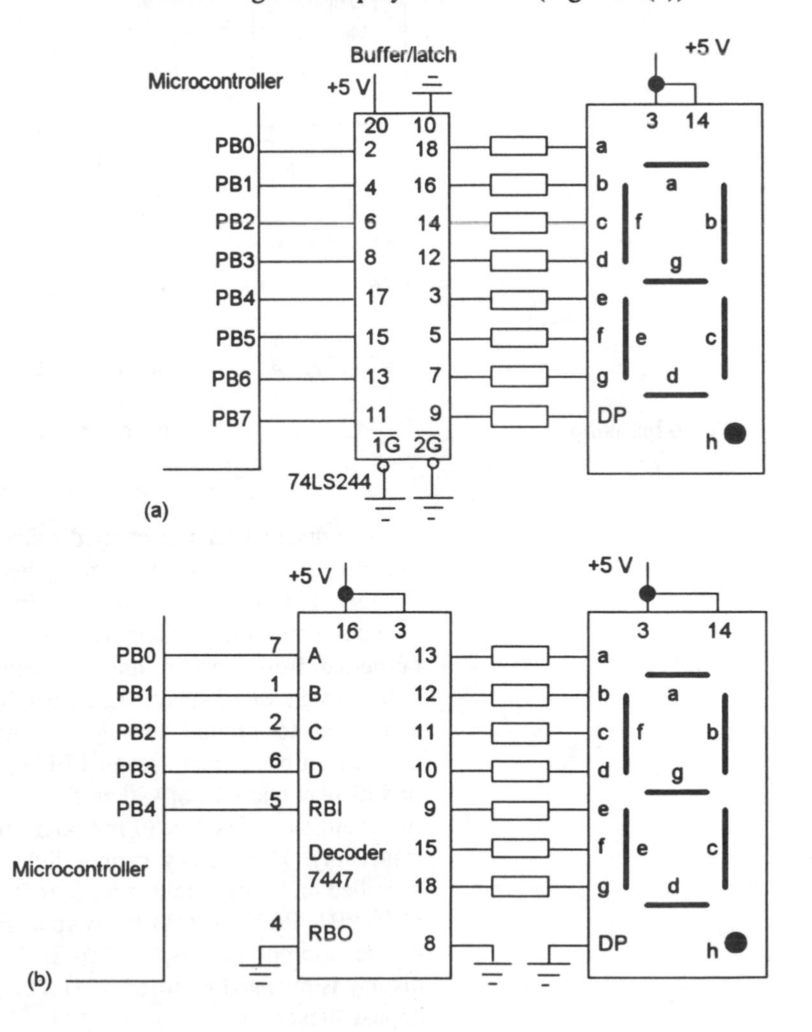

Fig. 11.8 Driving a display

With a four-number display, if the number 15 is to be displayed we generally do not want it to appear as 0015 but just 15 with the first two display elements blank. The term *blanking* is used when none of the segments are lit and this is achieved with a decoder such as the 7447 by the *ripple blanking input* RBI being set low. When RBI is low and the BCD inputs A, B, C and D are low then the output is blanked. If the input is not zero the ripple blanking output RBO is high regardless of the RBI status. The RBO of the first digit in the display can be connected to the RBI of the second digit, and the RBO of the second connected to the RBI of the third, thus allowing only the final 0 to be blanked (Fig. 11.9).

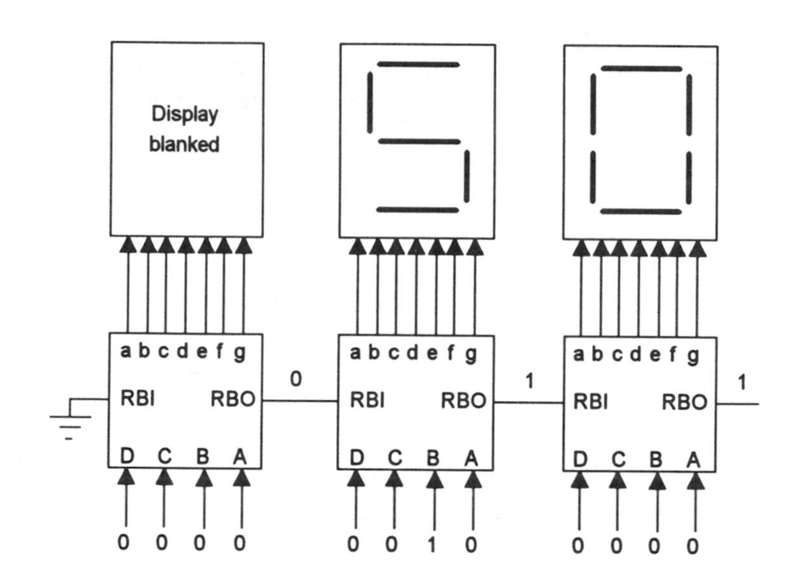

Fig. 11.9 Ripple blanking

With displays having many display elements, rather than use a decoder for each element, multiplexing is used with a single decoder. Figure 11.10 shows the circuit for multiplexing a four-element common cathode type of display. The BCD data is outputted from port A and the decoder presents the decoder output to all the displays. Each display has its common cathode connected to ground through an npn transistor such as the 2N2222 (if each of the seven LED elements, plus decimal point, in a display takes 10 mA, then the maximum current flowing into the common cathode is 80 mA and this has to be be taken by the transistor). The display cannot light up unless the transistor is switched on by an output from port B. Thus by switching between PB0, PB1, PB2 and PB3 the output from port A can be switched to the appropriate display. To maintain a constant display, a display is repeatedly turned on sufficiently often for the display to appear flicker-free.

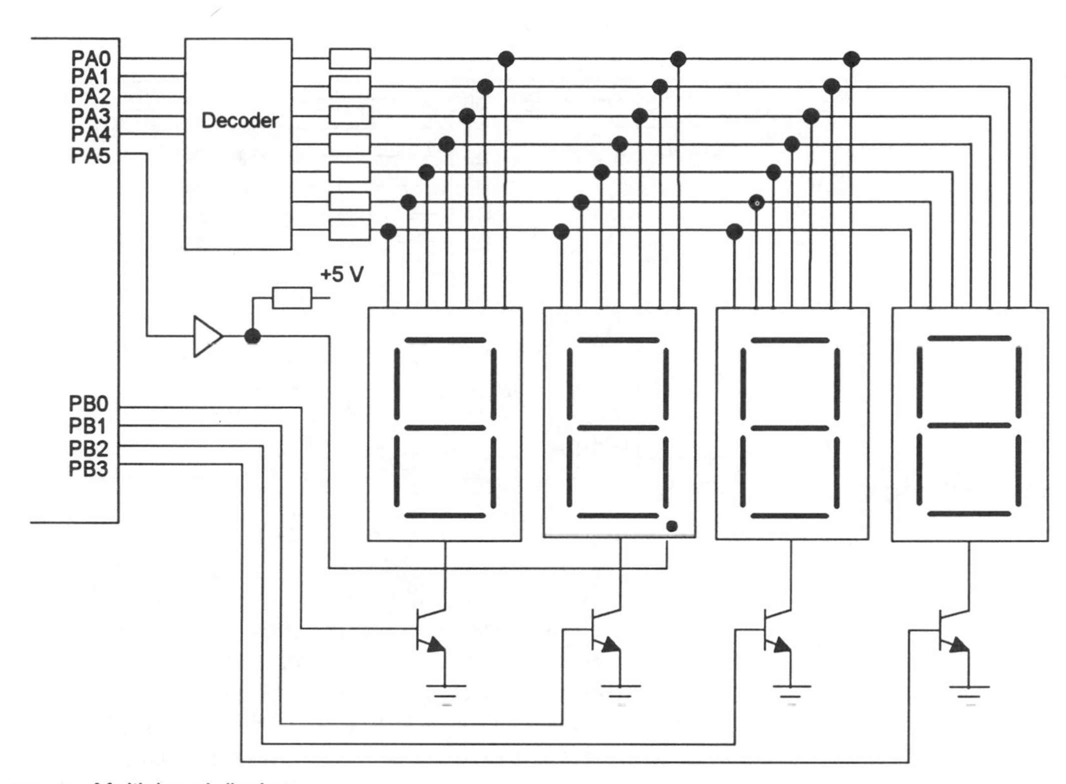

Fig. 11.10 Multiplexed display

11.4 Interfacing analogue

Many sensors produce analogue signals which have to be converted into digital signals for microprocessors. Likewise, the digital output from microprocessors often has to be converted to analogue for many actuators. Some microcontrollers have integral analogue-to-digital converters and so, when initialised to use these inputs, they can have direct analogue inputs without the need for an external analogue-to-digital converter. The next two sections look at signal conversion.

11.4.1 Analogue-to-digital conversion

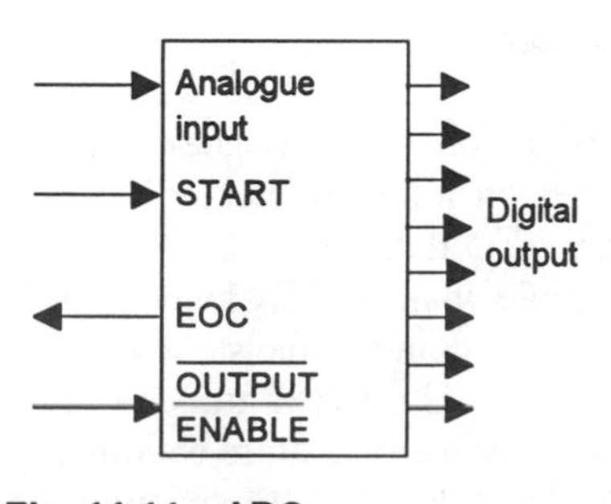

Fig. 11.11 ADC

Figure 11.11 shows the basic form of an analogue-to-digital converter (ADC). A low-to-high pulse is applied to the ADC START pin in order to start the conversion. This causes the END OF CONVERSION (EOC) signal to go low. After starting the conversion, several clock cycles have to elapse before it is completed; when completed the EOC signal goes high and the digital data is available on the ADC output lines. A low on the OUTPUT ENABLE (OE) or READ input to the ADC will then transfer the digital output for it to be read.

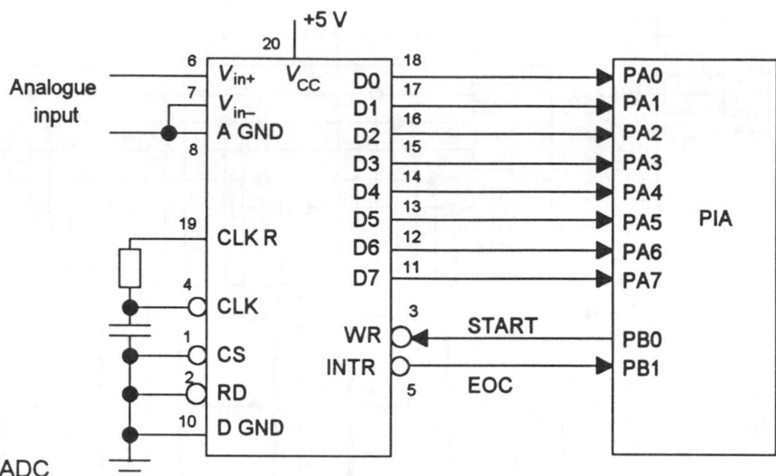

Fig. 11.12 Interfacing an ADC

To illustrate the connections between an ADC and a microprocessor system, Fig. 11.12 shows an ADC0801 (no latch) connected to the PIA of a microprocessor system. The digital output from the ADC is connected to port A of a PIA, with its integral latch, and port B is used to provide the START signal and receive the EOC signal. This might be used as an interrupt signal to the microprocessor. The READ pin of the ADC is kept low. The program follows this sequence:

1. Initialise the PIA so that, say, port A is input, port B bit 0 is an output and port B bit 1 is an input.
2. Output a 0 on bit PB0.
3. Output a 1 on bit PB0 to give the low-to-high transition to start the conversion.
4. Output a 1 on bit PB0.
5. Wait until PB1 goes low, indicating the end of the conversion.
6. Read the inputs on port A and store.

ADC0804 is a latched version of an analogue-to-digital converter and so can be connected, in a similar manner to Fig. 11.12, but directly to the microprocessor data bus.

Some ADCs have inputs for more than one analogue signal, e.g. the ADC0809 has eight analogue input channels. At any one time, just one of these analogue signals is selected and converted to digital. The channel is selected by using an address obtained by writing to three pins A, B and C (Table 11.1); these might be connected to three port B lines of a PIA.

Table 11.1 Address selection

	Address line		
Input channel	*C*	*B*	*A*
IN0	0	0	0
IN1	0	0	1
IN2	0	1	0
IN3	0	1	1
IN4	1	0	0
IN5	1	0	1
IN6	1	1	0
IN7	1	1	1

11.4.2 Digital-to-analogue conversion

Digital-to-analogue converters can have a fixed or variable voltage reference level, generated internally or externally. This controls the range over which the output signal can vary.

The term *unipolar* is used when the DAC input is simple binary and the resulting output voltage is some value between zero and the reference voltage. For example, we could have a DAC input of 0000 giving a DAC output of 0 V and 1111 giving 15/16 of the reference voltage. However, the term *bipolar* is used when the output is signed binary and so the output can have a positive or negative sign. Thus a twos complement input of 0111 might give +7/8 of the reference voltage and 1000 might give −8/8 of the reference voltage.

If a DAC has an internal latch, it may be interfaced directly to the data bus of a microprocessor. Figure 11.13 shows how the DAC MC1408 can be used for unipolar operation with a microprocessor system; the DAC has no internal latch and so might be used with a PIA to provide this facility. If an output voltage, rather than a current, is required from the DAC then a current-to-voltage converter circuit has to be used; a circuit involving a 741 op-amp is shown in Fig. 11.13.

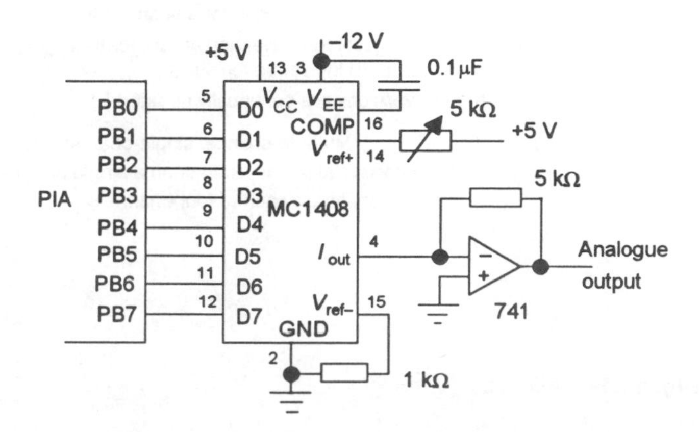

Fig. 11.13 MC1408

11.5 Microcontroller analogue interfaces

Many microcontrollers have integral analogue-to-digital converters. For example, the Motorola 68HC11 has an eight-channel, 8 bit, multiplexed input, successive approximations analogue-to-digital converter. The ADC uses two voltages: a high reference voltage V_{RH} which sets the analogue value for the digital data $FF and should be no higher than V_{DD}, i.e. 5 V; and a low reference voltage V_{RL} which sets the analogue value for the digital data $00 and is set to be no lower than V_{SS}, i.e. 0 V. The value of the analogue signal must fall between these two voltages, and the suggested span $V_{RH} - V_{LH}$ should be greater than about 2.5 V.

Bits 0 to 7 of port E are the analogue channel input pins. The multiplexer to select the channels is controlled by the A/D control/status register (ADCTL) (Fig. 11.14) and might be set to operate as a single-channel system involving just one of the port E pins or as a multichannel system with sampling of each channel in turn. When the ADCTL register is written to, four consecutive conversions are carried out and then, if SCAN is 1, there is a wait for the program to write to the ADCTL register again or, if SCAN is 0, another conversion cycle starts immed- iately. If MULT is 0 the four consecutive conversions are on a single channel, this having been selected by the CA, CB, CC, CD bits. If MULT is 1 the four consecutive conversions are one for each of the four channels. Each conversion takes 32 clock cycles. At the end of a conversion, the result is placed in a result register; the four registers are ADR1, ADR2, ADR3, ADR4.

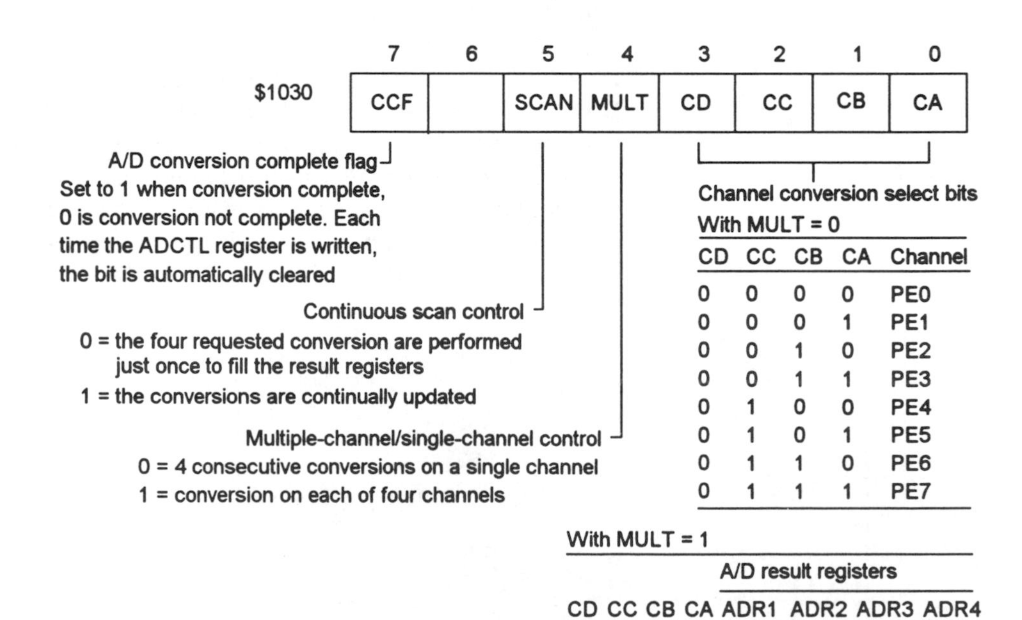

Fig. 11.14 ADCTL

For example, to obtain continuous conversion for the single channel PE4 we must have SCAN = 1, MULT = 0, CD = 0, CC = 1, CB = 0, CA = 0; we thus write 1000100 to the ADCTL register.

The procedure to use the 68HC11 for analogue inputs is:

1. Connect the required voltage levels to V_{RH} and V_{RL}.
2. Set the ADPU bit in the OPTION register (Fig. 11.15) to enable the A/D system and the CSEL bit to select the clock; 0 selects the E clock as the clock signal and 1 selects an on-chip *RC* oscillator.
3. Wait for the capacitors in the A/D system to become charged. This requires at least 100 μs.
4. Select the channels and operating mode by writing to the ADPU register. The conversion then starts after the ADCTL register is written to.
5. Wait until the CCF bit in the ADCTL register is set, then the conversion results can be collected from the ADR registers and stored in memory.

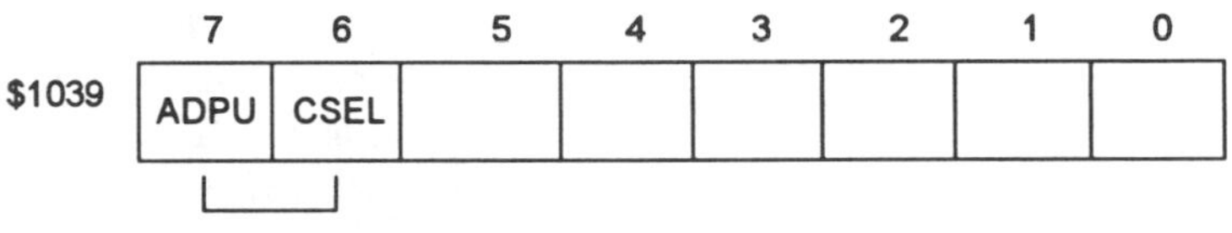

Fig. 11.15 OPTION

Here is an example of a program that will convert the analogue signal connected to PE0 into digital form, carrying out four conversions of the single channel and then stopping. To give the requisite time delay for capacitor charging, an E clock of 2 MHz has been assumed for the delay subroutine.

```
REGBAS  EQU   $1000          ; base address
OPTION  EQU   $39            ; offset of OPTION
ADCTL   EQU   $30            ; offset of ADCTL
ADR1    EQU   $31            ; offset of result register ADR1
ADR2    EQU   $32            ; offset of result register ADR2
ADR3    EQU   $33            ; offset of result register ADR3
ADR4    EQU   $34            ; offset of result register ADR4
        ORG   $00
RESULT  RMB   4              ; reserve four bytes to store results

        ORG   $C000          ; starting address of program
        LDX   #REGBAS
        BSET  OPTION,X,$80   ; set ADPU bit in OPTION register to start capacitor charging
        BCLR  OPTION,X,$40   ; select E-clock by making CSEL 0
        LDY   #30            ; count loop to give time delay
```

```
DELAY   DEY                     ; delay loop
        BNE     DELAY           ; repeat loop until count 0
        LDAA    #$00            ; initialise ADCTL: SCAN = 0, MULT = 0, PE0 selected
        STAA    ADCTL,X
AGAIN   LDAA    ADCTL,X         ; check CCF bit for completion of conversion
        BPL     AGAIN           ; wait until CCF bit set
        LDAA    ADR1,X          ; get first conversion result
        STAA    RESULT          ; save it in first reserved result byte
        LDAA    ADR2,X          ; get the second result
        STAA    RESULT+1        ; save it in second reserved result byte
        LDAA    ADR3,X          ; get the third result
        STAA    RESULT+2        ; save it in third reserved result byte
        LDAA    ADR4,X          ; get the fourth result
        STAA    RESULT+3        ; save it in fourth reserved result byte
        END
```

As an example of another microcontroller with ADC, consider the PIC16C74. Analogue inputs can be to eight channels: port A has RA0, RA1, RA2, RA3, RA5 and port E has RE0, RE1, RE2. With other PIC microcontrollers there are often just five channels, all on port A: RA0, RA1, RA2, RA3, RA5. The procedure is:

1. Registers ADCON1 (Fig. 11.16), TRISA and TRISE must be initialised in order to select the reference voltage to be used and to select which of the input channels are to be analogue. TRISA and TRISE E must have the relevant bits defined as inputs by setting them to 1.

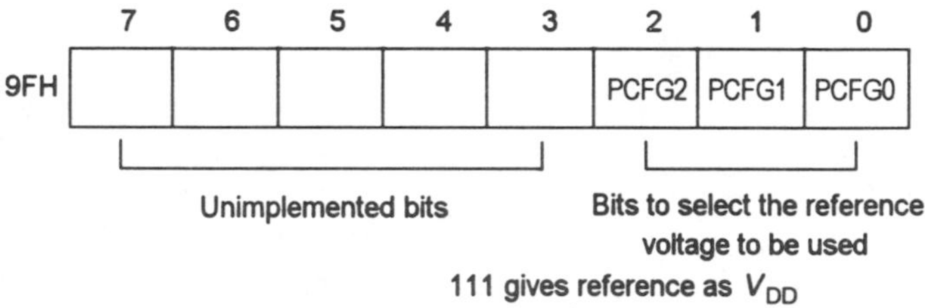

Fig. 11.16 ADCON1

2. Register ADCON0 (Fig. 11.17) must then be initialised to select the clock source for the conversion, to select the channels to be used and to initiate the conversion. The GO/DONE bit can be used to check whether conversion is complete. Thus the program instructions might be:

```
        bsf     ADCON0,2    ; start A/D conversion
ADLoop  btfce   ADCON0,2    ; is conversion finished?
        goto    ADLoop      ; if not, loop until finished
                            ; continue with rest of program
```

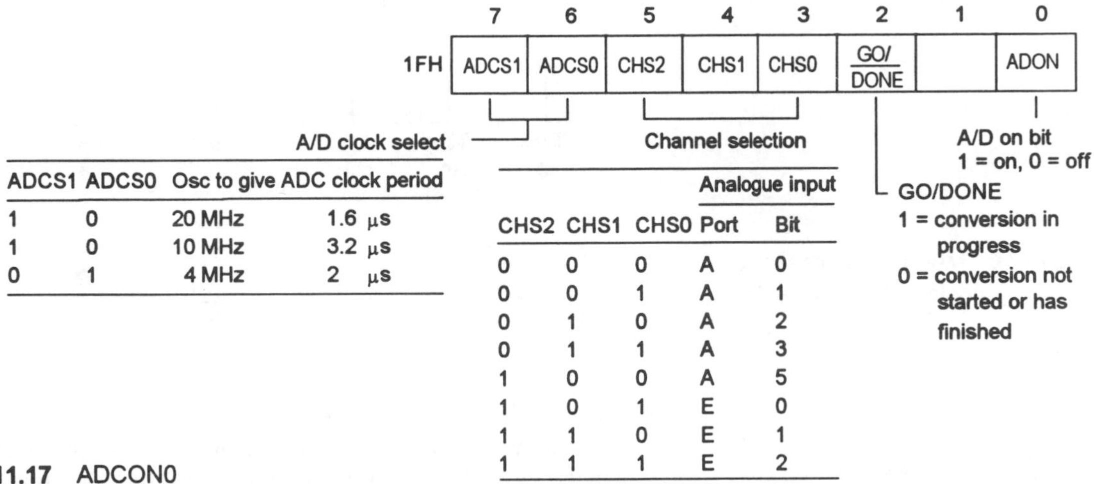

ADCS1	ADCS0	Osc to give ADC clock period	
1	0	20 MHz	1.6 μs
1	0	10 MHz	3.2 μs
0	1	4 MHz	2 μs

CHS2	CHS1	CHS0	Analogue input Port	Bit
0	0	0	A	0
0	0	1	A	1
0	1	0	A	2
0	1	1	A	3
1	0	0	A	5
1	0	1	E	0
1	1	0	E	1
1	1	1	E	2

Fig. 11.17 ADCON0

11.6 Interfacing timers

Programmable timer/counters are used with microprocessor systems to provide a wide range of timing and counting operations. They are available as chips, e.g. Motorola 6840 PTM, Intel 8253 PIT and Zilog Z8430, which can be connected to microprocessor systems or they are integral to some micro-controllers, e.g. Motorola 68HC11, Intel 8051 and PIC16C74.

The *Motorola 6840 PTM* (Fig. 11.18) has three independent 16-bit timers. Each timer is a 16-bit counter with a 16 bit latch, and when enabled, the counter decrements with each clock pulse supplied by either the E clock or an external clock input. When the count value reaches zero, a status register bit is set and an interrupt signal may be generated. The timers can be programmed to operate in a number of modes (Fig. 11.19):

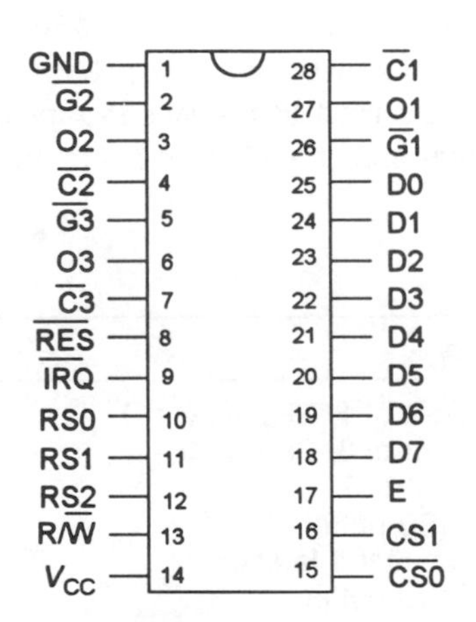

D0–D7	Data bus
C1–C3	Clock inputs for counters 1–3
G1–G3	Outputs for counters 1–3
CS0–1	Chip select inputs
RS0–2	Register select inputs
R/W	Read/write input
IRQ	Interrupt request output
RES	Reset input
E	Enable input

Fig. 11.18 6840 PTM

1. *Continuous mode*
   When the timer counts down to zero, it generates an interrupt signal. The counters are then reloaded from the latches each time they reach zero and the cycle repeated to give a continuous waveform.

2. *Single pulse output mode*
   The counter is loaded just once, so when the timer counts down to zero it produces a single interrupt signal. The result is a pulse width determined by the count value.

3. *Frequency comparison mode*
   The counter can be made to start and stop by an external signal applied to the gate input pin. The counter is loaded once and the counter reading gives the time for one period of the signal applied to the gate pin, i.e. between a falling edge and the next falling edge.

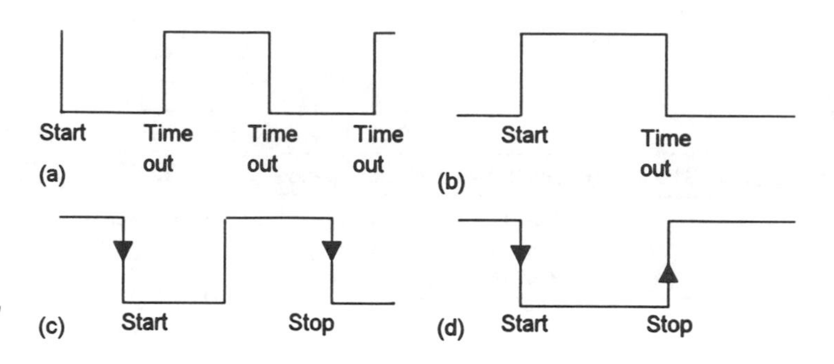

Fig. 11.19 Modes: (a) continuous pulse, (b) single pulse, (c) frequency, (d) pulse

Write	Read	Address
Counter 3 latch	LSB buffer	x + 7
MSB buffer	Counter 3	x + 6
Counter 2 latch	LSB buffer	x + 5
MSB buffer	Counter 2	x + 4
Counter 1 latch	LSB buffer	x + 3
MSB buffer	Counter 1	x + 2
Control reg. 2	Status	x + 1
Control reg. 3/1	Not used	x

Fig. 11.20 Memory map

4. *Pulse width comparison mode*
   The counter is loaded once, started by a falling edge and then stopped by the next rising edge, thus enabling the time of an external event to be determined.

The RS0, RS1 and RS2 inputs select the internal registers and these are then connected to address lines A0, A1, A2 of a microprocessor. By sending the appropriate address (Table 11.2) along these lines, registers can be read or written to. Figure 11.20 shows the resulting memory map. Thus if the PTM has a start address of $5000 then when reading, i.e. R/W = 1, address $5001 is the status register. Each timer has its own control register and latch. The MSB and LSB buffers are used to transfer the most significant and least significant eight bits of a 16-bit word to and from other internal 16-bit registers.

Table 11.2 Register select inputs

RS2	*RS1*	*RS0*	*R/W*	*Register*
0	0	0	0	Write control 1, CR2 bit 0 = 0
0	0	0	1	Write control 3, CR2 bit 0 = 1
0	0	1	0	Write control 2
0	1	0	0	Write MSB buffer
0	1	1	0	Write counter 1 latches
1	0	0	0	Write MSB buffer
1	1	1	0	Write counter 3 latches
0	0	1	1	Read status
0	1	0	1	Read counter 1
0	1	1	1	Read LSB buffer
1	0	0	1	Read counter 2
1	0	1	1	Read LSB buffer
1	1	0	1	Read counter 3
1	1	1	1	Read LSB buffer

Figure 11.21 shows how the bits in the control registers can be used to control the operation of the timers and Fig. 11.22 shows the interpretation of the flag settings that occur in the status register for interrupts.

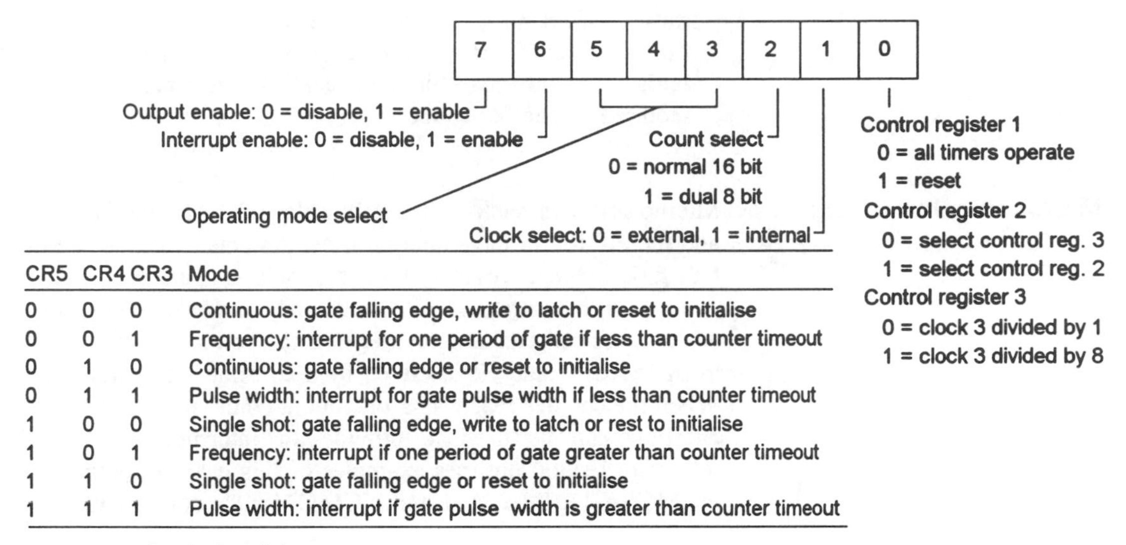

CR5	CR4	CR3	Mode
0	0	0	Continuous: gate falling edge, write to latch or reset to initialise
0	0	1	Frequency: interrupt for one period of gate if less than counter timeout
0	1	0	Continuous: gate falling edge or reset to initialise
0	1	1	Pulse width: interrupt for gate pulse width if less than counter timeout
1	0	0	Single shot: gate falling edge, write to latch or rest to initialise
1	0	1	Frequency: interrupt if one period of gate greater than counter timeout
1	1	0	Single shot: gate falling edge or reset to initialise
1	1	1	Pulse width: interrupt if gate pulse width is greater than counter timeout

Fig. 11.21 Control register

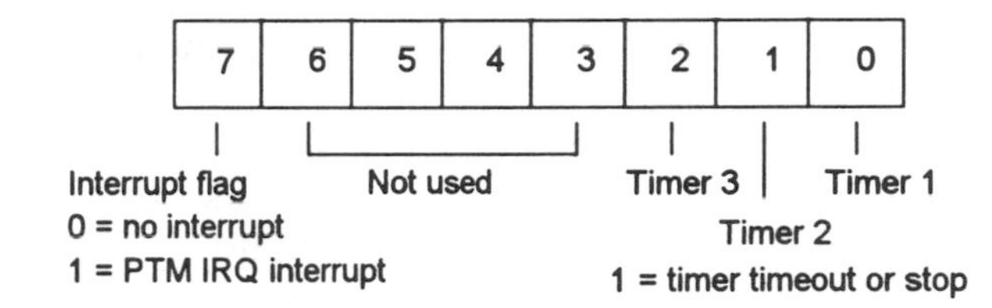

Fig. 11.22 Status register

The procedure for initialising the PTM is:

1. The reset pin of the PTM is generally connected to the reset pin of the microprocessor and is brought low to reset the PTM, then it is returned high.

2. The latches are then initialised by writing a 16 bit data word to them to give the beginning count value from which the count-down will start. If no word is written to them, they will assume the default value of FFFF after the reset. The larger this latch word, the longer it will be before the timeout occurs. For the internal clock of 1 MHz with the divide-by-1 clock option, it will take 2^{17} counts to countout from FFFF, a time of 0.13 s. With the divide-by-8 option it will take about 1 s.

3. A control word is then written to each timer control register. These should be written in the register sequence 3, 2, 1. For example, suppose we want to use timer 3 for continuous operation. We can select the divide-by-1 internal clock option, 16-bit counting mode, interrupt disabled and output enabled, by writing the word 10000010 to control register 3. So that we can then use control register 1 to enable the count to start, we

must then set bit 0 of control register 2 equal to 1 by writing the word 00000001. This then enables us to address control register 1 and clear bit 0 to start all the timers; the word required is then 00000000.

11.7 Microcontroller timers

Microcontrollers such as the Motorola 68HC11, the Intel 8051 and the PIC16C74 have internal timer systems which can be used for tasks which involve creating delays, periodic interrupt generation, measurement of periods and waveform generation. A basic timer consists of a counter that can be read from or written to by the CPU and it is driven by a constant frequency source. When the counter reaches its maximum count and overflows, the overflow can be used to provide an interrupt request. The following section outlines examples of this type of operation for the M68HC11, Intel 8051 and PIC16C74 microcontrollers.

11.7.1 Motorola 68HC11 microcontroller

The Motorola 68HC11 microcontroller has a timer system based on a 16-bit counter operating from the microcontroller clock signal (see Section 2.3, item 7). The output from the clock can be prescaled by setting the PR0 and PR1 bits in the timer interrupt register 1 (TMSK2) (Fig. 11.23) (see also Fig. 2.13 and Table 2.1).

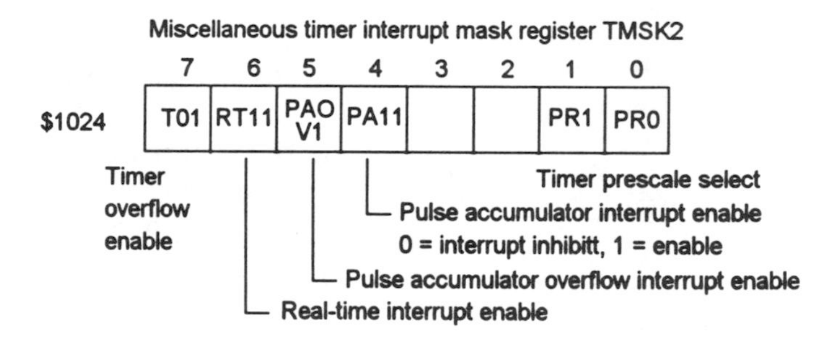

Fig. 11.23 TMSK2 register

For example, with a bus frequency of 2 MHz, PR0 set as 0 and PR1 set as 1, the prescale factor is 8 and each count takes 4 μs. The instructions that might be used for this factor are:

```
BCLR   TMSK2,X,$01 ; sets PR0 to 0
BSET   TMSK2,X,$02 ; sets PR1 to 1
```

The format of the BCLR and BSET instructions is BCLR (operand) (mask) to clear the bits of the operand set by the mask, with the mask being 0000 0001; and BSET (operand) (mask) to set the bits of the operand set by the mask, it being 0000 0010.

The clock starts running when the microcontroller is reset and the TCNT register thus starts at \$0000 and runs continuously thereafter until it reaches the maximum count of \$FFFF. On the next pulse the counter starts at \$0000 again and sets the timer overflow flag TOF in register TFLG2 (Fig. 11.24). Thus with the 2 MHz bus frequency and a prescale factor of 8, the counter overflows after 262.144 μs and sets TOF. It continues to count and cannot be reset by the program but its value can be read at any time. The TCNT is a double-byte register with the higher byte at address \$100E and the low byte at \$100F. The double byte can be read by the double-byte instructions LDD \$100E or LDX \$100E. If the instructions LDAA \$100E and LDAA \$100F had been used then, while the first instruction was being read, the low 8 bits of the counter would have incremented and thus changed by the time the second instruction had been implemented. The count would then have been in error.

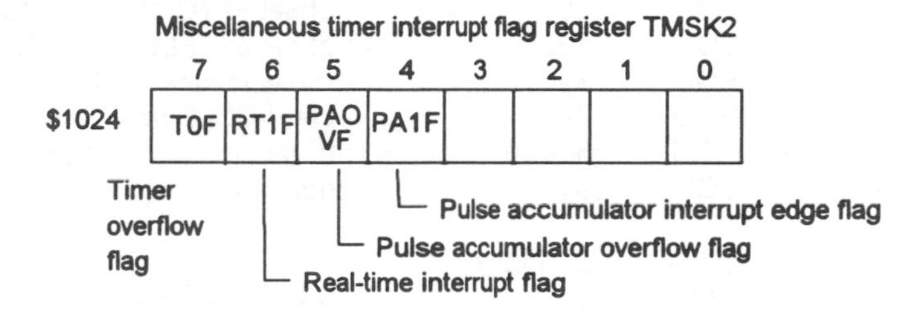

Fig. 11.24 TFLG2 register

The timer overflow flag TOF can be used to provide a time delay. Thus with the 2 MHz bus frequency and a prescale factor of 8, the counter overflows after 262.144 μs and provides a delay of 262.144 μs. The TOF bit must be reset by the program each time it is set by the counter; this can be done by writing a 1 to the TOF bit. Thus we might have the instructions:

```
LDAA  #$80
STAA  TFLG2,X
```

By looping though this delay a number of times, multiples of 262.144 μs delay times can be generated. The same arrangement can be used to generate periodic interrupts.

With this arrangement the timing operation just consists of the program waiting for the required number of timeover flags to occur. Another way of timing involves the use of the output-compare function. Port A of the microcontroller can be used for general inputs/outputs or for timing functions. The timer has output pins OC1, OC2, OC3, OC4 and OC5 with internal registers TOC1, TOC2, TOC3, TOC4 and TOC5. We can use the

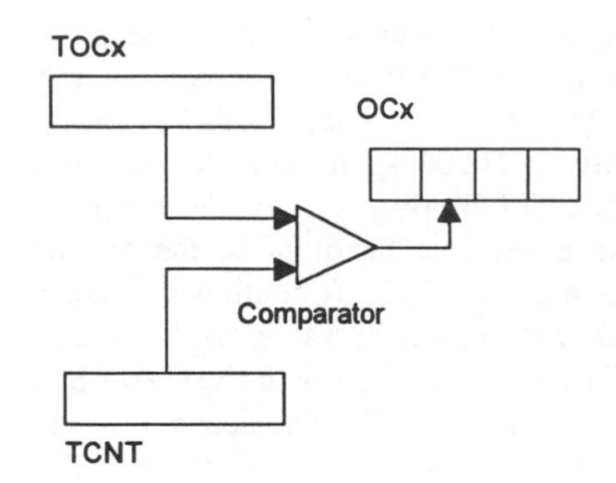

Fig. 11.25 Output compare

output-compare function to compare the values in the registers TOC1 to TOC5 with the value in the free-running counter TCNT. When a match occurs between a register and the counter then the corresponding OCx flag bit is set and output occurs through the relevant output pin. Figure 11.25 illustrates this. Thus by programming the TOCx registers, the times at which outputs occur can be set. The output-compare function can generate timing delays with higher accuracy than the timer overflow flag.

The following program illustrates how output-compare can be used to produce a time delay. The longest delay that can be generated in one output-compare operation is 32.7 ms when the E clock is 2 MHz. In order to generate longer delays, multiple output-compare operations are required. Thus we might have each output-compare operation producing a delay of 25 ms and repeating this 40 times to give a total delay of 1 s.

```
REGBAS   EQU    $1000          ; base address of registers
TOC2     EQU    $18            ; offset of TOC2 from REGBAS
TCNT     EQU    $0E            ; offset of TCNT from REGBAS
TFLG1    EQU    $23            ; offset of TFLGI from REGBAS
OC1      EQU    $40            ; mask to clear OC1 pin and OC1F flag
CLEAR    EQU    $40            ; clear OC2F flag
D25MS    EQU    50000          ; number of E clock cycles to generate a 25 ms delay
NTIMES   EQU    40             ; number of output-compare operations needed to give 1 s delay

         ORG    $1000
COUNT    RMB    1              ; memory location to keep track of the number of
                               ; output-compare operations still to be carried out

         ORG    $C000          ; starting address of the program
         LDX    #REGBAS
         LDAA   #OC1           ; clear OC1 flag
         STAA   TFLG1,X
         LDAA   #NTIMES        ; initialise the output-compare count
         STAA   COUNT
         LDD    TCNT,X
WAIT     ADDD   #D25MS         ; add 25 ms delay
         STD    TOC2,X         ; start the output-compare operation
         BRCLR  TFLG1,X OC1    ; wait until the OC1F flag is set
         LDAA   #OC1           ; clear the OC1F flag
         STAA   TFLG1,X
         DEC    COUNT          ; decrement the output-compare counter
         BEQ    OTHER          ; branch to OTHER if 1 s elapsed
         LDD    TOC2,X         ; prepare to start the next compare operation
         BRA    WAIT
OTHER                          ; the other operations of the program which occur after the
                               ; 1 s delay
```

Another example of a program involving the output-compare function is one to generate a square wave output, i.e. an output that is switched on for a period of time, then off for a period of time and this sequence continually repeated. The on time and the off time can be set to different values; the following program, however, has equal on and off times with each set to 2 ms. The clock frequency is assumed to be 2 MHz and the prescale factor is set to 1. Thus the number of cycles required for 2 ms is 4000. If we store this value in, say, TOC3 then every 4000 cycles the counter will reach this value and set the OC3 flag.

```
REGBAS  EQU    $1000
TOC3    EQU    $1A
TCTL1   EQU    $20
TMSK1   EQU    $22
TFLG1   EQU    $23
TCNT    EQU    $0E
PWIDTH  EQU    4000                 ; set the pulse width
                                    ; to give 2 ms
        ORG    $C000
        LDX    #REGBAS
        LDAA   #$20
        STAA   TFLG1,X              ; clear status flag
        LDAA   #$10
        STAA   TCTL1,X              ; output toggle OC3
        LDD    TCNT,X
AGAIN   ADDD   #PWIDTH              ; number of cycles
                                    ; to give 2 ms
        STD    TOC3,X
HERE    BRCLR  TFLG1,X,$20,HERE     ; wait until time
                                    ; elapsed
        LDAA   #$20
        STAA   TFLG1,X              ; clear status flag
        BRA    AGAIN
        END
```

The timer overflow flag can be used to generate an interrupt. To use a timer overflow interrupt, the TOI bit in register TMSK2 (Fig. 11.23) must be set to 1, the vector must be initialised and the interrupt unmasked.

11.7.2 Intel 8051 microcontroller

The Intel 8051 microcontroller has two internal 16 bit timer/counters, T0 and T1. Both are initialised by setting bits in the special function register TMOD (Fig. 11.26). TMOD is in effect two identical 4 bit registers, one for T0 and the other for T1. The timer is in the timer mode if it is counting the internal crystal-driven clock and in counter mode if it is counting transitions at a designated pin of the 8051. Thus for use as timers the C/T flag in TMOD must be 0. The timer/counter internal count registers are incremented every machine cycle, this being 1/12 of the crystal frequency. Counting or timing is turned on by setting bits in the TCON register (Fig. 11.27).

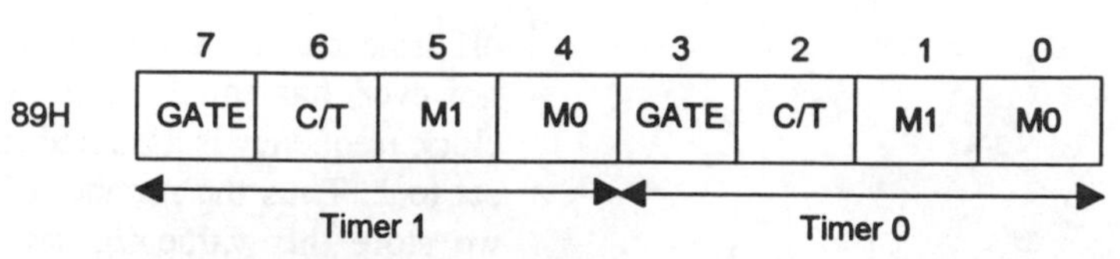

Gate: 0 = timer runs whenever TR0/TR1 set
1 = timer runs only when INT0/INT1 is high along with TR0/TR1

C/T: counter/timer select
0 = input from system clock
1 = input from TX0/TX1

M0 and M1 set the mode

M1	M0	Mode	
0	0	0	13 bit counter, lower 5 bits of TL0 and all 8 bits of TH0
0	1	1	16 bit counter
1	0	2	8 bit auto-reload timer/counter
1	1	3	TL0 is an 8 bit timer/counter controlled by timer 0 control bits. TH0 is an 8 bit timer controlled by timer 1 control bits. Timer 1 is off.

Fig. 11.26 TMOD register

	7	6	5	4	3	2	1	0
88H	TF1	TR1	TF0	TR0	IE1	IT1	IE0	IT0

TF0, TF1	Timer overflow flag; set by hardware when time overflows and cleared by hardware when the processor calls the interupt routine
TR0, TR1	Timer run control bits: 1 = timer on, 0 = timer off
IE0, IE1	Interrupt edge flag; set by hardware when external interrupt edge or low level detected and cleared when interrupt processed
IT0, IT1	Interrupt type set by software: 1 = falling edge triggered interrupt, 0 = low level triggered interrupt

Fig. 11.27 TCON register

Timer 0 has its low byte TL0 at address 8AH and its high byte TH0 at address 8CH; timer 1 has its low byte TL1 at address 8BH and its high byte TH1 at address 8DH.

As an illustration, consider the programming needed to set up timer 0 for use. The line:

```
MOV  TMOD,#00000001B
```

sets the TMOD register with the mode bit M1 to 0 and M1 to 1, i.e. mode 1 operation, so that it is set in mode 1 as a 16 bit timer; it sets C/T to 0 so that the input is from the internal clock; and it sets the gate to 0 so that the timer runs when TR0 is set. The line:

```
SETB  TR0
```

can then used to activate the timer by turning on TR0 in the TCON register. The timer can be stopped by the program line:

```
CLR TR0
```

In this program the timer is set up as a 16 bit timer, hence it overflows and sets the TF0 flag when the count reaches 2^{16} = 65 536. Thus with a 12 MHz crystal, giving a frequency into the counter of 1 MHz, the timer overflow flag is set after 65 536 μs. If we had set the mode in TMOD to mode 0, i.e. M1 = 0 and M0 = 0, then it would have been a 13 bit counter and the timer overflow would have occurred after 2^{13} = 8192 μs. If we had set the mode in TMOD to mode 2, i.e. M1 = 1 and M0 = 0, then it would have been an 8 bit counter and the timer overflow would have occurred after 2^8 = 256 μs. With the mode 3 operation, i.e. M1 = 1 and M0 = 1, we have an 8 bit counter which is auto- matically reloaded when the counter overflows.

If we want a timer to start from some initial count, the timer registers can be given an initial value. This will determine how long must elapse before overflow occurs. Suppose we want a delay of 1 ms and have a 1 MHz crystal. The frequency into the counter is 1/12 MHz. If we used mode 2 then the timer overflow would occur after $2^8/[(1/12) \times 10^6]$ s or 3.072 ms. To generate a delay of 1 ms we thus need to start the counter at some initial value so that it reaches overflow after 1 ms. A time of 1 ms is a count of $0.001 \times [(1/12) \times 10^6] = 83.3$. So we need to give the counter an initial value of $2^8 - 83.3$ or, near enough, 173. The program lines to achieve this are:

```
        MOV    TMOD,#%000000010   ; set timer 0 in
                                  ; mode 2
        MOV    TH1,#173           ; set initial count
        MOV    TL1,#173
        SETB   TR0                ; start the timer
LOOP    JNB    TF0,LOOP           ; wait for overflow
```

Another way of using an initial count to generate a time delay is to give the counter a negative initial value. Thus we might have:

```
MOV TH0,#0FCH
MOV TL0,#18H
```

This adds FC18, or in denary notation −1000, so that the clock reaches its maximum value after a count of 1000. To convert a denary number into its hexadecimal equivalent, repeated division by 16 is used. After each division the remainder, expressed as a hexadecimal digit, forms the hex number. Thus 1000/16 = 62 with remainder 8, 62/16 = 3 with remainder 14 and so the hex number is 03E8. To obtain the −1000 in hex, we derive the 15s complement (equivalent to the ones complement in binary arithmetic) by subtracting from FFFF to give FC17 and then obtain the 16s complement (equivalent to the twos complement in binary arithmetic) by adding 1 to give FC18.

As an illustration, consider the following program for the production of a 10 kHz pulsed square waveform at port P1.0, i.e. the output at that port is switched on for half a cycle then off for half a cycle with the cycle frequency being 10 kHz; this makes the duration of each off and each on equal to 50 μs. A 12 MHz crystal is assumed and so the clock frequency is 1 MHz. With the 8 bit timer the longest possible time interval before overflow is 2^8 = 256 μs. Since this is greater than the time interval required, we can use just 8 bits.

```
        ORG   8100H
        MOV   TMOD,#02H  ; sets mode 2, i.e. 8 bit auto-
                         ; reload
        MOV   TH0,#CE    ; –50 (decimal notation) reload
                         ; value in T0
        SETB  TR0        ; start the timer
LOOP    JNB   TF0,LOOP   ; wait for overflow
        CLR   TF0        ; clear the timer overflow flag
        CPL   P1.0       ; toggle port bit
        SJMP  LOOP       ; repeat
        END
```

There are two timer interrupts, and they are able to occur when either of the two timers overflows. When a timer overflows from all 1s to 0s, its timer overflow flag is set and an interrupt is generated if the interrupt for that particular timer is enabled by the interrupt enable register (Fig. 11.28). Thus if we are using timer 0 we need to enable ET0.

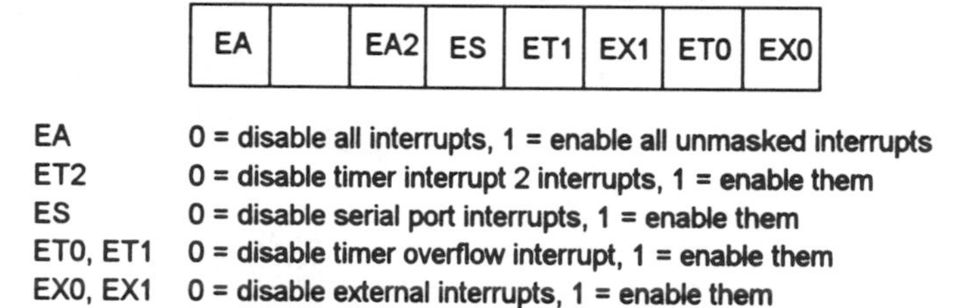

Fig. 11.28 IE register

For a program where an interrupt is to occur every 1 ms, we might have these program lines:

```
MSEC    MOV   TH1,#FCH   ; this resets timer for interrupts
        MOV   TL1,#18H
        INC   MSEC
        RETI

MAIN    MOV   TMOD,#1    ; set mode 1
```

```
        MOV     TH0,#FCH    ; load time value
        MOV     TL0,#18H
        SETB    TR0         ; start the timer
        SETB    ET0         ; enable timer interrupt
HERE    SJMP    HERE
        END
```

In C language the program might be:

```
#include<reg51.h>
unsigned inter msec;

void msec(void)
{
   TH1=–1000>>8; /* this resets the timer for interrupts */
   TL1=–1000&0x00FF;
   msec++;
}

void main(void)
{
   TMOD=0x01;
   TH0=~(1000/256);
   TL0=–(1000%256);
   TR0=1;
   ET0=1;
   while(1);
}
```

11.7.3 PIC timers

The PIC microcontroller PIC16C64A has, in addition to a watchdog timer, the three timers TMR0, TMR1 and TMR2 (see Section 2.5). TMR0 is an 8-bit counter which can be written to or read from and can be used to count external signal transitions or clock signals and generate an interrupt after a certain number of events or clock signals have occurred.

Selection of the clock source is made by the TOCS bit in the OPTION register (Fig. 11.29). Thus to use the internal clock signal the TOCS bit is set to 0. To assign this signal to TMRO, bit PSA has to be set to 0. If the prescalar is not selected (see Table 2.2) then the counter is incremented after every two clock cycles. Selecting a prescalar value by setting bits in the OPTION register (see Table 2.2) allows the count to be incremented after every 2, 4, 8, 16, 32, 64, 128 or 256 clock cycles. Suppose we want the count to be incremented every 2 cycles then we must make PS0, PS1 and PS2 equal to 0.

The counter sets an overflow flag T0IF in the INTCON (Fig. 11.30) register when it overflows and can cause an interrupt if that interrupt source has been enabled.

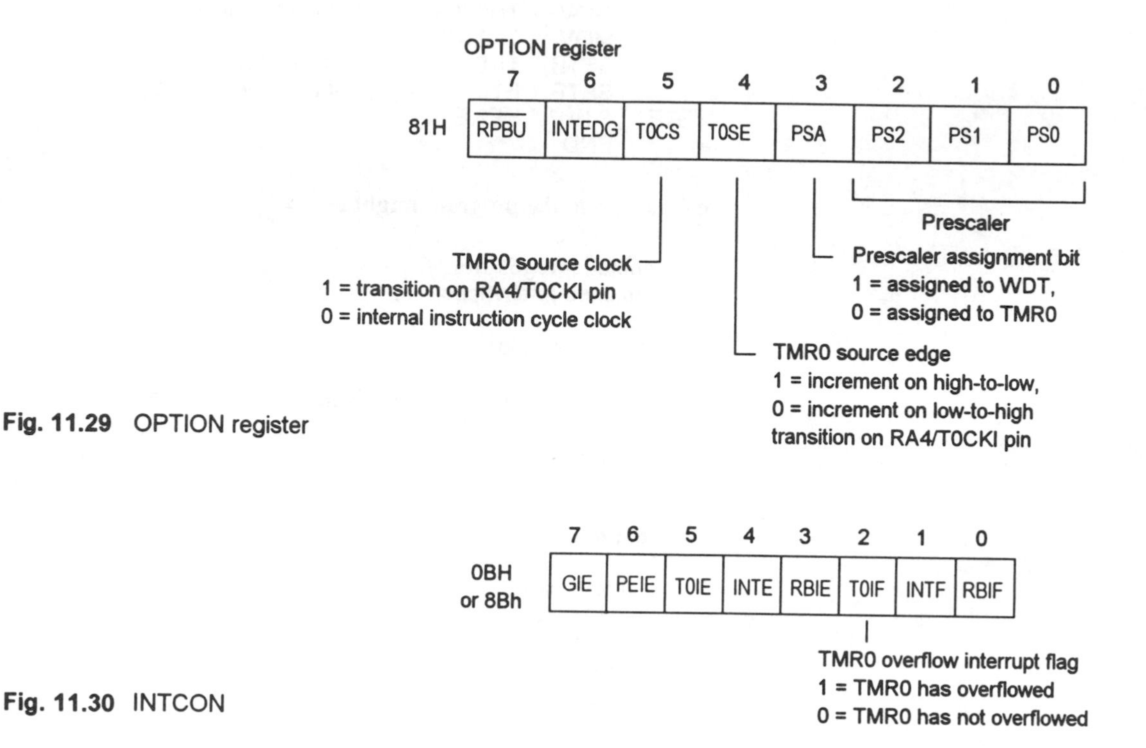

Fig. 11.29 OPTION register

Fig. 11.30 INTCON

The TMR0 counter will overflow when its count reaches $2^8 = 256$. With the prescalar set to divide by 256 then the number of cycles required to cause an overflow is 256×256. The PIC microcontroller divides the frequency of the oscillations it receives by 4 and uses it as the driving frequency for the counter. With an oscillator of 4 MHz then the frequency applied to the counter is 1 MHz and so the overflow occurs, from an initial counter setting of all 0s, after a time of $256 \times 256/1 \times 10^6 = 0.0655$ s = 65.5 ms.

If TMR0 is given an initial value then, for accurate time intervals, we can use the count that has to elapse before overflow. Suppose we wanted a time interval of 10 ms, then using the 4 MHz oscillator with the prescalar set to divide by 256, a count of $0.010 \times (4 \times 10^6/4)/256 = 39$ is required. Thus the counter is given an initial value of $256 - 39 = 217$. If we wanted 1 ms, one way of achieving this would be to repeat the count for the 10 ms overflow 10 times by using a loop. Note that if TMR0 is used to time from being written to, there will be a two-cycle delay before the counting starts.

TMR1 is a 16 bit counter and operates like the 8 bit TMR0 but with the added capability of being able to use a CCP (capture/compare/PWM) module. The capture mode can be used to indicate when a pulse of specific duration has been captured. The compare mode can be used to compare incoming pulses to a specified time duration. The pulse width modulated (PWM) waveform can be used for controlling the speed of d.c. motors.

TMR1 controls the timing of the output on the RC2/CCP1 pin (see Fig. 2.25). To use TMR1 to generate a positive-going signal on this pin requires the following initialisation. The RC2/CCP1 pin has to be set as an output by setting bit 2 to 0 in TRISC. The T1CON register (Fig. 11.31) has to have the bit TMR1ON, bit 0, set to 1 to enable the count input to TMR1, 0 disables it. Bits CCP1M0 and CCP1M1 in the CCP1CON (Fig. 11.32) determine the effect on the RC2/CCP1 pin of a compare. With the bits as 00 the pin is set on a compare, with 01 it is cleared on a compare, with 10 it is not affected on a compare. Thus to output a positive-going pulse we put the bits as 00. For the compare mode we also set bit 3, CCP1M3, in CCP1CON to 1. Thus the input to CCPICON is b'00001000'.

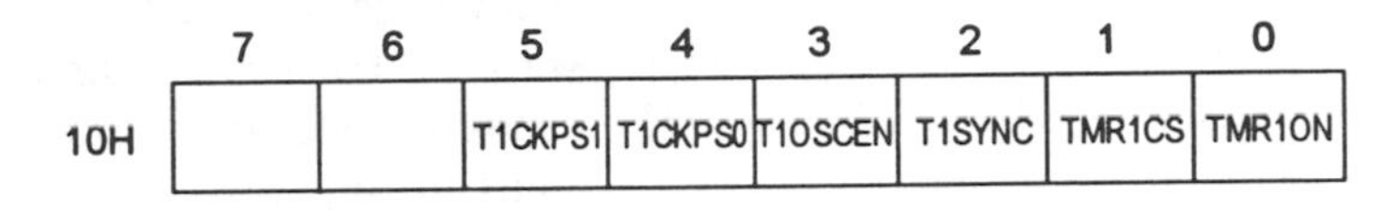

Fig. 11.31 T1CON

	7	6	5	4	3	2	1	0
17H			CCP1X	CCP1Y	CCP1M3	CCP1M2	CCP1M1	CCP1M0

Fig. 11.32 CCP1CON

We can then produce the positive-going signal at some specific time by starting the counter and comparing it with a value set for the time required. When the two counts are equal there is an output from the RC2/CCP1 pin. Here is the code sequence for this, with an output occurring when the TMR1 holding register has the value 5:

```
bcf      T1CON,TMR1ON   ; stop TMR1
clrf     TMR1H          ; clear MSB of TMR1 holding
                        ; register
clrf     TMR1L          ; clear LSB of TMR1 holding
                        ; register
clrf     CCPR1H         ; clear MSB of TMR1 compare
                        ; register
movlf    H'05'          ; move 5 to w register
movwf    CCPRIL         ; move 5 into LSB of TMR1
                        ; compare register
bcf      CCP1CON,0      ; set pin on compare
```

If we want to produce a positive-going pulse from the RC2/CCP1 pin then we can use the above procedure to obtain a positive-going signal, restart the timer when it occurs and then use the compare to clear the output when the second compare occurs:

```
bsf        T1CON,TMR1ON   ; begin TMR1
movlw      10             ; duration of pulse
movwf      CCPR1L         ; move 10 into LSB of TMR1
                          ; compare register
bsf        CCP1CON,0      ; 0 output on second compare
```

To use TMR1 to determine the duration of a positive-going pulse input to the RC2/CCP1 pin, we use it in its capture mode. The procedure is thus to set the RC2/CCP1 pin as an input by setting bit 2 to 1 in TRISC. The T1CON register (Fig. 11.24) has to have the bit TMR1ON, bit 0, set to 1 to enable the count input to TMR1, 0 disables it. Bits CCP1M0 and CCP1M1 in the CCP1CON (Fig. 11.32) determine the effect on the RC2/CCP1 pin of a capture. With the bits as 00 the pin gives the capture time of every falling edge to the pin, with 01 the capture time on every rising edge, with 10 the capture time of every 4th rising edge and with 11 the capture time of every 16th rising edge. For the capture mode we also set bit 2, CCP1M2, in CCP1CON to 1. Thus for a positive-going pulse we first capture the time of the rising edge by setting CCP1CON to b'00000101' and copy it to a register. Then we capture the time of the falling edge by setting CCP1CON to b'00000100' and subtract the first time from it to give the pulse duration.

The TMR2 timer is able to control the period of PWM outputs. The input from the oscillator to TMR2 is prescaled by bits 0 and 1 in the T2CON register (Fig. 11.33). The value in TMR2 is compared with the value in register PR2 and when it is greater then a signal is produced. The number loaded into the PR2 register has to be one less than the desired value at which the signal it required. The signal that occurs when TMR2 is one greater than PR2 can be routed through a postscalar, set by bits in the T2CON register so that interrupts occur after a specific number of these signals.

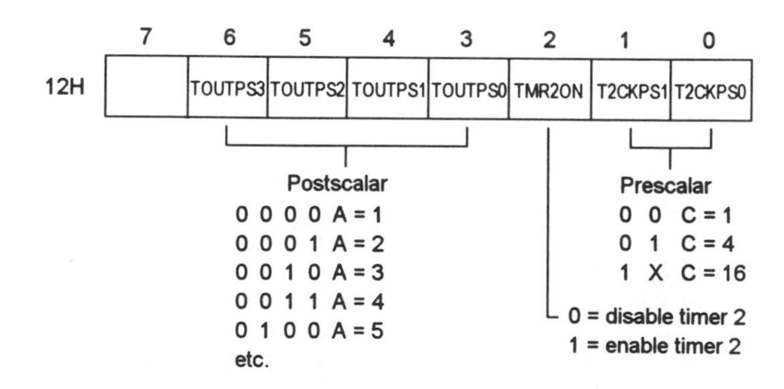

Fig. 11.33 T2CON

Suppose we have a 4 MHz oscillator, i.e. a signal to the timer of frequency 1 MHz and so every 1 μs, and require TMR2 to give an interrupt every 5 ms. If we set the prescalar to C = 4 then the count will increment every 4 μs. Suppose we load PR2 with the decimal number 249. When TMR2 reaches 250 then an overflow signal will be produced. This will occur after 250 × 4 = 1000 μs. If we use postscaling of 2 then an interrupt signal will be produced every 5000 μs = 5 ms. T2CON has thus to be set to b'00001101', bits 0 and 1 being for prescaling, bit 2 for enabling and bit 3 for postscaling. The initialisation instructions for the scaling are for bank 0 and are thus:

```
movlw 'b00001101'
movwf T2CON
bsf     INTCON,PEIE  ; enable interrupt path (Fig. 11.34)
```

and for the PR2 value and bank 1 they are:

```
movlw 249
movwf PR2
bsf     PIE1,TMR2IE  ; enable timer 2 path (Fig. 11.35)
```

Finally we also need to set:

```
bsf     INTCON,GIE  ; enable global interrupts (Fig. 11.34)
```

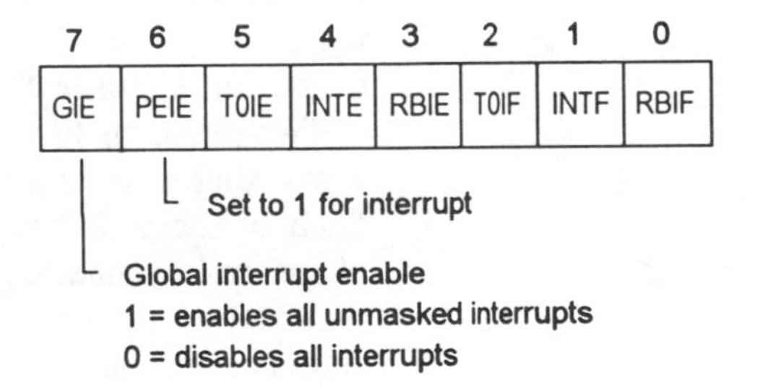

Fig. 11.34 INTCON

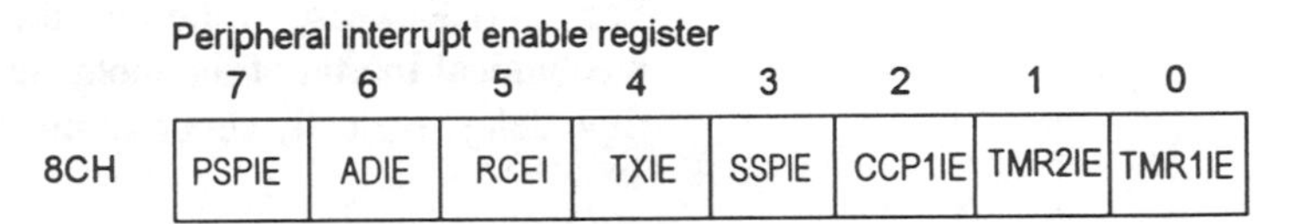

Fig. 11.35 PIE1

11.8 Interfacing stepper motors

Stepper motors (see Section 3.5.1) are widely used with microprocessor systems for the positional control of objects, giving a fixed number of degrees of rotation, i.e. steps, for each input pulse. The term *phase* is used for the number of independent pairs of motor windings between which current is switched in order to

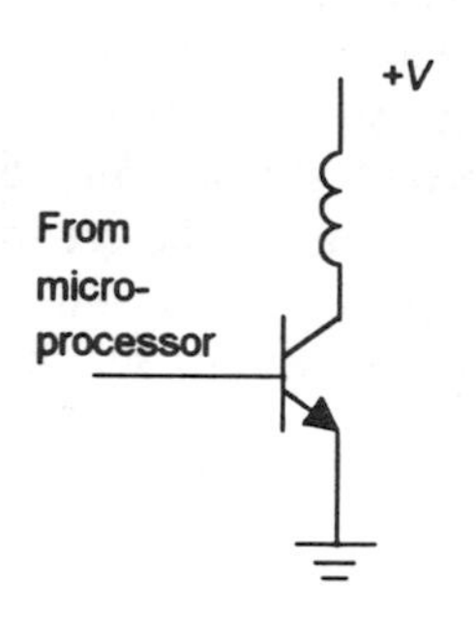

Fig. 11.36 Transistor switch

generate the step rotation. Driving a stepper motor involves applying a series of voltages to the coils of the motor; the stepper rotates each time the voltages are switched from one pattern to the next. Two-phase motors tend to be used for light-current applications.

11.8.1 Interfaces

Operating stepper motors with microprocessors involves writing the step pattern to a latch – an internal latch in the case of a microcontroller and possibly a PIA with a microprocessor system – to hold the voltages while they are used to activate the stepper coils. The coils, however, require larger currents than can be supplied by a microprocessor and the microprocessor has to be isolated from the motor to avoid damage from the large back e.m.f.s that can occur with the switching of the inductive motor windings.

The larger currents can be obtained by using the output voltage from the microprocessor to switch on a bipolar transistor (Fig. 11.36). Where large stepper motors are involved, the larger currents required for their operation require the use of a Darlington pair of transistors or a power MOSFET. Isolation can be provided by using a diode in the line, a resistor or an opto-isolator (Fig. 11.37). The diode offers a simple, cheap interface which is widely used. The optoisolator contains an LED and a phototransistor; the microprocessor provides the current through the LED and this transmits light to the phototransistor, causing it to activate. Optoisolators provide complete isolation.

Two-phase motors are termed *unipolar* when they have six connecting wires to generate the switching sequence (Fig. 11.38). Each of the coils has a centre-tap. With the centre-taps of the phase coils connected together, such a stepper motor can be switched with just four transistors. Table 11.3 gives the switching sequence for the transistors in order to produce the steps for clockwise rotation; the sequence is then repeated for further steps. For anticlockwise rotation the sequence is reversed. The mechanical inertia of the motor means that there has to be a short time delay, typically about 10 ms, between each step.

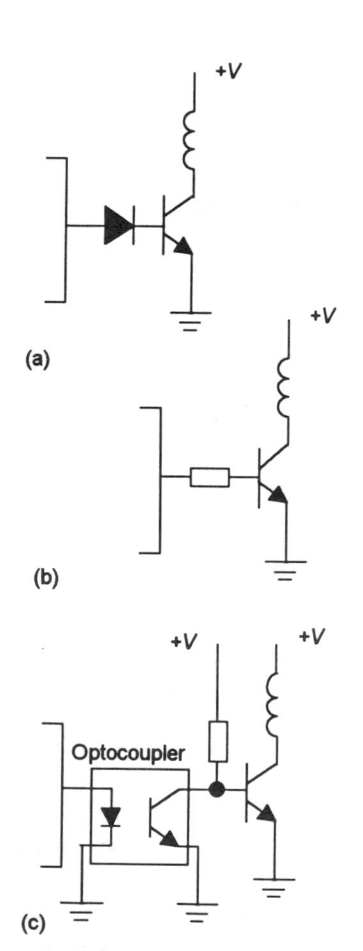

Fig. 11.37 Isolation

Table 11.3 Switching sequence for full-stepping unipolar stepper

	Transistors			
Step	*1*	*2*	*3*	*4*
1	On	Off	On	Off
2	On	Off	Off	On
3	Off	On	Off	On
4	Off	On	On	Off

Half-step rotations are obtained if, instead of using the above full-step sequence, the voltages are switched to the coils in such a way that the rotor stops midway between the full steps; this is known as *half-stepping*. Table 11.4 shows the sequence when the unipolar stepper is half-stepping.

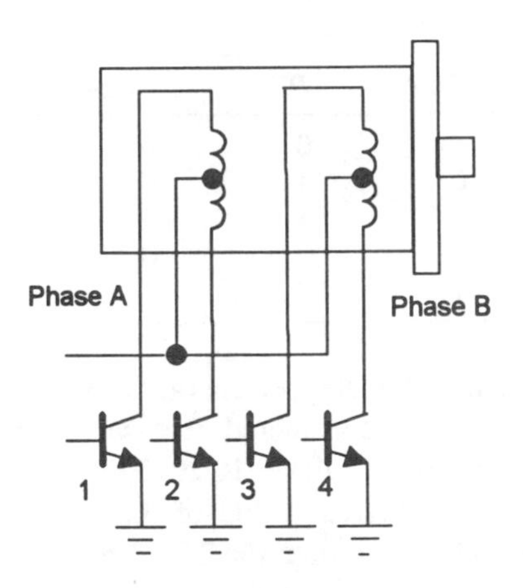

Fig. 11.38 Unipolar motor

Table 11.4 Half-steps for unipolar stepper

	Transistors			
Step	*1*	*2*	*3*	*4*
1	On	Off	On	Off
2	On	Off	Off	Off
3	On	Off	Off	On
4	Off	Off	Off	On
5	Off	On	Off	On
6	Off	On	Off	Off
7	Off	On	On	Off
8	Off	Off	On	Off

A technique known as *mini-stepping* can be used for very small step angles. This involves dividing each step into a number of equal substeps and using different currents to the coils so that the rotor moves to intermediate positions between normal step positions.

A program to generate a continuous sequence of step pulses to operate a stepper motor could thus have the algorithm:

1. Start
2. State the sequence of outputs needed to obtain the required step sequence
3. Set to initial step position
4. Advance a step
5. Jump to delay routine to give time for the step to be completed. In operating a stepper motor, delays have to be used between each instruction to advance by a step; this allows time for that step to occur before the next program instruction
6. Is this the last step in the step sequence for one complete rotation? If not continue to next step, if yes loop back to 3
7. Continue until infinity

Here is a possible program for a two-phase stepper in the full-step configuration and controlled by the microcontroller M68HC11 using outputs from PB0, PB1, PB2 and PB3. A look-up table is used for the output code sequence necessary to drive the stepper in the step sequence; Table 11.5 shows the data used to provide the look-up table.

Table 11.5 Stepping sequence

	The outputs required from Port B				
Step	*PB0*	*PB1*	*PB2*	*PB3*	*Code*
1	1	0	1	0	A
2	1	0	0	1	9
3	0	1	0	1	5
4	0	1	1	0	6
1	1	0	1	0	4

The code sequence required for full-step stepper operation is thus A, 9, 5, 6, A. A time delay of 10 ms is considered necessary. For a system with a 2 MHz clock, a 10 ms delay is 20 000 clock cycles. To obtain such a delay, the current value of the TCNT register is found and 20 000 is added to it, then the TOC2 register is loaded with this new value.

```
REGBAS    EQU     $1000
PORTB     EQU     $4                        ; output port
TFLG1     EQU     $23                       ; timer interrupt flag register 1
TCNT      EQU     $0E                       ; timer counter register
TOC2      EQU     $18                       ; output compare 2 register
TEN_MS    EQU     20000                     ; 10 ms on clock

          ORG     $0000
STTBL     FCB     $A                        ; this is the look-up table
          FCB     $9
          FCB     $5
          FCB     $6
ENDTBL    FCB     $A                        ; end of look-up table

          ORG     $C000
          LDX     #REGBAS
          LDAA    #$80
          STAA    TFLG1,X                   ; clear flag
START     LDY     #STTBL
BEG       LDAA    0,Y                       ; start with first position in table
          STAA    PORTB,X
          JSR     DELAY                     ; jump to delay
          INY                               ; increment in table
          CPY     #ENDTBL                   ; is it end of table?
          BNE     BEG                       ; if not, branch to BEG
          BRA     START                     ; if yes, go to start again

DELAY     LDD     TCNT,X
          ADDD    #TEN_MS                   ; add a 10 ms time delay
          STD     TOC2,X
HERE      BRCLR   TFLG1, X, $80, HERE       ; wait till time delay has elapsed
          LDAA    #$80
          STAA    TFLG1,X                   ; clear flag
          RTS
          END
```

If half-step stepper operation had been required, as in Table 11.4, the code sequence would have been A, 8, 9, 1, 5, 4, 6, 2.

11.8.2 Drivers

An alternative to using software to sequence the operation of the coils of a stepper motor is to use a hardware driver. Figure 11.39 shows the connections with the SAA 1027 driver for a four-phase stepper. The three inputs are controlled by applying high or low signals to them. When the set terminal is held high, the output from the integrated circuit changes state each time the trigger terminal goes from low to high. The sequence repeats itself at four-step intervals but can be reset to the zero condition at any time by applying a low signal to the trigger terminal. When the rotation input is held low there is clockwise rotation, when high it is anticlockwise.

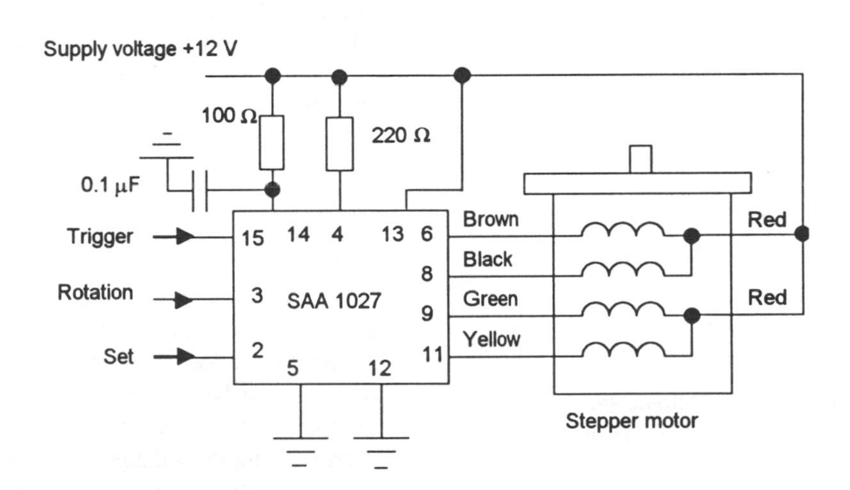

Fig. 11.39 SAA 1027 driver

11.9 Interfacing power

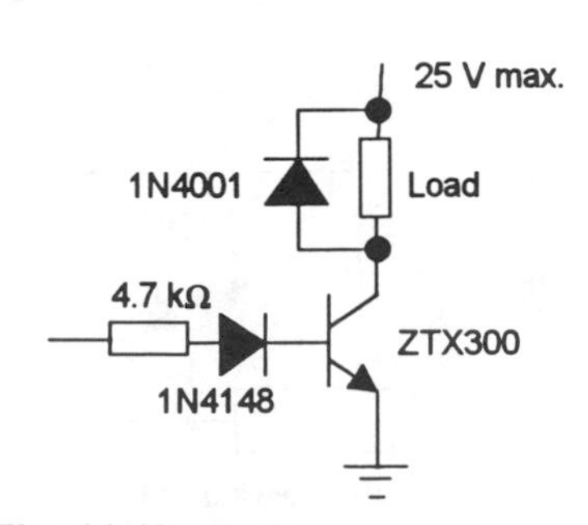

Fig. 11.40 Transistor driver

Microcontrollers and peripheral interfaces are not able to supply the high current needed to drive external devices such as light bulbs, heaters and motors. The following items indicate some ways in which this problem may be addressed:

1. *Transistor drivers*
   Figure 11.40 shows how a transistor can be used to drive an external load. A ZTX300 npn transistor might be used; this has a maximum collector current of 500 mA, which is the maximum load current. An alternative is to use a Darlington pair of transistors (Fig. 11.41); the Darlington TIP122 gives a maximum load current of 5 A. Multichannel driver integrated circuits are available, e.g. the ULNS2803A with eight separate

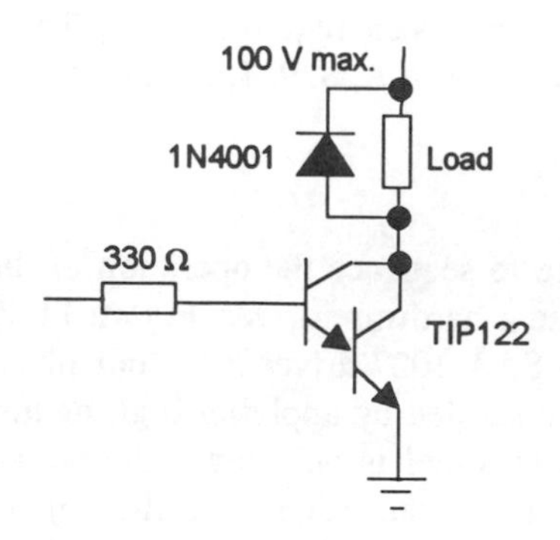

Fig. 11.41 Darlington driver

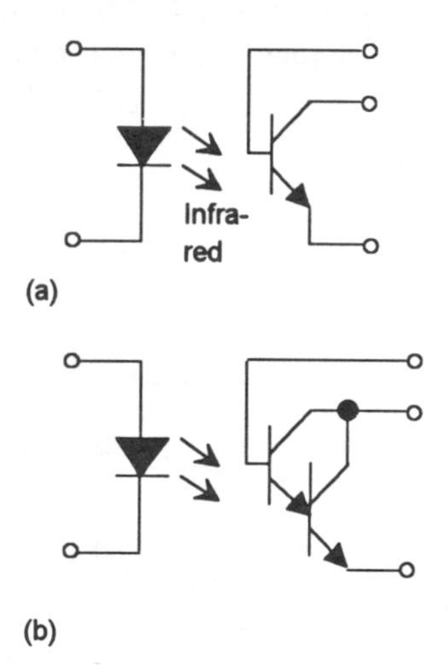

Fig. 11.42 Optoisolators: (a) transistor, (b) Darlington

Darlington drivers. Special versions, e.g. the ULN-2001N, are available for inductive loads such as lamps or relays and have seven Darlington arrays giving up to 500 mA each and with internal diodes to allow for the suppression of transients. Outputs can be paralleled to give higher currents. Other versions include latches, e.g. the Sprague UCN5801A.

2. *Optoisolator drivers*
Optoisolators provide electrical isolation with the maximum current that can be used with a load determined by the phototransistors. With *optoisolators* or, as they are sometimes called, *optocouplers,* the output from the microprocessor is applied to an LED which emits infrared radiation. This radiation is detected by a phototransistor, or triac, and gives rise to currents in its circuit which replicate the changes occurring in the current applied to the LED. The *transfer ratio* is used to specify the ratio of the output current to the input current. For example, a simple transistor optoisolator (Fig. 11.42(a)) might have a a transfer ratio of 20% and an output current limited to 7 mA. The output current is thus smaller than the input current but there is complete isolation. However, a Darlington optoisolator (Fig. 11.42(b)) might have a transfer ratio of 300% and a maximum output current of 100 mA; such an optoisolator will thus give an output current three times larger than the input current. A high-gain Darlington optoisolator, e.g. the Siemens 6N139, might have a transfer ratio of 800% and maximum output current of 60 mA. Another form of optoisolator uses a triac (Fig. 11.43(a)) to detect the infrared radiation. This conducts on either half of an a.c. cycle and can thus be used with alternating current circuits; a typical device has a maximum r.m.s. current of 100 mA and can be used with mains voltage. A commonly used form for this type of optocoupler incorporates a zero-crossing unit with the triac (Fig. 11.43(b)). This only turns on the triac when the voltage goes through zero, reducing the transients and preventing electromagnetic interference. A typical zero-crossing optocoupler has a maximum r.m.s. current of 100 mA and can be used with mains voltage.

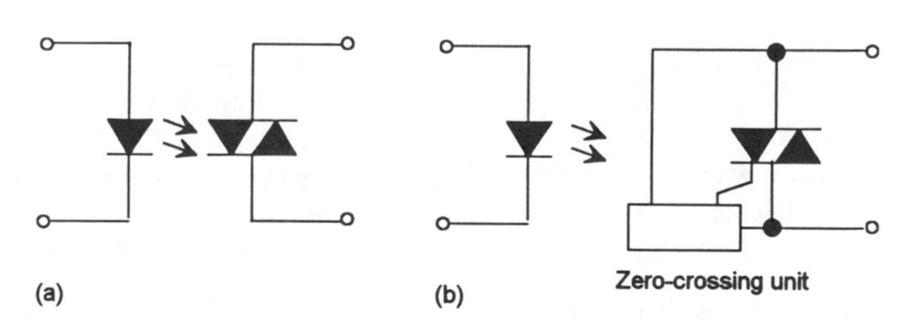

Fig. 11.43 Triac optocouplers

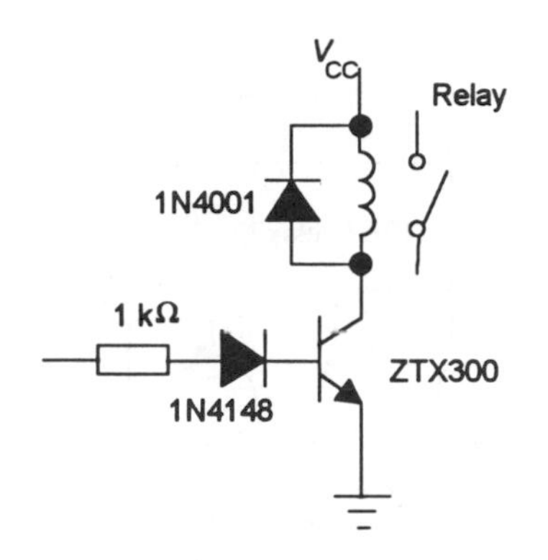

Fig. 11.44 Relay driver

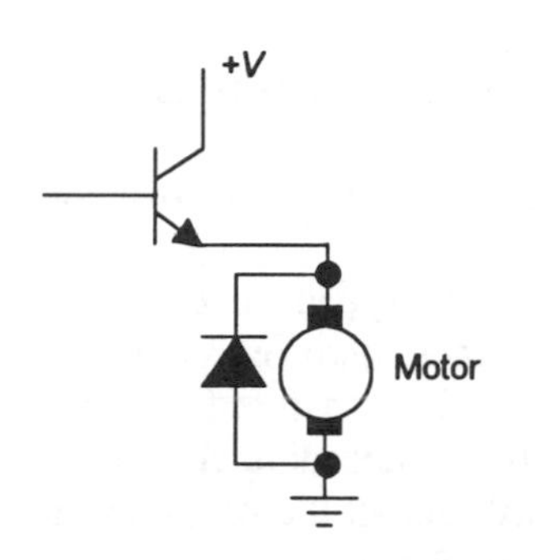

Fig. 11.45 Motor speed control

Optoisolators can be used to drive low power load circuits directly or they can be used used to operate a relay and so drive higher power load circuits.

3. *Relay drivers*
Relays can be used in conjunction with transistors or optocouplers to enable their relatively small current output to be used for switching much larger currents. A typical reed relay is suitable for use at input voltages from 3.8 to 11 V with single-pole or double-pole make actions to control maximum currents of 1 A and voltages of 100 V. Relay coils with higher voltage and current ratings can be used for higher power applications. Figure 11.44 shows the type of circuit that might be used with a simple transistor driver and relay.

4. *DC motor drivers*
DC motors can be driven by transistor or relay circuits. A basic transistor circuit which can be used to control the speed of a motor is shown in Fig. 11.45. The transistor is switched on and off by means of the signal applied to its base. By varying the time for which the transistor is on, so the average current applied to the motor can be varied; it is an example of pulse wave modulation. Such a circuit can only drive the motor in one direction; a circuit involving four transistors, termed an H-circuit, will enable the motor to be operated in both forward and reverse directions with speed control in each direction. Such a circuit is usually supplied with logic gates so that only two input signals are required to control the speed and direction of rotation; Fig. 11.46 shows one form.

Figure 11.47 shows how relays might be used to control the power to a motor and its direction of rotation.

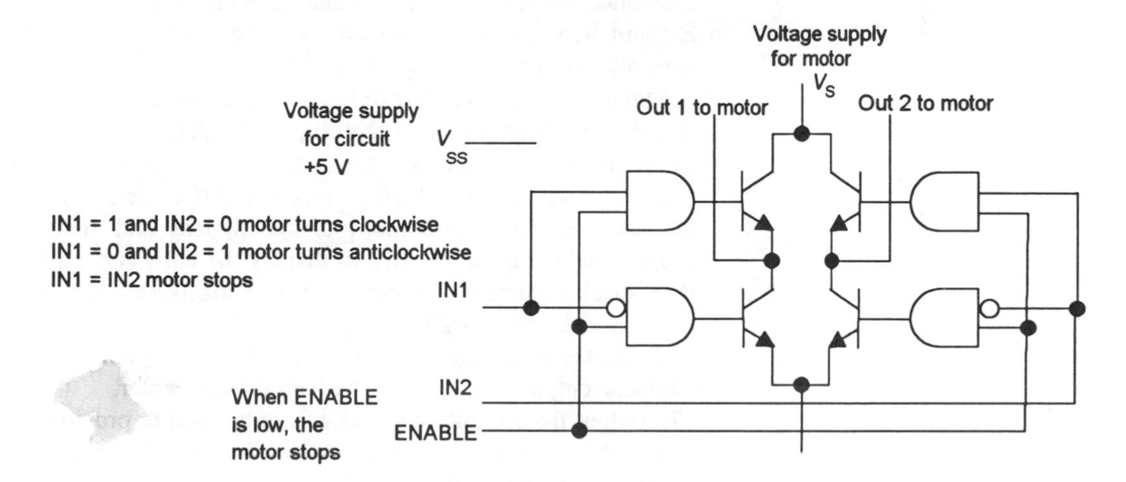

Fig. 11.46 Motor drive circuit

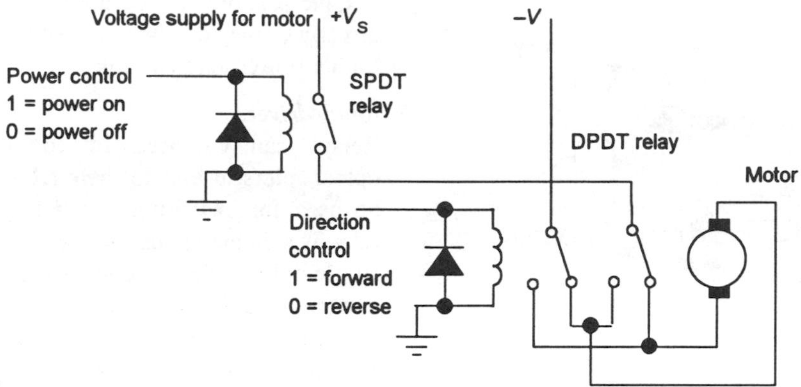

Fig. 11.47 Control by relays

Problems

1. Why are switches generally connected to inputs of microprocessor systems by pull-up resistors?
2. Explain how the problem of switch bouncing can be overcome by means of (a) hardware, (b) software.
3. Explain how the active key in a 16-key keypad can be detected by using a decoding chip interfaced to a microcontroller.
4. Write a program in C for a 16-key keypad interfaced to an Intel 8051 microcontroller by a 74C922 decoding chip so that, depending on the key pressed, it will output the ASCII symbol 0, 1, 2, 3, 4, 5, 6, 7, 8, 9, A, B, C, D, E or F.
5. An LED when forward-biased requires a current of 15 mA and has a voltage drop across it of 1.7 V. It is to be connected from a +5 V voltage supply in series with a current-limiting resistor and an inverter buffer to the input port of a microcontroller. What should be the value of the resistor?
6. Explain how a decoder can be used to interface a microcontroller with a seven-segment LED display.
7. A Motorola microcontroller 68HC11 is to be used to drive, via decoder and multiplexer, a five-digit LED display connected in the common cathode arrangement. Port D is to be used to supply the inputs to the display units and port B the signals to the decoder. Give a diagram of the system and write a program which could be used to display the number 5 on the third display element. To obtain a 5 on a display element, the input to it should be $6D.
8. Describe the arrangements that could be used to interface the analogue output from a sensor with a microprocessor.
9. The output from a microprocessor is to be used to provide an analogue current to actuate some device. Describe the arrangements that could be used.
10. Write a program for use with a Motorola 68HC11 to obtain a single reading from a single-channel analogue input.

11. What should be the word written to the ADCTL register of a Motorola 68HC11 microcontroller if it is to be used for one multiple-channel conversion of the inputs on PE0, PE1, PE2 and PE3?
12. What should be the word written to the ADCON0 register of a PIC16C74 microcontroller to initialise and initiate conversion if it is to be used for an analogue input on port A RA0 with an oscillator of 10 MHz giving a clock period of 3.2 μs?
13. For a Motorola 68HC11 microcontroller with an E clock of 1 MHz, if the PR0 bit is set to 0 and the PR1 bit is set to 0, what will be the overflow period?
14. For a Motorola 68HC11 microcontroller write a program using the output-compare function to generate a time delay of 1 s if the E clock frequency is 2 MHz and the prescale factor is set to 1.
15. Write the program lines needed to set up timer 0 in the Intel 8051 microcontroller as a timer which overflows after a count of 13 bits and then turns it on.
16. Write the program line needed to set up timer 1 in the Intel 8051 microprocessor as a timer which overflows after 16 bits.
17. Write the program lines needed to initialise timer 0 in the Intel 8051 microcontroller to overflow after a count of 100.
18. Devise a program for the Intel 8051 microcontroller to produce a 1 kHz square wave output from port P1.0. Assume a 12 kHz crystal.
19. The TMR0 timer of a PIC16C64A microcontroller is to be used to overflow after 30 ms when used with a 4 MHz oscillator and a prescalar setting of divide by 256. What initial value should it be given?
20. Write the program lines needed to generate a 100 μs positive-going pulse on the RC2 pin of a PIC16C64A micro-controller. Assume a 4 MHz clock.
21. A small d.c. motor running off 12 V in just one direction is to be switched on and off by the output from a microcontroller. What interface might be used?
22. Write an algorithm that could be used with a microcontroller operating a stepper motor and driving it for 10 steps in one direction.
23. One application of a DAC with a microprocessor system is to generate waveforms by transforming a sequence of digital values from an output port to an analogue signal. Design a circuit to produce a ramp waveform. How could the design be modified to produce a sine wave output?

12 Testing systems

12.1 Introduction

This chapter is a brief discussion of the techniques that can be used to test and detect faults in microprocessor-based systems. As with other electronic systems, faults can occur in components through a variety of mechanisms and lead to partial or complete failure of a system. The microprocessor will have been tested by the manufacturer, but the problems inherent in testing such a complex system mean that faults may only later manifest themselves due to patterns of usage that were not investigated during testing. Faults may also occur as a result of system components changing their characteristics with time, or even failing, and so affecting performance.

12.1.1 Software or hardware fault?

With microprocessor-based systems there is the problem of distinguishing between software faults and hardware faults when a system malfunctions or ceases to run. For small systems the procedure is to use a set of test programs to check the running of the system. If the test programs do not run then there is likely to be a hardware fault ather than a software fault.

12.2 System testing

Software can be used by a microprocessor-based system to institute a self-test program for correct functioning. Such programs are often initiated during the start-up sequence of a system when it is first switched on. For example, printers include microprocessors in their control circuits and generally the control program stored in ROM also includes test routines. Thus when first switched on it goes through these test routines and is not ready to receive data until all tests indicate the system is fault-free.

12.2.1 ROM testing

ROM devices are used to store fixed instructions which remain unaltered during program execution. This property means they can be tested using a *checksum test*. A checksum test totals all the data bytes stored in the ROM and compares the result with a checksum that is already stored. If there is a difference then the ROM is faulty; if they agree it is considered to be fault-free. As a simple illustration, suppose we have a ROM which contains just the two hexadecimal numbers 07 and 08. Adding these numbers gives 0E and this is the checksum number stored in the last location in ROM for testing purposes; the last ROM location is reserved for the checksum. During the test, the sum of the numbers in ROM is compared with the checksum and if they differ a fault is assumed to have occurred.

12.2.2 RAM testing

Unlike ROM, the contents of RAM are not fixed and thus a checksum test cannot be used. To test RAM, data has to be written into each location and then read back; if the data read back agrees with what was written then the location is assumed to be fault-free. A basic RAM test, the so-called *checkerboard test*, involves writing data patterns to RAM into every memory location with adjacent bits at opposite logic levels, analogous to the alternation between black and white squares on a chess board; the patterns used are hex 55, i.e. 0101 0101 and AA, i.e. 1010 1010. The values stored are then read back to check that they corresponds to the data sent.

12.2.3 Input/output testing

The standard approach for input testing is to feed in known signals through input ports and check them by means of a test program. For output testing, known signals can be sent from the microprocessor to the output ports and the output checked by perhaps using some form of display unit such as a bank of LEDs.

12.2.4 Watchdog timer

A *watchdog timer* is basically an internal timer that the system must reset before it times out. If the timer is not reset in time then an error is assumed to have occurred. When a microprocessor executes instructions from its memory, a nearby electrical disturbance might momentarily upset the processor data bus and the wrong byte may be accessed. Alternatively a software bug can cause the processor to get into problems when it returns from a subroutine. The consequence of such faults is that the system may crash with possibly dangerous consequences for actuators controlled by the microprocessor. To avoid this happening with critical systems, a watchdog timer is used to reset the microprocessor.

The microcontroller MC68HC11 includes an internal watchdog timer, called *computer operating properly* (COP), to detect software processing errors. When the COP timer has been started it is necessary for the main program to reset the COP periodically before it times out. If the watchdog timer times out before being set to start timing all over again then a COP failure reset occurs. The COP timer can be reset to zero time by writing a $55 to the COP reset register (COPRST) at address $103A followed later in the program by writing a $AA to clear the COP timer. If the program hangs up in between the two instructions then COP times out and results in the COP failure reset routine being executed. The assembly language program has the following lines:

```
LDAA    #$55     ; reset timer
STAA    $103A    ; writing $55 to COPRST
                 ; other program lines
LDAA    #$AA     ; clearing timer
STAA    $103A    ; writing $AA to COPRST
```

The COP operating period is set by setting CR1 and CR2 in the OPTION register (Fig. 12.1), address $1039, to either 0 or 1. For example, with CR1 set to 0 and CR2 set to 0 and a bus frequency of 2 MHz, a timeout of 16.384 ms might be given; whereas with CR1 set to 1 and CR2 set to 0, a timeout of 262.14 ms is given.

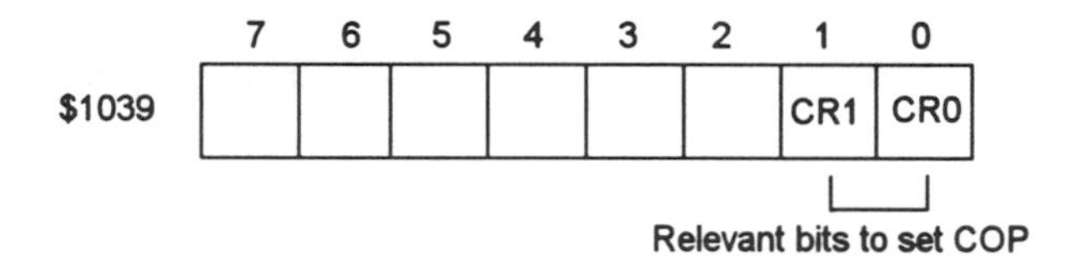

CR1	CR0	E clock divided by 215 divided by	Crystal frequency 8 MHz / Bus frequency 2 MHz / COP timeout	Crystal frequency 4 MHz / Bus frequency 1 MHz / COP timeout
0	0	1	16.384 ms	32.768 ms
0	1	4	65.536 ms	131.072 ms
1	0	16	262.144 ms	524.288 ms
1	1	64	1.049 s	2.097 s

Fig. 12.1 OPTION

12.3 Data signal corruption

Error detection techniques try to detect when a data signal has been corrupted and has an error as a result of noise. One such technique is *parity checking*. With this method an extra bit is added to a message to make the total number of 1s an even number when *even parity* is used or an odd number when *odd parity* is used. For even parity, the character 1010000 would have a zero parity bit placed after its most significant bit, i.e. 01010000; for odd parity, it would have a one, i.e. 11010000. This method can detect the presence of a single error in the message but not the presence of two errors which result in no change in parity. With even parity and the character 11010000, a single error in, say, the third bit would be detected in 1101100 because the parity check bit would be wrong. But it would not be detected if there were also an error in the first bit since 1101110 would have the correct parity bit. If no error is detected then the signal is acknowledged as being error-free by the return of the ACK character to the sending terminal; if an error is detected the signal NAK is used. This is called an *automatic repeat request* (ARQ). The NAK signal then results in the retransmission of the message.

12.3.1 Block parity

The efficiency of error detection can be increased by the use of *block parity*. The message is divided into a number of blocks and each block has a block check character added at the end of the block. For example, with the following block, a check bit for even parity is placed at the end of each row and a further check bit at the foot of each column.

	Information bits				*Check bit*
First symbol	0	0	1	1	0
Second symbol	0	1	0	0	1
Third symbol	1	0	1	1	1
Fourth symbol	0	0	0	0	0
Block check bits	1	1	0	0	0

At the receiver the parity of each row and each column is checked and any single error is detected by the intersection of the row and column containing the error check bit.

12.3.2 Cyclic redundancy checking

Another form of error detection is *cyclic redundancy checking* (CRC). At the transmitting terminal the binary number representing the data being transmitted is divided by a predetermined number using modulo-2 arithmetic. The remainder from the division is the CRC character which is transmitted with the data. At the receiver the data plus the CRC character are divided by the same number. If no transmission errors have occurred there is no remainder.

A common CRC code is CRC-16, 16 bits being used for the check sequence. The 16 bits are considered to be the coefficients of a polynomial with the number of bits equal to the highest power of the polynomial. The data block is first multiplied by the highest power of the polynomial, i.e. x^{16} and then divided by the CRC polynomial

$$x^{16} + x^{12} + x^5 + 1$$

using modulo-2 arithmetic, i.e. $x = 2$ in the polynomial. The CRC polynomial is thus 10001000000100001. The remainder of the division by this polynomial is the CRC.

As an illustration, suppose we have the data 10110111 or polynomial

$$x^7 + x^5 + x^4 + x^2 + x^1 + 1$$

and a CRC polynomial of

$$x^5 + x^4 + x^1 + 1$$

or 110011. The data polynomial is first multiplied by x^5 to give

$$x^{12} + x^{10} + x^9 + x^7 + x^6 + x^5$$

and so 1011011100000. Dividing this by the CRC polynomial gives:

```
            11010111
110011 | 1011011100000
         110011
          110011
          110011
           100100
           110011
            101110
            110011
             111010
             110011
              01001
```

and so a remainder of 01001, which then becomes the CRC code transmitted with the data.

12.4 Common faults

Here are some of the commonly encountered faults that can occur with specific types of components and systems.

12.4.1 Input/output hardware

1. *Sensors*
   A simple test is to substitute the sensor with a new one and see what effect this has on the results given by the system. If the results change then it is likely that the original sensor was faulty; if the results do not change then the fault is elsewhere in the system. It is also possible to check that the voltage and current sources are supplying the correct voltages and currents, whether there is electrical continuity in connecting wires, that the sensor is correctly mounted and used under the conditions specified by the manufacturer's data sheet, etc.

2. *Switches and relays*
   Dirt and particles of waste material between switch contacts is a common cause of incorrect functioning of mechanical switches. A voltmeter used across a switch should indicate the applied voltage when the contacts are open and very nearly zero when they are closed. Mechanical switches used to detect the position of some item, e.g. the presence of a workpiece on a conveyor, can fail to give the correct responses if the alignment is incorrect or if the actuating lever is bent.

   Inspection of a relay can disclose evidence of arcing or contact welding. The relay should then be replaced. If a relay fails to operate then a check can be made for the voltage across the coil. If the correct voltage is present then coil continuity can be checked with an ohmmeter. If there is no voltage across the coil then the fault is likely to be the switching transistor used with the relay.

3. *Motors*
   Both d.c. and a.c. motors need correct lubrication. The brushes on d.c. motors do experience wear and can require changing. Setting of new brushes needs to be in accordance with the manufacturer's specification. A single-phase capacitor-start a.c. motor that is sluggish in starting probably needs a new starting capacitor. The three-phase induction motor has no brushes, commutator, slip rings or starting capacitor, and short of a severe overload, the only regular maintenance it requires is periodic lubrication.

4. *Hydraulic and pneumatic systems*
   Dirt is a common cause of faults with hydraulic and pneumatic systems. Small particles of dirt can damage seals, block orifices, cause valve spools to jam, etc. Thus filters should be regularly checked and cleaned, components should only be dismantled in clean conditions, and oil should be regularly

checked and changed. With an electrical circuit a common method of testing is to measure the voltages at a number of test points. Likewise, with a hydraulic and pneumatic system there needs to be points at which pressures can be measured. Damage to seals can result in hydraulic and pneumatic cylinders leaking, beyond normal levels, and this will produce a drop in system pressure when the cylinder is actuated. Leakage can be remedied by replacing the seals in the cylinders. The vanes in vane-type motors are subject to wear and can then fail to make a good seal with the motor housing; this leads to a loss of motor power. The vanes can be replaced. Leaks in hoses, pipes and fittings are common faults.

12.4.2 Microprocessor systems

Typical faults in microprocessor systems are:

1. *Chip failure*
   Chips are fairly reliable but occasionally there can be failure.
2. *Passive component failure*
   Microprocessor systems will usually include passive components such as resistors and capacitors. Failure of any of these components can cause system malfunction.
3. *Open circuits*
   Open circuits can result from a break in a signal path or in a power line. Typical reasons for these faults are unsoldered or faulty soldered joints, fracture of a printed circuit track, a faulty connection on a connector and breaks in cables.
4. *Short circuits*
   Short circuits between points on a board which should not be connected often arise as a result of surplus solder bridging the gaps between neighbouring printed circuit tracks.
5. *Externally introduced interference*
   Externally induced pulses will affect the operation of the system since they will be interpreted as valid digital signals. Such interference can originate from the mains supply having spikes as a result of other equipment sharing the same mains circuit and being switched on or off. Filters in the mains supply to the system can be used to remove such spikes.
6. *Software faults*
   Despite extensive testing it is still quite feasible for software to contain bugs and, under particular input or output conditions, they might cause a malfunction.

In microprocessor systems there are signals occurring simultaneously on several parallel lines and they may be changing at a rapid rate. This means that conventional troubleshooting items, like multimeters and oscilloscopes, have limited use. Here are some hardware fault-finding techniques used with microprocessor systems:

1. *Visual inspection*
   Just carefully looking at a faulty system may reveal the source of a fault, e.g. an integrated circuit which is loose in its holder or surplus solder bridging tracks on a board.

2. *Multimeter*
   This is of limited use with microprocessor systems but can be used to check for short- or open-circuit connections and the correct functioning of power supplies.

3. *Oscilloscope*
   The oscilloscope is essentially limited to where repetitive signals occur and the most obvious such signal is the clock signal. Most of the other signals with a microprocessor system are not repetitive and depend on the program being executed.

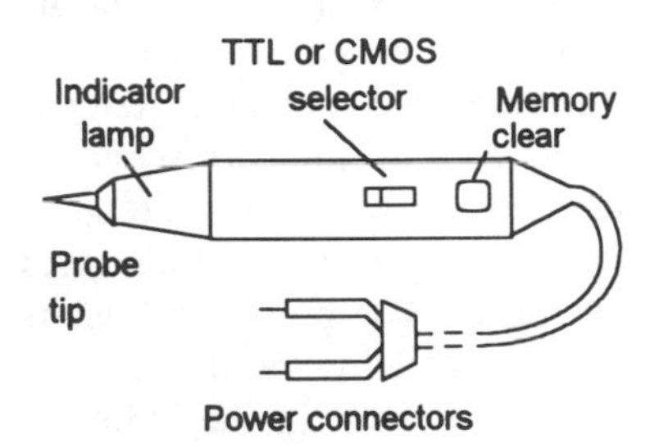

Fig. 12.2 Logic probe

4. *Logic probe*
   The logic probe is a hand-held device (Fig. 12.2), shaped like a pen, which can be used to determine the logic level at any point in the circuit to which it is connected. The selector switch is set for TTL or CMOS operation and when the probe tip is touched to the point in question, the indicator lamp indicates whether it is below the logic level 0 threshold, above the logic 1 threshold or a pulsating signal. A pulse-stretching circuit is often included with the probe in order to stretch the duration of a pulse to allow sufficient time for it to operate the indicator lamp and the effect to be noticed. A memory circuit can be used for detecting a single pulse; the memory clear button is pressed to turn off the indicator lamp and then any change in logic level is registered by the lamp.

   A logic probe can thus be used to determine whether a logic gate is correctly functioning. Control bus lines can be checked to determine that they are functioning and not held permanently low, for example. A chip enable line might be checked to ensure that it is operating and selecting an item.

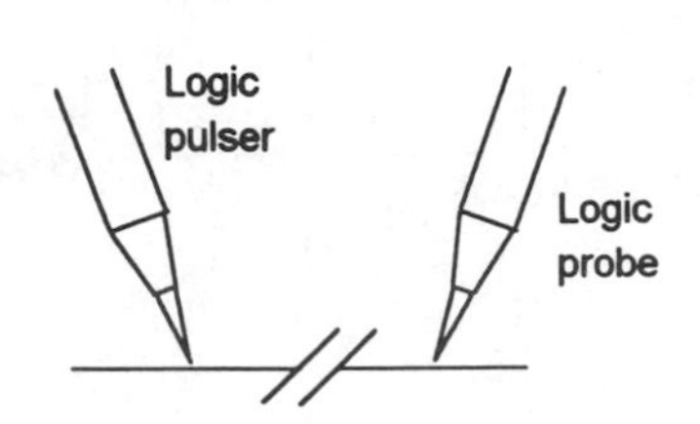

Fig. 12.3 Continuity testing

5. *Logic pulser*
   The logic pulser is a hand-held pulse generator, shaped like a pen, that is used to inject controlled pulses into circuits; this might be a single pulse or a burst of pulses. The pulser probe tip is pressed against a node in the circuit and the button on the probe pressed to generate a pulse. It is often used with the logic probe to check the functions of logic gates and the continuity of printed circuit tracks (Fig. 12.3).

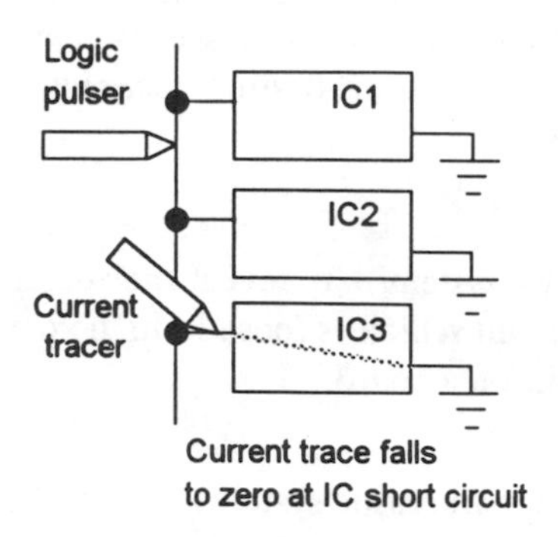

Fig. 12.4 Use of a current tracer

6. *Current tracer*
   The current tracer is similar to the logic probe but it senses pulsing current in a circuit rather than voltage levels. The tip of the current tracer is magnetically sensitive and is used to detect the changing magnetic field near a conductor carrying a pulsing current. The current tracer tip is moved along printed circuit tracks to trace out the low impedance paths along which current is flowing (Fig. 12.4). It can thus be used to check for 'stuck' gates or to check printed circuit tracks for short circuits, perhaps resulting from solder bridges.

7. *Logic clip*
   A logic clip is a device which clips to an integrated circuit and makes contact with each of the integrated circuit pins. The logic state of each pin is then shown by LED indicators, one for each pin.

8. *Logic comparator*
   The logic comparator tests integrated circuits by comparing them to a good (reference) integrated circuit (Fig. 12.5). Without removing the integrated circuit being tested from its circuit, each input pin is connected in parallel with the corresponding input pin on the reference integrated circuit; likewise each output pin is connected with the corresponding output pin on the reference integrated circuit. The two outputs are compared with an EXCLUSIVE-OR gate, which then gives an output when the two outputs differ. The pulse stretcher is used to extend the duration of the signal fed to the indicator so that pulses of very short duration will result in the indicator being on for a noticeable period.

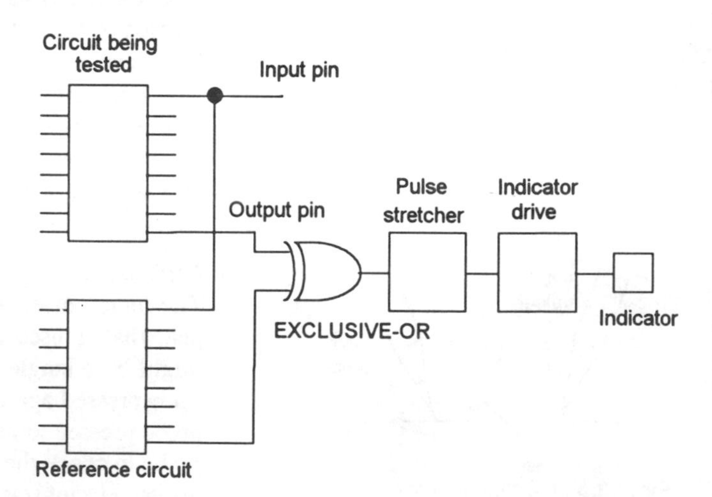

Fig. 12.5 Logic comparator

9. *Signature analyser*
   With analogue systems, fault-finding usually involves tracing through the circuitry and examining the waveforms at various nodes; waveforms are compared with what would be expected, enabling faults to be identified and located. With digital systems the procedure is more complex since trains of pulses at nodes all look very similar. To identify whether there is a fault, the sequence of pulses is converted into a more readily identifiable form, e.g. 258F, which is termed the *signature*. The signature obtained at a node can then be compared with the signature which should occur. When using the signature analyser with a circuit, it is often necessary for the circuit to have been designed so that data bus feedback paths can be broken easily for the test to stop faulty digital sequences being fed back during the testing. A short program, which is stored in ROM, is activated to stimulate nodes and enable signatures to be obtained. The microprocessor itself can be tested if the data bus is broken to isolate it from memory and it is then made to free-run and give a no operation (NO) instruction to each of its addresses in turn. The signatures for the microprocessor bus in this state can then be compared with those expected.
10. *Logic analyser*
   The logic analyser is used to simultaneously sample and store in a first-in first-out (FIFO) memory the logic levels of bus and control signals in a unit under test. The FIFO memory has typically 1024 or 2048 individual storage locations, each 32 bits wide. As each new word is clocked into the memory, all previously captured data moves on one place to make room for it. The data word moved out from the opposite end of the FIFO memory is lost. Thus, at any instant, the FIFO memory can contain the logic states of bus and control lines during the previous 1024 or 2048 clock periods. The point in the program at which the data capture starts or finishes is selected by the user through setting up a trigger word. The analyser compares the trigger word with the incoming data and only starts to store data when the word occurs in the program. Data capture then continues for a predetermined number of clock pulses and is then stopped. The stored data may then be displayed as a list of binary, octal, decimal or hex codes, or as a time display in which the waveforms are displayed as a function of time, or as a mnemonic display.

12.4.3 Systematic fault-location methods

Systematic fault-location methods can be used for systems that may be considered as a sequence of blocks. Here are some of them:

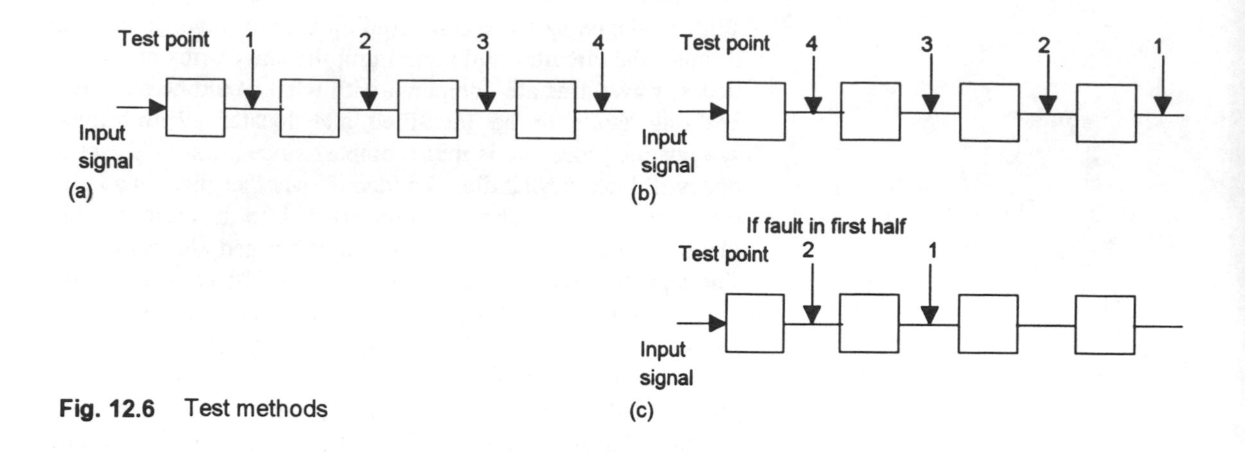

Fig. 12.6 Test methods

1. *Input to output*
   A suitable input signal is injected into the first block of the system and then measurements are made in sequence, starting from the first block, at the output of each block in turn until the faulty block is found (Fig. 12.6(a)).
2. *Output to input*
   A suitable input signal is injected into the first block of the system and then measurements are made in sequence, starting from the last block, at the output of each block in turn until the faulty block is found (Fig. 12.6(b)).
3. *Half-split*
   A suitable input signal is injected into the first block of the system. The blocks constituting the system are split in half and each half is tested to determine in which half the fault lies. The faulty half is then split into half and the procedure repeated (Fig. 12.6(c)).

Problems

1. Explain how self-testing can be used by a microprocessor-based system to check its ROM and RAM.
2. Explain how a watchdog timer is used to indicate the presence of faults.
3. What is the reason for adding parity bits to messages?
4. What bit should be added to 0101110 as an odd parity check?
5. Explain how cyclic redundancy checking it used to determine the presence of errors in messages.
6. Why is an oscilloscope of limited use in fault-finding with microprocessor-based systems?

13 Systems

13.1 Introduction

This chapter illustrates how the components required for a complete microprocessor-based system, i.e. input systems, microprocessors and microcontrollers, programming and output systems, can be brought together. The applications considered are for systems involving temperature sensors; one of them is a system involving one of three LEDs being switched on according to the temperature and the other is a digital thermometer for monitoring room temperature.

13.2 The design cycle

The design process for developing a microprocessor-based system can be considered as a number of stages:

1. *The need*
   The design process begins with a need, perhaps from a customer or client.
2. *Analysis of the problem*
   Before developing a design it is necessary to find out the true nature of the problem, i.e. to determine *exactly* what the end product is required to do. This is an important stage in that not defining the problem accurately can lead to wasted time on designs that will not meet the need.
3. *Preparation of a specification*
   Following the analysis of the problem, a specification of the requirements can be prepared. This will state the problem, any constraints placed on the solution, and the criteria which may be used to judge the quality of the design. All the functions required of the design, together with any desirable features, should be specified. Thus there might be a statement of dimensions, sensitivity required, accuracy, input and output requirements, interfaces, power requirements, operating environment, relevant standards and codes of practice, etc.

4. *Generation of possible solutions*
   Outline solutions are prepared which are worked out in sufficient detail to indicate the means of solving the specified problem. It also means finding out how similar problems were solved in the past; there is no sense in reinventing the wheel.

5. *Selection of a suitable solution*
   The various possible solutions are evaluated and the most suitable one selected.

6. *Designing the hardware and software*
   The detail of the selected solution has now to be worked out. This might require the development of a detailed block diagram of the system showing how the various elements are to be interconnected, with all the integrated circuit pin numbers identified, a decision having been made as to whether a microprocessor or microcontroller is to be used and which one from the chosen family will provide the required facilities. The development of a pseudocode program (see Section 4.2.1) might be used to indicate the structure involved in the required program.

7. *Build and test the hardware*
   The hardware might be assembled on a prototype board where circuitry can be easily constructed and altered; the board consists of rows of solderless sockets in which there are spring clips to grip any pins or connecting wires. In wiring up a board, a useful method is to first insert all integrated circuits into sockets, making sure all pins are straight, with the integrated circuits laid out in essentially the same positions as on the circuit diagram designed above. Then insert any other components. Colour-coded wires can be used to make the interconnections; these should be cut to a length which allows them to lie flat on the board and they should be routed round components. A systematic approach to the wiring is essential: you might first wire all V_{CC} and ground pins, then the data and address lines; use different coloured wires for V_{CC}, ground, data and address connections.

8. *Write and test the software*
   The use of *modular programming* (see Section 4.3) allows the programming task to be broken down into subtasks or modules so that programs can be written, tested and debugged for each module (see Chapter 9) before the modules are assembled to give the complete program. You might then use a simulator (see Section 9.2) or an emulator (see Section 9.4) to test and debug the software.

9. *Test the system*
   Test the completed system.

13.3 Temperature sensors

This chapter is concerned with applications requiring the use of temperature sensors. Possible temperature sensors for microprocessor systems which can give an electrical output and can be used for temperatures in a range about room temperature, are thermocouples, thermistors and integrated circuit sensors based on thermodiodes/transistors. All give analogue signals and will require an analogue-to-digital converter. If we have a signal which is proportional to the temperature and use an 8 bit ADC with a temperature range of, say, 0 to 40°C, then the resolution is $40/(2^8 - 1) = 0.16$°C. For greater accuracy we might prefer to use a 12 bit ADC with a resolution of $40/(2^{12} - 1) = 0.01$°C. Microcontrollers typically have 8 bit ADCs, so if a microcontroller were used for a system, to obtain 12 bit resolution would require a digital port with an external 12 bit ADC.

Now consider the various possible sensors and their signal conditioning:

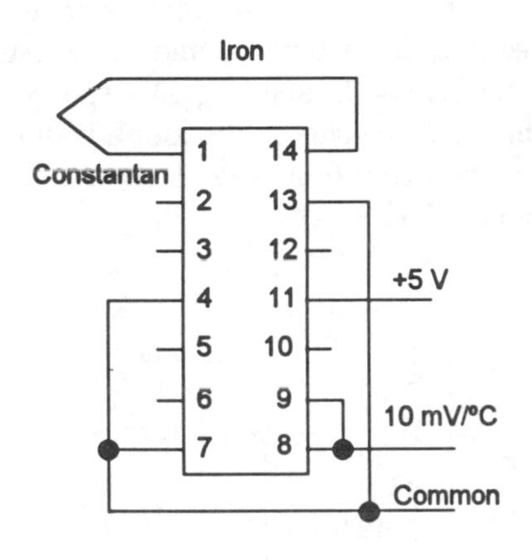

Fig. 13.1 AD594

1. *Thermocouples*

   Thermocouples suffer from the disadvantage of giving very small e.m.f.s, requiring a cold junction or cold junction compensation (this allows the cold junction to be at room temperature and to change with that temperature) and being basically non-linear. Although, over the range considered, a thermocouple can be chosen which is essentially linear. Integrated circuits are available which combine amplification with cold junction compensation, e.g. the Analog Devices AD594 which, when used with a +5 V supply, gives an output with a constantan–iron thermocouple of 10 mV/°C.

2. *Thermistor*

   A thermistor gives a large resistance change per degree change and this can readily be converted into a voltage change. Figure 13.2 shows a simple circuit that can be used; the output voltage V_{out} is:

$$V_{out} = \frac{R_T}{R + R_T} V_{CC}$$

   A problem with this potential divider circuit is that the output voltage is not a linear function of the thermistor resistance. However, since the resistance itself is not a linear function of the temperature, the non-linearity of the circuit might be acceptable. An alternative circuit, which does output a linear function of the thermistor resistance change, is to use the thermistor as one arm of a Wheatstone bridge and then amplify the out-of-balance voltage. The non-linearity of the thermistor does, however, mean that a look-up table is likely to be the best way of programming.

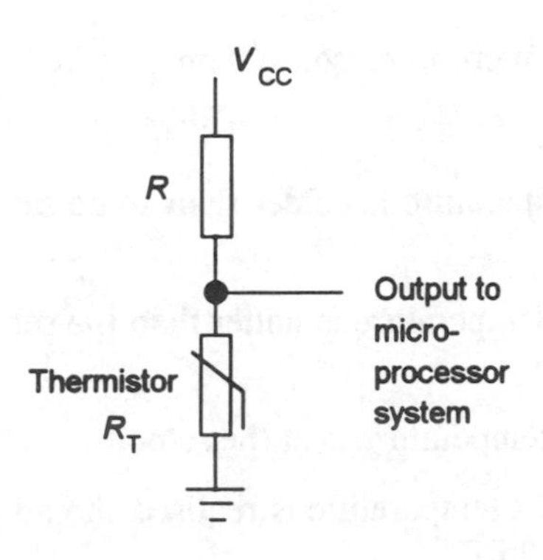

Fig. 13.2 Thermistor circuit

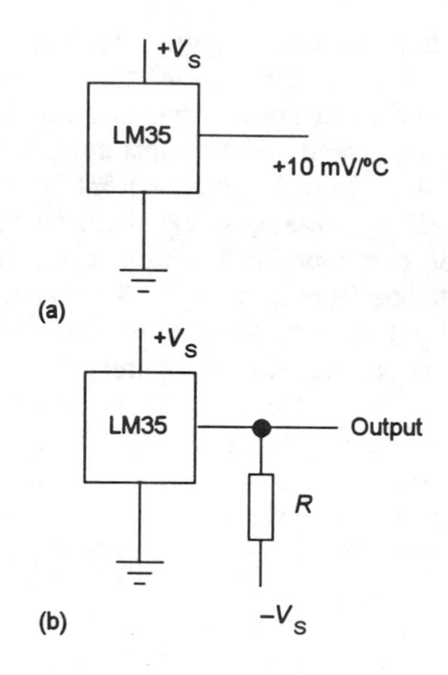

Fig. 13.3 LM35

3. *Integrated circuit sensor*
   An integrated temperature sensor, such as the LM35 from National Semiconductor, gives an output voltage which is directly proportional to the temperature. The chip does not require any external calibration to achieve accuracies of ±0.4°C at +25°C and can operate in the range –40 to +110°C. It draws very little current from the supply, only 56 μA. To operate over the range 12 to 150°C the circuit in Fig. 13.3(a) can be used; to operate over its full range then National Semiconductors recommend the circuit shown in Fig. 13.3(b) with R chosen to be $V_S/0.000\,05\ \Omega$. Therefore, with $V_S = 12$ V the resistance is 240 kΩ. The output is then 0 mV at 0°C and +10 mV/°C.

   Often when using such a sensor to provide the input to a microprocessor, the voltage is amplified so that over the required temperature range it varies between 0 and +5 V. An op-amp can be used, e.g. the CA3140E, and Fig. 13.4 shows a possible circuit. We might therefore choose the amplification so that the output varies between 0 and 5 V when the temperature changes from 0 to 40°C.

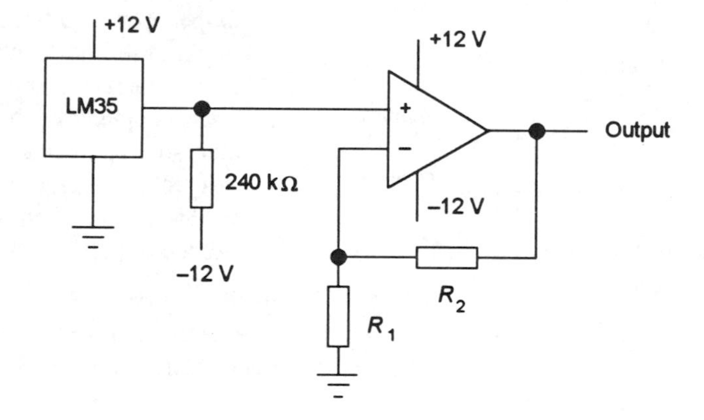

Fig. 13.4 LM35

13.4 Temperature indicator

Consider the requirement for a microprocessor system to give a temperature indicator which will:

1. Switch on one LED if the temperature is colder than some set temperature.
2. Switch on another LED if the temperature is hotter than the set temperature.
3. Switch on another LED if the temperature is at the setpoint.
4. The accuracy with which the set temperature is realised should be about ±1°C for a setpoint of 25°C.

The sensor is required to give a signal when a particular temperature is reached. A possible arrangement is to use an LM35 sensor which gives 10 mV/°C with a particular voltage value as the setpoint. Consider using the simple circuit of Fig. 13.3(a). The voltage signal from the sensor is an analogue signal and thus analogue-to-digital conversion is required. For a setpoint of 25°C the output from the sensor will be 250 mV. With the full range of input signal being 5 V then the fraction of 8 bit ADC output is $(0.25/5) \times 255 = 12.75$ and so the setpoint can be taken as a decimal input of 13. A change of 1 in 255 is a change of $5/255 = 0.020$ V which is 2°C, so the input to the microprocessor will only change every 2°C, thus giving an accuracy of ±1°C. Note that using the simple circuit of Fig. 13.3(a) gives a full-range input which is far greater than required; using the circuit of Fig. 13.4 would enable the temperature range to be restricted and the accuracy increased. An 8 bit ADC without amplification of the sensor signal is, however, adequate for the accuracy required. This means that a microcontroller with an internal 8 bit ADC can be used. Figure 13.5 shows a possible system with a PIC16C74. Note that the port B outputs have internal pull-up resistors.

Because there is no need to have a high accuracy for the oscillator frequency, the simplest method is used – just a capacitor and a resistor. For an oscillator frequency of about 4 MHz, i.e. an internal clock rate of 1 MHz, a resistor of 4.7 kΩ and a capacitor of 33 pF might be used. A push-button reset is included. When the button is not pressed the MCLR pin is high; the 10 kΩ resistor is to prevent short-circuiting when the button is pressed. A protective circuit is also included which creates a short time delay when power is first switched on, allowing time for the power to reach a safe level to operate the microcontroller. During this time the circuit operates a reset.

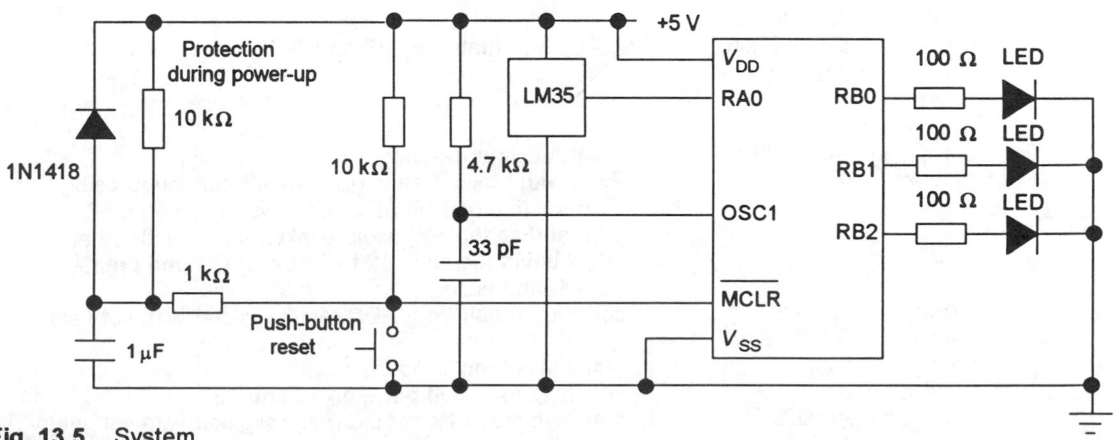

Fig. 13.5 System

LEDs might be used which have a maximum current of 20 mA and give a voltage drop of 2 V, hence a series resistor is required, although LEDs are available with built-in resistors so they can be directly connected across 5 V. To limit the current through an LED to below its maximum when connected to 5 V, we need to drop 3 V across a resistor and so a resistance of 2/0.020 = 100 Ω is required.

The program might consist of an initialisation module, an analogue-to-digital conversion module with an interrupt service routine for the sensors to switch on the relevant LED.

```
            list        P=PIC16C74A
            include     "C:\MPLAB\PIC74A.INC"

Ledcold     equ         b'00000001'     ; port b mask for LED cold output
Ledok       equ         b'00000010'     ; port b mask for LED OK output
Ledhot      equ         b'00000100'     ; port b mask for LED hot output

            org         0
            goto        Start

Start       call        Init            ; initialisation routine
Main        bsf         ADCON0,2        ; start of analogue-to-digital conversion
            goto        Main            ; keep looping until interrupted

Init        clrf        porta           ; reset input/output ports
            clrf        portb
            bsf         STATUS,5        ; select bank 1
            movlw       b'00001'        ; set RA0 as input
            movwf       TRISA
            clrf        TRISB           ; set up port B for outputs
            movlw       b'00000001'     ; set up ADCON1
            movwf       ADCON1
            movlw       b'00000111'     ; set up timing
            movwf       OPTION_REG      ; TMR0 prescaled to divide by 256
            bcf         STATUS,5        ; go to bank 0
            movlw       b'01000001'     ; set up A/D register with power on, osc. divider to get
                                        ; ADC period
            movwf       ADCON0
            movlw       b'11000000'     ; set up interrupts for GIE and PEIE
            movwf       INTCON
            return

isr         bcf         ADCON0,1        ; reset A/D interrupt flag
            movlw       d'12'           ; 25°C with LM35 means 0.25 V; with full range being 5 V
                                        ; then fraction of 8-bit ADC output is (0.25/5) x 256 =
                                        ; 12.8 and so the set result is taken as 13  with 12 and
                                        ; lower being too cold, 12 to 13 being OK and greater
                                        ; than 13 too hot
            subwf       ADRES,w         ; compare result from ADC result register with set value
            btfss       STATUS,w
            goto        Cold            ; result less than 12 to LED cold
            movlw       d'13'           ; checking for result between 12 and 13
            subwf       ADRES,w         ; compare result from ADC result register with set value
            btfss       STATUS,w
            goto        Ok              ; result close enough to set value to LED OK
```

```
        goto    Hot        ; result more than set value, go to LED hot
Cold    movlw   ledcold    ; output to LED cold
        movwf   portb
        retfie             ; return and enable global interrupt
Ok      movlw   ledok      ; output to LED OK
        movwf   portb
        retfie             ; return and enable global interrupt
Hot     movlw   ledhot     ; output to LED hot
        movwf   portb
        retfie             ; return and enable global interrupt
        End
```

An alternative might be to use the temperature sensor with an ADC, e.g. ADC0804 (see Section 11.4.1), and process the output by a microprocessor system with RAM and ROM, based on a Z80 perhaps. The LEDs might then be connected in the manner shown in Fig. 11.7(b).

The above task might be regarded as a simple preliminary to the design of a temperature-controlled heating system – the output could then be used to switch a heater on or off, via a suitable interface.

13.5 Digital thermometer

Consider the task of designing a digital thermometer with the specification:

1. To display room temperature on the Celsius scale.
2. The required temperature range is 0 to about 40°C and the readings should be given to the first decimal place, i.e. a three-digit display. High accuracy is not required.
3. The thermometer should be able to be run off batteries.

The sensor that might be used is the LM35 integrated circuit with the signal conditioning shown in Fig. 13.4 so that the output from the sensor circuit varies between 0 and +5 V for the required range. The op-amp used, e.g. the CA3140E, will have a gain of:

$$A_V = \frac{R_1 + R_2}{R_1} = 1 + \frac{R_2}{R_1}$$

If we select the temperature range as 0 to 42.5°C (this is convenient for an 8 bit ADC since 255/42.5 = 6 and so we just have to divide the output of the ADC by 6 to obtain the temperature in °C) then the gain required is 5/0.425 = 11.765 and so R_2/R_1 = 10.765. Thus, using standard resistors, we might choose R_1 = 4.7 kΩ and R_2 = 51 kΩ as being close enough for the accuracy required. A change in 1 bit will result from a change in temperature of 1/6 or about 0.2°C; the LM35 has an accuracy of about ±0.4°C.

For a system with an 8-bit analogue-to-digital converter used to interface with the sensor circuit, we might choose an analogue-to-digital latched converter such as the ADC0809 with a ROM chip such as the Intel 8355, a RAM chip such as the Intel 8156 and a microprocessor such as the Intel 8085A. Alternatively we might choose a microcontroller with integral analogue-to-digital conversion, ROM and RAM, e.g. the Motorola 68HC11 or the Intel 8051. The advantage of using a microcontroller in such an embedded system is there are fewer wire connections to be made by the user and so less chance of faults developing as a result of faulty wiring; also the system is more compact. A disadvantage is that, without modifying the system and adding extra chips, you are limited to the configurations of ROM and RAM supplied by the chip manufacturers.

A three-digit display, with decimal point, is required and thus three LED seven-segment displays, either common anode or common cathode (see Sections 3.4.1), might be used. These might be used with software or hardware decoding (see Section 11.3.1) to generate the required codes for the numbers. Software decoding might use a look-up table to arrive at the codes. Hardware decoding has the advantage of simplifying the programming. We might have one decoder/driver for each digit or we might use multiplexing with just one (see Fig. 11.10).

In considering the display part of the system, we need to determine how far the display is likely to be from the microprocessor or microcontroller system and whether the distances involved are such that a serial interface is required. With a parallel interface we might use a decoder such as the 7447 with a 7475 latch, or the multiplexed decoder 74C917. With a serial interface we might use the multiplexed serial interface/LCD encoder/driver MC14499 (Fig. 13.6). This can drive a four-digit display and accepts a 20 bit input of 16 bits for the four-digit display with 4 bits for the decimal point; Fig. 13.7 shows the serial input sequence. At any one instant, one of the four digits or the decimal point can be illuminated. Time multiplexing results in each being turned on and off many times per second and so give the appearance of all being simultaneously illuminated. To enter data, ENABLE must be made low and then set high so that the data can be latched by the MC14499.

Signal	Pin	Pin	Signal
d	1	18	V_{DD}
c	2	17	e
b	3	16	f
a	4	15	g
DATA	5	14	h
OSC	6	13	CLOCK
IV	7	12	$\overline{\text{ENABLE}}$
III	8	11	I
V_{SS}	9	10	II

DATA = serial data input
a, b, c, d, e, f, g, h = outputs to seven segment display
I, II, III, IV = character select outputs
OSC = oscillator input, to use internal oscillator connect a capacitor to set the frequency

Fig. 13.6 MC14499

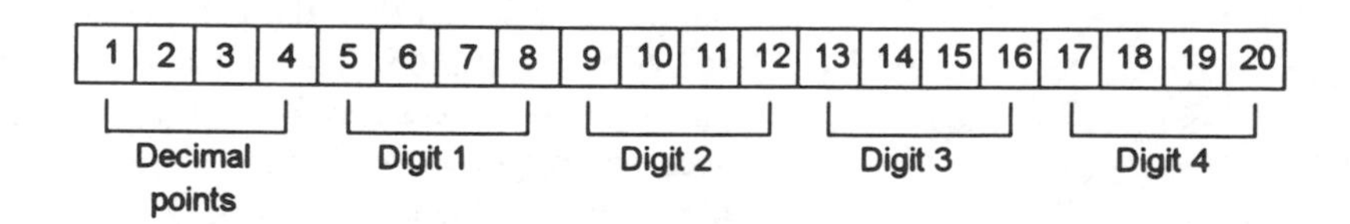

Fig. 13.7 Data input

As is apparent from the above, there are a number of possible solutions to the problem of developing a digital thermometer. To illustrate one possible option, Fig. 13.8 shows a system involving the microcontroller 68HC11, the multiplexed serial interface/LCD encoder/driver MC14499 and a common cathode LED display. The system shows a manual reset switch; the RESET pin has to be set low for a reset. Problems can arise during system power-up when V_{DD} is below the minimum operating level, so the low voltage inhibitor circuit MC34064 is used to hold RESET low whenever V_{DD} is below the minimum operating level. MC34164 is also a low voltage sensing device, and together with its associated resistor and capacitor, it provides an external manual and power-on reset.

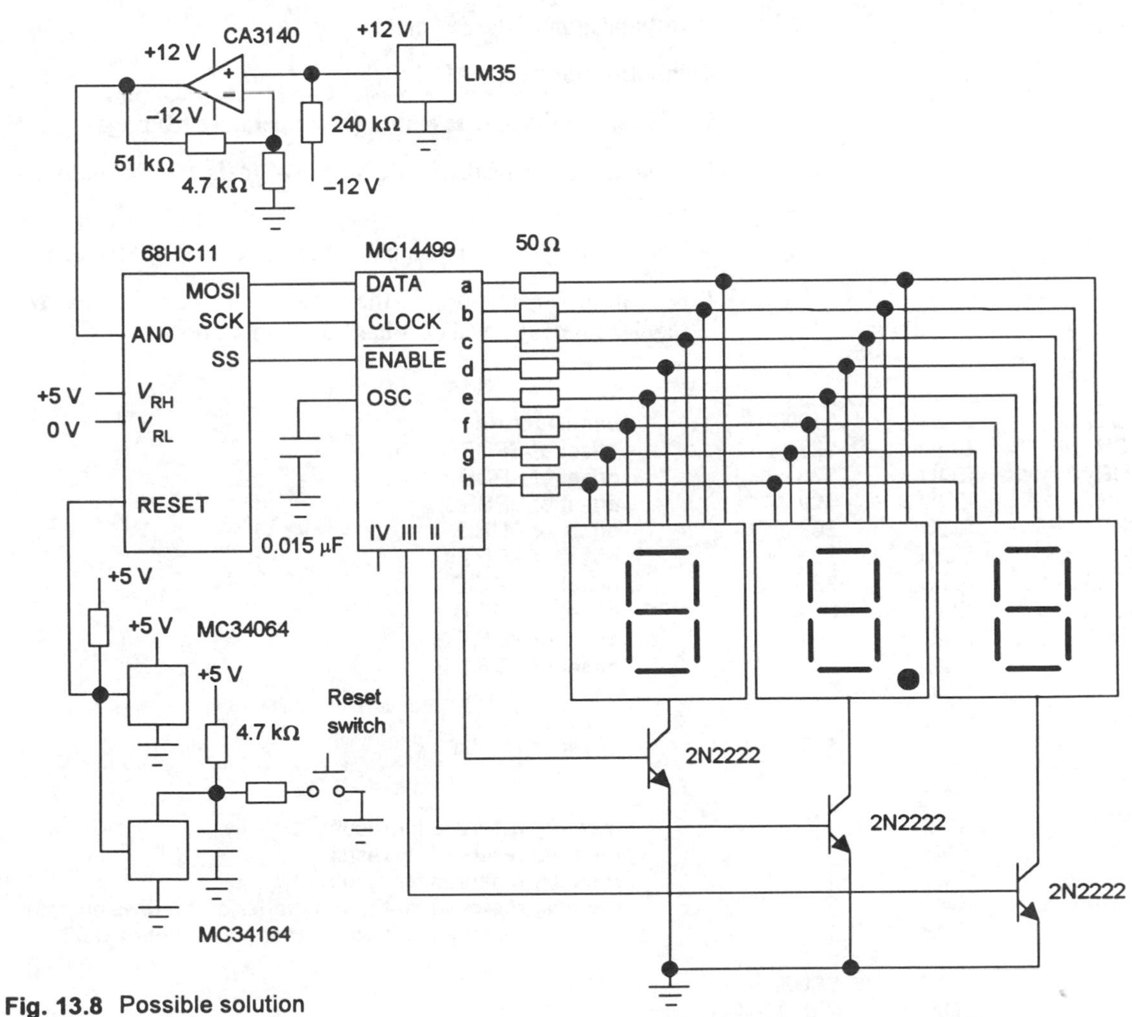

Fig. 13.8 Possible solution

If the chosen LED display has a current specification of 10 mA and a voltage drop of 2 V, then because the multiplexing means that the display is only on for one-fifth of the time, the peak current to give an average of 10 mA is 50 mA; the maximum output current of the MC14499 is 40 to 50 mA. The output from the MC14499 is 1 V below the power supply. With a 5 V power supply, the output to the display is 4 V. This means we need to drop 2 V across a resistor and so, if we restrict the maximum current to 40 mA, a series resistance value of 2/0.040 = 50 Ω is required. The transistor will need to be able to take the maximum current of eight LEDs, the seven segments plus a decimal point, and so it needs a peak current rating of 320 mA. The 2N2222 has a maximum current rating of 800 mA.

The program for such a system will consist of:

1. Initialisation of the SPI system.
2. Initialisation of the ADC.
3. Converting the A/D result into a temperature reading.
4. Separating the reading to give the signals for the individual digits.
5. Transmitting the serial signal to the MC14499 and the display.
4. Repeating the reading of the temperature and its display at regular intervals; every 1 s has been chosen here.

```
REGBAS   EQU   $1000        ; base address
SPCR     EQU   $28          ; offset of SPCR
SPDR     EQU   $2A          ; offset of SPDR
SPSR     EQU   $29          ; offset of SPSR
DDRD     EQU   $09          ; offset of DDRD
ADR1     EQU   $31          ; offset of ADR1
OPTION   EQU   $39          ; offset of OPTION
ADCTL    EQU   $30          ; offset of ADCTL
PORTB    EQU   $04          ; offset of PORT B
PORTD    EQU   $08          ; offset of PORT D
TCNT     EQU   $0E          ; offset of TCNT
TOC2     EQU   $18          ; offset of TOC2
TFLG1    EQU   $23          ; offset of TFLG1

         ORG   $00
BYTE1    RMB   1            ; memory reserved for result
BYTE2    RMB   1            ; memory reserved for result
BYTE3    RMB   1            ; memory reserved for result
REMAIN   RMB   2            ; memory reserved for the remainder of the division
OC2CNT   RMB   1            ; memory reserved to hold comparison count of OC2

         ORG   $C000
         LDX   #REGBAS
         LDAA  #%00000010   ; store 00000010 in BYTE1 to give the decimal point
         STAA  BYTE1
```

```
                                         ; initialise SPI
            LDAA     #%00111000          ; value to set SPI pin directions: SS, MOSI, SCK to be
                                         ; outputs, MISO to be input
            STAA     DDRD,X
            LDAA     #%01010110          ; value to enable SPI, falling edge, master mode, port D
                                         ; normal and 128 Kbits/s
            STAA     SPCR,X
                                         ; enable ADC
            BSET     OPTION,X,$80        ; set ADPU bit in OPTION to start capacitor charging
            BCLR     OPTION,X,$40        ; select E clock by making CSEL 0
            LDY      #30                 ; count loop to give time delay for charging
DELAY       DEY                          ; delay loop
            BNE      DELAY               ; repeat loop until count 0
FOREVER     LDAA     #$00                ; initialise ADCTL: SCAN = 0, MULT = 0, PE0 selected
            STAA     ADCTL,X
AGAIN       LDAA     ADCTL,X             ; check CCF bit for completion of conversion
            BPL      AGAIN               ; wait until CCF bit set
            LDAB     ADR1,X              ; read the temperature signal
                                         ; convert to a temperature value
            CLRA
            LDX      #6                  ; divide by 6 to give ºC
            IDIV
            STD      REMAIN              ; save the reminder from the division in double acc.
            XGDX                         ; store integer
                                         ; separating the digits for the display
            LDX      #10                 ; separate upper integer from lower integer
            IDIV
            LSLB                         ; shift lower integer to upper 4 bits of accumulator B
            LSLB
            LSLB
            LSLB
            STAB     BYTE3               ; BYTE3 has upper bits upper integer and lower 4 bits 0
            XGDX                         ; move upper integer into B
            STAB     BYTE2               ; BYTE2 has upper integer
            LDD      REMAIN
            LDAA     #10                 ; multiply remainder by 10
            MUL
            LDX      #6
            IDIV                         ; divided by 6 to derive the first decimal place digit
            XGDX
            ADDB     BYTE3               ; move the decimal digit into lower 4 bits of BYTE3
            STAB     BYTE3
                                         ; transmitting the data to the MC14499 and the display
            BCLR     PORTD,X,$20         ; SS pin made low ready for transfer to MC14499
            LDAA     BYTE1               ; send BYTE1 out
            STAA     SPDR,X
            BRCLR    SPSR,X,$80          ; wait until the 8 bits have been outputted
            LDAA     BYTE2               ; send BYTE2 out
            STAA     SPDR,X
            BRCLR    SPSR,X,$80          ; wait until the 8 bits have been outputted
            LDAA     BYTE3               ; send BYTE3 out
            STAA     SPDR,X
            BRCLR    SPSR,X,$80          ; wait until the 8 bits have been outputted
            BSET     PORTD,X,$20         ; make SS pin high so MC14499 can latch the data for
                                         ; the display
                                         ; the temperature is to be monitored every 1 s and the
                                         ; display updated, the following gives the delay
```

```
            LDAB    #100            ; each output compare gives 10 ms delay and so
                                    ; 100 delays will generate 1 s
            STAB    OC2CNT
            LDX     #REGBAS
            BCLR    TFLG1,X,$BF     ; clear the OC2F bit in TFLG1
            LDD     TCNT,X
REPEAT      ADDD    #2000           ; for time delay of 10 ms
            STD     TOC2,X
WAIT        BRCLR   TFLG1,X,$40     ; check whether OC2F flag set
            BCLR    TFLG1,X,$BF     ; clear the OC2F flag
            LDD     TOC2,X
            DEC     OC2CNT
            BNE     REPEAT
                                    ; repeat the temperature measurement and its display
            BRA     FOREVER
            END
```

Figure 13.9 shows another possible solution for the digital thermometer. It is based on using the Motorola 6802 micorporcessor. This has an internal clock and 128 bytes of internal RAM. EPROM is provided by the 2K Intel 2716. A common anode LED display is shown; because of lack of space on the page, only two display elements have been shown. It has been assumed there is a software, rather than hardware, conversion of the binary signal to binary coded decimal form, hence code for the display will be used. A 74LS138 1-of-8 decoder is used to provide the address decoding for the chips, although just three of the outputs are used. The input from the sensor can be of the same form as in Fig. 13.7 and is via the 8 bit analogue-to-digital converter ADC0809. The 6821 peripheral interface adapter is used to provide the output interface.

Subroutines BCD, to convert binary to BCD, and CONVERT, to convert BCD to code for the display, might be:

```
            ORG   F000
TENS        EQU   0000          ; BCD values
UNITS       EQU   0001
DEC         EQU   0002
RAM1        EQU   0003          ; look-up table vector address
RAM2        EQU   0004
DISTENS     EQU   0005          ; BCD code for display
DISUNITS    EQU   0006
DISDEC      EQU   0007
BINARY      EQU   0008          ; for use in binary to BCD

BCD         CLR   TENS
            CLR   UNITS
            CLR   DEC
LOOPTENS    LDAA  BINARY
            SUBA  #64           ; subtract 100
            BCS   LOOPUNITS     ; did borrow occur and so number less than 100?
            STAA  BINARY        ; no, save result as new  binary
            LDAA  TENS          ; increment tens digit until a borrow occurs
            INCA
```

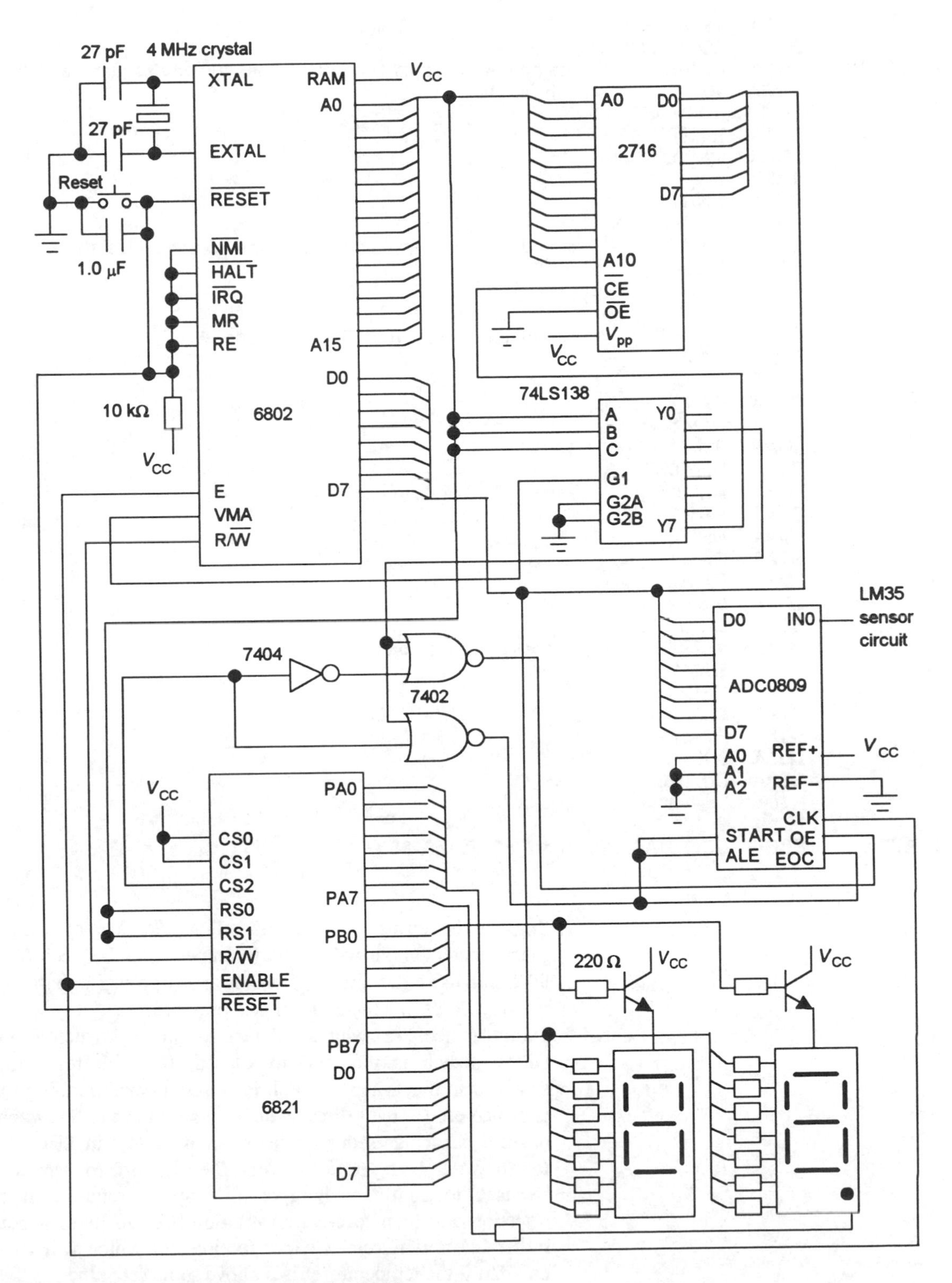

Fig. 13.9 A possible solution using the 6802

```
           STAA  TENS
           BRA   LOOPTENS
LOOPUNITS  LDAA  BINARY      ; the number in binary is now less than 100 and so just the units
           SUBA  #0A         ; subtract 10
           BCS   LOOPDEC
           STAA  BINARY
           LDAA  UNITS
           INCA
           STAA  UNITS
           BRA   LOOPUNITS
LOOPDEC    LDAA  BINARY      ; the number in binary is now  less than 10 and so just the dec.
           STAA  DEC
           RTS

CONVERT    LDX   #TABLE      ; subroutine to convert BCD tens to code
           STX   RAM1
           LDAA  TENS
           STAA  RAM2
           LDX   RAM1
           LDAA  0,X
           STAA  DISTENS
           LDX   #TABLE      ; convert BCD units to code
           STX   RAM1
           LDAA  UNITS
           STAA  RAM2
           LDX   RAM1
           LDAA  0,X
           STAA  DISUNITS
           LDX   #TABLE      ; convert BCD dec. to code
           STX   RAM1
           LDAA  DEC
           STAA  RAM2
           LDX   RAM1
           LDAA  0,X
           STAA  DISDEC
           RTS

TABLE      FCB   C0, F9, A4, B0, 99, 92, 82, F8, 80, 88
```

Problems

1. Suggest the forms that systems might take for (a) a digital thermometer which will display temperatures between 0 and 99°C and use a thermistor as sensor and (b) a digital barometer which will display the atmospheric pressure.
2. Design systems (a) which will turn on an LED when a push-button switch is momentarily closed, (b) with three input switches so that when a switch is closed a corresponding LED is turned on, (c) with three switches which have to be switched on in a particular sequence in order to switch an LED on, a fourth switch being used to switch the LED off, (d) which can be used to continuously give an angular rotation in one direction and then reverse the rotation back to its start point, rather like a windscreen wiper motion, (e) which will switch on a fan if the temperature rises above some set value.

Appendix: Logic gates

The following are the truth tables and symbols used for logic gates. Different sets of standard circuit symbols have been used with the main form having originated in the United States; an international standard form (IEEE/ANSI) has, however, now been developed which removes the distinctive shape used for a symbol and uses a rectangle with the logic function written inside it. Both formats are given here.

AND gate

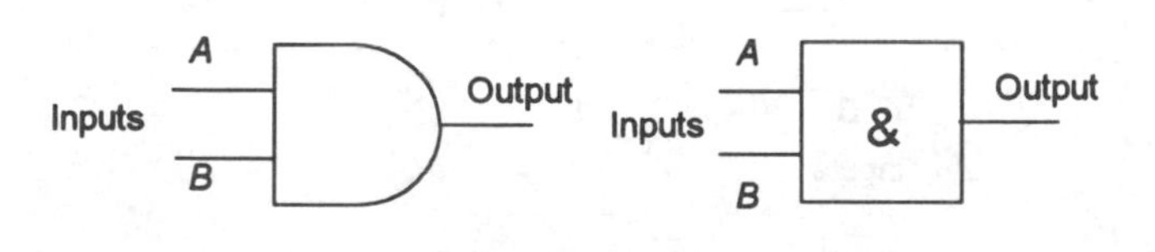

Input		
A	*B*	*Output*
0	0	0
0	1	0
1	0	0
1	1	1

OR gate

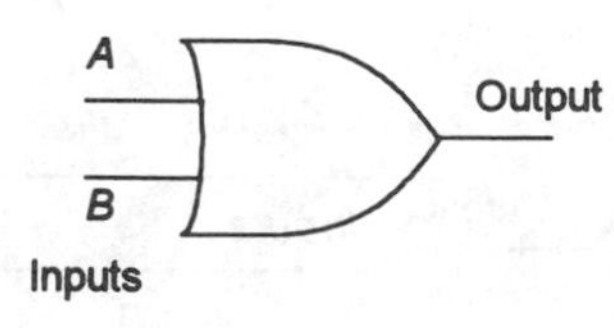

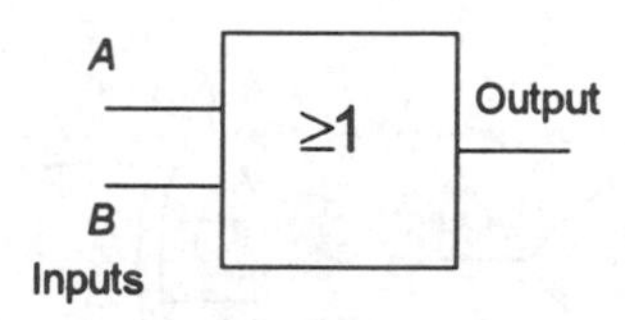

Input		
A	*B*	*Output*
0	0	0
0	1	1
1	0	1
1	1	1

NOT gate

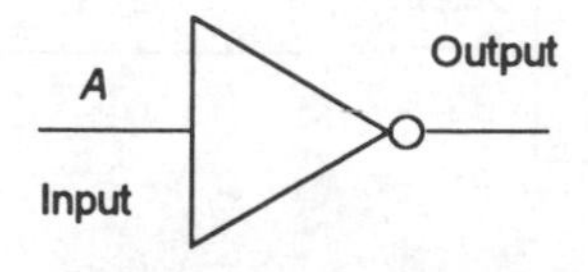

A

1

Output

Input

Input A	*Output*
0	1
1	0

NAND gate

This can be considered as an AND gate followed by a NOT gate.

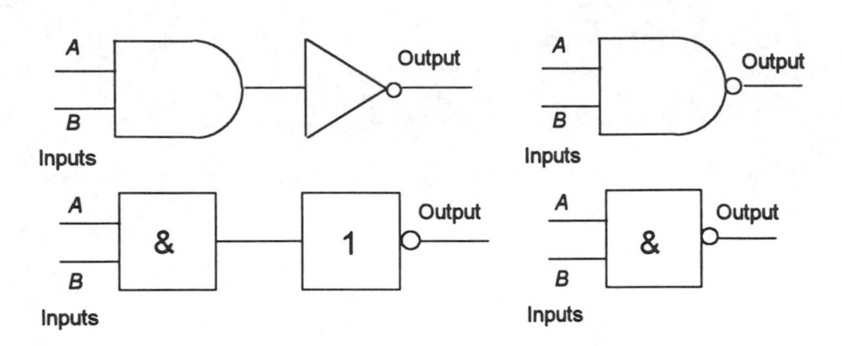

Inputs		
A	*B*	*Output*
0	0	1
0	1	1
1	0	1
1	1	0

NOR gate

This can be considered as an OR gate followed by a NOT gate.

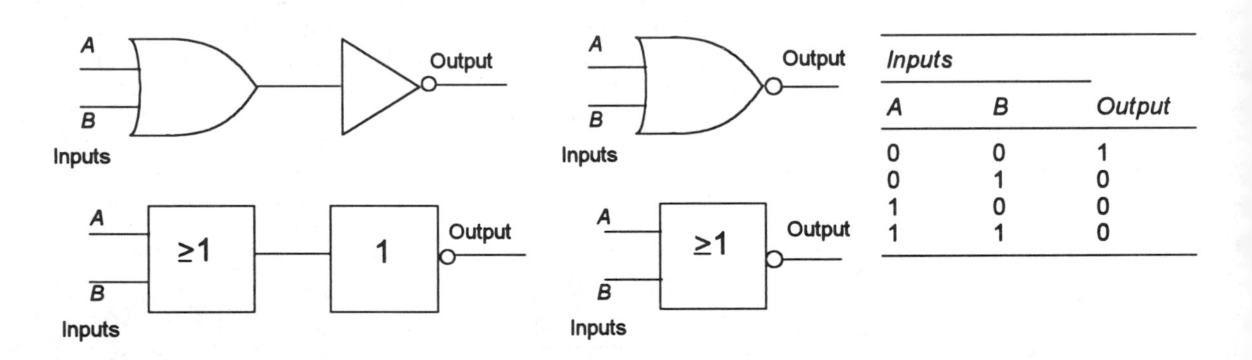

Inputs		
A	*B*	*Output*
0	0	1
0	1	0
1	0	0
1	1	0

EXCLUSIVE-OR (XOR) gate

This can be considered as an OR gate with a NOT gate applied to one of its inputs; alternatively it can be considered as an AND gate with a NOT gate applied to one of its inputs.

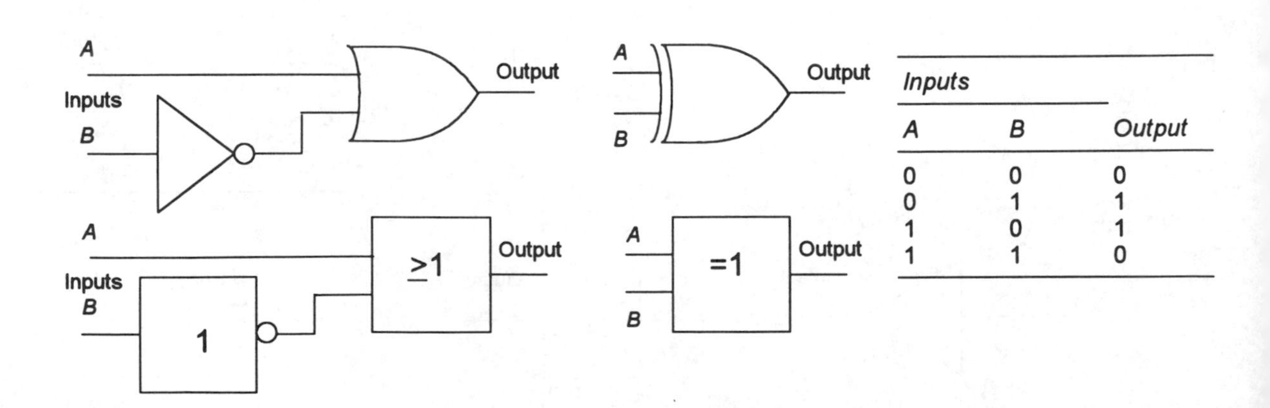

Inputs		
A	*B*	*Output*
0	0	0
0	1	1
1	0	1
1	1	0

Further reading

Chapter 2

Bennet R.H. *The 8051 Family of Microcontrollers* (Prentice Hall 1995)

Cady F.M. *Software and Hardware Engineering, Motorola M68HC11* (Oxford University Press 1997)

Intel Corp. *8-bit Embedded Controllers* (Intel Corp. 1990)

Intel Corp. *Embedded Applications* (Intel Corp. 1990)

Motorola *M68HC11 Reference Manual* (Motorola 1991)

Motorola *M68HC11A8 Technical Data* (Motorola 1991)

Peatman J.B. *Design with PIC Microcontrollers* (Prentice Hall 1998)

Predko M. *Programming and Customizing the PIC Microcontroller* (McGraw-Hill 1998)

Spasov P. *Microcontroller Technology* (Prentice Hall 1996, 1992)

Yeralan S. and Ahluwalia A. *Programming and Interfacing the 8051 Microcontroller* (Addison-Wesley 1993)

Chapter 3

Chowanietz E. *Automobile Electronics* (Newnes 1995)

Denton T. *Automobile Electrical and Electronic Systems* (Arnold 1995)

Gray C.B. *Electrical Machines and Drive Systems* (Longman 1989)

Kenjo T. *Stepping Motors and their Microprocessor Controls* (Oxford University Press 1984)

Kenjo T. *Power Electronics for the Microprocessor Age* (Oxford University Press 1990)

Rankl W. and Effing W. *Smart Card Handbook* (John Wiley 1997)

Tisal J. *GSM Cellular Radio Telephony* (John Wiley 1997)

Chapter 7

Aitkin P. and Jones B.L. *Teach Yourself C Programming in 21 Days* (Sams Publishing 1995)

Bronson G. *C for Engineers and Scientists* (West 1993)

Schultz T. *C and the 8051,* vols 1, 2 (Prentice Hall 1998)

Van Sickle T. *Programming Microcontrollers in C* (High Text 1994)

Chapter 9

Motorola *M68HC11EVB Evaluation Board User's Manual* (Motorola 1986)

Predko M. *Programming and Customizing the PIC Microcontroller* (McGraw-Hill 1998)

Predko M. *Programming and Customizing the 8051 Microcontroller* (McGraw-Hill 1999)

Answers

Chapter 1

1. The width of the data bus and hence the number of bits that can be simultaneously processed
2. (a) 11011, (b) 11111, (c) 10 1010
3. (a) 1B, (b) 1F, (c) 2A
4. (a) 0001 0111 0001, (b) 0010 1100 0000
5. (a) 0001 0000, (b) 0001 0110
6. (a) 1111 1001, (b) F9
7. (a) 01 1111, (b) 10 0010
8. $0.101\ 001 \times 2^3$
9. (a) Z, N, C and V are all zero, (b) Z = 1, N = 1, C = 1, V = 0
10. (a) Tempory storage for data or addresses, (b) store instructions, (c) store addresses
11. ALE
12. +5 V d.c.
13. Ground is pins 1 and 21; +5 V is pin 8
14. (a) 6, (b) 7, 8, 9, 10, 12, 13, 14, 15, (c) 1, 2, 3, 4, 5, 30 to 40
15. The pin is active when taken low, e.g. a bar over a W on a read/write line indicates that the line is taken low for the write operation
16. Both A15 and A16 are high, hence CS3 goes low and selects that chip
17. (a) The microprocessor writes to the data bus; (b) it reads the data bus
18. 8
19. 8K × 8
20. More because several simple instructions would be needed to do the same job

Chapter 2

1. See Section 2.1
2. See Fig. 2.1 and associated text
3. (a) E, (b) C, (c) D, (d) B
4. (a) 0, (b) 1
5. See Section 2.3, item 4
6. See Section 2.4, item 2
7. High to reset pin

8. (a) See Fig. 2.19, (b) see Fig. 2.21
9. See Section 2.5
10. See Section 2.5, item 1
11. RA0,1,2,3,5; RE0,1,2

Chapter 3

1. When the card has been positioned in the machine and contacts established, check the authenticity of the card. If not valid then reject, if valid then read the balance; if the balance is sufficient then debit the fare, if not sufficient then reject; if fare debited then authorise the transaction
2. To institute a sequence of events; a step in the sequence is triggered either as a result of time elapsed since the previous step or by a feedback signal to indicate that the previous step has been completed.
3. Timing wheel with the teeth producing voltage pulses in a coil as each tooth passes it
4. Pull-up resistors, see Fig. 3.20
5. Use a decoder to select batches of 8
6. See Section 3.3.1 and Fig. 3.22
7. See Section 3.3.1 and Fig. 3.23
8. $1/(2^{16} - 1)$
9. See Section 3.4.1 and Fig. 3.34
10. To convert BCD into a suitable signal for the display
11. See Section 3.6
12. See Section 3.5.2

Chapter 4

1. See Section 4.1.1
2. As in Fig. 4.2
3. See Fig. A.1
4. See Fig. A.2
5. See (a) Fig. 4.5 and (b) Fig. 4.6 plus associated codes
6. See Section 4.3
7. See Section 4.3.1
8. Sequence, loop, conditional
9. See (a) Fig. 4.10, (b) Fig. 4.13, (c) Fig. 4.16 with C1 = C and C2 ≠ C
10. (a) An iteration of B while C is true, (b) elementary operations which occur in the sequence 1 followed by 2 so we have:

```
DO 1
Operation A
DO 2
```

11. If C is true then B occurs
12. See (a) Fig. 4.28, (b) Fig. 4.16, (c) Fig. 4.13
13. See Fig. A.3
14. See Fig. A.4
15. See Fig. A.5

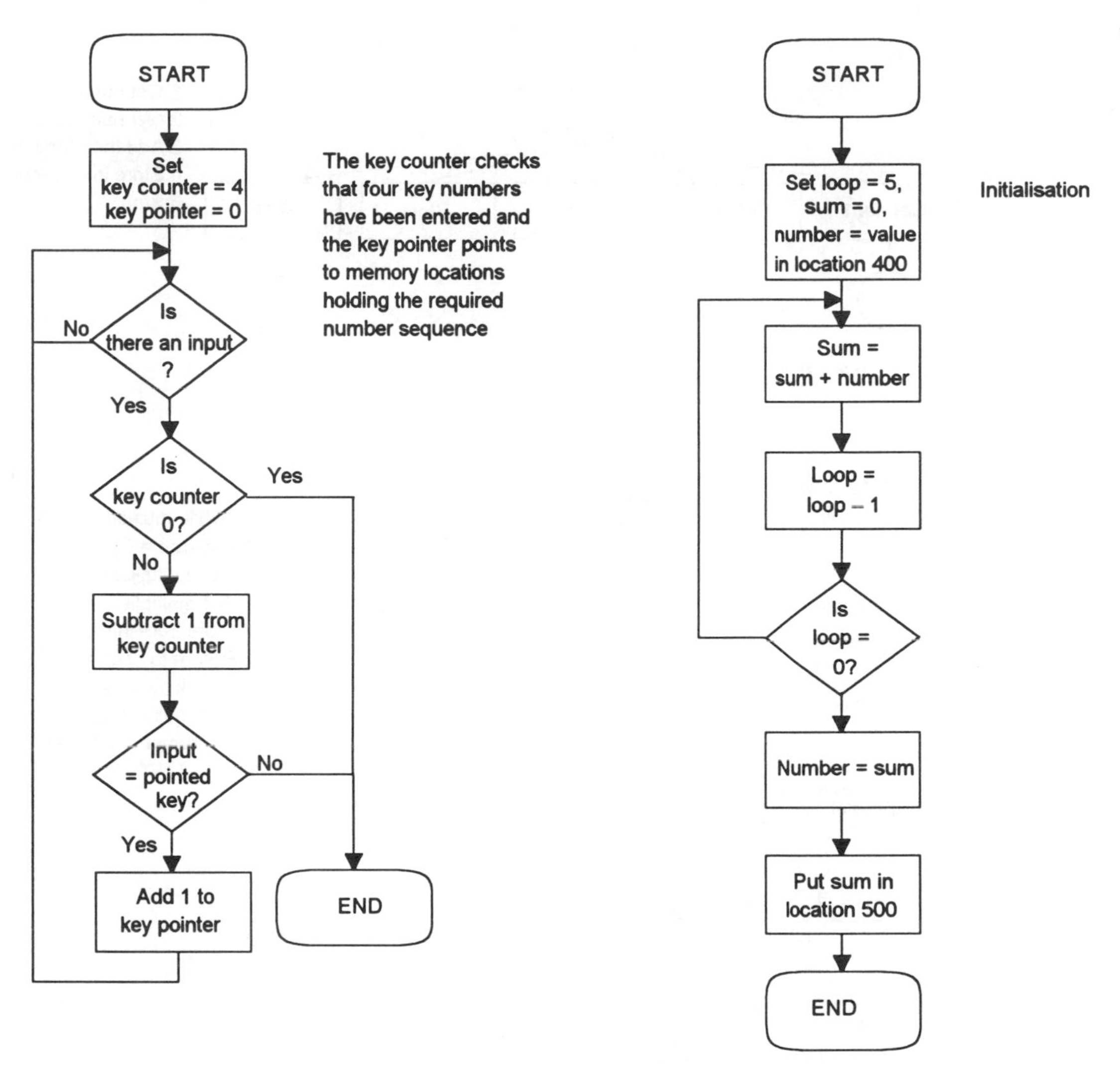

Fig. A.1 Problem 3 Chapter 4

Fig. A.2 Problem 4 Chapter 4

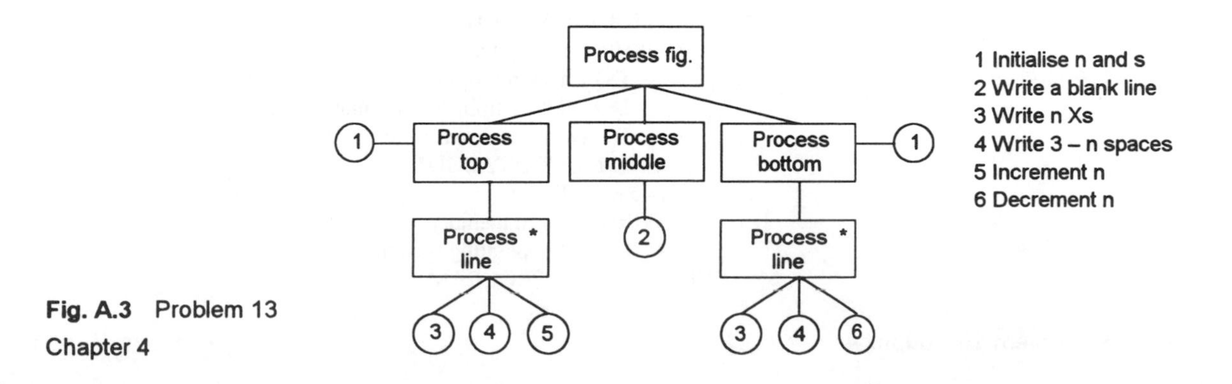

Fig. A.3 Problem 13 Chapter 4

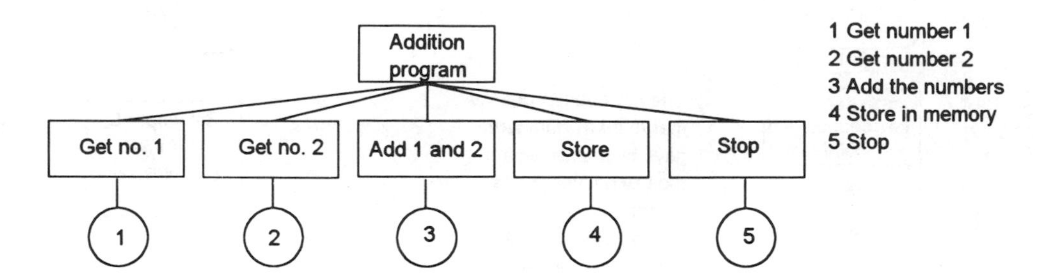

Fig. A.4 Problem 14 Chapter 4

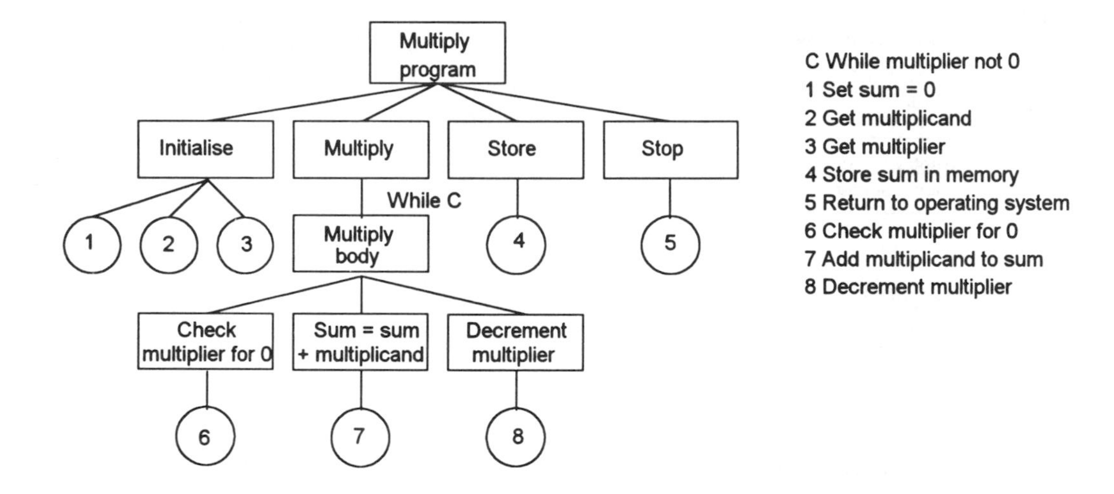


```
 MULIPLY PROGRAM
DO set sum = 0
    DO Get multiplicand
    DO Get multiplier
    MULTIPLY
      MULTIPLY BODY
      WHILE Multiplier not 0
        DO Check multiplier for 0
        DO Add multiplicand to running sum
        DO Decrement multiplier
      END MULTIPLY BODY
    END MULTIPLY
    DO Store sum in memory
    DO Return to operating system
END MULTIPLY PROGRAM
```

Fig. A.5 Problem 15 Chapter 4

```
16. CAR ALARM
    IF the key is in the ignition
    THEN
        IF the door is open
        THEN
          DO sound alarm
        ENDIF door open
    ELSE the key not in the ignition
        IF the lights are on
        THEN
          DO sound alarm
        ENDIF lights on
    ENDIF key in ignition
    END CAR ALARM
```

```
17. FLASH LED
    DO Switch on LED
    PULSE BODY
        1s TIME DELAY
          DO Initialise delay counter
          DELAY LOOP BODY
            DELAY LOOP
            WHILE count not zero
              DO decrement count by 1
              DO check for count = 0
            END DELAY LOOP
          END DELAY LOOP BODY
      END 1s TIME DELAY
      DO Change state of LED
    END PULSE BODY
    END FLASH LED
```

Chapter 5

1. (a) Place decimal 10 into A, (b) copy contents of memory address $1000 into A, (c) place decimal 10 into A, (d) copy contents of memory address $1000 into B, (e) place decimal 10 into double accumulator D, (f) add A to B and store result in A, (g) add 8 bit B to 16 bit register X and store result in X, (h) add decimal 10 and the C flag to accumulator A and store result in A, (i) add contents of address $10 and C flag to A and store result in A, (j) subtract B from A and store result in A, (k) subtract decimal 10 and C bit from A and store result in A, (l) subtract contents of address $10 and C flag from A and store result in A
2. (a) Copy contents of R7 to A, (b) copy contents of A to R7, (c) copy contents of address 20H to A, (d) move decimal 20 into A, (e) move hex 2E into A, (f) move contents of address 2EH to R3, (g) add contents of R5 to A with result in A and overflow in carry, (h) add decimal 20 to A with result in A and overflow in carry, (i) add contents of address 20 to A, result in A, overflow in carry, (j) subtract decimal 20 with borrow from A with result in A, underflow in borrow

3. (a) Copy decimal 5 into A, (b) copy data from address 1000 into A, (c) copy data from B into A, (d) copy A into memory addressed by contents of BC register pair, (e) copy value addressed by IX index register plus offset value 5 into A, (f) add register B to A and store result in A, (g) add data from address 1000 to A, (h) subtract B from A and store result in A
4. (a) Move 6 into w, (b) move w into FSR, (c) clear w, (d) move Reg1 into w, (e) add 6 to w
5. (a) Load acc. with data in C000, (b) AND acc. with number F0, (c) store in C001
6. (a) Set A to zero, (b) A = 1110 1000, C = 0, (c) A = 1111 1011, C = 0, (d) A = 0111 1101, C = 1
7. (a) Set A to zero, (b) A = 1110 1000, (c) A = 0101 1110, (d) A = 1001 1110, C = 0
8. (a) A = 0000 1110, C = 0, (b) A = 1000 0101, C = 1, (c) A = 0011 0010, C = 0
9. (a) INC, (b) DEC, (c) TAB, (d) STAA, (e) BLT
10. (a) INC A, (b) DEC A, (c) XCH A,Rn, (d) JZ rel
11. (a) INC A, (b) DEC A, (c) JMP, (d) CPL
12. (a) incf Reg,f, (b) decfsz Reg,f, (c) goto label, (d) comf Reg,f
13. (a) 1101 0111, (b) 0100 0001, (c) 0110 1001
14.
```
LDAA $00 ; load contents of address $00 into A
ADDA $01 ; add contents of address $01 to A
STAA $02 ; store sum in A at address $02
```
15.
```
LDAA $00 ; load contents of addres $00 into A
LDAB $01 ; load contents of address $01 into A
STAA $01 ; store A in $01
STAB $00 ; store B in $00
```
16.
```
MOV A,#10H ; put 0 in accumulator
MOV A,#10H ; put 10H in accumulator
MOV A,#20  ; put decimal 20 in accumulator
```
17.
```
MOV A,2000H  ; copy contents of address 2000H into acc.
CPL  A       ; complement accumulator
ADD  A,B     ; add B to A to form twos complement
MOV 2020H,A  ; store result at 2020H
```
18.
```
LD   A,(1900) ; load data from address 1900H into acc.
ADD A,3       ; add 3 to accumulator
LD   (1901),A ; store result at address 1901H
```
19.
```
LD   A,B    ; copy B to A
ADD A,20H   ; add 20H to A
LD   B,A    ; copy A to B
```
20.
```
LDA  $0080
ASL  A
CLC
ADC  $0080
STA  $0081
```
21.
```
LDA  $C000
ORA  #$0F
STA  $C000
```
22.
```
LD   A,0C80H
AND  A,FOH
LD   0C80H,A
```

23.
```
movlw  10
movwf  Reg
addwf  Reg,w
```
24.
```
movlw b'00001111'
movwf Reg
```
25. The accumulator is loaded with the data at address 2000H
26. The address of the start of the user RAM is 1800H

Chapter 6

1. See Section 6.2, loop gives repeated addition
2. Causes the program to jump to address 0 and thus the monitor program
3. If location $00 contents are 0 branch to there and store 0 in $01, else load contents of $01 into $00
4. Move value at P1.0 into carry flag, move carry flag to P1.1 and keep on repeating by looping to start
5. The program could be:

```
START   EQU    $C100
END     EQU    $C120
SUM     EQU    $C121
        ORG    $C000
        LDX    #START     ; X at start
        LDD    #0000      ; clear A and B
ADD     ADDB   0,X        ; add byte to B
        ADCA   #00        ; add 1 to A if c = 1
        INX               ; go to next
        CPX    #END       ; end of block?
        BLS    ADD        ; if not repeat
        STD    SUM        ; store result
        END
```

6. The program could be:

```
NUM1    EQU    1900H          ; high byte of number 1
NUM2    EQU    1902H          ; high byte of number 2
SUM     EQU    1904H          ; high byte of sum
        ORG    1800H
START   LD     A,(num1+1)     ; get low byte of 1
        LD     B,A            ; store it
        LD     A,(num2+1)     ; get low byte of 2
        ADD    A,B            ; add low byte of 1
        LD     (sum+1),A      ; save the sum low byte
        LD     A,(num1)       ; get high byte of 1
        LD     B,A            ; store it
        LD     A,(num2)       ; get high byte of 2
        ADC    A,B            ; add high byte of 1
        LD     (sum),A        ; save the sum high byte
        RST    30H
        END
```

7. The program could be:

```
        ORG    $E000
SHIFT   LSLA                  ; shift left
```

```
        DECB              ; decrement B
        BNE     SHIFT     ; loop if B not zero
HERE    BRA     HERE      ; stop
        END
```

8. See Section 6.3
9. See Section 6.4
10. Contents of AF transferred to BC
11. See Section 6.4.1; to allow a subroutine to be used with different data
12. Sends abc
13. Multiplying the total number of cycles for each instruction in the loop by the clock period
14. See Fig. 6.5 and associated text
15. A possible solution is:

```
        LDX     #20000    ; use X as loop counter
LOOP    NOP
        NOP
        DEX
        BNE     LOOP      ; repeat until loop count 0
        END
```

16. A possible solution is:

```
        LDAB    #100      ; B is outer loop counter
OUTER   LDX     #20000    ; X is inner loop counter
INNER   NOP
        NOP
        DEX               ; decrement inner count
        BNE     INNER     ; branch to inner loop
        DECB              ; decrement outer loop
        BNE     OUTER     ; branch to outer loop
        END
```

17. A possible solution is:

```
REGBAS  EQU     $1000     ; base address
PORTB   EQU     $04       ; port B address relative
                          ; to the base
        ORG     $C000
        LDX     #BASE
        LDAA    #$01
AGAIN   STAA    PORTB,X   ; output for LED off
        JSR     DELAY     ; jump to time delay
        ROLA              ; move 1 to next bit
        BRA     AGAIN     ; repeat again
        END

DELAY   LDY     #$FFFF    ; time delay count
LOOP    DEY               ; decrement count
        BNE     LOOP      ; repeat until count is 0
        RTS               ; return from delay
```

18. A possible solution is:

```
BCDBAS  EQU     $B600     ; base address of table
        ORG     $E000
        LDX     #BCDTAB   ; point to table
```

```
            LDAB    $%00100000   ; load in B the binary
                                 ; number to convert
            ABX                  ; add offset
            LDAA    $00,X        ; load table entry into A
```

19. A possible solution is:

```
REGBAS      EQU     $1000        ; base address of
                                 ;  registers
PORTE       EQU     $0A          ; offset for port E
            LDX     #REGBAS      ; load base address
            LDAA    PORTE,X      ; read port E
```

20. A possible solution is:

```
REGBAS      EQU     $1000        ; base address of
                                 ;  registers
PORTB       EQU     4            ; offset for port B
            LDX     #REGBAS      ; load base address
            LDAA    #$04         ; load 04
            STAA    PORTB,X      ; output the data
```

21. A possible solution is:

```
        org     0
        clrf    PORTD           ; clear bits in port D
        bsf     STATUS,RP0      ; get bank 1
        clrf    TRISD           ; set to 0 for output
        bcf     STATUS,RP0      ; return to bank 0 for
                                ; output
```

22. The header file is:

```
STATUS      EQU     H'0003'
PORTA       EQU     H'0005'
PORTB       EQU     H'0006'
PORTC       EQU     H'0007'
PORTD       EQU     H'0008'
PORTE       EQU     H'0009'
TRISA       EQU     H'0085'
TRISB       EQU     H'0086
TRISC       EQU     H'0087'
TRISD       EQU     H'0088'
TRISE       EQU     H'0089'
```

23. A possible program is:

```
            ORG     8100H
            SETB    P4.0        ; set for input
LOOP        MOV     C,P4.01     ; read input and store in
                                ; carry flag
            MOV     P4.0,C      ; transfer state of carry flag
            sjmp    LOOP
            END
```

24. A possible program is:

```
            ORG     8100H
            SETB    P4.1        ; set for input
            SETB    P4.2        ; set for input
LOOP        MOV     C,P4.1      ; read input and store in
                                ; carry flag
            ORL     C,P4.2      ; logic OR
            MOV     P4.0,C      ; transfer either input to
                                ; the output
            SJMP    LOOP
            END
```

Chapter 7

1. (a) The variable counter is an integer, (b) the variable num is assigned the value 10, (c) the word 'Name' is displayed, (d) the display is 'Number 12', (e) include the file stdio.h, (f) a comment which does not constitute part of the program
2. ```
main( )
{
old_value( );
correction( );
new_value( );
}
```
3. (a) Calls up the library necessary for the printf( ) function, (b) indicates the beginning and end of a group of statements, (c) starts a new line, (d) the phrase 'problem 3'
4. The number is 12
5. answer is the integer 2. This is because it is restricted to an integer response
6. (a) 1, (b) 0, (c) 1, (d) 10, (e) 0, (f) 3
7. (a) 1000 1000, (b) 1101 1111, (c) 0101 0111
8. ```
#include <stdio.h>

in main(void);
{
int len, width;
printf("Enter length:  ");
scanff("%d", &len);
printf("enter width:  ");
scanf("%d", &width);
printf("Area is %d", lens * width);
return 0;
{
```
9. Similar to program example given in Section 7.5.3
10. Divides first number by second number unless second is 0
11. ```
include <stdio.h>

main( )
{
float voltage;
printf("enter voltage value: ");
scanf("%f", &voltage);
if(voltage<19)
    printf("voltage is satisfactory\n");
else
    printf("voltage is low\n");
}
```
12. ```
# define Limit 100.0
# include <stdio.h>

main( )
{
int code_num;
float value;
printf("Type in sensor num and value:  ");
scanf("%d%f", &code_num, &value);
```

```
if(value>Limit)
    printf("Sensor %d is over the limit\n", code_num);
}
```

13. /*This program determines the roots of a quadratic equation of the form $ax^2 + bx + c = 0$*/

```
#include <math.h>
#include <stdio.h>

main( )
{
double a, b, c, disc, root1, root2;
printf("\nEnter values for a, b, and c:     ");
scanf("%f %f %f", &a, &b, %c);
if(a = = 0.0 && b = = 0.0)
    printf("The equation has no roots");
else if(a = = 0.0)
    printf("The equation has the single root x = %f, -c/b);
else
{
    disc = pow(b,2,0) - 4 * a * c; /*calculate discriminant*/
    if(disc >0.0
  {
    disc = sqrt(disc);
      root1 = (-b + disc)/(2 * a);
      root2 = (-b - disc)/(2 * a);
      printf("\nThe two roots are %f and %f", root1, root2);
    }
    else if (disc < 0.0)
      printf("Both roots are imaginary");
    else
      printf("\nBoth roots are equal to %f", -b(2 * a));
}
```

14.

```
# include <stdio.h>

main( )
{
int temp[8], sum, i;
float average;
sum = 0;
for(i = 0, x <7; ++i)
{
    printf/("Enter a value for element number %d:  ", i);
    scanf("%d", &temp[i]);
}
printf("The values stored are:\n");
for(i = 0; x < 7; ++i)
    printf("%d", temp[i]);
average = sum/8.0;
printf("%\nThe average is %f\n", average);
}
```

15.

```
#include <stdio.h>

int main(void)
{
int temp[31], i, min, max, avg;
int days;
printf("How many days in the month?  ");
```

```
scanf("%d", %days(;
for(i = 0; i < days; i++)
     {
        printf("Enter noonday temp for day %d:  ", i+1);
        scanf("%d", &temp[i]);
     }
avg = 0; /*initialise average*/
for(i = 0; i < days; i++) avg = avg + temp[i];
printf("Average temp:  %d\n", avg/days);

min = 100; /*initialise min with some value below which
                  all minimum values will come */
max = 0; /* initialise max */
for(i = 0; i < days; i++)
     {
        if (min > temp[i]) min = temp[i];
        if (max < temp[i]) max = temp[i]);
     }
printf("Minimum temp: %d\n", min);
printf("Maximum temp:  %d\n", max);

return 0;
}
```

16. The address of the variable named sum
17. The first two elements 1 and 2
18. (a)

```
#include <math.h>
#include <stdio.h>

int main(void)
{
double val = 1.0;
do
{
     printf("%f %f\n", val, log(val));
     val++;
}
while (val<11.0);

return 0;
}
```

(b)

```
#include <math.h>
#include <stdio.h>

int main(void)
{
double val = -1.0;
do
{
     printf(%sine of %f is %f\n", val, sin(val));
     val += 0.1;
}
while(val<= 1.0);

return 0;
}
```

Chapter 8

1. See Section 8.2; to save having to write out definitions for microcontroller registers and control bits
2. Initially the motor is off. Then if stop motor off, else if start motor on. Definitions required: motoroff, motoron, TRUE, stop, start
3. PORTA = PORTA & 0xbf;
   P1 = P1 & 0xbf;
4. PORTA = PORTA | 0x0a;
   P1 = P1 | 0x0x;
5. PORTA = PORTA ^ 0x08;
   P1 = P1 ^ 0x08;
6. PORTA = PORTA <<1;
7. BIT0 = BIT0 & ~ON;
8. FLAG = FLAG | BIT0;
9. FLAG = FLAG & BIT0;
10. FLAG = FLAG &~ BIT0;
11. A possible program is:

```
#include <reg51.h>
#define STEPPER P1
main( )
{
        do
        {
            STEPPER = 0x0a;
                DELAY( );
            STEPPER = 0x09;
                DELAY( );
            STEPPER = 0x05;
                DELAY( );
            STEPPER = 0x09;
                DELAY( );
            STEPPER = 0x05;
                DELAY( );
            STEPPER = 0x0a;
                DELAY( );
        }
        while(1);
}
```

12. A possible program is:

```
#include <reg51.h>
sbit LED = P1^1; /* pin for LED */
main( )
{
        do
        {
            LED = 0; /* turn LED off */
            DELAY( );
            LED = 1; /* turn LED off */
            DELAY( );
        }
        while(1);
}
```

13.

```
unsigned char tab[ ] = {32, 34, 36, 37, 39, 41, 43, 45};
unsigned char F,C;
unsigned char CtoF(unsigned char degC);
```

```
{
   return tab[degC];
}
```

Chapter 9

1. See Section 9.2
2. See Section 9.3
3. See Section 9.3.1, item 4
4. 1
5. Exposure to UV light
6. See Section 9.5.1
7. See Section 9.5.2: to deny electrical access by any external means to the on-chip memory
8. To prevent exposure to the UV in sunlight and artificial light and so erasure
9. EEPROM is electrically erasable and individual bytes, rows or bulk erasure can be used; EPROM is UV erasable and only bulk erasable
10. 1
11. (a) Both PPROG BYTE and ERASE, (b) both PPROG ROW and ERASE, (c) PPROG EELAT, (d) PPROG EEPGM
12. See Section 9.5.3
13. See Section 9.5.3

Chapter 10

1. See Section 10.3
2. High, low, floating
3. See Section 10.4.2
4. See Section 10.4.3
5. See Section 10.5.3
6. SETB EX0
7. SETB EA
8. (a) EI, (b) CLI
9. SETB EA
10. SETB IT0
SETB IT1
11. bsf INTCON,GIE
bsf INTCON,INTF
12. bsf OPTION,INTEDG
13. See Section 10.5.3, item 3
14. CRA 00110100, CRB 00101111
15. The program might read:

```
LDAA    #$00     ; load 0s
STAA    $2000    ; make side A input port
LDAA    #$FF     ; load 1s
STAA    $2000    ; make side B output port
LDAA    #$34     ; load control register value
STAA    $2000    ; select port A data register
LDAA    #$2F     ; load control register value
STAA    $2002    ; select port B data register
```

16. The program might read:

```
         LDAA   #$00     ; load 0s
         STAA   $2000    ; make side A input port
         LDAA   #$FF     ; load 1s
         STAA   $2000    ; make side B output port
         LDAA   #$05     ; load control register value
         STAA   $2000    ; select port A data register
         LDAA   #$34     ; load control register value
         STAA   $2002    ; select port B data register
READ     LDAA   $2000    ; read port A
         LDAA   DELAY    ; load time delay subroutine
         BRA    READ
         END
```

17. The program might read:

```
LD     A,4FH      ; input mode
OUT    (07H),A    ; port A control register
LD     A,CFH      ; bit mode
OUT    (06H),A    ; port B control register
LD     A,1FH      ; bit pattern
OUT    (06H),A    ; port B control register
```

18. (a) 80H, (b) 90H, (c) 81H
19. See Fig. 10.29 and associated text
20. See Section 10.7
21. (a) 7 bit + even parity + 2 stop bits, (b) 7 bit + odd parity + 2 stop bits, (c) 8 bit + no parity + 2 stop bits
22. Bits 0 and 1 of the mode register, see Fig. 10.43
23. See Fig. 10.46 and associated text
24. The program might be:

```
REGBAS   EQU    $1000      ; base address
SPDR     EQU    $2A        ; offset of SPDR
SPCR     EQU    $28        ; offset of SPCR
SPSR     EQU    $29        ; offset of SPSR
DDRD     EQU    $09        ; offset of DDRD
         ORG    $00
         LDX    #REGBAS
         LDAA   #$38       ; enable SPI outputs
         STAA   DDRD,X     ; set directions of SPI pins
         LDAA   #$57       ; SPI master, CPHA = 1,
                           ; CPOL = 0, /32 clock rate
         STAA   SPCR,X
         LDAA   DATA       ; load the data
         STAA   SPDR,X     ; start SPI transfer
POLL     TST    SPCR,X     ; wait for transfer to be
                           ; completed
         BPL    POLL
         LDAA   SPDR,X     ; get data from slave
DONE     BRA    DONE
```

25. SCP1 = 1, SCP0 = 1, SCR2 = 0, SCR1 = 0, SCR0 = 0
26. Bit 4 of SCI control register 1, see Fig. 10.53
27. The program might be:

```
REGBAS   EQU    $1000      ; base address
BAUD     EQU    $2B        ; offset of BAUD
SCCR1    EQU    $2C        ; offset of SCCR1
SCCR2    EQU    $2D        ; offset of SCCR2
         ORG    $00
```

```
        LDX     #REGBAS
        LDAA    #$30        ; baud rate to 9600
        STAA    BAUD,X      ; initialise BAUD register
        LDAA    #$00        ; 8 data bits
        STAA    SCCR1,X     ; initialise SCCR1
        LDAA    #$0C        ; enable transmitter and
                            ; receiver, disable interrupts
        STAA    SCCR2,X     ; initialise SCCR2
```

28. Bits 6 and 7 to be 0 in SCON (see Fig. 10.57)
29. The program might be:

```
MOV     TMOD,#20H     ; B00100000
MOV     TH1,#E3       ; TH1 = 13
MOV     TCON,#00H     ; B01000000
MOV     SCON.#52H     ; B01010010
SETB    TR1
```

30. The program might be:

```
void serint(void)
{
        TMOD = 0x20;/*timer 1 mode 2*/
        TH1 = 0xFD;/* 9600 baud*/
        TCON = 0x40;*/start baud clock*/
        SCON = 0x50;*/enable receiver*/
        IE = 0x90;*/enable serial interrupts*/
}
```

31. SPRG = 64, BRGH = 1
32. TRISC bit 6 = 1, bit 7 = 1; TXSTA bit 5 = 1, bit 1 = 1; RCSTA bit 7 = 1, bit 4 = 1; INTCON OEIE = 1, GIE = 1
33. Conversion of signal levels, see Section 10.8.1
34. See Section 10.8.3
35. Yes

Chapter 11

1. See Section 11.2
2. See Section 11.2.1
3. See Fig. 11.5 and associated text
4. The program might be:

```
# include <reg51.h>
unsigned char code ASCIIbtn( ) = {"0123456789ABCDEF"};
void display(unsigned char ascii);
unsigned char readkey(void)
{
  while(P1.4); /* wait for DAV going low*/
  while ((P1.4) = = 0); /*wait for DAV going high*/
  return P1 & 0x0F;
}
void main(void)
{
  while(1)
  {
    display(ASCIIbtn(readkey( ) );
  }
}
```

5. 220 Ω

6. See Fig. 11.8 and associated text
7. See Fig. 11.10 for basic arrangement. A possible program is:

```
REGBAS   EQU   $1000      ; base address
PORTB    EQU   $04        ; offset for port B
PORTD    EQU   $08        ; offset for port D
DDRD     EQU   $09        ; offset of DDRD
         ORG   $C000
         LDX   #REGBAS
         LDAA  #$3F       ; value to be written into
                          ; DDRD
         STAA  DDRD,X     ; port D output
         LDAA  #$6D       ; segment pattern for 5
         STAA  PORTB,X    ; output segment pattern
         LDAA  #$08       ; value to set pin PD3
         STAA  PORTD,X    ; show  5 on 3rd display
         END
```

8. See Section 11.4.1, latch plus ADC
9. PIA, DAC, current-to-voltage converter; see Fig. 11.13
10. A possible program is:

```
REGBAS   EQU   $1000            ; base address
OPTION   EQU   $39              ; offset of OPTION
ADCTL    EQU   $30              ; offset of ADCTL
ADR1     EQU   $31              ; offset of ADR1
ADR2     EQU   $32              ; offset of ADR2
ADR3     EQU   $33              ; offset of ADR3
ADR4     EQU   $34              ; offset of ADR4
         ORG   $00
RESULT   RMB   4                ; reserve 4 bytes for
                                ; results

         ORG   $C000            ; starting address of
                                ; program
         LDX   #REGBAS
         BSET  OPTION,X,$80     ; set ADPU to start
         BCLR  OPTION,X,$40     ; select E clock
         LDY   #30              ; count loop for delay
DELAY    DEY                    ; delay loop
         BNE   DELAY            ; repeat until count 0
         LDAA  #$20             ; initialise ADCTL
         STAA  ADCTL,X
AGAIN    LDAA  ADCTL,X          ; check CCF
         BPL   AGAIN            ; wait until CCF set
         LDAA  ADR1,X           ; get 1st result
         STAA  RESULT           ; save in 1st byte
         LDAA  ADR2,X           ; get 2nd result
         STAA  RESULT+1         ; save in 2nd byte
         LDAA  ADR3,X           ; get 3rd result
         STAA  RESULT+2         ; save in 3rd byte
         LDAA  ADR4,X           ; get 4th result
         STAA  RESULT+3         ; save in 4th byte
         END
```

For a single value, any of the results can be used.

11. 00010000
12. 01000100
13. 65.54 ms

14. A possible program will involve a number of output-compare operations such as 40 operations with each creating a delay of 25 ms.

```
REGBAS   EQU    $1000         ; base address of registers
TOC2     EQU    $18           ; offset of TOC2 from REGBAS
TCNT     EQU    $0E           ; offset of TCNT from REGBAS
TFLG1    EQU    $23           ; offset of TFLG1 from REGBAS
OC2      EQU    $40           ; mask to select OC2 and OC2F
CLEAR    EQU    $40           ; value to clear OC2F flag
DELAY25  EQU    5000          ; number of E clock cycles to give 25 ms
ONESEC   EQU    40            ; number of output-compare operations required for 1 s
COUNT    RMB    1             ; memory location for number of output-compare operations
         ORG    $C000         ; starting address for program
         LDX    #REGBAS
         LDAA   #OC2          ; clear OC2 flag
         STAA   TFLG1,X
         LDAA   ONESEC        ; initialise output-compare count
         STAA   COUNT
         LDD    TCNT,X
DELAY    ADDD   #DELAY25      ; add 25 ms delay
         STD    TOC2,X        ; start the output-compare operation
         BRCLR  TFLG1,X OC2   ; delay until OC2F flag set
         LDAA   #OC2          ; clear OC2F flag
         STAA   TFLG1,X
         DEC    COUNT         ; decrement the output-compare count
         BEQ    HERE          ; branch to HERE when 1 s elapsed
         LDD    TOC2,X        ; start next output-compare operation
         BRA    DELAY
HERE     BRA    HERE
         END
```

15. MOV TMOD,#00000000B
    SETB TR0
16. MOV TMOD,#00010000B
17. MOV TH0,#0FFH
    MOV TH0,9CH
18. A possible program is:

```
        ORG    8100H
        MOV    TMOD,#01H    ; 16-bit timer mode
LOOP    MOV    TH0,#0FEH    ; –500 high byte
        MOV    TL0,#0CH     ; –500 low byte
        SETB   TR0          ; start timer
WAIT    JNB    TF0,WAIT     ; wait for overflow
        CLR    TR0          ; stop timer
        CLR    TF0          ; clear timer overflow flag
        CPL    P1.0         ; change port bit
        SJMP   LOOP         ; repeat loop
        END
```

19. 139
20. A possible program is:

```
Init    clrf    TRISC        ; set bits of port C as
                             ; outputs
        movlw   H'01'        ; enable count input
        movwf   T1CON
        movlw   H'09'        ; clear on compare
        movwf   CCP1CON
```

```
Pulse   bcf     T1CON,TMR1ON   ; stop TMR1
        clrf    TMR1H          ; clear MSB
        clrf    TMR1L          ; clear LSB
        clrf    CCPR1H         ; clear MSB of
                               ; compare register
        movlf   H'01'
        movwf   CCPR1L         ; move 1 into LSB of
                               ; compare register
        bcf     CCP1CON,0      ; set pin on compare
Pulse1  bcf     STATUS,GIE     ; disable interrupts
        btfsc   STATUS,GIE     ; during time
        goto    Pulse1
        bsf     T1CON,TMR1ON   ; begin TMR1
        movlw   101            ; duration of pulse
        movwf   CCPRIL
        bsf     CCP1CON,0      ; 0 output on second
                               ; compare
        bsf     STATUS,GIE     ; re-enable interrupts
```

21. Probably a resistor plus a Darlington pair
22. As the algorithm in Section 11.8.1 but with item 6 written for 10 steps
23. As Fig. 11.13 with a program which gives a digital output that is incremented. For the sine wave, a look-up table can be used to obtain the sequential digital values

Chapter 12

1. See Section 12.2
2. See Section 12.2.4
3. To check if any corruption has occurred
4. Add a 1 in the MSB position
5. See Section 12.3.2
6. See Section 12.4.2; the signals are not repetitive and they are concerned with a number of parallel lines on which signals change at rapid rates

Chapter 13

1. (a) A possible solution is to use a potential divider circuit with a thermistor and supply the output to an A/D input of a microcontroller such as the Intel 8051. The output from the microcontroller can then be used to drive two seven-segment LED displays. The program can use a look-up table with the temperature being stored in binary coded decimal format for direct output through two ports to the display, one port being used for the low digit and one for the high digit. (b) The semiconductor transducer the MPX2100AP might be used with an instrumentation amplifier, e.g. the MC68HC11, to give an analogue input to the A/D input of a microcontroller. The MPX2100AP is a silicon diaphragm with integral strain gauges and resistors in the silicon; it gives a differential voltage output which is directly proportional to the differential pressure applied to the two sides of the diaphragm. The AP on

MPX2100AP indicates that the version suggested for this application measures the external pressure relative to a zero pressure, i.e. vacuum, sealed in the cavity on one side of the diaphragm. The output can then be used to drive an LED display.

2. (a) A possible solution is shown in Fig. A.6 with a PIC microcontroller, and here is a possible program:

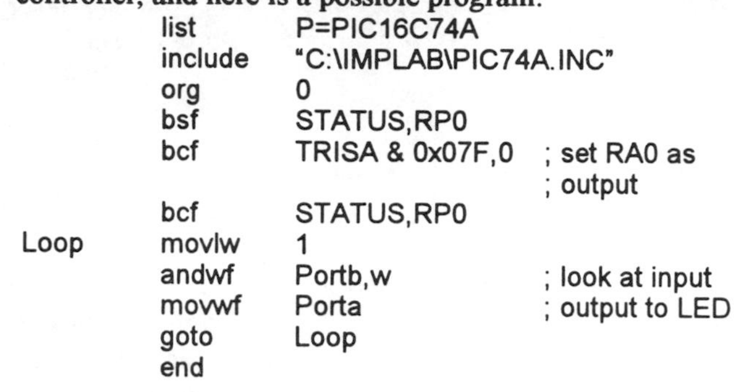

```
        list      P=PIC16C74A
        include   "C:\IMPLAB\PIC74A.INC"
        org       0
        bsf       STATUS,RP0
        bcf       TRISA & 0x07F,0   ; set RA0 as
                                    ; output
        bcf       STATUS,RP0
Loop    movlw     1
        andwf     Portb,w           ; look at input
        movwf     Porta             ; output to LED
        goto      Loop
        end
```

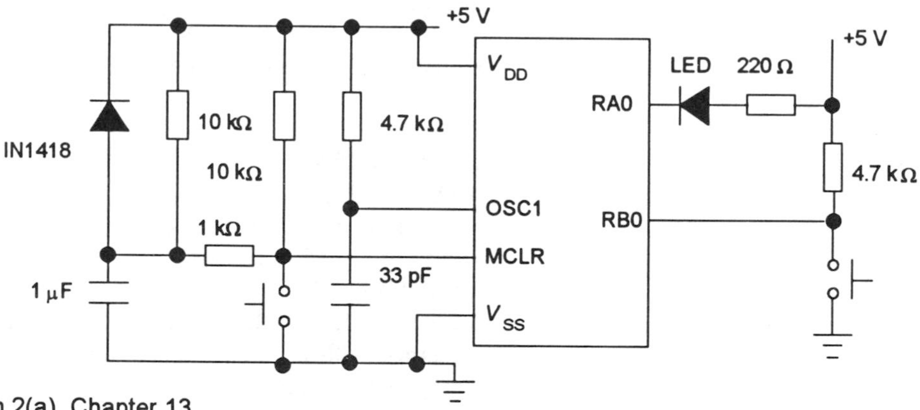

Fig. A.6 Problem 2(a), Chapter 13

(b) A possible solution is shown in Fig. A.7 with a Motorola 68HC11 microcontroller. A possible program is:

```
REGBASE  EQU    $1000
PORTB    EQU    $04          ; offset of port B
PORTC    EQU    $03          ; offset of port C
DDRC     EQU    $07          ; offset of DDRC
         ORG    $C000
         LDX    #REGBASE
         LDAA   #$FF
         STAA   PORTB,X      ; switch off LEDs
         LDAA   #00
         STAA   DDRC,X
LOOP     LDAA   PORTC,X      ; inputs from switches
         STAA   PORTB,X      ; turn on
                             ; corresponding LEDs
         BRA    LOOP         ; repeat loop
         END
```

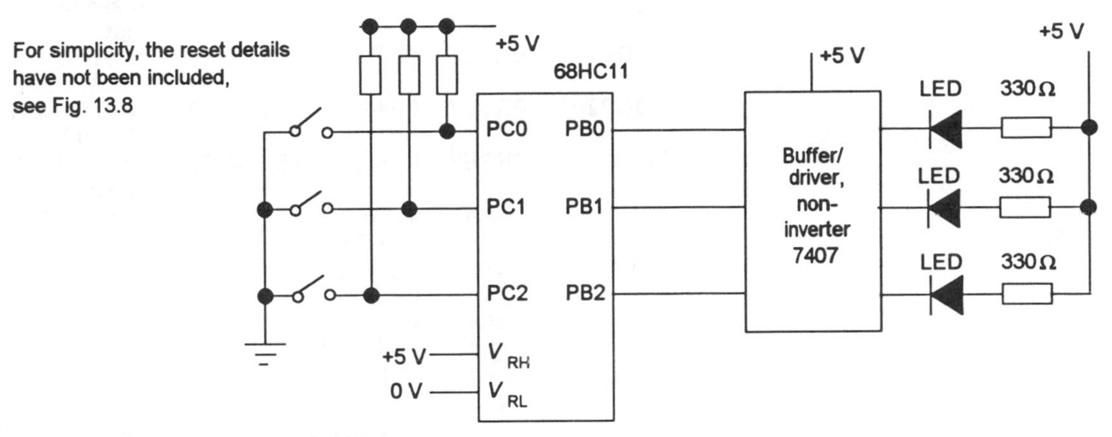

Fig. A.7 Problem 2(b) Chapter 13

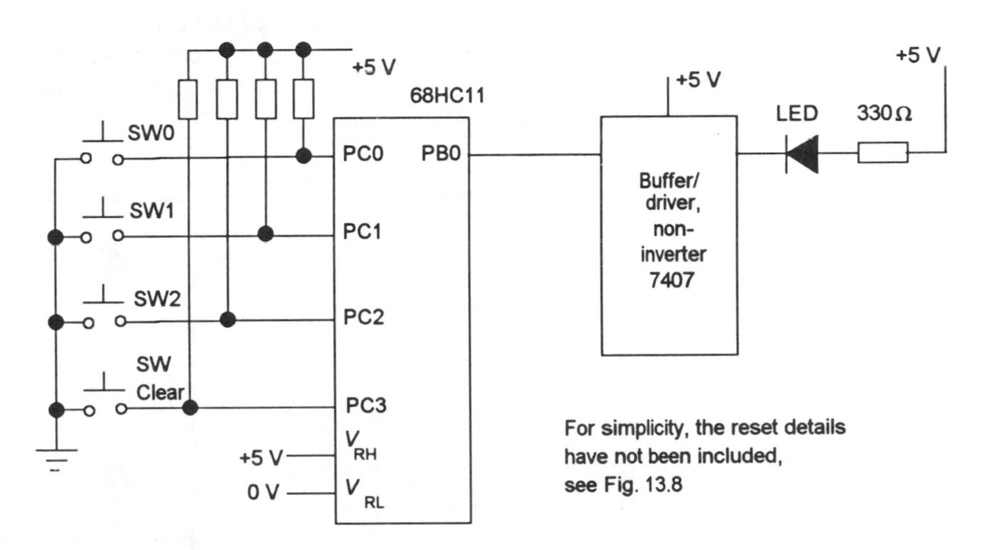

Fig. A.8 Problem 2(c) Chapter 13

(c) A possible solution is shown in Fig. A.8 with a Motorola 68HC11 microcontroller. A possible program is:

```
REGBASE  EQU    $1000
PORTC    EQU    $3                     ; offset for
                                       ; port C
PORTB    EQU    $4                     ; offset for
                                       ; port B
DDRC     EQU    $7                     ; offset for
                                       ; DDRC
         ORG    $C000
         LDX    #REGBASE
         LDAB   #$FF
         STAB   PORTB,X                ; switch LEDs
                                       ; off
         LDAA   #00
```

```
        STAA   DDRC,X                  ; make port C
                                       ; input
LOOP1   BRSET  PORTC,X,$0,LOOP1        ; is SW0
                                       ; closed?
LOOP2   BRSET  PORTC,X,$1,LOOP2        ; AND is SW1
                                       ; closed?
LOOP3   BRSET  PORTC,X,$2,LOOP3        ; AND is SW2
                                       ; closed?
        LDAA   #$FE                    ; turn on LED
        STAA   PORTB,X
CLEAR   BRSET  PORTC,X,$80,CLEA        ; is SW clear
               R                       ; closed?
        LDAA   #$FF                    ; turn off LED
        STAA   PORTB,X
HERE    BRA    HERE
        END
```

(d) A possible design, giving just the interface details, is shown in Fig. A.9 using an Intel 8051 microcontroller along with a unipolar-connected stepper motor; the microcontroller outputs the drive pattern to obtain the required rotation in half-steps. An alternative is to use a hardware driver. A possible program is:

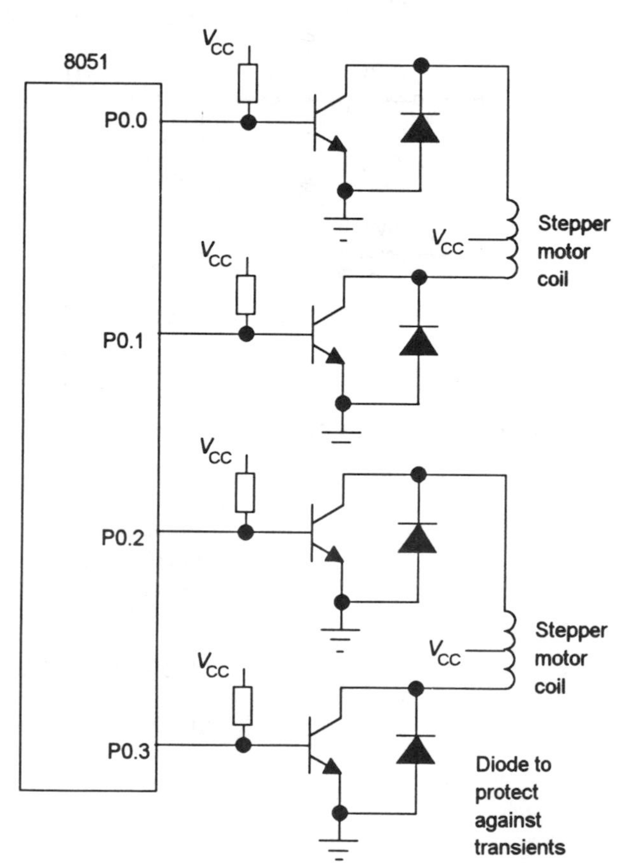

Fig. A.9 Problem 2(d) Chapter 13

```
#include <reg51.h>
void delay( )
{
     TH0=0x01; /*to give 20 ms time delay*/
     TL0=0x00;
     TF0=0;
     TR0=1;
     while(TF0==0);
     TR0=0;
}

unsigned char steptab[ ] =
     {0xa, 0x8, 0x9, 0x1, 0x5, 0x4, 0x6, 0x2};

main( )
{
     unsigned char ptr=0; /*step counter */
     unsigned char cntr; /*loop counter */
     bit DEFLAG; /*direction flag */
     TMOD=0x21;
     DFLAG=0; /*initial direction*/
     while(1)
        {
          for(cntr=0;cntr<10;cntr++)
          {
          P1=steptab[ptr & 0x7];
          delay( ); /*time delay */
          if(DEFLAG==0) ptr++; /*increment step counter */
          else ptr--; /*decrement step counter */
          }
        DFLAG=!(DFLAG); /*change direction */
        }
}
```

(e) A possible design is a microcontroller interfacing with a temperature sensor, as in Fig. 13.8, and outputting via the circuit shown in Fig. A.10. The program is similar to the program in Section 13.4: initialisation to set the analogue input port and a single output, an interrupt service routine so that the fan comes on at some temperature and off at another, with an output to the fan port connection

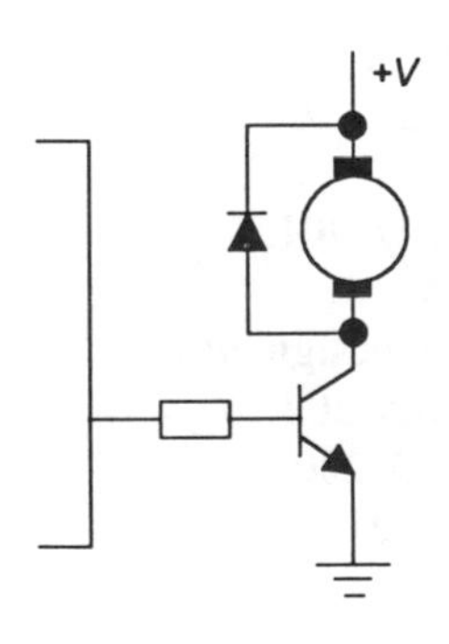

Fig. A.10 Problem 2(e) Chapter 13

Index

IC number index